Communications
in Computer and Information Science   1560

More information about this series at https://link.springer.com/bookseries/7899

Guangtao Zhai · Jun Zhou · Hua Yang · Ping An · Xiaokang Yang (Eds.)

Digital TV and Wireless Multimedia Communications

18th International Forum, IFTC 2021
Shanghai, China, December 3–4, 2021
Revised Selected Papers

 Springer

Editors
Guangtao Zhai (ID)
Shanghai Jiao Tong Univeristy
Shanghai, China

Jun Zhou (ID)
Shanghai Jiao Tong University
Shanghai, China

Hua Yang
Shanghai Jiao Tong University
Shanghai, China

Ping An (ID)
Shanghai University
Shanghai, China

Xiaokang Yang
Shanghai Jiao Tong University
Shanghai, China

ISSN 1865-0929   ISSN 1865-0937 (electronic)
Communications in Computer and Information Science
ISBN 978-981-19-2265-7   ISBN 978-981-19-2266-4 (eBook)
https://doi.org/10.1007/978-981-19-2266-4

This Springer imprint is published by the registered company Springer Nature Singapore Pte Ltd.
The registered company address is: 152 Beach Road, #21-01/04 Gateway East, Singapore 189721, Singapore

Preface

This volume constitutes selected papers presented at IFTC 2021: The 18th International Forum of Digital Multimedia Communication, held in Shanghai, China, during December 3–4, 2021.

IFTC is a summit forum in the field of digital media communication. The 18th IFTC served as an international bridge for extensively exchanging the latest research advances in digital media communication around the world. The forum also aimed to promote technology, equipment, and applications in the field of digital media by comparing the characteristics, frameworks, and significant techniques and their maturity, analyzing the performance of various applications in terms of scalability, manageability, and portability, and discussing the interfaces among varieties of networks and platforms.

The conference program included invited talks focusing on the metaverse delivered by four distinguished speakers from Harvard University (USA), Bilkent University (Turkey), Shanghai Jiao Tong University (China), and Huazhong University of Science and Technology (China), as well as an oral session of six papers, a poster session of 23 papers, and 12 papers in a special session on electric big data. The topics of these papers range from audio/image processing to telecommunications as well as big data. This book contains the 41 papers selected for IFTC 2021.

The proceeding editors wish to thank the authors for contributing their novel ideas and visions that are recorded in this book, and all reviewers for their contributions. We also thank Springer for their trust and for publishing the proceedings of IFTC 2021.

IFTC 2021 was co-hosted by the Shanghai Image and Graphics Association (SIGA), the China International Industry Fair (CIIF 2020), and the Shanghai Association for Science and Technology, and it was co-sponsored by Shanghai Jiao Tong University (SJTU), the Shanghai Telecom Company, the Shanghai Institute for Advanced Communication and Data Science (SICS), Shanghai University of Engineering Science, and the Shanghai Key Laboratory of Digital Media Processing and Transmission.

December 2021

Guangtao Zhai
Jun Zhou
Hua Yang
Ping An
Xiaokang Yang
Xianyang Xue
Yue Lu

Organization

General Chairs

Xiaokang Yang	Shanghai Jiao Tong University, China
Ping An	Shanghai University, China
Ning Liu	Shanghai Jiao Tong University, China
Guangtao Zhai	Shanghai Jiao Tong University, China

Program Chairs

Xiangyang Xue	Fudan University, China
Jun Zhou	Shanghai Jiao Tong University, China
Yue Lu	East China Normal University, China
Hua Yang	Shanghai Jiao Tong University, China

Tutorial Chairs

Yugang Jiang	Fudan University, China
Yuming Fang	Jiangxi University of Finance and Economics, China
Jiantao Zhou	University of Macau, China

International Liaisons

Weisi Lin	Nanyang Technological University, Singapore
Patrick Le Callet	Nantes Université, France
Lu Zhang	INSA Rennes, France

Finance Chairs

Yi Xu	Shanghai Jiao Tong University, China
Hao Liu	Donghua University, China
Beibei Li	Shanghai Polytechnic University, China
Xuefei Song	Shanghai Ninth People's Hospital, China

Publications Chairs

Hong Lu	Fudan University, China
Feiniu Yuan	Shanghai Normal University, China

Xianming Liu	Harbin Institute of Technology, China
Liquan Shen	Shanghai University, China

Award Chairs

Zhijun Fang	Shanghai University of Engineering Science, China
Xiaolin Huang	Shanghai Jiao Tong University, China
Hanli Wang	Tongji University, China
Yu Zhu	East China University of Science and Technology, China

Publicity Chairs

Wenjun Zhang	Shanghai Jiao Tong University, China
Bo Yan	Fudan University, China
Gang Hou	Central Research Institute of INESA, China

Industrial Program Chairs

Yiyi Lu	China Telecom, Shanghai, China
Guozhong Wang	Shanghai University of Engineering Science, China
Chen Yao	Third Research Institute of the Ministry of Public Security, China
Yan Zhou	Renji Hospital, China

Arrangements Chair

Cheng Zhi	SIGA, China

Program Committee

Ping An	Shanghai University, China
Lianghui Ding	Shanghai Jiao Tong University, China
Yuming Fang	Jiangxi University of Finance and Economics, China
Zhijun Fang	Shanghai University of Engineering Science, China
Shuang Fen	Communication University of China, China
Zhongpai Gao	Shanghai Jiao Tong University, China
Ke Gu	Beijing University of Technology, China
Dazhi He	Shanghai Jiao Tong University, China

Jianling Hu	Soochow University, China
Menghan Hu	East China Normal University, China
Xiaolin Huang	Shanghai Jiao Tong University, China
Yugang Jiang	Fudan University, China
Beibei Li	Shanghai Polytechnic University, China
Hao Liu	Donghua University, China
Peng Liu	Shandong University, China
Xianming Liu	Harbin Institute of Technology, China
Zhi Liu	Shandong University, China
Hong Lu	Fudan University, China
Yue Lu	East China Normal University, China
Ran Ma	Shanghai University, China
Xiongkuo Min	Shanghai Jiao Tong University, China
Da Pan	Communication University of China, China
Peng Qi	Tongji University, China
Liquan Shen	Shanghai University, China
Yi Xu	Shanghai Jiao Tong University, China
Ci Wang	East China Normal University, China
Guozhong Wang	Shanghai University of Engineering Science, China
Hanli Wang	Tongji University, China
Jia Wang	Shanghai Jiao Tong University, China
Minyu Wang	Shandong University, China
Yongfang Wang	Shanghai University, China
Meng Wu	Northwestern Polytechnical University, China
Xiangyang Xue	Fudan University, China
Rong Xie	Shanghai Jiao Tong University, China
Bo Yan	Fudan University, China
Chao Yang	Shandong University, China
Hua Yang	Shanghai Jiao Tong University, China
Xiaokang Yang	Shanghai Jiao Tong University, China
Chen Yao	Third Research Institute of the Ministry of Public Security, China
Haibing Yin	Hangzhou Dianzi University, China
Feiniu Yuan	Shanghai Normal University, China
Guangtao Zhai	Shanghai Jiao Tong University, China
Chongyang Zhang	Shanghai Jiao Tong University, China
Xiaoyun Zhang	Shanghai Jiao Tong University, China
Yujin Zhang	Shanghai University of Engineering Science, China
Xiaoli Zhao	Shanghai University of Engineering Science, China

Jiantao Zhou	University of Macau, China
Jun Zhou	Shanghai Jiao Tong University, China
Wenhan Zhu	Shanghai Jiao Tong University, China
Yu Zhu	East China University of Science and Technology, China
Yucheng Zhu	Shanghai Jiao Tong University, China

Contents

Image Analysis

Image Analysis

Multi-level Prediction for Overlapped Parcel Segmentation

Zhequan Zhou[1]($\boxtimes$), Shujing Lyu[2,3]($\boxtimes$), and Yue Lu[2,3]($\boxtimes$)

[1] School of Computer Science and Technology, East China Normal University,
Shanghai, China
zqzhou@stu.ecnu.edu.cn
[2] School of Communication and Electronic Engineering,
East China Normal University, Shanghai, China
{sjlv,ylu}@cs.ecnu.edu.cn
[3] Shanghai Key Laboratory of Multidimensional Information Processing,
Shanghai, China

Abstract. In this paper, we propose a new instance segmentation framework based on a multi-level prediction mechanism, aiming at segmenting overlapped parcels. In this framework, one location on FPN's feature maps can predict a set of overlapped instances through a multi-level head architecture according to their overlapping order. Besides, to avoid the inherent limit of bounding boxes in object overlapping scenes, our approach is bounding-box free. And we also provide a dataset for overlapped parcel instance segmentation named OLParcel. On a Mask RCNN baseline, our network can improve 4.25% AP, 4.26% recall, and 7.11% MR^{-2} on our dataset.

Keywords: Instance segmentation · Parcel sorting · Overlap

1 Introduction

Lots of advanced instance segmentation methods have been proposed [2,6,12,15, 23,25,27] and have achieved remarkable performances on many popular datasets, such as COCO [14] and PASCAL VOC [5]. However, they still have limitations in some stacked or overlapped scenarios. Such as in parcel sorting application, parcels on the conveyor belt are randomly stacked and highly overlapped with each other. As a result, these advanced instance segmentation frameworks still face challenges when predicting these parcels. Figure 1 shows a typical failure case in this scene: Mask RCNN [6] fails to predict a parcel highly overlapped with others (indicated by a red dash box). This kind of failure is mainly ascribed to two reasons. The first reason is that bounding boxes aren't suitable for these scenes, since highly overlapped objects are likely to have highly overlapped bounding boxes. Therefore, it is difficult for a network to generate distinguishing prediction for each proposal. Besides, these predictions are prone to be mistakenly suppressed by box-based Non-maximum Suppression (NMS). The second reason is the lack of a special mechanism to explicitly handle this overlapping situation.

© Springer Nature Singapore Pte Ltd. 2022
G. Zhai et al. (Eds.): IFTC 2021, CCIS 1560, pp. 3–17, 2022.
https://doi.org/10.1007/978-981-19-2266-4_1

For example, when Mask RCNN tries to predict these parcels in Fig. 1(a), there is an intractable ambiguity: it is not clear w.r.t which parcel to be predicted in these overlapped regions.

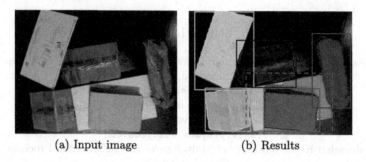

(a) Input image   (b) Results

Fig. 1. Instance segmentation results of baseline (Mask RCNN [6]).

Some works have tried to address this issue in objects overlapping scenes from several different perspectives, such as new loss functions [26,29] and sophisticated NMS [1,9–11,16]. However, as we will analyze later (Sect. 2), since these proposed methods still base on bounding boxes, it's still difficult for them to distinguish highly overlapped parcels like in Fig. 1. Therefore, to avoid the limit of bounding boxes in object overlapping scenes, our approach is bounding-box free. Further, to resolve the prediction ambiguity in overlapping regions, a multi-level prediction mechanism is proposed to explicitly handle overlapping situation based on parcels' overlapping order.

Besides, we also contribute an overlapped parcel instance segmentation dataset, named OLParcel, which contains 1,539 images with 8,631 parcels in them. Section 4.1 shows more information about OLParcel.

2   Related Work

2.1   Bounding Box in Instance Segmentation

In the instance segmentation task, many methods use bounding boxes as an intermediate representation before generating final masks.

Bounding Box in Generating Proposals. Proposal-based instance segmentation frameworks [6,12,15] need first generate lots of proposals. These region proposals can be regarded as a large set of bounding boxes spanning the full image. However, the overlap of objects increases the difficult in object localization when generating proposals. Some object detection works [26,29] designed new loss functions to address this problem. They enforce proposals to be close to their corresponding ground truths or introduce extra penalties to push proposals away from other ground truths. The quality of detections is improved with the help of these new loss functions. However, since box-based NMS is still used in these frameworks, the issue that overlapped objects may be mistakenly suppressed remains unresolved.

Bounding Box in Generating Masks. Many instance segmentation frameworks like Mask RCNN and its variants [6,12,15] generate final masks by performing binary segmentation inside their proposals. This kind of instance segmentation methods is called box-based method. However, since highly overlapped instances have highly overlapped proposals, it is difficult for them to generate distinguishing predictions for these proposals.

Bounding Box in Post-processing. The effectiveness of naïve box-based NMS is based on the assumption that multiple instances rarely occur at the same location, which is no longer satisfied in the object overlapping scenes. Many improved NMS strategies have been proposed to resolve this issue. For example, Soft-NMS [1] and Softer-NMS [8] suggest decaying the confidence score of the neighboring predictions rather than directly discard them. Jan et al. [10] and Lu et al. [18] proposed a new neural network to perform NMS. Other works such as Tnet [9] and AdaptiveNMS [16], proposed to predict different NMS thresholds for different bounding boxes. Although these works improve the detection performance in object overlapping scenes, it is still difficult to distinguish highly overlapped objects as in Fig. 1 due to their highly overlapped bounding boxes.

In conclusion, based on the above analyses, we argue that one key issue in object overlapping scenes lies in the inherent limit of bounding boxes: highly-overlapped objects always have highly-overlapped bounding boxes. Therefore, we try to build a bounding-box free framework via building our approach based on box-free methods like CondInst [23] and using mask-based NMS in post-processing. Instead of encoding instances into bounding boxes, these box-free methods encode them into "mask coefficients" [2] or "generating filters" [23], which is a much more flexible and accurate way.

2.2   Multiple Instance Prediction

In this paper, we propose a multi-level prediction mechanism to predict a set of overlapped parcels. This idea of multiple instance prediction is not totally new. Some previous works have implied the idea of multiple instance prediction.

Multiple Instance Prediction via Different Object Aspect Ratios. Some networks [6,17,19,20] set various anchor boxes of different aspect ratios at each location. These anchor boxes can be viewed as pre-defined proposals or sliding windows. As a result, this kind of method can predict multiple objects of different aspect ratios at a location with these anchor boxes. However, these pre-defined anchor boxes result in many hyper-parameters. The tuning of these hyper-parameters is very tricky.

Multiple Instance Prediction via Different Object Sizes. Most instance segmentation frameworks have been equipped with feature pyramid network (FPN) [13] to predict objects of different sizes. Therefore, the overlaps caused by different object sizes have been alleviated with this multi-level prediction on many datasets such as COCO [14] and PASCAL VOC [5]. However, in single-class

datasets like our OLParcel, CityPersons [28] or CrowdHuman [22], when objects
are in the same category and have similar size, it is unpractical to resolve overlapping situations only through FPN.

In conclusion, we argue that it's difficult to distinguish overlapped objects
only through their sizes and aspect ratios. It inspires us to design a special
mechanism to explicitly handle this overlapping situation according to the characteristics of overlapped parcels, such as overlapping order.

3   Our Approach: Multi-level Prediction

We propose a multi-level prediction mechanism based on parcels' overlapping
order to resolve the ambiguity about which parcel is to be predicted in the overlapped regions. Parcel Level (PL for short) is defined to describe the overlapping
order of parcels in this paper. Furthermore, to predict parcels of different PLs,
we extend output heads of the instance segmentation framework to multi-level
heads.

The details of our approach are introduced as follows.

3.1   Parcel Level

Algorithm 1. Compute occlusion relations of two parcels

Input:
   M_i is the i-th parcel's mask
   M_j is the j-th parcel's mask
Output:
   $\mathcal{R}$ is a integer representing for occlusion relations between parcel i and parcel j.

1: compute Convex full of M_i: $\mathcal{C}_i = Convex(M_i)$
2: compute Convex full of M_j: $\mathcal{C}_j = Convex(M_j)$
3: compute Intersection over Union between $\mathcal{C}_i$ and $\mathcal{C}_j$: $U_{ij} = \mathcal{C}_i \cap \mathcal{C}_j$
4: **if** $U_{ij} < thr$ **then**
5:     $\mathcal{R} = 0$
6: **else**
7:     compute intersection area between $\mathcal{C}_i$ and $\mathcal{C}_j$: $I_{ij} = \mathcal{C}_i \cap \mathcal{C}_j$
8:     compute intersection area between I_{ij} and M_i: $\mathcal{A}_i = Area(I_{ij}, M_i)$
9:     compute intersection area between I_{ij} and M_j: $\mathcal{A}_j = Area(I_{ij}, M_j)$
10:    **if** $\mathcal{A}_i < \mathcal{A}_j$ **then**
11:        $\mathcal{R} = 1$
12:    **else**
13:        $\mathcal{R} = 0$
14:    **end if**
15: **end if**
16: **return** $\mathcal{R}$

Parcel Level (PL) represents the top-down order of a parcel in overlapped scene. In an image, $PL(i,(x,y))$ means the level of i-th parcel at image location (x,y). It can be computed based on the ground-truth masks of the image. To obtain a parcel's PL, we should know how many parcels are stacked upon it. We decompose this problem into sub problems that how to compute occlusion relations of any two overlapped parcels, namely which one is occluder and which one is occludee. We approximately consider the convex hull calculated by a parcel's visible parts as its non-occluded shape. In the rest paper, we use M_i to denote the ground-truth mask of i-th parcel and C_i to denote the convex hull calculated by M_i. We design Algorithm 1 to compute occlusion relations of two parcels.

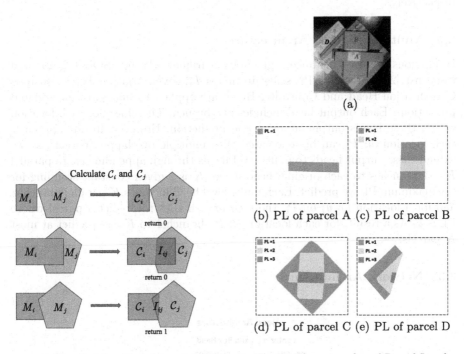

(a)

(b) PL of parcel A (c) PL of parcel B

(d) PL of parcel C (e) PL of parcel D

Fig. 2. Algorithm 1.   **Fig. 3.** The examples of Parcel Level.

The key idea of Algorithm 1 is shown in Fig. 2: for i-th parcel and j-th parcel, we first calculate their convex hulls C_i and C_j; if the Intersection over Union (IoU) between C_i and C_j is larger than a threshold (0.05 by default), we consider these two parcels to be overlapped with each other, otherwise the algorithm returns 0 (the first row in Fig. 2); then we calculate the intersection area I_{ij} of C_i and C_j; if j-th parcel is an occludee, the I_{ij} should be in M_i and not in M_j, and the algorithm also returns 0 (the second row in Fig. 2); if i-th parcel is an occludee, the algorithm returns 1 (the third row in Fig. 2). We label Algorithm 1 as $\mathcal{S}$.

Formally, the PL of i-th parcel at image location (x, y) can be formulated as,

$$PL(i, (x, y)) = \begin{cases} 1 + \sum_{j}^{j \neq i} \mathcal{I}(\mathcal{C}_j, (x, y)) * \mathcal{S}(M_i, M_j), & (x, y) \in \mathcal{C}_i \\ 0, & (x, y) \notin \mathcal{C}_i \end{cases} \quad (1)$$

where $\mathcal{I}$ is a function judging if a location (x, y) is in a parcel's convex hull; $\mathcal{I}$ returns 1 when the location is in the convex hull of this parcel, otherwise returns 0; $\mathcal{S}$ is Algorithm 1. In training phase, we use the PL labels generated by Algorithm 1 and Eq. 1 to train our network.

Figure 3 shows examples of PL. In Fig. 3(a), there are four parcels: parcel A, parcel B, parcel C, and parcel D. The remains show these four parcels' PLs respectively.

3.2 Multi-level Head Architecture

In previous box-free instance segmentation frameworks like SOLOv2 [27] and CondInst [23], on each FPN's feature maps P_i, several output heads, such as Classification Head and Controller Head, are applied to make instance-related predictions. Each output head includes one branch. Therefore, for each location on P_i, these heads output at most one prediction. However, in our approach, each location on P_i can be associated with multiple overlapped parcels, so we extend these output heads to multi-level heads through appending extra parallel $K - 1$ branches to each original head where K is a given constant standing for the maximum PL we predict. Each multi-level head includes K parallel branches, and for a location (x, y) on P_i, the k-th branch tries to predict a parcel whose PL is k. As a result, for each location on P_i, branch 1 to K can predict at most K parcels.

3.3 Network Architecture

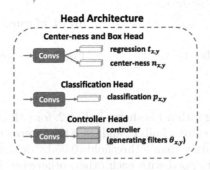

Fig. 4. Head architecture of CondInst.

We choose CondInst [23] as a baseline network to build our framework. Figure 4 shows the head architecture of CondInst. In CondInst, there are three output

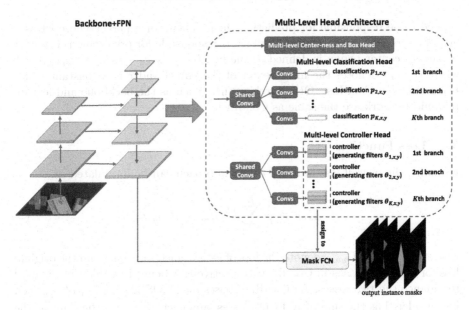

Fig. 5. Network architecture.

heads: Center-ness and Box Head, Classification Head, and Controller Head. Our framework is achieved by extending these output heads to multi-level heads. Figure 5 illustrates our method based on CondInst. The multi-level head architecture in the upper right corner of Fig. 5 includes three multi-level heads: Multi-level Center-ness and Box Head, Multi-level Classification Head, and Multi-level Controller Head (Multi-level Center-ness and Box Head is folded in this figure for the limitation of space). Each multi-level head includes K parallel branches. Following CondInst, each branch is composed of four 3×3 convolutions and a final output layer. Since the parameters in multi-level heads are K times compared to original output heads, we share the first few layers among K branches in each multi-level head to make network parameter-efficient. In our paper, the first one layer is shared on the trade-off between accuracy and computational cost.

For an input image $I \in \mathbb{R}^{H \times W \times 3}$, the goal of our work is to predict the pixel-level mask for each parcel. The ground-truths in our work are defined as $\{(M_i, \mathcal{K}_i)\}$, where $M_i \in \{0, 1\}^{H \times W}$ is the mask for i-th parcel and $\mathcal{K}_i \in \{0, \ldots, K\}^{H \times W}$ is this parcel's PL.

In CondInst, each location on the FPN's feature maps P_i either is associated with a parcel, thus being a positive sample, or is considered a negative sample. In our approach, each location can be associated with multiple parcels. More specifically, let us consider the feature maps $P_i \in \mathbb{R}^{H \times W \times C}$. As shown in previous works, a location (x, y) on the feature maps can be mapped back onto the image as $\left(\lfloor \frac{s}{2} \rfloor + xs, \lfloor \frac{s}{2} \rfloor + ys\right)$ where s is down-sampling ratio of P_i. If the mapped location falls in the center regions of some parcels, the location is considered to be responsible for predicting them. Then, for a parcel whose PL is k at $\left(\lfloor \frac{s}{2} \rfloor + xs, \lfloor \frac{s}{2} \rfloor + ys\right)$, the k-th branch is responsible for predicting this parcel. A parcel's center region is defined as the box $(c_x - rs, c_y - rs, c_x + rs, c_y + rs)$, where (c_x, c_y) denotes the mass center of the parcel and r is a constant scalar being 1.5 as in CondInst. Other architectures such as the backbone and feature pyramid network are the same as CondInst.

3.4   Loss Function

Formally, the overall loss function of our approach can be formulated as,

$$L_{overall} = \frac{1}{K} \sum_{k=1}^{K} L_{output}^k + \lambda L_{mask}, \qquad (2)$$

where L_{output}^k and L_{mask} denote the loss of k-th branch's outputs and the original loss for instance masks in CondInst, respectively. λ being 1 in this work is used to balance the two losses. As CondInst bases on FCOS [24], $\sum_{k=1}^{K} L_{output}^k$ can be considered as the sum of K FCOS losses, and each L_{output}^k is the same as the L_{fcos} in FCOS paper.

3.5   Inference

In inference, given an input image, we forward it through the network to obtain outputs including classification confidence $p_{k,x,y}$, center-ness scores $n_{k,x,y}$, box prediction $t_{k,x,y}$, and generated filters $\theta_{k,x,y}$ where k is represent for k-th branch. We first follow steps in CondInst to obtain new classification score $p_{k,x,y}$ by multiplying original classification confidence $p_{k,x,y}$ with the corresponding center-ness score. Then we use a confidence threshold of 0.05 to filter out predictions with low confidence. Afterwards, for each PL k, the top 100 predictions outputted by k-th branch are used to compute masks. The steps computing masks are the same as CondInst. As a result, there are totally 100K predictions to be used to compute masks. In post-processing, we choose Matrix-NMS proposed in SOLOv2 [27], which based on predicted masks and has similar performance but faster compared to naïve mask-based NMS. These 100k computed masks are sent to Matrix-NMS, and re-scored $p_{k,x,y}$ is obtained. Finally, we choose the masks with $p_{k,x,y} > 0.05$ as final predictions.

4   Experiments

In this section, we evaluate our method from different perspectives.

4.1 Dataset: OLParcel

In this study, we collect a parcel dataset in overlapped scene and name it OLParcel.

The OLParcel dataset contains a total of 1,539 images, including 8,631 parcels. All images are stored in PNG format with the resolution of 360×954. OLParcel is partitioned into a training set and a testing set, the former containing 860 images with 4,856 parcels, and the latter containing 679 images with 3,775 parcels.

Table 1 lists the "Parcel Level Density" about OLParcel. The PLs of only 0.49% parcels are bigger than 2. So we set the max PL as 2, that is $K = 2$, in our experiments.

Table 1. Parcel Level Density in OLParcel

OLParcel	$PL = 1$	$PL = 2$	$PL \geq 3$
Training	87.93%	11.64%	0.43%
Testing	86.33%	13.11%	0.56%
Total	87.23%	12.28%	0.49%

4.2 Evaluation

Following previous works [3,16,22], AP, $recall$ and MR^{-2} [4] are used to evaluate network performances. Besides, for evaluating networks' performance on overlapped parcels more effectively, we design following two additional criterion:

- Overlapped Parcel Average Precision (AP_{OL}), which is only for overlapped parcels. For each prediction, we first calculate IoU with all ground-truths. Then, if the ground-truth having max IoU with this prediction is overlapped, we consider this prediction is responsible for predicting this overlapped parcel and call it overlapped prediction. Finally, we obtain AP_{OL} only using overlapped ground-truths and overlapped predictions.
- Overlapped Parcel Recall ($Recall_{OL}$), which is similar as AP_{OL}. We obtain $Recall_{OL}$ only using overlapped ground-truths and overlapped predictions.

4.3 Experiments on OLParcel

Implementation Details. We employ standard ResNet-50 [7] as the backbone and train it with image scale (shorter side) randomly sampled from [288, 448], which reduces overfitting. Left-right flipping data augmentation is also used during training. Inference is on a single scale of 360 pixels. We use a mini-batch size of 8 images on one GPU and train the model for 20k iterations. The initial learning rate is 0.005 and is decreased by 10 at the 10k iteration and 15k iteration. The backbone is initialized from the pre-trained model on ImageNet [21] classification. Other network settings is the same as original paper [23]. All naïve box-based NMS overlap IoU thresholds are set to 0.6 by default.

Comparison to Baselines. In this experiment, we compare the performance of our method with CondInst [23] and Mask RCNN [6], which are representative works categorized into box-free method and box-based method, respectively. For CondInst, we use the official open-source implementation in AdelaiDet[1]. And for Mask RCNN, we use the official open-source implementation in detectron2[2]. The initial learning rates of CondInst and Mask RCNN are 0.005 and 0.01 respectively. Other settings are the same as our approach.

Table 2. Comparisons of different methods using naïve box-based NMS with different IoU thresholds

IoU*	Method	AP	AP_{OL}	Recall	$Recall_{OL}$	MR^{-2}
0.5	Mask RCNN [6]	91.27	86.90	92.13	88.75	17.71
	CondInst [23]	90.36	87.04	91.36	88.15	18.57
	Ours	92.25	89.10	93.22	90.07	15.93
0.6	Mask RCNN [6]	92.21	89.58	93.75	91.22	16.79
	CondInst [23]	92.17	88.86	93.27	90.98	15.96
	Ours	94.02	92.46	95.50	94.09	**14.66**
0.7	Mask RCNN [6]	92.91	90.12	94.65	92.56	17.83
	CondInst [23]	92.90	90.96	94.70	93.04	18.51
	Ours	94.72	93.16	96.66	95.75	15.09
0.8	Mask RCNN [6]	93.14	90.45	95.60	94.01	20.86
	CondInst [23]	93.18	90.75	95.79	94.66	21.55
	Ours	**95.02**	**93.61**	**97.54**	97.05	16.91
0.9	Mask RCNN [6]	91.38	86.74	96.11	94.78	30.14
	CondInst [23]	92.39	88.86	96.48	95.71	26.42
	Ours	93.27	90.86	97.83	**97.49**	23.35

Table 2 shows comparisons of different methods using naïve box-based NMS with different IoU thresholds. We observe that at the same IoU threshold, our method improves about 1–2% in AP, 1–2% in $recall$, and 3–7% in MR^{-2} compared to CondInst and Mask RCNN. And for more challenge metrics AP_{OL} and $recall_{OL}$, our method obtains 2–3% and 2–4% gains respectively, which indicate the effectiveness of our multi-level prediction mechanism designed for segmenting overlapped parcels. We also observe that compared with default IoU threshold setting (0.6), slightly enlarging the IoU threshold (from 0.6 to 0.8) may help to recall more instances, so AP and $recall$ increase slightly; however, the MR^{-2} index suffers from significantly drops, indicating that high IoU threshold introduces more false predictions with high confidences.

---

[1] https://github.com/aim-uofa/AdelaiDet.
[2] https://github.com/facebookresearch/detectron2.

Table 3. Comparisons of different NMS strategies

NMS	Method	AP	AP_{OL}	$Recall$	$Recall_{OL}$	MR^{-2}
Box-NMS	Mask RCNN [6]	92.21	89.58	93.75	91.22	16.79
	CondInst [23]	92.17	88.86	93.27	90.98	15.96
	Ours	94.02	92.46	95.50	94.09	14.66
Matrix-NMS	Mask RCNN [6]	91.12	89.34	91.54	90.65	16.94
	CondInst [23]	91.49	88.23	92.53	89.81	16.01
	Ours	**96.46**	**95.93**	**98.01**	**97.73**	**9.68**

Table 3 lists the comparison results of different methods with different NMS strategies. The Box-NMS refers to naïve box-based NMS. Compared to use Box-NMS in post-processing, our Matrix-NMS based method improves 2.44% in AP, 2.51% in $recall$, and 4.98% in MR^{-2}, validating the effectiveness of discarding bounding boxes. Surprisingly, for CondInst and Mask RCNN, their performances are slightly dropped when using Matrix-NMS, which suggests that without suitable mechanism designed for overlapped objects, only using mask-base NMS isn't beneficial to performances.

(a) Input   (b) CondInst (c) Mask RCNN(d) Ours: PL=1(e) Ours: PL=2   (f) Ours

Fig. 6. Visual comparison of the baselines and our approach.

Figure 6 shows visual results of baseline models and our approach. The first column are input images. The second column are the CondInst's results. The third column are the Mask RCNN's results. The fourth column are our approach's results produced by $1st$ branch. The fifth column are our approach's results produced by $2nd$ branch. The last column are our approach' results. The score threshold for visualization is 0.3. The failure cases are indicated in red dash boxes. As shown in Fig. 6(b) and 6(c), the baseline models face challenges on predicting overlapped parcels, but our method still works well. In addition, from Fig. 6(d) and Fig. 6(e), we observe that i-th branch is prone to predict these parcels whose PLs are i at parcels' center locations. It's because we label the central regions of parcels as positive samples when training the network.

Comparison with Previous Crowded Detection Works. To our knowledge, there is no instance segmentation work in object overlapping scenes. But some detection works in crowded scene have been proposed which are similar with our work. Therefore, in this experiment, we give a comparison with two object detection works—Soft-NMS [1] and CrowdDet [3]—using object detection metrics. CrowdDet is the state-of-the-art method in crowded detection. We re-implement the Soft-NMS according to original paper [1]. For CrowdDet, we use the official open-source implementation[3]. Both methods use the initial learning rate 0.01. Other settings are the same as our approach.

Table 4 shows the comparison results. For our instance segmentation method, we can obtain predicted bounding boxes through outputs of box branch or predicted masks, so we report our results based on both ways (the last row and the second to the last row in Table 4, respectively).

According to Table 4, our method improves about 1–2% in AP, 1–3% in $recall$, and 5–8% in MR^{-2} compared to CrowdDet and Soft-NMS, which further indicates our approach is very effective to deal with these scenes again.

Table 4. Comparison with previous crowded detection works

Method	AP	$Recall$	MR^{-2}
FPN + Soft NMS [1]	94.88	97.67	20.55
CrowdDet (with RM) [3]	94.22	96.00	17.85
Ours (predicted masks)	95.62	**98.04**	13.85
Ours (box branch)	**95.71**	97.96	**12.68**

4.4 Ablation Studies

In this section, we study the impact of different shared layer numbers in multi-level heads.

As mentioned in Sect. 3.2, in each multi-level head, we share the first few layers between branches to make network parameter-efficient. It's easy to see that the shared layers try to capture the common features among different PLs and the latter layers try to capture specialized features only used in a single PL. Table 5 shows the results. The AP and MR^{-2} improves slowly with the decrease of shared layer number, but $recall$ decreases slightly. After shared layer number reduces to one, the gains become much small, and thus setting the number of shared layers to one is a nice choice.

---

[3] https://github.com/Purkialo/CrowdDet

Table 5. Results with different number of shared layers in multi-level heads

Number	AP	AP_{OL}	Recall	$Recall_{OL}$	MR^{-2}
4	96.25	95.06	**98.38**	**98.06**	13.24
3	96.30	95.60	98.04	97.69	11.01
2	96.26	95.56	97.70	97.37	10.33
1	**96.46**	**95.93**	98.01	97.73	**9.68**
0	96.39	95.92	97.83	97.57	9.75

5 Conclusion

In this work, we propose a new instance segmentation framework based on a multi-level prediction mechanism for segmenting overlapped parcels. The multi-level prediction mechanism is implemented by extending prediction heads to multiple branches. In addition, bounding-box is abandoned to improve the segmentation performance of overlapped parcels. Finally, the experimental results have demonstrated the effectiveness of our proposed method.

Theoretically, our approach also can be applied to other box-free instance segmentation frameworks like SOLOv2. This still needs to be done.

References

1. Bodla, N., Singh, B., Chellappa, R., Davis, L.S.: Soft-NMS-improving object detection with one line of code. In: Proceedings of the IEEE Conference on Computer Vision and Pattern Recognition, pp. 5561–5569 (2017)
2. Bolya, D., Zhou, C., Xiao, F., Lee, Y.J.: YOLACT: real-time instance segmentation. In: Proceedings of the IEEE/CVF International Conference on Computer Vision, pp. 9157–9166 (2019)
3. Chu, X., Zheng, A., Zhang, X., Sun, J.: Detection in crowded scenes: one proposal, multiple predictions. In: Proceedings of the IEEE/CVF Conference on Computer Vision and Pattern Recognition, pp. 12214–12223 (2020)
4. Dollar, P., Wojek, C., Schiele, B., Perona, P.: Pedestrian detection: an evaluation of the state of the art. IEEE Trans. Pattern Anal. Mach. Intell. **34**(4), 743–761 (2011)
5. Everingham, M., Eslami, S.A., Van Gool, L., Williams, C.K., Winn, J., Zisserman, A.: The pascal visual object classes challenge: a retrospective. Int. J. Comput. Vis. **111**(1), 98–136 (2015)
6. He, K., Gkioxari, G., Dollár, P., Girshick, R.: Mask R-CNN. In: Proceedings of the IEEE Conference on Computer Vision and Pattern Recognition, pp. 2961–2969 (2017)
7. He, K., Zhang, X., Ren, S., Sun, J.: Deep residual learning for image recognition. In: Proceedings of the IEEE Conference on Computer Vision and Pattern Recognition, pp. 770–778 (2016)
8. He, Y., Zhu, C., Wang, J., Savvides, M., Zhang, X.: Bounding box regression with uncertainty for accurate object detection. In: Proceedings of the IEEE/CVF Conference on Computer Vision and Pattern Recognition, pp. 2888–2897 (2019)

9. Hosang, J., Benenson, R., Schiele, B.: A convnet for non-maximum suppression. In: Rosenhahn, B., Andres, B. (eds.) GCPR 2016. LNCS, vol. 9796, pp. 192–204. Springer, Cham (2016). https://doi.org/10.1007/978-3-319-45886-1_16

10. Hosang, J., Benenson, R., Schiele, B.: Learning non-maximum suppression. In: Proceedings of the IEEE Conference on Computer Vision and Pattern Recognition, pp. 4507–4515 (2017)

11. Huang, X., Ge, Z., Jie, Z., Yoshie, O.: NMS by representative region: Towards crowded pedestrian detection by proposal pairing. In: Proceedings of the IEEE/CVF Conference on Computer Vision and Pattern Recognition, pp. 10750–10759 (2020)

12. Huang, Z., Huang, L., Gong, Y., Huang, C., Wang, X.: Mask scoring R-CNN. In: Proceedings of the IEEE/CVF Conference on Computer Vision and Pattern Recognition, pp. 6409–6418 (2019)

13. Lin, T.Y., Dollár, P., Girshick, R., He, K., Hariharan, B., Belongie, S.: Feature pyramid networks for object detection. In: Proceedings of the IEEE Conference on Computer Vision and Pattern Recognition, pp. 2117–2125 (2017)

14. Lin, T.-Y., et al.: Microsoft COCO: common objects in context. In: Fleet, D., Pajdla, T., Schiele, B., Tuytelaars, T. (eds.) ECCV 2014. LNCS, vol. 8693, pp. 740–755. Springer, Cham (2014). https://doi.org/10.1007/978-3-319-10602-1_48

15. Liu, S., Qi, L., Qin, H., Shi, J., Jia, J.: Path aggregation network for instance segmentation. In: Proceedings of the IEEE Conference on Computer Vision and Pattern Recognition, pp. 8759–8768 (2018)

16. Liu, S., Huang, D., Wang, Y.: Adaptive NMS: Refining pedestrian detection in a crowd. In: Proceedings of the IEEE/CVF Conference on Computer Vision and Pattern Recognition, pp. 6459–6468 (2019)

17. Liu, W., et al.: SSD: single shot multibox detector. In: Leibe, B., Matas, J., Sebe, N., Welling, M. (eds.) ECCV 2016. LNCS, vol. 9905, pp. 21–37. Springer, Cham (2016). https://doi.org/10.1007/978-3-319-46448-0_2

18. Qi, L., Liu, S., Shi, J., Jia, J.: Sequential context encoding for duplicate removal. In: Proceedings of the 32nd International Conference on Neural Information Processing Systems, pp. 2053–2062 (2018)

19. Redmon, J., Farhadi, A.: YOLO9000: better, faster, stronger. In: Proceedings of the IEEE Conference on Computer Vision and Pattern Recognition, pp. 7263–7271 (2017)

20. Ren, S., He, K., Girshick, R., Sun, J.: Faster R-CNN: towards real-time object detection with region proposal networks. IEEE Trans. Pattern Anal. Mach. Intell. **39**(6), 1137–1149 (2016)

21. Russakovsky, O., et al.: ImageNet large scale visual recognition challenge. Int. J. Comput. Vis. **115**(3), 211–252 (2015)

22. Shao, S., et al.: CrowdHuman: a benchmark for detecting human in a crowd. arXiv preprint arXiv:1805.00123 (2018)

23. Tian, Z., Shen, C., Chen, H.: Conditional convolutions for instance segmentation. In: Vedaldi, A., Bischof, H., Brox, T., Frahm, J.-M. (eds.) ECCV 2020. LNCS, vol. 12346, pp. 282–298. Springer, Cham (2020). https://doi.org/10.1007/978-3-030-58452-8_17

24. Tian, Z., Shen, C., Chen, H., He, T.: FCOS: fully convolutional one-stage object detection. In: Proceedings of the IEEE/CVF International Conference on Computer Vision, pp. 9627–9636 (2019)

25. Wang, X., Kong, T., Shen, C., Jiang, Y., Li, L.: SOLO: segmenting objects by locations. In: Vedaldi, A., Bischof, H., Brox, T., Frahm, J.-M. (eds.) ECCV 2020.

LNCS, vol. 12363, pp. 649–665. Springer, Cham (2020). https://doi.org/10.1007/978-3-030-58523-5_38

26. Wang, X., Xiao, T., Jiang, Y., Shao, S., Sun, J., Shen, C.: Repulsion loss: detecting pedestrians in a crowd. In: Proceedings of the IEEE Conference on Computer Vision and Pattern Recognition, pp. 7774–7783 (2018)

27. Wang, X., Zhang, R., Kong, T., Li, L., Shen, C.: SOLOv2: dynamic and fast instance segmentation. Adv. Neural Inf. Process. Syst. **33**, 17721–17732 (2020)

28. Zhang, S., Benenson, R., Schiele, B.: CityPersons: a diverse dataset for pedestrian detection. In: Proceedings of the IEEE Conference on Computer Vision and Pattern Recognition, pp. 3213–3221 (2017)

29. Zhang, S., Wen, L., Bian, X., Lei, Z., Li, S.Z.: Occlusion-aware R-CNN: detecting pedestrians in a crowd. In: Proceedings of the European Conference on Computer Vision (ECCV), pp. 637–653 (2018)

Knowledge Distillation for Action Recognition Based on RGB and Infrared Videos

Zhenzhen Quan[1], Qingshan Chen[1], Kun Zhao[2], Zhi Liu[1](✉),
and Yujun Li[1](✉)

[1] School of Information Science and Engineering, Shandong University,
Qingdao 266237, Shandong, China
{liuzhi,liyujun}@sdu.edu.cn
[2] Inspur Electronic Information Industry Co., Ltd., Jinan 250101, Shandong, China

Abstract. Most internet videos and surveillance system videos are based on RGB images. In recent years, with the popularization of infrared imagers, infrared images have been gradually used in surveillance systems. The combination of infrared and RGB images brings many advantages to the field of video surveillance. In this paper, we propose a knowledge distillation method based on RGB and infrared videos to classifying person actions. The teacher network is trained by employing RGB videos, and the student network is trained by using infrared data. We learn the RGB action knowledge in the teacher network through knowledge distillation, and reduce the difference between the RGB and infrared modality by narrowing the difference between the significant characteristics of the RGB images and the infrared images. We make an experimental comparison on NTU RGB+D dataset. The outcomes demonstrate that the approach we put forward is superior to the most cross-sectional and most advanced action recognition methods based on infrared.

Keywords: Action recognition · Infrared · RGB · Knowledge distillation

1 Introduction

Action recognition is one of the key technologies of intelligent video surveillance systems, and it is also one of the research hotspots in the field of computer vision. The primary assignment is to voluntarily identify human behavior from video sequences. In addition to being applied to video surveillance systems, effective behavior recognition technology can also be extensively used in video retrieval, man-machine interaction and other fields.

So far, most internet videos and surveillance system videos are based on RGB. In recent years, with the popularization of infrared imagers, infrared spectroscopy images have been gradually used in surveillance systems [1–4]. In the military field, small target recognition based on infrared images is an

© Springer Nature Singapore Pte Ltd. 2022
G. Zhai et al. (Eds.): IFTC 2021, CCIS 1560, pp. 18–29, 2022.
https://doi.org/10.1007/978-981-19-2266-4_2

important task of the military early warning system. In civil use, infrared images also have a broad application, including unmanned driving technology and unmanned aerial vehicle technology, which require detection, identification and screening of surrounding environmental information. The combination of infrared and RGB image brings many advantages to the field of video surveillance. Infrared image is a direct reflection of the thermal radiation energy of the object, and has the advantages of strong anti-interference ability and high sensitivity. Using infrared images, we can clearly observe the situation ahead in a completely dark night or on a battlefield with dense clouds, which are difficult to show in RGB images. However, infrared images also have some shortcomings, such as the lack of clear appearance and texture characteristics of the imaged objects. In addition, there is strong noise and background clutter interference inside the infrared imager receiver, which makes infrared images have the problems of long-scale contrast, low signal to noise ratio and coarse resolution, while RGB graphics can overcome the existing problems of infrared images to a certain extent [5,6].

Therefore, the combination of infrared and RGB images is of great significance in applications such as intelligent monitoring. Action recognition based on infrared and RGB videos aim to use the complementarity of the two spectrum video images of infrared and RGB, and to train the model to identify the behavior information of interest in the video. Compared with the vigorous development of action recognition algorithms based on RGB, the existing infrared and RGB image action recognition algorithms have fewer related algorithms and lack of data, and they are rarely used in practical applications. However, this method of combining multiple spectral images is gradually becoming a research field that is urgently needed in reality, and has received more and more attention.

Knowledge distillation can distill knowledge from a large network to a small one, improving the accuracy of the small network. Its biggest advantage is that it reduces network parameters, achieves model compression, and has strong portability. Therefore, in order to leverage the advantages of RGB images and knowledge distillation, we put forward a knowledge distillation method based on RGB images and infrared images.

The contributions of this paper are as follows:

(1) In order to reduce network resources and make up for the lack of infrared datasets, we construct a knowledge distillation network, using the commonly RGB action recognition network as the teacher network, and infrared data to feed small student network. The RGB modality behavior information can be learned through distillation loss.
(2) To take full advantage of supplementary knowledge of RGB videos and to further narrow the difference between RGB modality and infrared modality, we consider minimize the difference between the significant characteristics of RGB videos and infrared videos.
(3) We carry out extensive experiments on the NTU RGB+D, and the outcomes demonstrate that our raised algorithm is efficient and feasible.

The organization of this paper is: Related works is retrospected in Sect. 2. The raised method is recommended in Sect. 3. The outcomes and related discussions are introduced in Sect. 4. At last, the conclusion is in Sect. 5.

2 Related Work

2.1 Action Recognition Based on RGB and Infrared

Action recognition based on RGB modality has been extensively studied in past few years [7,8]. Karpathy et al. [9] put forward a means of processing the input into a low-resolution stream and a high-resolution stream, which significantly decreases the training time of the CNN without affecting the accuracy. Simonyan et al. [10] raised the two-stream convolution network to train multi-frame density optical flow, and utilized the multi-task training method to combine the two action classification datasets for purpose of increasing training data, and ultimately achieved better results on both datasets. Tran et al. [11] introduced an approach to use deep 3-dimensional convolutional networks (3D ConvNets) for the sake of learning spatiotemporal features. Donahue et al. [12] designed Long-term Recurrent Convolutional Networks (LRCNs) combining convolutional layers and long-term recursion, which is a type of structure for image recognition and description. TSN [13] used a sparse sampling strategy to utilize the information of the entire video. Lin et al. [14] proposed a universal and efficient time-domain drift module (TSM), which has the characteristics of high efficiency and high performance. In addition, there are also networks including TEA [15] and ACTION-Net [16] that consider motion characteristics and have achieved good results.

Recently, many methods including optical flow method [17], spatiotemporal interest points [18], and motion history maps [5], have been applied for infrared action recognition. In addition, some methods based on deep learning have also been raised for infrared action recognition. Gao et al. [19] constructed an Infrared Action Recognition (InfAR) dataset, which is captured at different times. The effective of InfAR dataset on low-level features and deep convolutional neural network (CNN) is also verified. Jiang et al. [20] introduced the discriminative code layer and the corresponding discriminative code loss function to design a neoteric two-stream 3D CNN architecture. They obtained better performance than the method raised in [19]. However, 3D convolutional neural network had high requirements for computing ability. Wang et al. [21] put forward to use CNN to study convolutional features, and use trajectory-constrained sample and pooling strategy to aggregate convolutional features to form a descriptor. And Liu et al. [22] introduced three-stream TDDs (TSTDDs) method to inquire feature maps from CNN.

2.2 Knowledge Distillation

Hinton et al. [23] first introduced the concept of knowledge distillation, which is to distill knowledge from a large network onto a small one. The process of knowledge distillation is obtained by constructing the distillation loss. Adriana et al.

[24] was mainly aimed at extending the knowledge distillation method proposed by Hinton [23], allowing the student network to be deeper and narrower than the teacher network, using the output of the teacher network and the features of the middle layer as hints to improve the training process and the performance of the student network. Lopez-Paz et al. [25] introduced theoretical and causal insights on the internal workings of generalized distillation, and extended it to unsupervised, semi-supervised and multi-task learning environments, and illustrated its effectiveness in various numerical simulations of synthetic and real data. [26] proposed a feature fusion method based on canonical correlation analysis (CCA) and knowledge distillation. The generated features were the approximation and weight regularization of the features generated by CCA. This method utilized to the scene classification with RGB and infrared images. Considering that knowledge distillation has the advantage of distilling knowledge to small networks and greatly reducing network parameters, we plan to put forward a knowledge distillation method to classify RGB and infrared action videos.

3   Method

Our goal is to assist the training in the student network with infrared data by leveraging the knowledge distilled from the teacher network with RGB data. The method framework is shown in Fig. 1. RGB videos is used as input to train the teacher network, and infrared video is employed as input to train a small one. The difference between the two modalities is reduced by minimizing the loss of salient features. The raised method learn RGB modality behavior features from teacher network to improve the accuracy of infrared action recognition.

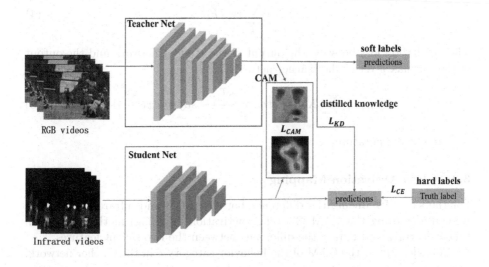

Fig. 1. The architecture of the proposed method.

3.1 Knowledge Distillation

Let $f_k^T(x, y)$ denote the k-th unit on the last convolutional layer of the teacher network, and $f_k^S(x, y)$ denote the k-th unit on the last convolutional layer of the student network.

The total activation degree F_k^T after global average pooling for teacher network is:

$$F_k^T = \sum_{x,y} f_k^T(x, y) \tag{1}$$

where x and y are the input and output of convolutional layer, k is the k-th unit on the convolutional layer, and T represent the teacher network.

The total activation degree F_k^S after global average pooling for student network is:

$$F_k^S = \sum_{x,y} f_k^S(x, y) \tag{2}$$

Therefore, for the action category given by the teacher network, the corresponding category score of the softmax layer is:

$$S_c^T = \sum_k w_k^{cT} F_k^T \tag{3}$$

where w_k^{cT} is the weight value of the k-th unit under the corresponding behavior category of the teacher network, and this value indicates the importance of F_k^T under the behavior category c.

For the behavior category c given by the student network, the corresponding category score of the softmax layer is:

$$S_c^S = \sum_k w_k^{cS} F_k^S \tag{4}$$

The distillation loss between the output of the student network and the output of the softmax layer of the teacher network is:

$$L_{KD} = \sum_c KL(softmax(\frac{S_c^T}{\tau}) - softmax(\frac{S_c^S}{\tau})) \tag{5}$$

τ represent temperature.

3.2 Class Activation Mapping

For the sake of reducing the difference between RGB and infrared modalities, we consider using the CAM [27] (class activation mapping) method to obtain salient features and reduce the difference between the two salient features.

Consider M_c^T is the CAM of the behavior category c in the teacher network, each space element is:

$$M_c^T(x, y) = \sum_k w_k^{cT} f_k^T(x, y) \tag{6}$$

where $M_c^T(x, y)$ denote the degree of significance for category c at the spatial position (x, y) of an image.

Combining (2) and (3), we can get:

$$S_c^T = \sum_{x,y} M_c^T(x, y) \tag{7}$$

Define $M_c^S(x, y)$ is the CAM of the behavior category c in the student network, the CAM loss is mean square error loss between the CAM of the teacher network and the CAM of the student network.

$$L_{CAM} = \sum_{i=1}^{m} \left\| \frac{M_{ci}^T(x, y)}{\|M_{ci}^T(x, y)\|_2} - \frac{M_{ci}^S(x, y)}{\|M_{ci}^S(x, y)\|_2} \right\|_2^2 \tag{8}$$

And the standard cross-entropy loss L_{CE} is

$$L_{CE} = -\sum_{c} q_c \log P_c^S \tag{9}$$

where q_c is the truth label for the behavior category c, $P_c^S = \frac{\exp(S_c^S)}{\sum_c \exp(S_c^S)}$ is the probability of the corresponding behavior category c output by the softmax layer of the student network.

Therefore, the total loss is the sum of the CAM loss L_{CAM}, the distillation loss L_{KD} and the standard cross-entropy loss L_{CE}.

$$L = L_{CE} + \alpha \tau^2 L_{KD} + \beta L_{CAM} \tag{10}$$

The process of the method can be split into next steps:

(1) Give the truth label q_c and the hyper-parameters α, τ, β;
(2) Train the teacher network F^T;
(3) Obtain the category score S_c^T and S_c^S, the degree of significance $M_c^T(x, y)$ and $M_c^S(x, y)$;
(4) Obtain the cross-entropy loss L_{CE} between q_c and the output of F^S, the CAM loss L_{CAM} of F^T and F^S, and the distillation loss L_{KD} of F^T and F^S;
(5) Train F^S with minimize L.

4 Experimental Results

4.1 Dataset

The proposed method is evaluated on a large dataset NTU RGB+D [28]. NTU RGB+D dataset consists of sixty action classes and more than fifty-six thousand videos in total, which is taken by 3 Kinect V2 cameras at the same time. For each sample, the dataset includes RGB videos, depth map sequences, 3D skeletal data, and infrared (IR) videos. RGB videos resolutions are 1920×1080, while depth maps and IR videos are in 512 × 424. The 3D skeletal data includes 3D coordinates of twenty five body joints per frame. We select ten classifications (A001-A010) of RGB and infrared data to evaluate our method, including drinking, eating, tooth brushing, washing hair, drop, pickup, throw, sitting down, standing up, and clapping. After extracting images from the RGB video and infrared video in the dataset, some action examples are shown in Fig. 2.

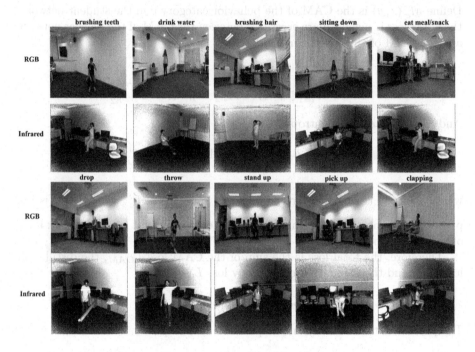

Fig. 2. Examples of NTU RGB+D dataset.

4.2 Experimental Settings

In our experiments, we randomly split NTU RGB+D dataset into training and testing sets. We randomly select 80% of the samples in each class as training samples, and the rest samples as testing. We utilize the RGB videos in NTU RGB+D dataset to train teacher network. According to the TSN method [13], we divide RGB videos into 3 segments, and send them to the teacher network [14] for training. Then we use the trained teacher network to train the student model by using infrared videos as input based on the network architecture in Fig. 1.

We employ ResNet50 as the backbone for the teacher network and ResNet18 for the student network due to the small parameters. The temperature is set to 4 because the student network is relatively small, and there is unnecessary to acquire too much negative knowledge from the teacher network. The training parameters for the NTU RGB+D are: 50 training epochs, initial learning rate 0.001 (decays by 0.1 at epoch 20 and 40), weight decay 5e−4, batch size 16, segment 8, and dropout 0.8. All the experiments are preformed on two NVIDIA RTX 2080Ti GPUs using PyTorch [29]. We set hyper-parameters α and β in Sect. 4.4.

4.3   Evaluations on NTU RGB+D Dataset

We evaluate the proposed method by using the NTU RGB+D dataset. Compared with the knowledge distillation method [23], the method combining knowledge distillation and CAM has a better effect. Table 1 exhibits the consequences.

Table 1 exhibits that the raised method is superior to HOG + SVM, TSTDDs, knowledge distillation and attention transfer method. Both method based on knowledge distillation and our method are better than the result of the student network. The best result of knowledge distillation method achieves the accuracy of 74.69 from experiments which hyper-parameter α is set in $\{0.01, 0.1, 1\}$, 3.5% higher than baseline method (accuracy is up to 71.20). It proves that we can get useful RGB information from RGB action recognition network for infrared action recognition. Our method gets 76.03 accuracy when hyper-parameters α and β are set in $\{0.1, 1\}$, 4.83% higher than baseline. This shows that the knowledge distillation and CAM method have better effects by reducing the difference between RGB and infrared and learning the key feature representations of RGB modality.

Table 1. Recognition results (%) of different methods on NTU RGB+D dataset.

Method	NTU RGB+D
HOG [30] + SVM	48.92
TSTDDs [22]	72.36
TSN [13] + ResNet18 (Student Network)	71.20
Knowledge Distillation [23] ($\alpha = 0.1$)	74.69
Attention Transfer [31]	74.58
Ours	**76.03**

4.4   Ablation Study

The consequence of the teacher network and student network is exhibited in Table 2. The outcome of the teacher network represents the accuracy of RGB behavior recognition. Due to the high resolution of the RGB image, the behavior characteristics can be clearly obtained, so the recognition rate of the teacher network is much higher. Knowledge distillation method is higher than the student network trained result, indicating that it has learned useful information about action. After adding to reduce the significant feature difference between

RGB and infrared modality, the recognition rate is up to 76.03. It is said that the significant feature includes modal difference. After adding the distillation method, the recognition rate of the student network is still very different from the recognition rate of the teacher network. The reason is that the parameters of the student network are twice as small as the teacher network. The advantage of using a small network is that it can reduce parameters and improve portability.

There are two hyper-parameters α and β in Eq. (9). For the sake of understanding how they affect the performance, we employ a grid-search means to carry on the parameter sensitivity analysis on NTU RGB+D dataset. The parameter α and β take their values from $\{0.01, 0.1, 1\}$. Table 3 demonstrates the performance of our method. From the table, we can get the optimum values is $\{0.1, 1\}$. It means that the significant characteristics should be more important than knowledge distillation, because the significant characteristics greatly contributes to multi-modal feature fusion.

Table 2. Comparisons of different models. The teacher network, student network, knowledge distillation, knowledge distillation and CAM.

Method	NTU RGB+D
TSM [14] + ResNet50 (Teacher Network)	90.53
TSN [13] + ResNet18 (Student Network)	71.20
Ours (W/O CAM)	74.69
Ours (W/O Knowledge Distillation)	74.48
Ours	**76.03**

Table 3. Parameters sensitivity analysis of α and β on NTU RGB+D dataset.

α	β	NTU RGB+D
0.01	1	75.61
0.1	**1**	**76.03**
1	1	72.95
1	0.1	72.54
1	0.01	72.13

5   Conclusion

In this paper, we propose a knowledge distillation method based on RGB and infrared videos to classifying human actions. We employ RGB videos to train the teacher network, while infrared videos to train the student network. We can learn RGB action feature information in the teacher network through knowledge distillation, and reduce the difference between the two modalities by narrowing the difference between the significant characteristics of the RGB images and the infrared images. Effectiveness experiments on action recognition dataset NTU RGB+D demonstrate the effectiveness of our method. In the future, we will consider how to better integrate the low-level feature of RGB and infrared modality.

Acknowledgements. This paper is partially supported by the Major Fundamental Research of Shandong Provincial Natural Science Foundation under Grant ZR2019ZD05, the Key Research & Development Project of Shandong Province under Grant 2019JZZY020119, and Shandong Provincial Natural Science Foundation Intelligent Computing Joint Fund under Grant ZR2020LZH013. The NTU RGB+D Action Recognition Dataset we employed made by the ROSE Lab at the Nanyang Technological University, Singapore.

References

1. Gao, C., Wang, L., Xiao, Y., Zhao, Q., Meng, D.: Infrared small-dim target detection based on Markov random field guided noise modeling. Pattern Recogn. **76**, 463–475 (2018)
2. Wang, L., Gao, C., Jian, J., Tang, L., Liu, J.: Semantic feature based multi-spectral saliency detection. Multimed. Tools Appl. **77**(3), 3387–3403 (2017). https://doi.org/10.1007/s11042-017-5152-5
3. Meng, H., Pears, N., Bailey, C.: A human action recognition system for embedded computer vision application. In: 2007 IEEE Conference on Computer Vision and Pattern Recognition, pp. 1–6. IEEE (2007)
4. Tian, Y., Cao, L., Liu, Z., Zhang, Z.: Hierarchical filtered motion for action recognition in crowded videos. IEEE Trans. Syst. Man Cybern. Part C (Appl. Rev.) **42**(3), 313–323 (2011)
5. Bobick, A.F., Davis, J.W.: The recognition of human movement using temporal templates. IEEE Trans. Pattern Anal. Mach. Intell. **23**(3), 257–267 (2001)
6. Bobick, A.F., Wilson, A.D.: A state-based approach to the representation and recognition of gesture. IEEE Trans. Pattern Anal. Mach. Intell. **19**(12), 1325–1337 (1997)
7. Gan, C., Yao, T., Yang, K., Yang, Y., Mei, T.: You lead, we exceed: labor-free video concept learning by jointly exploiting web videos and images. In: Proceedings of the IEEE Conference on Computer Vision and Pattern Recognition, pp. 923–932 (2016)
8. Peng, X., Wang, L., Wang, X., Qiao, Y.: Bag of visual words and fusion methods for action recognition: comprehensive study and good practice. Comput. Vis. Image Underst. **150**, 109–125 (2016)
9. Karpathy, A., Toderici, G., Shetty, S., Leung, T., Sukthankar, R., Fei-Fei, L.: Large-scale video classification with convolutional neural networks. In: Proceedings of the IEEE Conference on Computer Vision and Pattern Recognition, pp. 1725–1732 (2014)
10. Simonyan, K., Zisserman, A.: Two-stream convolutional networks for action recognition in videos. arXiv preprint arXiv:1406.2199 (2014)
11. Tran, D., Bourdev, L., Fergus, R., Torresani, L., Paluri, M.: Learning spatiotemporal features with 3D convolutional networks. In: Proceedings of the IEEE International Conference on Computer Vision, pp. 4489–4497 (2015)

12. Donahue, J., et al.: Long-term recurrent convolutional networks for visual recognition and description. In: Proceedings of the IEEE Conference on Computer Vision and Pattern Recognition, pp. 2625–2634 (2015)
13. Wang, L., et al.: Temporal segment networks: towards good practices for deep action recognition. In: Leibe, B., Matas, J., Sebe, N., Welling, M. (eds.) ECCV 2016. LNCS, vol. 9912, pp. 20–36. Springer, Cham (2016). https://doi.org/10.1007/978-3-319-46484-8_2
14. Lin, J., Gan, C., Han, S.: TSM: temporal shift module for efficient video understanding. In: Proceedings of the IEEE/CVF International Conference on Computer Vision, pp. 7083–7093 (2019)
15. Li, Y., Ji, B., Shi, X., Zhang, J., Kang, B., Wang, L.: Tea: temporal excitation and aggregation for action recognition. In: Proceedings of the IEEE/CVF Conference on Computer Vision and Pattern Recognition, pp. 909–918 (2020)
16. Wang, Z., She, Q., Smolic, A.: Action-Net: multipath excitation for action recognition. In: Proceedings of the IEEE/CVF Conference on Computer Vision and Pattern Recognition, pp. 13 214–13 223 (2021)
17. Weinzaepfel, P., Revaud, J., Harchaoui, Z., Schmid, C.: DeepFlow: large displacement optical flow with deep matching. In: Proceedings of the IEEE International Conference on Computer Vision, pp. 1385–1392 (2013)
18. Laptev, I.: On space-time interest points. Int. J. Comput. Vis. **64**(2), 107–123 (2005)
19. Gao, C., et al.: Infar dataset: infrared action recognition at different times. Neurocomputing **212**, 36–47 (2016)
20. Jiang, Z., Rozgic, V., Adali, S.: Learning spatiotemporal features for infrared action recognition with 3D convolutional neural networks. In: Proceedings of the IEEE Conference on Computer Vision and Pattern Recognition Workshops, pp. 115–123 (2017)
21. Wang, L., Qiao, Y., Tang, X.: Action recognition with trajectory-pooled deep-convolutional descriptors. In: Proceedings of the IEEE Conference on Computer Vision and Pattern Recognition, pp. 4305–4314 (2015)
22. Liu, Y., Lu, Z., Li, J., Yang, T., Yao, C.: Global temporal representation based CNNs for infrared action recognition. IEEE Signal Process. Lett. **25**(6), 848–852 (2018)
23. Hinton, G., Vinyals, O., Dean, J.: Distilling the knowledge in a neural network. arXiv preprint arXiv:1503.02531 (2015)
24. Romero, A., Ballas, N., Kahou, S.E., Chassang, A., Gatta, C., Bengio, Y.: FitNets: hints for thin deep nets. arXiv preprint arXiv:1412.6550 (2014)
25. Lopez-Paz, D., Bottou, L., Schölkopf, B., Vapnik, V.: Unifying distillation and privileged information. arXiv preprint arXiv:1511.03643 (2015)
26. Peng, X., Li, Y., Wei, X., Luo, J., Murphey, Y.L.: RGB-NIR image categorization with prior knowledge transfer. EURASIP J. Image Video Process. **2018**(1), 1–11 (2018)
27. Zhou, B., Khosla, A., Lapedriza, A., Oliva, A., Torralba, A.: Learning deep features for discriminative localization. In: Proceedings of the IEEE Conference on Computer Vision and Pattern Recognition, pp. 2921–2929 (2016)
28. Shahroudy, A., Liu, J., Ng, T.-T., Wang, G.: NTU RGB+D: a large scale dataset for 3D human activity analysis. In: Proceedings of the IEEE Conference on Computer Vision and Pattern Recognition, pp. 1010–1019 (2016)
29. Paszke, A., et al.: Pytorch: an imperative style, high-performance deep learning library. In: Advances Neural Information Processing Systems, vol. 32, pp. 8026–8037 (2019)

30. Dalal, N., Triggs, B.: Histograms of oriented gradients for human detection. In: 2005 IEEE Computer Society Conference on Computer Vision and Pattern Recognition (CVPR 2005), vol. 1, pp. 886–893. IEEE (2005)
31. Zagoruyko, S., Komodakis, N.: Paying more attention to attention: improving the performance of convolutional neural networks via attention transfer. arXiv preprint arXiv:1612.03928 (2016)

A Text Classification Method Based Automobile Data Management

Lutao Wang[1], Zhenyu Chen[1(✉)], Lisha Wu[1], Cuiling Jia[2], and Jinlong Hao[2]

[1] Big Data Center, State Grid Corporation of China, Beijing, China
czy9907@126.com
[2] Beijing China-Power Information Technology Co., Ltd., Beijing 100089, China

Abstract. The state grid has a large number of assets, the physical part of these assets involves many categories, such as power equipment, real estate, vehicles and so on. The state grid needs to record and manage these assets, which involves the process of storing equipment and assets with specific IDs. However, because the type of equipment and assets are not uniformly coded across provinces, and various text descriptions vary from one to another, making this management and recording process is very difficult and complex. FastText is a text-based classifier, its N-gram model can read the sequential information between words and is faster than most other models, so we decide to use FastText to solve this problem, that is, through the classification of text to record various equipment and assets. It is suitable for the need for automatic identification of equipment and assets in this project. The purpose of this method is to ensure the correct correspondence with the type of equipment and assets according to the standard rules of technical object types of the state grid. FastText has a good classification accuracy, and so far, the method has achieved good results in the automotive category.

Keywords: Feature extraction · Natural language processing (NLP) · Classification

1 Introduction

From 2012 to now, a large number of new technologies and solutions have emerged in the AI field. Deep Learning has the problems that need to be dealt with and faced are becoming more and more complex, from machine vision to speech recognition. More complex applications have emerged, requiring more advanced technical solutions.

In many natural language processing (NLP) applications, text classification refers to the process by which a computer maps a piece of text containing information to a predetermined category or categories. The application scenarios of text classification include: identifying whether an email is harassment or advertising and marketing spam, classifying article categories, film reviews and product reviews. The main process of text classification is: first, the text data of the preprocessing model. Shallow learning models usually require manual methods to obtain good sample features, and then use classic machine learning algorithms to classify them. However, unlike shallow models,

© Springer Nature Singapore Pte Ltd. 2022
G. Zhai et al. (Eds.): IFTC 2021, CCIS 1560, pp. 30–41, 2022.
https://doi.org/10.1007/978-981-19-2266-4_3

deep learning integrates feature engineering directly into the output by learning a set of nonlinear transformations, thereby integrating feature engineering into the model fitting process [1].

In-text processing technology, counting from the large unmarked corpus and using a continuous representation of words is one of the mainstream methods of natural language processing. For example, distributed semantics is responsible for analyzing the characteristics of these methods, and learning word embedding forward neural network predicts the word pairs around the word. A simple logarithmic bilinear model can be used to learn the statistical rules of words in a large corpus. Most of the vocabularies in these technologies come from different vectors and have no internal word structure.

For some languages, they are not rich representations. For example, some languages may have dozens of variations for a verb, and these words corresponding to the change rarely appear or do not appear in the training corpus, which brings certain difficulties to natural language processing. By improving the traditional vector representation, these languages can be expressed more abundantly [2]. In general, FastText is used for text classification while generating word embedding. Word2Vec generally does not carry the morphological features of the word, because the morphological information of the word is lost because they are converted into different ids. FastText uses Word2Vec to generate a vector for each word in the corpus and uses character-level n-grams to represent each word. The linear classifier in text classification is designed to minimize the l loss on N documents, which is shown in Eq. 1:

$$L = \sum_{n=1}^{N} \mathcal{l}(y_n, BAx_n) \tag{1}$$

where, x_n is a pack of one-hot vectors, y_n is the label of the nth document. In the case of a large vocabulary and a large output space, and the matrices A and B are very large.

Compared with Word2Vec's larger number of predicted words, the number of labels in paper [3] is huge, all using hierarchical softmax, which is shown in Fig. 1, each input word/N-gram corresponds to each vector, and used to obtain the text vector. These vectors are used to predict, the most simplified form is softmax. In this article, in addition to word vectors, a large number of N-gram vectors are also introduced. Therefore, a hash bucket is used to map several N-grams to the same vector to reduce the computational cost.

It is pointed out in paper [4] two main feature extraction methods: weighted words (bag-of-words) and word embedding learn from word sequences to consider their occurrence information. The feature of weighted words (bag-of-words) is based on counting the words in the document, so it belongs to the unsupervised model word representation scoring scheme that generates word vectors. The word embedding model needs a large number of test data sets for training and is limited, and the pre-trained word embedding vector is not suitable for words that are missing in the text data corpus. In terms of dimensionality reduction methods, it mainly includes T-SNE, mainly used for data visualization of text and documents; improving the prediction performance of the extracted features LDA; random projection with faster calculation speed than PCA; autoencoder that requires more data for training.

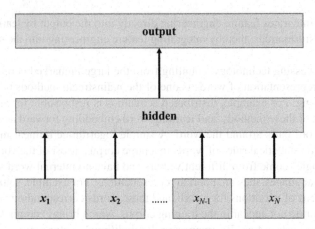

Fig. 1. Data flow diagram

Starting from the car data, the base model is trained to detect anomalies in the data where the technical object type is "car". The algorithm model is used to obtain a classifier to determine whether a certain equipment asset is a car based on the car data.

The first approach is to use traditional classifiers, data features needed to be found artificially and must be done by people very familiar with the relevant business.

The second approach is traditional machine learning methods such as SVM and Random Forest, this requires good data quality and does not guarantee classification results to be well enough.

The last approach is frontier machine learning models that are deep neural networks, we applied FastText for this task, as the full model doesn't spend a big amount of memory and could speed up the training process.

Furthermore, FastText does not need a trained word vector, it can do the word vector training itself, which is shown in Fig. 2. Where each word is represented as a character N-gram packet. A vector representation is associated with each character N-gram. Also, it can learn the training task in a very short time and perform high-speed prediction work, which is perfectly suited to our requirements.

In-text processing tasks, a document is usually regarded as a sequence of words [5]. The collection of all words in a training set is called a vocabulary or feature set, and these documents are usually represented by arrays. A file is represented by a binary vector, assigned a value of 1 if the document contains a characteristic word. Experiments show that sensory does not produce any significant result classification improvement. The main difference between the task document for building a classifier and other tasks is the representation of the document. The particularity of the text classification problem is that the number of vector representation text feature selection and/or feature transformation learning algorithm features is very large, and it is difficult to apply many complex text learning algorithms for classification.

The FastText hierarchical loss puts all labels and words in a Huffman tree, and the lower the frequency of occurrence, the closer the word is to the leaf end. It is that the predicted words at each position of the tree are more correct. This method allows

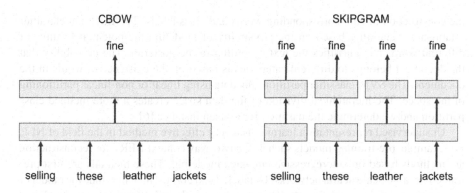

CBOW   SKIPGRAM

fine   fine   fine   fine   fine

selling   these   leather   jackets   selling   these   leather   jackets

I am selling these fine leather jackets

Fig. 2. The word representations: skip-gram and cbow

FastText to greatly improve the speed of training and prediction, and because it includes the N-gram model, it takes into account the order of words, which effectively improves accuracy. In practice, the type of object that needs to be processed is the main basis for identifying equipment assets, and spaces, random characters, or error codes may be entered. The coding of the types of equipment assets of each province stored in the data center of the State Grid is more complicated. Although FastText added the N-gram model to increase the order information between words, the overall context length is limited, which makes it impossible to capture more order information for words larger than the context window size.

This paper proposes our improved algorithm to analyze the text classification model. The improved algorithm is faster for sub-word embedding. The purpose of this method is to ensure that the types of technical objects and equipment assets correspond correctly by the state grid technical object types standard rules. The improved method further accelerates the training speed and testing speed while maintaining high precision.

2 Data Management and Abnormal Data Detection

Text is a special kind of sparse, high-dimensional data. The low frequency of most words requires quantitative data directly on the text using most methods. In the classification problem, the probability value is assigned to the test instance, or a specific label is explicitly assigned to the instance.

The text classification problem assumes the classification value of the label, although continuous values can also be used as the label. Other variants of the classification problem allow to sort test instances for different class selections or allow multiple label instances to be assigned to tests. The problem classification of text and the classification of records are closely related to fixed-value features, word frequency also plays a helpful role in the process of classification, and the typical domain size of text data is much larger than the typical set-value classification problem. The rule-based classifier determines the most likely types of different word types that are most likely to be related to it and requires the construction of rule-corresponding words and class labels. The Bayesian classifier establishes a classifier based on the probability of modeling the potential features of different words and classifies the text according to the posterior. The probability that the document belongs to different categories is based on the existence of words in the document. The SVM classifier partitions the data using linear or non-linear partitioning of the space. The hierarchical division of the data space creates a more inclined class partition and we determine the partition for a given instance [6].

Unsupervised representation learning is a very effective method in the field of NLP. For example, pre-training models such as the two-way context BERT for reconstruction are methods based on autoregressive language modeling. These methods are first pre-trained on large-scale neural networks. Unlabeled text corpus, then fine-tune the model or representation of downstream tasks. However, because BERT assumes that the predicted token is independent of every other token that is not shielded, BERT cannot use the product rule to model the joint probability in a modeling language like AR. In addition, it ignores the dependence between the mask positions and there is a pre-training fine-tune difference.

The artificial symbols used by BERT during pre-training have no fine-tuning time in actual data. In the traditional AR model, using a fixed forward or backward decomposition order, the new XLNet [7] is a generalized autoregressive pre-training method, which is shown in Fig. 3. XLNet maximizes the expected log-likelihood of all possible permutations of a sequence decomposition order of the two-way context is learned by maximizing all the expected possibilities. Each position learns to use the information from all positions in the context, that is, to capture the two-way context. In addition, the autoregressive objective also provides a natural way to use the product rule to decompose the joint probability of the predicted token, and XLNet integrates ideas from the most advanced autoregressive model Transformer-XL to pre-training.

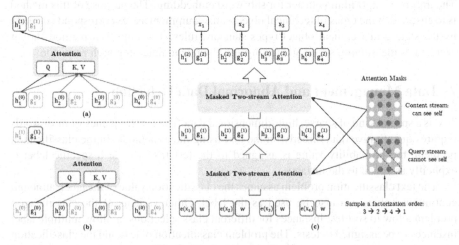

Fig. 3. Content stream attention

Support vector machine is an early solution to pattern recognition problems, which can be used to deal with classification problems [8]. SVM is mainly based on equality constraints rather than classical inequalities and conforms to the least-squares formula constraints. The classifier is shown in Eq. 2.

$$y(x) = sign\left[\sum_{k=1}^{N} a_k y_k \psi(x, x_k) + b\right] \quad (2)$$

where, α_k is a positive real constant and b is a real constant. The typical one $\psi(\cdot,\cdot)$ has the following options $\psi(x \cdot x_k) = x_k^T x \cdot \psi(x, x_k) = \left(x_k^T x + 1\right)^d$.

The RBF SVM function is shown in Eq. 3:

$$\psi(x, x_k) = \exp\left\{-\|x - x_k\|_2^2 \big/ \sigma^2\right\} \quad (3)$$

The kernel parameters can be selected according to the optimization. The support value is proportional to the error of the data point. Most of the values are equal to zero. Therefore, people would rather talk about the support value range in the case of least squares.

The support vector machine maps the data to a higher-dimensional input space and constructs an optimal separation hyperplane in this space. This involves solving the secondary programming problem, and the gradient-based neural network training method. On the other hand, the architecture has many local minima. The core selects functions and parameters so that the limit on the dimension is minimized [9–11]. When there is no prior knowledge about a specific classification task, the performance of complex features cannot be improved, and the text document is converted into a vector. In high-dimensional space, the correlation of many features is very low.

Feature reduction is very heavy for training classifiers with good generalization and reducing computational cost [12–14]. Document vectors are usually defined in a space of thousands of dimensions, and each dimension corresponds to a word feature. The standard learning architecture turns the input into a feature vector, the purpose is that the data can be separated/aggregated or processed in other ways. However, it is difficult for text and image data to be explicitly represented by feature vectors, which means that feature extraction is complex and requires sufficient knowledge [15–18].

3 Proposed Structure

In all learning tasks, there are many pre-training ways. However, the initial attempt in the NLP field is to fine-tune the induction transfer and then adjust the language model. Inductive transfer learning was first used in the field of computer vision including object detection [19, 20].

The main way is to fine-tune the model that has been formed, most of which are concentrated in the first layer of the transfer model. In NLP, a method that goes beyond transfer is proposed. The mainstream method is to pre-train to capture additional embedding context through other tasks, use different embedding and then use levels as features.

The Universal Language Model is shown in Fig. 4. Language modeling can be regarded as a source task, it captures many aspects of the language related to downstream

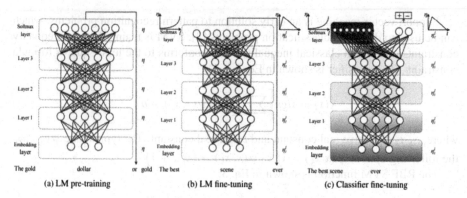

(a) LM pre-training   (b) LM fine-tuning   (c) Classifier fine-tuning

Fig. 4. Universal Language Model

tasks, such as long-term dependence, etc. In addition, the pre-trained LM can be a trait that can easily adapt to the target.

It has achieved the most advanced results in a series of NLP tasks, demonstrating the great potential of the fine-tuning method [21]. The BERT-base is shown in Fig. 5. The sequence has one or two fragments. The first tag of the sequence is always [CLS], which contains special classification embedding, and the other special tag [SEP] is used to separate fragments. A simple softmax classifier is:

$$p(c|h) = \text{softmax}(Wh) \qquad (4)$$

where, W is a task-specific parameter matrix. Further pre-training: BERT is trained in a general domain, which has a different data distribution from the target domain. Multi-task fine-tuning: In the absence of a pre-trained LM model, multi-task learning has shown its effectiveness in utilizing knowledge shared between multiple tasks. When there are multiple tasks available in the target domain, an interesting question is whether fine-tuning BERT on all tasks at the same time still brings benefits.

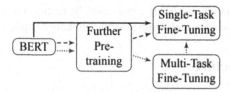

Fig. 5. Fine-tuning BERT

In [22], they use a small set of field-specific features to extract biographical and text from the author. The proposed method effectively classifies text into a set of pre-defined general classes. Therefore, a greedy strategy is used to select the feature set, which usually follows the defined class. These features require knowledge of the source of information to classify tweets into selected categories.

Given a large number of unlabeled examples, articles, websites, and other sources of information that often exist, it would be useful to take advantage of this additional information fashion in some automated fashion. The classification results produced by this method exceed those obtained without additional unlabeled data. In [23], they introduced another use of this broader background knowledge that helps classification. It neither categorizes background knowledge nor directly compares it with any training or test examples. Instead, it takes advantage of the fact that knowing certain words that appear at the same time may help to learn, and this can be found in a large amount of text in the domain.

We use the Latent Semantic Index (LSI). LSI is considered particularly useful-fighting ambiguity and synonyms, which makes classification tasks more difficult. The idea here is to use background text to re-describe the data when creating this new one, rather than relying only on training data.

Figure 6 shows a unified architecture that stacks CNN and LSTM in a semantic sentence model [24]. The combination of CNN and LSTM can be seen in some computer vision tasks, such as image captioning and speech recognition). Most of these models use multi-layer CNN and train CNN and RNN separately or throw a fully connected output to convert the CNN layer into RNN as input. This architecture applies CNN to text data and feeds continuous window features directly to LSTM, enabling LSTM to learn remote dependence from higher-order sequential features. The sequence-based model is sufficient to capture the combined semantics of many NLP tasks, so CNN is directly built on the sequence outside the parse tree on the word.

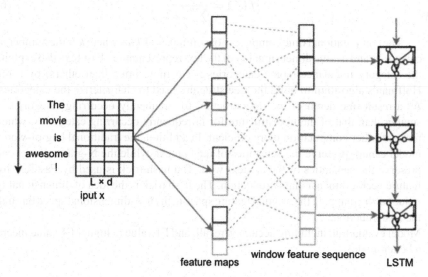

Fig. 6. C-LSTM for sentence modeling

The proposed description text of the device asset is used to determine whether it is true for the sedan. The following is the workflow:

1. Pre-processing of description text, including word separation, de-duplication, removal of numeric symbols, etc.

2. Generating word vector features: This ignores the internal morphological features of words, e.g., "book" and "books", both of which have more common characters, i.e., their internal morphology is similar, but in traditional Word2Vec, this internal morphological information is lost because they are converted to different ids. To overcome this problem, FastText uses character-level N-grams to represent a word. For the word "book", suppose the value of n is 3, then its trigram has: " < bo", "boo", "ook", "ok >", where " <" means prefix and " >" means suffix. So, we can use this trigram to represent the word "book".

3. Input the features to the model for training, and get the classification model.

   In the above figure represents the feature vector of the i-th word in the text, and the negative log-likelihood function of this model is as follows:

$$-\frac{1}{N} \sum_{n=1}^{N} y_n \log(f(BAx_n)) \tag{5}$$

B is the weight coefficient of function A. The matrix A in the above equation is the word lookup table, and the whole model is to find out all the word representations and then take the average value to represent the text representation, and then input this text representation into the linear classifier, which is the softmax function of the output layer.

$$f(Z_j) = \frac{e^{z_j}}{\sum_{i=1}^{n} e^{z_i}} \tag{6}$$

The computational time complexity of softmax is $O(kh)$, where k is the number of categories and h is the dimensionality of the text representation. FastText also exploits the category imbalance (some categories occur more often than others) by using Huffman's algorithm to build the tree structure used to characterize the categories. As a result, the depth of the tree structure for frequently occurring categories is smaller than that of the tree structure for infrequently occurring categories, which makes further computation more efficient. In addition, the traditional bag-of-words model cannot preserve the semantics of the context, while the N-grams model can preserve the semantics of the context well. The hash trick is used by FastText for feature vector dimensionality reduction. The hash trick is the idea of dimensionality reduction by mapping the original feature space to the low-dimensional space through the hash function.

4. Model evaluation, including accuracy, recall, and F1 value (a higher F1 value means a better model).

4 Experiments

4.1 Dataset

The dataset includes 23,777 positive samples (is sedan) and 6,223 negative samples (not sedan). 80% of the data (rounded) is used as the training set for training, 10% (rounded) as the validation set, and the other 10% (rounded) as the test set.

4.2 Experimental Results

FastText's hierarchical loss puts all labels, that is, all words, into a Huffman tree. The less frequent words are closer to the leaf end. Suppose we have 10,000 words in the dictionary, and the simple softmax is a classification problem of 10,000 categories; suppose that one of our target words is 01001 position on the Huffman tree (for example, we use 0 for the left subtree and 1 for the right subtree). Then the non-class problem on this sample is five binary classification problems, and it is expected that the predicted word will be more inclined to the correct direction at each position on this path. This method makes FastText greatly increase the speed of training and prediction, since the N-gram model is added, and the order of words is considered, which effectively improves the accuracy.

Table 1. The testing score on FastText

	Precision	Recall	f1-score	Number of test data
False	0.922	0.904	0.913	1855
True	0.908	0.926	0.917	7145
Weighted avg.	0.915	0.901	0.908	9000

Table 2. The testing score on improved network

	Precision	Recall	f1-score	Number of test data
False	0.936	0.928	0.932	1855
True	0.934	0.949	0.941	7145
Weighted avg.	0.935	0.944	0.939	9000

The scores of model training and testing results are shown in Table 1 and Table 2. It can be seen from the two tables that the proposed improved method has some improvements in accuracy and F1 score over FastText. Although FastText added the n-gram model to increase the sequence information between words, the length of the global context points to words with a larger context window size, and no more sequence information can be captured. Therefore, this paper uses the method of adding and averaging the FastText mapping layer to improve the sum of squares and averaging.

5 Conclusion

The FastText's hierarchical loss puts all the labels, that is, all the words, inside a Huffman tree, and the less frequently they appear, the closer the words are to the leaf end. Suppose we have 10,000 words inside the lexicon, simple softmax is a 10,000-class classification problem; assume that one of our target words at the top of the Huffman tree is 01001 position (for example, we use 0 for the left subtree, 1 for the right subtree) then the non-class problem on this sample is a 5 binary classification problem, expect the predicted word in this path each position is more inclined to the correct direction. This approach allows FastText to greatly increase the speed of training and prediction and effectively improves the accuracy due to the inclusion of the n-gram model.

Although FastText adds the n-gram model to increase the order information between words, the length of the entire context is limited, which makes it unable to capture more order information of words larger than the context window size. Hierarchical softmax is a loss function that is close to softmax and much faster to compute. Each intermediate node has a trained binary decision activation (e.g., sigmoid) and predicts whether we should go left or right. In the validation, we initially found that although FastText incorporates the n-gram model to increase the order information between words, the overall context length is limited resulting in the inability to capture more order information for words larger than the context window size. When we want to assign a file to multiple tags, we can still use softmax loss and play with the parameters of prediction. However, playing around with these parameters can be tricky and unintuitive because the probabilities must sum to 1. A convenient way to handle multiple tags is to use separate binary classifiers for each tag.

In this paper, the FastText algorithm is applied to the data management process of State Grid with good results. In the future, we will continue to use the FastText algorithm to optimize the model parameters and find better methods for text NLP processing, such as trying to stitch word vectors to form two-dimensional information so that more information can be extracted using CNNs commonly used for images.

Acknowledgement. This work was funded by the "Research on data quality governance technology based on big data approximate computing and artificial intelligence" program of the Big Data Center, State Grid Corporation of China (SGCC).

References

1. Bojanowski, P., Grave, E., Joulin, A., et al.: Enriching word vectors with subword information. Trans. Assoc. Comput. Linguist. **5**, 135–146 (2017)
2. Joulin, A., Grave, E., Bojanowski, P., et al.: FastText.zip: compressing text classification models. arXiv preprint arXiv:1612.03651 (2016)
3. Joulin, A., Grave, E., Bojanowski, P., et al.: Bag of tricks for efficient text classification. arXiv preprint arXiv:1607.01759 (2016)
4. Kowsari, K., Jafari Meimandi, K., Heidarysafa, M., et al.: Text classification algorithms: a survey. Information **10**(4), 150 (2019)
5. Ikonomakis, M., Kotsiantis, S., Tampakas, V.: Text classification using machine learning techniques. WSEAS Trans. Comput. **4**(8), 966–974 (2005)
6. Aggarwal, C.C., Zhai, C.X.: A survey of text classification algorithms. In: In: Aggarwal, C., Zhai, C. (eds.) Mining Text Data, pp. 163–222. Springer, Boston (2012). https://doi.org/10.1007/978-1-4614-3223-4_6
7. Yang, Z., Dai, Z., Yang, Y., et al.: XLNet: generalized autoregressive pretraining for language understanding. Adv. Neural Inf. Process. Syst. **32** (2019)
8. Suykens, J.A.K., Vandewalle, J.: Least squares support vector machine classifiers. Neural Process. Lett. **9**(3), 293–300 (1999)
9. Svetnik, V., et al.: Random forest: a classification and regression tool for compound classification and QSAR modeling. J. Chem. Inf. Comput. Sci. **43**(6), 1947–1958 (2003)

10. Tsoumakas, G., Katakis, I.: Multi-label classification: an overview. Int. J. Data Warehous. Min. (IJDWM) **3**(3), 1–13 (2007)
11. Yu, B.: An evaluation of text classification methods for literary study. Literary Linguist. Comput. **23**(3), 327–343 (2008)
12. Gao, X., Hoi Steven, C.H., Zhang, Y., et al.: SOML: sparse online metric learning with application to image retrieval. In: Twenty-Eighth AAAI Conference on Artificial Intelligence, pp. 1206–1212 (2014)
13. Zhang, Y., Gao, X., Chen, Z., et al.: Learning salient features to prevent model drift for correlation tracking. Neurocomputing **418**, 1–10 (2020)
14. Tang, G., Gao, X., Chen, Z., Zhong, H.: Unsupervised adversarial domain adaptation with similarity diffusion for person re-identification. Neurocomputing **442**, 337–347 (2021)
15. Lodhi, H., Saunders, C., Shawe-Taylor, J., et al.: Text classification using string kernels. J. Mach. Learn. Res. **2**(Feb), 419–444 (2002)
16. Gao, X., Hoi Steven, C.H., Zhang, Y., et al.: Sparse online learning of image similarity. ACM Transactions on Intelligent Systems and Technology **8**(5), 64:1–64:22 (2017)
17. Zhang, Y., Gao, X., Chen, Z., et al.: Mining spatial-temporal similarity for visual tracking. IEEE Trans. Image Process. **29**, 8107–8119 (2020)
18. Xia, Z., Hong, X., Gao, X., et al.: Spatiotemporal recurrent convolutional networks for recognizing spontaneous micro-expressions. IEEE Trans. Multimed. **22**(3), 626–640 (2020)
19. Howard, J., Ruder, S.: Universal language model fine-tuning for text classification. arXiv preprint arXiv:1801.06146 (2018)
20. Kim, S.B., Han, K.S., Rim, H.C., et al.: Some effective techniques for naive bayes text classification. IEEE Trans. Knowl. Data Eng. **18**(11), 1457–1466 (2006)
21. Sun, C., Qiu, X., Xu, Y., Huang, X.: How to fine-tune BERT for text classification. In: Sun, M., Huang, X., Ji, H., Liu, Z., Liu, Y. (eds.) CCL 2019. LNCS, vol. 11856, pp. 194–206. Springer, Cham (2019). https://doi.org/10.1007/978-3-030-32381-3_16
22. Sriram, B., Fuhry, D., Demir, E., et al.: Short text classification in twitter to improve information filtering. In: Proceedings of the 33rd International ACM SIGIR Conference on Research and Development in Information Retrieval, pp. 841–842 (2010)
23. Zelikovitz, S., Hirsh, H.: Using LSI for text classification in the presence of background text. In: Proceedings of the Tenth International Conference on Information and Knowledge Management, pp. 113–118 (2001)
24. Zhou, C., Sun, C., Liu, Z., et al.: A C-LSTM neural network for text classification. arXiv preprint arXiv:1511.08630 (2015)

A Multi-stream Fusion Network for Multi-task Image Restoration

Fei Tao[1], Wuzhen Shi[1(✉)], Liting Chen[1], and Yutao Liu[2]

[1] College of Electronics and Information Engineering, Shenzhen University,
Shenzhen, China
`taofei2021@email.szu.edu.cn, wzhshi@szu.edu.cn`

[2] School of Computer Science and Technology, Ocean University of China,
Qingdao, China

Abstract. Image contains a lot of effective information. However, due to the limitation of image acquisition technology and the interference of acquisition environment, motion and other factors, the acquired image will appear multiple distortion problems simultaneously, such as low resolution, motion blur and noise, which affect our acquisition of information. Therefore, it is an important task to solve the multi-distortion problem, so as to obtain a high-resolution, noiseless and clear image. In this paper, we propose a multi-stream fusion network (dubbed MSFNet) to deal with the multi-distortion problem of deblurring, denoising and super-resolution. Each stream of the proposed method handles a task individually to strengthen the optimization of the corresponding task. A multi-feature fusion module is used to establish the relationship between different tasks, which realizes the joint optimization of multi-tasks. Experimental results show that the proposed MSFNet achieves better quantitative and qualitative performance than the two-stage image restoration method.

Keywords: Multi-stream fusion network · Multi-task restoration · Deblur · Super-resolution · Denoise

1 Introduction

In the process of image transmission and reception, due to the limitation of equipment, environment, target movement, preservation conditions and other factors, the images we obtain will have multiple distortion phenomena such as blur, low resolution, noise and so on. For example, images acquired at night are often accompanied by low resolution and noise due to poor light. However, most of the existing image restoration methods are only suitable for a single distortion problem. These existing image super-resolution methods [1–3], denosing methods [4–6], and debluring methods [7,8] cannot obtain good image reconstruction results from a distorted image with low resolution, blur and heavy noise. This is because these methods do not consider the relationship among

G. Zhai et al. (Eds.): IFTC 2021, CCIS 1560, pp. 42–54, 2022.
https://doi.org/10.1007/978-981-19-2266-4_4

different distortion problems. Therefore, divide-and-conquer not only increases the computational complexity, but also can not obtain the ideal image restoration results.

Recently, some researchers have begun to pay attention to the problem of multi-distortion image restoration, trying to establish the relationship between different distortion problems to obtain better image reconstruction results. For example, Zhang et al. [9] proposed a gated fusion network for joint image deblurring and super-resolution. However, it is obvious that many images will have problems of low resolution, blur, and noise at the same time. In this case, before using Zhang's method [9], image denoising is required to obtain good image restoration results. This two-stage strategy does not establish the relationship between the denoising task and other tasks.

In order to deal with the problem of multi-distortion image restoration with low resolution, blur, and noise better, this paper proposes a multi-stream fusion network. Each stream of the proposed method handles a task individually to strengthen the optimization of the corresponding task. A multi-feature fusion module is used to establish the relationship between different tasks, which realizes the joint optimization of multi-tasks. Instead of processing multiple image restoration tasks superimposed on each other simply, the proposed method performs a joint multi-task optimisation. This not only improves the performance of the network by sharing features, but also helps to improve the output of the network by constraining each other in the correlation relationship, and effectively prevents overfitting, as well as avoiding secondary degradation and distortion of the valid information caused by simple superposition, so that the image restoration presents better results. Our experimental results show that the proposed MSFNet achieves better quantitative and qualitative performance than the two-stage image restoration method.

To sum up, our main contributions include:

- A multi-stream fusion network is proposed for multi-distortion image restoration that can handle distorted images with simultaneous motion blur, low-resolution and serious noise.
- A multi-feature fusion module is introduced to establish the relationship between different tasks, which makes joint optimization of multiple tasks possible.
- Extensive experiments are done to show that the proposed multi-stream fusion network obtains better quantitative and qualitative results than the simple two-stage image restoration method.

2 Related Work

2.1 Image Deblurring

Some image deblurring methods assume that the blur is uniform [10–12]. That is, they believe that every pixel of the image is blurred by the same blur kernel. However, this assumption in a real scene is difficult to achieve, because the different depths of different positions in the scene and the motion of the foreground target will cause different pixel to have different degrees of blur. In order to achieve better deblurring effect, recent methods mainly focus on non-uniform deblurring [13–15]. Some non-uniform deblurring methods estimate blur kernels based on the depth of the scene [13, 14] or the segmentation result of the image [15]. Due to the high computational complexity of kernel estimation, some studies have explored image deblurring methods based on end-to-end networks [16]. Some recent work has also added attention mechanism to the image deblurring network [7, 8].

2.2 Image Super-Resolution

Deep learning-based methods have become the mainstream of image super-resolution. The pioneer deep learning-based single image super-resolution methods is the SRCNN model proposed by Dong et al. [17] in 2014, which simply cascades three convolution layers for extracting features, processing non-linear mappings and reconstructing images, respectively. Due to the powerful learning ability of deep networks, such a simple network can obtain better image reconstruction results than traditional methods with lower computational complexity. The input of SRCNN is the result of bicubic interpolation of low resolution image, which not only makes the amplification process not optimized, but also increases the computational complexity due to the increase of input dimension. To solve this problem, Dong et al. [18] further proposed a fast version of SRCNN (called FSRCNN), whose network directly takes low-resolution images as input and uses a deconvolution layer to achieve resolution increase. Both SRCNN and FSRCNN only have a small number of layers. In order to train a very deep network, Kim et al. [19] proposed a so-called VDSR model, which speeds up network training by learning residuals. In addition, Kim et al. [1] proposed a so-called VDCN model [1] by combining the recurrent neural network with convolutional neural networks, which further deepened the network and improved the quality of image super-resolution. In 2017, Christian Ledig et al. [20] applied adversarial networks to image super-resolution, which attempts to reconstruct images that are more in line with human visual characteristics rather than simple signal reconstruction.

2.3 Image Denoising

Image denoising is an important technique in the field of image processing, and how to retain the original image feature information while denoising is one of the current research objectives of image denoising.

Traditional Denoising Methods. Traditional image denoising includes spatial domain methods and transform domain methods. The spatial method mainly uses a filter template to filter the neighborhood area of all pixels. Common spatial methods include: mean filter, Wiener filter, median filter, weighted median filter, bilateral filter, etc. The transform domain method mainly presents different characteristics based on the coefficients of the image and noise in the transform domain. Common transform domain methods are: Fourier transform, cosine transform and wavelet transform.

Deep Learning Based Approach. Burger et al. [21] used a multi-layer perceptron (MLP) method to achieve image denoising. Subsequently, Goodfellow et al. [22] proposed an image denoising method based on a generative adversarial network, in which a generative model is used to generate noise-free images in an end-to-end manner, and a discriminative model is used to distinguish generated images and real images. The generated images are more close to real images with the help of generative adversarial training. In 2017, Zhang et al. proposed the DnCNN network [23], which combines Batch Normalization (BN) [24] and Residual Learning [25]. Because it emphasizes the complementary role of residual learning and batch normalization in image restoration, DnCNN brings fast convergence and good performance with deeper network structure. In addition, DnCNN uses batch normalization to normalize the training data to make the training network converge faster, and residual learning can solve the problems of gradient dispersion and information loss, and the denoising effect is significant. In 2018, Zhang et al. [?] proposed FFDNet, which has low computational complexity and highlights the importance of noise level maps in balancing noise reduction and detail preservation. In 2019, Jia et al. [?] proposed the FOCNet model, which is based on the discretization of fractional differential equations, and at the same time introduces multi-scale feature interaction, strengthens the control of dynamic systems, and performs well in image denoising.

3   Proposed Method

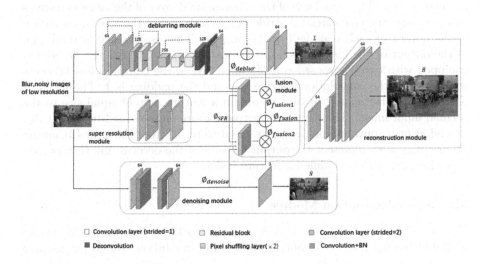

Fig. 1. The architecture of the proposed multi-stream fusion network.

The proposed network contains three branches (deblurring, super-resolution, denoising) and five modules (deblurring module, super-resolution module, denoising module, gate fusion module, reconstruction module). The architecture of the proposed multi-stream fusion network is shown in Fig. 1. The input of the network is a distorted image with simultaneous blur, low resolution and serious noise. The deblurring branch maps the input distorted image to an unblurred image (but with noise). The denoising branch maps the input distorted image into a noise-free image (but blurry). The super-resolution branch maps the input distorted image into a noise-free, unblurred, high-resolution image by fusing the information of the deblurring branch and the denoising branch. The gate fusion module adaptively learns the relationship between different branch features and effectively merges them to generate high-resolution clear images. In the training process, the three branches have corresponding losses to supervise the optimization of the network. Next, we will introduce each module in detail.

3.1 Deblurring Module

The main task of the deblurring module is to independently perform the deblurring process on the original input image and extract the deblurring features. This module uses an asymmetric residual encoder-decoder architecture to expand the perceptual field, where the encoder consists of three scales with similar structures, each with eight residual blocks and one convolutional layer with an activation function. The residual block of this module is two convolutional layers with an activation function ReLU in between. The number of input channels of each residual block is equal to the number of output channels. The convolutional stride is 1 that will not change the spatial resolution of the image.

The convolution kernel size of the first scale convolution layer is 7×7, the convolutional stride is 1, and padding is 3, so the original image size is preserved in the first scale. The kernel size of the convolutional layer of the latter two scales is 3×3, and the convolutional stride is 2, which makes the spatial resolution of the output of each scale half of the original. That is, the spatial resolution of the output of the encoder is a quarter of the input images. The decoder is equipped with two transposed convolutional layers, the convolutional kernel is set to 4×4, the convolutional stride is 2 and the padding is 1. The image is enlarged by a factor of 2 in turn to obtain a feature map of equal size to the original input image. The number of output feature map channels is 64. Finally, two additional convolutional layers are used to reconstruct the clear LR image. We use ϕ_{deblur} to represent the output features of the decoder and then output it to the gated fusion module for feature fusion.

3.2 Super-Resolution Module

The super-resolution module uses 8 residual blocks to independently extract high dimensional features to obtain image super-resolution. We do not use any pooling or strided convolutional layers. The output channels of both convolution and residual block are set to 64, so that the number of extracted feature channels is equal to the number of deblurred channels. The residual block of this module is set up with two convolutional layers, both with a convolutional kernel of 3×3 and a step size of 1. A LeakyReLU layer with a leaky value of 0.2 is added in the middle as the activation function. We express the extracted features as ϕ_{SFR}. The output features have two functions: one is to be used as the input of the gated fusion module to adaptively generate the weight map of other branch information, the other is to be used as an important super-resolution feature to fuse with the features of other branches to obtain the input of the final reconstruction module.

3.3 Denoising Module

The module uses a DnCNN network [23] as a denoising module for extracting denoising features $\phi_{denoise}$. In particular, the module is a 17-layer network containing three types of layers. The first layer is a convolutional layer with a 3×3 kernel, plus a ReLU layer as the activation function to generate the initial feature map. In layer 2 to 16, each layer contains one convolutional layer, one batch normalization (BN) layer and an activation layer ReLU. The input and output channels of the convolutional layer are 64 and the size of the convolutional kernel remains 3×3. The output here is used as the denoised feature $\phi_{denoise}$, which is feed into the multi-feature gate fusion module. In the 17th layer, we use a convolutional layer to reconstruct a noiseless image, without setting a activation function. The output of this network is a residual image, so finally the residual image is subtracted from the noise image to obtain the denoised image $\hat{N}$.

3.4 Multi-feature Fusion Module

This module integrates information from all three branches. Firstly, it fuses the deblurred feature ϕ_{deblur}, the super-resolution feature ϕ_{SFR} and the original input image ϕ_{blur_noise}. These features are first concatenated together, and then pass through two convolutional layers to generate a weight map, which is used to multiply with the deblurred features ϕ_{deblur} pixel by pixel to obtain the fused features $\phi_{fusion1}$.

$$\phi_{fusion1} = G_{gate}(\phi_{SFR}, \phi_{deblur}, \phi_{blur\_noise}) \otimes \phi_{deblur} \qquad (1)$$

Secondly, this multi-feature fusion module fuses the denoised features $\phi_{denoise}$, the super-resolution features ϕ_{SFR} and the original input image ϕ_{blur_noise}. These features are first concatenated together, and then pass through two convolutional layers to generate a weight map, which is used to multiply with the denoised features $\phi_{denoise}$ pixel-by-pixel to obtain the fused features $\phi_{fusion2}$.

$$\phi_{fusion2} = G_{gate}(\phi_{SFR}, \phi_{denoise}, \phi_{blur\_noise}) \otimes \phi_{denoise} \qquad (2)$$

G_{gate} denotes the importance map generating function. Finally, these fused features are summed with the super-resolved features to obtain the final fusion feature ϕ_{fusion}.

$$\phi_{fusion} = \phi_{fusion1} + \phi_{fusion2} + \phi_{SFR} \qquad (3)$$

3.5 Reconstruction Module

The module consists of 8 residual blocks, 4 convolutional layers and 2 pixel-shuffling layers. The residual block here is the same as that of the deblurring module, with two convolutional layers and an activation function ReLU in between. The number of input channels is equal to the number of output channels. The convolutional kernel is 3 × 3 and the stride is set to 1. The fused features from the gate fusion module are processed as input directly into the residual block. This is followed by a convolutional layer for increasing the number of channels from 64 to 256, with the aim of increasing the image resolution by a factor of 2 in the next pixel-shuffling layer. The image is then processed in the same way so that the final resolution is 4 times the size of the original image. Finally, the image is reconstructed using two convolutional layers. In this module, we use a LeakyReLU function with the leaky value of 0.2 as activation function, which is placed after the pixel-shuffling layer.

3.6 Loss Function

To make the network converge better during training, we choose the mean square error MSE as the loss function.

$$MSE = \frac{1}{H \times M} \sum_{i=1}^{H} \sum_{j=1}^{M} (X(i,j) - Y(i,j))^2 \qquad (4)$$

It is used to calculate the error between the predicted restoration image and the real image. The proposed multi-feature fusion network generates three output images, i.e. the deblurred low resolution image $\hat{L}$, the denoised low resolution image $\hat{N}$ and the noiseless, unblurred, high resolution image $\hat{H}$. For each blurred, noisy and low resolution image ϕ_{blur_noise}, there are a noisy low resolution image as deblurred label, a blurred low resolution image as denoised label and a noiseless, unblurred, high resolution image as the final super-resolution label. Therefore, in order to balance the loss of different branches, we have the following loss function:

$$LOSS = L_{SR}(\hat{H}, H) + \alpha L_{deblur}(\hat{L}, L) + \beta L_{denoise}(\hat{N}, N) \qquad (5)$$

L_{SR}, L_{deblur}, $L_{denoise}$ denotes the mean square error value between the output image and the labeled image. After comparing the results of several experiments, we found that when $\alpha = 0.5$, $\beta = 0.1$, the model can achieve better results.

4   Experimental Results

In this chapter, we first introduce training details and data processing methods, and then conduct quantitative and qualitative comparative analysis.

4.1   Training Details

In order to facilitate network training, we set the training process as three steps. The first two steps disable the multi-feature fusion module, and its initial learning rate is set to 10^{-4}. In the first step, 25 epochs are set, and the learning rate is halved every 7 iterations. In the second step, 60 epochs are set, and the learning rate is multiplied by 0.1 after 30 epochs. In the third step of training, the multi-feature fusion module is added, the epoch is set to 55, the learning rate is set to 5×10^{-5}, and the learning rate is multiplied by 0.1 after 25 epochs. The batch size for training is set to 8.

4.2   Datasets

Both networks mentioned in this paper use the GOPRO dataset [16] to generate the training dataset and the test dataset. The training dataset and the test dataset are processed differently. For the processing of the training dataset, the GOPRO dataset contains 2103 blurred and clear high resolution image pairs used for training. To generate more training data, we resized each high resolution image pair using three random scales within [0.5, 1.0]. We then cropped the high resolution image pairs into 256×256 blocks in stride of 128 to obtain a blurred high resolution block H_{blur} (not needed during training) and a clear high resolution block H. We use the bicubic downsampling method to reduce H_{blur} and H by 4 times to generate a blurred low resolution block L_{blur} and a clear low resolution block L, and L_{blur} adds Gaussian noise with a variance of 25 through the Matlab function "imnoise" as the input L_{blur_noise} of the proposed network. L plus with noise is used as the deblurring label, while L_{blur} is used as the denoising label N. The processing of the test dataset is relatively simple. As no labels are required, the processed L_{blur_noise} is directly used as the multi-distortion image with simultaneous motion blur, low resolution and serious noise. The clear high-resolution noiseless image H is used as the ground-true for comparison.

4.3 Quantitative Comparison

To compare with the proposed method, we set up a comparison experiment in which the same test dataset is denoised with a DnCNN pre-training network model [23] and then deblurred and super-resolved with a joint deblurring and super-resolving pre-training network model [9], called two-stage image restoration method. The two-stage image restoration method has a permanent loss of some detailed features in the first stage of the denoising process, resulting in poor results in the second stage of the joint deblurring and super-resolution. The proposed method emphasizes the optimization of three tasks at the same time, and establishes the relationship between different tasks through a multi-feature gate fusion module, so that the proposed method can obtain better image reconstruction results.

Many quantitative comparison metrics that are more in line with human visual characteristics have been proposed [26, 26–30]. However, PSNR and SSIM are still the most commonly used metrics. Therefore, PSNR and SSIM are used as the quantitative comparison metrics in this paper. The comparison is made between the proposed method and the two-stage image restoration method. Figure 2 and Fig. 3 show the PSNR and SSIM comparisons of the 567 test data sets between the proposed method and the two-stage method. As shown in Fig. 2, the proposed method performs better in PSNR metric. The average PSNR of the proposed method is 21.22479 dB, which is 1.26899 dB higher than the 19.9558 dB of the two-stage image restoration. As shown in Fig. 3, the SSIM metric shows that the proposed method has an average SSIM of 0.6714179, which is 0.072599 higher than the two-stage image restoration method of 0.5988189. Both PSNR and SSIM metrics show the proposed method has higher quantitative value than the compared method.

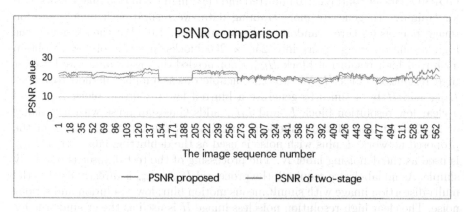

Fig. 2. PSNR comparison of the proposed method and the two-stage image restoration method

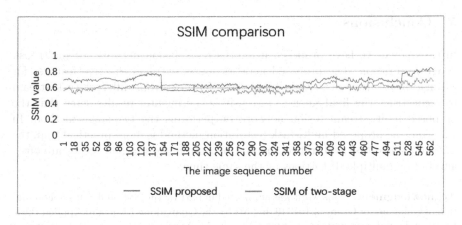

Fig. 3. SSIM comparison of the proposed method and the two-stage image restoration method

4.4 Qualitative Comparison

Figure 4 shows the visual comparison of our proposed MSFNet and the two-stage image restoration method. The first column is the ground-true high resolution image, the second column is the input multi-distortion image with motion blur, low resolution and serious noise, the third column is the reconstructed results of the two-stage method, and the forth column is our result. As shown, The input image is severely distorted. The two-stage method cannot obtain the desired reconstruction result. In contrast, our method effectively restores more image details.

Fig. 4. Visual comparison of our proposed method and the two-stage image restoration method

5   Conclusions

In this paper, we have proposed a multi-stream fusion network for multi-task image restoration. The proposed network firstly extracts effective features for a single restoration task, then fuses these features from different task stream to reconstruct the final images. Extensive experimental results show that the proposed multi-stream fusion network outperforms the two-stage method. In addition, the proposed multi-task restoration method is more practical than the common single-task restoration method because images in real scenes are often affected by multiple distortions at the same time.

Acknowledgment. This work was supported in part by the National Science Foundation of China under Grant 62101346, in part by the Guangdong Basic and Applied Basic Research Foundation under Grant 2021A1515011702 and in part by the Stable Support Plan for Shenzhen Higher Education Institutions under Grant 20200812104316001.

References

1. Kim, J., Lee, J.K., Lee, K.M.: Accurate image super-resolution using very deep convolutional networks. In: 2016 IEEE Conference on Computer Vision and Pattern Recognition (CVPR), pp. 1646–1654 (2016)
2. Gu, J., Lu, H., Zuo, W., Dong, C.: Blind super-resolution with iterative kernel correction. In: 2019 IEEE/CVF Conference on Computer Vision and Pattern Recognition (CVPR), pp. 1604–1613 (2019)
3. Soh, J.W., Cho, S., Cho, N.I.: Meta-transfer learning for zero-shot super-resolution. In: 2020 IEEE/CVF Conference on Computer Vision and Pattern Recognition (CVPR), pp. 3513–3522 (2020)
4. Liu, D., Wen, B., Jiao, J., Liu, X., Wang, Z., Huang, T.S.: Connecting image denoising and high-level vision tasks via deep learning. IEEE Trans. Image Process. **29**, 3695–3706 (2020)
5. Jia, X., Liu, S., Feng, X., Zhang, L.: FOCNet: a fractional optimal control network for image denoising. In: 2019 IEEE/CVF Conference on Computer Vision and Pattern Recognition (CVPR), pp. 6047–6056 (2019)
6. Zhang, K., Zuo, W., Zhang, L.: FFDNet: toward a fast and flexible solution for CNN-based image denoising. IEEE Trans. Image Process. **27**(9), 4608–4622 (2018)
7. Zhang, Y., et al.: Image deblurring based on lightweight multi-information fusion network. In: 2021 IEEE International Conference on Image Processing (ICIP), pp. 1724–1728 (2021)
8. Zhang, J., Zhang, C., Wang, J., Xiong, Q., Zhang, Y., Zhang, W.: Attention driven self-similarity capture for motion deblurring. In: 2021 IEEE International Conference on Multimedia and Expo (ICME), pp. 1–6 (2021)
9. Zhang, X., Dong, H., Hu, Z., Lai, W.-S., Wang, F., Yang, M.-H.: Gated fusion network for joint image deblurring and super-resolution. arXiv preprint arXiv:1807.10806 (2018)
10. Xu, L., Zheng, S., Jia, J.: Unnatural l0 sparse representation for natural image deblurring. In: Proceedings of the IEEE Conference on Computer Vision and Pattern Recognition, pp. 1107–1114 (2013)

11. Schmidt, U., Rother, C., Nowozin, S., Jancsary, J., Roth, S.: Discriminative non-blind deblurring. In: Proceedings of the IEEE Conference on Computer Vision and Pattern Recognition, pp. 604–611 (2013)
12. Pan, J., Sun, D., Pfister, H., Yang, M.-H.: Blind image deblurring using dark channel prior. In: Proceedings of the IEEE Conference on Computer Vision and Pattern Recognition, pp. 1628–1636 (2016)
13. Hu, Z., Xu, L., Yang, M.-H.: Joint depth estimation and camera shake removal from single blurry image. In: Proceedings of the IEEE Conference on Computer Vision and Pattern Recognition, pp. 2893–2900 (2014)
14. Paramanand, C., Rajagopalan, A.N.: Non-uniform motion deblurring for bilayer scenes. In: Proceedings of the IEEE Conference on Computer Vision and Pattern Recognition, pp. 1115–1122 (2013)
15. Hyun Kim, T., Ahn, B., Mu Lee, K.: Dynamic scene deblurring. In: Proceedings of the IEEE International Conference on Computer Vision, pp. 3160–3167 (2013)
16. Nah, S., Hyun Kim, T., Mu Lee, K.: Deep multi-scale convolutional neural network for dynamic scene deblurring. In: Proceedings of the IEEE Conference on Computer Vision and Pattern Recognition, pp. 3883–3891 (2017)
17. Dong, C., Loy, C.C., He, K., Tang, X.: Learning a deep convolutional network for image super-resolution. In: Fleet, D., Pajdla, T., Schiele, B., Tuytelaars, T. (eds.) ECCV 2014. LNCS, vol. 8692, pp. 184–199. Springer, Cham (2014). https://doi.org/10.1007/978-3-319-10593-2_13
18. Dong, C., Loy, C.C., Tang, X.: Accelerating the super-resolution convolutional neural network. In: Leibe, B., Matas, J., Sebe, N., Welling, M. (eds.) ECCV 2016. LNCS, vol. 9906, pp. 391–407. Springer, Cham (2016). https://doi.org/10.1007/978-3-319-46475-6_25
19. Kim, J., Lee, J.K., Lee, K.M.: Deeply-recursive convolutional network for image super-resolution. In: Proceedings of the IEEE Conference on Computer Vision and Pattern Recognition, pp. 1637–1645 (2016)
20. Ledig, C., et al.: Photo-realistic single image super-resolution using a generative adversarial network. In: Proceedings of the IEEE Conference on Computer Vision and Pattern Recognition, pp. 4681–4690 (2017)
21. Burger, H.C., Schuler, C.J., Harmeling, S.: Image denoising: can plain neural networks compete with BM3D? In: 2012 IEEE Conference on Computer Vision and Pattern Recognition, pp. 2392–2399. IEEE (2012)
22. Goodfellow, I., et al.: Generative adversarial networks. Commun. ACM **63**(11), 139–144 (2020)
23. Zhang, K., Zuo, W., Chen, Y., Meng, D., Zhang, L.: Beyond a gaussian denoiser: residual learning of deep CNN for image denoising. IEEE Trans. Image Process. **26**(7), 3142–3155 (2017)
24. Ioffe, S., Szegedy, C.: Batch normalization: accelerating deep network training by reducing internal covariate shift. In: International Conference on Machine Learning, pp. 448–456. PMLR (2015)
25. He, K., Zhang, X., Ren, S., Sun, J.: Deep residual learning for image recognition. In: Proceedings of the IEEE Conference on Computer Vision and Pattern Recognition, pp. 770–778 (2016)
26. Liu, Y., Gu, K., Zhang, Y., Li, X., Zhai, G., Zhao, D., Gao, W.: Unsupervised blind image quality evaluation via statistical measurements of structure, naturalness, and perception. IEEE Trans. Circ. Syst. Video Technol. **30**(4), 929–943 (2020)
27. Liu, Y., Gu, K., Wang, S., Zhao, D., Gao, W.: Blind quality assessment of camera images based on low-level and high-level statistical features. IEEE Trans. Multimed. **21**(1), 135–146 (2019)

28. Liu, Y., Gu, K., Li, X., Zhang, Y.: Blind image quality assessment by natural scene statistics and perceptual characteristics. ACM Trans. Multimed. Comput. Commun. Appl. (TOMM) **16**(3), 1–91 (2020)
29. Liu, Y., Gu, K., Zhai, G., Liu, X., Zhao, D., Gao, W.: Quality assessment for real out-of-focus blurred images. J. Vis. Commun. Image Represent. **46**, 70–80 (2017)
30. Liu, Y., Li, X.: No-reference quality assessment for contrast-distorted images. IEEE Access **8**, 84 105–84 115 (2020)

Intelligent Figure Replacement Platform Based on Deep Learning

Ying Ma, Di Zhang$^{(\boxtimes)}$, Hongfei Wang, Haozhe Hon, and Long Ye

Key Laboratory of Media Audio and Video (Communication University of China), Ministry of Education, Beijing 100024, China
{dizhang,cuchhz,yelong}@cuc.edu.cn

Abstract. We introduce an intelligent platform to automatically replace the figures in video. The platform consists of three parts: figure replacement, content synthesis and interactive output. The original figure can be replaced by target figure captured with green screen background. The synthesized video is harmonized to fit the original video style. Actor can interactive with the output video to achieve better artistic effects. For the input video, we used Siammask and the STTN algorithm to key out the targeted figure and synthesize the background. Then, we use green screen keying in UE4 to get new figures in green screen background. Finally, we use the RainNet algorithm to harmonize the style of the foreground and background. Different from the existing methods which require manual manipulation on the video, our platform enhances the video production efficiency while lowers the requirement of video creation skills.

Keywords: UE4 · Green screen · Figure replacement · Video restoration · Style transfer

1 Introduction

Since the birth of film in 1888, the video entertainment industry has been continuing to pursue better viewing and experience for users. However, due to the limitation of environment and venue, audiences can only "watch" and cannot interact with actors. At present, there are video inpainting and compositing technologies on the market that cannot achieve a satisfactory effect. For example, Tiktok is a platform that can achieve the effect of changing faces of characters. But the created video has a large color difference with the original background, which does not have a strong sense of reality [1]. In comparison, virtual studio system can realize the function to put person with the virtual background. Virtual studio uses computer image processing and traditional chroma key graphics technology, analog lens tracking technology is applied to analyze the motion parameters of the camera push, pull, shake and move [2].

Traditional keying techniques, often used as industrial production tools, are criticized by their minimal reliance on algorithms, one need to prepare green screens (chroma keying) or foreground-free frames (interpolation keying) upfront for technical use in post, and the application field is usually narrow. When deep learning based keying

© Springer Nature Singapore Pte Ltd. 2022
G. Zhai et al. (Eds.): IFTC 2021, CCIS 1560, pp. 55–70, 2022.
https://doi.org/10.1007/978-981-19-2266-4_5

algorithms were proposed, Poisson Matting [3] and BayesMatting [4, 5] relied good keying effect on well-trained models. They also require fewer runtime parameters and are suitable for most scenes. However, when the foreground and background colors are very similar, the infrastructure of the mask cannot differentiate between noise, foreground and background and will not give the desired keying effect.

As the figures are subtracted, large holes appear in the video. To get a restored background, these holes need to be filled. Image inpainting algorithms based on deep learning can be divided into 3 categories: partial differential equation-based restoration techniques, image decomposition-based inpainting methods, and texture synthesis-based image inpainting algorithms. The BSCB (Bertamlio Sapiro Caselles Ballester) model proposed by Bertalmio et al. [6] is based on a partial differential equation restoration algorithm with better restoration results for small-scale broken images. The inpainting method based on image decomposition decomposes the image into two parts: structure and texture [7, 8], and this method has better results for restoring images with larger defective areas. The basic idea of texture synthesis-based image inpainting algorithms is to find the image block that is most similar to the missing information part from the unbroken area. The most representative of these algorithms is the Criminisi algorithm [9]. The basic idea of video inpainting is to cut the video into frames. The missing information in each frame is then filled in. Dahun Kim et al. [10] proposed single-frame restoration and adjacent-frame borrowing to get good results in inpainting missing information in videos. However, such work may cause errors in video inpainting due to angle changes or camera switching in continuous video. However, such work may cause errors in video inpainting due to angle changes or camera switching in continuous video. Based on GAN, image inpainting shows good performance. The paper [11] proposes SPDNorm, which dynamically balances the realism and diversity in the hole region, making the generated content more diverse toward the center of the hole and closer to the adjacent image content at the hole boundary. In addition, the authors propose perceptual diversity loss, which facilitates PD-GAN (proposed by the authors based on vanilla GAN) to generate diverse results.

After the video synthetization, due to some differences between the inserted characters and the original video background style, the video needs to be stylized and unified. Traditional non-parametric image style transfer methods are mainly based on the drawing of physical models and the synthesis of textures. The non-parametric image style transfer method can only extract the underlying features of the image, but not the high-level abstract features. When processing images with complex colors and textures, the final image synthesis results are rough and difficult to meet the actual needs. Deep learning image style transfer methods mainly include image-based iteration and model-based iteration. The maximum mean difference-based image iteration method proposed by Gatys et al. [12, 13] synthesizes images with high quality, good controllability, easy to tune the reference and without training data. Correspondingly, these algorithms have long computation times and are highly dependent on pre-trained models. Model-based iterative algorithms are computationally fast and are currently the mainstream technology for industrial application software. Iterative methods based on generative models proposed by Johnson [14] can generate corresponding models for specific styles. Iterative methods based on image reconstruction decoders proposed by Li et al. [15] can effectively avoid the parameters adjustment.

In this paper, we propose a platform to replace the figures in the video automatically. Once the video is imported, the user can select the figure to be keyed out. Then the background video without the original figure will be synthesized with the figure captured by green screen. The style transfer technology helps to migrate the style information of the background to the foreground figure video, so as to achieve a natural integration of the figure and the original video. Finally, the harmonic video will be viewed by the actor to achieve interactive effect.

2 Proposed Intelligent Figure Replacement Platform

The structure of the intelligent figure replacement platform proposed in this paper is shown in Fig. 1.

The system can be divided into three parts: figure replacement, content synthesis, and interactive output. The figure replacement part provides a pre-processed video signal for the content synthesis stage, including the keying out of the original figure and the inpainting of the background. The content synthesis part is based on UE4, where the green screen video is keyed to get the foreground video and alpha matte. This video renders with the background video to get the unharmonized video, which is fed into the video modulation network together with the alpha matte to get the stylized and harmonized video. The interactive output part displays the unharmonized and modulated video generated in the fusion stage in two different ways. For the unmodulated video, it is displayed as a return signal in real-time to provide a reference for the actor. For the modulated video, the corresponding encoding parameters can be selected and stored locally depending on the application scenario.

The details of figure replacement, content synthesis, and interactive output, are described in the following parts separately.

2.1 Figure Replacement

2.1.1 Background Content Generation

In the early stages of building this system, we manually keyed each frame of the video for a specific figure, leaving holes when the figures are keyed out. In order to get a complete background video, people should fill in the holes according to the adjacent frames or other background information. The task became even difficult when dealing with large amounts of video. So we turned our attention to deep learning network to implement the video-inpainting operation automatically. In this section, we chose SiamMask [16] and STTN [17] to imply video-inpainting.

A. Original figure keying

The first step in processing the video is to key out the original figure in the video. For the keying operation, we have chosen the Siammask algorithm. SiamMask is a unified framework for Visual Object Tracking (VOT) and Video Object Segmentation (VOS). It is based on a fully convolutional network for object tracking with the addition of mask

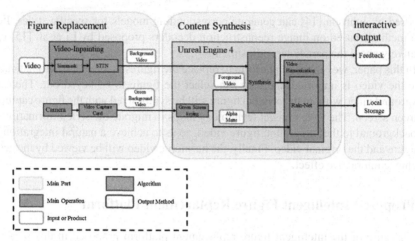

Fig. 1. The structure of the intelligent figure replacement platform

branches to achieve target segmentation. Meanwhile it enhances the loss of the network for optimization (Table 1). Comparing SiamMask with the remaining five trackers on the VOT-2018 benchmark. SiamMask gives a more excellent result. Once the network has been trained, SiamMask can automatically track and segment the target object, it relies only on the target object framed in the initial frame (Fig. 2).

Table 1. Comparison with other trackers under the EAO, Accuracy, and Robustness metrics on VOT-2018

	SiamMask	DaSiamRPN [18]	SiamRPN [19]	SA_Siam_R [20]	CSRDCF [21]	STRCF [22]
EAO	0.380	0.326	0.244	0.337	0.263	0.345
Accuracy	0.609	0.569	0.490	0.566	0.466	0.523
Robustness	0.276	0.337	0.460	0.258	0.318	0.215
Speed	55	160	200	32.4	48.9	2.9

Framework

It predicts $w \times h$ binary masks via a simple two-layer neural network h_ϕ and the learning parameter ϕ. The predicted mask is denoted by m_n corresponding to the n th RoW

$$m_n = h_\phi(g_\theta^n(z, x)).$$

In the two leftmost images, the top left image is the template and the searched video is the image with multiple people below the template, the template needs to be resized to (127, 127, 3) and the searched video need to be resized to (255, 255, 3). The size of the search can be set to other values but the value of the template needs to be fixed at 127. The template image is the f_θ output (15, 15, 256) feature map through Siamese Net,

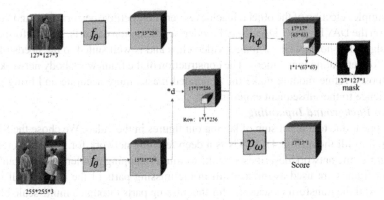

Fig. 2. Schematic illustration of the original figure keying framework

and the search image is outputted (31, 31, 256) feature map through f_θ. The two feature maps obtained are inter-correlated to obtain a (17, 17, 256) feature map.

The obtained feature map can be connected to two branches, and two layers of 1 × 1 channel transform convolution are done on each branch. The size of the feature map does not change at this point. When received on the second branch, the branch of the mask is convolved with two layers of h_ϕ of the neural network to obtain a feature map of (17, 17, 63 × 63). Another branch class score is the confidence level of each row. We need to select the row items with the highest score value in the 17 × 17 map based on the data obtained from the class score to generate our target mask. However, since the accuracy of the directly predicted mask branch is not very satisfactory, the authors proposed the refine module as shown in Fig. 3 to improve the accuracy of the segmentation, thus obtaining a more accurate mask.

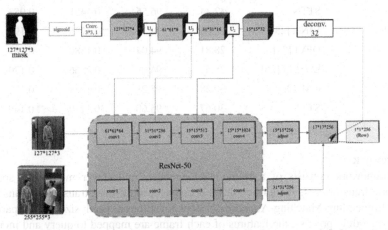

Fig. 3. Schematic illustration of the stacked refinement modules

The framework implements both video target tracking and video target segmentation tasks, and the model is simple and versatile while being easy to interact with, requiring only a simple selection of the object. It achieves very competitive performance and fastest speeds on the DAVIS-2016, DAVIS-2017 video segmentation datasets. The performance of the algorithm holds well for longer video clips and is well suited to the needs of our system for generating long videos. The construction of the framework body network and the proposed refine module make the generated masks more accurate and bring great convenience to the subsequent experiments.

B. Video Background Inpainting

Holes appear due to the last step of keying out figures in the video. We chose the STTN algorithm to fill them (Fig. 4). STTN is a deep learning network for video restoration. The algorithmic network describes a 'multi-to-multi' mapping problem. The distant and adjacent frames are used as input to fill in the missing parts of the video in all input frames. And the transformer searches for the missing parts through a multi-scale block-based attention module. This module includes both temporal and spatial dimensions. In Table 2, STTN was evaluated quantitatively and qualitatively with the remaining four algorithmic networks using standard fixed masks and real moving object masks. And excellent results were obtained in the evaluation.

Table 2. Quantitative comparisons with other algorithmic networks on Youtube-VOS [27] and DAVIS [28]. The higher the value of PSNR and SSIM, the better the result. The lower the value of E_{warp} and VFID, the better the result.

Models		PSNR	SSIM	Ewarp	VFID
Youtube-vos	VINet [23]	29.2	94.34	0.1490	0.072
	DFVI [24]	29.16	94.29	0.1509	0.066
	LGTSM [25]	29.74	95.04	0.1859	0.070
	CAP [26]	31.58	96.07	0.1470	0.071
	STTN	32.34	96.55	0.1451	0.053
DAVIS	VINet [23]	28.96	94.11	0.1785	0.199
	DFVI [24]	28.81	94.04	0.1880	0.187
	LGTSM [25]	28.57	94.09	0.2566	0.170
	CAP [26]	30.28	95.21	0.1824	0.182
	STTN	30.67	95.60	0.1779	0.149

Framework

The framework consists of a frame-level encoder, multi-layer multi-head spatial-temporal transformers, and a frame-level decoder. A multi-head transformer runs multiple "Embedding-Matching-Attending". Steps for different patch sizes run in parallel. In the encoding process, the features of each frame are mapped to query and memory (i.e., key-value pairs) for further retrieval, using $f_1^T = \{f_1, f_2, ..., f_T\}$, where $f_i \in R^{h \times w \times c}$ denotes the features encoded from the frame-level encoder or former transformers, h and w are the height and width of the input image. c represents the number of channels the features are mapped as key and memory embedded in the Transformer, it enables the

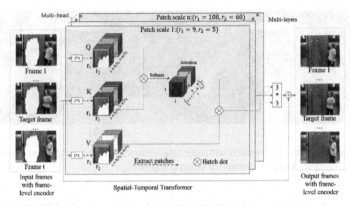

Fig. 4. Overview of the video background inpainting framework

correspondence of each region to be modeled in a different semantic space. In the matting process, the region similarity is calculated by matching the query and key between the spatial blocks extracted from all frames.

The spatial blocks of shape $R_1 * R_2 * c$ are first extracted from the query features of each frame to obtain $N = T * h/r_1 * w/r_2$ blocks. A similar operation is performed to extract the blocks (i.e. key-value pairs) in the memory. The similarity between the blocks can be computed by matrix multiplication through reshaping the query block and the key module into one-dimensional vectors respectively. After modeling the correspondence of all the spatial blocks in the Attending stage, the query values of each block can be obtained by weighting the relevant fast values. The most similar regions of the missing parts of each frame are detected and transformed to obtain the final restored video.

Video frame restoration algorithms before this framework are mostly divided into two types, one uses the frame attention mechanism to synthesize the missing parts by weighting adjacent frames. The second gradually fills the missing parts with similar pixels from the border to the inner similar pixels through the pixel-level attention mechanism, but both methods have limitations. We have tried other algorithms that use these two methods for restoration results. In the network, a deep generative model is used to learn the transformation of the spatio-temporal domain, and then the joint temporal and spatial dimensions are trained. The final video restoration is completed. The problem of video restoration is effectively targeted. It also worked well in this system experiment. It can be observed that the network is much better in terms of complementation (Fig. 5).

2.1.2 Green Screen Video Acquisition

The video signal obtained through the camera shooting is mainly transmitted to the camera's own memory card through the SDI data line. However, since the system needs to input the acquired video into the UE4 for real-time processing, and be able to synthesize video output to the two monitors in real time, the video signal cannot be stored in the camera's own memory card. In contrast, it needs to input the video signal directly into the UE4. However, as the SDI format is an unencoded baseband video signal, the SDI interface cannot directly transmit the compressed digital signal, and its code stream

(a)   (b)

Fig. 5. (a) Shows the results obtained with other algorithms for video completion, and (b) shows the results obtained with our algorithm for video completion

directly stores the luminance and chrominance values of each sampling point, ordinary hosts cannot parse such signals, and the hosts need to install additional video capture cards. In this system, the Blackmagic Decklink 4K Extreme 12G capture card are chosen. It is capable of 4K input and output via the 12G-SDI interface and can handle DCI 4K images up to 25p at 4096 x 2160 resolution. It can also capture images at 10bit YUV or full color bandwidth 12bit RGB. The capture card is installed. On the PCI slot of the computer host and the SDI cable is used to connect the output of the camera to the SDI port of the video capture card. After the capture card can work properly, open the UE4 get the green screen video captured by the camera in UE4.

2.2 Content Synthesis

2.2.1 Uncoordinated Video Production

UE4 is chosen as the platform to build the entire project. Due to its extensibility and compatibility, it helps to achieve high integration of the project. At this stage, our idea is to import the background video and the green screen video into UE4 as material assets, and set the background as the bottom layer. Therefore, it brings three main tasks in the next process:

Firstly, extracting the foreground subject from the green screen video and simply place it in front the background video;
Secondly, generating the Alpha channel from the keyed subject as a mask for the subsequent video harmonization;
And finally, directly splicing the foreground and background as footage to provide material for the video harmonization.

At the beginning, we tried to implement the green screen keying by programming the blueprint for the instance, after researched and actually operated two blueprint keying methods, the results were not very satisfactory. Method 1 and the keying effect are shown in Fig. 6(a).

The image keyed out by this method has a situation where the green screen cannot be completely deducted, and there is a significant improvement after reducing the overall opacity, but the opacity of the subject would also be lost, which is not a very ideal effect. Method 2 and the keying effect are shown in Fig. 6(b).

Compared with the first one, the method has been improved in opacity, but the parameters still cannot be adjusted to achieve the appropriate effect, and the intensity of the keying is slightly larger, resulting in part of the subject's reflective parts are also deducted, while there will be the problem of excessive gamma value of the main body.

Finally, after capturing the green screen video through capture card, a plug-in of the capture card is found which has its own function with color keying diagram. After a slight adjustment of the parameters, we generated a more satisfactory result. Compared with the results of the previous blueprint keying, the opacity and gamma value issues have been significantly improved, and the intensity is also controlled within an acceptable range, but there are still some defects in the local opacity. Effects is shown in Fig. 6(c).

After solving the green screen keying, the alpha matte is set out to generate immediately, where the pure white subject superimposed to the black background formed by the picture. So according to our vision, as long as the green screen keyed out transformed into pure white then the work is basically completed. On the basis of the capture card plug-in, what only needed is to turn on the Alpha channel switch in the above-mentioned green keyed parameter panel.

Finally, to synthesize the inharmonic video and the mask video, two video playback boards are set up in UE4, one for placing the keyed foreground subject, and the other for placing the produced pure white foreground. The two boards both contain two layers of image, the bottom layer is used for the background, while the top layer with alpha channel is used for foreground. The cameras that focused on the boards will output the captured image. The layout is shown in Fig. 6(d).

2.2.2 Harmonic Video Creation

After the synthesis of the video, a big gap between the tone of the foreground figure and background video can be clearly observed, the foreground figure looks very abrupt. We initially tried to adjust the values of color temperature, exposure, and contrast in UE4 to allow the foreground figure to blend into the background for a better result. However, when the background was changed, the parameters had to be changed again. It is tedious and complicated. So the algorithmic network was chosen to achieve the final coordination of the video. To achieve this effect, we first fed the resulting composite video and the previously obtained alpha matte into the prepared video harmonization network, but during the green screen keying phase of UE4, there was an overall loss of opacity in the video, resulting in a loss of opacity in the final alpha matte that caused a certain amount of greyness. Therefore, a binarization process is added to the alpha matte in the harmonic network to produce the ideal foreground mask, thus providing a better result when harmonize the video. The Rain-Net network is chosen to achieve this task. The video transferred to the monitor is not harmonized, but a composite video of the foreground and background video. Once the position of the character has been determined, the harmonized unification will be manipulated to the video through RainNet network. It achieves the desired effect of color uniformity and harmonized looking video.

Although the RainNet network takes a long time to run. The RainNet [29] algorithmic network still provides us with a well-performing image harmonization network in which different images are described and transformed by defining the visual style of the image as visual attributes such as lighting, color temperature, saturation, and hue texture. This

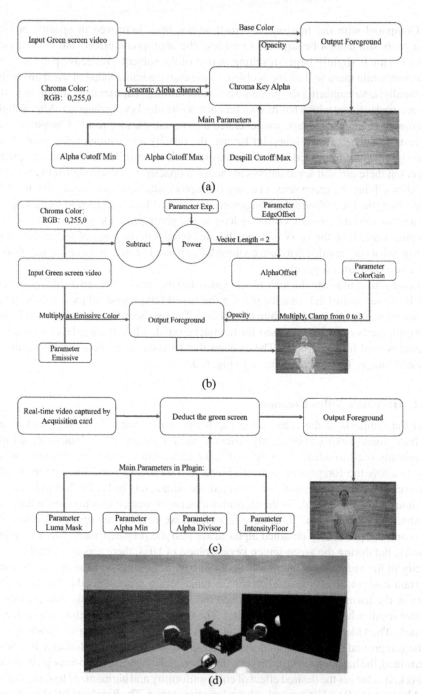

Fig. 6. (a) Is method 1 and the keying effect, (b) is method 2 and the keying effect, (c) is method 3 and keying effect, (d) is Layout of output synthetic video and alpha matte

Framework

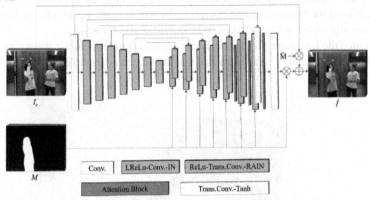

Fig. 7. Structure of the harmonic video creation framework

makes the synthesized images look more realistic and ensures a uniform visual style between the foreground and the background (Fig. 7).

Framework

We have previously rescaled the alpha image obtained from UE4 by binarizing it to obtain the alpha matte map of the real input to the network, with the Foreground set to I_f and the background set to I_b. The foreground mask is the alpha matte we have got is denoted by M, which indicates the region to be harmonized in the composite image I_c. Accordingly, the background mask is $\overline{M} = 1 - M$. The object composition process is formulated as $I_c = M \circ I_f + (1 - M) \circ I_b$, where $\circ$ is the Hadamard product. In this paper, the harmonization model is defined as generator G, and the harmonized image as $\hat{I} = G(I_c, M)$, where G is a learnable model that is expected to optimize for making $\hat{I}$ close to the ground truth image I by $||G(I_c, M) - I||_1$.

The simple and effective normalization module proposed in this network has a much better performance than previous normalization methods. It is very stable and works well when harmonizing successive images. And it is very accurate in representing images through defined visual styles.

2.3 Interactive Output

2.3.1 Real-Time Return of Synthetic Video

With the video board built in UE4, we are able to present the video to be returned and output in the screen. In order to make the footage given at the beginning of the work we create the camera asset, aligned its spatial position to the screens that are going to return, and edit the level blueprint of UE4 in able to set the main viewing angle to this camera at beginning of the work (as shown in Fig. 8).

At the same time, it is important that the output on the hardware needs to be seen by the users in real time. To accomplish this, we use two additional sets of display devices, one is placed in front of the green screen to receive feedback at any time, the other one is facing to the audiences for them to get the feedback in real time.

A HDMI divider is used to connect the three monitors except for the primary display which used for monitoring and operating the whole systems, with the same source, the system allows two output screens to be operated synchronously.

Once the hardware problem is resolved, it is simple to adjust the position and size of the default window so as to ensure that the screen is displayed perfectly.

Fig. 8. Layout of real-time return video

2.3.2 Harmonic Video Local Storage

The algorithm which used for harmonization in our entire project called the rain-net network, which is a color fusion algorithm for pictures, so the idea is to output the captured video in UE4 as a picture set frame by frame, color fusion for each picture, and then synthesize the video to save it locally.

The first problem we encountered is that UE4 could not capture two frames and save them at the same time. But the uncoordinated video and the mask are both needed, therefore we need to create a new video playback version and compositing the two frames together for playback (as shown in Fig. 9).

Fig. 9. Layout of uncoordinated video and the mask

After integrating the algorithms of image cutting and binarizing the mask, we synthesized the video from Rain-net and finally realize a system including green screen video capture, video harmonization and local storage (Fig. 10).

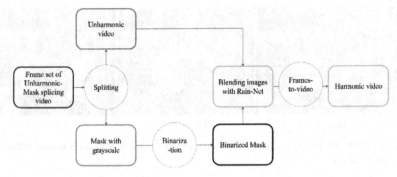

Fig. 10. Video reconciliation process

3 Experimental Results

The studio is located in the State Key Laboratory of Media Convergence and Communication, Communication University of China, Beijing, China, the studio covers an area of 25 square meters. To achieve a high-quality keying effect, only two green screens are kept, one facing the camera and the other covering the ground, and a green screen was chosen that was easy to smooth out the folds and had a uniform color. Several fill lights are placed on top of the green screen to lighten the figures, brighten their skin tones and remove any shadows left by the green screen. At the front of the green screen, a monitor is placed on each side of the camera, one facing the green screen and the other facing the operation floor. And monitor is placed on the operation floor, the layout of the studio is shown in Fig. 11. The type of TV camera we use is RED SCARLET X, and the UE4 is deployed on a 16G RAM, intel i7 CPU2.4GHz server.

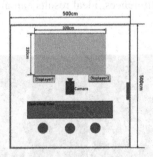

Fig. 11. The layout of the studio, with the brown part representing the walls and the green part representing the green screen (Color figure online)

The original video is shown in Fig. 12(a), a background video with inpainted background is generated as in Fig. 12(b). Figure 12(c) indicates the final replacement result after style harmonization.

The camera captures the actor standing in front of the green screen, as shown in Fig. 13(a). The captured video is passed to UE4 for processing. The position of the actor and the background can be observed in the real-time display as shown in Fig. 13 (b).

(a)   (b)   (c)

Fig. 12. (a) Is the original video, (b) is the video-inpainting video, and (c) is output video after video harmonization

(a)   (b)

Fig. 13. Shot in the studio

The same operation has been done with the other videos in the same way and got the following results in Fig. 14. It can be seen from our experiment that the platform is more suitable for processing long videos and videos with small background changes. For videos with large color differences, ideal results can also be obtained through this platform.

(a)   (b)

Fig. 14. Original video and output video

The results show that our foreground figure blends in perfectly with the background video, successfully replacing the original figure in the video.

4 Conclusion

We propose an intelligent figure replacement platform. Our platform allows the target figure to perfectly replace the original figure in the video, and harmonies the new figure to the tone of the original video to get a lifelike blending effect. Through this platform, a large amount of manpower is reduced, it will boost the efficiency of video production. It also lowers the requirements for video creation skills, making it possible for more people to make their own videos. In the future, we will continue to improve our platform for more applications, such as replacing the figure with characters from any type of scenes.

References

1. Omar, B., Dequan, W.: Watch, share or create: the influence of personality traits and user motivation on TikTok mobile video usage. Int. J. Interact. Mob. Technol. **14**(4) (2020)
2. Sun, J., Jiang, H.: Introduction to the virtual studio system. Res. Digit. Media **34**(06), 70–72 (2017)
3. Sun, J., Jia, J., Tang, C.-K., Shum, H.-Y.: Poisson Matting, Microsoft Research Asia, Hong Kong University of Science and Technology
4. Chuang, Y.-Y., Curless, B., Salesin, D.H., Szeliski, R.: A Bayesian Approach to Digital Matting. Department of Computer Science and Engineering, University of Washington, Seattle
5. Jia, Y., Hu, S., Martin, R.R.: Video completion using tracking and fragment merging. Vis. Comput. **21**, 601–610 (2005)
6. Bertalmio, M., Saprio, G., Caselles, V., et al.: Image inpainting. In: Proceedings of ACM SIGGRAPH, pp. 417–424 (2000)
7. Gu, J., Peng, S., Wang, X.: Digital image inpainting using Monte Carlo method. In: International Conference on Image Processing, pp. 961–964 (2004)
8. Aujol, J.-F., Aubert, G., Blanc-Féraud, L., Chambolle, A.: Image decomposition application to SAR images. In: Griffin, L.D., Lillholm, M. (eds.) Scale Space Methods in Computer Vision, pp. 297–312. Springer, Heidelberg (2003). https://doi.org/10.1007/3-540-44935-3_21
9. Criminisi, A., Perez, P., Toyama, K.: Region filling and object removal by exemplar-based image inpainting. IEEE Trans. Image Process. **13**(9), 1200–1212 (2004)
10. Kim, D., Woo, S., Lee, J.Y., et al.: Deep video inpainting. In: 2019 IEEE/CVF Conference on Computer Vision and Pattern Recognition (CVPR). IEEE (2019)
11. Liu, H., Wan, Z., Huang, W., et al.: PD-GAN: probabilistic diverse GAN for image inpainting. In: Proceedings of the IEEE/CVF Conference on Computer Vision and Pattern Recognition, pp. 9371–9381 (2021)
12. Gatys, L.A., Ecker, A.S., Bethge, M.: A neural algorithm of artistic style. arXiv preprint arXiv:1508.06576 (2015)
13. Gatys, L.A., Bethge, M., Hertzmann, A., et al.: Preserving color in neural artistic style transfer. arXiv preprint arXiv:1606.05897 (2016)
14. Johnson, J., Alahi, A., Fei-Fei, L.: Perceptual losses for real-time style transfer and super-resolution. In: Leibe, B., Matas, J., Sebe, N., Welling, M. (eds.) ECCV 2016. LNCS, vol. 9906, pp. 694–711. Springer, Cham (2016). https://doi.org/10.1007/978-3-319-46475-6_43
15. Li, Y., Fang, C., Yang, J., et al.: Universal style transfer via feature transforms. arXiv preprint arXiv:1705.08086 (2017)
16. Wang, Q., Zhang, L., Bertinetto, L., et al.: Fast online object tracking and segmentation: a unifying approach. In: Proceedings of the IEEE/CVF Conference on Computer Vision and Pattern Recognition, pp. 1328–1338 (2019)

17. Zeng, Y., Fu, J., Chao, H.: Learning joint spatial-temporal transformations for video inpainting. In: Vedaldi, A., Bischof, H., Brox, T., Frahm, J.-M. (eds.) Computer Vision – ECCV 2020, pp. 528–543. Springer International Publishing, Cham (2020). https://doi.org/10.1007/978-3-030-58517-4_31

18. Zhu, Z., Wang, Q., Li, B., Wei, W., Yan, J., Hu, W.: Distractor-aware siamese networks for visual object tracking. In: Ferrari, V., Hebert, M., Sminchisescu, C., Weiss, Y. (eds.) ECCV 2018. LNCS, vol. 11213, pp. 103–119. Springer, Cham (2018). https://doi.org/10.1007/978-3-030-01240-3_7

19. Li, B., Yan, J., Wu, W., Zhu, Z., Hu, X.: High performancevisual tracking with siamese region proposal network. In: IEEE Conference on Computer Vision and Pattern Recognition (2018)

20. He, A., Luo, C., Tian, X., Zeng, W.: Towards a better match in siamese network based visual object tracker. In: Leal-Taixé, L., Roth, S. (eds.) ECCV 2018. LNCS, vol. 11129, pp. 132–147. Springer, Cham (2019). https://doi.org/10.1007/978-3-030-11009-3_7

21. Lukezic, A., Vojir, T., Zajc, L.C., Matas, J., Kristan, M.: Discriminative correlation filter with channel and spatial reliability. In: IEEE Conference on Computer Vision and Pattern Recognition (2017)

22. Li, F., Tian, C., Zuo, W., Zhang, L., Yang, M.-H.: Learning spatial-temporal regularized correlation filters for visualtracking. In: IEEE Conference on Computer Vision and Pattern Recognition (2018)

23. Kim, D., Woo, S., Lee, J.Y., Kweon, I.S.: Deep video inpainting. In: CVPR, pp.5792–5801 (2019)

24. Xu, R., Li, X., Zhou, B., Loy, C.C.: Deep flow-guided video inpainting. In: CVPR, pp. 3723–3732 (2019)

25. Chang, Y.L., Liu, Z.Y., Lee, K.Y., Hsu, W.: Learnable gated temporal shift modulefor deep video inpainting. In: BMVC (2019)

26. Lee, S., Oh, S.W., Won, D., Kim, S.J.: Copy-and-paste networks for deep videoinpainting. In: ICCV, pp. 4413–4421 (2019)

27. Xu, N., et al.: YouTube-VOS:a large-scale video object segmentation benchmark. arXiv (2018)

28. Caelles, S., et al.: The 2018 DAVIS challenge on video object segmentation. arXiv (2018)

29. Chen, X., Feng, K., Liu, N., et al.: RainNet: a large-scale dataset for spatial precipitation downscaling. arXiv preprint arXiv:2012.09700 (2020)

Feature Aligned Ship Detection Based on RepPoints in SAR Images

Cong'an Xu[1,2], Hang Su[1(✉)], Long Gao[1], Jun'feng Wu[1], Wen'jun Yan[1], and Jian'wei Li[3]

[1] Information Fusion Institute, Naval Aviation University,
Yantai 264000, Shandong, China
`shpersonal_email@163.com`
[2] Advanced Technology Research Institute, Beijing Institute of Technology,
Jinan 250300, Shandong, China
[3] Troops of 92877, Shanghai 201100, China

Abstract. Ship detection in synthetic aperture radar (SAR) image is an important and challenging task. A number of methods based on deep learning have been proposed for the ship detection task and achieved remarkable performance. However, existing methods still suffer from some problems, such as feature misalignment, multi-scale, small target missing, etc., which lead to low detection accuracy. To solve these problems, we propose a feature-aligned anchor-free ship detection algorithm based on the RepPoints method. The model consists of a feature pyramid networks (FPN) backbone, a feature alignment module, and a refinement detection head. Specifically, the FPN backbone is used to extract multi-scale features, then the feature alignment module is used to perform coarse-grained location prediction. After that, the deformable convolution (DConv) is used for the fine-grained feature alignment based on the coarse prediction. Finally, a score map and refined location prediction are generated on the aligned feature map. Experimental results on the publicly available SAR image dataset SSDD demonstrate the effectiveness of the proposed method.

Keywords: SAR image · Ship detection · Feature alignment · Anchor-free · Coarse to fine

1 Introduction

Synthetic aperture radar (SAR) has the characteristics of all-day and all-weather operation, and is widely used in military and civil fields. As an important branch of SAR image interpretation, ship detection is of great significance to port supervision, fishery supervision and military investigation. Traditional detection methods are usually based on manually designed features or statistical models, which

Supported by the National Natural Science Foundation of China (Grant No. 61790550, No. 61790554, No. 61971432, No. 62022092) and the Young Elite Scientists Sponsorship Program by CAST.

© Springer Nature Singapore Pte Ltd. 2022
G. Zhai et al. (Eds.): IFTC 2021, CCIS 1560, pp. 71–82, 2022.
https://doi.org/10.1007/978-981-19-2266-4_6

have poor generalization ability and low detection accuracy in complex scenes, and cannot meet the requirements of high-precision detection of ship in SAR images. The detection method based on deep learning has the advantages of strong feature extraction ability, strong generalization ability and high detection accuracy without manual feature design, and has gradually replaced the traditional methods [4].

Since Li et al. [5] discloses the first SAR image ship detection dataset SSDD, many algorithms have been proposed to address the SAR ship detection task. For example, Li et al. proposes an improved Faster R-CNN algorithm. This method consists of two stages: firstly, it uses the RPN network to generate a proposal, then the refined detection is performed on the proposal. This algorithm obtains relatively better performance by aligning features with the RPN network. However, the two-stage algorithms are complex in the detection stage, thus not satisfying the real-time monitoring requirement. To address this problem, one-stage algorithms which can directly predict categories and location information are proposed. For example, inspired by DSOD, Deng et al. [3] proposes a ship detection algorithm training from scratch. Based on depthwise convolution, Zhang et al. [15] improves the speed of ship detection in SAR images by an end-to-end network structure. These methods have faster speed, but the performance is relatively low because they neglect to align the feature.

Based on these algorithms, the 1.5-stage algorithms are proposed to address the feature misalignment as well as keep relatively fast speed. A representative method is RepPoints [13], which predicts the location in the coarse prediction stage, and takes the learned position as the offset to generate aligned features. But as far as we see, there is no work trying to use the 1.5-stage algorithm on the SAR ship detection task.

To address the feature misalignment problem in SAR ship detection task, we propose a feature-aligned anchor-free method based on the RepPoints algorithm. This method can improve the detection accuracy by aligning the feature, as well as improve the detection efficiency by using the 1.5-stage structure. We conduct three experiments on a publicly available SAR ship detection dataset, and the results verify the effectiveness of the proposed method.

The main contributions of this paper are as follows:

1. This paper introduces the DConv method to address the feature misalignment problem in the ship detection task.
2. Based on RepPoints, this paper proposes a SAR image ship detection algorithm, and obtains state-of-the-art (SOTA) results compared to previous algorithms.

2 Related Works

2.1 Deep Learning Based Object Detection Algorithms

Based on the number of stages, previous methods can be generally split into three categories: one-stage algorithm, two-stage algorithm, and 1.5-stage algorithms. One-stage algorithms, represented by SSD [7] and YOLO [8], can directly predict categories and location information. However, these methods suffer from the feature misalignment problem, making the detection accuracy relatively low. The two-stage algorithms such as Faster R-CNN [9] firstly generate a proposal through the RPN network, then perform the refined detection based on the proposal. These methods can address the feature alignment problem by RoIPooling or RoIAlign methods. However, the two-stage algorithm is complex and slow in the detection stage, which does not meet the real-time monitoring requirement. Based on these studies, 1.5-stage algorithms are proposed to solve the problem of feature misalignment as well as keep relatively fast speed. For example, based on SSD, RefineDet [14] first makes coarse predictions of locations and then refines predictions, but the prediction refine stage is still made on mis-aligned features. The RepPoints algorithm firstly realizes feature alignment by using the DConv [2], then obtains the fine-grained predictions on the aligned features. By introducing the DConv, this method can align features well and thus obtain remarkable performance on a variety of detection tasks.

2.2 Feature Misalignment

Feature misalignment mainly refers to that the predicted location has changed greatly relative to the original position, but the classification and regression still use the original position features for prediction. As shown in Fig. 1, the red box is the ground truth bounding box, and the blue box is the predicted bounding box. The predicted bounding box is close to the ground truth, but its receptive field is not aligned with the predicted position in the original image, which will lead to the decrease of detection accuracy.

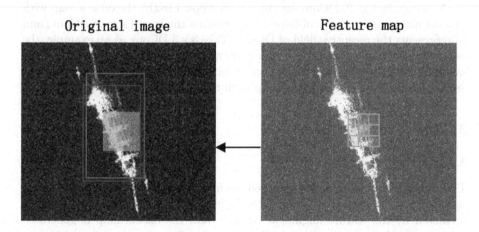

Fig. 1. Feature misalignment in SAR ship detection. (Color figure online)

For two-stage detection algorithms, in the first stage, coarse regression is carried out through the RPN network to generate a proposal; in the second stage, the proposal in the first stage is unified to the same size through RoIAlign and refined regression and classification are carried out. Through the proposal generated in the RPN and RoIAlign operation, the two-stage algorithm has greatly alleviated the problem of feature misalignment. However, for one-stage algorithms, the feature misalignment problem is more serious because there is no RPN and RoIAlign operation.

2.3   Deformable Convolution

The vanilla convolution has a fixed shape and can obtain a fixed size receptive field. Different from vanilla convolution, deformable convolution realizes convolution of arbitrary shape by adding offsets, and can obtain receptive field of any shape. Specifically, taking 3×3 convolution weighted by $\mathbf{w}$ as an example, for grid $\mathcal{R}$ on the input feature map $\mathbf{x}$, where $\mathcal{R} = \{(-1,-1),(-1,0),\ldots,(0,1),(1,1)\}$, the corresponding position $\mathbf{p}$ on the output feature map $\mathbf{y}$ can be calculated as:

$$\mathbf{y}\left(\mathbf{p}\right) = \sum_{\mathbf{p}_n \in \mathcal{R}} \mathbf{w}\left(\mathbf{p}_n\right) \cdot \mathbf{x}\left(\mathbf{p} + \mathbf{p}_n\right) \tag{1}$$

However, for DConv, the grid $\mathcal{R}$ will be added to offsets $\Delta\mathcal{R}$, and the output becomes

$$\mathbf{y}\left(\mathbf{p}\right) = \sum_{\mathbf{p}_n \in \mathcal{R}, \Delta\mathbf{p}_n \in \Delta\mathcal{R}} \mathbf{w}\left(\mathbf{p}_n\right) \cdot \mathbf{x}\left(\mathbf{p} + \mathbf{p}_n + \Delta\mathbf{p}_n\right) \tag{2}$$

In this way, DConv can achieve convolution of arbitrary shapes.

As shown in Fig. 2, DConv has two main steps. Firstly, the offsets map with channel number of $2 \times k^2$ is obtained. k represents the kernel size of DConv, and k^2 represents the receptive field of DConv. Take 3×3 DConv as an example, the number of channels of the offsets map is 18, which corresponds to the offsets of 9 sampling points during convolution operation. Finally, DConv generates aligned feature map on the input feature map with the offsets map.

3   The Proposed Method

3.1   Overall Architecture

The overall architecture of the proposed method is shown in Fig. 3. Firstly, multi-scale features are extracted by the FPN Backbone. Then, the location is coarsely predicted by the feature alignment module, and the offsets map is generated according to the coarse prediction. Based on the offsets map, an aligned feature map is generated through the DConv. Finally, refined location regression and classification are carried out on the aligned feature map. During training stage, the losses of coarse prediction of location and fine prediction of location and category are calculated.

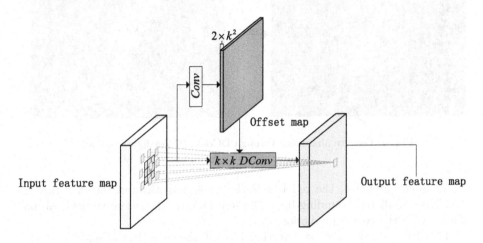

Fig. 2. Deformable convolution.

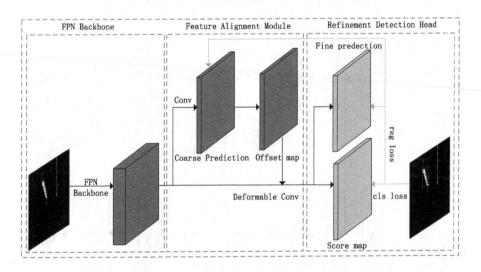

Fig. 3. Overall architecture.

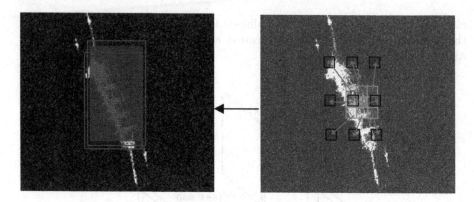

Fig. 4. Feature alignment through DConv. (Color figure online)

As shown in Fig. 4, the red box is the ground truth, and the blue box is the coarse predicted bounding box. Through DConv, the receptive field can be aligned with the coarse prediction.

The detailed structure of detection head is shown in Fig. 5, and the same detection head is added to the feature map of each layer. The features extracted by FPN backbone in this paper are the same as the RetinaNet [6].

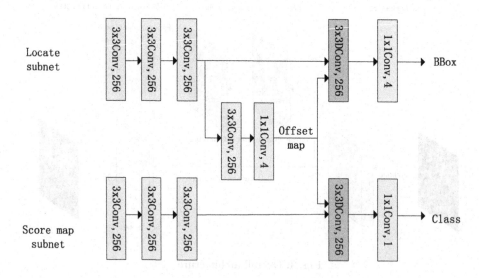

Fig. 5. Detailed structure of the detection head.

3.2   Bounding Box Representation

In this paper, the bounding box is represented by the top-left point and the down-right point. In the coarse prediction stage, the offsets map evenly samples nine points through the coarse predicted bounding box with channel 18.

3.3   Loss Function

Focal loss function (FL) is used to balance positive and negative samples for classification, and Smooth L1 loss function $(Smooth_{L1})$ is used for regression loss both in coarse stage and refine stage. The over all losses are calculated as:

$$losses = \lambda_1 Smooth_{L1}(b_{coarse}, b_*) + \lambda_2 Smooth_{L1}(b_{fine}, b_*) + \lambda_3 FL(cls_{pred}, cls_*)$$

$$(3)$$

where, b_* represents the ground truth bounding box, b_{coarse} represents the coarse predicted bounding box, b_{fine} represents the fine predicted bounding box, cls_* represents the label of the ground truth, and cls_{pred} represents the predicted label. λ_1, λ_2, and λ_3 are the weight of the losses.

4   Experiments and Results

In this section, we evaluate the proposed method in two aspects: (1) compare with previous methods to show the effectiveness of our method; (2) conduct the ablation study to show the stability when using different backbone networks and number of channels in the detection head.

4.1   Dataset and Evaluation Metrics

SSDD is the first public SAR ship detection dataset, which contains SAR images with different resolutions, polarization modes and scenarios. All algorithms uses the same 80% samples as the training set and the rest 20% samples as the testing set. Here, image names with the index suffix of 1 and 9 are selected as the testing set, and the others as the training set. AP, AP_{50}, AP_{75}, AP_s, AP_m, AP_l, number of parameters and FPS are used as evaluation metrics. The meaning of the evaluation metrics is shown in Table 1.

4.2   Implementation Details

The Pytorch is employed on an NVIDIA RTX1080Ti GPU for all algorithms. In order to ensure comparison fairness, all experiments are implemented under the MMDetection toolbox [1]. The resolution of input images is uniformly set to 512×512 both in training and testing stages, and the batch size is set to 8. The ResNet-50 is used as the backbone network with the channel number in detection head setting to 256. Stochastic gradient descent (SGD) serves as the optimizer, with a learning rate of 0.01, a momentum of 0.9, and a weight decay of 0.0001. The training epoch is set to 24, and the learning rate is reduced by 10 times per epoch from 16-epoch to 22-epoch to ensure an adequate loss reduction. The NMS threshold is set to 0.5. λ_1, λ_2, and λ_3 are set to 0.5, 1.0 and 1.0.

Table 1. Meaning of evaluation metrics.

Metric	Meaning
AP	AP for IoU $= 0.5::0.05::0.95$
AP_{50}	AP for IoU $= 0.50$
AP_{75}	AP for IoU $= 0.75$
AP_s	AP for small objects: area $< 32^2$ (IoU $= 0.50:0.05:0.95$)
AP_m	AP for medium objects: $32^2 <$ area $< 96^2$ (IoU $= 0.50:0.05:0.95$)
AP_l	AP for large objects: area $> 96^2$ (IoU $= 0.50:0.05:0.95$)
Params	Number of parameters (MB)
FPS	Frames per second

4.3 Results

To verify the superiority of the proposed method, we compare it with other 6 competitive CNN-based SAR ship detectors such as Faster R-CNN, RetinaNet, and YOLOv3. As shown in Table 2, the proposed method obtains the SOTA results while maintains advantages in parameters and FPS. The best results are marked in bold.

Table 2. Results of different algorithms.

Method	Backbone	AP	AP_{50}	AP_{75}	AP_s	AP_m	AP_l	Params	FPS
Faster R-CNN [9]	ResNet-50	0.588	0.917	0.682	0.540	0.662	**0.653**	41.12	36.1
RetinaNet [6]	ResNet-50	0.491	0.855	0.519	0.421	0.607	0.483	36.1	41.2
YOLOV3 [8]	DarkNet-53	0.497	0.920	0.503	0.475	0.538	0.419	61.52	**61.5**
Guide Anchoring [12]	ResNet-50	0.458	0.846	0.459	0.396	0.576	0.391	37.19	31.2
CenterNet [16]	ResNet-50	0.149	0.429	0.066	0.109	0.203	0.300	72.08	54.1
FCOS [11]	ResNet-50	0.243	0.563	0.179	0.11	0.426	0.608	**31.84**	49.1
Ours	ResNet-50	**0.604**	**0.949**	**0.694**	**0.559**	**0.671**	0.605	36.6	35.5

4.4 Ablation Study

To show the influence of the backbone network, we conduct the experiments with different backbone networks, and the results are shown in Table 3. We can see that the backbone network with deeper layers and more parameters can obtains better feature expression, thus obtaining better performance. Generally the proposed method obtains relatively stable detection results among different backbone networks, validating the robustness of the proposed method. Specifically, the ResNet-101 achieves similar results to ResNet-50, while the number of parameters increases and speed decreases. ResNet18 has advantages in terms of number of parameters and FPS while maintaining detection accuracy. The backbone network for mobile deployment, MobileNetV2 [10], has a much lower accuracy, and the result of FPS is not optimal.

Table 3. Results with different backbone networks.

Backbone	AP	AP_{50}	AP_{75}	AP_s	AP_m	AP_l	Params	FPS
ResNet-101	**0.605**	**0.956**	0.684	0.557	**0.681**	**0.628**	55.59	27.4
ResNet-50	0.604	0.949	**0.694**	**0.559**	0.671	0.605	36.6	35.5
ResNet-18	0.584	0.942	0.669	0.541	0.654	0.537	20.11	**44.7**
MoblileNetV2	0.537	0.907	0.583	0.509	0.589	0.540	**13.21**	39.9

To analyze the influence of the number of channels, we also test different channels in the detection head based on the ResNet-18. As show in Table 4, the best result is obtained when setting the number of channels to 256.

Table 4. Results with different number of channels.

Number of channels	AP	AP_{50}	AP_{75}	AP_s	AP_m	AP_l	Params	FPS
512	0.580	0.931	0.664	**0.545**	0.638	**0.580**	44.52	29.3
256	**0.584**	**0.942**	**0.669**	0.541	**0.654**	0.537	20.11	44.7
128	0.550	0.910	0.604	0.518	0.611	0.527	13.64	46.2
64	0.541	0.903	0.624	0.516	0.592	0.471	11.85	50.2
32	0.480	0.854	0.509	0.464	0.532	0.341	**11.32**	**51.0**

4.5 Visualization of Detection Results

In this section, we visualize detection results under different scenarios. Figure 6 visualizes detection results under offshore scenarios, and Fig. 7 visualizes detection results under inshore scenarios. The first line is the ground truth, and the second line is the detection results. As we can see from the figures, the proposed method can accurately detect ship under offshore scenarios of different resolution. However, due to the interference of the shore, there are some false detection results under the inshore scenarios.

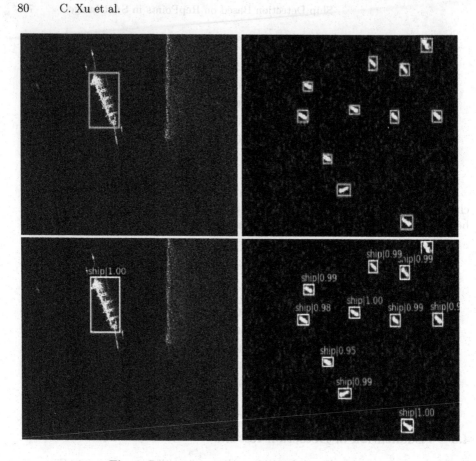

Fig. 6. Detection results under offshore scenarios.

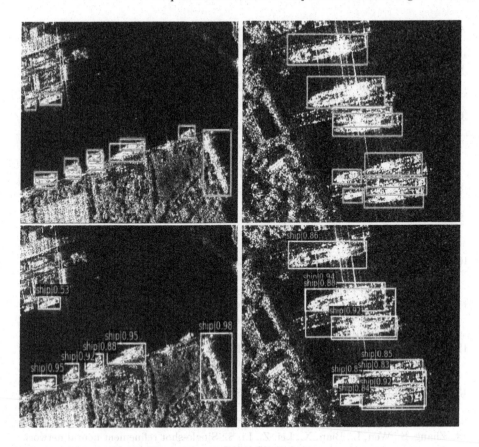

Fig. 7. Detection results under inshore scenarios.

5 Conclusions

To solve the problem of feature misalignment in the SAR ship detection, this paper proposes a feature-aligned anchor-free ship detection algorithm. Compared with previous algorithms, the proposed method achieves SOTA results on the SSDD dataset, and maintains advantages both in parameter numbers and speed.

References

1. Chen, K., et al.: MMDetection: open MMLab detection toolbox and benchmark. ArXiv abs/1906.07155 (2019)
2. Dai, J., et al.: Deformable convolutional networks. In: 2017 IEEE International Conference on Computer Vision (ICCV), pp. 764–773 (2017)
3. Deng, Z., Sun, H., Zhou, S., Zhao, J.: Learning deep ship detector in SAR images from scratch. IEEE Trans. Geosci. Remote Sens. **57**, 4021–4039 (2019)

4. He, F., He, Y., Liu, Z., Xu, C.: Research and development on applications of convolutional neural networks of radar automatic target recognition. J. Electron. Inf. Technol. **41**(1), 119–131 (2020)

5. Li, J., Qu, C., Shao, J.: Ship detection in SAR images based on an improved faster R-CNN. In: 2017 SAR in Big Data Era: Models, Methods and Applications (BIGSARDATA), pp. 1–6 (2017)

6. Lin, T.Y., Goyal, P., Girshick, R.B., He, K., Dollár, P.: Focal loss for dense object detection. IEEE Trans. Pattern Anal. Mach. Intell. **42**, 318–327 (2020)

7. Liu, W., et al.: SSD: single shot multibox detector. In: Leibe, B., Matas, J., Sebe, N., Welling, M. (eds.) ECCV 2016. LNCS, vol. 9905, pp. 21–37. Springer, Cham (2016). https://doi.org/10.1007/978-3-319-46448-0_2

8. Redmon, J., Farhadi, A.: YOLOv3: an incremental improvement. ArXiv abs/1804.02767 (2018)

9. Ren, S., He, K., Girshick, R.B., Sun, J.: Faster R-CNN: towards real-time object detection with region proposal networks. IEEE Trans. Pattern Anal. Mach. Intell. **39**, 1137–1149 (2015)

10. Sandler, M., Howard, A.G., Zhu, M., Zhmoginov, A., Chen, L.C.: MobileNetV2: Inverted residuals and linear bottlenecks. In: 2018 IEEE/CVF Conference on Computer Vision and Pattern Recognition, pp. 4510–4520 (2018)

11. Tian, Z., Shen, C., Chen, H., He, T.: FCOS: fully convolutional one-stage object detection. In: 2019 IEEE/CVF International Conference on Computer Vision (ICCV), pp. 9626–9635 (2019)

12. Wang, J., Chen, K., Yang, S., Loy, C.C., Lin, D.: Region proposal by guided anchoring. In: 2019 IEEE/CVF Conference on Computer Vision and Pattern Recognition (CVPR), pp. 2960–2969 (2019)

13. Yang, Z., Liu, S., Hu, H., Wang, L., Lin, S.C.F.: RepPoints: point set representation for object detection. In: 2019 IEEE/CVF International Conference on Computer Vision (ICCV), pp. 9656–9665 (2019)

14. Zhang, S., Wen, L., Bian, X., Lei, Z., Li, S.: Single-shot refinement neural network for object detection. In: 2018 IEEE/CVF Conference on Computer Vision and Pattern Recognition, pp. 4203–4212 (2018)

15. Zhang, T., Zhang, X., Shi, J., Wei, S.: Depthwise separable convolution neural network for high-speed SAR ship detection. Remote Sens. **11**, 2483 (2019)

16. Zhou, X., Wang, D., Krähenbühl, P.: Objects as points. ArXiv abs/1904.07850 (2019)

A Novel Cutting Double k-Clique Spanning Tree Method for Coalition Detection from Brain Functional Networks

Kai Liu[1], Hongbo Liu[2], and Zhaolin Wan[2(✉)]

[1] School of Information Science and Technology, Dalian Maritime University, Dalian, China
dlhslk@dlmu.edu.cn
[2] College of Artificial Intelligence, Dalian Maritime University, Dalian, China
{lhb,zlwan}@dlmu.edu.cn

Abstract. Network science is a useful tool to investigate brain functional networks. In particular, community detection could be considered as a representative framework to identify brain functional coalitions. However, brain functional networks generally demonstrate dense structure feature and imbalanced coalition scale. It causes high-complexity and imbalance problems for community detection. In this paper, a novel method, named Cutting Double k-Clique Spanning Tree (COUSIN) method, for coalition detection from brain functional networks has been proposed. The local nodes are characterized into k-cliques as essential substructures. Then the k-cliques with each degressively order k hierarchically merge and form two spanning trees of the given network. A cutting strategy is used to drop coalitions from the double spanning tree. Experiments of robustness verification are executed on simulated networks. The experimental tests on real datasets exhibit prominent performance of community detection of the proposed method. The obtained coalitions from actual brain functional networks indicate the application value of the method in neuroscience.

Keywords: k-Clique · Coalition detection · Brain functional networks

1 Introduction

Brain functional networks are constructed through dividing brain into regions of interest (ROIs) and measuring temporal correlations between fMRI signals of them [1]. Brain functional coalition is composed of groups of specific ROIs with same cognitive function. Identifying such localized structure helps to unmask working pattern of the human brain [2].

Network science is a useful tool in investigation of network type data [3]. In particular, community detection as outstanding sub-topic of network science is applied to mine medium-scale structure from given network [4]. The nodes prefer to group with other nodes by high connection or similar function. It indicates

G. Zhai et al. (Eds.): IFTC 2021, CCIS 1560, pp. 83–95, 2022.
https://doi.org/10.1007/978-981-19-2266-4_7

that community detection could be considered as an alternative method for coalition detection from brain functional networks.

Network science mainly focuses on networks with sparse edges. And the works of community detection general hypothesize that communities with similarity scale. However, brain functional networks demonstrate high density structure and imbalanced coalition scale. This raises high-complexity and imbalance problems for community detection. There are few community detection methods devoted to handling the problems simultaneously.

In this paper, a novel method, named Cutting Double k-Clique Spanning Tree (COUSIN) method, for coalition detection from brain functional networks has been proposed. The local property for close-connected nodes is characterized by the k-clique which is the maximal complete subgraph with k-order. A double k-clique spanning tree, made of two spanning trees, forms the robust reconfiguration of the given network. Cutting the edges from the tree, the coalitions would emerge. COUSIN is composed of the following four steps:

1. The enumeration of all k-cliques is executed in a fast and parallel method. We present a recursive and backtracking mode to enumerate the k-cliques without redundancy.
2. The construction of double k-clique spanning tree is generated by two spanning trees with the aid of k-clique property. The max-clique turns into root of spanning tree. Then degressively choose and merge cliques with each order k to form two spanning trees. The double k-clique spanning tree could be combined by the two spanning trees.
3. The coalitions are obtained through sequential cutting edges from the double k-clique spanning tree. Modularity is used to guide cutting strategy. The edges among the coalitions will be removed in early cutting steps.
4. Small-scale groups of nodes are absorbed into the existing huge coalition. The result reflects multiple scale property of coalitions.

2   Related Works

Abundant accomplishments about the community detection based on graph partition theorems have appeared [5,6]. Here we review some excellent researches. The Kernighan-Lin algorithm is an iterative heuristic algorithm for partitioning the given network into two disjoint subsets of similar size with a minimal number of cutting edges [7]. It initiates from a random partition of two subsets, and repeats the step of exchanging pairs of nodes on descent direction of cutting cost. Girvan-Newman (GN) algorithm reallocates weight of every edge by the number of shortest paths between pair of nodes that pass the edge. Then it iteratively executes two steps: remove the edge with highest weight and recalculate weight of edges in the remaining network. In the iteration, it also checks the connectivity of the network that the disconnected community structure will emerge through the cutting strategy. These methods run very fast, but they limit in two partitions which always results in two communities with equal scale.

Some methods are going to optimize the modularity in a hierarchical way e.g. Louvain algorithm and Fast-Newman algorithm [8,9]. They repeatedly group the nodes into a small number of communities. Then the communities are merged by optimizing modularity locally. The emergence of the optimal communities occurs in the maximum modularity. Structural Clustering Algorithm for Networks (SCAN) algorithm is based on the local similarity between pair of nodes [10]. It links the nodes with similar neighbor structure. Combinatorial Structural Clustering (CSC) algorithm uses a triangle pattern to approach the communities [11]. These methods could get multiple communities from the given networks. But they usually have not good performance in imbalanced networks especially those with outliers. Imbalance problem refers to the situation that scales of communities are different. This can be unequal number of nodes or unequal density of edges. Outlier refers to the node with weak connection with communities.

We have proposed a novel self-adaptive skeleton approach to detect self-organized coalitions from brain functional networks, named k-CLIque Merging Evolution (CLIME) algorithm, which effectively tackles the problems of scale imbalance, outliers and hard-examples [12]. However, this method would not adapt the condition with high-complexity problem especially when with vast scale of network.

Cutting edges from spanning tree of the given network is a fast and simple method for community detection [13]. When an edge has been cut, a group of nodes that can be considered as a community will drop from the spanning tree. A good cutting strategy can approach the valid community structure, but this is generally very hard to do [14]. That is because 1) An effective cutting strategy is hard to choose. It usually cut the edge within community and drops only a part of the community or even a meaningless one. 2) The construction of spanning tree is sometimes unstable. It is hard to generate a favorable spanning tree to represent the structure of the network. In most cases, there is no modular structure beside the edges.

3 Cutting Double k-Clique Spanning Tree Method

The detail of the Cutting Double k-Clique Spanning Tree (COUSIN) Method will be described in this section. It includes four parts: enumeration of all k-cliques, construction of double k-clique spanning tree, cutting double k-clique spanning tree and absorbing k-clique leaves.

3.1 Enumeration of All k-Cliques

For a graph $G =< V, E >$ and its adjacency matrix W, if there exists a subgraph l that satisfies

$$\begin{cases} |l| = k; \\ W(i,j) = 1, \forall i,j \in l, i \neq j; \\ W(z,a) = 0, \forall a \in G \setminus l, \exists z \in l; \end{cases} \tag{1}$$

we call l is a k-clique in G. The number of nodes in l is k. Every pair of nodes (i,j) in l is connected. And for any node a outside of l should disconnect to at least one node in l.

The set of all k-cliques M is enumerated based on the recursive backtracking mode, shown in Algorithm 1. M is a $n \times m$ Boolean matrix where n is the label of nodes and m is the label of the maximal cliques. M_i is the column vector of M, represents the i-th k-clique. M is joint by the subsets $M^{(j)}$ which are the subset of k-cliques with same order j. $\Gamma(v)$ is the neighbour set of node v. $\oplus$ is the concatenation operation of two sets.

The algorithm is initialized by setting V as the node set of the given network G. Sort V in a degeneracy ordering. In the beginning, for each node v in the ordering V, R is the current searched node v, P is the neighbors of v that are later in the ordering and X is the neighbors of v that are earlier in the ordering. The subfunction $MaxClique(R, P, X)$ is a recursive function. R storages the chosen clique nodes. P storages the neighbors of P, which may join into R. X storages the nodes which have been found in previous iteration. If and only if P and X are both empty sets, R will be outputted as a k-clique. Otherwise, R is not a k-clique or it has been outputted in previous searches that will not output.

3.2 Construction of Double k-Clique Spanning Tree

The k-cliques form the basic element in our method. Due to the strong local connection property of k-clique, we have more confidence that there is a large probability of the cliques with high order k appearing within coalition. On the contrary, only a few cliques with low order k could appear among coalitions.

The k-clique mode is used to generate the robust representative of the network, named double k-clique spanning tree. The generation process is shown in Algorithm 2. We first determine the maximum clique as the root of the first spanning tree $T^{(1)}$. Then choose a k-clique which belongs to high order clique subset to merge into the spanning tree. The merging operation is shown in Fig. 1. We also remove the used k-cliques from M, aiming to generate the second spanning tree $T^{(2)}$ without overlapped k-clique. At last, the two spanning trees would merge into the double k-clique spanning tree T.

3.3 Cutting Double k-Clique Spanning Tree

Double k-clique spanning tree is an applicable reconfiguration of the given network. Cutting edges from the double k-clique spanning tree is very easy to obtain suitable coalition partition. The cutting strategy is shown in Algorithm 3. We use the inverse order related to the spanning process to cut the edges. The single edges $M^{(2)}$ in T are firstly cut. When edge has been cut from T, there may appear component of node groups that are disconnected to other nodes. We determine the component as a coalition. In every cutting step, calculate the modularity Q to measure quality of the coalition partition [15]. d_v is the degree of node v. $\chi(Z_v, Z_s)$ is an indicator of whether the pair of nodes v and s belongs to same coalition. The optical coalition partition occurs when we get a maximal modularity Q.

Algorithm 1: Enumeration of all k-Cliques

1: **Input:** adjacency matrix W;
2: **Output:** k-clique matrix M.
3: **for** each node v in a degeneracy ordering **do**
4:   $V \leftarrow V \setminus \{v\}; R \leftarrow \{v\}$;
5:   $P \leftarrow \Gamma(v) \cap V; X \leftarrow \Gamma(v) \setminus V$;
6:   $MaxClique(R, P, X)$;
7: **end for**
8: **for** $j = 1$ to max **do**
9:   **if** $|M_i| == j$ **then**
10:     $M^{(j)} \leftarrow M^{(j)} \oplus M_i$;
11:   **end if**
12: **end for**
13: $M \leftarrow [M^{(max)}, \cdots, M^{(2)}]$;
14:
15: **Function:**$MaxClique(R, P, X)$
16: **if** $P == \emptyset$ and $X == \emptyset$ **then**
17:   $M_i \leftarrow R; i++$;
18: **else**
19:   $P' \leftarrow P \cup X$;
20:   $u_p \leftarrow \underset{u_p \in P'}{\arg\max} |\Gamma(u_p) \cap P|$;
21:   **for** $u \in \Gamma(u_p) \cap P$ **do**
22:     $MaxClique(R \cup \{u\}, P \cap \Gamma(u), X \cap \Gamma(u))$;
23:     $P \leftarrow P \setminus \{u\}$;
24:     $X \leftarrow X \cup \{u\}$;
25:   **end for**
26: **end if**

Algorithm 2: Construction of Double k-Clique Spanning Tree

1: **Input:** k-clique matrix M;
2: **Output:** double k-clique spanning tree matrix T.
3: Initialize $T^{(1)} = \emptyset$;
4: **for** $j = max$ to 2 **do**
5:   **while** choose a k-clique l from $M^{(j)}$ **do**
6:     **if** $|T^{(1)} \cup l| > |T^{(1)}|$ **then**
7:       $T^{(1)} \leftarrow T^{(1)} \cup l$;
8:       $M^{(j)} \leftarrow M^{(j)} \setminus l$;
9:     **end if**
10:   **end while**
11: **end for**
12: $T^{(1)}$ replaced by $T^{(2)}$, repeat the algorithm;
13: $T \leftarrow T^{(1)} \cup T^{(2)}$.

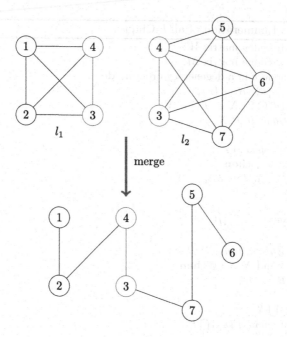

Fig. 1. Two k-cliques merge to tree.

Algorithm 3: Cutting Double k-Clique Spanning Tree

1: **Input:** double k-clique spanning tree matrix T;
2: **Output:** coalition partition C.
3: **for** $j = 2$ to max **do**
4:     **while** choose an edge e from $T \cap M^{(j)}$ **do**
5:         $T \leftarrow T \setminus e$;
6:         Check the connectivity of T and determine the disconnected groups as Z.
7:         $Q \leftarrow \frac{1}{2|E|} \sum\limits_{v,s \in V} [E_{vs} - \frac{d_v d_s}{2|E|}] \chi(Z_v, Z_s)$.
8:     **end while**
9: **end for**
10: $C \leftarrow \arg\max_Z Q(Z)$

3.4 Absorbing k-Clique Leaves

Due to the cutting process starting on the minor k-cliques, there always drop some single nodes or small groups of nodes, which can be seen as the leaves cut from the double k-clique spanning tree. Thus these nodes should be judged as outliers or absorbed into other coalitions. The absorbing method is shown in Algorithm 4. A truncation threshold δ is used to divide the coalition partition C into leaf set L and branch set B. Then the leaves are absorbed into the branches through their connectivity to them.

Algorithm 4: Absorbing k-Clique Leaves

1: **Input:** truncation threshold δ, coalition partition C;
2: **Output:** corrected coalition partition C.
3: **for** $C_i \in C$ **do**
4:    **if** $|C_i| < \delta$ **then**
5:        $B \leftarrow B \oplus C_i$;
6:    **else**
7:        $L \leftarrow L \oplus C_i$;
8:    **end if**
9: **end for**
10: **for** $B_i \in B$ **do**
11:    $o \leftarrow \arg\max_{j} |\Gamma(B_i) \cap L_j|$;
12:    $L_o \leftarrow L_o \cup B_i$;
13: **end for**
14: $C \leftarrow L$;

---

4   Experimental Evaluation

In order to evaluate the efficiency of COUSIN, both series of synthetic topological datasets and public datasets are used in this section.

4.1   Synthetic Experiments

The Girvan-Newman benchmark, constructing synthetic network with labels, is a criterion to measure the performance of community detection method [16]. But this method only considers the balance situation which the communities have the equal size. We extend this method to match our imbalance problem. The synthetic imbalanced network is composed of 200 nodes partitioned into 4 coalitions, C_1, C_2, C_3 and C_4, of size 20, 40, 60 and 80, respectively. For each community, it is an Erdos Renyi (ER) graph which every node is connected by the inter-coalition probability p to the other nodes within the same coalition. And the four coalitions are mixed through that each node is connected by the inner-coalition probability q to the nodes outside of its coalition. That is, for any node pair (v_s, v_t), $v_s \in C_i, v_t \in C_j$, the probability of edge $e(v_s, v_t) = 1$ is formulated as

$$P\left(e(v_s, v_t) = 1\right) = \begin{cases} p, & i = j; \\ q, & i \neq j. \end{cases} \qquad (2)$$

The average degree for nodes of each coalition is $(T - 1)p + (200 - T - 1)q$, where T is size of the coalition. The model validation technique adapted is independent experiments. Each experiments are repeatedly for 100 times to approach an average accuracy in different parameter condition. The assessment criteria is ARI.

We discuss a typical synthetic scene under the condition that fix $p = 0.4$ with different $q = \{(5, \cdots, 70) \times 10^{-3}\}$. For the node in C_1, the expected number of edges linking within the coalition is 8. And the expected numbers of edges linking with remainder of the network (any one of C_2, C_3, C_4) are $0.9, \cdots, 12.6$. For one node from the remainder, the expected numbers of edges linking with C_1 are $0.1, \cdots, 1.4$.

The comparison of COUSION with FN and LPA algorithms is shown in Fig. 2. FN algorithm is the Fast Newman algorithm which successively merges the node into community by maximizing modularity [17]. LPA algorithm is the Label Propagation Algorithm that propagates labels throughout the given network and forms communities in the process of label propagation [18]. FN algorithm could accurately detect C_3 and C_4 in every situations. But with the increasement of q, it always misclassifies the minor communities C_1 and C_2 as one community. It prefers to regard the two communities as one community to approach high modularity rather than separate them. LPA algorithm could detect the 4 communities with a high ARI under the condition of $q < 10^{-2}$. However, ARI drops rapidly when $p > 10^{-2}$. That is because a high q means a large number of edges across communities. These edges hinder label propagation within the community. Finally, it results in considering the network as one community. However, our COUSIN algorithm could effectively identify the structure of the four communities.

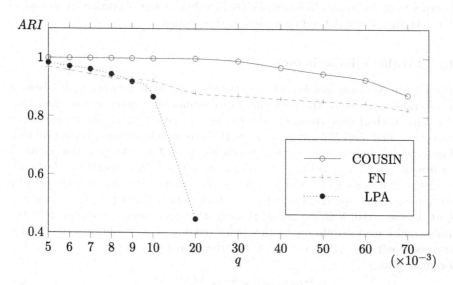

Fig. 2. Synthetic experiments

4.2 Public Experiments

We employ two public network datasets, American College Football dataset and Dolphin Social Network dataset, to verify the effect of our method.

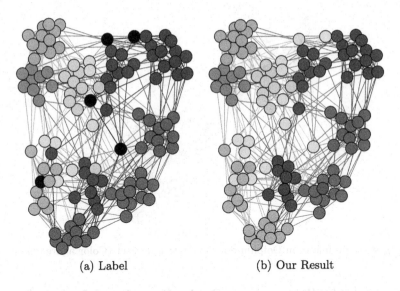

(a) Label   (b) Our Result

Fig. 3. Experiment on American College Football Dataset

The American College Football dataset describes the competitive relation among Division IA colleges represented by a network that includes 115 nodes and 613 edges. The network also contains a prior label, 12 "conferences", representing ground truth for each node. The label could be used to check the accuracy of our method. The result compared with the label is shown in Fig. 3. Each color represents one community and we obtain 11 communities from the network which miss one conference compared to the label. Although two conferences have been incorporated into one community by our method, these nodes are dispersed in the network so they can be seen as one community. And run our method many times, we can also find the two separated conferences which are just the same as the label. But we still think the result we got shown in the figure is a more suitable community structure for the dataset.

The Dolphin Social Network illustrates the frequent relation among bottle nose dolphins living off Doubtful Sounds in New Zealand which includes 62 nodes and 159 edges. The data does not provide a common label. Thus, we run our method on it and show an acceptable result shown in Fig. 4. Each color represents one community. The nodes in the same community have more frequent associations than with the ones outside of the community.

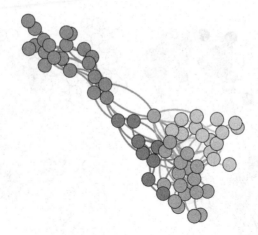

Fig. 4. Experiment on Dolphin Social Network dataset (Color figure online)

5   Detect Coalitions from Brain Functional Networks

The brain FMRI data are collected by Chen from Dalian Zhongshan Hospital [11]. The data are characterized by Power 264 brain atlas which divided brain into 264 ROIs as nodes in brain functional networks [19]. The edges are measured by Pearson correlation coefficient of FMRI time series between each pair of ROIs [20].

One paradigm of adjacency matrix A for brain functional networks is shown in Fig. 5. The dense structure of the network demonstrates the efficiency feature that low economic costs on message passing path of brain.

The adjacency matrix A is binarized by a binarization threshold ϵ. The binarization process is formulated as follow:

$$W = \mathbb{1}(A > \epsilon). \tag{3}$$

The value in A larger than ϵ is regarded as 1, otherwise 0. The brain functional networks is expressed by the unweighted and undirected network with adjacency matrix W.

We conduct our method on W to detect coalitions. We demonstrate 3 primary coalitions in Fig. 6. Each coalition relate to specific cognitive functions, e.g. visual system (green nodes), motor and somatosensory network (yellow nodes) and default mode network (red nodes).

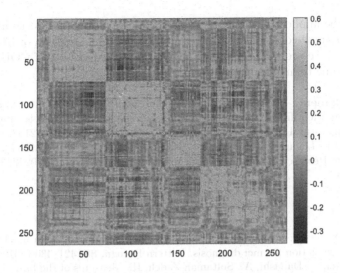

Fig. 5. One paradigm of adjacency matrix for brain functional networks

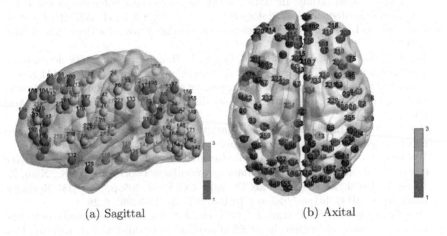

(a) Sagittal   (b) Axital

Fig. 6. Coalitions detected by COUSIN (Color figure online)

6 Conclusion

In this paper, we propose a coalition detection method, called COUSION, to identify coalition structure from brain functional networks. The enumeration of k-cliques is executed in a fast and parallel mode. The maximum cliques form the roots of spanning tree. And it generates double k-clique spanning tree along with decrease direction of k. The cutting strategy cuts the edges in inverse direction of generation process. The connected components are regarded as coalition by maximizing modularity index.

The synthetic experiments demonstrate the effectiveness of COUSION on approaching coalition structure. We also test the method on public network datasets. The application of COUSION in brain functional networks illustrates that the obtained coalitions reveal potentially functional relation of ROIs.

In future, we are interest in designing an extended version of COUSION to adapt dynamic brain functional networks.

Acknowledgment. The authors would like to thank Drs. Liang Chen and Shigang Feng for their scientific collaborations in this research work. This work is supported by the National Natural Science Foundation of China (Grant Nos. 61772102, 62176036, 62102059), the Liaoning Collaborative Fund (Grant No. 2020-HYLH-17), and the Fundamental Research Funds for the Central Universities (No. 3132022225 and No. 3132021245).

References

1. Zhang, Y., et al.: Strength and similarity guided group-level brain functional network construction for mci diagnosis. Pattern Recogn. **88**, 421–430 (2019)
2. Golbabaei, S., Dadashi, A., Soltanian-Zadeh, H.: Measures of the brain functional network that correlate with Alzheimer's neuropsychological test scores: an FMRI and graph analysis study. In: 38th Annual International Conference of the IEEE Engineering in Medicine and Biology Society (EMBC), pp. 5554–5557. IEEE (2016)
3. Barabási, A.-L., et al.: Network Science. Cambridge University Press, Cambridge (2016)
4. Javed, M.A., Younis, M.S., Latif, S., Qadir, J., Baig, A.: Community detection in networks: a multidisciplinary review. J. Netw. Comput. Appl. **108**, 87–111 (2018)
5. Peng, R., Yao, Y.: Comparison of community structure partition optimization of complex networks by different community discovery algorithms. Informatica **44**(1) (2020)
6. Bai, Y., Yuan, J., Liu, S., Yin, K.: Variational community partition with novel network structure centrality prior. Appl. Math. Model. **75**, 333–348 (2019)
7. Weihong, Y., Yuehui, Y., Guozhen, T.: Recursive Kernighan-Lin Algorithm (RKL) scheme for cooperative road-side units in vehicular networks. In: Li, K., Xiao, Z., Wang, Y., Du, J., Li, K. (eds.) ParCFD 2013. CCIS, vol. 405, pp. 321–331. Springer, Heidelberg (2014). https://doi.org/10.1007/978-3-642-53962-6_28
8. Que, X., Checconi, F., Petrini, F., Gunnels, J.A.: Scalable community detection with the Louvain algorithm. In: IEEE International Parallel and Distributed Processing Symposium, pp. 28–37. IEEE (2015)
9. Newman, M.E.: Modularity and community structure in networks. Proc. Natl. Acad. Sci. U.S.A. **103**(23), 8577–8582 (2006)
10. Xu, X., Yuruk, N., Feng, Z., Schweiger, T.A.: SCAN: a structural clustering algorithm for networks. In: ACM SIGKDD International Conference on Knowledge Discovery and Data Mining, vol. 12, pp. 824–833. Association for Computing Machinery, New York (2007)
11. Chen, L., Liu, H., Zhang, W., Zhang, B.: Combinatorial structural clustering (CSC): a novel structural clustering approach for large scale networks. In: Madureira, A.M., Abraham, A., Gamboa, D., Novais, P. (eds.) ISDA 2016. AISC, vol. 557, pp. 427–436. Springer, Cham (2017). https://doi.org/10.1007/978-3-319-53480-0_42
12. Liu, K., et al.: Self-adaptive skeleton approaches to detect self-organized coalitions from brain functional networks through probabilistic mixture models. ACM Trans. Knowl. Discov. Data **15**(5), 1–38 (2021)

13. Saoud, B., Moussaoui, A.: Community detection in networks based on minimum spanning tree and modularity. Phys. A **460**, 230–234 (2016)
14. Wang, Z., Hou, M., Yuan, G., He, J., Cui, J., Zhu, M.: Hierarchical community detection in social networks based on micro-community and minimum spanning tree. IEICE Trans. Inf. Syst. **102**(9), 1773–1783 (2019)
15. Brandes, U., et al.: On modularity clustering. IEEE Trans. Knowl. Data Eng. **20**, 172–188 (2008)
16. Lancichinetti, A., Fortunato, S., Radicchi, F.: Benchmark graphs for testing community detection algorithms. Phys. Rev. E **78**(4), 046110 (2008)
17. Newman, M.E., Girvan, M.: Finding and evaluating community structure in networks. Phys. Rev. E **69**(2), 026113 (2004)
18. Gui, Q., Deng, R., Xue, P., Cheng, X.: A community discovery algorithm based on boundary nodes and label propagation. Pattern Recogn. Lett. **109**, 103–109 (2018)
19. Power, J.D., et al.: Functional network organization of the human brain. Neuron **72**(4), 665–678 (2011)
20. Feng, W., Zhu, Q., Zhuang, J., Yu, S.: An expert recommendation algorithm based on Pearson correlation coefficient and FP-growth. Clust. Comput. **22**(3), 7401–7412 (2019)

Risk Attention Network: Weakly-Supervised Learning for Joint Tumor Segmentation and Survival Prediction

Jianeng Liu[1,2], Yinsheng Chen[3], Jing Yan[4], Zhenyu Zhang[4], Huailing Zhang[5], and Zhi-Cheng Li[1,2(✉)]

[1] Shenzhen Institute of Advanced Technology, Chinese Academy of Sciences, Shenzhen, China
zc.li@siat.ac.cn
[2] University of Chinese Academy of Sciences, Beijing, China
[3] Sun Yat-sen University Cancer Center, Guangzhou, China
[4] The First Affiliated Hospital of Zhengzhou University, Zhengzhou, China
[5] Guangdong Medical University, Dongguan, China

Abstract. Deep neural networks trained on medical images have shown good potential in survival prediction. However, the majority of image-based survival analysis relies on accurate voxel-level annotations. In this paper, we present a Risk Attention Network (RAN) for concurrent survival prediction and tumor segmentation from brain MRI in a weakly supervised approach with survival labels only. By incorporating risk attention blocks (RABs), the proposed RAN learns a pyramidal risk-aware feature hierarchy for better semantic and spatial predictions. By adapting RAN trained for survival prediction in an end-to-end manner, the network concurrently learns risky regions from risk activation maps (RAMs) to generate voxel-level tumor segmentation. The model is trained on a multicenter dataset and achieves both accurate survival prediction (C-index 0.63) and competitive segmentation performance (Dice score 0.79) compared with supervised method on the test dataset. The model is available at Mendeley data library.

Keywords: Convolutional neural network · Survival prediction · Weakly supervised segmentation · Attention mechanism · Glioma

1 Introduction

Survival analysis aims to model the duration of time from the beginning of follow-up until an event of interest (e.g. death, disease progression or recurrence)

Supported by the National Natural Science Foundation of China (U20A20171, 81730048), GuangDong Basic and Applied Basic Research Foundation (2020B15151 20046), Youth Innovation Promotion Association of the Chinese Academy of Sciences (2018364), and Guangdong Key Project (2018B030335001).

G. Zhai et al. (Eds.): IFTC 2021, CCIS 1560, pp. 96–107, 2022.
https://doi.org/10.1007/978-981-19-2266-4_8

occurs [1], which is an important subfield of statistics. An accurate survival prediction is of critical importance for optimal therapeutic decision and follow-up plan making. Through survival prediction, covariates associated with patients survival can also be determined. Survival data may contain censored instances caused by either time limitation or loss to follow-up, where the event of interest of these censored instances cannot be observed after a certain time point [2]. In such a case, prediction models based on standard statistical or machine learning algorithm are no longer suitable. Specific survival models are required to deal with such censored time-to-event data.

Traditionally, various statistical methods have been widely studied to handle the censoring problem. The most popular survival model is Cox proportional hazards model [3], where the patient's risk is assumed as a linear combination of covariates. However, it is overly simplistic for real world survival data. To handle censored problem with complex real word data, complicated machine learning approaches have been developed to complement or compete with traditional statistical survival models [4–6]. Among current machine learning-based survival models, deep neural networks have shown superior performance in survival prediction using clinical data and pathological images as input [7–10]. The main advantage of deep learning-based approaches is its ability to automatically learn the survival model by its own from the a wide variety of input data. So far, few convolutional neural network (CNN)-based survival analysis has been done using MRI or CT images [11–13]. One important reason is the lack of annotated data. Most existing image-based survival models rely on accurate annotation of regions of interest (ROI). Supervised ROI segmentation requires large voxel-level annotated datasets, which is time-consuming and costly. This motivates us to develop survival models without pre-acquired ROI annotations. To develop a CNN-based survival model that can obviate the need of tumor segmentation has undoubted clinical benefits.

Learning survival models directly from MRI or CT images is more challenging than from ROI, because most area in the image is healthy tissue that is not much associated with survival. To address this challenge, we consider learning to focus on the tumor area while ignore the irrelevant healthy part. We rethink this challenging task from a weakly supervised learning perspective. Among weakly supervised image recognitions, the most attractive one is learning to segment voxel-level object with image-level classification labels only [14]. Those methods employ a CNN trained for classification to produce class-specific attention maps used for segmentation. Inspired by this technique, we consider segmenting the tumor by a specific CNN trained for risk regression with survival labels merely. We infer that learning risk-aware features for survival prediction could identify the risky regions, while learning regional features from the localized risky areas could also improve the survival prediction. In other words, survival prediction and risky region localization reinforce each other. Although promising, it is a more challenging task, requiring to learn risk-aware features showing where and how much the risk is. To this end, feature crucially matters.

In this paper, we for the first time present Risk Attention Network (RAN), a deep convolutional neural network learning a pyramidal risk-aware feature hierarchy, which is (1) end-to-end trainable for survival prediction using whole-brain MR images without pre-segmented ROI, and (2) able to concurrently produce voxel-level tumor segmentation in a weakly-supervised approach trained with survival labels only. These two properties are made possible with following contributions:

(1) *Pyramid network structure*: RAN is built based on a pyramidal hierarchy to learn multi-scale features with strong semantics at all scales. The multi-scale features are fused to achieve accurate predictions.
(2) *Risk attention block*: To learn risk-aware features, risk attention blocks (RABs) are incorporated in RAN, where a multi-level attention branch and a channel attention branch are mixed for better feature representations.
(3) *Risk activation map*: To learn risky regions, risk activation maps (RAMs) are generated by weighting the activation maps at each scale. RAM identifies highly risky regions with high resolution, enabling voxel-level tumor segmentation. It also provides a good visual explanation of why and what RAN predicts.

2   Methods

For a patient i, survival data can be represented as a triplet (x_i, T_i, δ_i), including a P-dimension covariate vector x_i, a censored or observed survival time T_i, and a status indicator δ_i which is 1 for an observed event (death) and 0 in case of censoring. Then, the instantaneous rate of event occurrence at time t, or the hazard in a Cox model, is modeled as

$$h(t|x_i) = h_0(t)exp(\beta^T x_i), \tag{1}$$

where $h_0(t)$ is the baseline hazard, and β is the coefficient vector. $r(x_i) = \beta^T x_i$ is referred to as the *risk* function, which is simplified as a linear combination of covariates in Cox.

2.1   Risk Attention Network Framework

Instead of using a simplistic linear model, we aim to learn the risk function directly from images via a specific network. The framework of the proposed network, RAN, is illustrated in Fig. 1. The image data is used as network input (x_i). The survival data, (T_i, δ_i), is used as the labels for model training. The output $\hat{r}_\theta$ is the estimated risk, wherein θ is the network weight parameters waiting to be learned. Besides the survival prediction task, we can jointly perform the tumor segmentation using RAN. At the same time of learning the risk, from the last convolutional layers we can calculate the RAMs, from which the tumor segmentation can be computed.

The architecture design follows our first *hypothesis* that multi-scale and semantically-strong feature representation could enable both survival prediction and weakly-supervised tumor segmentation. RAN is constructed based on a

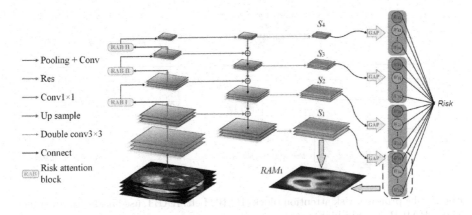

Fig. 1. Architecture of the proposed risk attention network (RAN).

multi-scale architecture, taking the pyramid feature network (FPN) as a backbone [15]. RAN comprises a bottom-up path containing three RABs, a top-down path, and a feature fusion structure. In the bottom-up pathway, ResNet is used as a backbone network for feature extraction [16]. Based on the gradually reduced spatial size of the learned feature maps, the ResNet in the bottom-up path here can be divided into 4 stages. A RAB is placed at each bottleneck between two adjacent stages to learn risk-aware features. Therefore, we have in total 3 RABs in our network. The feature maps along the top-down pathway are adjusted to have equal size by gradually upsampling using a factor 2-based nearest neighbor interpolation. Lateral connections are used to merge the upsampled semantically-stronger top feature map with the corresponding spatially-finer bottom map by element-wise addition, generating 4 merged maps at different scales. At each lateral connection a 1 × 1 convolution is appended to obtain equal channel dimensions.

Then, these multi-scale merged features are fused for a better prediction. Before fusion, two 3 × 3 convolutions are performed to refine each merged feature, generating four feature maps $\{S_1, S_2, S_3, S_4\}$, as shown in Fig. 1. Global average pooling (GAP) is performed on $\{S_1, S_2, S_3, S_4\}$ respectively, generating four feature vectors. Each vector is followed by a fully-connected layer and a sigmoid node, yielding the final estimated risk $r(x_i)$. Besides predicting the risk, RAMs showing tumor localizations are also calculated as the weighted sum of the activation maps at different four scales. As shown in Subsect. 3, the finest RAM calculated from S_1, denoted as RAM_1, represents the optimal tumor localization. Finally, the tumor can be segmented from RAM_1 by a fixed threshold. Next, we will describe in detail each component of the proposed RAN network.

2.2 Risk Attention Block

Our second *hypothesis* is that using attention mechanism to emphasize the highly risky regions could improve the prediction/localization ability of the pyramidal network. We observe that tumors with different survivals exhibit fine-grained

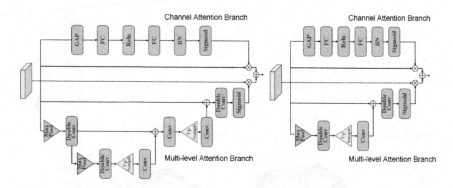

Fig. 2. The proposed risk attention block (RAB). Left: RAB I, used in the lowest stage; Right: RAB II, used in higher stage.

variances in both overall appearances and local patterns. In other words, tumors with different survival change in texture gradually, both globally and locally. Thusly, RAN should have the ability of capturing both global and subtle differences within the tumor area, which reflects the gradual change of risk.

To this end, the RAB is presented, as shown in Fig. 2. The multi-level attention branch emphasizes highly risky regions at different scales using a mini-pyramidal bottom-up top-down structure. Specifically, given an input feature map F, in RAB I the multi-level branch learns an attention map M_1 by fusing features at three scales, yielding an element-wise weighted feature $A_1 = F \cdot M_1$. In RAB II an attention map M_2 is learnt by fusing features at two scales and the corresponding output is $A_2 = F \cdot M_2$.

According to the spatial size of input feature maps, RAB I is embedded in the lowest stage while RAB II is used in higher stages (Fig. 1). The channel attention branch further selects channel-wise features using the channel-attention SENet [17]. The output of RAB is an element-wise sum of the risk-aware features from the two branches.

2.3 Risk Activation Map

With image-level classification labels only, one can generate a discriminative class activation map, or CAM, for approximate localization of objects belonging to that class by using a GAP layer [14]. However, traditional CAM is computed from feature maps extracted in the last convolutional layer of a CNN. In such a case, CAM has much lower resolution and less spatial context and therefore cannot be directly used for voxel-level segmentation.

In our study, we propose a risk activation map (RAM) technique by weighting the activation maps from different scales using multiple GAPs. Our purpose is to make use high resolution features as well as rich spatial context by multi-scale fusion. Given the last convolutional feature maps at scale scl as $S_{scl} \in \{S_1, S_2, S_3, S_4\}$, the k-th feature map in S_{scl} is denoted as $S_{scl}^k, k = 1, 2, ..., K$ and its spatial element is $S_{scl}^k(x, y)$, where (x, y) is the spatial location. At each scale, S_{scl} is fed into a GAP layer, yielding a K-dimensional vector, where the k-th element is

$$s_{scl}^k = \sum_{(x,y)} S_{scl}^k(x,y). \tag{2}$$

The vectors at all scales are then concatenated as a $4K$-dimensional vector, followed by a fully-connected layer. A sigmoid node on the top is applied for final risk prediction. The input of the sigmoid can be defined as

$$z = \sum_{scl=1}^{4} z_{scl}, \tag{3}$$

Here z_{scl} can be calculated as

$$z_{scl} = \sum_{k=1}^{K} w_{scl}^k s_{scl}^k. \tag{4}$$

Here w_{scl}^k is the weight learnt from the fully-connected layer, measuring the importance of the feature map S_{scl}^k in risk prediction. Therefore, the RAM at each scale RAM_{scl} can be given by weighting the feature maps at that scale. The element in RAM_{scl} is

$$RAM_{scl}(x,y) = \sum_{k=1}^{K} w_{scl}^k S_{scl}^k(x,y). \tag{5}$$

The optimal segmentation can be calculated from the finest RAM as $Y = T(UP(RAM_4))$, where UP upsamples RAM to the size of original image and T denotes a fixed thresholding operation.

2.4   Survival Loss Function

The proposed dual-task network can be trained in an end-to-end manner. The survival loss function can be defined as the regularized negative log-partial likelihood as

$$L(\theta) = -\frac{1}{N_0} \sum_{i=1}^{N} \delta_i \cdot \left[\hat{r}_\theta(x_i) - \log \sum_{j:T_j>=T_i} \exp(\hat{r}_\theta(x_j))\right] + \alpha \|\theta\|_2^2, \tag{6}$$

where N is the number of all included patients, N_0 is the number of patients who are still alive, and j is from the set of all patients whose survival time T_j is longer than T_i (maybe including censored patients). ℓ_2-norm is used to alleviate overfitting with a weight α.

3   Experiments

Data and Setup. A cohort of 649 glioma patients is collected, comprising 163 from the Brain Tumor Segmentation (BraTS) challenge database [18] and 486

Table 1. Performance comparison of survival prediction.

Models	LASSO-Cox Radiomics	DeepConvSurv	RAN
Training C-index	0.637	0.656	0.675
Test C-index	0.610	0.612	0.632

from two local institutions: The First Affiliated Hospital of Zhengzhou University and Sun Yat-sen University Cancer Center. The cohort is divided using stratified random sampling into a training set of 519 patients and a test set of 130 patients in a ratio of 4:1. All patients have overall survival data and pretreatment brain MRI including T1-weighted, T1-weighted contrast-enhanced, T2-weighted and T2-weighted FLAIR (T1w, T1c, T2w and FLAIR). All local MR images were acquired with 1.5 and 3.0-T MRI machines (uMR 780, United Imaging, Shanghai, China; Trio TIM or Magnetom Verio, Siemens Healthcare, Erlangen, Germany; and Discovery MR 750, GE Healthcare, Milwaukee, Wisconsin). The exclusion criteria are incomplete MRI sequences or poor imaging quality. Overall survival is calculated as the duration from surgery to death or the end of follow-up. Patients still alive at the last follow-up or lost to follow-up are considered as censored.

Here we briefly describe the manual delineation standard to generate the segmentation ground truth for both BraTs data and local data. BraTS provides manual delineations of the whole tumor for segmentation evaluation. According to the BRATS guideline, we first delineate the whole tumor area as the hyperintensity regions with homogeneous signal distribution in the white matter on T2w images. FLAIR images are used to cross-check the extension of the whole tumor. Then, the solid tumor core is segmented by assessing hyperintensities in T1c together with the inhomogeneous component of the hyperintense lesion visible in T1w and the hypointense regions visible in T1w. Next, the edema area can be obtained by subtracting the solid tumor core from the whole tumor area.

For each local patient, the tumor is delineated by two experts according to the BRATS guideline. The two annotations for a local patient are merged using STAPLE [19] to generate segmentation ground truth. The same preprocessing pipeline as used in BraTS is applied on the MRI from local institutions, including N4 distortion correction, skull stripping, 1mm isotropic voxel resampling, rigid registration and histogram matching. For each patient, 4 transverse slices with the largest tumor area are selected from T1w, T1c, T2w and FLAIR respectively and are resized into 224×224. ResNet-50 is used as the basic unit. The network is trained from scratch using Adam optimizer with a learning rate of 10^{-4}, a batch size of 16, and a regularization weight of 0.01. We use random rotation, shear and zoom for data augmentation.

Survival Prediction Performance. We compare the proposed RAN with two state-of-the-art survival models, the LASSO-Cox radiomics model [20] and the DeepConvSurv model [22]. Both models require the segmented tumor for feature extraction. For LASSO-Cox, from the segmented tumor high-throughput

Table 2. Performance comparison of tumor segmentation.

Methods	Training data set			Test data set		
	DICE	Sensitivity	Specificity	DICE	Sensitivity	Specificity
RAM_1	0.866	0.821	0.989	0.792	0.803	0.977
U-net	0.930	0.975	0.998	0.822	0.901	0.995

hand-crafted radiomics features are extracted, and a LASSO-Cox model is built, as described in [20]. Here intensity features, shape features, and texture features are extracted from the segmented tumor area using an open-source package pyradiomics (version 2.2.0; https://pyradiomics.readthedocs.io) [21]. For DeepConvSurv, the ROI containing the segmented tumor is resized into 128×128 and fed into a CNN trained with survival loss, as detailed in [22]. The output of all survival models is the predicted risk score regarding overall survival. A standard measure, the Harrell's C-index, is used to assess the performance of survival analysis [9, 20, 22], where 1 means perfect fitting and 0.5 equals random guess. C-index has a similar meaning of the regular area under the ROC curve (AUC). The results in Table 1 shows the superior performance of RAN, where the C-index of RAN reaches 0.675 in the training set and 0.632 in the test set. Our results verify that the proposed RAN is able to predict survival with high accuracy directly from whole-brain MRI data without a pre-delineated ROI. Interestingly, our method achieves better prediction than traditional radiomics model and DeepConvSurv model that are established based on accurately segmented tumor areas. One possible reason is that diffuse glioma has been demonstrated not as a focal but a systemic disease of the whole brain [23, 24]. Therefore, it is a reasonable hypothesis that imaging features from whole-brain MRI might be better predictor of tumor prognosis. In other words, learning a risk score from merely the tumor area may be not enough.

Tumor Segmentation Performance. We compare the proposed RAN with a fully-supervised standard U-net trained with DICE loss [25]. The U-net is trained from scratch using the Adam optimizer with a learning rate of 10^{-4} and a batch size of 16. For RAN, the optimal segmentation can be generated from RAM_1 using an empirical threshold of 127. According to the BraTS guideline, the segmentation is evaluated in terms of DICE score, sensitivity and specificity, whose definitions can be found in [18]. The results in Table 2 verify that our weakly-supervised RAN achieves competitive performance compared with fully-supervised model. Four examples are illustrated in Fig. 3, showing the powerful localization ability of the RAM technique. The RAMs also provide a good visual explanation of *what* and *why* RAN predicts. Except RAM_1, the other RAMs from coarser scales fail to generate an accurate segmentation. To lend insight into failure modes, fours examples (corresponding to the four examples in Fig. 3) of the coarser RAMs calculated from $\{S_2, S_3, S_4\}$ and the average RAM over all four scales is shown in Fig. 4. It indicates that as the resolution reduces, the localization ability of RAM becomes weaker.

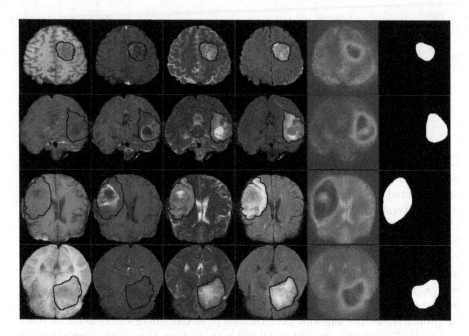

Fig. 3. Column 1–4: preprocessed T1w, T1c, T2w and FLAIR images overlapped with the segmentation ground truth shown in purple contour. Column 5: RAM_1 calculated from the first scale overlapped with FLAIR image. Colume 6: Segmentation result calculated from RAM_1 using a fixed thresholding operation.

Table 3. Model performance with different ablation settings.

Multi-level attention	Channel attention	Survival prediction	Tumor segmentation		
		C-index	DICE	Sensitivity	Specificity
No	No	0.598	0.641	0.725	0.878
No	Yes	0.603	0.675	0.715	0.891
Yes	No	0.613	0.790	0.800	0.943
Yes	Yes	0.632	0.792	0.803	0.977

Ablation Experiments. To evaluate the importance of the proposed risk attention mechanism, ablation experiments are performed. We evaluate three settings, including RAN based on reduced RABs with only multi-level attention, RAN with only channel attention, or RAN without RAB. Table 3 shows the ablation results obtained on the test data set. The overall performance of the RAN without RAB lags far behind the original RAN. By adding channel attention, the DICE increases from 0.641 to 0.675, while the C-index are just slightly better. The multi-level attention improves the performance significantly with a DICE of 0.790 and a C-index of 0.613, which is on par with the original RAN. The results verify our hypothesis that tumor segmentation and survival prediction are mutually correlated and can reinforce each other. Two examples of RAM_1 and corresponding segmentation for each ablation model is shown in Fig. 5.

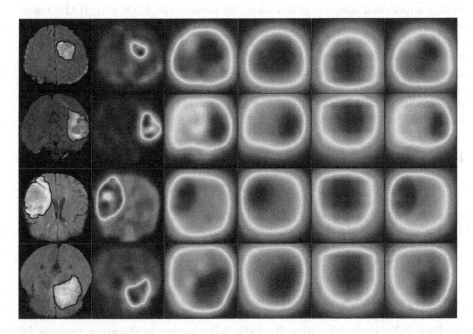

Fig. 4. Column 1: preprocessed FLAIR images overlapped with the segmentation ground truth shown in purple contour. Column 2–5: RAM_1, RAM_2, RAM_3, and RAM_4 calculated from each of the four scales. Column 6: the average RAM calculated over all four scales.

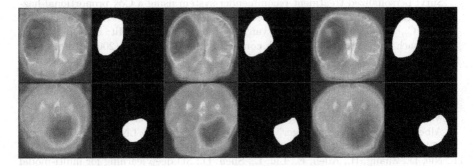

Fig. 5. RAM_1 and corresponding segmentations of the ablation models. From left to right: the results of a reduced RAN without RAB, without channel attention, and without multi-level attention.

4   Conclusion

This study is initially motivated by a practical requirement of developing a CNN-based survival model without the costly ROI annotations. Inspired by the weakly supervised image segmentation, we present the RAN with RABs based on a pyramidal architecture to learn risk-aware features. RAN is trained with survival labels only and achieves accurate risk prediction. Concurrently, a high resolution RAM is calculated, and a voxel-level segmentation of the tumor can be directly obtained from the RAM using a simple fixed thresholding. This study not only presents a promising way to predict survival directly from medical images without delineating ROI, but also show a potential of segmenting the tumor using a CNN trained with survival labels only.

References

1. Wang, P., Li, Y., Reddy, C.K.: Machine learning for survival analysis: a survey. ACM. Comput. Surv. **51**(6), Article 10 (2019)
2. Klein, J.P., Moeschberger, M.L.: Survival Analysis: Techniques for Censored and Truncated Data. Springer, Heidelberg (2005)
3. Cox, D.R.: Regression models and life-tables. J. Roy. Stat. Soc. Ser. B (Methodol.) **34**(2), 187–202 (1972)
4. Ishwaran, H., Kogalur, U.B., Blackstone, E.H., Lauer, M.S.: Random survival forests. Ann. Appl. Stat. **2**(3), 841–60 (2008)
5. Tibshirani, R.: The lasso method for variable selection in the Cox model. Stat. Med. **16**(4), 385–395 (1997)
6. Park, S.Y., Park, J.E., Kim, H., Park, S.H.: Review of statistical methods for evaluating the performance of survival or other time-to-event prediction models (from conventional to deep learning approaches). Korean J. Radiol. **22**(10), 1697–1707 (2021)
7. Katzman, J.L., Shaham, U., Cloninger, A., Bates, J., Jiang, T., Kluger, Y.: DeepSurv: personalized treatment recommender system using a Cox proportional hazards deep neural network. BMC Med. Res. Methodol. **18**(1), 1–12 (2008)
8. Lee, C., Zame, W.R., Yoon, J., van der Schaar, M.: DeepHit: a deep learning approach to survival analysis with competing risks. In: AAAI (2008)
9. Mobadersany, P., Yousefi, S., Amgad, M., et al.: Predicting cancer outcomes from histology and genomics using convolutional networks. P. Natl. Acad. Sci. USA **115**(13), E2970–E2979 (2018)
10. Li, R., Yao, J., Zhu, X., Li, Y., Huang, J.: Graph CNN for survival analysis on whole slide pathological images. In: Frangi, A.F., Schnabel, J.A., Davatzikos, C., Alberola-López, C., Fichtinger, G. (eds.) MICCAI 2018. LNCS, vol. 11071, pp. 174–182. Springer, Cham (2018). https://doi.org/10.1007/978-3-030-00934-2_20
11. Nie, D., Zhang, H., Adeli, E., Liu, L., Shen, D.: 3D deep learning for multi-modal imaging-guided survival time prediction of brain tumor patients. In: Ourselin, S., Joskowicz, L., Sabuncu, M.R., Unal, G., Wells, W. (eds.) MICCAI 2016. LNCS, vol. 9901, pp. 212–220. Springer, Cham (2016). https://doi.org/10.1007/978-3-319-46723-8_25
12. Kim, H., Goo, J.M., Lee, K.H., Kim, Y.T., Park, C.M.: Preoperative CT-based deep learning model for predicting disease-free survival in patients with lung adenocarcinomas. Radiology **296**(1), 216–224 (2020)

13. Yan, J., Zhao, Y., Chen, Y., et al.: Deep learning features from diffusion tensor imaging improve glioma stratification and identify risk groups with distinct molecular pathway activities. EBioMedicine **72**, 103583 (2021)
14. Zhou, B., Khosla, A., Lapedriza, et al.: Learning deep features for discriminative localization. In: CVPR, pp. 2921–2929. IEEE (2016)
15. Lin, T.Y., Dollár, P., Girshick, et al.: Feature pyramid networks for object detection. In: CVPR, pp. 2117–2125. IEEE (2017)
16. He, K., Zhang, X., Ren, S., Sun, J.: Deep residual learning for image recognition. In: CVPR, pp. 770–778. IEEE (2016)
17. Hu, J., Shen, L., Sun, G.: Squeeze-and-excitation networks. In: CVPR, pp. 7132–7141. IEEE (2018)
18. Menze, B.H., Jakab, A., et al.: The multimodal brain tumor image segmentation benchmark (BRATS). IEEE Trans. Med. Imaging **34**(10), 1993–2024 (2015)
19. Warfield, S.K., Zou, K.H., Wells, W.M.: Simultaneous truth and performance level estimation (STAPLE): an algorithm for the validation of image segmentation. IEEE Trans. Med. Imaging **23**(7), 903–921 (2004)
20. Li, Q., Bai, H., Chen, Y., et al.: A fully-automatic multiparametric radiomics model: towards reproducible and prognostic imaging signature for prediction of overall survival in glioblastoma multiforme. Sci. Rep. **7**(1), 14331 (2017)
21. van, Griethuysen, J.J.M., Fedorov, A., Parmar, C., et al.: Computational radiomics system to decode the radiographic phenotype. Cancer Res. **77**(21), e104–e107 (2017)
22. Zhu, X., Yao, J., Huang, J.: Deep convolutional neural network for survival analysis with pathological images. In: IEEE BIBM, pp. 544–547 (2016)
23. Sahm, F., Capper, D., Jeibmann, A., et al.: Addressing diffuse glioma as a systemic brain disease with single-cell analysis. JAMA Neurol. **69**, 523–526 (2012)
24. Osswald, M., Jung, E., Sahm, F., et al.: Brain tumour cells interconnect to a functional and resistant network. Nature **528**, 93–98 (2015)
25. Ronneberger, O., Fischer, P., Brox, T.: U-net: convolutional networks for biomedical image segmentation. In: Navab, N., Hornegger, J., Wells, W.M., Frangi, A.F. (eds.) MICCAI 2015. LNCS, vol. 9351, pp. 234–241. Springer, Cham (2015). https://doi.org/10.1007/978-3-319-24574-4_28

Automatic Detection of Obstructive Sleep Apnea Based on Multimodal Imaging System and Binary Code Alignment

Ruoshu Yang[1], Ludan Zhang[1], Yunlu Wang[1], Menghan Hu[1($\boxtimes$)], Qingli Li[1], and Xiao-Ping Zhang[2]

[1] Shanghai Key Laboratory of Multidimensional Information Processing, School of Communication and Electronic Engineering, East China Normal University, Shanghai 200062, China
mhhu@ce.ecnu.edu.cn

[2] Department of Electrical, Computer and Biomedical Engineering, Ryerson University, Toronto, Canada

Abstract. There are many patients with obstructive sleep apnea syndrome, which has caused concern. When it occurs, the nasal airflow disappears, and the breathing action of the chest and abdomen still exists. Therefore, we propose a multimodal imaging system in tandem with binary code alignment to remotely and automatically detect the obstructive sleep apnea. The RGB-thermal imaging module is applied to monitor the breathing conditions in the nose or mouth area. The depth camera is utilized to monitor the undulating state of the chest cavity. The obtained respiratory waveform is afterwards subjected to the limiting filter to suppress noisy signals that are not related to the mission objective. The signals derived from thermal camera and depth camera are pooled together for binary code alignment. When these two synchronously acquired bimodal signals do not match well, the obstructive sleep apnea is present. Our method achieves the satisfactory performance with accuracy, precision, recall and F1 of 91.38%, 96.15%, 86.21%, and 90.91%, respectively. This indicates that the proposed multimodal imaging system coupled with binary code alignment has a potential for non-contact and automatic detection of obstructive sleep apnea.

Keywords: Obstructive Sleep Apnea (OSA) · RGB-thermal imaging · Depth imaging · Limiting filter processing · Binary code alignment

1 Introduction

With the increasing public awareness of sleep-related diseases, sleep apnea syndrome (SAS) has become a public health and economic challenge [1]. It has been found that there is a causal relationship between the occurrence of sleep apnea

R. Yang and L. Zhang—These authors contributed equally to this work.

© Springer Nature Singapore Pte Ltd. 2022
G. Zhai et al. (Eds.): IFTC 2021, CCIS 1560, pp. 108–119, 2022.
https://doi.org/10.1007/978-981-19-2266-4_9

and some diseases, such as hypertension, coronary heart disease, arrhythmia, stroke and heart rhythm failure [2]. In addition, sleep apnea is associated with poor sleep quality, daytime fatigue, lethargy, neuropsychiatric disorders (such as cognitive impairment and depression), and impaired quality of life [3,4]. Obstructive sleep apnea (OSA) is the most common form of apnea. It affects nearly one billion people worldwide, and its prevalence exceeds 50% in some countries [5].

Most cases of obstructive sleep apnea have not been diagnosed and treated even in developed countries [6]. This is partly due to the laborious procedures required for sleep apnea diagnostic testing. Although the Polysomnography (PSG) system provides detailed and highly accurate results, there are some disadvantages. It is a necessary condition for patients to spend the night in the sleep laboratory and requires sleep technicians to participate in the study. Besides, the data needs to be scored manually to produce results [1]. These requirements make the patient feel uncomfortable and cause the process to be slow and expensive [7]. Therefore, it may be beneficial to provide reliable sleep apnea diagnosis with fewer and simpler measurement techniques without the need for a dedicated sleep laboratory [8].

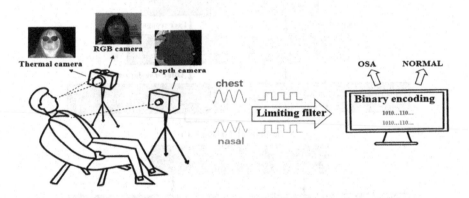

Fig. 1. Application pipeline of the proposed approach.

Obstructive sleep apnea syndrome requires simultaneous detection of oral or nasal airflow and chest wall movements. The use of a mask, barometer, differential pressure sensor and hot wire anemometer sensor will make the patient feel bulky or uncomfortable during the whole process [1]. The commonly used respiratory inductance plethysmography (RIP) measures chest movement by wrapping it around the patient's chest, which can also affect sleep comfort. Although the contact measurement technology can also make the respiratory signal have higher waveform stability and less noise, the contact measurement method always requires many sensors to be connected to the human body, which brings a physical and psychological burden to the user and leads to error in the experimental results. Therefore, the non-contact measurement method is more suitable for detecting abnormal breathing patterns, and there is an urgent need to develop a non-contact and user-friendly monitoring program [9]. This paper proposes a non-contact multimodal automatic detection method for OSA. The application pipeline of this paper is shown in Fig. 1.

The contributions of the current work are twofold:

- Considering the characteristics of OSA, we built a multimodal imaging system for automatic OSA detection, including RGB-thermal camera and depth camera. The RGB-thermal camera and depth camera can respectively capture the temperature change signals in nose region and chest heaving signals in thoracic region caused by breathing.
- To achieve remote and automatic OSA detection, a signal processing method that combines limiting filtering and binary code alignment is proposed to accurately draw the conclusion from the obtained bimodal signals. The limiting filtering can turn sine waves into square waves, and the binary code alignment can recode the two curves to draw the final judgement.

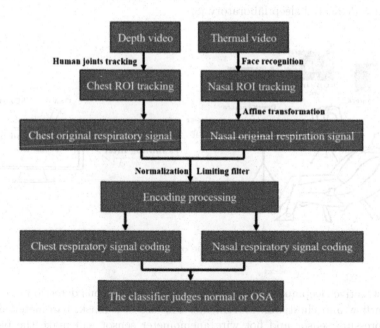

Fig. 2. Workflow of signal extraction and signal processing.

2   Methods

The flow of our method is shown in Fig. 2. First of all, the human body video is obtained through the depth video, RGB video and thermal video. In depth videos, the region of Interest (ROI) of the chest is determined by tracking the joints of the human body automatically, so as to obtain the original breathing signal of the chest. The ROI of the nose is determined by real-time face recognition on the RGB video, and then converted to thermal video by affine transformation to obtain the corresponding ROI, so as to obtain the original respiratory signal of the nose. Then the original respiratory signal of the nose and chest are respectively passed through a limiting filter. Finally, the two signals derived from thermal video and depth video are pooled together for binary code alignment. If they can be aligned, the classifier judges that the person is normal, otherwise, the classifier judges that it occurs apnea events during sleep, which suggests the person may have OSA.

2.1   Signal Extraction

Temperature Fluctuation Curve. Owing to the few geometric and texture facial details, it may be relatively difficult to detect the nose region in thermal image [10]. Therefore, it is necessary to apply affine transformation to map RGB face detection results to thermal image. Face detection is based on the discriminant regression method [11], and 66 landmark points are obtained. We choose the 31st, 32nd, 34th, and 36th landmark points to determine the ROI that completely covers the nose area. Then, the corresponding ROI on the thermal image is determined by affine transformation [7]. The formula is as follows:

$$T = \begin{bmatrix} cos(\theta) & -sin(\theta) & t1 \\ sin(\theta) & cos(\theta) & t2 \\ 0 & 0 & 1 \end{bmatrix},
\tag{1}$$

$$\begin{bmatrix} x' \\ y' \\ 1 \end{bmatrix} = T \begin{bmatrix} x \\ y \\ 1 \end{bmatrix},
\tag{2}$$

where T is the transformation matrix, θ is the angle of rotation, $t1$ and $t2$ are the amount of translation, and x and y are the horizontal and vertical coordinates of the landmark points. The horizontal and vertical coordinates of the four landmark points in ROI of thermal image are obtained from the horizontal and vertical coordinates of the RGB landmark points through a transformation matrix.

After that, the following formula is used to calculate the average gray value of the ROI in the thermal image to obtain the temperature fluctuations of the entire inhalation and expiration cycle.

$$\bar{g} = \frac{1}{n} \sum_{x=1}^{n} g(x),
\tag{3}$$

where $g(x)$ is the gray value of each pixel in the ROI, and n means that there are n pixels in the ROI.

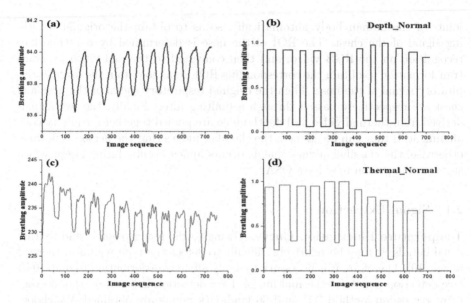

Fig. 3. Multi-mode limiting filter processing for normal mode: (a) the original waveform of the depth image; (b) the depth waveform processed by the limiting filter; (c) the original waveform of the thermal image; (d) the waveform of thermal image processed by the limiting filter.

Thoracic Heaving Curve. The depth camera is applied to obtain the thoracic undulation curve. Microsoft Azure Kinect provides a program interface that can be used for body tracking, through which the 3D position in each joint is returned. Through programming, the four key points of the chest area are tracked, and then the ROI used for extracting depth signals can be determined via these vertices. After that, we map the 3D position around the desired chest to a 2D depth image [12]. The ROI can be tracked automatically regardless of the movement of the subject. The Python plotting library Matplotlib [13] displays signals in real time. By calculating the average value of the depth data in each frame of a specific ROI, we can extract the respiratory signal. The formula is as follows:

$$\bar{Y}(k) = \frac{1}{n} \sum_{i,j \in N} Y(i,j,k),\tag{4}$$

where $Y(i, j, k)$ represents the depth data of the pixel (i, j) in the frame k; N represents the pixel coordinate vector of each ROI, and n represents the number of pixels in a certain ROI. A moving average filter with a data span of 5 is used to smooth all the frames of $Y(k)$ to eliminate sudden changes in the waveform.

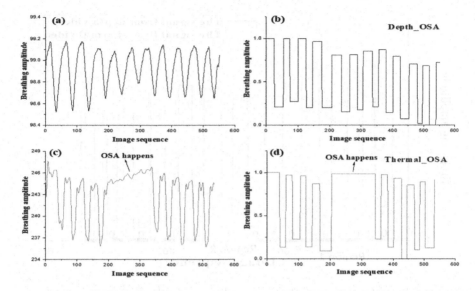

Fig. 4. Multi-mode limiting filter processing for OSA mode: (a) the original waveform of the depth image; (b) the depth waveform processed by the limiting filter; (c) the original waveform of the thermal image; (d) the waveform of thermal image processed by the limiting filter.

2.2 Binary Code Alignment Processing

Limiting Filter. Due to the difference of sensor accuracy, the depth image is ideal with less noise, but thermal image has more noise and lower accuracy, and we found that almost all noises are relatively small. The noise waveforms with small amplitude are caused by factors such as air flow, light and dark alternation. These noises are difficult to avoid, so we decided to use limiting filter to process the two waveforms.

To filter the small amplitude waveform area into a stable value, the idea of limiting amplitude filtering is adopted to enhance the ability to suppress extremely low amplitude noise, while ensuring that the true value of the normal amplitude signal is better tracked. If the difference between y_i and $y_{i-1} < A$, then the current sampling y_i is invalid; if the difference between y_i and $y_{i-1} \geq A$, y_i is valid; the current value is discarded, and the previous sampling value y_{i-1} is used to replace the sampled value y_i this time. The limiting operation formula is as follows:

$$y_i = \begin{cases} y_i & \mid y_i - y_{i-1} \mid \geq A \\ y_{i-1} & \mid y_i - y_{i-1} \mid < A \end{cases}. \tag{5}$$

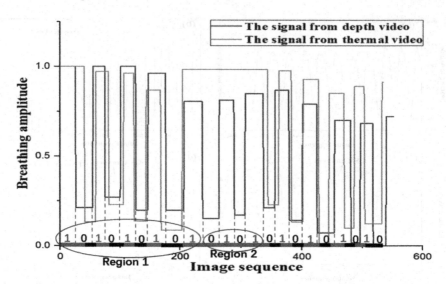

Fig. 5. OSA waveform: we write the binary code of the depth image waveform in figure, and divide each area coded as "1" and coded as "0", and compare whether the coding of the thermal image waveform contains the coding of the depth image waveform in the divided area. In the figure, the red on the X-axis represents the thermal image code as "1", and the black represents the thermal image code as "0". From the figure, if the area coded as "1" should contain the red part, the area coded as "0" should contain the black part. As shown in region 1, the two signals respectively extracted from depth video and thermal video match, meaning that the breathing sequence is normal. As shown in region 2, the two signals respectively extracted from depth video and thermal video mismatch, meaning that the apnea occurs.

The min-max normalization method is used to process numerical features and convert them into values in the range of [0, 1]. The formula is as follows:

$$y_i' = \frac{y_i - min(y_i)}{max(y_i) - min(y_i)}, \tag{6}$$

among them, y_i' is the normalized number, y_i is the original number, and $min(y_i)$ and $max(y_i)$ are the minimum and maximum values of the feature respectively.

As shown in Fig. 3 and Fig. 4, after the processing, it can effectively overcome the impulse interference caused by accidental factors, reduce the difference between thermal image and depth image due to different instruments, and enlarge the difference caused by disease characteristics. The difference here means that there is no respiratory signal in thermal image when sick, and the depth camera signal still exists, just like Fig. 4.

Binary Code Alignment. After normalization, the data of thermal image and depth image are subjected to the same recoding process, which are shown in Fig. 5 and Fig. 6. The position of the data mutation is obtained, and the encoding processing is carried out between two adjacent positions, and the encoding is determined by the following rule:

$$s = \begin{cases} 1 & y'_i \geq 0.5 \\ 0 & y'_i < 0.5 \end{cases}, \tag{7}$$

where y'_i is the signal data after normalization, s is the coded value. The location of the depth image's data mutation is mapped to that of the thermal image. We determine whether the code between the adjacent data mutation points mapped on the thermal image contains the code number intercepted by the depth camera, and then repeat this operation. When there are two consecutive data mismatches during the judgment process, that is to say, the data is not aligned, it ends early and it is judged that there is a diseased condition. If there is no mismatch until the end of the existing waveform, it is judged as no symptoms.

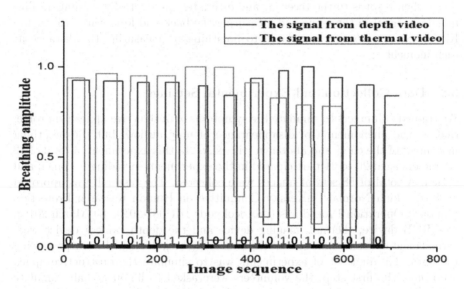

Fig. 6. Normal waveform: the coding of the thermal image waveform contains the coding of the depth image in the divided area, indicating that they are all matched.

3   Experiments

3.1   Hardware and Principle

RGB-Thermal Camera Hardware and Principle. In this experiment, a thermal imager (MAG62, Magnity Electronics Co. Ltd., Shanghai, China) and an RGB camera with a resolution of 640 * 480 were used. According to the previous work [14], we placed the thermal imager and the RGB camera in parallel to obtain almost the same field of view. Two cameras can simultaneously collect thermal video and RGB video. The alternation of inhalation and exhalation will cause the nostril region (ROI) to produce observable radiation intensity or temperature changes. Due to the dynamic nature of this process, the observable intensity or temperature varies with time and location. The heat flow dynamics at the nostril level can be observed in the measurement sequence of the thermal images. These sequences are further processed to extract waveforms related to respiration.

Depth Camera Hardware and Principle. Our experiment uses Azure Kinect (released by Microsoft in 2019) to record the depth images of the experimenter's breathing. The Microsoft Kinect used to obtain the depth image sequence is a kind of TOF sensor [8], which is based on the Light Det [15]. The optical TOF system is mainly composed of an optical transmitter and a receiver. The transmitter sends out a modulated signal, which bounces off objects in the scene, then returns to the receiver, and estimates the depth by sending an illumination signal in the scene and measuring the back and forth time [16]. Azure Kinect extracts waveforms related to breathing by measuring the distance at each moment.

3.2 Data Collection and Experimental Settings

We trained volunteers to simulate the symptoms of obstructive apnea syndrome, that is, the phenomenon of disappearance of nose airflow, but the breathing movement of the chest and abdomen still exists. In this experiment, a total of 12 volunteers aged 20 to 31 participated in the experiment, including 6 women and 6 men. A total of 58 sets of images were collected. The research was approved by East China Normal University Committee on Human Research Protection Standard Operation Procedures (protocol code HR 087-2019, 1st March 2019). The RGB device, thermal imaging device and the depth camera device were turned on at the same time so that the data could be well aligned while processing the data. The first set of experiments was to simulate the obstructive apnea syndrome: the first step, the volunteers were asked to lie on a chair, simulate a sleeping scene, and breathe several times naturally; the second step was to simulate the phenomenon of disease, and they were asked not to breathe through the nose, but the chest cavity was still undulating, and then breathed abnormally for several times; the third step was to simulate the phenomenon of gradually returning to normal breathing. They breathed normally for several times and then ended. Then we conducted the second set of experiments, and simulated the normal situation without disease: volunteers breathed normally from beginning to end, and the time of the two sets of experiments was basically the same.

4 Results and Discussion

We conducted three sets of experiments using three methods, and calculated the accuracy, precision, recall and F1 respectively. Table 1 shows the performance indicators of the three methods. Our method achieves the best performance and its accuracy, precision, recall and F1 are 91.38%, 96.15%, 86.21%, and 90.91%, respectively.

For the processing method, we compared the binary code alignment method with the 10-second detection method. The performance comparison is shown in Table 1. The 10-second detection method is based on the characteristics of obstructive sleep apnea syndrome, that is, the disappearance of airflow in the nose for at least 10 s. This method only focuses on the signal extracted from thermal videos. If there exists at least 10 s airflow disappearance, this signal was judged as OSA, otherwise it was judged as normal. However, this method is only effective under extremely ideal conditions. Under real conditions, patients usually experience a struggle during the disappearance of nasal airflow that lasts at least 10 s. Many factors, such as the movement of the volunteer's head, the alternation of light and dark, and the flow of air, may cause errors in this judgment method, and the coding method can avoid the influence of these uncertain factors and make judgments more precisely.

Table 1. Performance comparison of different processing methods for the OSA detection.

Processing	Accuracy (%)	Precision (%)	Recall (%)	F1 (%)
Limiting filtering + coding	91.38	96.15	86.21	90.91
Limiting filtering + 10s check	79.31	85.42	70.69	77.36
Band-pass filtering + coding	52.59	53.06	44.83	48.60

For the filtering method, we compared our limiting filtering and band-pass filtering. Due to the problem of noise caused by the natural inaccuracy of thermal images, after band-pass filtering, there is still a lot of interfering data. The limiting filtering can make the data closer to the characteristics of the disease through processing and can achieve very accurate results. Therefore, it can be proved that the combination of our limiting filtering method and binary code alignment method has a great contribution to the detection of obstructive sleep apnea syndrome.

From the experimental results, we observed that the recall value was relatively low, which indicated that the accuracy of this classifier to determine whether a patient was sick was not high. So we checked the original images and data, and found that when a volunteer was simulating the condition of a patient, the original data of thermal image was not much different from that of the non-diseased, so we speculated that this might be a mistake of the volunteer in the simulation experiment.

This experiment is conducted under relatively ideal experimental conditions. Therefore, the characteristics of the simulated patient's disease are different from those of the real patient, and simulation errors are prone to occur. Moreover, each experiment of the volunteers only lasts one to two minutes, while under real sleep conditions, patients may experience unpredictable struggles that last longer.

Therefore, our next step is to improve the experiment to achieve a complete real-time monitoring and detection method. We will try to contact the hospital to find enough patients with obstructive sleep apnea syndrome to conduct the experiment in a real sleep environment to help our classification method provide more realistic reference data.

5   Conclusion

This paper proposes a non-contact automatic monitoring method based on the characteristics of obstructive apnea syndrome, which is a multimodal detection method that combines RGB-thermal image and depth image. We filter the noise through the limiting filter to obtain a more accurate respiratory waveform, and then detect it through binary code alignment. Our method can achieve good performance and its accuracy, precision, recall and F1 are 91.38%, 96.15%, 86.21%, and 90.91%, respectively. Through comparative analysis, the method of combining limiting filtering and binary code alignment has certain advantages.

Acknowledgments. This work is sponsored by the National Natural Science Foundation of China (No. 61901172, No. 61831015, No. U1908210), the Shanghai Sailing Program (No.19YF1414100), the "Chenguang Program" supported by Shanghai Education Development Foundation and Shanghai Municipal Education Commission (No. 19CG27), the Science and Technology Commission of Shanghai Municipality (No. 19511120100, No. 18DZ2270700, No. 14DZ2260800), the foundation of Key Laboratory of Artificial Intelligence, Ministry of Education (No. AI2019002), the Fundamental Research Funds for the Central Universities and Sichuan Science and Technology Program (2021JDGD0002).

References

1. Shokoueinejad, M., et al.: Sleep apnea: a review of diagnostic sensors, algorithms, and therapies. Physiol. Meas. **38**, R204–R252 (2017)
2. Javaheri, S., et al.: Sleep apnea. J. Am. Coll. Cardiol. **69**(7), 841–858 (2017)
3. Kapur, V.K., et al.: Clinical practice guideline for diagnostic testing for adult obstructive sleep apnea: an American academy of sleep medicine clinical practice guideline. J. Clin. Sleep Med. **13**(03), 479–504 (2017)
4. Randerath, W., et al.: Challenges and perspectives in obstructive sleep apnoea. Eur. Respiratory J. **52**(3), 1702616 (2018)
5. Benjafield, A.V., et al.: Estimation of the global prevalence and burden of obstructive sleep apnoea: a literature-based analysis. Lancet Respir. Med. **7**(8), 687–698 (2019)
6. Jaiswal, S.J., Owens, R.L., Malhotra, A.: Raising awareness about sleep disorders. Lung India: Off. Organ Indian Chest Soc. **34**(3), 262 (2017)
7. Mendonça, F., Mostafa, S.S., Ravelo-García, A.G., Morgado-Dias, F., Penzel, T.: Devices for home detection of obstructive sleep apnea: a review. Sleep Med. Rev. **41**, 149–160 (2018)

8. Massaroni, C., Nicolò, A., Sacchetti, M., Schena, E.: Contactless methods for measuring respiratory rate: a review. IEEE Sens. J. **21**(11), 12821–12839 (2020)
9. Collop, N.A., et al.: Obstructive sleep apnea devices for out-of-center (OOC) testing: technology evaluation. J. Clin. Sleep Med. **07**(05), 531–548 (2011)
10. Sarfraz, M.S., Stiefelhagen, R.: Deep perceptual mapping for thermal to visible face recognition. arXiv preprint arXiv:1507.02879 (2015)
11. Asthana, A., Zafeiriou, S., Cheng, S., Pantic, M.: Robust discriminative response map fitting with constrained local models. In: Proceedings of the IEEE Conference on Computer Vision and Pattern Recognition, pp. 3444–3451 (2013)
12. Wang, Y., et al.: Unobtrusive and automatic classification of multiple people's abnormal respiratory patterns in real time using deep neural network and depth camera. IEEE Internet Things J. **7**(9), 8559–8571 (2020)
13. Hunter, J.D.: Matplotlib: a 2D graphics environment. IEEE Ann. Hist. Comput. **9**(03), 90–95 (2007)
14. Hu, M.-H., Zhai, G.-T., Li, D., Fan, Y.-Z., Chen, X.-H., Yang, X.-K.: Synergetic use of thermal and visible imaging techniques for contactless and unobtrusive breathing measurement. J. Biomed. Opt. **22**(3), 1–11 (2017)
15. Benetazzo, F., Freddi, A., Monteriù, A., Longhi, S.: Respiratory rate detection algorithm based on RGB-D camera: theoretical background and experimental results. Healthc. Technol. Lett. **1**(3), 81–86 (2014)
16. Hussmann, S., Ringbeck, T., Hagebeuker, B.: A performance review of 3D TOF vision systems in comparison to stereo vision systems. Stereo Vis. **372** (2008)

Application and Research of Deep Learning in Wheel Tread Defect Detection

Jiaxin Wang[1], Hongtao Li[2(✉)], Zheng Liang[3], Xiaoguang Huang[1], and Juan Wang[4]

[1] State Grid Information and Telecommunication Group Co., LTD., Beijing, China
[2] China Construction Second Engineering Bureau Ltd., East China Company, Shanghai, China
2839969235@qq.com
[3] China Shandong Foreign Trade Vocational College, Qingdao, China
[4] Institute of Cloud Computing and Big Data, China Academy of Information and Communications Technology, Beijing, China

Abstract. The surface problems of wheels include peeling, cracks and scratches, etc. In the process of automatic detection, it is of practical significance to acquire real-time wheel tread images through image collectors on rails and make quick and effective analysis. This paper studies the application of deep learning in wheel tread defect detection, and classifies and identifies common wheel tread defect images such as cracks, peeling, scratches and pits. Firstly, through data set enhancement, the wheel tread defect gallery is created, which contains 35,000 pictures, including nine kinds of defect pictures and one kind of normal pictures, with an average of 3,500 pictures in each category, and the resolution of each image is processed into 224×224. Then, the initial results of wheel tread detection by six classic models are compared, including VGG16, VGG19, ResNet18, ResNet34, ResNet50 and ResNet101. In the experiment process, the training efficiency is improved through transfer learning. The results show that the ResNet50 model has higher performance and better effect in identifying wheel tread defects. The loss function combining the Center loss and Softmax loss is adopted, and Adam is adopted as the optimization algorithm. The experimental results show that, compared with traditional machine vision recognition method and the original ResNet50 network, the method adopted in this paper has achieved good results in recognition accuracy and real-time performance.

Keywords: Deep learning · ResNet · Wheel tread defect

1 Introduction

According to the official website, at present, the running distance of China's railways has reached 120,000 km, including 19,000 km of high-speed rail transportation. By 2025, most of the planned routes will be built and put into use. By then, the total railway transportation mileage in China will reach about 180,000 km, and there will be more than 20% of high-speed railways covering more than 80% of large, medium and small cities in China. The rapid expansion of railway has also brought a lot of safety risks. If the train wheels are used for a long time, the wheelset will easily produce defects such as tread abrasion, tread peeling, tread wear, web hole crack, rim crack, etc. If the wheelset has problems, it will cause hidden dangers to the safe running of the train. The impacts include: the vibration of the train will increase when it is running, which will damage the rails, make the rails age prematurely and increase the maintenance cost. Since the rail transit began to be used, the inspection and maintenance of wheels has been regarded as the top priority in the world.

The wheel detection is mainly static and dynamic. Static detection means that the train stops at the detection workshop and manually detects the wheels. The static detection equipment is relatively simple, but it is laborious and inefficient. People who rely on manual detection for a long time will be tired and cause detection errors. Static detection includes: eddy current method [1], photoelectric method [2], electromagnetic ultrasound [3], mechanical detection [4] and other methods; Dynamic detection means that when the train is running normally, the detection equipment on the frame or the equipment on the rail is used to detect the wheels in real time, with high efficiency and high accuracy, and the effect is remarkable in practical application. Dynamic monitoring mainly includes: shock load method [5], image measurement method [6], track circuit interruption time method [7], vibration acceleration detection method [8]. Also, there are many other research methods [9,10] and related applications [11,12] for other fields of detection and recognition [13,14].

Wheel defect detection can be regarded as an image processing problem. At present, the application of deep learning in image recognition is becoming more and more mature, and the effect is getting better and better. In this paper, the mainstream image recognition algorithm in deep learning is applied to wheel tread defect detection, and the experimental results show that the comprehensive efficiency and accuracy ResNet50 model is the best. Based on ResNet [15] model, the loss function combining the Center loss and Softmax loss is adopted, and Adam is used as the optimization algorithm to achieve better results.

2   Method

2.1   Data Processing

(1) Common Wheel Tread Defects

The wheel structure is determined by the wheel diameter, rim tread, hub size, rotation, web shape, hub torque and shape. The wheel shown below is shown in Fig. 1. Common defects of wheelset include brake peeling, fatigue peeling, abrasion peeling, continuous peeling, hot crack at the root of the wheel rim, abrasion on the tread, pressing into pockmarks, melting strain on the tread, brake hot crack, etc. The following are nine tread defects identified in this paper, as shown in Fig. 2.

Fig. 1. Wheel structure diagram

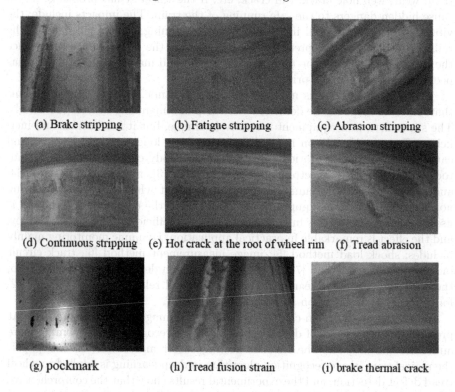

(a) Brake stripping   (b) Fatigue stripping   (c) Abrasion stripping

(d) Continuous stripping (e) Hot crack at the root of wheel rim (f) Tread abrasion

(g) pockmark   (h) Tread fusion strain   (i) brake thermal crack

Fig. 2. Wheel tread defect map

(2) Tread Defect Dataset Enhancement

Due to the limited number of collected data sets of wheel tread defects, in order
to reduce the risk of over-fitting in the process of deep learning, a huge data
set is needed for training. Therefore, it is very important to enhance the input
image data, which can improve the accuracy and generalization ability of the
network model. Commonly used methods for data enhancement include scaling
transformation, random cropping, translation transformation, flipping and random rotation transformation, noise interference and many other methods. In this
paper, a variety of data combination enhancement methods are used to expand
the data set to train convolutional neural network. The network expands the
data set by flipping the original picture first, which will double the data set.
Then, the expanded data set is scaled, interfered by noise, cut and rotated, so

that the collected picture is expanded by 10 times. In this way, the training set of wheel tread defect images has been expanded from 3500 to 35000. Figure 3 shows some datasets.

Fig. 3. Partially processed atlas

(3) Treatment Results

A total of 35,000 tread defect pictures were processed. Each tread image is processed into an image of the same size, that is, an image with a resolution of 224×224, and then the image is named in a unified format so that the program can identify the configuration label. The training set contains 32,000 tread pictures (3,200 in each category). The test set contains 3000 pictures. The following datasets are divided into Table 1.

Table 1. Data set partition table

Tread type	Training set	Testing set
Brake stripping	3200	300
Fatigue stripping	3200	300
Abrasion stripping	3200	300
Continuous stripping	3200	300
Hot crack at the root of wheel rim	3200	300
Tread abrasion	3200	300
Tread fusion strain	3200	300
Pockmark	3200	300
Brake thermal crack	3200	300
Normal	3200	300

2.2 Application Transfer Learning

Due to the limited number of images of wheel tread defects collected in this study, transfer learning is used to improve the performance of network training. Transfer learning reduces the assumption that test and training data sets must be independent of each other, so that researchers can deal with the problem of insufficient pictures in the training process through transfer learning [16]. The classic public data sets used for deep learning include Pascal VOC, COCO, ImageNet, etc. Among them, ImageNet [17] data set has many categories and a huge number, which is the most frequently used data set in deep learning image processing research at present, and is maintained by a dedicated team, and has high authority in the industry.

Because the generalization ability of the structure trained by ImageNet dataset has been greatly improved, and at the same time, the features in ImageNet dataset are abundant, and the features of many pictures are very similar to those of wheel tread defects. Therefore, the transfer learning method in this paper is to pre-train ResNet50 with ImageNet data set, and optimize the parameters of ResNet50 by collecting and making wheel tread defect data set on the basis of pre-training, so that it can be used in wheel tread defect detection. Pre-training process mainly includes network pre-training, filtering ImageNet dataset and configuring deep learning environment. The process of transfer learning is shown in Fig. 4.

Transfer learning is to improve the learning from the target domain to the distribution P2 by using the learned distribution P1 of the learning tasks in the source domain, so that P2 has better generalization. The generalization training process of the distribution P2 depends on the distribution P1 and the target data set, which is an indispensable means to save a lot of repetitive training work in supervised learning [18,19].

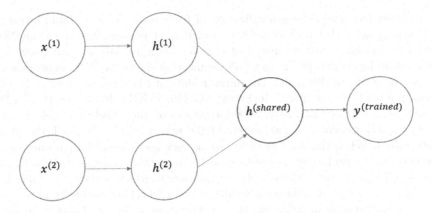

Fig. 4. Architecture representation of transfer learning

During learning, $h^{(shared)}$ is the source domain of shared knowledge. During training, the neural network layer represented by the source domain can be frozen as needed, and only the non-feature extraction classification layer can be trained. $x^{(1)}$ and $x^{(2)}$ represent the bottom input structure, $x^{(1)}$ and $x^{(2)}$) represent the trainable target areas according to the input structure, and $h^{(shared)}$ represents the pre-training knowledge areas that have been frozen and shared, and the final training results will be fine-tuned automatically under the task of multiple task iterations.

2.3 Comparison of Identification Results of Different Models

Because PyTorch is highly modular and has a very concise network library, there are rich network models that can be called by simple code, which greatly reduces the workload of users. The software and hardware configuration of the server used in this experiment is shown in Table 2.

Table 2. Server configuration

Package	Configuration
Power	Dell precision Tower 5820 950 w
CPU	Intel Xeon 14core E5-2680V4 (2.4 GHz, 9.6GT/s)
Memory	128G (32 GB * 4) DDR4 2666 MHZ ECC-REG
System hard disk	2.5 in. 512G SSD
Data hard disk	3.5 in. 8T 7200 RPM
Display card	two Geforce GTX 3090
OS	Linux Ubuntu 18.04
Language	python3.7
Framework	PyTorch 1.6

In order to expand the generalization of features, we need to build a transfer learning network for VGG network and ResNet network and use ImageNet model as the basic feature model of transfer learning. We need to freeze all convolution layers except the last Full Connections layer for VGG network and ResNet network. In this paper, the initial results of wheel tread detection by six classical models are compared, including VGG16, VGG19, ResNet18, ResNet34, ResNet50 and ResNet101. After 20000 iterations on the wheel tread defect data set in the experiment, the parameters of the network basically reach the ideal state values. When the number of iterations increases again, the parameters of the network are no longer changed, basically in a stable state, and the network is in a convergent state. The specific recognition accuracy is shown in Table 3.

Table 3 lists the identification results of train wheel tread defects in several different convolution models, and the identification accuracy of several models is very high. The detection accuracy of VGG16 model on this data set is 0.732, and the recognition rate of VGG19 model on this data set is 0.751. ResNet model performs best on this data set, and the recognition rate of ResNet18 is as high as 0.810. The recognition rate of ResNet34 is 0.825, and the recognition accuracy of ResNet50 is 0.840, which further deepens the layer number of ResNet model, that is, when using ResNet101 model, its recognition rate drops slightly to 0.832. To sum up the recognition performance of each model, we can find that ResNet50 has the highest recognition rate, so we use ResNet50 as the basic network of tread defect detection and optimize it.

Table 3. Results of different model recognition

Model	VGG16	VGG19	ResNet18	ResNet34	ResNet50	ResNet101
Time-consuming of training model convergence	40 min	46 min	52 min	60 min	71 min	135 min
Average test time per image	6 s	6.5 s	7 s	7.6 s	9.2 s	11.3 s
ACC	0.732	0.715	0.810	0.825	0.840	0.832

2.4   Loss Function

Convolutional network can evaluate the modeling degree of convolutional neural network model by learning loss function. If the actual result differs greatly from the measured value, the loss function will get a large loss value [20]. After a series of function optimization operations, the loss function can reduce the predicted error to very small or even zero [21]. In this paper, based on the improvement of ResNet50 algorithm, the loss function Center loss is applied, and the accuracy is significantly improved by combining with the Softmax loss function.

In the dataset of wheel tread defects, although the defects are different, the specificity between samples is not high. Center loss can effectively solve this problem: Center loss continuously optimizes the distance between the feature center's corresponding category and the depth feature center during the training process by learning the feature's category center. Under the combined action of the Center loss function and the Softmax loss function, the model is trained. In order to give full play to the two loss functions, a hyper parameter is set to balance. The soft loss function increases the feature interval between different classes, while the Center loss function gathers the features of the same class to its feature center, which narrows the interval between the features of the same class. With the application of these two loss functions, we can understand that the Softmax loss function is used to increase the distance between classes, and the Center loss function is used to reduce the distance within classes. By combining the two loss functions, the features learned are more cohesive, and the recognition accuracy is high.

Softmax:

$$p_j = \frac{e^{a_j}}{\sum_{k=1}^{T} e^{a_k}}$$

where, a_j represents the output value of the j-th node, and T is the number of output nodes, that is, the number of classifications. The output values of multi-classifications can be converted into probability distributions ranging from $[0, 1]$ to 1 by Softmax function. Softmax Loss:

$$L_s = -\sum_{j=1}^{T} y_j \log p_j$$

where, p_j represents the probability value of output node j corresponding to Softmax layer, $y_j \in \mathbf{y}$, and $\mathbf{y}$ represents a vector of $1 \times T$. Because only one of the T columns inside $\mathbf{y}$ is 1 and the others are 0, this formula has a simpler form:

$$L_s = -\ln p_j$$

Center Loss:

$$L_c = \frac{1}{2} \sum_{i=1}^{m} ||x_i - c_{y_i}||^2$$

where, c_{y_i} represents the feature center of the class corresponding to this sample, and m represents the size of each batch. This formula indicates that the sum of squares of the distance between each sample feature and feature center in batch is as small as possible, that is, it is responsible for intra-group gaps. In order to minimize the distance between classes and maximize the distance between classes, this paper combines Softmax Loss with Center Loss:

$$L = L_s + \lambda * L_c = -\sum_{i=1}^{m} \log \frac{e^{W_{y_i}^T x_i + b_{y_i}}}{\sum_{i=1}^{m} e^{W_{y_i}^T x_i + b_{y_i}}} + \frac{\lambda}{2} \sum_{i=1}^{m} ||x_i - c_{y_i}||^2$$

In this formula, L_s represents the Softmax Loss value, L_c represents the Center Loss value, m represents the number of samples contained in mini-batch, n represents the total number of categories of tread defect atlas, and the super parameter λ is used to control the ratio between the Softmax loss function and the Center loss function. If λ is set to 0, only the Softmax loss function works, that is, the auxiliary function Center loss is not used.

In this experiment, the use of Center loss in ResNet50 combined with Softmax loss function is used to replace the standard cross entropy loss. This replacement can reduce the weight of easily identifiable samples, so that more attention can be paid to the hard-to-identify samples when training the model, and the recognition rate of hard-to-identify samples can be improved, and the overall performance of the model can also be improved. A comparison is made between using the Center loss combined with the Softmax loss function and using the standard cross office function from two aspects of loss value and accuracy. The experimental results are shown in Table 4. In this experiment, the standard cross entropy function is replaced by the use of Center loss combined with Softmax loss function in ResNet50. This replacement can reduce the weight of easy-to-identify samples, so that more attention can be paid to the hard-to-identify samples when training the model, so that the recognition rate of the hard-to-identify samples can be improved, and the overall performance of the model can also be improved. In this paper, we compare the use of Center loss combined with Softmax loss function and standard cross entropy function from two aspects of loss value and accuracy. The experimental results are shown in Table 4.

Table 4. Loss function comparison result

Type	Sensitive	Specific	Precision	Accuracy
ResNet50 using standard cross entropy function	84.4%	86.5%	87%	85.5%
ResNet50 using Center los combine Softmax loss function	81.8%	92.1%	93.2%	86.3%

From Table 4, it can be seen that the recognition rate of the model using Center loss combined with Softmax loss function in wheel tread defect recognition is 86.3%, and the recognition accuracy of the two functions is similar. Obviously, the test loss value has dropped a lot, and the test loss value using the standard cross entropy function model is 0.18, while the test loss value of the model using Center loss combined with Softmax loss function is only 0.08. Therefore, choose the Center loss combined with the Softmax loss function.

2.5   Optimization Algorithm

The quality of convolutional neural network model training and the choice of optimizers have a direct relationship with the quality of network model training, which has a very important influence. At present, there are many optimization algorithms that can optimize the problems existing in the network, and it is very important to choose the appropriate optimization algorithm to improve the performance of the model. To ensure that other factors are the same, the results obtained by using different optimization algorithms to train the model on ResNet50 will be different. We apply these algorithms to the experiment for analysis below. The experimental network is the improved ResNet50 model, and other parameters are set the same. The performance of these optimization algorithms is analyzed from the recognition accuracy. Figure 5 shows the performance analysis of the optimization algorithm. As shown in the Fig. 5, after analyzing the five optimization algorithms, the SGD method has the worst optimization effect, followed by Adagrad method, while Adam optimization algorithm has the best effect and the highest accuracy in model optimization, achieving the highest recognition accuracy, with the recognition rate of wheel tread defects reaching 85.20%, so Adam optimization algorithm is selected.

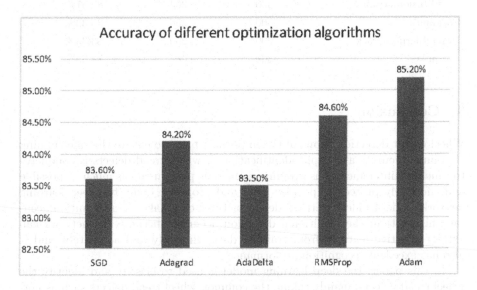

Fig. 5. Analysis of optimization algorithm performance

2.6   Result

The ResNet50 network using the Center loss combined with the Softmax loss function is shown in Table 5 for the recognition results of the tread defect test samples.

From Table 5, it can be seen that the recognition rate of normal tread is 88.33%, and the recognition accuracy rate of brake peeling, hot crack at the root of the rim, tread abrasion, tread melting strain, and pressing into pockmarks also exceeds 85%, and other recognition rates also exceed 80%.

Table 5. Recognition result

Tread type	Sample number	Correct number	Accuracy rate
Brake stripping	300	255	85.00%
Fatigue stripping	300	248	82.67%
Abrasion stripping	300	251	83.67%
Continuous stripping	300	247	82.53%
Hot crack at the root of wheel rim	300	257	85.67%
Tread abrasion	300	260	86.67%
Tread fusion strain	300	263	87.67%
Pockmark	300	256	85.33%
Brake thermal crack	300	250	83.33%
Normal	300	265	88.33%

3   Conclusion

Wheel defeat detection is one of the important parts to ensure the safe running of trains. Accurate and rapid identification of wheel tread defects is conducive to timely maintenance, thus avoiding dangerous phenomena as much as possible and effectively protecting people's lives and property. Using the deep learning network model to identify tread defect pictures can make the recognition accuracy higher than the traditional detection accuracy, because the network can extract effective features from training data efficiently and accurately, and it also has excellent recognition performance.

In this paper, the deep learning model is used to classify and identify the wheel tread defects, mainly taking the common wheel tread defects such as normal, crack, peeling, scratch and pitting as research pairs, comparing the models of VGG16, VGG19, ResNet18, ResNet34, ResNet50 and ResNet101, finally using ResNet50, and using the loss function combining Center loss and Softmax loss, so that The experimental results show that, compared with the traditional machine vision recognition method and the original ResNet50 network, the method adopted in this paper has achieved better results in recognition accuracy and real-time performance in wheel tread defect recognition. Although deep neural network and wheel tread recognition have been studied in this paper, there are still some shortcomings due to the limitations of data set and experimental conditions, which can be improved in the following three aspects: (1) Expand the dataset. (2) Optimize the neural network structure model. (3) Transplant the trained network model to low-power embedded devices to realize real-time identification of wheel tread defects.

References

1. Rockstroh, B., Kappes, W., Walte, F., et al.: Ultrasonic and eddy-current inspection of rail wheels and wheel set axles. In: 17th World Conference on Nondestructive Testing, pp. 25–28 (2008)
2. Xue, W., Guohua, X.X.Z: Wheel flats detecting methods based on wavelet resilient neural network. China Mech. Eng. **20** (2003)
3. Peng, J.P., Wang, L., Gao, X.R., et al.: Design of defect inspection instrument for wheel tread based on EMAT technology. Instr. Tech. Sens. **1**, 18–20 (2009)
4. Gao, X.D., Wu, N.Y., Ao, Y.H., Li, G.H., et al.: Development of automatic wheelset detection system of wagon. Electr. Drive Locomot. **2** (2003)
5. Decker, M., Steffen, R., Juergen, F., Bernd, B.: System for testing the operational integrity of a sample subject. In: Particular for a Wheelset of Railway Vehicles. EP (2011)
6. Li, J., Wang, J., Wang, S.: A novel method of fast dynamic optical image stabilization precision measurement based on CCD. Optik **122**(7), 582–585 (2011)
7. Zhang, Y., Wang, L., Gao, X., et al.: A review of wheel tread damage detection technologies in and out of China. Locomot. Roll. Stock Technol. **1**, 1–4 (2002)
8. Chen, X.: Research on on-line monitoring and diagnosis system for urban rail transit vehicles. Electron. Meas. Technol. **42**(20), 104–109 (2016)
9. Li, W., Chen, Z., Gao, X., et al.: Multimodel framework for indoor localization under mobile edge computing environment. IEEE Internet Things J. **6**(3), 4844–4853 (2019)
10. Gao, X., Chen, Z., Tang, S., et al.: Adaptive weighted imbalance learning with application to abnormal activity recognition. Neurocomputing **173**, 1927–1935 (2016)
11. Tang, G., Gao, X., Chen, Z., Zhong, H.: Unsupervised adversarial domain adaptation with similarity diffusion for person re-identification. Neurocomputing **442**, 337–347 (2021)
12. Zhang, Y., Gao, X., Chen, Z., et al.: Learning salient features to prevent model drift for correlation tracking. Neurocomputing **418**, 1–10 (2020)
13. Zhang, Y., Gao, X., Chen, Z., et al.: Mining spatial-temporal similarity for visual tracking. IEEE Trans. Image Process. **29**, 8107–8119 (2020)
14. Xia, Z., Hong, X., Gao, X., et al.: Spatiotemporal recurrent convolutional networks for recognizing spontaneous micro-expressions. IEEE Trans. Multimed. **22**(3), 626–640 (2020)
15. He, K., Zhang, X., Ren, S., et al.: Deep residual learning for image recognition. In: Proceedings of the IEEE Conference on Computer Vision and Pattern Recognition, pp. 770–778 (2016)
16. Kan, M., Shan, S., Chen, X.: Multi-view deep network for cross-view classification. In: Proceedings of the IEEE Conference on Computer Vision and Pattern Recognition, pp. 4847–4855 (2016)
17. Girshick, R.: Fast R-CNN. In: Proceedings of the IEEE International Conference on Computer Vision, pp. 1440–1448 (2015)
18. Gao, X., Hoi, S.C.H., Zhang, Y., et al.: Sparse online learning of image similarity. ACM Trans. Intell. Syst. Technol. **8**(5), 64:1–64:22 (2017)
19. Gao, X., Hoi, S.C.H., Zhang, Y., et al.: SOML: sparse online metric learning with application to image retrieval. In: Twenty-Eighth AAAI Conference on Artificial Intelligence, pp. 1206–1212 (2014)

132   J. Wang et al.

20. Kausar, A., Jamil, A., Nida, N., et al.: Two-wheeled vehicle detection using two-step and single-step deep learning models. Arab. J. Sci. Eng. **45**(12), 10755–10773 (2020)
21. Yan, Z.Q., Zeng, Q.Z., Zhang, Q.L.: Overview on research and application of machine vision technology in wood industry. Wood Process. Mach. **4** (2013)

An Invoice Recognition System for Robotic Process Automation Based on HOG

Cunliang Han[✉], Xiaojun Zhang, Huijuan Jiao, Min Wang, and Tiantian Han

State Grid Huitongjincai (Beijing) Information Technology Co., Ltd., Beijing, China
mengsjtl@163.com

Abstract. Nowadays, innovations and reforms in China's power industry become inevitable trends. The application of robotic process automation (RPA) creates favorable conditions for promoting the digital transformation of finance, which is of great practical significance for improving the competitiveness of electric power enterprises in China. In the process of using RPA, the information on paper invoices needs to be transformed into digital forms that can be recognized by computers, which would be time-consuming and labor-intensive manually. To solve this problem, this paper studies the usage of image recognition technology to recognize paper invoices. First, image acquisition and preprocessing of invoice images are performed. Second, text positioning and character cutting are used. Finally, character recognition methods based on histogram of oriented gradient features are implemented to extract information in the invoices, so that the invoice information can be accurately extracted and labor consumption can be greatly reduced. Experimental results show the effectiveness of the method.

Keywords: Pattern recognition · Text localization · Information processing · Character recognition · Histogram of oriented gradient feature

1 Introduction

In recent years, some experts and scholars have done meaningful research and exploration for invoice image processing. In their study on invoice recognition, Cui *et al.* used the structural features of numbers and thus identifying Arabic numerals on invoices [1], this method has a relatively high recognition rate, but is not real time and only clear and neat Arabic numerals can be recognized. Li *et al.* proposed to use the Naive Bayes to build a Naive Bayes classification model to divide each pixel in the image into two classes, and effectively achieve the separation of each color region of color images [2].

Han *et al.* proposed an image binarization enhancement algorithm using Monte Carlo simulation for binarization segmentation of images with complex background and uneven brightness [3]. Shen *et al.* integrated the Otsu method and Bernsen algorithm for real time binarization to solve the image processing problem under uneven illumination conditions [4]. Bu *et al.* proposed to use the frame line removal algorithm to eliminate the interference of frame lines on character recognition [5]. Ouyang *et al.* proposed to use the maximum symmetric surround algorithm to achieve the recognition and correction

© Springer Nature Singapore Pte Ltd. 2022
G. Zhai et al. (Eds.): IFTC 2021, CCIS 1560, pp. 133–147, 2022.
https://doi.org/10.1007/978-981-19-2266-4_11

of the stamp by clustering analysis of image targets [6]. Xu *et al.* proposed the Improve-Zxing algorithm to achieve three-point localization of QR codes [7], which enables the localization and recognition of QR codes on invoices. Luo proposed to use upward-first region growing method to search for interlinear white space for text line segmentation and image correction [8]. Cao *et al.* proposed a moving benchmark point algorithm to locate the text information area of bank notes [9]. Jin *et al.* proposed to use the binarization method for adaptive character segmentation and recognition of numbers in invoices based on vertical projection and contour features to improve the segmentation efficiency and accuracy of image strings [10]. Wang *et al.* used a deep learning-based OCR text recognition method to solve the problem of inefficient processing of massive images in the banking industry [11].

In an article on invoice recognition and management system based on image analysis, Yang and Yang proposed a Web-side invoice recognition and management system using OpenCV.js open source graphics function library and Tesseract.js optical character recognition [12]. The combination of image processing and the Web can easily and quickly convert a large number of paper documents into electronic data on the Web, creating a new economic model. BP neural network was proposed to identify characters contaminated by stamps in invoices in an article published by Jiang *et al.* [13].

After analyzing the financial reimbursement challenges in universities, He [14] proposed to directly adopt OCR technology to recognize the invoice images and extract the key information in the invoices to reduce the manual entry process in the online reimbursement process. Ru *et al.* proposed a CNN-RNN based approach to recognize medical invoice characters, this paper fused two deep learning networks CNN and RNN to get CNN-RNN to improve the recognition rate [15]. Thus, computer vision based methods [23, 24] and applications [25, 26] are paid important attention on both of academic and industry communities [19, 22] in recent years.

Although there have been many research results for invoice image recognition, there are still problems in accuracy, completeness, efficiency and intelligence of the recognition procedure. This paper synthesizes related research results and practices, integrates invoice image processing techniques, adopts binarization, morphological processing and several other methods for invoice image pre-processing, adopts multilayer autoencoders + SVM algorithm for text localization, character cutting based on projection method, and the last step is character recognition based on HOG features to achieve efficient extraction of invoice image information.

2   Invoice Image Capture and Pre-processing

Compared with the methods listed above, the accuracy and recognition speed are greatly improved. The overall architecture is shown in Fig. 1.

2.1   Invoice Image Acquisition

Image acquisition is the process of capturing the actual environment or target, converting it into corresponding image data, and at the same time storing the image data according to a certain encoding pattern. Image acquisition can be done by hardware devices such as

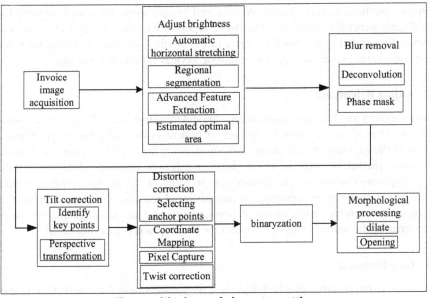

Text positioning and character cutting

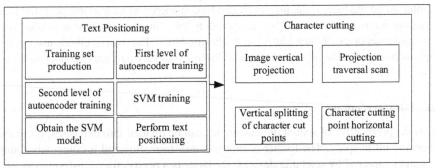

Character recognition based on HOG features

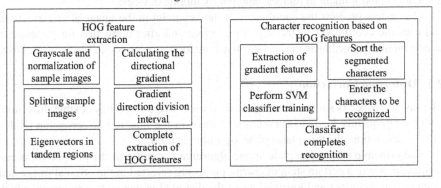

Fig. 1. Overall architecture of invoice image recognition

scanners, overhead cameras, mobile devices, and image capture software. Capturing the actual scene generally on the use of hardware equipment tools, software capture system is generally applied to the window object of the monitor. Because mobile devices are more convenient to use, this paper uses mobile devices for image capturing.

2.2 Adjust Brightness

When shooting in an environment where the environment is too bright or too dark, it is easy to produce transitional exposure or underexposure, resulting in poor image quality of the captured invoice image. Before adjusting the brightness, it is necessary to determine whether the brightness of the image needs to be adjusted, which is called the image exposure evaluation. The module first performs automatic horizontal stretching of the image, then region segmentation and advanced feature extraction, and performs region analysis on the results of region segmentation and advanced features, followed by estimating the optimal region, adjusting the S-curve, and preserving details.

2.3 Blur Removal

According to the requirements of this project, we consider only the case that the face of the invoice is blurred. The background blurring is not considered. If the final image is not blurred on the face of the invoice, it can be considered as a clean image. If the face of the invoice is blurred, it can be considered as "all" blurred. The blur is divided into two main categories: "bokeh blur" and "dithering blur". The main methods used in the implementation for the blur removal and dithering recovery part are deconvolution and phase masking.

2.4 Tilt Correction

From the perspective of spatial dimension, tilt can be divided into two cases: tilt in the plane and tilt in space. The former is an affine transformation and is commonly found in images captured by scanning devices; the latter is a perspective transformation, and this kind is predominant in images captured by mobile devices.

The system predicts the coordinates of the key point in the image after correction, and uses the coordinates of the key point before and after correction for perspective transformation according to the "perspective transformation principle" mentioned above.

2.5 Distortion Correction

The invoice paper is soft and the captured invoice image often has flexible distortion, which subsequently leads to curved text content in the image. For correction of this flexible aberration, the thin plate spline algorithm is used.

The principle of the thin plate spline algorithm is similar to the perspective transformation, where a certain stem of anchor points are selected in the original image and scattered on the upper and lower edges of the distorted image text or rectangle, which clips the text area from above and below, followed by coordinate mapping and pixel acquisition to correct the distorted text area in the original image.

An example of processed image is shown in Fig. 2.

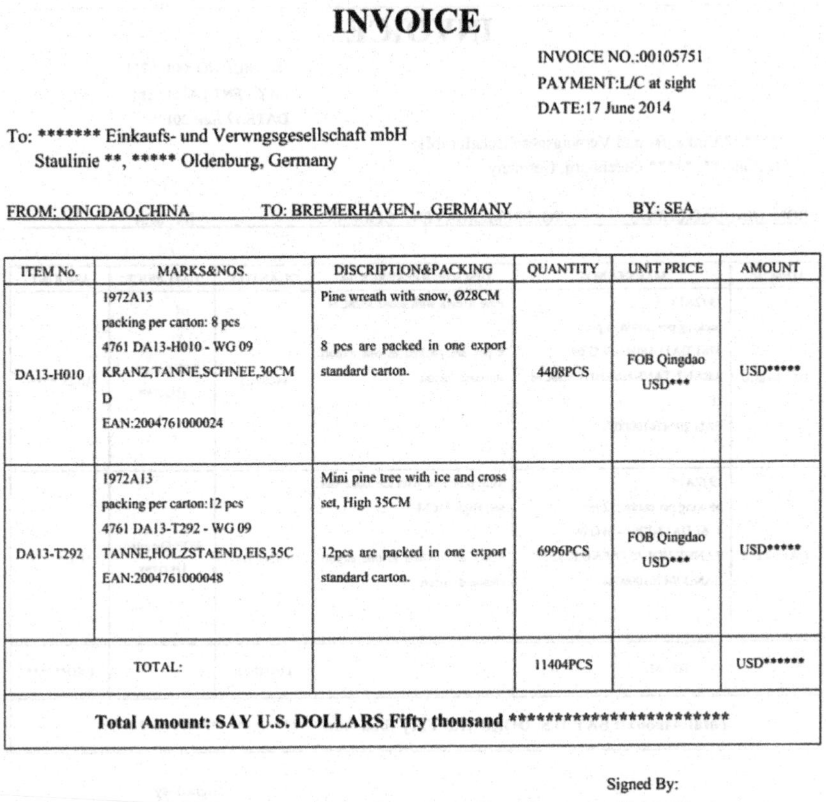

INVOICE

INVOICE NO.:00105751
PAYMENT:L/C at sight
DATE:17 June 2014

To: ******* Einkaufs- und Verwngsgesellschaft mbH
Staulinie **, ***** Oldenburg, Germany

FROM: QINGDAO,CHINA   TO: BREMERHAVEN, GERMANY   BY: SEA

ITEM No.	MARKS&NOS.	DISCRIPTION&PACKING	QUANTITY	UNIT PRICE	AMOUNT
DA13-H010	1972A13 packing per carton: 8 pcs 4761 DA13-H010 - WG 09 KRANZ,TANNE,SCHNEE,30CM D EAN:2004761000024	Pine wreath with snow, Ø28CM 8 pcs are packed in one export standard carton.	4408PCS	FOB Qingdao USD***	USD*****
DA13-T292	1972A13 packing per carton:12 pcs 4761 DA13-T292 - WG 09 TANNE,HOLZSTAEND,EIS,35C EAN:2004761000048	Mini pine tree with ice and cross set, High 35CM 12pcs are packed in one export standard carton.	6996PCS	FOB Qingdao USD***	USD*****
	TOTAL:		11404PCS		USD******

Total Amount: SAY U.S. DOLLARS Fifty thousand ************************

Signed By:

Fig. 2. Preliminary treatment effect

2.6 Binarization

Image binarization is the process of converting a color image or a multi-gray image into only black and white images. In this paper, the adaptive thresholding binarization method is used to threshold each cell block of the image according to the local features by the Adaptive-Method algorithm.

The invoice image after binarization is shown in Fig. 3.

2.7 Morphological Processing

After binarization, further processing of the image is required, such as noise removal, character enhancement, and handling of problems such as character concatenation. A common method is morphological processing, which is used in various fields of image processing research.

Morphological processing is an effective and convenient tool often used in digital image processing. The basic conversion operations are erode and dilate, and the combination of these two operations can lead to two common types of processing: open and closed operations. The following is the description of dilate and open operations.

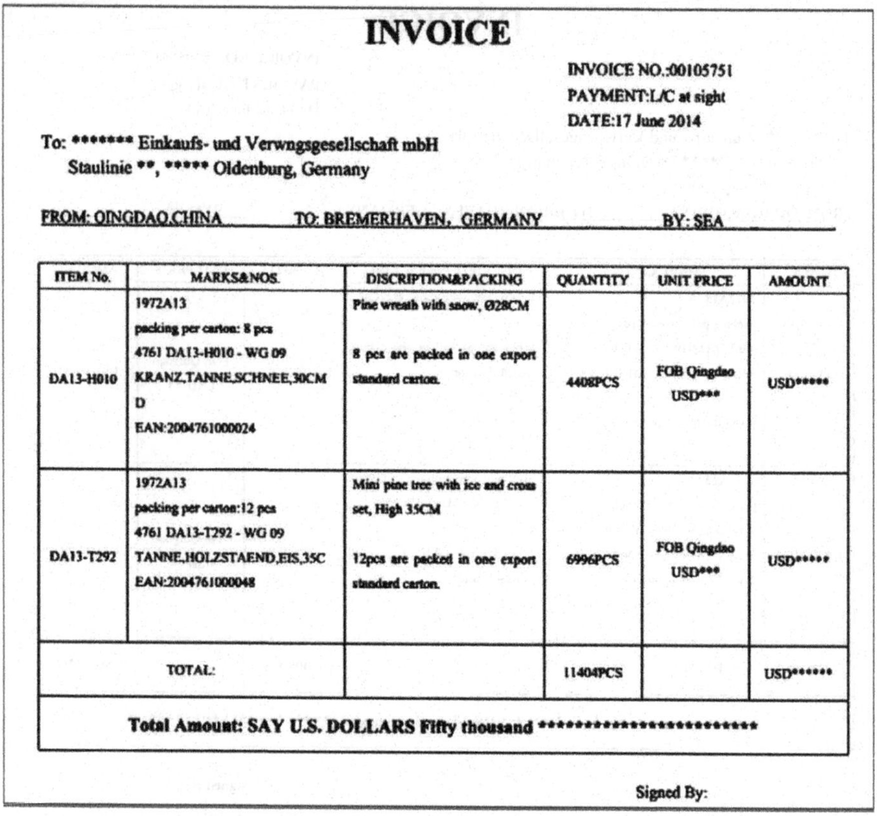

INVOICE

INVOICE NO.:00105751
PAYMENT:L/C at sight
DATE:17 June 2014

To: ******* Einkaufs- und Verwngsgesellschaft mbH
Staulinie **, ***** Oldenburg, Germany

FROM: QINGDAO,CHINA   TO: BREMERHAVEN, GERMANY   BY: SEA

ITEM No.	MARKS&NOS.	DISCRIPTION&PACKING	QUANTITY	UNIT PRICE	AMOUNT
DA13-H010	1972A13 packing per carton: 8 pcs 4761 DA13-H010 - WG 09 KRANZ,TANNE,SCHNEE,30CM D EAN:2004761000024	Pine wreath with snow, Ø28CM 8 pcs are packed in one export standard carton.	4408PCS	FOB Qingdao USD***	USD*****
DA13-T292	1972A13 packing per carton:12 pcs 4761 DA13-T292 - WG 09 TANNE,HOLZSTAEND,EIS,35C EAN:2004761000048	Mini pine tree with ice and cross set, High 35CM 12pcs are packed in one export standard carton.	6996PCS	FOB Qingdao USD***	USD******
	TOTAL:		11404PCS		USD*******

Total Amount: SAY U.S. DOLLARS Fifty thousand ************************

Signed By:

Fig. 3. Binarization effect

Dilate. The dilate operation is the opposite of erosion, which is the operation of convolving the image with the kernel and calculating the maximum value. It can be understood that the image is traversed by sliding the kernel, and if the kernel intersects with the current pixel image region, the kernel shape is inflated, which makes the highlighted areas in the image grow gradually and makes its boundary features more obvious, and also plays the role of connecting "bridges".

Open Operations. The open operation is a re-dilate of the image erosion. The open operation is mainly used to remove noise; it is also used to separate adjacent areas, similar to the effect of erosion; it can also make the contour edge features of highlight areas more prominent.

When using the connected component algorithm for localization, it is often necessary to dilate the image so that the characters are connected by dilating, which facilitates the fusion of text regions. In the following, the invoice number, payment, and date areas are expanded to connect the characters. This operation will cause the image to be blurred to facilitate the next operation.

The effect is shown in Fig. 4.

Fig. 4. Dilating effect

In the character cutting, if the projection method is used for cutting, the characters pressed against the border line will cause the characters to be connected, which is not good for cutting. We use Open operation for the unit price and amount area. This operation will facilitate the next operation.

The effect is shown in Fig. 5.

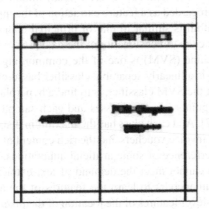

Fig. 5. Open operation effect

The use of morphological post-processing makes the character features of the invoice images more visible and reduces interference.

The flow of invoice image acquisition and pre-processing is shown in Fig. 6.

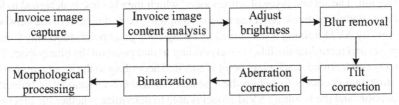

Fig. 6. Process of invoice image acquisition and preprocessing

3   Text Positioning and Character Segmentation

3.1   Text Positioning

The task of text localization is to frame out the location of the region where the text is located in the image and intercept it. In this paper, a multilayer autoencoder + SVM algorithm is used for localization.

Sparse autoencoder is an unsupervised machine learning algorithm that continuously adjusts the parameters of the autoencoder by calculating the error between the output of the autoencoder and the original input, and finally trains the model. The autoencoder can be used to compress the input information and extract useful input features.

The autoencoder is always unsupervised learning, and its output results in its own, i.e., a process of reconstructing the input data once completed. Therefore, there is no need to label the data, and the network training can be completed by parameter adjustment through the error between the output and the input.

In this process, first the input data is encoded, and the result of encoding can be decoded, so the intermediate layer of the encoding result is another representation of the input data. Moreover, since the number of neurons in the middle layer is less than that in the input layer, it can be regarded as a feature extraction of the input in the middle layer. The effect of this algorithm is similar to that of principal component analysis, which uses this feature to reduce the dimensionality of the data [16].

Support Vector Machine (SVM) is one of the common algorithms in the field of machine learning. SVM is a linearly separable classifier based on samples. For a given sample point, the goal of the SVM classifier, is to find a hyperplane in the sample space that divides the sample points into two classes and each sample point has the farthest distance to that plane [17]. And each class has the maximum distance to the hyperplane.

Due to the variety of invoice vouchers and the rich content of the layout may also be accompanied by the interference of some artificial annotations, conventional concate-nated domain algorithm cannot meet the demand of text extraction. In this paper, we use multilayer sparse autoencoder to learn the features of the area where the pixel is located, extract the high-level features of the location of the pixel, and use SVM to train the features and determine whether the point is located in the text area.

The training set is made first, and then the first layer of autoencoder training is started. Invoice images are obviously color differentiated, so here the images of the training set are RGB maps. This training is unsupervised learning and does not require the use of labels. After learning is completed, the coding part of the network is taken. The first layer of encoder learns the features within the module with that pixel point as the center region. The second layer of autoencoder, which then begins, is designed to learn module-to-module features. After learning is complete, the coding part of the network is taken. Finally, SVM training is performed by taking 100k pixel points randomly from the training set and recording the label corresponding to that point on the binary map. SVM is a supervised learning. Each pixel point is encoded according to the input requirements of the first two encoders to obtain the features. Then the SVM model is trained for classification, and the resulting SVM model is able to determine whether the pixel point is located in the text region.

The flow is shown in Fig. 7.

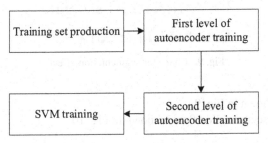

Fig. 7. Text localization based on multi-layer sparse self-encoding + SVM

The network is trained by the above steps and the effect of text localization is tested by using the trained network. The results after processing by the algorithm are shown in Fig. 8.

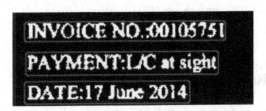

Fig. 8. Algorithm processing results

The effect is similar to binarization, but only the desired text area is processed. The characters of the completed image are not clear because the content of the learning is the area where the text is located, rather than a detailed binarization process, so it will blur the expansion of the situation, without affecting the positioning effect. This method is relatively complex in terms of calculation and long processing time, but it can achieve good results, and with the development of equipment, its calculation time can be effectively reduced.

3.2   Character Segmentation

Character segmentation is the process of taking a successfully located text region and cutting it into individual characters. The most commonly used segmentation algorithms are based on the projection method and are widely used in the field of character segmentation.

First, the vertical projection of the positioned image is performed, i.e., the number of pixel points present in each column is calculated, and then the scan is started from left to right, and the cutting points of all characters are obtained after several iterative scans. Then the vertical segmentation is performed according to the character cutting-points obtained earlier. Finally, similarly, the vertically segmented characters are cut horizontally, i.e., into individual character images.

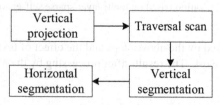

INVOICE NO.:00105751

PAYMENT:L/C at sight

DATE:17 June 2014

Fig. 9. Character segmentation effect

The effect is shown in Fig. 9.
The character segmentation flow is shown in Fig. 10.

Vertical projection	→	Traversal scan

Horizontal segmentation	←	Vertical segmentation

Fig. 10. Character cutting process

4   Character Recognition Based on HOG Features

In this paper, we use histogram of gradient features for character recognition. The histogram of gradient (HOG) feature is a feature descriptor used for object detection in computer vision and image processing [18]. HOG features combined with SVM are widely used in various image recognition fields, and this algorithm is also suitable for character recognition.

The processing steps and principles are as follows. First, the sample image is grayed out and normalized as input, and the image gradient information is obtained by calculating the directional gradient with the gradient operator. Then the sample image is segmented into several units of pixels. The gradient directions are divided equally into intervals of corresponding numbers, and a multi-dimensional feature vector is obtained by performing histogram statistics inside each cell for the gradient directions of all pixels in their directional intervals. Next, individual cell cells are combined into large, spatially connected intervals. The feature vectors of all cells in a region are concatenated and normalized to obtain the HOG features of the interval. Finally, all blocks are concatenated to complete the HOG feature extraction.

The process is shown in Fig. 11.

After HOG features are extracted from the character images, they are fed into the SVM multi-class classifier for character recognition.

The cut characters are first normalized and classified, then divided into a training set and a test set, and then each character is extracted with gradient features by the HOG algorithm. Then the SVM classifier is trained using the features as well as the previously completed labels. Finally, the characters to be recognized are input and the HOG features

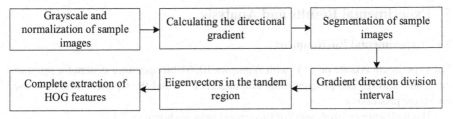

Fig. 11. Extract HOG features

are extracted, and the recognition is completed by the classifier trained in the previous step.

The process is shown in Fig. 12.

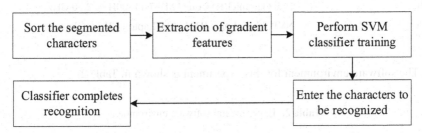

Fig. 12. HOG feature recognition character

The pseudo code for the HOG feature calculation implementation is shown below,

```
given I: an image of gradient orientation
initialize H ← 0
for all positions (p, q) inside of the image do
    i ← I (p, q)
    k ← the small region including (p, q)
    for all offsets (x, y) such that corresponds neighbors do
        if (p + x, q + y) is inside of the image then
            j ← I (p + x, q + y)
            H (k, i, j, x, y) ← H (k, i, j, x, y) + 1
        end if
    end for
end for
```

5   Experimental Results and Analysis

5.1   Experimental Environment

The experiment is done on a PC with Windows 10, 64-bit operating system for programming and testing. The programming language is C++ and the OpenCV library is used for image processing.

The hardware environment for this experiment is shown in Table 1.

Table 1. Experimental hardware environment

Hardware section	Performance parameters
RAM	Samsung DDR4 3200 MHz 16 GB
CPU	11th Gen Intel(R) Core(TM) i7-11800H @ 2.30 GHz
GPU	NVIDIA GeForce RTX 3060 Laptop GPU 6 GB

The software environment for this experiment is shown in Table 2.

Table 2. Experimental software environment

Software section	Performance parameters
Operating system	Windows10
Development tools	VS2019, MFC
Open-source library	OpenCV 3.4.14, mupdf, libxl 6 GB

5.2   Experimental Results

The experimental results are shown in Table 3.

Table 3. Recognition results of different scale data sets

Quantity	Original image accuracy %	Noise (5%) accuracy %	Noise (10%) accuracy %	Time
200	100	99.5	99.0	14.2 s
300	99.6	99.0	98.6	21.1 s
500	99.8	99.2	99.0	35.2 s

It can be seen that this method has a high recognition rate. When adding Salt Pepper noise to the character image and then recognizing it, it still has a high recognition rate when the random noise covers 5% of the image as well as the random noise covers 10% of the image, which shows its strong anti-interference ability.

This method is compared with the Tesseract-OCR-based complex invoice adaptive recognition method of Sun *et al.* [19], the invoice recognition method based on improved LeNet-5 convolutional neural network of Yin *et al.* [20], and the invoice image processing and recognition method based on intelligent management of accounting information of Li [21]. Experimental results of several invoices are analyzed and the results are listed in Table 4.

It can be seen that the recognition rate of the Tesseract-OCR-based complex invoice adaptive recognition method is not high and time consuming in all cases. The invoice recognition method based on improved LeNet-5 convolutional neural network takes less time, but the recognition rate is slightly lower than the method in this paper. The recognition rate of the invoice image processing and recognition method based on intelligent management of accounting information is lower than this method and time consuming.

This method is also compared with Tencent Cloud OCR, Baidu Cloud OCR and the native Tesseract-OCR engine, and the experimental data of 200 invoices are compared. The results are listed in Table 5.

Table 4. Comparison of the results of using this method with the methods in other papers for the identification of 200 invoices

Identification method	Original image accuracy %	Noise (5%) accuracy %	Noise (10%) accuracy %	Time
Proposed method	100	99.5	99.0	14.2 s
Tesseract -OCR based adaptive recognition of complex invoices	92	89	81	19.6 s
Invoice recognition based on improved LeNet-5 convolutional neural network	99.5	98.5	96.0	12.4 s
Image processing and recognition of bills based on intelligent management of accounting information	98.5	95.0	93.5	24.1 s

Table 5. Comparison of the results of using this method with the existing commercial application of ocr method for the identification of 200 invoices

Identification method	Original image accuracy %	Noise (5%) accuracy %	Noise (10%) accuracy %	Time
Proposed method	100	99.5	99.0	14.2 s
Baidu cloud OCR	99.5	95.0	92.5	16.5 s
Tencent cloud OCR	100	97.0	94.0	18.3 s
Tesseract-OCR	76.0	58.0	36.5	32.6 s

It can be seen that the Tesseract-OCR method does not have an advantage in recognition rate and efficiency in all cases. Tencent Cloud OCR and Baidu Cloud OCR perform better in recognition rate without noise, but the time required is slightly longer than our method. Tencent Cloud OCR and Baidu Cloud OCR have lower recognition rates than our method when adding pretzel noise.

6 Conclusion

This paper investigates invoice image recognition in robotic process automation. Through processing steps such as invoice image acquisition and pre-processing, text positioning and character segmentation, and character recognition based on HOG features, the purpose of recognizing information on paper invoices is achieved, and a high recognition rate can still be achieved in the presence of noise interference. However, the method still has a few cases of recognition errors, and there is still room for optimization.

References

1. Cui, W.C., Ren, L., Liu, Y., et al.: Invoice number recognition algorithm based on numerical structure characteristics. J. Data Acquis. Process. **32**(01), 119–125 (2017)
2. Li, Z., Cong, L.: Research on color image binarization method based on Naive Bayes. Digit. Print. **1**(01), 17–21 (2020)
3. Han, Z., Su, B., Li, Y.G., et al.: An enhanced image binarization method incorporating with Monte-Carlo simulation. J. Cent. South Univ. **26**(6), 1661–1671 (2019). https://doi.org/10.1007/s11771-019-4120-9
4. Shen, Z., Wang, Z.: Research on binarized image processing under uneven illumination conditions. Electron. Compon. Inf. Technol. **4**(02), 99–100 (2020)
5. Bu, F., Hu, Q., Wang, Y.: A valid frame line removal algorithm for financial document. Comput. Knowl. Technol. **12**(23), 148–150 (2016)
6. Ouyang, H., Fan, D., Li, D.: Invoice seal identification based on multi-feature fusion decision. Comput. Eng. Des. **39**(09), 2842–2847 (2018)
7. Xu, A., Zhu, J., Chen, Y.: Research on recognition technology based on QR code of fuzzy invoice. Mod. Bus. Trade Ind. **40**(30), 212–213 (2019)
8. Luo, X.: Document image rectification method based on lines space. Comput. Eng. **1**(4), 277–280 (2017)
9. Cao, Y., Wang, J., Du, G.: Location algorithm on bank bill image. J. Liaoning Univ. Technol. (Nat. Sci. Ed.) **37**(05), 281–283 (2017)
10. Jin, H., Xia, T., Wang, B.: Study of adaptive character segmentation and extraction algorithm. J. Xi' an Univ. Technol. **1**(4), 399–402 (2016)
11. Wang, Y., Li, Z., Yang, G.: Research and application of OCR based on deep learning in banks. Appl. Res. Comput. **37**(S2), 375–379 (2020)
12. Yang, R., Yang, J.: Invoice recognition and management system with image analysis. Comput. Era (10), 4–8 (2020)
13. Jiang, C., Lu, T., Min, F., et al.: Invoice text detection and recognition based on neural network. J. Wuhan Inst. Technol. **41**(06), 586–590 (2019)
14. He, W.: A new exploration of financial reimbursement in universities based on OCR technology. Commer. Account. **10**, 79–81 (2020)
15. Ru, M., Xie, K., Wen, F.: CNN-RNN recognition method for pin-printed medical invoices. J. Changjiang Univ. (Nat. Sci. Ed.) **16**(10), 106–112 (2019)

16. Zhang, H.: Research and implementation of documents recognition technology in complex background. Univ. Electron. Sci. Technol. China **1**(02), 238–248 (2017)
17. Fang, L., Gong, W.: Similar character of license plate recognition method based on multi-classification SVM. Comput. Digit. Eng. **45**(07), 1411–1415 (2017)
18. Wu, Y.: Human motion detection and tracking based on video sequences. Xihua Univ. **1**(07), 353–364 (2015)
19. Sun, R., Qian, K., Xu, W., et al.: Adaptive recognition of complex invoices based on tesseract-OCR. J. Nanjing Univ. Inf. Eng. (Nat. Sci. Ed.) **13**(03), 349–354 (2021)
20. Yin, Z., Jiang, B., Yang, Y.: Research on invoice recognition based on improved LeNet-5 convolutional neural network. Equip. Manuf. Technol. (05), 148–150+163 (2021)
21. Li, Z.: Bill image processing and recognition based on intelligent management of accounting information. Henan Sci. **38**(09), 1394–1399 (2020)
22. Tang, G., Gao, X., Chen, Z., Zhong, H.: Unsupervised adversarial domain adaptation with similarity diffusion for person re-identification. Neurocomputing **442**, 337–347 (2021)
23. Gao, X., Hoi Steven, C.H., Zhang, Y., et al.: Sparse online learning of image similarity. ACM Trans. Intell. Syst. Technol. **8**(5), 64:1-64:22 (2017)
24. Zhang, Y., Gao, X., Chen, Z., et al.: Mining spatial-temporal similarity for visual tracking. IEEE Trans. Image Process. **29**(16), 8107–8119 (2020)
25. Xia, Z., Hong, X., Gao, X., et al.: Spatiotemporal recurrent convolutional networks for recognizing spontaneous micro-expressions. IEEE Trans. Multimedia **22**(3), 626–640 (2020)
26. Gao, X., Hoi Steven, C.H., Zhang, Y., et al.: SOML: sparse online metric learning with application to image retrieval. In: Twenty-Eighth AAAI Conference on Artificial Intelligence, pp. 1206–1212 (2014)

Quality Assessment

Memorability Based No-Reference Quality Assessment for Multiply-Distorted Images

Han Zhang[1], Yongfang Wang[1(✉)], Yumeng Xia[1], and Zhijun Fang[2]

[1] School of Communication and Information Engineering, Shanghai University, Shanghai 200444, China
yfw@shu.edu.cn

[2] School of Electronic and Electrical Engineering, Shanghai University of Engineering Science, Shanghai 201620, China

Abstract. In the paper, we proposed an effective no-reference image quality assessment (NR-IQA) model based on image memorability for multiply-distortion images, which is motivated by the image memorability property that the distortion happened in high memorable areas is more obvious to human perception. In our proposed method, we first extract memorable feature through attention-driven memorability predictor. Besides, structure feature is captured based on local binary pattern in gradient domain since human visual system (HVS) is susceptible to structure degradation. Considering that memorable and structure features are less sensitive to luminance change, luminance feature is extracted by the entropy of first derivative of image which improves the performance of our method significantly. Finally, we use support vector regression (SVR) to learn the mapping from feature space to quality space. A large number of experiments on two benchmark multiply-distorted datasets verify the advantage and efficiency of our proposed NR-IQA model compared with the state-of-the-art methods.

Keywords: Image memorability · Local binary pattern · Entropy of first derivative · Image quality assessment

1 Introduction

With the developing of distance education and traffic monitoring techniques rapidly, there are higher requirements for high-quality images and videos. In real communication system, the degradation of visual information is bound to occur during the image processing including capture, compression and transmission. Therefore, it's very necessary to accurately predict image quality in kinds of multimedia applications.

During the past period of time, many image quality assessment (IQA) methods have been proposed for for the field of multimedia. Generally, there are two kinds of IQA models: subjective and objective [1]. Subjective IQA approaches need sufficient judgement of human perception, which are time-consuming, labor-intensive, and impractical. While objective IQA algorithm establishes the model by function fitting or machine learning, and calculates the image according to the human opinion score to obtain the

© Springer Nature Singapore Pte Ltd. 2022
G. Zhai et al. (Eds.): IFTC 2021, CCIS 1560, pp. 151–163, 2022.
https://doi.org/10.1007/978-981-19-2266-4_12

evaluation value of the image. Hence, researchers have paid more attention to objective IQA methods.

Objective IQA algorithms can be divided into three categories [2]: full-reference (FR), reduced-reference (RR) and no-reference (NR). FR-IQA models have the most development with high evaluation accuracy where reference images are completely available. The algorithms such as SSIM [3], IW-SSIM [4], MS-SSIM [5], consider structure similarity between the pristine and distorted image to measure image content degradation. In addition, some researchers utilized phase congruency, gradient magnitude and color information to model the difference between the reference and distorted images, such as FSIM [6], VSI [7], PSIM [8], in which low-level features have been effectively used. FR-IQA methods are also proposed by using some advance visual and neural tactics, such as IGM [9], NQM [10], VSNR [11]. RR-IQA models transmit part of the information of the pristine image through an auxiliary channel, such as [12, 13, 14]. RR-IQA models presented in [12] and [13] based on the natural statistics features of images. While in [14], the orientation selectivity (OS) based RR-IQA is built for visual content representation.

Although FR and RR algorithms offer an effective way to evaluate the quality, NR-IQA approaches are more valuable and desirable in image application because it estimates image quality only with the distorted stimulus without the pristine image. Typically, NR-IQA methods are classified into training-free and training-based methods. Training-free models does not rely on image prior knowledge to predict the quality of distorted images. A. Mittal [15] established a completely blind IQA method, which does not use any prior knowledge, but uses the statistical features in natural images. However, it has following disappointed shortcoming: different natural pristine images may have very different statistical distribution, while images with different degrees of distortion may have the same statistical distribution. BPRI [35] uses a blind IQA framework based on pseudo-reference image (PRI) to measure the distance from the distorted image to PRI and model the distortion features. And in BMPRI [36], similarity scores is performed on the distorted image and multiple pseudo-reference images (MPRIS) to predict the final quality. With the development of brain theory, In [16], an effective algorithm is proposed which use free energy principle for IQA of multiply distorted images. A natural scene statistic (NSS) algorithm based on the image discrete cosine transform (DCT) is proposed in [17] for IQA. BRISQUE [18] used scene statistics of locally normalized luminance value to calculation the loss of naturalness of the distorted images in spatial domain. Zhai et al. [37] introduces comparative perceptual quality assessment (C-PQA), and uses free energy minimization to establish a framework to determine the relative quality of two images.

In this paper, a new NR-IQA algorithm based on image memorability for multiply-distortion image is proposed, which is inspired from human brain mechanism of understanding the internal memorability of images [25]. To be specific, we attempt to mine the memorable information of image by simulating the theory of Bora and Phillip [19] and validate its effectiveness in NR-IQA model. The rest of the paper is as follows. In Sect. 2, we introduce our proposed algorithm. In Sect. 3, we show our experiment results. Finally, we conclude in Sect. 4.

2 Proposed Memorability Based NR-IQA Method

In real image communication system, images always suffer from hybrid distortions, thus this paper presents a model for multiply-distorted images. The basic flow of the model is showed in Fig. 1. First of all, the memorable feature is represented by extracting spatial envelop properties descriptor with attention-driven pooling strategy [25]. Secondly, considering that structure feature is the primary factor of human visual system (HVS) to understand visual contents, local binary pattern in gradient domain (GLBP) is used to capture structure information. Thirdly, since memorable feature structure feature are insensitive to luminance degradation in image, we apply entropy of first derivative (EFD) of images to measure luminance distortion. Finally, the SVR [26] with RBF kernel is utilized to learn the mapping from feature space to quality measure. The image quality score is

$$Q = \text{SVR}(f_M, f_S, f_L) \tag{1}$$

where f_M, f_S, f_L are memorable, structure and luminance feature, respectively.

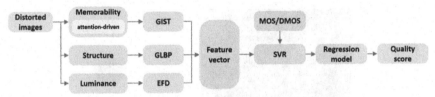

Fig. 1. Our NR-IQA framework for multiply-distorted images.

2.1 Memorable Feature Extraction Based on Saliency

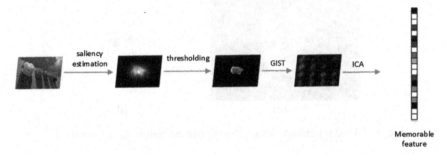

Fig. 2. Proposed attention-driven framework for extracting memorable feature.

Recently, many researches have focused on human brain mechanism of understanding the intrinsic memorability of image. Phillip [20] presented a memory game to collect memory information for extensive images and determined which images are sensitive to long-term memory. Then, they mined this memory information to determine which features have an impact on memory and trained memorability predictors on simple images features such as SIFT [21], HOG [22] and GIST [23]. Khosla et al. [24] proposed a probabilistic framework by combined local and global images features, which uses a data-driven method to model the local region that may be lost in the image. Bora et al. [25] further proposed an effective memorability predictor by combining an attention-driven strategy with simple features (for example HOG and GIST).

Figure 2 shows our attention-driven pooling based capture method for memorable feature. Firstly, we use algorithm [27] that can effectively simulate human eye gaze to get the saliency map of the image. Through the threshold binarization of the saliency graph, a binary mask representing the region of interest is generated. The interest region of image I can be defined as

$$I_m = I * B \tag{2}$$

where B is the binary map. In the paper, we adopted OTSU algorithm [33] to achieve optimal threshold. Figure 3 shows some examples of the interest region I_m of input image.

(a)   (b)

(c)   (d)

Fig. 3. (a) and (c), Pristine image. (b)–(d) Interest regions I_m of (a) and (c).

Secondly, we obtain a global descriptor of interest region I_m by extracting GIST feature [23]. The Gabor filters with different scales and orientations are used to filter image to generate GIST feature maps. The Gabor filters are deduced as

$$G_{\theta_i}^l = Kexp\left(-\frac{x_{\theta_i}^2 + y_{\theta_i}^2}{2\sigma^{2(l-1)}}\right) \cdot \exp\left(2\pi j\left(u_0 x_{\theta_i} + v_0 y_{\theta_i}\right)\right) \tag{3}$$

$$x_{\theta_i} = x\cos(\theta_i) + y\sin(\theta_i) \tag{4}$$

$$y_{\theta_i} = -x\sin(\theta_i) + y\cos(\theta_i) \tag{5}$$

where l is the scale of filter, (x, y) indicates coordinates, K is a positive constant, $\theta_i = \frac{\pi(i-1)}{\theta_l}$ ($i = 1, 2, ..., \theta_l$) and θ_l means the number of orientations at each scale, v_0 is the wavelength of each filter and u_0 determines the direction of the Gabor kernel function. Then, feature maps are defined as

$$F = G_{\theta_i}^l * I_m \tag{6}$$

These feature maps are divided into 4*4 blocks, and the average values in each block form a column vector as GIST feature G.

Finally, the dimensionality reduction operation to GIST feature is completed through independent component analysis (ICA) [32] which selects latent independent components from the mixed observation signals. The objective of ICA is to separate memorability feature from the GIST feature by finding a decomposition matrix W. Thus, the memorability feature is defined as

$$f_M = W \cdot G \tag{7}$$

2.2   Structure Feature Extraction Based on GLBP

Fig. 4. (a) Pristine image of MDID2013. (b) Distorted image of MDID2013. (c)–(d) GLBP maps of (a) and (b).

Local binary pattern (LBP) calculated in gradient domain (GLBP) can extract structural information effectively [28], as shown in Fig. 4. The first step of GLBP is calculating the gradient map by using P operator. Next step is calculating the LBP for each pixel on the gradient map. Then the GLBP at each pixel is

$$GLBP_{P,R} = \begin{cases} \sum_{i=0}^{P-1} s(g_i - g_c), u(GLBP_{P,R}) \leq 2 \\ P + 1, others \end{cases} \quad (8)$$

where P represents the number of neighbor and R means the radius of neighborhoods. g_c and g_i are the gradient magnitudes of the central pixel and its adjacent pixels, respectively. u means a uniform index. GLBP patterns with u value less than two will be counted.

$$u(GLBP_{P,R}) = \|s(g_{P-1} - g_c) - s(g_0 - g_c)\| + \sum_{i=0}^{P-1} \|s(g_i - g_c) - s(g_{i-1} - g_c)\| \quad (9)$$

When the u value is higher than two, the GLBP value is defined as $P + 1$. Although the value of u reduce the kinds of the GLBP patterns, most of the structural features can be obtained from uniform patterns [28] in the experiment. The thresholding function $s(\cdot)$ is defined as

$$s(g_i - g_c) = \begin{cases} 1, g_i - g_c \geq 0 \\ 0, g_i - g_c < 0. \end{cases} \quad (10)$$

The last step is to accumulate the gradient magnitudes of pixels with the same GLBP value, then generate the gradient weighted GLBP histogram as structure feature fs

$$h_{glbp}(k) = \sum_{i=1}^{N} \omega_i f(GLBP_{P,R}(i), k) \quad (11)$$

$$f(x, y) = \begin{cases} 1, x = y \\ 0, others \end{cases} \quad (12)$$

where N represents the number of image pixels, k means the possible GLBP patterns and ω_i denotes the gradient magnitude of each pixel which is assigned to the GLBP value as weight. h_{glbp} stands for structure feature fs. HVS can get more information from multi-scale images. And we achieve this by performing 2x down sampling in each dimension.

2.3 Luminance Feature Extraction Based on EFD

Generally, the visual quality of visual scene [34] is very sensitive to the change of brightness. However, Fig. 5 shows the GLBP and GIST feature mapping between the corresponding distorted-image before and after luminance reduction. From Fig. 5, we find that GLBP and GIST feature map are similar in different luminance level, which also indicate the structure and memorability feature is not sensitive to the luminance distortion. Therefore, we proposed to adopt entropy of first derivative (EFD) [34] of images as luminance feature. After verification, this method can effectively improve the performance of the model.

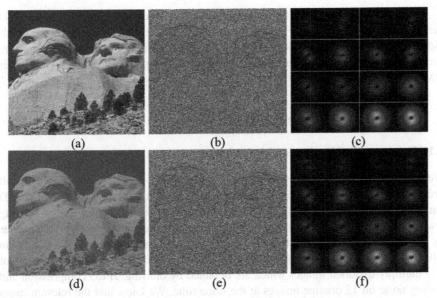

Fig. 5. (a) Pristine image. (b) GLBP map of (a). (c) GIST map of (a). (d) Distorted image. (e) GLBP map of (d). (f) GIST map of (d).

Fig. 6. (a) EFD = 0.9728, DMOS = 0.125. (b) EFD = 0.8994, DMOS = 0.506.

The EFD of an image is given by

$$D(x, y) = \frac{\partial^2 I(x, y)}{\partial x \partial y} \tag{13}$$

$$EFD = \sum_{i=0}^{n} p_i \log p_i \tag{14}$$

where D is the first derivative of images, and p_i means the gray-level i probability. p_i is calculated by

$$p_i = \frac{N_i}{N} \tag{15}$$

where N_i is the pixel number of gray-level i, N is the total number of pixel. EFD denotes luminance feature f_L. Figure 6 shows the EFD value of an image and corresponding differential mean opinion score (DMOS) value with different luminance distortion. From Fig. 6, we find that higher EFD value of an image suggest better contrast and lower DMOS.

3 Experiments Results and Discussions

3.1 Databases and Evaluation Methodology

We will conduct comparative experiments on two multiply-distorted datasets, which will provide strong evidence for the effectiveness of our NR-IQA algorithm. The LIVEMD dataset [29] contains 15 high-quality reference images with rich content, colors, lighting level and background configurations. 15 pristine images are used to generate 225 images by GB+JPEG (Gaussian Blur followed by JPEG compression) and GB+GN (Gaussian Blur followed by white noise) respectively. The MDID2013 database [16] consists of 324 multiply-distorted images which are obtained by blurring, JPEG compression and adding noise on 12 pristine images at the same time. We know that the relevant mean opinion score (MOS) or DMOS of each distorted-image in the above datasets which represent subjective visual quality.

We use the Pearson linear correlation coefficient (PLCC), Spearman rank order correlation coefficient (SRCC), Kendall rank-order correlation coefficient (KRCC) and root mean square error (RMSE) to evaluate our model. The values of PLCC, SRCC and KRCC are close to 1, indicating that they are more consistent with human perception. A smaller RMSE value indicates that the method has better performance.

3.2 Training

Our proposed method uses the LIBSVM package [30]. Specifically, we choose radial basis function (RBF) kernel when using ε-SVR, which is helpful for better experiments. For the simulation, we adjusted the proportion of training-testing dataset, used 80% of the distorted images for training, and tested the remaining 20% images. Such a process was randomly repeated 1000 times and reported median performance. We compare our method with fourteen IQA models, including FR metrics: PSNR [31], VSNR [11], NQM [10], SSIM [3], FSIM [6], VSI [7], IGM [9], PSIM [8]; RR metrics: RRED [12], RREDLOG [13], OSVP [14] and NR metrics: BRISQUE [18], NIQE [15], SISBLIM [16].

The predicted performance is shown in Table 1 on the MDID2013 dataset, where the three best indicators are highlighted in bold. As can be seen in Table 1, PSIM, BRISQUE and our model achieved the best performance. PSIM calculates gradient magnitude on multi-scales to characterize the structure information of distorted image. BRISQUE normalizes the luminance coefficient in scene statistics locally to quantify the latent loss of naturalness in the image. Thus, the two methods yield better performance than other metrics. Owing to using memorable feature, our proposed method captures more precise perceptual feature than other models.

Table 1. Performance comparison on MDID2013.

IQA index	PLCC	SRCC	KRCC	RMSE
PSNR [31]	0.556	0.560	0.394	0.042
VSNR [11]	0.366	0.358	0.245	3.254
NQM [10]	0.434	0.402	0.263	3.482
SSIM [3]	0.561	0.450	0.314	0.042
FSIM [6]	0.570	0.582	0.390	0.054
VSI [7]	0.528	0.570	0.389	0.043
IGM [9]	0.805	0.833	0.624	**0.035**
PSIM [8]	0.833	**0.862**	**0.663**	0.069
RRED [12]	0.820	0.806	0.601	0.528
REDLOG [13]	**0.850**	0.837	0.639	0.470
OSVP [14]	0.701	0.644	0.429	0.204
BRISQUE [18]	**0.875**	**0.862**	0.633	**0.024**
NIQE [15]	0.577	0.545	0.379	0.042
SISBLIM [16]	0.796	0.808	**0.690**	0.694
Proposed	**0.893**	**0.873**	**0.673**	**0.022**

Table 2. Performance comparison on LIVEMD.

IQA index	PLCC	SRCC	KRCC	RMSE
PSNR [31]	0.771	0.677	0.500	10.868
VSNR [11]	0.625	0.629	0.448	8.881
NQM [10]	**0.910**	**0.900**	**0.721**	7.901
SSIM [3]	0.707	0.720	0.543	**6.969**
FSIM [6]	0.893	0.864	0.673	8.499
VSI [7]	0.879	0.841	0.645	9.021
IGM [9]	0.886	0.850	0.658	8.769
PSIM [8]	0.885	0.851	0.660	8.816
RRED [12]	0.900	0.887	0.707	7.984
REDLOG [13]	0.860	0.827	0.635	9.464
OSVP [14]	0.664	0.516	0.359	14.148
BRISQUE [18]	**0.923**	**0.893**	**0.722**	**7.198**
NIQE [15]	0.838	0.773	0.580	10.32
SISBLIM [16]	0.895	0.878	0.692	8.427
Proposed	**0.943**	**0.933**	**0.778**	**6.244**

The performance comparison on LIVEMD dataset is showed in Table 2, and from which we can see that the best three methods on LIVEMD database are NQM, BRISQUE and our NR-IQA algorithm. In order to fit human perception, NQM supposes the degradation process as linear frequency attenuation followed by additive Gaussian noise. It is worth noting that the result of all methods on LIVEMD is better than that on MDID2013 since the degradation situation in MDID2013 is more complex. And the proposed NR model outperforms all competing IQA metrics on LIVEMD database as well.

Table 3. Overall performance comparison on two datasets.

IQA index	PLCC	SRCC	KRCC	RMSE
PSNR [31]	0.681	0.628	0.456	6.336
VSNR [11]	0.517	0.516	0.363	6.526
NQM [10]	0.711	0.692	0.529	6.051
SSIM [3]	0.646	0.607	0.447	**4.069**
FSIM [6]	0.758	0.746	0.555	4.964
VSI [7]	0.732	0.728	0.538	5.263
IGM [9]	0.852	0.843	0.644	5.113
PSIM [8]	0.863	**0.856**	0.661	5.155
RRED [12]	**0.867**	0.853	0.663	4.863
REDLOG [13]	0.856	0.831	0.637	5.699
OSVP [14]	0.679	0.570	0.388	8.311
BRISQUE [18]	**0.903**	**0.880**	**0.685**	**4.195**
NIQE [15]	0.729	0.678	0.496	6.018
SISBLIM [16]	0.854	0.849	**0.691**	5.190
Proposed	**0.922**	**0.908**	**0.734**	**3.640**

As is shown in Table 3, we calculate the weighted-average indicators over two databases of fifteen metrics. The weights are distributed according to how many distorted images are in the data set. Our model has a good correlation with human perceived quality. At the same time, that our proposed method is robust does not depend on the datasets.

3.3 Contributions of Features

In Table 4, PLCC value comparison of different composition of features is listed. We can observe that our model can have better result with the usage of memorable feature and luminance feature.

Table 4. PLCC comparison for different composition of features.

Composition of features	MDID2013	LIVEMD
Structure	0.879	0.933
Structure + luminance	0.884	0.938
Structure + memorable	0.890	0.942
Structure + memorable + luminance	**0.893**	**0.943**

4 Conclusion

In this paper, considering that image quality degradation has highly correlated with image memorability, a memorability based blind IQA is proposed for multiply-distortion images. To further improve the performance, we also introduce structure and luminance features which meet the characteristics of human perceptual. Finally, the results on two multiply-distortion datasets demonstrate that the proposed model is better than other fourteen state-of-the-art methods even including some full reference visual quality assessment methods. Thanks to the continuous mining and utilization of human perceived memory features, IQA model based on memorability will have further improvement in the future work. At the same time, exploring the memorability between frames of audio-visual signals is more likely to conform to the memorable feature of human perception, which will also be an attempt in this field.

Acknowledgment. This work was supported by National Natural Science Foundation of China under Grant No. 61671283, 61301113.

References

1. Mittal, A., Saad, M.A., Bovik, A.C.: A completely blind video integrity oracle. IEEE Trans. Image Process. **25**(1), 289–300 (2016)
2. Liu, T.J., Liu, K.H.: No-reference image quality assessment by wide-perceptual-domain scorer ensemble method. IEEE Trans. Image Process. **27**(3), 1138–1151 (2018)
3. Wang, Z., Bovik, A.C., Sheikh, H.R., Simoncelli, E.P.: Image quality assessment: from error visibility to structural similarity. IEEE Trans. Image Process. **13**(4), 600–612 (2004)
4. Wang, Z., Li, Q.: Information content weighting for perceptual image quality assessment. IEEE Trans. Image Process. **20**(5), 1185–1198 (2011)
5. Wang, Z., Simoncelli, E.P., Bovik, A.C.: Multiscale structural similarity for image quality assessment. In: The Thrity-Seventh Asilomar Conference on Signals, Systems and Computers, pp. 1398–1402. IEEE (2010)
6. Zhang, L., Zhang, D., Mou, X., Zhang, D.: FSIM: a feature similarity index for image quality assessment. IEEE Trans. Image Process. **20**(8), 2378–2386 (2011)
7. Zhang, L., Shen, Y., Li, H.: VSI: a visual saliency-induced index for perceptual image quality assessment. IEEE Trans. Image Process. **23**(10), 4270–4281 (2014)
8. Gu, K., Li, L., Lu, H., Min, X., Lin, W.: A fast reliable image quality predictor by fusing micro- and macro-structures. IEEE Trans. Ind. Electron. **64**(5), 3903–3912 (2017)

9. Wu, J., Lin, W., Shi, G., Liu, A.: Perceptual quality metric with internal generative mechanism. IEEE Trans. Image Process. **22**(1), 43–54 (2013)
10. Damera-Venkata, N., Kite, T.D., Geisler, W.S., Evans, B.L., Bovik, A.C.: Image quality assessment based on a degradation model. IEEE Trans. Image Process. **9**(4), 636–650 (2000)
11. Chandler, D.M., Hemami, S.S.: VSNR: a wavelet-based visual signal-to-noise ratio for natural images. IEEE Trans. Image Process. **16**(9), 2284–2298 (2007)
12. Soundararajan, R., Bovik, A.C.: RRED indices: reduced reference entropic differencing for image quality assessment. IEEE Trans. Image Process. **21**(2), 517–526 (2012)
13. Golestaneh, S.A., Karam, L.J.: Reduced-reference quality assessment based on the entropy of DNT coefficients of locally weighted gradients. In: 2015 IEEE International Conference on Image Processing (ICIP), pp. 4117–4120. IEEE (2015)
14. Wu, J., Lin, W., Shi, G., et al.: Orientation selectivity based visual pattern for reduced-reference image quality assessment. Inf. Sci.: Int. J. **351**, 18–29 (2016)
15. Mittal, A., Soundararajan, R., Bovik, A.: Making a completely blind image quality analyzer. IEEE Sig. Process. Lett. **20**(3), 209–212 (2013)
16. Gu, K., Zhai, G., Yang, X., Zhang, W.: Hybrid no-reference quality metric for singly and multiply distorted images. IEEE Trans. Broadcast. **60**(3), 555–567 (2014)
17. Saad, M.A., Bovik, A.C., Charrier, C.: Blind image quality assessment: a natural scene statistics approach in the DCT domain. IEEE Trans. Image Process. **21**(8), 3339–3352 (2012)
18. Mittal, A., Moorthy, A.K., Bovik, A.C.: No-reference image quality assessment in the spatial domain. IEEE Trans. Image Process. **21**(12), 4695–4708 (2012)
19. Isola, P., Parikh, D., Torralba, A., Oliva, A.: Understanding the intrinsic memorability of images. NIPS **24**, 2429–2437 (2011)
20. Isola, P., Xiao, J., Torralba, A., Oliva, A.: What makes an image memorable? In: CVPR 2011, pp. 145–152. IEEE, Providence (2011)
21. Lazebnik, S., Schmid, C., Ponce, J.: Beyond bags of features: spatial pyramid matching for recognizing natural scene categories. In: CVPR 2006, pp. 2169–2178. IEEE (2006)
22. Felzenszwalb, P.F., Girshick, R.B., McAllester, D., Ramanan, D.: Object detection with discriminatively trained part-based models. IEEE Trans. Pattern Anal. Mach. Intell. **32**(9), 1627–1645 (2010)
23. Oliva, A., Torralba, A.: Modeling the shape of the scene: a holistic representation of the spatial envelope. Int. J. Comput. Vis. **42**(3), 145–175 (2001). https://doi.org/10.1023/A:101113963 1724
24. Khosla, A., Xiao, J., Torralba, A., Oliva, A.: Memorability of image regions. NIPS **25**, 305–313 (2012)
25. Celikkale, B., Erdem, A., Erdem, E.: Visual attention-driven spatial pooling for image memorability. In: 2013 IEEE Conference on Computer Vision and Pattern Recognition Workshops, Portland, OR, pp. 976–983 (2013)
26. Schölkopf, B., Smola, A.J.: Learning with Kernels: Support Vector Machines, Regularization, Optimization, and Beyond. MIT Press, Cambridge (2002)
27. Erdem, E., Erdem, A.: Visual saliency estimation by nonlinearly integrating features using region covariances. J. Vis. **13**(4), 11 (2013)
28. Li, Q., Lin, W., Fang, Y.: No-reference quality assessment for multiply-distorted images in gradient domain. IEEE Sig. Process. Lett. **23**(4), 541–545 (2016)
29. Jayaraman, D., Mittal, A., Moorthy, A.K., Bovik, A.C.: Objective quality assessment of multiply distorted images. In: Proceedings of IEEE Asilomar Conference on Signals, Systems and Computers, pp. 1693–1697. IEEE, Pacific Grove (2012)
30. Chang, C.C., Lin, C.J.: LIBSVM: a library for support vector machines. ACM Trans. Intell. Syst. Technol. (TIST) **2**(3), 1–27 (2011)
31. Hore, A., Ziou, D.: Image quality metrics: PSNR vs. SSIM. In: 2010 20th International Conference on Pattern Recognition, pp. 2366–2369. IEEE, Istanbul (2010)

32. Hyvarinen, A., Oja, E.: A fast fixed-point algorithm for independent component analysis. Neural Compon. **9**(7), 1483–1492 (1997)
33. Sezgin, M., Sankur, B.: Survey over image thresholding techniques and quantitative performance evaluation. J. Electron. Imaging **13**(1), 146–168 (2004)
34. Hammed, A., Ali, M.: No-reference quality assessment using the entropy of first derivative of blurred images in HSV color space. Int. J. Mod. Phys. Appl. **4**(1), 175–180 (2015)
35. Min, X., Gu, K., Zhai, G., Liu, J., Yang, X., Chen, C.W.: Blind quality assessment based on pseudo-reference image. IEEE Trans. Multimedia **20**(8), 2049–2062 (2017)
36. Min, X., Zhai, G., Gu, K., Liu, Y., Yang, X.: Blind image quality estimation via distortion aggravation. IEEE Trans. Broadcast. **64**(2), 508–517 (2018)
37. Zhai, G., Zhu, Y., Min, X.: Comparative perceptual assessment of visual signals using free energy features. IEEE Trans. Multimedia **23**, 3700–3713 (2021)

A CNN-Based Quality Assessment Method for Pseudo 4K Contents

Wei Lu, Wei Sun, Wenhan Zhu, Xiongkuo Min, Zicheng Zhang, Tao Wang,
and Guangtao Zhai[✉]

Institute of Image Communication and Network Engineering, Shanghai Jiao Tong
University, Shanghai 200240, China
{SJTU-Luwei,zhaiguangtao}@sjtu.edu.cn

Abstract. Recently, there has been a growing interest in Ultra High-Definition (UHD) content, which brings a better visual experience for end-users. However, quite a few contents with 4K resolution are upscaled from High-Definition (HD) contents and suffer degradations in quality, such as blur, texture shift, etc. These pseudo 4K contents can not deliver the expected quality of experience (QoE) to end-users while requiring a high transmission bit rate in the meantime, which inevitably results in a waste of bandwidth resources. Hence, we develop a novel deep learning-based no reference (NR) image quality assessment (IQA) model for recognition and quality evaluation of real and fake 4K images. To reduce the computational overhead for a 4K image, we first select three representative patches with high texture complexity by the Grey-Level Co-occurrence Matrix (GLCM) based measure. Next, the convolutional neural network (CNN) is adopted to extract the quality-aware features of three representative patches. Specifically, we extract different levels of features from intermediate layers of CNN and concatenate them into a more effective quality-aware feature representation. Finally, the shallow fully connected (FC) network is utilized to aggregate the features into the quality score and the overall quality score of the 4K image is calculated as the average value of three patches' quality scores. The experimental results show that the proposed method outperforms all compared NR IQA metrics on the 4K IQA database.

Keywords: Image Quality Assessment (IQA) · Pseudo 4K content · No Reference (NR) · Deep learning

1 Introduction

Due to the rapid popularization of 4K television, the speed-up of broadband networks, and the audience's demand for high-quality TV content, there has been an increasing interest in Ultra High-Definition (UHD) content with 4K resolution (3840×2160 pixels) in recent years. As a more advanced technology than High-Definition (HD), 4K UHD technology could deliver a more detail-rich, immersive visual experience to viewers [1]. Nowadays, most broadcasters

© Springer Nature Singapore Pte Ltd. 2022
G. Zhai et al. (Eds.): IFTC 2021, CCIS 1560, pp. 164–176, 2022.
https://doi.org/10.1007/978-981-19-2266-4_13

and online video websites could provide video content at 4K UHD resolution. However, it is common that video frames with a resolution lower than 4K UHD level are upscaled to 4K UHD resolution in the video acquisition, production, post-production, and distribution pipelines [2]. The pseudo UHD content, which is generated using upsampling or super-resolution (SR) algorithms, has the 4K resolution format but suffers degradations in quality. As depicted in Fig. 1, the pseudo 4K image blurs in details clearly compared with the real 4K image. What's more, the pseudo 4K UHD content cannot deliver the expected quality of experience (QoE) to end-users, but it requires a high transmission bit rate, which inevitably results in a waste of bandwidth resources. Hence, it is necessary to separate the real 4K image from the pseudo 4K image interpolated from low resolution (LR).

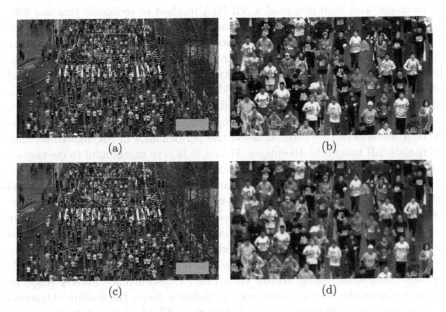

Fig. 1. An example of quality degradations in pseudo 4K image. (a) is the real 4K image and (c) is the pseudo 4K image upscaled from 720p, (b) and (d) are the images cropped from (a) and (c) respectively.

In the past two decades, as one of the basic technologies in image processing, image quality assessment (IQA) has attracted great attention from researchers and plenty of IQA methods have been proposed. Objective IQA algorithms could be categorized according to the availability of the distortion-free reference image, namely full reference (FR) IQA, reduced reference (RR) IQA, and no reference (NR) IQA [3]. Because the reference image cannot be obtained in many situations, NR IQA is more valuable for practical applications but also a more challenging topic. In terms of distortion types, NR IQA methods can be further divided into distortion-specific and general-purpose ones [4]. General-purpose algorithms extract the general quality features which have the ability to describe various distortions, while distortion-specific algorithms utilize the quality features suited for the quality degradations caused by a specific distortion process [5]. General-purpose NR IQA methods could be divided into three categories: natural scene statistics (NSS)-based methods [6], human visual system (HVS)-based methods [7] and learning-based methods [8].

Nevertheless, most existing IQA metrics are designed for LR images with synthetic or authentic distortions and can not effectively evaluate 4K UHD images with a very high resolution [9]. Furthermore, the degradations in quality of pseudo 4K images upscaled from low resolution ones have their characteristics, such as blur and texture shift, etc. Recently, Zhu *et al.* [9] constructed a dataset consisting of real 4K images and fake 4K images upscaled by fourteen SR methods, and then proposed a NR IQA method to recognize real and fake 4K images and evaluate their quality. Rishi *et al.* [2] built a database comprised of 10824 4K images and developed a two-stage authentic resolution assessment (ARA) algorithm for the classification of real and fake 4K contents. However, Rishi's method cannot predict the quality of 4K images, and the performance of the method proposed by Zhu *et al.* could be improved in terms of quality evaluation accuracy. Moreover, compared with the classification task, the regression task of 4K image quality has broader application scenarios. For example, the 4K IQA method can be used to assess the performance of SR algorithms that interpolate LR images to 4K images. Hence, it is very meaningful to develop an efficient 4K IQA model for high resolution image quality evaluation.

In this paper, we propose an efficient deep learning-based NR IQA model for classification and quality evaluation of both real and fake 4K UHD images. The proposed IQA method contains three parts: patch selection module, feature extraction module, and quality evaluation module. Firstly, the patch selection module selects three representative patches to reduce the computational complexity of the algorithm by an effective and efficient region of interest (ROI) selection algorithm, which utilizes Grey-Level Co-occurrence Matrix (GLCM) [10] to measure the texture complexity of patches. Next, the feature extraction module uses the convolutional neural network (CNN) because of its strong feature representation abilities. Specifically, we apply global average pooling to the feature maps extracted by each stage of CNN and concatenate these features to derive the quality-aware feature representation. Finally, we measure the perceptual quality of 4K UHD images via the fully connected (FC) layer in the quality evaluation module which consists of two layers of FC networks. To analyze the performance of the proposed model, we compare our model with popular NR IQA metrics as well as the IQA metrics designed for 4K images on the 4K IQA database in [9]. Experimental results demonstrate that the proposed model outperforms all compared methods. The code of the proposed model will be released for promoting the development of NR IQA for true and pseudo 4K UHD contents[1].

---

[1] Code access: https://github.com/luwei-1998/4K_IQA.

2   Proposed Method

In this section, our proposed NR 4K IQA model is described in detail. The framework of the proposed model is depicted in Fig. 2, which contains three parts: patch selection module, feature extraction module, and quality evaluation module. To reduce the computational cost of 4K IQA algorithms, we select three representative patches from each 4K image via the texture complexity measures. Then, we extract quality-aware features by a CNN backbone. Finally, these features are aggregated into the quality score for the regression task and the class probabilities for the classification task.

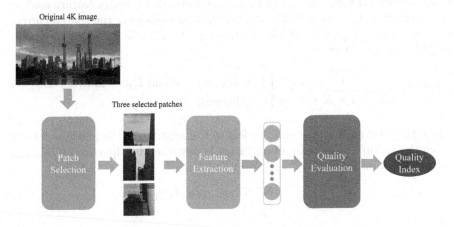

Fig. 2. The framework of the proposed NR 4K IQA model.

2.1   Patch Selection Module

It is improper to extract features on the whole 4K image due to high computation cost brought by 4K resolution. Therefore, we attempt to extract non-overlapped patches from the 4K image and select the three most representative patches for feature extraction. Given a 4K UHD image I, we first extract $H \times V$ patches through scanning the image I both horizontally and vertically with stride size s, where H, V, and s are respectively set as 15, 8, and 256 in the paper. The width and height of each patch $P_{i,j}$ are w, where $w = 235$ and $i \in 1, 2, 3, \ldots, H, j \in 1, 2, 3, \ldots, V$. Next, because the patches with high texture complexity are more sensitive to the upscaling operations, we calculate the texture complexity for every patch to select representative patches, which could be expressed as:

$$TC_{i,j} = F(P_{i,j}) \tag{1}$$

where $F(\cdot)$ is texture complexity function and $TC_{i,j}$ is the texture complexity value for patches $P_{i,j}, i \in 1, 2, 3, \ldots, H, j \in 1, 2, 3, \ldots, V$. Finally, we choose the three representative patches P_1, P_2, P_3 which have maximum texture complexity values:

$$P_1, P_2, P_3 = \underset{P_{h1,v1}, P_{h2,v2}, P_{h3,v3}}{\arg\max} (F(P_{h1,v1}) + F(P_{h2,v2}) + F(P_{h3,v3})) \quad (2)$$

where $P_{h1,v1}, P_{h2,v2}, P_{h3,v3}$ are three different patches in $\{P_{i,j}\}, i \in 1, 2, 3, \dots, H$, $j \in 1, 2, 3, \dots, V$. As for the texture complexity function $F(\cdot)$, we select the contrast of GLCM, which is a common texture complexity descriptors in pattern recognition.

Contrast of GLCM. As one of important methods for image feature analysis and extraction, GLCM describes the textures by measuring the spatial correlation properties of gray scale. Given an image I with size $M \times N$, the GLCM could be computed as:

$$GLCM(k,l) = \frac{1}{M \times N} \sum_m \sum_n \begin{cases} 1, & \text{if } I(m,n) = k \text{ and } I(m + \Delta m, n + \Delta n) = l \\ 0, & \text{otherwise} \end{cases}$$
$$(3)$$

where the pixel $(m + \Delta m, n + \Delta n)$ refers to the neighbor of the pixel (m, n) in I. Then the texture complexity of an image is described by the contrast $f_{contrast}$ of the GLCM as follows:

$$f_{contrast} = \sum_k \sum_l (k - l)^2 GLCM(k, l) \quad (4)$$

2.2   Feature Extraction Module

Compared with the handcrafted features, the features extracted by CNN are more powerful and more suitable for various contents and distortions [11,12]. Commonly adopted backbones such as VGG [13] and ResNet [14] are designed for image classification tasks and extract high-level semantic features, but the perceived visual quality is also affected by low-level visual features. Therefore, it is not the best choice to directly use the popular CNN architecture as the backbone of the NR IQA task. Based on the notion that different stages of CNN extract the features of different levels, Zhao et al. [15] proposed the perceptual similarity, which calculated the L2 distance for each pair of feature maps extracted by the different layers of the CNN. Inspired by the above method, our method adopts ResNet as the backbone and utilizes the features extracted from intermediate layers to obtain a more effective quality-aware feature representation. The framework of the feature extraction module is illustrated in Fig. 3.

   To balance the computational efficiency and the predictive performance of the method, the ResNet-18 pre-trained on the ImageNet [16] is chosen as the backbone to extract features. As depicted in Fig. 3, the architecture of ResNet-18 could be divided into five stages, namely, *conv1*, *conv2_x*, *conv3_x*, *conv4_x*, and $conv5\_x$. In each of the above stages except for $conv1$, there are several convolutional layers in series to deepen the network. The feature maps from different stages of ResNet including $conv2\_x$, $conv3\_x$, $conv4\_x$, and $conv5\_x$ are extracted, referred to as F_{conv2_x}, F_{conv3_x}, F_{conv4_x}, F_{conv5_x}, respectively. The dimension of the feature maps is halved after each stage while the number of feature channels is doubled. Next, we employ the spatial global average pooling to these feature maps to obtain features from low level to high level. Finally, the features of different levels are concatenated into the final quality-aware representation, which is expressed as:

$$F_{final} = \text{cat}\left(gap(F_{conv2\_x}), gap(F_{conv3\_x}), gap(F_{conv4\_x}), gap(F_{conv5\_x})\right) \quad (5)$$

where $gap(\cdot)$ means the spatial global average pooling and $cat(\cdot)$ denotes the concatenation operation.

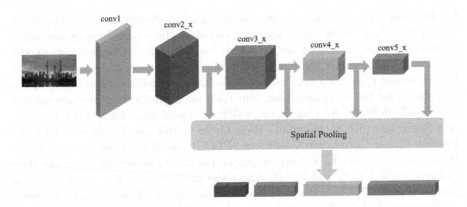

Fig. 3. The framework of feature extraction module.

2.3   Quality Evaluation Module

After extracting the quality-aware features, we adopt the shallow fully connected network to aggregate them into the quality score. We calculate the mean score value of three patches as the overall quality score of the 4K image. As for the classification task, we obtain the class probabilities with two fully connected layers composed of 128 neurons and 2 neurons respectively. The cross entropy is used as the loss function of the proposed model, which can be computed as:

$$L = -[y_{predict} \log y_{label} + (1 - y_{predict}) \log(1 - y_{label})] \quad (6)$$

where $y_{predict}$ is the positive probability predicted by the proposed model and y_{label} is the ground-truth positive probability. In terms of the regression task, the quality score is derived by two fully connected layers composed of 128 neurons and 1 neuron respectively. We adopt the euclidean distance as the loss function:

$$L = \|q_{predict} - q_{label}\|^2 \quad (7)$$

where $q_{predict}, q_{label}$ refer to the predicted quality score and the ground-truth quality score respectively.

3 Experiment Evaluation

In this section, we first illustrate the experimental setup and evaluation criteria. Then we compare our proposed model with current popular general IQA methods and the state-of-art 4K IQA methods on the real and pseudo 4K images database [9]. After that, we present the performance of different texture complexity measures. Finally, we validate the effectiveness of the proposed model through extensive ablation studies.

3.1 Experiment Protocol

Evaluation Criteria. To compare the methods' performance in the classification of the real and fake 4K images, we calculate three performance measures: Precision, Recall, and Accuracy, in which real and fake 4K images correspond to positive and negative samples respectively. The values of these indicators are between 0 and 1, the larger the values, the better the classification accuracy of the models. As for the regression task, four common evaluation criteria are applied to evaluate different IQA methods, which are Spearman Rank Order Correlation Coefficient (SRCC), Kendall's Rank Order Correlation Coefficient (KRCC), Pearson Linear Correlation Coefficient (PLCC) and Root Mean Squared Error (RMSE). SRCC and KRCC represent the prediction monotonicity of the IQA method, while PLCC and RMSE reflect the prediction accuracy. The value of SRCC, KRCC, PLCC is between 0 and 1, and an excellent model is supposed to obtain the values of these measures close to 1 and the value of RMSE close to 0.

Experiment Setup. The proposed method is validated on the 4K IQA dataset consisting of 350 real 4K images and 2802 pseudo 4K images. The database is divided into a training set of 80% real and fake 4K images and a test set of 20% real and fake 4K images. To ensure complete separation of training and testing contents, we assign the 4K images belonging to the same scene to the same set. In our experiment, we train and test our proposed model on a server with Intel Xeon Silver 4210R CPU @ 2.40 GHz, 128 GB RAM, and NVIDIA GTX 3090 GPU, and our proposed model is implemented in PyTorch [17]. The Adam optimizer [18] with the initial learning rate 0.0001 is used to train the proposed model. The learning rate decays with a multiplicative factor of 0.9 for every 10 epochs and the epochs are set at 50. The batch size is set at 32. The 4K IQA database is randomly split 10 times, and the average value of the above evaluation criteria is computed as the final result.

Compared Methods. We compare the proposed model with thirteen NR IQA models, which could be divided into two categories: general-purpose NR IQA methods and distortion-specific methods. The general-purpose methods include NIQE [19], QAC [8], IL-NIQE [20], LPSI [21], HOSA [22], BRISQUE [6], BPRI [23], BMPRI [24], NFERM [25] and GMLF [26]. The distortion-specific methods include CPBD [27], Zhu's method [9] and Rishi's method [2]. Among the thirteen NR IQA methods, NIQE, IL-NIQE, and CPBD do not need to be trained on the training set, while the remaining methods are retrained on the database. Notably, Rishi's method can only complete the classification task, so we could only compare its accuracy indicators with others.

3.2 Performance Comparison with Other IQA Methods

Table 1 illustrates the performance results of the proposed method and the other existing 13 NR IQA methods and the top 1 performance results in each column are marked in bold. From Table 1, we can make several observations. First, we can clearly see that the proposed model outperforms other NR IQA metrics and it leads by a significant margin, which indicates that the proposed model is much more effective at evaluating the quality of 4K pseudo images than the state-of-art NR IQA metrics which are based on handcrafted features. Next, compared with the quality regression task, the classification task of real and pseudo 4K images is relatively unchallenging. Most of the popular IQA metrics do well in distinguishing the authenticity of 4K images. Finally, some NR IQA metrics based on handcrafted features perform better than Rishi's method, which adopts a light CNN to extract features. It can be concluded that the features extracted by shallow CNN are not sufficient to deal with the distortions of pseudo 4K image caused by various SR algorithms, which indirectly confirms the necessity of the features extracted from different stages of deeper CNN.

Moreover, in order to make quantitative statements about the performance of different IQA methods, we employ the statistical significance test in [28] to measure the difference between the predicted quality scores and the subjective ratings. Figure 4 presents the results of the statistical significance test for the proposed method and other NR IQA metrics. It can be easily found that the performance of our proposed 4K IQA model on the 4K image database is statistically superior to all compared state-of-the-art NR IQA metrics.

3.3 Performance of Different Texture Complexity Measures

In this section, we mainly analyze the performance of different texture complexity measures in the patch selection module. The feature extraction module is set as the same as in Sect. 2.2. We select four effective and efficient measures, two of which are used in the previous 4K IQA work: variance [2] and local variance [9], and two of which are common texture complexity descriptors in pattern recognition: entropy of gray difference histogram and contrast of GLCM. In order to verify their effectiveness, the random method is used to form a contrast. Besides,

Table 1. Performance comparison of the proposed model and thirteen NR IQA methods, where P_T, P_F, R_T, R_F refer to the precision and recall of positive and negative samples respectively.

Metrics	SRCC	KRCC	PLCC	RMSE	P_T	P_F	R_T	R_F	Accuracy
BPRI	0.3506	0.2956	0.5614	13.5928	0.9097	0.9729	0.7771	0.9904	0.9667
BMPRI	0.3594	0.2308	0.6534	12.4345	0.5890	0.9441	0.5486	0.9522	0.9074
BRISQUE	0.6651	0.5061	0.6696	12.2003	0.8795	0.9477	0.5629	0.9904	0.9429
CPBD	0.5963	0.4315	0.6194	12.8950	0.5522	0.9349	0.4686	0.9525	0.8988
NFERM	0.6708	0.4990	0.6662	12.2497	0.9653	0.9299	0.3971	0.9982	0.9315
GMLF	0.2387	0.1594	0.2376	14.2550	0.3433	0.9196	0.3600	0.9140	0.8525
HOSA	0.7153	0.5299	0.7173	11.4445	0.6613	0.9496	0.5914	0.9622	0.9210
NIQE	0.5223	0.3797	0.5691	13.5061	0.7550	0.9442	0.5371	0.9782	0.9293
IL-NIQE	0.3819	0.2593	0.3437	15.4249	0.1469	0.9081	0.4600	0.6663	0.6434
LPSI	0.5782	0.5051	0.7629	10.6193	0.7188	0.9942	0.7886	0.9936	0.9708
QAC	0.6866	0.5204	0.6427	12.5836	0.4868	0.892	0.2114	0.9722	0.8877
Rishi's	–	–	–	–	0.6757	0.9634	0.7086	0.9575	0.9299
Zhu's	0.8613	0.6927	0.8948	7.3045	0.9939	0.9908	0.9257	0.9993	0.9911
Proposed	**0.9500**	**0.8284**	**0.9836**	**2.2717**	**1.0000**	**0.9995**	**0.9957**	**1.0000**	**0.9996**

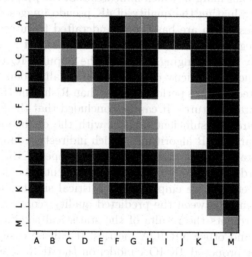

Fig. 4. Statistical significance comparison between the proposed model and other NR IQA metrics. A black/white block (i, j) means the method at row i is statistically worse/better than the one at column j. A gray block (m, n) means the method at row m and the method at n are statistically indistinguishable. The metrics denoted by A-M are of the same order as the compared metrics in Table 1

we also compare the computational complexity of all the methods in terms of the execution speed. The execution time is computed as the average time of 10 times measuring the texture complexity for 120 patches of a 4K image.

Table 2. Performance comparison of texture complexity measures.

$F(\cdot)$	Time(s)	SRCC	KRCC	PLCC	RMSE
Random	–	0.9121	0.7656	0.9737	2.8726
Variance	0.0312	0.9378	0.8073	0.9813	2.4021
Local variance	0.224	0.9231	0.7702	0.9753	2.8126
Hist entropy	**0.0282**	0.9294	0.7863	0.9759	2.7226
GLCM contrast	0.1105	**0.9500**	**0.8284**	**0.9836**	**2.2717**

The experimental results for different texture complexity measures are depicted in Table 2 and the top 1 performance results in each column are marked in bold. Firstly, we can clearly see that all the texture complexity measures perform better than the random method, which complies with the principle that the patches with more complex textures are more sensitive to upscaling operations. Secondly, the contrast of the GLCM performs the best among these measures and has a moderate computation cost, which indicates that it is effective and efficient in calculating texture complexity. Therefore, the contrast of the GLCM is employed in the patch selection module of our proposed method.

3.4 Ablation Experiments

In this section, we conduct the ablation experiment to further validate the contribution of features extracted from different intermediate layers of CNN. We select five feature extraction modules for the ablation experiment, which are:

- BL: The baseline model ResNet.
- BL_{345}: The baseline model with features from $F_{conv3\_x}, F_{conv4\_x}, F_{conv5\_x}$
- BL_{245}: The baseline model with features from $F_{conv2\_x}, F_{conv4\_x}, F_{conv5\_x}$
- BL_{235}: The baseline model with features from $F_{conv2\_x}, F_{conv3\_x}, F_{conv5\_x}$
- BL_{all}: The proposed model.

The results are listed in Table 3. It is observed that our proposed model is superior to the other three models and achieves a higher correlation with subjective perceptive scores. The absence of features extracted from any one of the intermediate layers leads to performance degradation. Besides, the experimental results indicate that the low-level features extracted from shallow convolution layers contribute relatively little to the high-level features extracted from deeper convolution layers.

Table 3. Performance comparison of five models for ablation study.

Model	SRCC	KRCC	PLCC	RMSE
BL	0.9386	0.8003	0.9774	2.6984
BL_{345}	0.9475	0.8185	0.9831	2.3333
BL_{245}	0.9453	0.8131	0.9804	2.4846
BL_{235}	0.9423	0.8038	0.9768	2.7374
BL_{all}	**0.9500**	**0.8284**	**0.9836**	**2.2717**

4   Conclusion

In this paper, we propose a novel deep learning-based NR IQA model for the quality evaluation of real and pseudo 4K UHD images. To reduce the computation cost of the algorithms, we first select three representative patches from a 4K image with the GLCM-based texture complexity measure. Then we employ a CNN to derive a more effective quality-aware feature representation for each patch. Specifically, we apply global average pooling to the feature maps extracted from each stage of CNN and then concatenate these features into the final feature representation. Finally, the shallow fully connected network is adopted to aggregate the quality-aware features into the quality score and the mean value of quality scores for three patches serves as the overall quality. Experimental results demonstrate that the proposed model outperforms other NR IQA metrics both in classification and regression tasks and leads by a significant margin. In the future, we intend to extend this work to recognize the captured and generated contents.

Acknowledgements. This work was supported in part by National Key R&D Program of China (No. 2019YFB1405900), and in part by the Open Research Project of the State Key Laboratory of Media Convergence and Communication, Communication University of China, China (No. SKLMCC2020KF003).

References

1. Wang, J., Li, S.: Investigation and design of 4K ultra high definition television production and broadcasting system. In: 2020 IEEE 5th Information Technology and Mechatronics Engineering Conference (ITOEC), pp. 579–582 (2020). https://doi.org/10.1109/ITOEC49072.2020.9141900
2. Shah, R.R., Akundy, V.A., Wang, Z.: Real versus fake 4K-authentic resolution assessment. In: ICASSP 2021–2021 IEEE International Conference on Acoustics, Speech and Signal Processing (ICASSP), pp. 2185–2189. IEEE (2021)
3. Zhai, G., Sun, W., Min, X., Zhou, J.: Perceptual quality assessment of low-light image enhancement. ACM Trans. Multimed. Comput. Commun. Appl. (TOMM) **17**(4), 1–24 (2021)
4. Sun, W., Min, X., Zhai, G., Gu, K., Ma, S., Yang, X.: Dynamic backlight scaling considering ambient luminance for mobile videos on LCD displays. IEEE Trans. Mob. Comput. **21**(1), 110–124 (2022)

5. Zhai, G., Min, X.: Perceptual image quality assessment: a survey. Sci. China Inf. Sci. **63**(11), 1–52 (2020). https://doi.org/10.1007/s11432-019-2757-1
6. Mittal, A., Moorthy, A.K., Bovik, A.C.: No-reference image quality assessment in the spatial domain. IEEE Trans. Image Process. **21**(12), 4695–4708 (2012)
7. Zhai, G., Wu, X., Yang, X., Lin, W., Zhang, W.: A psychovisual quality metric in free-energy principle. IEEE Trans. Image Process. **21**(1), 41–52 (2011)
8. Xue, W., Zhang, L., Mou, X.: Learning without human scores for blind image quality assessment. In: Proceedings of the IEEE Conference on Computer Vision and Pattern Recognition, pp. 995–1002 (2013)
9. Zhu, W., Zhai, G., Min, X., Yang, X., Zhang, X.P.: Perceptual quality assessment for recognizing true and pseudo 4K content. In: ICASSP 2021–2021 IEEE International Conference on Acoustics, Speech and Signal Processing (ICASSP), pp. 2190–2194. IEEE (2021)
10. Haralick, R.M., Shanmugam, K., Dinstein, I.H.: Textural features for image classification. IEEE Trans. Syst. Man Cybern. **6**, 610–621 (1973)
11. Sun, W., Min, X., Zhai, G., Ma, S.: Blind quality assessment for in-the-wild images via hierarchical feature fusion and iterative mixed database training. arXiv preprint arXiv:2105.14550 (2021)
12. Sun, W., Wang, T., Min, X., Yi, F., Zhai, G.: Deep learning based full-reference and no-reference quality assessment models for compressed UGC videos. In: 2021 IEEE International Conference on Multimedia & Expo Workshops (ICMEW), pp. 1–6. IEEE (2021)
13. Simonyan, K., Zisserman, A.: Very deep convolutional networks for large-scale image recognition. arXiv preprint arXiv:1409.1556 (2014)
14. He, K., Zhang, X., Ren, S., Sun, J.: Deep residual learning for image recognition. In: Proceedings of the IEEE Conference on Computer Vision and Pattern Recognition, pp. 770–778 (2016)
15. Zhao, G., Huang, J.: DeepSim: deep learning code functional similarity. In: Proceedings of the 2018 26th ACM Joint Meeting on European Software Engineering Conference and Symposium on the Foundations of Software Engineering, pp. 141–151 (2018)
16. Deng, J., Dong, W., Socher, R., Li, L.J., Li, K., Fei-Fei, L.: ImageNet: a large-scale hierarchical image database. In: 2009 IEEE Conference on Computer Vision and Pattern Recognition, pp. 248–255. IEEE (2009)
17. Paszke, A., et al.: Automatic differentiation in PyTorch (2017)
18. Kingma, D.P., Ba, J.: Adam: a method for stochastic optimization. arXiv preprint arXiv:1412.6980 (2014)
19. Mittal, A., Soundararajan, R., Bovik, A.C.: Making a "completely blind" image quality analyzer. IEEE Signal Process. Lett. **20**(3), 209–212 (2012)
20. Zhang, L., Zhang, L., Bovik, A.C.: A feature-enriched completely blind image quality evaluator. IEEE Trans. Image Process. **24**(8), 2579–2591 (2015)
21. Wu, Q., Wang, Z., Li, H.: A highly efficient method for blind image quality assessment. In: 2015 IEEE International Conference on Image Processing (ICIP), pp. 339–343. IEEE (2015)
22. Xu, J., Ye, P., Li, Q., Du, H., Liu, Y., Doermann, D.: Blind image quality assessment based on high order statistics aggregation. IEEE Trans. Image Process. **25**(9), 4444–4457 (2016)
23. Min, X., Gu, K., Zhai, G., Liu, J., Yang, X., Chen, C.W.: Blind quality assessment based on pseudo-reference image. IEEE Trans. Multimed. **20**(8), 2049–2062 (2017)
24. Min, X., Zhai, G., Gu, K., Liu, Y., Yang, X.: Blind image quality estimation via distortion aggravation. IEEE Trans. Broadcast. **64**(2), 508–517 (2018)

25. Gu, K., Zhai, G., Yang, X., Zhang, W.: Using free energy principle for blind image quality assessment. IEEE Trans. Multimed. **17**(1), 50–63 (2014)
26. Xue, W., Mou, X., Zhang, L., Bovik, A.C., Feng, X.: Blind image quality assessment using joint statistics of gradient magnitude and Laplacian features. IEEE Trans. Image Process. **23**(11), 4850–4862 (2014)
27. Narvekar, N.D., Karam, L.J.: A no-reference perceptual image sharpness metric based on a cumulative probability of blur detection. In: 2009 International Workshop on Quality of Multimedia Experience, pp. 87–91 (2009). https://doi.org/10.1109/QOMEX.2009.5246972
28. Sheikh, H.R., Sabir, M.F., Bovik, A.C.: A statistical evaluation of recent full reference image quality assessment algorithms. IEEE Trans. Image Process. **15**(11), 3440–3451 (2006)

Image Quality Assessment Based on Sparse Reference Information

Xinkang Lian[1,2,3,4,5], Shuangyi Xie[1,2,3,4,5], Shuang Shi[1,2,3,4,5(✉)],
Chengxu Zhou[1,2,3,4,5], and Nan Guo[1,2,3,4,5]

[1] Engineering Research Center of Intelligent Perception and Autonomous Control,
Ministry of Education, Beijing, China
`shuangs0502@foxmail.com`
[2] Beijing Key Laboratory of Computational Intelligence and Intelligent System,
Beijing, China
[3] Beijing Laboratory of Smart Environmental Protection, Beijing, China
[4] Faculty of Information Technology, Beijing University of Technology,
Beijing, China
[5] Beijing Artificial Intelligence Institute, Beijing, China

Abstract. The last few years have seen the appearance of a new sparse reference-based free energy principle, which demonstrates that an input visual signal was always strived to be comprehend by the human visual system (HVS) through removing the undetermined portions. By this inspiration, we in this paper put forward an image quality assessment (IQA) model based on sparse reference information. In essential, as compared with the classical good-performance FEDM model that was developed with a linear local autoregressive (AR) model, the proposed sparse reference (SR) IQA model is a simplified version of FEDM, achieving comparable performance but hundreds of times faster implementation. More specifically, this paper introduces the extremely sparse random sampling method into the FEDM model. Experimental results on the most well-known LIVE IQA database illustrate the effectiveness along with efficiency of our SR-IQA model as compared with the typical full-reference IQA models and the cutting-edge SR IQA models.

Keywords: Free energy theory · Human visual system (HVS) · Image quality assessment (IQA) · Sparse reference (SR)

1 Introduction

Contemporarily, human consumers receive tens of thousands of video frames or images every moment. The ensuing issue is that the visual quality of those images that is to be corrupted by stochastic noise, blurriness, JPEG compression, etc. require a huge number of workers to guarantee. Therefore, it is extremely urgent to monitor and control the quality of images or video sequences through

S. Shi—This paper was supported in part by the NSFC under Grants 62076013, 62021003, and 61890935.

hiring few employees simultaneously [1]. With strong capacity to approach the human perception to visual quality, the method of image quality assessment (IQA) is typically deemed to be a perfect choice to address this issue.

Nowadays, the mainstream IQA models are roughly divided into subjective IQA and objective IQA. The former has great significance since it records the images to be accessed and their subjective quality ratings of human beings (e.g. LIVE [2]) to verify the accuracy of objective IQA models. But subjective IQA is laborious, time-consuming, expensive and not appropriate for a majority of real-time applications. Consequently, a vast amount of mathematical models were designed to quickly and accurately assess the image quality to form the increasing number of objective IQA models [44–49].

In the light of weather the original reference image is available or not, the objective IQA models can be further divided into 3 categories. The first category is full-reference (FR) IQA models, whose presupposition relies on the entirely known original image signals [3–16], such as mean squared error (MSE), structural similarity index (SSIM) [3], feature similarity (FSIM) [4], analysis of distortion distribution-based SSIM (ADD-SSIM) [7], perceptual similarity (PSIM) [9], etc. However, we can hardly acquire the lossless image signals in many cases, and the results obtained from their evaluation are quite different from the subjective perceived quality of the images, which limits the FR methods unable to work well. As a result, the sparse-reference (SR) IQA models, just using part of the lossless image as the needed features, are enthusiastically carried out by the researchers, pushing the SR-IQA into the phase of rapid development of higher performance era [17–22]. For example, the free energy based distortion metric (FEDM) [17] was illuminated based on the principle of free energy to try to simulate and fit the human brain's internal generative (IG) model [23,24]. The quality assessment metric of contrast (QMC) [20] was developed by incorporating image signature-based saliency preservation [25] and entropy increment [26] together with a straightforward linear function.

Resulted from the limitation of portability, implementation cost and the requirement of the whole lossless image, just very few of the booming developed IQA models (e.g. SSIM and MSE) have been successfully embedded into the existing processing systems for images/videos. Naturally whether we can develop an efficient and valid IQA model to overcome the shortcomings described above or not is an extremely vital issues needed to be addressed. To this aim, this paper makes great efforts to develop a sparse reference information-based IQA model (SRIQA) with extremely sparse random sampling method. SRIQA is a simplified version of FEDM, possessing the property of strong portability and less computational burden and thus having potential and huge application prospects. Furthermore, SRIQA requires just one number as the SR feature, which even acts as a no-reference (NR) IQA model because that number can be precisely encoded with quite few bits in the file of the header.

The layout of this paper is organized below. We firstly review the free energy based brain principle and then illustrate our proposed SRIQA model in the second section. We conducted experiments on LIVE [2] to verify the excellent accuracy of our proposed IQA model with mainstream FR IQA models and relevant SR-IQA models, and further analyzed the reason why the proposed SRIQA implements highly faster than its original version of FEDM in the third section. Finally, we draw some concluding remarks in the last section.

2 The Proposed SRIQA Model

Today many current IQA models primarily devoted themselves to extract low level features, e.g., image gradient, phase congruency, and structural information. Nevertheless, we hold the belief that it should be highly connected between the visual quality of images and the human brain's psychological and physiological mechanisms of perception. During recent years, the team of Prof. Friston has provided a milestone principle namely the free energy based brain theory [23,24], which explains and unifies some significant brain principles in physical and biological sciences with regard to human thinking, perception, learning and action. The hypothesis of Bayesian brain [27], which has been broadly applied in ensemble learning, is similar to the free energy based brain theory, whose fundamental premise is that the human brain realizes the cognitive process on account of a model called internal generative IG model. Merely relying on this phenomenon, the human brain can takes advantage of a constructive manner to predict those encountered scenes.

In fact, the above mentioned process (the constructive model) can be considered as a probabilistic model made up of a prior term and likelihood term. Toward deducing the posterior possibility of the external visual input signal, the HVS inverts the likelihood term. In spite of the fact that the brain conducts much more complicated mechanism far beyond most of our current level of knowledge, it can be reasonably assumed that it is fairly natural that there exist a discrepancy between the brain's IG model and the encountered scene. Zhai *et al.* [28,29] found such discrepancy gap is strongly related to the quality of human perceptions, and thus the quality of images can be measured.

In specifically, we assume that the Θ of the IG model is parametric toward the perception of external visual input signal, and we can explain the perceived scenes through changing the vector $\boldsymbol{\xi}$ of parameters. As for an external visual image V, its 'surprise' is defined (determined by entropy) based on the integration of the joint distribution $P(V,\boldsymbol{\xi}|\Theta)$ over the space of the model parameters $\boldsymbol{\xi}$

$$-\log P(V|\Theta) = -\log \int P(V,\boldsymbol{\xi}|\Theta)d\boldsymbol{\xi}. \tag{1}$$

The expression in math is hard to be understood, hence we introduce an auxiliary term $Q(\boldsymbol{\xi}|V)$ into Eq. (1) and redefine the equation to be:

$$-\log P(V|\Theta) = -\log \int Q(\boldsymbol{\xi}|V)\frac{P(V,\boldsymbol{\xi}|\Theta)}{Q(\boldsymbol{\xi}|V)}d\boldsymbol{\xi}. \tag{2}$$

Note that $Q(\boldsymbol{\xi}|V)$ is an auxiliary posterior distribution of the parameters of the IG model for the external input visual signal V. It can be considered as an approximate posterior to the real posterior of the model parameters $P(\boldsymbol{\xi}|V)$.

The human brain always tries to decrease the discrepancy gap between the real posterior $P(\xi|V)$ and the approximate posterior $Q(\xi|V)$ through changing the parameter ξ in $Q(\xi|V)$ for searching the best explanation of the perceived external visual image V. Employing the Jensen's inequality to Eq. (2), the following relationship can be easily derived:

$$-\log P(V) \leq - \int Q(\xi|V) \log \frac{P(V,\xi)}{Q(\xi|V)} d\xi. \tag{3}$$

On the basis of the definition in statistical thermodynamics [30], we can easily know the right part of Eq. (3) is the upper bound of 'free energy', which is defined by

$$J(\xi) = - \int Q(\xi|V) \log \frac{P(V,\xi)}{Q(\xi|V)} d\xi. \tag{4}$$

Obviously, it is the free energy, a discrepancy measure between the input visual image and its optimal explanation deduced by the IG model that can be on behalf of itself to be a natural proxy for measuring the psychically quality of images. According to this, a perceptual distance between the lossless image V_r and its corrupted one V_d to be the absolute difference of the two images in free energy is defined as follows:

$$Q_{\text{FEDM}}(V_r, V_d) = \left| J(\hat{\xi}_r) - J(\hat{\xi}_d) \right| \tag{5}$$

with

$$\hat{\xi}_r = \arg \min_{\xi_r} J(\xi|\Theta, V_r),$$

$$\hat{\xi}_d = \arg \min_{\xi_d} J(\xi|\Theta, V_d).$$

We in this work select Θ with a linear AR model due to its simplicity and its capacity to approximate a broad range of natural scenes through changing its parameters [31–34]. We can define the AR model to be

$$x_j = \chi^k(x_j)\beta + \tau_j \tag{6}$$

where x_j is a pixel in question, $\chi^k(x_j)$ is a vector that includes k nearest neighbors of x_j, $\beta = (\beta_1, \beta_2, ..., \beta_k)^T$ is a vector of AR coefficients, and τ_j is white noise term with zero mean. Hence, the lossless image V_r's free energy is measured by the entropy between the lossless image and its corresponding predicted one V_p by

$$J(V_r) = - \sum_{i=0}^{255} P_i(\tilde{V}_r) \log P_i(\tilde{V}_r) \tag{7}$$

where $P_i(\tilde{V}_r)$ presents the probability density of grayscale i in $\tilde{V}_r$, which can be derived by

$$\tilde{V}_r = V_r - V_p = V_r - R(V_r) \tag{8}$$

with

$$R(x_j) = \chi^k(x_j)\boldsymbol{\beta}_{est} \tag{9}$$

where $\boldsymbol{\beta}_{est}$ is the best choice of AR coefficients for x_j adopting the least square method. In such a manner, the free energy of the distorted image V_d is correspondingly defined.

The performance indicators of PLCC, SROCC and RMSE of the five algorithms have been displayed respectively in Tables 1, 2 and 3. According to the data, FDEM obtains quite well performance, but it takes a long time to run. More importantly, instructing and optimizing real-time applications is the most valuable function of the IQA model. In practical application, FEDM and other image/video processing systems do not consider the principle of free energy, but embed AR prediction model. As a result, the above facts lead to a serious issue, that is, the system can achieve good performance, but also cannot be ported. In order to cope with this issue, this paper adopts the widely studied extremely sparse random sampling method to improve FEDM, and proposes the SRIQA method with short time-consuming, high efficiency and strong practicability. In order to address this issue, we improve the FEDM with the extremely sparse random sampling method to achieve the effective, fast and practical SRIQA model.

To be specific, we compute the model parameter Θ using the extremely sparse random sampling way, and renew the free energy of the used reference image V_r as

$$J'(V_r) = -\sum_{i=0}^{255} P_i(\tilde{V}_r') \log_2 P_i(\tilde{V}_r') \tag{10}$$

where $P_i(\tilde{V}_r')$ means the probability density of grayscale i in $\tilde{V}_r'$ computed by

$$\tilde{V}_r' = V_r - V_p' = V_r - F(V_r) \tag{11}$$

where $F(V_r)$ is obtained by employing the 'imwrite' command with the extremely sparse random sampling method in Matlab. In the same way, the free energy $J'(V_d)$ of the V_d (distorted image) can also be obtained. Eventually, the SRIQA is computed by importing the $J'(V_r)$ and $J'(V_d)$ into Eq. (5). Our proposed extremely sparse random sampling method mainly conducts sampling 28 times from 1/1000 pixels of the input image to the entire image. The experimental results verify that we obtain the special performance at 3/1000 and 6/100 sampling value, which can be explained in Sect. 3. We defined that the performance of 3/1000 sampling value called SRIQA, and of 6/100 sampling value called SRIQA+. It is worth noting that the extremely sparse random sampling method runs fairly fast and can be widely integrated into the majority of image/video processing systems so that it can make the SRIQA more flexible and portable.

3   Results of Experiments

We selected five typical IQA algorithms to conduct comparative experiment, among which the FR algorithms are PSNR and SSIM, and the SR algorithms

Table 1. PLCC of four classical models in [3, 17, 22] and our SRIQA model on five image subsets distorted by the way of JEPG2000, JEPG, AGWN, Blur and Fast-fading in the database of LIVE.

Pearson linear correlation coefficient (PLCC)						
Algorithm	JP2K	JPEG	AGWN	Blur	FF	Average
PSNR [3]	0.8996	0.8879	0.9858	0.7835	0.8895	0.8893
SSIM [3]	0.9410	0.9504	0.9695	0.8743	0.9428	0.9356
FEDM [17]	0.9262	0.9211	0.9256	0.7359	0.8532	0.8724
SDM [22]	0.9447	0.9569	0.9789	0.9252	0.9316	0.9475
SRIQA (pro.)	0.9174	0.9206	0.8894	0.7590	0.8529	0.8678
SRIQA+ (pro.)	0.9256	0.9212	0.9236	0.7375	0.8532	0.8722

Table 2. SROCC of four classical models in [3, 17, 22] and our SRIQA model on five image subsets distorted by the way of JEPG2000, JEPG, AGWN, Blur and Fastfading in the database of LIVE.

Spearman rank-order correlation coefficient (SROCC)						
Algorithm	JP2K	JPEG	AGWN	Blur	FF	Average
PSNR [3]	0.8954	0.8809	0.9854	0.7823	0.8907	0.8869
SSIM [3]	0.9355	0.9449	0.9629	0.8944	0. 9413	0.9358
FEDM [17]	0.9200	0.9230	0.9152	0.7594	0.8229	0.8681
SDM [22]	0.9439	0.9447	0.9729	0.9342	0.9384	0.9468
SRIQA (pro.)	0.9098	0.9199	0.8782	0.7780	0.8252	0.8622
SRIQA+ (pro.)	0.9197	0.9234	0.9131	0.7617	0.8246	0.8685

Table 3. RMSE of four classical models in [3, 17, 22] and our SRIQA model on five image subsets distorted by the way of JEPG2000, JEPG, AGWN, Blur and Fast-fading in the database of LIVE.

Root mean-squared error (RMSE)						
Algorithm	JP2K	JPEG	AGWN	Blur	FF	Average
PSNR [3]	11.017	14.653	4.7027	11.478	13.015	10.973
SSIM [3]	8.5349	9.9070	6.8533	8.9643	9.4963	8.7512
FEDM [17]	7.3813	9.5935	8.1619	9.2857	10.7773	9.0399
SDM [22]	8.2737	9.2445	5.7166	7.0095	10.357	8.12026
SRIQA (pro.)	7.9027	9.7787	9.9642	9.0373	10.7961	9.4958
SRIQA+ (pro.)	7.3977	9.5942	8.2867	9.2712	10.7780	9.0656

Table 4. PLCC of our proposed SRIQA models, conducting extremely sparse random sampling 28 times, on five image subsets distorted by various distortion types in the database of LIVE.

Random Sampling	JPEG 2000	JPEG	White Noise	Gaussian Blur	Fast-fading	Mean PLCC	Computation Time	Computation efficiency
1/1000	0.9021	0.9183	0.8298	0.7532	0.8530	0.8513	0.9886	194.2
2/1000	0.9122	0.9020	0.8715	0.7539	0.8505	0.8580	1.1830	162.3
3/1000	0.9174	0.9206	0.8894	0.7590	0.8529	**0.8678**	**1.3780**	**139.3**
4/1000	0.9191	0.9156	0.8959	0.7532	0.8526	0.8673	1.5666	122.5
5/1000	0.9186	0.9225	0.9037	0.7493	0.8552	0.8699	1.7599	109.1
6/1000	0.9202	0.9186	0.9070	0.7424	0.8477	0.8672	1.9527	98.3
7/1000	0.9195	0.9202	0.9091	0.7441	0.8529	0.8692	2.1451	89.5
8/1000	0.9220	0.9170	0.9099	0.7423	0.8506	0.8683	2.3376	82.1
9/1000	0.9201	0.9193	0.9124	0.7442	0.8496	0.8691	2.5310	75.8
1/100	0.9228	0.9182	0.9128	0.7411	0.8503	0.8690	2.7224	70.5
2/100	0.9238	0.9181	0.9200	0.7418	0.8528	0.8713	4.6436	41.3
3/100	0.9253	0.9217	0.9206	0.7383	0.8502	0.8712	6.5702	29.2
4/100	0.9255	0.9211	0.9218	0.7402	0.8503	0.8718	8.4732	22.7
5/100	0.9261	0.9208	0.9230	0.7384	0.8520	0.8721	10.3900	18.5
6/100	0.9256	0.9212	0.9236	0.7375	0.8532	**0.8722**	**12.3143**	**15.6**
7/100	0.9259	0.9220	0.9236	0.7377	0.8533	0.8725	14.2522	13.5
8/100	0.9254	0.9210	0.9231	0.7389	0.8529	0.8723	16.1710	11.9
9/100	0.9257	0.9218	0.9238	0.7382	0.8537	0.8726	18.0893	10.6
1/10	0.9255	0.9228	0.9240	0.7385	0.8506	0.8723	19.9936	9.6
2/10	0.9260	0.9213	0.9249	0.7358	0.8529	0.8722	39.1718	4.9
3/10	0.9261	0.9209	0.9252	0.7364	0.8534	0.8724	58.3404	3.3
4/10	0.9258	0.9213	0.9252	0.7365	0.8531	0.8724	77.4257	2.5
5/10	0.9259	0.9210	0.9253	0.7359	0.8532	0.8723	96.5608	2.0
6/10	0.9261	0.9211	0.9255	0.7357	0.8533	0.8723	115.6321	1.7
7/10	0.9262	0.9210	0.9255	0.7357	0.8533	0.8723	134.7134	1.4
8/10	0.9261	0.9212	0.9255	0.7359	0.8532	0.8724	153.9539	1.2
9/10	0.9261	0.9210	0.9256	0.7360	0.8532	0.8724	172.9504	1.1
1	0.9262	0.9211	0.9256	0.7359	0.8532	0.8724	191.9450	1.0

are FEDM, SDM and our proposed SRIQA. We adopted the nonlinear regression (given by VQEG [35]) based logistic function of five-parameter to correspond to subjective scores and objective predictions of the five models:

$$\text{Quality}(q) = \rho_1 \left(\frac{1}{2} - \frac{1}{1 + e^{\rho_2(s_o - \rho_3)}} \right) + \rho_4 s_o + \rho_5 \tag{12}$$

where $Quality(q)$ is the corresponding score of input score q, the s_o refers to the original scores of IQA, and the ρ_1 to ρ_5 are five free parameters, assigned in the curve fitting process. We used the three classical evaluation indices suggested by VQEG, namely pearson linear correlation coefficient (PLCC), spearman rank-

Table 5. SROCC of our proposed SRIQA models, conducting extremely sparse random sampling 28 times, on five image subsets distorted by various distortion types in the database of LIVE.

Random Sampling	JPEG 2000	JPEG	White Noise	Gaussian Blur	Fast-fading	Mean SROCC	Computation Time	Computation efficiency
1/1000	0.8920	0.9173	0.8153	0.7635	0.8238	0.8424	0.9886	194.2
2/1000	0.9045	0.9033	0.8588	0.7702	0.8188	0.8511	1.1830	162.3
3/1000	0.9098	0.9199	0.8782	0.7780	0.8252	**0.8622**	**1.3780**	**139.3**
4/1000	0.9127	0.9175	0.8867	0.7745	0.8234	0.8630	1.5666	122.5
5/1000	0.9109	0.9231	0.8937	0.7710	0.8253	0.8648	1.7599	109.1
6/1000	0.9117	0.9208	0.8979	0.7635	0.8206	0.8629	1.9527	98.3
7/1000	0.9119	0.9193	0.9001	0.7651	0.8204	0.8634	2.1451	89.5
8/1000	0.9156	0.9181	0.8997	0.7611	0.8183	0.8626	2.3376	82.1
9/1000	0.9138	0.9207	0.9021	0.7660	0.8243	0.8654	2.5310	75.8
1/100	0.9145	0.9181	0.9035	0.7625	0.8200	0.8637	2.7224	70.5
2/100	0.9167	0.9189	0.9084	0.7649	0.8226	0.8663	4.6436	41.3
3/100	0.9197	0.9222	0.9101	0.7599	0.8200	0.8664	6.5702	29.2
4/100	0.9192	0.9222	0.9120	0.7616	0.8242	0.8678	8.4732	22.7
5/100	0.9200	0.9232	0.9121	0.7603	0.8213	0.8674	10.3900	18.5
6/100	0.9197	0.9234	0.9131	0.7617	0.8246	**0.8685**	**12.3143**	**15.6**
7/100	0.9194	0.9241	0.9127	0.7613	0.8243	0.8684	14.2522	13.5
8/100	0.9197	0.9224	0.9123	0.7609	0.8229	0.8676	16.1710	11.9
9/100	0.9202	0.9249	0.9131	0.7615	0.8241	0.8688	18.0893	10.6
1/10	0.9192	0.9244	0.9136	0.7618	0.8248	0.8688	19.9936	9.6
2/10	0.9203	0.9234	0.9146	0.7582	0.8218	0.8677	39.1718	4.9
3/10	0.9199	0.9232	0.9145	0.7589	0.8225	0.8678	58.3404	3.3
4/10	0.9197	0.9231	0.9146	0.7599	0.8223	0.8679	77.4257	2.5
5/10	0.9197	0.9231	0.9148	0.7594	0.8239	0.8682	96.5608	2.0
6/10	0.9204	0.9231	0.9153	0.7583	0.8228	0.8680	115.6321	1.7
7/10	0.9204	0.9230	0.9149	0.7591	0.8230	0.8680	134.7134	1.4
8/10	0.9201	0.9230	0.9148	0.7593	0.8227	0.8680	153.9539	1.2
9/10	0.9201	0.9231	0.9152	0.7597	0.8223	0.8681	172.9504	1.1
1	0.9200	0.9230	0.9152	0.7594	0.8229	0.8681	191.9450	1.0

order correlation coefficient (SROCC), and root mean-squared error (RMSE) to further assess the prediction accuracy of the five typical models on the most commonly used LIVE dataset. We tabulated the obtained data in Tables 1, 2 and 3. In the implementation, we inserted the extremely sparse random sampling method into the SRIQA model proposed in this paper. We then detected the performance of algorithm on five types of distortion (Fast-fading, JPEG2000 compression, Gaussian Blur, JPEG compression, White Noise,) obtaining the performance values of five typical metrics, calculation time and efficiency. The final values of PLCC, SROCC, Kendall Rank-order Correlation Coefficient (KRCC), and RMSE are displayed separately in Tables 4, 5, 6 and 7.

Table 6. KRCC of our proposed SRIQA models, conducting extremely sparse random sampling 28 times, on five image subsets distorted by various distortion types in the database of LIVE.

Random Sampling	JPEG 2000	JPEG	White Noise	Gaussian Blur	Fast-fading	Mean KRCC	Computation Time	Computation efficiency
1/1000	0.6992	0.7423	0.6203	0.5757	0.6241	0.6523	0.9886	194.2
2/1000	0.7218	0.7244	0.6688	0.5877	0.6170	0.6639	1.1830	162.3
3/1000	0.7243	0.7461	0.6943	0.5937	0.6291	**0.6775**	**1.3780**	**139.3**
4/1000	0.7336	0.7428	0.7057	0.5923	0.6274	0.6804	1.5666	122.5
5/1000	0.7280	0.7515	0.7126	0.5902	0.6322	0.6829	1.7599	109.1
6/1000	0.7267	0.7474	0.7186	0.5816	0.6239	0.6796	1.9527	98.3
7/1000	0.7292	0.7461	0.7220	0.5826	0.6251	0.6810	2.1451	89.5
8/1000	0.7342	0.7450	0.7205	0.5812	0.6232	0.6808	2.3376	82.1
9/1000	0.7320	0.7492	0.7232	0.5843	0.6316	0.6841	2.5310	75.8
1/100	0.7325	0.7449	0.7262	0.5810	0.6239	0.6817	2.7224	70.5
2/100	0.7367	0.7454	0.7337	0.5833	0.6289	0.6856	4.6436	41.3
3/100	0.7394	0.7512	0.7345	0.5778	0.6257	0.6857	6.5702	29.2
4/100	0.7402	0.7508	0.7379	0.5799	0.6303	0.6878	8.4732	22.7
5/100	0.7418	0.7519	0.7385	0.5795	0.6266	0.6876	10.3900	18.5
6/100	0.7405	0.7540	0.7402	0.5818	0.6316	**0.6896**	**12.3143**	**15.6**
7/100	0.7389	0.7542	0.7391	0.5808	0.6295	0.6885	14.2522	13.5
8/100	0.7405	0.7520	0.7387	0.5799	0.6295	0.6881	16.1710	11.9
9/100	0.7409	0.7547	0.7400	0.5803	0.6310	0.6894	18.0893	10.6
1/10	0.7395	0.7547	0.7410	0.5803	0.6308	0.6893	19.9936	9.6
2/10	0.7408	0.7526	0.7421	0.5772	0.6274	0.6880	39.1718	4.9
3/10	0.7402	0.7526	0.7425	0.5784	0.6282	0.6884	58.3404	3.3
4/10	0.7392	0.7526	0.7425	0.5780	0.6280	0.6881	77.4257	2.5
5/10	0.7396	0.7526	0.7427	0.5780	0.6308	0.6888	96.5608	2.0
6/10	0.7403	0.7524	0.7435	0.5768	0.6287	0.6884	115.6321	1.7
7/10	0.7401	0.7521	0.7427	0.5782	0.6289	0.6884	134.7134	1.4
8/10	0.7401	0.7519	0.7425	0.5778	0.6285	0.6882	153.9539	1.2
9/10	0.7395	0.7526	0.7433	0.5784	0.6284	0.6884	172.9504	1.1
1	0.7399	0.7525	0.7431	0.5782	0.6287	0.6885	191.9450	1.0

We designed the SRIQA model by using extremely sparse random sampling method. The SRIQA samples the random input image pixels, analysing the sampled image with the free energy theory. The performance of the 28 times sampling are all shown in Tables 4, 5, 6 and 7. In these tabulations, the first column in the table represents the sampling range of the input image, where the random sampling value of "1" represents sampling of the whole picture, namely the FEDM model. The SRIQA performs optimal when sampling the whole image, but needs the longest time and has the lowest efficiency. By analyzing Tables 4, 5, 6 and 7, we found that with the reduction of sampling range, the PLCC, SROCC, and KRCC values decreased, while RMSE values increased, indicating

Table 7. RMSE of our proposed SRIQA models, conducting extremely sparse random sampling 28 times, on five image subsets distorted by various distortion types in the database of LIVE.

Random Sampling	JPEG 2000	JPEG	White Noise	Gaussian Blur	Fast-fading	Mean RMSE	Computation Time	Computation efficiency
1/1000	8.7185	9.8137	12.3390	9.2395	10.8648	10.1951	0.9886	194.2
2/1000	8.0039	10.6364	10.5883	9.0770	10.8511	9.8314	1.1830	162.3
3/1000	7.9027	9.7787	9.9642	9.0373	10.7961	**9.4958**	**1.3780**	**139.3**
4/1000	7.7540	9.8888	9.6009	9.0869	10.9845	9.4630	1.5666	122.5
5/1000	7.8530	9.4448	9.2362	9.0641	10.7379	9.2672	1.7599	109.1
6/1000	7.7031	9.8269	9.0815	9.1553	11.0605	9.3655	1.9527	98.3
7/1000	7.7033	9.5944	8.9696	9.1957	10.7483	9.2423	2.1451	89.5
8/1000	7.5926	9.8301	8.9764	9.1749	10.8890	9.2926	2.3376	82.1
9/1000	7.6933	9.7290	8.8479	9.1682	10.9325	9.2742	2.5310	75.8
1/100	7.5592	9.7544	8.8031	9.2260	10.9864	9.2658	2.7224	70.5
2/100	7.4508	9.7216	8.4239	9.2056	10.7679	9.1140	4.6436	41.3
3/100	7.4235	9.5746	8.4421	9.2356	10.8883	9.1128	6.5702	29.2
4/100	7.4157	9.6028	8.3822	9.2444	10.9299	9.1150	8.4732	22.7
5/100	7.3852	9.6226	8.3021	9.2409	10.8127	9.0727	10.3900	18.5
6/100	7.3977	9.5942	8.2867	9.2712	10.7780	**9.0656**	**12.3143**	**15.6**
7/100	7.3972	9.5497	8.2726	9.2624	10.7730	9.0510	14.2522	13.5
8/100	7.4162	9.5915	8.3105	9.2333	10.7747	9.0653	16.1710	11.9
9/100	7.3855	9.5519	8.2586	9.2702	10.7538	9.0440	18.0893	10.6
1/10	7.4061	9.5075	8.2645	9.2455	10.8932	9.0634	19.9936	9.6
2/10	7.3905	9.6044	8.1952	9.2835	10.7870	9.0521	39.1718	4.9
3/10	7.3888	9.6106	8.1791	9.2718	10.7786	9.0458	58.3404	3.3
4/10	7.4033	9.5906	8.1766	9.2705	10.7883	9.0459	77.4257	2.5
5/10	7.3912	9.6088	8.1776	9.2861	10.7806	9.0489	96.5608	2.0
6/10	7.3828	9.6036	8.1663	9.2854	10.7755	9.0427	115.6321	1.7
7/10	7.3772	9.6010	8.1654	9.2881	10.7827	9.0429	134.7134	1.4
8/10	7.3817	9.5857	8.1658	9.2866	10.7790	9.0398	153.9539	1.2
9/10	7.3853	9.6006	8.1610	9.2841	10.7811	9.0424	172.9504	1.1
1	7.3813	9.5935	8.1619	9.2857	10.7773	9.0399	191.9450	1.0

that the SRIQA performance become deteriorated. By analysing Tables 4, 5, 6 and 7, we fund the same interesting phenomenon, which has highly research value and the corresponding values have been bolded, and derived the following two conclusions: 1) In the case of slight performance loss, it greatly improves the computational efficiency, up to about 140 times of the benchmark at 3/1000 sampling value; 2) In the case of little performance loss, the computational efficiency is improved to 15.6 times of the benchmark at the 6/100 sampling value. In addition to the very encouraging results, our SRIQA has also quite well performance of lower computational complexity and better portability than the FEDM model, due to the adopted extremely sparse random sampling method, which greatly improves the work efficiency and have been broadly embedded into the majority of the current applications.

4   Applications in Other Fields

With the rapid development of image procession, the sparse reference-based IQA technology can be implemented in numerous practical applications. The first application is abnormality detection in industry, especially the smoke detection in industrial scenarios which has received an amount of attention from researchers in recent years [36–38]. The process of abnormality detection relies on images, which make the detected target visible, and can enable the staff to monitor the abnormal situation in time and then avoid bad things from happening. The second application is atmospheric pollution monitoring and early warning [39,40], the image-based method contains more visual features, thus enabling efficient and accurate air pollution monitoring. The third application field is three-dimensional vision and display technologies [41,42]. The currently popularized three-dimensional technology, making the image no longer confined to the plane of the screen [43] and making the audience has a feeling of immersion, is based the image procession technology. All in all, there are several advantages of sparse reference-based IQA technology, so it is necessary to extend this technology to different fields.

5   Conclusion

This paper has proposed a new sparse reference-based free energy metric by utilizing sparse random sampling method. The extremely sampling method has been widely used in majority of typical image/video processing systems. According to the recently presented free energy theory, the HVS abandons the uncertain part to perceive the input image in the visual neural system. We in this design adopt the maturely develop sparse random sampling technique to effectuate SRIQA. Different from traditional free energy based models, this model conducts extremely sparse random sampling on the input image and analyzing the sampled pixels instead of the whole image, which greatly improves the computational efficiency and practicability.

References

1. Bovik, A.C.: Automatic prediction of perceptual image and video quality. Proc. IEEE **101**(9), 2008–2024 (2013)
2. Sheikh, H.R., Wang, Z., Cormack, L., Bovik, A.C.: LIVE image quality assessment Database Release 2. http://live.ece.utexas.edu/research/quality
3. Wang, Z., Bovik, A.C., Sheikh, H.R., Simoncelli, E.P.: Image quality assessment: from error visibility to structural similarity. IEEE Trans. Image Process. **13**(4), 600–612 (2004)

4. Zhang, L., Zhang, L., Mou, X., Zhang, D.: FSIM: a feature similarity index for image quality assessment. IEEE Trans. Image Process. **20**(8), 2378–2386 (2011)
5. Liu, A., Lin, W., Narwaria, M.: Image quality assessment based on gradient similarity. IEEE Trans. Image Process. **21**(4), 1500–1512 (2012)
6. Wu, J., Lin, W., Shi, G., Liu, A.: Perceptual quality metric with internal generative mechanism. IEEE Trans. Image Process. **22**(1), 43–54 (2013)
7. Gu, K., Wang, S., Zhai, G., Lin, W., Yang, X., Zhang, W.: Analysis of distortion distribution for pooling in image quality prediction. IEEE Trans. Broadcast. **62**(2), 446–456 (2016)
8. Gu, K., et al.: Saliency-guided quality assessment of screen content images. IEEE Trans. Multimed. **18**(6), 1098–1110 (2016)
9. Gu, K., Li, L., Lu, H., Min, X., Lin, W.: A fast reliable image quality predictor by fusing micro- and macro-structures. IEEE Trans. Industr. Electron. **64**(5), 3903–3912 (2017)
10. Gu, K., Qiao, J., Min, X., Yue, G., Lin, W., Thalmann, D.: Evaluating quality of screen content images via structural variation analysis. IEEE Trans. Vis. Comput. Graph. **24**(10), 2689–2701 (2018)
11. Li, L., Zhou, Y., Gu, K., Lin, W., Wang, S.: Quality assessment of DIBR-synthesized images by measuring local geometric distortions and global sharpness. IEEE Trans. Multimed. **20**(4), 914–926 (2018)
12. Wang, S., Gu, K., Zeng, K., Wang, Z., Lin, W.: Objective quality assessment and perceptual compression of screen content images. IEEE Comput. Graphics Appl. **38**(1), 47–58 (2018)
13. Di Claudio, E.D., Jacovitti, G.: A detail-based method for linear full reference image quality prediction. IEEE Trans. Image Process. **27**(1), 179–193 (2018)
14. Tang, Z., Zheng, Y., Gu, K., Liao, K., Wang, W., Yu, M.: Full-reference image quality assessment by combining features in spatial and frequency domains. IEEE Trans. Broadcast. **65**(1), 138–151 (2019)
15. Min, X., Zhai, G., Gu, K., Yang, X., Guan, X.: Objective quality evaluation of dehazed images. IEEE Trans. Intell. Transp. Syst. **20**(8), 2879–2892 (2019)
16. Chen, W., Gu, K., Lin, W., Yuan, F., Cheng, E.: Statistical and structural information backed full-reference quality measure of compressed sonar images. IEEE Trans. Circ. Syst. Video Technol. **30**(2), 334–348 (2020)
17. Zhai, G., Wu, X., Yang, X., Lin, W., Zhang, W.: A psychovisual quality metric in free-energy principle. IEEE Trans. Image Process. **21**(1), 41–52 (2012)
18. Rehman, A., Wang, Z.: Reduced-reference image quality assessment by structural similarity estimation. IEEE Trans. Image Process. **21**(8), 3378–3389 (2012)
19. Gu, K., Zhai, G., Yang, X., Zhang, W.: A new reduced-reference image quality assessment using structural degradation model. In: Proceedings of IEEE International Symposium on Circuits and Systems, pp. 1095–1098, May 2013
20. Gu, K., Zhai, G., Yang, X., Zhang, W., Chen, C.W.: Automatic contrast enhancement technology with saliency preservation. IEEE Trans. Circ. Syst. Video Technol. **25**(9), 1480–1494 (2015)
21. Chen, W., Gu, K., Min, X., Yuan, F., Cheng, E., Zhang, W.: Partial-reference sonar image quality assessment for underwater transmission. IEEE Trans. Aerosp. Electron. Syst. **54**(6), 2776–2787 (2018)
22. Liu, Y., Zhai, G., Gu, K., Liu, X., Zhao, D., Gao, W.: Reduced-reference image quality assessment in free-energy principle and sparse representation. IEEE Trans. Multimed. **20**(2), 379–391 (2018)
23. Friston, K., Kilner, J., Harrison, L.: A free energy principle for the brain. J. Physiol. Paris **100**, 70–87 (2006)

24. Friston, K.: The free-energy principle: a unified brain theory? Nat. Rev. Neurosci. **11**, 127–138 (2010)
25. Gu, K., Zhai, G., Lin, W., Liu, M.: The analysis of image contrast: from quality assessment to automatic enhancement. IEEE Trans. Cybern. **46**(1), 284–297 (2016)
26. Hou, X., Harel, J., Koch, C.: Image signature: highlighting sparse salient regions. IEEE Trans. Pattern Anal. Mach. Intell. **34**(1), 194–201 (2012)
27. Knill, D.C., Pouget, A.: The Bayesian brain: the role of uncertainty in neural coding and computation. Trends Neurosci. **27**(12), 712–719 (2004)
28. Gu, K., Zhai, G., Yang, X., Zhang, W.: Using free energy principle for blind image quality assessment. IEEE Trans. Multimed. **17**(1), 50–63 (2015)
29. Gu, K., Zhou, J., Qiao, J., Zhai, G., Lin, W., Bovik, A.C.: No-reference quality assessment of screen content pictures. IEEE Trans. Image Process. **26**(8), 4005–4018 (2017)
30. Feynman, R.P.: Stastical Mechanics: A Set of Lecture, 2nd edn. Westview, Boulder (1998)
31. Sekita, I., Kurita, T., Otsu, N.: Complex autoregressive model for shape recognition. IEEE Trans. Pattern Anal. Mach. Intell. **14**(4), 489–496 (1992)
32. Nakatani, Y., Sasaki, D., Iiguni, Y., Maeda, H.: Online recognition of handwritten Hiragana characters based upon a complex autoregressive model. IEEE Trans. Pattern Anal. Mach. Intell. **21**(1), 73–76 (1999)
33. Gu, K., Zhai, G., Lin, W., Yang, X., Zhang, W.: No-reference image sharpness assessment in autoregressive parameter space. IEEE Trans. Image Process. **24**(10), 3218–3231 (2015)
34. Gu, K., Lin, W., Zhai, G., Yang, X., Zhang, W., Chen, C.W.: No-reference quality metric of contrast-distorted images based on information maximization. IEEE Trans. Cybern. **47**(12), 4559–4565 (2017)
35. VQEG: Final report from the video quality experts group on the validation of objective models of video quality assessment. http://www.vqeg.org/
36. Gu, K., Zhang, Y., Qiao, J.: Ensemble meta-learning for few-shot soot density recognition. IEEE Trans. Industr. Inf. **17**(3), 2261–2270 (2021)
37. Liu, H., Lei, F., Tong, C., Cui, C., Wu, L.: Visual smoke detection based on ensemble deep CNNs. Displays **69**, 102020 (2021)
38. Gu, K., Xia, Z., Qiao, J., Lin, W.: Deep dual-channel neural network for image-based smoke detection. IEEE Trans. Multimed. **22**(2), 311–323 (2020)
39. Gu, K., Liu, H., Xia, Z., Qiao, J., Lin, W., Thalmann, D.: $PM_{2.5}$ monitoring: use information abundance measurement and wide and deep learning. IEEE Trans. Neural Netw. Learn. Syst. **32**(10), 4278–4290 (2021)
40. Gu, K., Xia, Z., Qiao, J.: Stacked selective ensemble for $PM_{2.5}$ forecast. IEEE Trans. Instrum. Meas. **69**(3), 660–671 (2020)
41. Ye, P., Wu, X., Gao, D., Deng, S., Xu, N., Chen, J.: DP3 signal as a neuro-indictor for attentional processing of stereoscopic contents in varied depths within the 'comfort zon'. Displays **63**, 101953 (2020)
42. Gao, Z., Zhai, G., Deng, H., Yang, X.: Extended geometric models for stereoscopic 3D with vertical screen disparity. Displays **65**, 101972 (2020)
43. Sugita, N., et al.: Effect of viewing a three-dimensional movie with vertical parallax. Displays **58**, 26 (2019)
44. Min, X., Gu, K., Zhai, G., Liu, J., Yang, X., Chen, C.W.: Blind quality assessment based on pseudo-reference image. IEEE Trans. Multimed. **20**(8), 2049–2062 (2018)
45. Min, X., Zhai, G., Gu, K., Liu, Y., Yang, X.: Blind image quality estimation via distortion aggravation. IEEE Trans. Broadcast. **64**(2), 508–517 (2018)

46. Min, X., Ma, K., Gu, K., Zhai, G., Wang, Z., Lin, W.: Unified blind quality assessment of compressed natural, graphic, and screen content images. IEEE Trans. Image Process. **26**(11), 5462–5474 (2017)
47. Min, X., et al.: Quality evaluation of image dehazing methods using synthetic hazy images. IEEE Trans. Multimed. **21**(9), 2319–2333 (2019)
48. Sun, W., et al.: MC360IQA: the multi-channel CNN for blind 360-degree image quality assessment. In: IEEE International Symposium on Circuits and Systems, pp. 1–5 (2019)
49. Min, X., et al.: Screen content quality assessment: overview, benchmark, and beyond. ACM Comput. Surv. **54**(9), 1–36 (2021)

Perceptual Quality Evaluation
of Corrupted Industrial Images

Yafei Gong[1,2,3,4,5], Chenchen Peng[6], Jing Liu[1,2,3,4,5(✉)], Chengxu Zhou[1,2,3,4,5], and Hongyan Liu[1,2,3,4,5]

[1] Faculty of Information Technology, Beijing University of Technology, Beijing, China
18829523037@163.com
[2] Engineering Research Center of Intelligent Perception and Autonomous Control, Ministry of Education, Beijing, China
[3] Beijing Laboratory of Smart Environmental Protection, Beijing, China
[4] Beijing Key Laboratory of Computational Intelligence and Intelligent System, Beijing, China
[5] Beijing Artificial Intelligence Institute, Beijing, China
[6] Faculty of Science, Beijing University of Technology, Beijing, China

Abstract. In recent years, computer vision applied in industrial application scenarios has been attracting attention. A lot of work has been made to present approaches based on visual perception, ensuring the safety during the processes of industrial production. However, much less effort has been done to assess the perceptual quality of corrupted industrial images. In this paper, we construct an Industrial Scene Image Database (ISID), which contains 3000 distorted images generated through applying different levels of distortion types to each of the 50 source images. Then, the subjective experiment is carried out to gather the subjective scores in a well-controlled laboratory environment. Finally, we perform comparison experiments on ISID database to investigate the performance of some objective image quality assessment algorithms. The experimental results show that the state-of-the-art image quality assessment methods have difficulty in predicting the quality of images that contain multiple distortion types.

Keywords: Image quality assessment · Industrial image · Database · Subjective test

1 Introduction

With the explosive growth of digital images, image-based vision technology has been implemented in numerous industrial scenarios, such as smoke detection [1,2], security monitoring [3], workpiece inspection [4], and so on. In general, the automated image acquisition devices are far more accurate and efficient than humans when it comes to collecting industrial scene images [5]. In addition, the better the quality of the images collected by the device, the higher the accuracy

© Springer Nature Singapore Pte Ltd. 2022
G. Zhai et al. (Eds.): IFTC 2021, CCIS 1560, pp. 191–202, 2022.
https://doi.org/10.1007/978-981-19-2266-4_15

192 Y. Gong et al.

of the detection of various situations. However, the quality of image is inevitably distorted because of the existence of various distortions during the process of image acquisition, compression and transmission. Specifically, lossy image compression degrades the quality of image due to the presence of blurring and ringing effects; limited channel bandwidth enforces the image to discard some information in the process of image transmission, which results in degradation of image quality. Therefore, it is imperative to conduct extensive subjective and objective experiments to evaluate the perceptual quality of corrupted industrial images, further serving as a trial bed for future image enhancement technology research.

Image quality assessment (IQA) method is one of the basic techniques in image processing, which analyzes the characteristics of images to assess the degree of distortion. The results can be further applied to other areas of image processing, such as image enhancement [6,7], image compression [8] and image dehazing [9,10]. According to whether someone is involved or not, the IQA method can be distinguished into subjective evaluation approach and objective evaluation approach. The former uses the human as the observer to evaluate images, aiming to truly reflect the human visual perception [11,12]. While the latter is to construct a mathematical model that reflects the subjective perception of human eyes, and thus gives results based on numerical calculations.

The subjective assessment method is commonly considered as the ultimate quality standard, yet it has the shortcomings of being time-consuming and expensive, as well as being impractical for real-time processing systems. Thus, a large amount of researchers have dedicated themselves to explore efficient objective quality assessment algorithms. Depending on whether the information from original image is referenced or not, objective IQA approaches are further separated into three kinds, i.e., full-reference (FR) IQA method [13,14], reduced-reference (RR) IQA method [15,16], no-reference (NR) IQA method [17–21]. The FR IQA algorithm assumes that the original image signal is completely known. Then the quality of distorted image can be obtained by quantifying the difference between the original image and the distorted image. The RR IQA method only extracts part of the image information for reference. The NR IQA approach directly calculates the distorted image perceptual quality without giving a reference image.

For FR IQA metrics, traditional peak signal to noise ratio (PSNR), defined by mean square error (MSE) [22], is extensively applied in the field of image compression. However, since the PSNR sometimes correlates poorly with human visual characteristics, an increasing number of researchers have made great efforts to develop some assessment algorithms based on human perception, such as the structural similarity (SSIM) [23], visual information fidelity (VIF) [24], and visual signal-to-noise ratio (VSNR) [25], etc. It is very difficult to attain distortion-free images due to the distortion introduced by the external environment and the internal camera sensor. Therefore people prefers to use the NR IQA approach to evaluate the distorted images quality. Most of the blind IQA models, such as the NIQE [26], the NFERM [27], the ARISM [28], etc., are constructed on the basis of natural scene statistic (NSS) or human visual system (HVS).

We establish a database called Industrial Scene Image Database (ISID) by introducing different levels of distortion into 50 source images in this paper.

Then, we implement the subjective experiment on the ISID to obtain the quality scores. It is well acknowledged that the sophisticated objective IQA algorithm is close consistent with human judgments, which is robust enough for the prediction of the distortion. Therefore, to find out the performance of some objective IQA algorithms, the comparison experiments are further performed on the ISID. The experiment results indicate that the existing quality assessment algorithms are only moderately related with the subjective ratings and could not perform well in predicting the quality of distorted images.

The remaining structure of this paper is illustrated below. Section 2 gives the process of database construction and subjective experiment. Section 3 details the objective quality metric for the ISID by different FR and NR approaches and analyses on comparison experiments. In the end, general conclusion is provided in Sect. 4.

2   Subjective Quality Assessment

To make the research about quality assessment, we construct a particular image database that consists of various distorted industrial scene images.

2.1   Database Construction

Fifty distortion-free industrial scene pictures were collected at different times, in different environment and weather conditions to construct the ISID database, as shown in Fig. 1. Among them, there are 35 images with 1920×1080 pixels and another 15 images with 1080×1920 pixels. The content of the collected images mainly includes workers, workshops, assembly lines, flare, close-up shots, and so on.

To simulate the random noise, blurring, spatial shifts, and compression artifacts arising from image processing, we introduced 11 kinds of different degrees of distortion into the original images to generate distorted images. These distortions respectively are Gaussian blur, lens blur, motion blur, JPEG compression, Gaussian noise, H.264/AVC, H.265/HEVC, brightness change, darkness change, mean shift, and contrast change. Gaussian noise often occurs in the process of image acquisition, therefore it is widely used in the construction of databases. Gaussian blur, lens blur, motion blur and mean shift are introduced because industrial scenes are too complicated and need to take into account issues, such as lens shake, movement of the captured object and abnormal lens focusing. Compression coding technique can minimize the quantity of data information used to represent image data, and is widely employed in image transmission and storage. Current compression methods that are utilized to preserve the images perceptual quality mainly are JPEG compression, H.264/AVC, H.265/HEVC, etc. In addition, most block coding-based compression technology inevitably introduces block artifacts, so we chose the above techniques to create the distorted images. At last, the changes in brightness and contrast of images significantly affect people's viewing experience. In order to better explore the factors that have a

Fig. 1. Two sample photos in industry that used to construct the ISID database

considerable impact on HVS, namely contrast change, brightness change, and darkness change, we introduced them for the database construction.

Brightness change and darkness change contain three levels of distortion, ranging from undetectable distortion to high levels of impairment, while the remaining types of distortion are set to six levels. Finally, through the introduction of different types and degrees of distortion, fifty distorted images were generated from the original images, so as to establish the ISID database. Our constructed database consists of 3000 distorted images, where the distortion in the image mainly includes common noise, artifacts, and blur in the real world.

2.2 Subjective Experiment

In this section, we conducted subjective experiment on the established database to collect the image subjective quality evaluation scores.

In accordance with International Telecomminications Union (ITU) recommendation [29], the single-stimulus (SS) is adopted in our experiment. Since it is difficult to acquire the completely distortion-free images as the reference image in real applications, the SS method is recently applied to construct the image database [30]. All the test images were displayed on three 23.8-in Hp monitors with the best resolution of 2560×1440, where the above monitors can rotate to meet the requirement of two resolutions. Fifty college students, whose ages range from 20 to 26 years old, participated in our subjective experiment. They all have the normal or corrected vision. At the beginning of the subjective test, the viewing distance was set to 2 or 2.5 times of the height of screen, and the environment in which the experiments were conducted was under moderate illumination and low noise conditions. The subjective scores were collected through the MATLAB graphical user interface (GUI), which is shown in Fig. 2. Considering the huge number of pictures in our database, the GUI can switch and score images through the keyboard to improve the efficiency of experiment. The image quality score can be automatically saved in the form by clicking the *Submit* button. For test images, five image quality levels are set, including "poor", "bad", "fair", "good", "excellent", which correspond to subjective scores of 1 to 5. The lower the score, the worse the perceived quality.

Before the formal subjective experiment, all participants had understood the objective of the experiment and the procedure of test. The whole experiment consists of two parts. In the first part, we conducted a short pre-training session to instruct participants on how to score the quality of different images. The other part is the formal test, where participants rate the images using the GUI. In order to avoid unnecessary errors due to visual fatigue, each participant would take 5 min break every 30 min.

2.3 Subjective Score Processing and Analysis

To get more precise subjective scores, we would eliminate the highest and lowest scores for every image. Then, the mean opinion score (MOS) is calculated as the ground truth of image quality. For each picture, the MOS value can be calculated by the following formula:

$$MOS_j = \sum_{i=1}^{N} \frac{P_{ij}}{N} \tag{1}$$

where P_{ij} represents the score of ith participant to j^{th} image, N is the number of participants. To show the MOS values distribution clearly, we draw the MOS distribution histogram, which is shown in Fig. 3. It can be observed that the MOS values are evenly distributed in different score intervals, which means that the images in ISID database contain various types and degrees of distortion.

3 Experiment

In this section, we will further survey the performance of existing mainstream objective IQA methods to assess the ISID database's images perceptual quality.

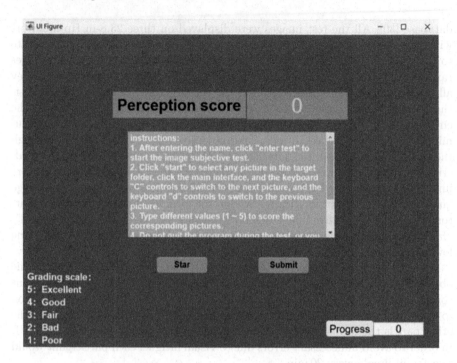

Fig. 2. Graphical user interface utilized to rate image quality

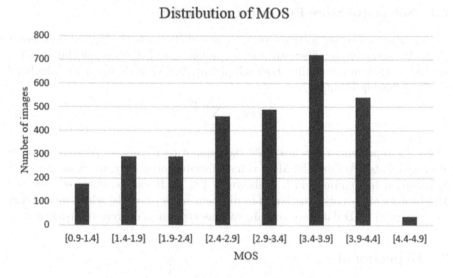

Fig. 3. The histogram distribution of MOS values

3.1 Performance Metrics

Based on the recommendation of the video quality experts group [31], this paper utilized a five-parameter monotonic logistic function to fit the prediction results of the IQA model, so as to decrease the nonlinearity of the prediction values. The above logistic function is shown as the following:

$$W(x) = \beta_1(0.5 - \frac{1}{1 + e^{\beta_2(x-\beta_3)}}) + \beta_4 x + \beta_5 \tag{2}$$

where x and W represent the subjective scores and mapping scores, respectively. When calculating performance, we firstly selected five commonly used metrics, i.e., Pearson Linear Correlation Coefficient (PLCC), Spearman Rank-Order Correlation Coefficient (SROCC), Kendall Rank Correlation Coefficient (KRCC), Root Mean-Squared Error (RMSE), and Mean Absolute Error (MAE). Among them, SROCC and KROCC are often used to measure the linear correlation between two vectors, which can assess the prediction monotonicity. PLCC estimates the linearity and consistency of objective IQA models. RMSE measures the IQA methods' prediction accuracy by calculating the error between the MOS values and the prediction results. MAE predicts the mean absolute error. The five indices mentioned above can be expressed as follows:

$$SROCC = 1 - \frac{6\sum\limits_{n=1}^{N} k_i^2}{N(N^2 - 1)} \tag{3}$$

$$PLCC = \frac{\sum\limits_{i=1}^{N}(h_i - \overline{h})(g_i - \overline{g})}{\sqrt{\frac{1}{N}\sum\limits_{i=1}^{N}(h_i - \overline{h})^2(g_i - \overline{g})^2}} \tag{4}$$

$$KRCC = \frac{N_c - N_k}{0.5N(N - 1)} \tag{5}$$

$$RMSE = \sqrt{\frac{1}{N}\sum\limits_{i=1}^{N}(g_i - h_i)^2} \tag{6}$$

$$MAE = \frac{1}{N}\sum\limits_{i=1}^{N}|g_i - h_i| \tag{7}$$

where c and k are the consistent data and the inconsistent data, respectively; g_i is the subjective quality score of the ith image; h_i is the prediction output of the objective quality evaluation model after nonlinear mapping; $\overline{h}$ and $\overline{g}$ are the average values of h and g. Among these indices, the larger the value of KRCC and PLCC, the better the predict performance; while the smaller the value of RMSE, the higher the accuracy.

Table 1. Performance comparison of fifteen state-of-the-art FR IQA models on the ISID dataset.

Metrics	PLCC	SROCC	KRCC	RMSE	MAE
MSE	0.3645	0.3512	0.2299	0.8565	0.6825
PSNR	0.3634	0.3413	0.2285	0.8569	0.6827
SSIM	0.5695	0.5701	0.4052	0.7561	0.5730
MS-SSIM	0.7115	0.6921	0.4920	0.6463	0.4959
VIF	**0.8504**	**0.8511**	**0.6535**	**0.4840**	**0.3667**
FSIM	0.6444	0.5789	0.4166	0.7034	0.5519
FSIMC	0.6502	0.5854	0.4216	0.6988	0.5483
GSI	0.5293	0.4680	0.3352	0.7804	0.6227
GMSM	0.8036	0.7858	0.5807	0.5474	0.4105
GMSD	0.8320	0.8030	0.6056	0.5103	0.3754
LTG	0.8319	0.8123	0.6105	0.5104	0.3776
VSI	0.5944	0.5356	0.3847	0.7397	0.5841
ADD-SSIM	0.7761	0.7546	0.5666	0.5800	0.4192
ADD-GSIM	0.7903	0.7668	0.5807	0.5636	0.4100
PSIM	0.8301	0.7908	0.5904	0.5129	0.3844

3.2   Comparison Experiment and Result Analysis

In this section, we selected 20 kinds of objective quality evaluation approaches to assess the images in our established database. Among them, there are 15 FR IQA algorithms, i.e., PSNR, MSE, SSIM, multi-SSIM (MS-SSIM) [32], VIF, feature similarity (FSIM) [33], FSIMC, gradient similarity index (GSI) [34], gradient magnitude similarity (GMSM), gradient magnitude similarity deviation (GMSD) [35], local-tuned-global model (LTG) [36], visual saliency induced index (VSI) [37], analysis of distribution for pooling in SSIM (ADD-SSIM) [38], ADD-GSIM, and perceptual similarity (PSIM) [39]. The remaining 5 methods are NR IQA algorithms, i.e., accelerated screen image quality evaluator (ASIQE), blind image quality measure of enhanced images (BIQME) [40], blind/referenceless image spatial quality evaluator (BRISQUE) [41], natural image quality evaluator (NIQE), and six-step blind metric (SISBLIM). The comparison experiment results of FR IQA methods and NR IQA methods are respectively shown in Table 1 and Table 2, where the one with the best performance is marked in bold.

It can be easily found that the VIF has obtained the best performance in the ISID database compared to other FR IQA algorithms. Specifically, the SROCC VALUE and PLCC value of the VIF are up to 85%. The reason for this is because the VIF simultaneously consider the NSS and the HVS to evaluate the perceptual quality of images. The GMSM, and PSIM is mainly based on the pooling strategy of standard deviation, which significantly improves the efficiency and accuracy of approaches. SSIM and its variants measure the contrast and

Table 2. Performance comparison of five state-of-the-art NR IQA models on the ISID dataset.

Metrics	PLCC	SROCC	KRCC	RMSE	MAE
ASIQE	0.5816	0.5602	0.3849	0.7482	0.6015
BIQME	0.1058	0.0673	0.0449	0.9146	0.7700
BRISQUE	0.7084	0.6965	**0.5076**	0.6492	0.5018
NIQE	0.6951	**0.7054**	0.4984	0.6613	0.5200
SISBLIM	**0.7184**	0.6540	0.4689	**0.6399**	**0.4990**

structural information loss of distorted images by a top-down method, therefore it also achieves a competitive performance. The PSNR evaluates the perceptual quality of images through the bottom-up method, but its performance is poor due to the low correlation with the HVS.

As shown in Table 2, NIQE and BRISQUE measure the deviation degree between the original image and the distorted image on the basis of the NSS model, so its SROCC value and PLCC value exceed 69%. Inspired by the free energy based brain theory and early human visual model [42–44], the SISBLIM systematically incorporates the single quality prediction of different types distortion and combined effects of various distortion, thus it outperforms other NR IQA algorithms. Through the analysis of the experiment results, it can be found that most existing IQA methods are not suitable for evaluating the perceptual quality of images that contain a large number of distortions. Therefore, it is imperative to propose a novel efficient IQA algorithm to evaluate the distorted images.

4   Conclusion

In this paper, we firstly build an image database named ISID, which is consist of 3000 distorted images that are produced by applying different types and degrees of distortion to the 50 source images. Secondly, we conduct the subjective experiment to gather the subjective score of distorted industrial images. At last, some comparison experiments are carried out on the ISID database to investigate the performance of objective IQA algorithms. The results of experiment demonstrate that most objective IQA approaches can't assess the perceptual quality of distorted images in our established database. In the future work, we will make effort to present a particular objective quality method for distorted industrial images based on the plausible modification of the well-performing SISBLIM.

References

1. Gu, K., Zhang, Y., Qiao, J.: Ensemble meta-learning for few-shot soot density recognition. IEEE Trans. Industr. Inf. **17**(3), 2261–2270 (2021)
2. Gu, K., Xia, Z., Qiao, J., Lin, W.: Deep dual-channel neural network for image-based smoke detection. IEEE Trans. Multimed. **22**(2), 311–323 (2020)
3. Li, L., Wang, G., Cormack, L., Bovik, A.C.: Efficient and secure image communication system based on compressed sensing for IoT monitoring applications. IEEE Trans. Multimed. **22**(1), 82–95 (2020)
4. de Araujo, P.R.M., Lins, R.G.: Computer vision system for workpiece referencing in three-axis machining centers. Int. J. Adv. Manuf. Technol. **106**, 2007–2020 (2020)
5. Kessler, M., Siewerdsen, J., Sonke, J.: Tu-C (SAM)-BRC-01: multimodality image acquisition, processing and display for guiding and adapting radiation therapy. Med. Phys. **38**(6), 3751 (2011)
6. Gu, K., Tao, D., Qiao, J., Lin, W.: Learning a no-reference quality assessment model of enhanced images with big data. IEEE Trans. Neural Netw. Learn. Syst. **29**(4), 1301–1313 (2018)
7. Gu, K., Zhai, G., Lin, W., Liu, M.: The analysis of image contrast: from quality assessment to automatic enhancement. IEEE Trans. Cybern. **46**(1), 284–297 (2016)
8. Min, X., Ma, K., Gu, K., Zhai, G., Wang, Z., Lin, W.: Unified blind quality assessment of compressed natural, graphic, and screen content images. IEEE Trans. Image Process. **26**(11), 5462–5474 (2017)
9. Min, X., Zhai, G., Gu, K., Yang, X., Guan, X.: Objective quality evaluation of dehazed images. IEEE Trans. Intell. Transp. Syst. **20**(8), 2879–2892 (2019)
10. Min, X., et al.: Quality evaluation of image dehazing methods using synthetic hazy images. IEEE Trans. Multimed. **21**(9), 2319–2333 (2019)
11. Gu, K., Zhai, G., Yang, X., Zhang, W.: Hybrid no-reference quality metric for singly and multiply distorted images. IEEE Trans. Broadcast. **60**(3), 555–567 (2014)
12. Gu, K., Liu, M., Zhai, G., Yang, X., Zhang, W.: Quality assessment considering viewing distance and image resolution. IEEE Trans. Broadcast. **61**(3), 520–531 (2015)
13. Gu, K., Wang, S., Zhai, G., Ma, S., Yang, X., Zhang, W.: Content-weighted mean-squared error for quality assessment of compressed images. Signal Image Video Process. **10**(5), 803–810 (2015). https://doi.org/10.1007/s11760-015-0818-9
14. Di Claudio, E.D., Jacovitti, G.: A detail-based method for linear full reference image quality prediction. IEEE Trans. Image Process. **27**(1), 179–193 (2018)
15. Gu, K., Zhai, G., Yang, X., Zhang, W.: A new reduced-reference image quality assessment using structural degradation model. In: Proceeding IEEE International Symposium on Circuits and Systems, pp. 1095–1098, May 2013
16. Liu, M., Gu, K., Zhai, G., LeCallet, P., Zhang, W.: Perceptual reduced-reference visual quality assessment for contrast alteration. IEEE Trans. Broadcast. **63**(1), 71–81 (2017)
17. Mittal, A., Moorthy, A.K., Bovik, A.C.: No-reference image quality assessment in the spatial domain. IEEE Trans. Image Process. **21**(12), 4695–4708 (2012)
18. Gu, K., Zhai, G., Yang, X., Zhang, W.: Using free energy principle for blind image quality assessment. IEEE Trans. Multimed. **17**(1), 50–63 (2015)
19. Min, X., Gu, K., Zhai, G., Liu, J., Yang, X., Chen, C.: Blind quality assessment based on pseudo-reference image. IEEE Trans. Multimed. **20**(8), 2049–2062 (2018)
20. Min, X., Zhai, G., Gu, K., Liu, Y., Yang, X.: Blind image quality estimation via distortion aggravation. IEEE Trans. Broadcast. **64**(2), 508–517 (2018)

21. Sun, W., Min, X., Zhai, G., Gu, K., Duan, H., Ma, S.: MC360IQA: a multi-channel CNN for blind 360-degree image quality assessment. IEEE J. Sel. Top. Signal Process. **14**(1), 64–77 (2020)
22. Wang, Z., Bovik, A.C.: Mean squared error: love it or leave it? A new look at signal fidelity measures. IEEE Signal Process. Mag. **26**(1), 98–117 (2009)
23. Wang, Z., Bovik, A.C., Sheikh, H.R., Simoncelli, E.P.: Image quality assessment: from error visibility to structural similarity. IEEE Trans. Image Process. **13**(4), 600–612 (2004)
24. Sheikh, H.R., Bovik, A.C.: Image information and visual quality. IEEE Trans. Image Process. **15**(2), 430–444 (2006)
25. Chandler, D.M., Hemami, S.S.: VSNR: a wavelet-based visual signal-to-noise ratio for natural images. IEEE Trans. Image Process. **16**(9), 2284–2298 (2007)
26. Mittal, A., Soundararajan, R., Bovik, A.C.: Making a completely blind image quality analyzer. IEEE Signal Process. Lett. **20**(3), 209–212 (2013)
27. Gu, K., Zhai, G., Yang, X., Zhang, W.: No-reference quality metric of contrast-distorted images based on information maximization. IEEE Trans. Cybern. **47**(12), 4559–4565 (2017)
28. Gu, K., Zhai, G., Lin, W., Yang, X., Zhang, W.: No-reference image sharpness assessment in autoregressive parameter space. IEEE Trans. Image Process. **24**(10), 3218–3231 (2015)
29. ITU: Methodology for the subjective assessment of the quality of television pictures. Recommendation, International Telecommunication Union/ITU Ratio communication Sector (2009)
30. Li, L., Zhou, Y., Lin, W., Wu, J., Zhang, X., Chen, B.: No-reference quality assessment of deblocked images. Neurocomputing **177**, 572–584 (2016)
31. Final report from the video quality experts group on the validation of objective models of video quality assessment VQEG, March 2000. http://www.vqeg.org/
32. Wang, Z., Simoncelli, E.P., Bovik, A.C.: Multiscale structural similarity for image quality assessment. In: Proceeding 37th Asilomar Conference on Signals, vol. 2, pp. 1398–1402, November 2003
33. Upadhyaya, V., Salim, M.: Compressive sensing based computed tomography Imaging: an effective approach for COVID-19 detection. Int. J. Wavelets Multiresolut. Inf. Process. **19**, 2150014 (2021)
34. Liu, A., Lin, W., Narwaria, M.: Image quality assessment based on gradient similarity. IEEE Trans. Image Process. **21**(4), 1500–1512 (2012)
35. Xue, W., Zhang, L., Mou, X., Bovik, A.C.: Gradient magnitude similarity deviation: a highly efficient perceptual image quality index. IEEE Trans. Image Process. **23**(2), 684–695 (2014)
36. Gu, K., Zhai, G., Yang, X., Zhang, W.: An efficient color image quality metric with local-tuned-global model. In: Proceeding IEEE International Conference on Image Processing, pp. 506–510, October 2014
37. Zhang, L., Shen, Y., Li, H.: VSI: a visual saliency-induced index for perceptual image quality assessment. IEEE Trans. Image Process. **23**(10), 4270–4281 (2014)
38. Appina, B., Dendi, S.V.R., Manasa, K., Channappayya, S.S., Bovik, A.C.: Study of subjective quality and objective blind quality prediction of stereoscopic videos. IEEE Trans. Image Process. **28**(10), 5027–5040 (2019)
39. Gu, K., Li, L., Lu, H., Min, X., Lin, W.: A fast reliable image quality predictor by fusing micro- and macro- structures. IEEE Trans. Industr. Inf. **64**(5), 3903–3912 (2017)

40. Gu, K., Zhou, J., Qiao, J., Zhai, G., Lin, W., Bovik, A.C.: No-reference quality assessment of screen content pictures. IEEE Trans. Image Process. **26**(8), 4005–4018 (2017)
41. Ospina-Borras, J.E., Benitez-Restrepo, H.D.: Non-reference quality assessment of infrared images reconstructed by compressive sensing. In: Proceeding of SPIE the International Society for Optical Engineering, pp. 9396 (2015)
42. Friston, K., Kilner, J., Harrison, L.: A free energy principle for the brain. J. Physiol.-Paris **100**, 70–87 (2006)
43. Friston, K.: The free-energy principle: a unified brain theory? Nat. Rev. Neurosci. **11**, 127–138 (2010)
44. Zhu, W., et al.: Multi-channel decomposition in Tandem with free-energy principle for reduced-reference image quality assessment. IEEE Trans. Multimed. **21**(9), 2334–2346 (2019)

No-Reference Image Quality Assessment Based on Image Naturalness and Semantics

Runze Hu[1(✉)], Wuzhen Shi[2], Yutao Liu[3], and Xiu Li[1]

[1] Tsinghua Shenzhen International Graduate School, Tsinghua University, Shenzhen, China
{hurunze,li.xiu}@sz.tsinghua.edu.cn
[2] College of Electronics and Information Engineering, Shenzhen University, Shenzhen, China
wzhshi@szu.edu.cn
[3] School of Computer Science and Technology, Ocean University of China, Qingdao, China

Abstract. Automatically providing feedback about the quality of natural images could be of great interest for image-driven applications. Toward this goal, this paper proposes a novel no-reference image quality metric capable of effectively evaluating the image quality without requring the information of the original image. The proposed method delivers a comprehensive analysis of the image quality through exploring its statistical natural properties and high-level semantics. Specifically, we adopt the NSS regularities based method to characterize the image naturalness, and take the semantic information of the image through the deep neural networks. The quality prediction model is then derived by SVR to analyze the relationship between these extracted features and the image quality. Experiments conducted on LIVEC and CID2013 databases manifest the effectiveness of the proposed metric as compared to existing representative image quality assessment techniques.

Keywords: Image quality assessment (IQA) · Deep neural network (DNN) · Naturalness

1 Introduction

Effectively analyzing the quality of images has become increasingly important to modern society. In the context of applications, image quality assessment (IQA) techniques are widely applied in monitoring the image quality in areas [1–3], such as image compression, video coding, and visual surveillance, etc. Hence, amongst the priorities of the research is the development of a reliable IQA technique capable of accurately and efficiently assessing the visual quality of the image. The subjective IQA method can deliver us the most reliable assessment results as it faithfully reflects the human visual perception. However, the subjective evaluation is labor-intensive and cannot be applied on the real-time systems, which makes it impractical for real-world applications. Comparatively, the objective IQA metrics that count on the mathematical models to mimic the perception of human observers are able to predict the image quality effectively. According to the accessibility of the distortion-free reference image, the objective IQA methods can be further classified into full-reference (FR), reduced-reference (RR) [4],

© Springer Nature Singapore Pte Ltd. 2022
G. Zhai et al. (Eds.): IFTC 2021, CCIS 1560, pp. 203–214, 2022.
https://doi.org/10.1007/978-981-19-2266-4_16

and no-refereence (NR) [5]. FR and RR IQA methods request either whole or partial information of the reference image which is generally not accessible in many real-world applications. Therefore, the NR IQA methods, which do not rely on the reference image, have the highest research potential.

Over the past decades, considerable works have been made to develop effective IQA methods [6]. The most representative and classical FR IQA methods are the peak signal-to-noise ratio (PSNR) and the structural similarity index (SSIM) [7] thanks to their virtues of high effectiveness and portability. In RR IQA methods, in [8], Charudatta et al. applied the discrete Fourier transform (DFT) to the wavelet-frequency co-occurrence matrix to extract partial information, including entropy, correlation and homogeneity, from the reference and distorted images. In [9], Qiang proposed a RR IQA method, in which a set of reduced-reference statistical features extracted et al. from the divisive normalization transformation (DNT) domain are compared for the distorted image and the reference image. The NR IQA method can be categorized into distortion-specific and universal methods [10, 11]. The former estimates the image quality by analyzing the degree of specific distortions, whereas the latter is not restricted to the distortion type. Yue et al. [12] proposed an effective blind quality metric to deal with the contrast-distorted images. In [13], Liu et al. estimated the degree of blurriness of the image based on the phase congruency and gradient magnitude features. In [14], Ye et al. designed a visual codebook to encode the image, in which the quality-aware features were extracted for quality evaluation. Hu et al. [15] proposed an NR IQA method to evaluate the quality of night-time images, where the low-level perceptual features were first extracted to describe the image basic properties, i.e. brightness and sharpness. The high-level semantic features are then extracted using the deep neural networks. All the extracted features are fused to generate a feature vector to be mapped to the image quality score. In [16], Li et al. deployed the general regression neural network to model the relationship between the extracted quality-aware features and the image quality score.

Although numerous existing NR IQA methods have demonstrated their effectiveness on some popular IQA databases, i.e. LIVEC, their capabilities of evaluating the quality of real-world images are still restricted. For example, the generalizability of many existing NR IQA methods is quite limited. These methods may succeed in a particular image database, yet fail to accurately evaluate the image quality on other databases. The reason for such a phenomenon may lie in that these NR IQA methods do not comprehensively analyze the distortion-related properties of the image. If an IQA method does not consider the image property that may be impacted by some distortions, it is quite difficult to deliver an accurate IQA result. Additionally, the distortions on the real-world images are rather complicated and hard to model, i.e. mixture of multiple distortions, leading to that the performance of existing NR IQA methods still remains unsatisfactory for evaluating the quality of real-world images. Therefore, it is essential to develop a more effective and reliable NR IQA method.

In this paper, we design a new NR IQA metric for authentically distorted images from two concerns, including image naturalness and semantics. Specifically, a distortion-free image possesses certain natural statistical characteristics that are related to different image contents [17]. However, the presence of distortions is capable of altering these statistical properties, leading to the image being less natural. Therefore, by measuring the deviation from these statistical properties, we can estimate the perceptual quality of the distorted image. In particular, we adopt the regularity of locally mean subtracted and contrast normalized (MSCN) coefficients [18] to describe the image naturalness. The distribution of MSCN coefficients for a natural image yields to the zero-mean generalized Gaussian distribution (GGD), while the GDD changes in the presence of distortions. Hence, we make use of the parameters that determine the distribution of MSCN coefficients to characterize the image naturalness. The semantics of an image reflects the interpretation and understanding of human beings on the image. The neglect of semantic information may lead to some inconsistent evaluation results with human subjective perception. In this work, we adopt the pre-trained deep neural networks (DNN) [19,20] to extract the semantic information from the image, which serves as high-level semantic features. Combining the extracted naturalness features with the high-level semantic features, we utilize the conventional support vector regression (SVR) method [21] to model the relationship between all the features and the subjective quality score. The entire process of the proposed NR IQA metric is illustrated in Fig. 1. From the experimental results on two authentic image databases, the proposed method demonstrates comparable performance to other mainstream IQA methods.

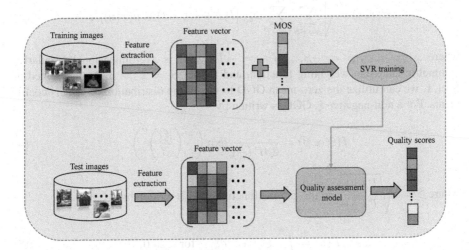

Fig. 1. Framework of the proposed NR IQA metric

2   Methodology

2.1   Characterization of the Image Naturalness

Naturalness is generally considered an essential attribute for the perceptual quality of real-world images. Intuitively, a high-quality image should look natural, and correspondingly, it possesses a high degree of statistical properties related to real-world contents. The presence of distortions in the image leads to deviations from the natural statistics. Thus, through measuring these deviations, we can estimate the perceptual quality of the image. In this work, we adopt the MSCN coefficients to characterize the image naturalness. Given an image I, the MSCN coefficients $\hat{I}$ of I are calculated as:

$$\hat{I} = \frac{I(x,y) - \mu(x,y)}{\sigma(x,y) + 1}, \tag{1}$$

where $I(x,y)$ indicates the pixel of I at the coordinate (x,y), $\mu(x,y)$ and $\sigma(x,y)$ are the mean and standard deviation of the image patch, respectively, and the center pixel of the image patch is located at $(x.y)$. The figure '1' in (1) is to prevent that the denominator closes to zero. $\mu(x,y)$ and $\sigma(x,y)$ are written by:

$$\mu(x,y) = \sum_{s=-S}^{S} \sum_{t=-T}^{T} \omega_{s,t} I(x+s, y+t) \tag{2}$$

and

$$\sigma(x,y) = \sqrt{\sum_{s=-S}^{S} \sum_{t=-T}^{T} \omega_{s,t} \left[I(x+s, y+t) - \mu(x,y) \right]^2}, \tag{3}$$

where $\omega = \{\omega_{s,t} | s = -S, ..., S, t = -T, ..., T\}$ is a 2-dimensional circularly-symmetric Gaussian weighting function, and we set $S = T = 3$. As mentioned in Sect. 1, we can utilize the zero-mean GGD to model the distribution of MSCN coefficients. For a non-negative ξ, GGD is written by

$$f(\xi; \alpha, \beta) = \frac{\alpha}{2\beta \Gamma\left(\frac{1}{\alpha}\right)} \exp\left(-\left(\frac{|\xi|}{\beta}\right)^{\alpha}\right) \tag{4}$$

where $\beta = \sigma \sqrt{\dfrac{\Gamma\left(\frac{1}{\alpha}\right)}{\Gamma\left(\frac{3}{\alpha}\right)}}$ and the gamma function $\Gamma(\cdot)$ is written by:

$$\Gamma(z) = \int_0^\infty \xi^{z-1} e^{-\xi} d\xi, \quad \text{for } z > 0. \tag{5}$$

The parameters α and β in (4) determine the distribution of MSCN coefficients, where α relates to the shape of the distribution and σ^2 in β indicates the variance. We calculate α and β using the moment-matching based method as detailed in [22]. Figure 2 shows the MSCN coefficients distributions of four images taken from the CID2013 database [23]. As observed, the quality of these images are perceptually different, and correspondingly, their MSCN coefficients distributions differ from each other.

2.2 Characterization of the Image Semantics

Apart from the naturalness of the image that demonstrates high potentiality in IQA, the high-level semantics is also considerably indicative to the image quality. Lacking

Fig. 2. The distributions of MSCN coefficients of four images from the CID2013 database

the analysis of the image semantics can result in inconsistent quality prediction with the human subjective perception. Therefore, the proposed method further exploits the semantic features of the image.

As indicated by the research of neuroscience [24,25], human beings perceive an image following two processes, which are recognizing and interpreting. The structural information, such as color, brightness and lines will be first perceived for object identification. After that, more complex spatial information related to the concept of objects, i.e., contour and regional shape, is obtained. By integrating the perceived structural and spatial semantic information, human brain is able to interpret the content of the image. However, the distortions not only degrade the quality of visual content, but also hinder the acquisition of high-level semantics. For example, the blurriness on the image edges and texture prevent extracting the structural semantics of the image. Hence, the high-level semantics can be considered an effective indicator of image quality. Here, we adopt the deep convolutional neural network (DCNN) model, which is originally trained on the ImageNet, to obtain the high-level semantics of the image. The DCNN behaves similarly to the aforementioned human visual process, in which it learns the semantic information of an image through cascading a number of network layers, such as the convolutional and pooling layers, and accordingly, the image semantic features can be obtained in the fully connected layers of the CNN.

In particular, given an image I, we feed its central patch P_o into the pretrained SqueezeNet [26] to extract the semantic features, denoted by:

$$F = D\left(P_o, l_o; \boldsymbol{W}\right), \tag{6}$$

where D refers to the DCNN model, l_o indicates the layer for extracting the semantic features, and $\boldsymbol{W}$ is the weights of the DCNN model. In implementation, we take the 1000-dimension outputs of the 'global avgpool' layer of the SqueezeNet as the high-level semantic information of the image for further quality evaluation. The procedure of the extraction of high-level semantic features is illustrated in Fig. 3.

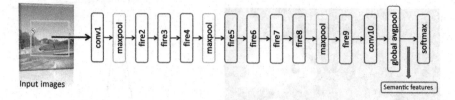

Input images

Semantic features

Fig. 3. Extraction of the high-level semantic features of images using the SqueezeNet.

2.3 Quality Evaluation

After obtaining all the features that are highly associated with the image quality, we adopt the SVR method to train the quality assessment to map from the feature space to the image quality score [27]. Specifically, we first integrate the naturalness features with the semantic features to produce a feature vector $\boldsymbol{\xi}$. Then the training data are generated by pairing the feature vector with the corresponding subjective MOS value, as in $\{(\boldsymbol{\xi}_1, M_1), (\boldsymbol{\xi}_2, M_2), \ldots, (\boldsymbol{\xi}_N, M_N)\}$, where $\boldsymbol{\xi}_n$ contains the features extracted from the n-th image for $n = 1, 2, \ldots, N$. The quality prediction model can be formulated as

$$M_n \approx Y(\boldsymbol{\xi}_n) = \langle \boldsymbol{a}, \boldsymbol{\xi}_n \rangle + b, \tag{7}$$

where $\langle \cdot \rangle$ indicates the inner product, $\boldsymbol{a}$ is the vector consisting of N coefficients of $\boldsymbol{\xi}_n$, and b is regarded as bias. We aim at solving $\boldsymbol{a}$ and b so that the difference between M_n and $Y(\boldsymbol{\xi}_n)$ reaches minimum. Toward this goal, we introduce two slack variables of ζ and ζ^*. $\boldsymbol{a}$ and b can be obtained by:

$$\min \frac{1}{2}||\boldsymbol{a}||^2 + C \left(\sum_{n=1}^{N} \zeta_n + \sum_{n=1}^{N} \zeta_n^* \right),$$
$$\text{s.t.} \ \langle \boldsymbol{a}, \boldsymbol{\xi}_n \rangle + b - M_n \leq \epsilon + \zeta_n \tag{8}$$
$$M_n - \langle \boldsymbol{a}, \boldsymbol{\xi}_n \rangle - b \leq \epsilon + \zeta_n^*$$
$$\zeta_n, \zeta_n^* \geq 0,$$

where C is a constant. Details of the derivation of SVR can be referred to [28].

3 Experiment Validation and Discussion

3.1 Performance Evaluation Protocols

We apply the proposed method on two classical databases to validate its prediction performance, which include the LIVEC [29] and CID2013 [23] databases. Both databases consist of authentically distorted images. In order to comprehensively evaluate the performance of the proposed method, we follow the suggestion from VQEG [30] to derive a nonlinear regression model of a five-parameter logistic function as:

$$M(Y) = \beta_1 \left(\frac{1}{2} - \frac{1}{1 + \exp\left(\beta_2 \cdot (Y - \beta_3)\right)} \right) + \beta_4 \cdot Y + \beta_5, \tag{9}$$

where M and Y indicate the subject MOS value and the predicted score, respectively. $\beta_1, ..., \beta_5$ are the fitted parameters. Four commonly used mathematical measures are adopted, i.e., the Pearsons linear correlation coefficient (PLCC), Spearman Rank order Correlation coefficient (SRCC), Kendalls rank correlation coefficient (KRCC) and root mean square error (RMSE), where SRCC and KRCC measure the rank correlation between M and Y. PLCC quantifies the linear correlation between M and Y. The error of the prediction of the proposed method can be quantified by RMSE. The closer the absolute value of these correlation coefficients (SRCC, KRCC, PLCC) is to 1 and the RMSE is to 0, the better performance the IQA method has.

3.2 Performance Comparison

We examine the performance of the proposed method through comparing it with five state-of-the-art NR IQA techniques, which includes DBCNN [31], NFERM [32], MEON [33], BRISQUE [34] and BMPRI [35]. All the methods yield to the same experimental settings, where each database was randomly split into training and test sets. The training set contains 80% images of the database which will be utilised to train the model, and the test set has the remaining 20% images for the purpose of model evaluation. We conduct the experimental process for 1000 times to produce 1000 evaluation results of SRCC, KRCC, PLCC and RMSE in order to minimize the influence of bias which is arisen from the randomness of data sampling. We take the average of the 1000 evaluation results and report it in Table 1, where the highest performance result on each evaluation index is highlighted with boldface.

In Table 1, we can clearly observe that the proposed method presents the best performance on these two databases, which strongly evidences the superiority and effectiveness of the proposed method. The learning-based method, such as the DBCNN, achieves relatively better performance, which implies the high-level perceptual information of image is an essential factor for the image quality evaluation. Comparatively, the method that only considers a limited number of image statistical properties, i.e. BRISQUE, is unable to deliver a satisfactory prediction performance.

3.3 Discussion

Ablation Study
The proposed method evaluates the image quality based on the two types of features, including the naturalness and semantics of the image. It is worth examining the individual contribution of each type of features in quality evaluation. If some features are insignificant, we can drop these features to improve the efficiency of the method. Toward this end, we derive the quality model for each type of features and evaluate its performance on both of the LIVEC and CID2013 databases. The same experimental procedures detailed in Sect. 3.2 were conducted. Experimental results with respect to SRCC, KRCC, PLCC and RMSE are clearly reported in Table 2. It is observed that both naturalness and high-level semantic features achieve moderate prediction performance as compared to the proposed method, which clearly demonstrates the importance

Table 1. Prediction performance in terms of SRCC, KRCC, PLCC, and RMSE on LIVEC and CID2013 databases. The highest performance on each index is emphasized with boldface.

Database	Index	DBCNN	NFERM	MEON	BRISQUE	BMPRI	Proposed
LIVEC	SRCC	0.6116	0.5181	0.3683	0.5228	0.4595	**0.7191**
	KRCC	0.4333	0.3548	0.2496	0.3639	0.3191	**0.5048**
	PLCC	0.6435	0.5493	0.4561	0.5610	0.5092	**0.7223**
	RMSE	15.4275	16.8604	17.9278	16.6950	17.3568	**13.9364**
CID2013	SRCC	0.7533	0.7079	0.3757	0.7353	0.6507	**0.8126**
	KRCC	0.5550	0.5234	0.2537	0.5453	0.4770	**0.6419**
	PLCC	0.7879	0.7179	0.4186	0.7375	0.6798	**0.8301**
	RMSE	13.8119	15.6191	20.4055	15.1526	16.4498	**11.2110**

Table 2. Performance evaluation of each type of features in the proposed method on LIVEC and CID2013 Databases.

Feature type	LIVEC				CID2013			
	SRCC	KRCC	PLCC	RMSE	SRCC	KRCC	PLCC	RMSE
Naturalness	0.3938	0.2726	0.4500	18.0117	0.4730	0.3393	0.5203	19.1724
High-level semantics	0.6215	0.4464	0.6433	14.6258	0.7509	0.5693	0.7447	14.9571
Proposed	0.7191	0.5048	0.7223	13.9364	0.8126	0.6419	0.8301	11.2110

of these two types of features in quality evaluation. What's more, the high-level semantic features deliver relative better performance than the naturalness, which indicates the high-level semantic features have a higher contribution to the proposed method than that from naturalness features. At last, the proposed method earns the best prediction performance, meaning that these two types of features play complementary roles in quality evaluation.

Generlization Capability Validation
The generalization capability is essential to the success of an NR IQA method as the real world is considerably complicated and models can easily encounter situations that are not learned from the training data [36]. An NR IQA model with effective generalization capability is always desired. Thus, we further assess the generalization capability of the proposed NR IQA method using the cross-database validation strategy. Specifically, we adopt the NR IQA method in Table 1 to build a quality prediction model on one image database and test this trained model on the other database. The performance of the generalization capability of the six NR IQA methods are reported in Table 3, where the best performance result is highlighted boldface.

Table 3. Generlization capability validation evaluated by SRCC, KRCC, PLCC and RMSE on LIVEC and CID2013 databases. The highest performance on each index is highlighted with bold-face.

Database	Index	DBCNN	NFERM	MEON	BRISQUE	BMPRI	Proposed
LIVEC (Trained on CID2013)	SRCC	0.4060	0.4054	0.2435	0.3816	0.3123	**0.4323**
	KRCC	0.2768	0.2793	0.1613	0.2624	0.2165	**0.2831**
	PLCC	0.4410	0.4574	0.2938	0.4348	0.3585	**0.4806**
	RMSE	18.2164	18.0484	19.4009	18.2774	18.9471	**17.9648**
CID2013 (Trained on LIVEC)	SRCC	0.6567	0.6515	0.3466	0.5806	0.5074	**0.6625**
	KRCC	0.4638	0.4601	0.2295	0.4189	0.3470	**0.4713**
	PLCC	0.6978	0.6470	0.3540	0.5708	0.5614	**0.7096**
	RMSE	16.2175	17.2630	21.1744	18.5903	18.7357	**15.9226**

From Table 3, we can observe that the performance of all these NR IQA methods has declined to a certain extent. Such a phenomenon is reasonable since there is a certain difference in the distribution between these two databases. When the test image is out of the distribution of the database that is initially adopted to train the model, the predicted quality score from this model could be uncertain, leading to the performance degradation of the model. This problem exists in all the supervised NR IQA methods that require the subjective MOS values to train the model. We can alleviate the problem by increasing the quantity and diversity of the training data [37,38]. In addition, it is observed that the performance of these NR IQA methods on the LIVEC database (trained on the CID2013) declines notably than that on the CID3013 database (trained on the LIVEC). This can be attributed to that the image quantity of CID2013 is less than the LIVEC. For supervised methods, in general, the more training data we provide, the better performance of the model has. Moreover, it is also observed from Table 3 that the proposed NR IQA method demonstrates the highest generalization capability among these NR IQA methods.

Computational Efficiency

The prediction accuracy of the proposed method has been analyzed comprehensively. We at last examine the computational efficiency of the proposed method, which is also an essential factor for practice [39,40]. An computationally-efficient IQA method is always desired as it potentially facilitates the functionality of real-time systems. In this paper, we count on the running time to quantify the efficiency of the proposed method. In particular, given an input image, we count the running time of the proposed method on the entire process of quality prediction of the image. The experiments were carried out on Matlab R2019b and our computer was configured with a 3.0 GHz Intel Core i5-9500 CPU and 8G RAM.

The experimental results are reported in Table 4. As observed, the proposed method achieves a comparable efficiency performance to other mainstream IQA methods, and its running time is less than one second, which shows great potential in practical applications. Though some IQA method, i.e. Brisque, is more efficient than the proposed method, its prediction accuracy remains unsatisfactory. There is always a trade-off between accuracy and computational efficiency. Our future work will focus on the improvement of the efficiency of the proposed method, while maintaining a high prediction accuracy. For example, we will explore more effective methods to characterize the image naturalness and seek some alternatives to the SVR method to improve the training process of the quality prediction model.

Table 4. Running time of NR IQA methods measured in seconds

DBCNN	NFERM	MEON	BRISQUE	BMPRI	Proposed
0.87	16.46	1.13	0.15	0.93	0.91

4 Conclusion

This paper tackles the challenge of no-reference quality assessment for authentically distorted images and hereby proposes an effective quality metric under the exploration of image naturalness and high-level semantics. In particular, the proposed method adopts MSCN coefficients to characterize the image naturalness and make use of the pre-trained deep convolutional neural networks to obtain semantic information of the image. These extracted perceptual features are then mapped to a single quality score of the image through the SVR method. Extensive experiments are carried out to validate the effectiveness of the proposed method in terms of prediction accuracy, generalization capability, and computational efficiency. The experimental results show the comparable performance of the proposed method to the mainstream NR IQA methods and also demonstrate its capability in practical applications.

Acknowledgments. This work was supported in part by the National Science Foundation of China under Grant 62101346, in part by the Guangdong Basic and Applied Basic Research Foundation under Grant 2021A1515011702 and in part by the Stable Support Plan for Shenzhen Higher Education Institutions under Grant 20200812104316001.

References

1. Liu, Y., et al.: Unsupervised blind image quality evaluation via statistical measurements of structure, naturalness, and perception. IEEE Trans. Circ. Syst. Video Technol. 30(4), 929–943 (2020)
2. Hu, R., Yang, R., Liu, Y., Li, X.: Simulation and mitigation of the wrap-around artifact in the MRI image. Front. Comput. Neurosci. 89 (2021)
3. Liu, Y., Gu, K., Wang, S., Zhao, D., Gao, W.: Blind quality assessment of camera images based on low-level and high-level statistical features. IEEE Trans. Multimed. 21(1), 135–146 (2019)
4. Liu, Y., Zhai, G., Gu, K., Liu, X., Zhao, D., Gao, W.: Reduced-reference image quality assessment in free-energy principle and sparse representation. IEEE Trans. Multimed. 20(2), 379–391 (2018)

5. Liu, Y., Gu, K., Li, X., Zhang, Y.: Blind image quality assessment by natural scene statistics and perceptual characteristics. ACM Trans. Multimed. Comput. Commun. Appl. (TOMM) 16(3), 1–91 (2020)
6. Zhai, G., Min, X.: Perceptual image quality assessment: a survey. Sci. China Inf. Sci. 63(11), 1–52 (2020). https://doi.org/10.1007/s11432-019-2757-1
7. Wang, Z., Bovik, A.C., Sheikh, H.R., Simoncelli, E.P.: Image quality assessment: from error visibility to structural similarity. IEEE Trans. Image Process. 13(4), 600–612 (2004)
8. Kulkarni, C.V., Dandawate, Y.H.: Reduced reference image quality assessment using wavelet coefficient co-occurrence matrix. Int. J. Eng. Emerg. Technol. (2021)
9. Li, Q., Wang, Z.: Reduced-reference image quality assessment using divisive normalization-based image representation. IEEE J. Sel. Top. Signal Process. 3(2), 202–211 (2009)
10. Liu, Y., Li, X.: No-reference quality assessment for contrast-distorted images. IEEE Access 8, 84 105–84 115 (2020)
11. Liu, Y., Fan, X., Gao, X., Liu, Y., Zhao, D.: Motion vector refinement for frame rate up conversion on 3d video. In: 2013 Visual Communications and Image Processing (VCIP), pp. 1–6. IEEE (2013)
12. Yue, G., Hou, C., Zhou, T., Zhang, X.: Effective and efficient blind quality evaluator for contrast distorted images. IEEE Trans. Instrum. Meas. 68(8), 2733–2741 (2019)
13. Liu, Y., Gu, K., Zhai, G., Liu, X., Zhao, D., Gao, W.: Quality assessment for real out-of-focus blurred images. J. Vis. Commun. Image Represent. 46, 70–80 (2017)
14. Ye, P., Doermann, D.: No-reference image quality assessment using visual codebooks. IEEE Trans. Image Process. 21(7), 3129–3138 (2012)
15. Hu, R., Liu, Y., Wang, Z., Li, X.: Blind quality assessment of night-time image. Displays 69, 102045 (2021)
16. Li, C., Bovik, A.C., Wu, X.: Blind image quality assessment using a general regression neural network. IEEE Trans. Neural Netw. 22(5), 793–799 (2011)
17. Moorthy, A.K., Bovik, A.C.: Blind image quality assessment: From natural scene statistics to perceptual quality. IEEE Trans. Image Process. 20(12), 3350–3364 (2011)
18. Mittal, A., Soundararajan, R., Bovik, A.C.: Making a "completely blind" image quality analyzer. IEEE Signal Process. Lett. 20(3), 209–212 (2013)
19. Hu, R., Monebhurrun, V., Himeno, R., Yokota, H., Costen, F.: A general framework for building surrogate models for uncertainty quantification in computational electromagnetics. IEEE Trans. Antennas Propag. 1 (2021)
20. Gu, K., Xia, Z., Qiao, J., Lin, W.: Deep dual-channel neural network for image-based smoke detection. IEEE Trans. Multimed. 22, 311–323 (2019)
21. Hu, R., Monebhurrun, V., Himeno, R., Yokota, H., Costen, F.: A statistical parsimony method for uncertainty quantification of FDTD computation based on the PCA and ridge regression. IEEE Trans. Antennas Propag. 67(7), 4726–4737 (2019)
22. Sharifi, K., Leon-Garcia, A.: Estimation of shape parameter for generalized gaussian distributions in subband decompositions of video. IEEE Trans. Circ. Syst. Video Technol. 5(1), 52–56 (1995)
23. Virtanen, T., Nuutinen, M., Vaahteranoksa, M., Oittinen, P., Häkkinen, J.: CID2013: a database for evaluating no-reference image quality assessment algorithms. IEEE Trans. Image Process. 24(1), 390–402 (2015)
24. Jiang, Q., Shao, F., Lin, W., Jiang, G.: Learning sparse representation for objective image retargeting quality assessment. IEEE Trans. Cybern. 48(4), 1276–1289 (2017)
25. Wu, J., Zeng, J., Dong, W., Shi, G., Lin, W.: Blind image quality assessment with hierarchy: degradation from local structure to deep semantics. J. Vis. Commun. Image Represent. 58, 353–362 (2019)

26. Iandola, F.N., Moskewicz, M.W., Ashraf, K., Han, S., Dally, W.J., Keutzer, K.: SqueezeNet: AlexNet-level accuracy with 50x fewer parameters and <1mb model size. CoRR, vol. abs/1602.07360 (2016). http://arxiv.org/abs/1602.07360
27. Hu, R., Monebhurrun, V., Himeno, R., Yokota, H., Costen, F.: An adaptive least angle regression method for uncertainty quantification in FDTD computation. IEEE Trans. Antennas Propag. 66(12), 7188–7197 (2018)
28. Burges, C.J.C.: A tutorial on support vector machines for pattern recognition. Data Min. Knowl. Discov. 2(2), 121–167 (1998)
29. Ghadiyaram, D., Bovik, A.C.: Massive online crowdsourced study of subjective and objective picture quality. IEEE Trans. Image Process. 25(1), 372–387 (2016)
30. Rohaly, A.M., Libert, J., Corriveau, P., Webster, A., et al.: Final report from the video quality experts group on the validation of objective models of video quality assessment. ITU-T Standards Contribution COM, pp. 9–80 (2000)
31. Zhang, W., Ma, K., Yan, J., Deng, D., Wang, Z.: Blind image quality assessment using a deep bilinear convolutional neural network. IEEE Trans. Circ. Syst. Video Technol. 30(1), 36–47 (2020)
32. Gu, K., Zhai, G., Yang, X., Zhang, W.: Using free energy principle for blind image quality assessment. IEEE Trans. Multimed. 17(1), 50–63 (2015)
33. Ma, K., Liu, W., Zhang, K., Duanmu, Z., Wang, Z., Zuo, W.: End-to-end blind image quality assessment using deep neural networks. IEEE Trans. Image Process. 27(3), 1202–1213 (2017)
34. Mittal, A., Moorthy, A.K., Bovik, A.C.: No-reference image quality assessment in the spatial domain. IEEE Trans. Image Process. 21(12), 4695–4708 (2012)
35. Min, X., Gu, K., Zhai, G., Liu, J., Yang, X., Chen, C.W.: Blind quality assessment based on pseudo reference image. IEEE Trans. Multimed. 1 (2017)
36. Zhai, G., Zhu, Y., Min, X.: Comparative perceptual assessment of visual signals using free energy features. IEEE Trans. Multimed. 23, 3700–3713 (2020)
37. Min, X., Ma, K., Gu, K., Zhai, G., Wang, Z., Lin, W.: Unified blind quality assessment of compressed natural, graphic, and screen content images. IEEE Trans. Image Process. 26(11), 5462–5474 (2017)
38. Min, X., Zhou, J., Zhai, G., Le Callet, P., Yang, X., Guan, X.: A metric for light field reconstruction, compression, and display quality evaluation. IEEE Trans. Image Process. 29, 3790–3804 (2020)
39. Min, X., et al.: Quality evaluation of image dehazing methods using synthetic hazy images. IEEE Trans. Multimed. 21(9), 2319–2333 (2019)
40. Zhang, J., et al.: HazDesNet: an end-to-end network for haze density prediction. IEEE Trans. Intell. Transp. Syst. (2020)

Reduced Reference Quality Assessment of Screen Content Images Rooted in Primitive Based Free-Energy Theory

Zhaolin Wan[1]([✉]), Xiguang Hao[2], Xiao Yan[2], Yutao Liu[3], Ke Gu[4],
and Lai-Kuan Wong[5]

[1] College of Artificial Intelligence, Dalian Maritime University, Dalian, China
zlwan@dlmu.edu.cn
[2] School of Information Science and Technology, Dalian Maritime University,
Dalian, China
[3] School of Computer Science and Technology, Ocean University of China,
Qingdao, China
[4] Faculty of Information Technology, Beijing University of Technology,
Beijing, China
[5] Faculty of Computing and Informatics, Multimedia University,
Persiaran Multimedia, Cyberjaya, Malaysia

Abstract. With the growing popularity of portable electronic devices, such as portable computer and cellular phone, a wide variety of digital screen content images (SCIs) have drastically invaded into our daily lives. Unlike natural scene images, SCIs are typically composed of graphic and textual images, with simpler shapes, and a larger frequency of thin lines, which may lead to different viewing experience. Therefore, an accurate quality metric for SCIs which could take into account its special properties is of particular interest. In this paper, we propose a novel reduced-reference method for assessing the perceptual quality of SCIs. Specifically, the principle of free energy models the perception and understanding of images as an active reasoning process, in which the brain attempts to explain the visual scene with an internal generative model. Sparse primitive cues are explored to model the human perception of the visual scene taking account of the unique properties of SCIs and the structure of primitives (atoms in the dictionary). The difference of the prediction discrepancies between the pristine and distorted images is defined as a measurement of the image quality. Experimental results show the effectiveness of the proposed metric and it performs favorably against state-of-the-arts on the benchmark screen image quality assessment database.

Keywords: Screen content image · Image quality assessment · Reduced-reference · Free-energy theory · Sparse primitive

© Springer Nature Singapore Pte Ltd. 2022
G. Zhai et al. (Eds.): IFTC 2021, CCIS 1560, pp. 215–226, 2022.
https://doi.org/10.1007/978-981-19-2266-4_17

1   Introduction

As its name implies, screen content images (SCIs) are the images which are shown on the display screens of computers, smart phones and some other electronic devices [1]. With the rapid development of electronic equipment, the amount of screen content is dramatically increasing. Meanwhile, Web conferencing, remote education, shared screen collaboration, etc., have drawn more and more attention in recent years [2]. Therefore, it is necessary to study a new processing strategy specifically for screen contents. In order to save resources and reduce consumption, SCIs are inevitably affected by various distortions during processing, which will lower the visual quality. As SCIs have different characteristics compared with natural scene images, there is an urgent need to explore new theories and techniques to effectively measure the quality of SCIs besides the traditional image quality assessment (IQA) methods [1]. However, the research of SCIs quality assessment is still quite limited so far.

Over the past decades, researchers have committed themselves to develop a large number of objective metrics for natural image quality assessment, including full-reference (FR) [3–10], reduced-reference (RR) [11–17] and no-reference (NR) [18–20], according to the accessibility of reference images. Among all FR IQA methods, PSNR and SSIM [3] are most widely used ones. PSNR measures the image quality by the difference of pixels, while SSIM estimates the quality of the distorted image by comparing the luminance, contrast and structural information. Zhang et al. [4] proposed an image quality evaluation method based on feature similarity, which takes phase consistency as the main feature and image gradient as an auxiliary feature. Liu et al. [5] proposed a quality evaluation method which calculates the gradient similarity of luminance and contrast between the original image and the distorted image. In [8], the authors proposed the Visual Signal-to-Noise Ratio (VSNR) method, which combines a low-level visual model based on wavelet decomposition and how the human visual system adaptively selects different spatial frequencies.

In most applications, the pristine image is not always accessible, then we can make use of only a fraction of information from the pristine image for quality evaluation, which is called RR approach. Rehman and Wang et al. [13] proposed RR-SSIM by extracting statistical features from divisive normalization transform (DNT) domain. In [14], the image quality was evaluated by the entropy of wavelet coefficients between two images. In [16], the QFTB metric measured the image quality using the phase and magnitude. Compared with the FR IQA methods that have been extensively researched, there are relatively few studies on RR IQA methods.

As an indirect translation of retinal information, vision works as an active process of the brain, which involves complicated psychological inference [21]. The free energy theory assumes that the human brain implements recognitive process, which is based on an internal generative mechanism (i.e. making use of a constructive model to predict visual signals). However, the real input and its prediction model of the brain are usually not identical, which may cause "surprise" for human perception. The discrepancy gap was closely related to the visual quality [22]. Motivated by the theory, Zhai *et al.* [22] proposed FEDM to predict the psychovisual quality, which leverages the free energy principle and the internal generative prediction is simulated by autoregressive (AR) model.

An ideal descriptive model should predict the visual signal better and make the free energy ("surprise") lower [22]. This is in accord with the Bayesian inference [23], that our brain works driven by uncertainties according to the optimal rules. As for the model which can best describe the visual signal, it should simulate the perceptual characteristics of human brain. The receptive fields of the brain are spatially localized, directional and bandpass, which can be simulated by sparse representation [24]. When neurons encode visual information at any given time point, only a small number of neurons are active, and most neurons are inhibited [25], which is also in line with the mechanism of sparse representation [26]. Therefore, we adopt sparse representation as the internal generative model of the brain for the purpose of image quality evaluation.

Based on the above analyses, we propose a novel RR method for assessing the perceptual quality of SCIs, which is rooted in primitive based free-energy theory. Since there are a variety of contents, such as natural images, icons, texts, buttons and graphics in SCIs, we adopt the traditional DCT dictionary for sparse representation, which can describe the textual and pictorial screen contents better. Sparse representation is first used as the internal generative model to predict the pristine and distorted images. Then the entropies between the distance of predictions for the pristine and distorted images are calculated based on the free energy principle. At last, the difference of the entropies between the pristine and distorted images is used as quality score.

2   The Proposed RR IQA Model for SCI

In this section, we will detail the proposed metric from three aspects: the free-energy principle, the primitive-based sparse representation, and the perceptual quality index. The framework is illustrated in Fig. 1.

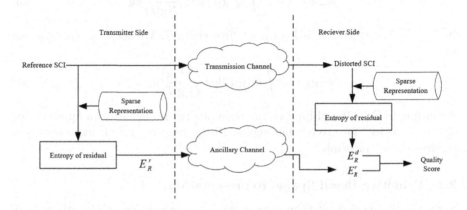

Fig. 1. The framework of the proposed RR IQA metric for SCI.

2.1 Free-Energy Principle

The free-energy principle suggests that the brain will reconstruct the received visual signal, seek the explanation of the most meaningful part, and discard the residual uncertain part. The reconstruction process is a probabilistic model in essence, including a similar item and a prior item. The visual perception infers the similar item based on the posterior probability of input signals. Because of the limited capability of the generative model, there will be a gap between the actual visual signal and the perceptual prediction made by the human brain (known as "surprise"). The discrepancy is correlated with the perception of visual signals by human brain, which can be used to measure image quality effectively.

For visual perception, the parameterized generative model $\mathcal{G}$ predicts input information by adjusting parameter $\mathbf{g}$. For image I, we use the term of $-\log P(I)$ to define its "surprise":

$$-\log P(I) = -\log \int P(I, \mathbf{g}) d\mathbf{g}. \tag{1}$$

Here, $P(I, \mathbf{g})$ represents the joint distribution of the model vector $\mathbf{g}$. Multiplying both the denominator and numerator in Eq. (1) by $Q(\mathbf{g}|I)$ at the same time, it could be rewritten as follows:

$$-\log P(I) = -\log \int Q(\mathbf{g}|I) \frac{P(I, \mathbf{g})}{Q(\mathbf{g}|I)} d\mathbf{g}, \tag{2}$$

where $Q(\mathbf{g}|I)$ is the auxiliary posterior probability distribution of the parameters corresponding to a given image, which can be considered as approximation of the true posterior of the parameters. When perceiving the input image I or adjusting the parameter g to look for the best solution, it aims to make the true posterior $P(\mathbf{g}|I)$ and its approximation $Q(\mathbf{g}|I)$ to be close. According to Jensen's inequality, Eq. (2) can be further translated into:

$$-\log P(I) \leq -\int Q(\mathbf{g}|I) \log \frac{P(I, \mathbf{g})}{Q(\mathbf{g}|I)} d\mathbf{g}. \tag{3}$$

In Eq. (3), the right side is known as "free energy". We use $F(\mathbf{g})$ to represent it:

$$F(\mathbf{g}) = -\int Q(\mathbf{g}|I) \log \frac{P(I, \mathbf{g})}{Q(\mathbf{g}|I)} d\mathbf{g}. \tag{4}$$

According to Eq. (3) and Eq. (4), the term of $F(\mathbf{g})$ is obviously an upper bound of the "surprise" for given input signal. Please refer to [22] for more details of the free energy principle.

2.2 Primitive-Based Sparse Representation

Sparse coding is derived from computational neuroscience, which attempts to find a concise representation of visual stimuli. It assumes that an image can be effectively represented by the combination of a few basis functions, and the combination of basis functions constitutes a dictionary. The dictionary needs to be adaptive to the image content and represent the internal structure of the image [27]. Specifically, for the input signal $x(x \in \mathbb{R}^n)$, it can be represented by dictionary $D(D \in \mathbb{R}^{n \times k})$ and the representation coefficient vector $\alpha(\alpha \in \mathbb{R}^k)$ satisfying $x \approx D\alpha$ and $\|x - D\alpha\|_2 \leq \epsilon$, where $\|\cdot\|_2$ is ℓ_2 norm and ϵ is the error accuracy. Typically, it is assumed that the dictionary D is redundant for the signal x, that is $k > n$.

Here, the sparse model can be regarded as the internal generative model of human brain. Compared with AR model, sparse representation is performed by image patch, not pixel, which is more efficient and reasonable and the time complexity can be significantly reduced. One pixel and its adjacent pixels in local region are self-similar. Many of the important forms of structure require higher-order than pixel statistics to characterize [28]. The visual primitives obtained through sparse representation can be regarded as the basic elements of perception, which contain a certain amount of structure information. Sparse coding based on structural primitives can reduce statistical higher-order dependencies of the representation to achieve efficient coding [29]. Furthermore, sparse representation has been proved to be consistent with the information representation of the primary visual cortex, and has direct physiological significance. Therefore, we use sparse representation as the internal generative model for image quality evaluation.

The dictionary for sparse representation can be a fixed dictionary, or one trained from certain signals. In general, for natural images, the dictionary trained over the image patches has better representation capacity. But SCIs are quite different from natural scene images, they always contain a variety of contents, such as natural images, icons, texts, buttons and graphics. These different contents have different structures, which is extremely challenging to be represented by one universal dictionary trained from some SCIs. Particularly, typical screen contents, such as website and text have a large number of letters. Most of the primitives in the dictionary trained from these types of SCIs carry certain structural information, which look like part of the letters, as shown in Fig. 2. These primitives cannot achieve perfect representation for other contents, such as graphics and natural images. Therefore, we adopt the traditional DCT dictionary, which is universal for all the parts of SCIs. Besides, SCIs are with larger area of smooth regions, which can be well reconstructed by only the DC primitive. In addition, the DCT dictionary is in no need to be sent to the receiver side and the time of training dictionary is saved.

The sparse representation of a given patch x_i is the process of searching for the atoms to produce the best approximation with dictionary D. The appropriate vector α_i is formulated as:

$$\alpha_i = \arg\min_{\alpha_i} \|x_i - D\alpha_i\|_2^2 \quad s.t. \quad \|\alpha_i\|_0 < L, \tag{5}$$

where L represents the degree of sparseness, that is, the number of non-zero coefficients, or the number of dictionary primitives for reconstructing each image

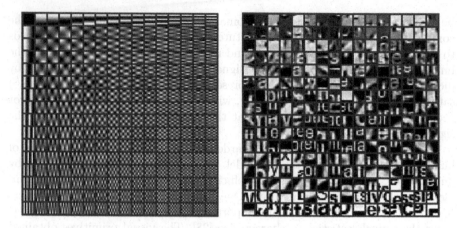

Fig. 2. Left: The DCT base dictionary; Right: Dictionary trained from SCI patches.

patch. To find the sparse representation, the orthogonal matching pursuit (OMP) algorithm [30] is usually exploited, which is simple and efficient in practice. The OMP algorithm greedily selects the primitive most similar to the residual during each iteration. Its reconstruction could reflect the layered perception that the brain will gradually process visual information, from the most basic to containing a certain structure and finally processing rich details.

2.3   The Perceptual Quality Index

It is believed that visual cognition is an active reasoning process that matches the internal generative model of the brain with visual sensory data. After obtaining the brain prediction of the input image, based on the free energy principle, the difference between the input and the generation model prediction is closely related to the image quality. To be precise, the quality of an image is quantified by the uncertainty of the difference in prediction [22]. Therefore, the degradation of image quality can be measured by predicting the uncertainty change of deviation. First, we define the difference between the input and the brain predicted image as the prediction residual:

$$R = I - I'. \tag{6}$$

Here, R represents the prediction residual, I represents the input, I' represents the prediction of I, and "$-$" represents the subtraction of the pixels at the corresponding positions of the two images. Entropy (E_R) can be used to measure the uncertainty of prediction difference (R). Therefore, we can compare the reference image with its corresponding distorted version by E_R and define its absolute difference as the perceptual quality index (Q):

$$Q = \left| E_R^r - E_R^d \right|, \tag{7}$$

where E_R^r represents E_R of the reference image, E_R^d represents E_R of the corresponding distorted image, and "$|\cdot|$" is absolute value operation. It should be noted that E_R can be simply represented by a single scalar, which is negligible and no transmission overhead is incurred.

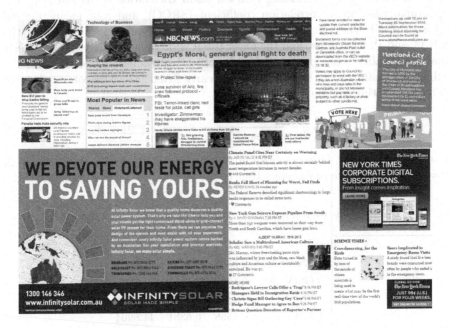

Fig. 3. The examples of the reference images in SIQAD database.

3   Experimental Results

In this section, we conduct extensive experiments on the SIQAD database [31] to test the effectiveness of our model. The SIQAD database consists of 980 distorted images generated from 20 references, which have a variety of colors, brightness and resolution, and there are many types of scenes, such as news pages, posters and so on. They are all obtained by screenshots directly. In SIQAD database, several kinds of distortion types are introduced to each reference images, such as distortions caused by imaging like Gaussian noise (GN), Gaussian blur (GB), motion blur (MB), contrast change (CC), or distortions by coding like JPEG compression, JPEG2000 compression (JP2K), and layer segmentation based coding (LSC). The examples of the reference images in the database are shown in Fig. 3.

In order to test the performance of our algorithm, we select two types of state-of-the-art IQA metrics as its competitors: one includes seven FR-IQA methods, i.e. FSIM [4], GSIM [5], PSIM [6], VSI [7], VSNR [8], IFC [9], and MAD [10];

the other one includes three RR-IQA methods, namely RRED [14], QFTB [16], and FEDM [22]. It should be noted that FR-IQA usually outperform RR-IQA in experiments because it make use of more reference information.

To evaluate the above IQA metrics, we employ three performance criteria as a common practice, including Pearson linear correlation coefficient (PLCC), Spearman rank-order correlation coefficient (SRCC), and root mean squared error (RMSE). The better the objective evaluation algorithm is, the higher the SRCC, and PLCC values, and the lower the RMSE value it has. VQEG suggests that the quality score predicted by the objective evaluation method and the subjective quality score should be non-linearly fitted [32]. The commonly used non-linear fitting function is:

$$q\left(z\right) = \beta_1 \left(\frac{1}{2} - \frac{1}{1 + \exp\left(\beta_2 \cdot \left(z - \beta_3\right)\right)}\right) + \beta_4 \cdot z + \beta_5, \tag{8}$$

where z is the raw object score and $q(z)$ is its fitted result. Meanwhile, β_j $(j = 1,2,3,4,5)$ are the parameters that could provide the most suitable fitting.

Table 1. The overall performance comparison on SIQAD database.

Model		PLCC	SRCC	RMSE
FR	FSIM [4]	0.5389	0.5279	2.0583
	GSIM [5]	0.5663	0.5551	11.7980
	PSIM [6]	0.7142	0.7056	10.0186
	VSI [7]	0.5568	0.5381	11.8904
	VSNR [8]	0.5982	0.5743	11.4706
	IFC [9]	0.6395	0.6011	11.0048
	MAD [10]	0.6191	0.6067	11.2409
RR	RRED [14]	0.5318	0.5358	12.1225
	QFTB [16]	0.3663	0.3360	13.3194
	FEDM [22]	0.6646	0.3049	10.6951
	Proposed	**0.7383**	**0.7076**	**9.6546**

In Table 1, we compare the performance of the listing metrics on the whole database by the criteria of PLCC, SRCC and RMSE, and highlight the metrics with best performance data in boldface. One can see that the proposed method usually achieves higher performance and significantly outperforms all competitors. Meanwhile, an advantage of our method is that only a single scalar is required to be transmitted, instead the size of the reference image. It should be noted that, our metric is the only approach which satisfies the following criteria: PLCC and SRCC are higher than 0.7 and RMSE is lower than 10, which proves its effectiveness and superiority.

In Table 2, we compare the state-of-arts on the SIQAD database by the evaluation criteria PLCC and SRCC. To show the results better, we also highlight the best metrics in boldface like Table 1. Among individual distortion types, our model achieves better performance than all the other testing RR-IQA metrics. Except for the SRCC indicator on the CC distortion type, the proposed metric all achieves the best performance. Especially on JPEG, JP2K, and LSC distortion types, both the PLCC and SRCC of the proposed metric are 0.2 higher than the second-best one. In general, compared by the start-of-art metrics, the proposed method has performed as the best IQA metric for SCIs in most cases. It could achieve better consistency with subjective scores and consistently stable performance under various types of distortion.

Table 2. The performance comparison on individual distortion types on SIQAD database.

Distortion type		RRED [14]	QFTB [16]	FEDM [22]	Proposed
GN	PLCC	0.8316	0.7406	0.7793	**0.8562**
	SRCC	0.8108	0.7220	0.7675	**0.8364**
GB	PLCC	0.7543	0.7067	0.7807	**0.8045**
	SRCC	0.7583	0.7032	0.7660	**0.7851**
MB	PLCC	0.7037	0.6288	0.4906	**0.7378**
	SRCC	0.6987	0.6431	0.4795	**0.7317**
CC	PLCC	0.4588	0.6412	0.7127	**0.7168**
	SRCC	0.4112	0.1078	0.5418	**0.4846**
JPEG	PLCC	0.4919	0.5864	0.4434	**0.7617**
	SRCC	0.5127	0.5667	0.4102	**0.7614**
JP2K	PLCC	0.5013	0.5321	0.3052	**0.7569**
	SRCC	0.4685	0.5407	0.2868	**0.7587**
LSC	PLCC	0.4669	0.4682	0.2942	**0.7261**
	SRCC	0.4513	0.4526	0.0988	**0.7255**

Figure 4 shows the distribution of subjective scores and objective scores on the SIQAD database, which visually shows the consistence of the prediction scores with the visual perception. In the figure, the blue "+" represents each image, and the red curve is the non-linear fitted curve. As can be seen from the figure, the blue "+" of the proposed method is evenly distributed on both sides of the fitted curve, and the fitted curve is close to a straight line. As for the other methods, the blue "+" distribution is relatively divergent, or the curve is irregular, indicating that it is difficult to fit between the objective score and the subjective score predicted by these methods. It proves that the proposed objective quality evaluation algorithm has a good correlation with the subjective quality score.

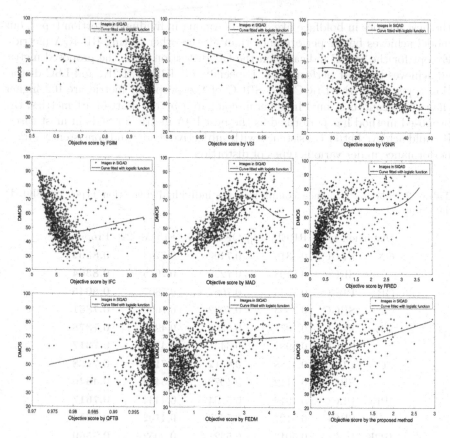

Fig. 4. Scatter plots of subjective scores (DMOS) against objective scores on SIQAD database.

4   Conclusions

In this study, motivated by free energy and sparse representation principles, a new RR IQA metric for SCIs is presented. Firstly, the traditional DCT dictionary is used for sparse representation to predict the reference and distorted image, which can better describe the screen content of text and image. Then, we evaluate the image quality by the entropy of the prediction difference. Extensive experiments on SIQAD database show that the proposed measure is consistent with the subjective quality evaluation of SCIs, and is better than the most advanced FR-IQA and RR-IQA measures.

Acknowledgement. This work is supported by the National Natural Science Foundation of China (Grant No. 62102059) and the Fundamental Research Funds for the Central Universities (No. 3132022225 and No. 3132021245).

References

1. Zhu, W., Ding, W., Xu, J., Shi, Y., Yin, B.: Screen content coding based on HEVC framework. IEEE Trans. Multimed. **16**(5), 1316–1326 (2014)
2. Zhan, M., Wang, W., Xu, M., Yu, H.: Advanced screen content coding using color table and index map. IEEE Trans. Image Process. **23**(10), 4399–4412 (2014)
3. Wang, Z., Bovik, A.C., Sheikh, H.R., Simoncelli, E.P.: Image quality assessment: from error visibility to structural similarity. IEEE Trans. Image Process. **13**(4), 600–612 (2004)
4. Zhang, L., Zhang, L., Mou, X., Zhang, D.: FSIM: a feature similarity index for image quality assessment. IEEE Trans. Image Process. **20**(8), 2378–2386 (2011)
5. Liu, A., Lin, W., Narwaria, M.: Image quality assessment based on gradient similarity. IEEE Trans. Image Process. **21**(4), 1500–1512 (2012)
6. Gu, K., Li, L., Lu, H., Min, X., Lin, W.: A fast reliable image quality predictor by fusing micro- and macro-structures. IEEE Trans. Ind. Electron. **64**(5), 3903–3912 (2017)
7. Zhang, L., Shen, Y., Li, H.: VSI: a visual saliency-induced index for perceptual image quality assessment. IEEE Trans. Image Process. **23**(10), 4270–4281 (2014)
8. Chandler, D.M., Hemami, S.S.: VSNR: a wavelet-based visual signal-to-noise ratio for natural images. IEEE Trans. Image Process. **16**(9), 2284–2298 (2007)
9. Sheikh, H.R., Bovik, A.C., de Veciana, G.: An information fidelity criterion for image quality assessment using natural scene statistics. IEEE Trans. Image Process. **14**(12), 2117–2128 (2005)
10. Larson, E.C., Chandler, D.M.: Most apparent distortion: full reference image quality assessment and the role of strategy. J. Electron. Imaging **19**(1), 011006-1–011006-21 (2010)
11. Liu, Y., Zhai, G., Gu, K., Liu, X., Zhao, D., Gao, W.: Reduced-reference image quality assessment in free-energy principle and sparse representation. IEEE Trans. Multimed. **20**(2), 379–391 (2018)
12. Wan, Z., Gu, K., Zhao, D.: Reduced reference stereoscopic image quality assessment using sparse representation and natural scene statistics. IEEE Trans. Multimed. **22**(8), 2024–2037 (2020)
13. Abdul, R., Wang, Z.: Reduced-reference image quality assessment by structural similarity estimation. IEEE Trans. Image Process. **21**(8), 3378–3389 (2012)
14. Soundararajan, R., Bovik, A.C.: RRED indices: reduced reference entropic differencing for image quality assessment. IEEE Trans. Image Process. **21**(2), 517–526 (2012)
15. Wan, Z., Qi, F., Liu, Y., Zhao, D.: Reduced reference stereoscopic image quality assessment based on entropy of classified primitives. In: IEEE International Conference on Multimedia and Expo (ICME), pp. 73–78 (2017)
16. Narwaria, M., Lin, W., McLoughlin, I.V., Emmanuel, S., Chia, L.T.: Fourier transform-based scalable image quality measure. IEEE Trans. Image Process. **21**(8), 3364–3377 (2012)
17. Wan, Z., Liu, Y., Qi, F., Zhao, D.: Reduced reference image quality assessment based on entropy of classified primitives. In: Data Compression Conference (DCC), pp. 231–240 (2017)
18. Liu, Y., Gu, K., Wang, S., Zhao, D., Gao, W.: Blind quality assessment of camera images based on low-level and high-level statistical features. IEEE Trans. Multimed. **21**(1), 135–146 (2019)

19. Liu, Y., Gu, K., Li, X., Zhang, Y.: Blind image quality assessment by natural scene statistics and perceptual characteristics. ACM Trans. Multimed. Comput. Commun. Appl. (TOMM) **16**(3), 1–91 (2020)
20. Liu, Y., et al.: Unsupervised blind image quality evaluation via statistical measurements of structure, naturalness, and perception. IEEE Trans. Circuits Syst. Video Technol. **30**(4), 929–943 (2020)
21. Sternberg, R.: Cognitive Psychology, 3rd edn. Thomson Wadsworth, Belmont (2003)
22. Zhai, G., Wu, X., Yang, X., Lin, W., Zhang, W.: A psychovisual quality metric in free-energy principle. IEEE Trans. Image Process. **21**(1), 41–52 (2012)
23. Knill, D.C., Pouget, A.: The Bayesian brain: the role of uncertainty in neural coding and computation. Trends Neurosci. **27**(12), 712–719 (2004)
24. Olshausen, B., Field, D.: Emergence of simple-cell receptive field properties by learning a sparse code for natural images. Nature **381**(6583), 607–609 (1996)
25. Hu, X., Zhang, J., Li, J., Zhang, B.: Sparsity-regularized Hmax for visual recognition. Plos One **9**(1), e81813 (2014)
26. Olshausen, B., Field, D.: Sparse coding with an overcomplete basis set: a strategy employed by v1? Vis. Res. **37**(23), 3311–3325 (1997)
27. Elad, M.: Sparse and Redundant Representations: From Theory to Applications in Signal and Image Processing. Springer, Heidelberg (2010)
28. Olshausen, B., Field, D.: Natural image statistics and efficient coding. Network **7**, 333–339 (1996)
29. Barlow, H.B.: Unsupervised learning. Neural Comput. **1**, 295–311 (1989)
30. Tropp, J.A., Gilber, A.A.: Signal recovery from random measurements via orthogonal matching pursuit. IEEE Trans. Inf. Theory **53**(12), 4655–4666 (2007)
31. Yang, H., Fang, Y., Lin, W.: Perceptual quality assessment of screen content images. IEEE Trans. Image Process. **24**(11), 4408–4421 (2015)
32. VQEG: Final report from the video quality experts group on the validation of objective models of video quality assessment, March 2000. http://www.vqeg.org/

Target Detection

Hidden Human Target Detection Model Inspired by Physiological Signals

Lejing Zhang, Yunlu Wang, Menghan Hu$^{(\boxtimes)}$, and Qingli Li

Shanghai Key Laboratory of Multidimensional Information Processing,
School of Communication and Electronic Engineering, East China Normal University,
Shanghai 200062, China
mhhu@ce.ecnu.edu.cn

Abstract. The current object detection algorithms will give unsatisfactory performance on the task of detecting hidden human targets. Therefore, in the current work, we propose a physiological signals powered hidden human targets detection model. The new proposals generation algorithm considering the spatio-temporal interdependent physiological features is first proposed to generate suitable candidate boxes. To eliminate the oddly shaped candidate boxes, we introduce a priori knowledge by combining the candidate box size and aspect ratio. The skin detection model is used to further reduce the number of candidate boxes. The custom-made dataset is established to validate the performance of the proposed model. The model we built yields the accuracy of 64% and 44% for indoor and outdoor environments, respectively. Compared to the YOLOv4, in terms of indoor and outdoor scenes, the developed model shows 30% and 16% improvement in accuracy. The results of the ablation experiments show the effectiveness of each component of the model.

Keywords: Occluded human detection · IPPG · Physiological signal measurement · Proposals generation

1 Introduction

For human target detection, if the images contain complete human target features, the current object detection algorithms such as YOLOv4 can give the perfect performance [1]. When human limbs are occluded by objects or humans deliberately hide themselves behind something, such as, walls, chairs, curtains and wood panels, these algorithms tend to fail. Aiming at this dilemma, we propose the model mainly utilizing Imaging PhotoPlethysmoGraphy (IPPG) to extract physiological signals from human body for distinguishing hidden human targets from background, thus overcoming shortcomings of the current object detection algorithms.

To the best of our knowledge, it is the first time that IPPG has been applied to the field of detecting hidden human targets. Previous researches about IPPG were mainly focused on measuring human heart rate stably and accurately [2–7].

© Springer Nature Singapore Pte Ltd. 2022
G. Zhai et al. (Eds.): IFTC 2021, CCIS 1560, pp. 229–238, 2022.
https://doi.org/10.1007/978-981-19-2266-4_18

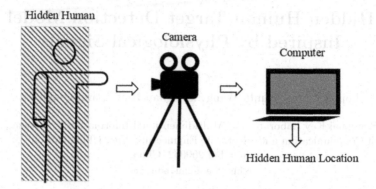

Fig. 1. Illustration of typical application scenario. The human target hides behind the occlusion, we capture the scene data by the RGB camera, and then the hidden human target is detected by the proposed model.

Allen [8] considered PPG to be an effective measurement tool to extract signals related to heartbeat. Recently, Jonathan [22] took use of white LED as light source to capture the heart rate with a cellphone, imposing FFT transform to obtain the heart rate value in power spectral density (PSD). Anchan [23] also took advantage of ambient light to measure the heart rate value with portable IPPG device. These advances in IPPG demonstrate the maturity and completeness in the measurement of signals related to heart beat with the use of the camera.

For the detection of occluded human targets, conventional sift, HOG, Haar operators were designed to describe some features and then combine a large number of weak classifiers to detect the targets as in [9–12]. With the improvement of computing power and neural network, the end-to-end models such as YOLOv4 are proposed to be the most remarkable methods in detection accuracy and speed [1,20,21]. YOLOv4 transforms the target detection problem into a regression problem with one stage compared with RCNN [13] and Faster-RCNN [14]. These neural networks for target detection are well established and mainly based on normal RGB camera. In terms of other occluded human detection means such as hyperspectral, far-infrared systems and FMCW radar are also commonly researched measures to detect the target in the past few years [15–19]. Nevertheless, these detection devices are expensive and complicated, which is a burden for people to apply in real life.

In real social life, it is of vital importance to utilize the available equipment to detect human targets under the occluded circumstances. For instance, in the process of military rescue and public security investigation, detecting occluded humans enables people to rescue and find suspects faster, which can improve work efficiency of government staff and reduce unnecessary human labor. The hypothetical application scenario is shown in Fig. 1.

The main contribution of our study is listed as follows:

1) We propose the new selective search algorithm inspired by physiological signal characteristics which considers both temporal and spatial characteristics of scenes to improve the effectiveness of hidden human target detection.
2) We propose the new IPPG signal extraction pipeline which simultaneously considers spatio-temporal interdependent relationship to raise the detection accuracy of hidden human targets.
3) We propose the physiological characteristics powered hidden human targets detection model, and the performance of the model is validated by the home-made dataset.

Section 2 is about the structure of the proposed model, and Sect. 3 conducts comparative experiments and ablation experiments. Section 4 is the conclusion of our study.

2   Proposed Detection Model

2.1   Pipelines of Hidden Human Detection Model Inspired by Physiological Signals

The procedure of our model is as follows. First, we generate an adequate number of regions of interest (ROI) in each collected image sequence by the proposed proposals generation method. Second, the IPPG algorithm is used to extract the physiological signals within each ROIs. Then, we remove the redundant boxes which are mostly background by skin detection algorithm. Ultimately, we get the final detection result and the location of occluded human targets. Figure 2 is the main structure of our model.

2.2   Dataset for Hidden Human Detection

To design the possible human hidden scenes, we chose commonly seen objects such as walls, cars, trees, curtains, and tables as the hiding places. The volunteers (4 males and 4 females) aged from 20–40 were squatting or standing, keeping still and hiding behind these shelters, with a small part of their bodies exposed. Such scenes were videotaped for a period of 20–30 s. Considering the influence of environmental light [9], the two circumstances i.e. indoor scene and outdoor scene were taken into account. The imaging device is a RGB camera and the frame rate of the camera is 30 frame per second. The resolution of the camera is 1520 × 720 pixel. A total of 100 image sequences are obtained. The typical images in this homemade dataset are shown in Fig. 3.

2.3   Proposals Generation Inspired by Physiological Signals

The classical selective search approach considers only four aspects i.e. color, texture, image size, and regional fitness. Unlike other non-living targets to be detected, the human targets have unique characteristics in terms of temporal

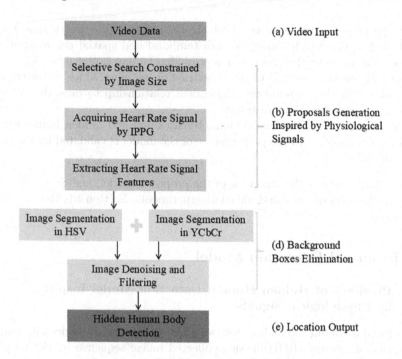

Fig. 2. Model pipeline of our raised algorithms for occluded human target detection. First, we need to generate a series of proposals for potential location. Then, we extract pure heart signal of different proposals by IPPG with ICA. Next, we can extract two heart signal features which can distinguish human body from background. Afterward, we filter out redundant boxes of background through skin pixel statistic information. Last, we get the location of hidden human targets.

sequence due to physiological activities. Inspired by this phenomenon, we propose a new selective search method. The proposed selective search method considers not only spatial features but also temporal features related to physiological activities i.e. physiological signals.

The classical selective search method generates thousands of candidate boxes at a time. If physiological signals are computed for these candidate boxes, the time complexity and spatial complexity can be imagined to be enormous. To alleviate model complexity, we introduce a priori knowledge by combining the candidate box size and aspect ratio. Therefore, the definition of the proposed proposals generation method is as follows:

$$s(r_i, r_j) = a_1 * s_c(r_i, r_j) + a_2 * s_t(r_i, r_j) + a_3 * s_s(r_i, r_j) + a_4 * s_f(r_i, r_j)$$
$$+ a_5 * s_r + a_6 * s_t \tag{1}$$

In the formula, $a_i \in \{0, 1\}$ represents whether the similarity is used or not. In our algorithm, we take all six aspects colour, texture, size, fill, aspect ratio, heart

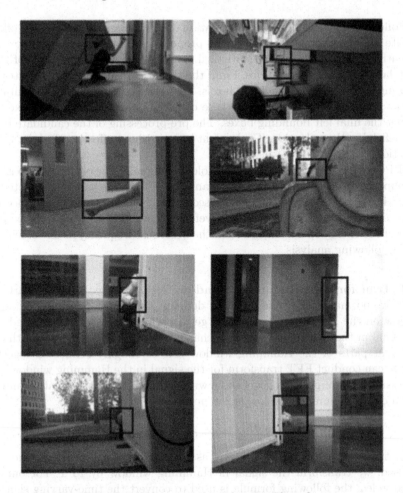

Fig. 3. Typical human body hidden scene of our dataset. The volunteers were squatting or standing, keeping still and hiding behind these shelters, with a small part of their bodies exposed. The region within the red box is the hidden human body area. (Color figure online)

rate threshold into consideration. $a_i = 1$, $s_c(r_i, r_j)$ denotes the colour similarity, $s_t(r_i, r_j)$ denotes the texture similarity, $s_s(r_i, r_j)$ denotes size similarity, and $s_f(r_i, r_j)$ denotes the fill similarity. The selective search method combines two similar regions together and seperates two dissimilar areas apart according to the upper defined regional similarity $s(r_i, r_j)$. In addition, we define s_r as the one of the constraints to generate proposals. If the potential length-width ratio of the proposal is smaller than 2, we take it into account, otherwise we remove it. As to the heart rate threshold s_t, we take 0.9 as the decision boundary. If the signal ratio is greater than 0.9, we continue to consider this candidate box; otherwise, we abandon this candidate box. From these six aspects, we generate a series of candidate boxes.

Collecting the bounding box information of the human category on the official website of ImageNet, we calculate the proportion of these candidate boxes to the entire image, and plot the statistical values of the size proportions of these candidate boxes as 10 categories. From the statistical values, we can master the size range of most of the candidate boxes. Then, we can obtain the size limitation for our bounding boxes. Imposing these constraints on the bounding boxes, we can get the final left bounding boxes. The pre-processing of the candidate boxes is beneficial to the reduction of redundant boxes without affecting the later target detection.

IPPG is applied to extract the physiological signals. The original video is first decomposed into R, G, and B three channels, and the G channel is selected for extracting the time-varying signal. Subsequently, Fourier transform is proceeded to obtain blood volume pulse wave waveform. Simultaneously, we find the peak value of the energy spectrum to obtain the heartbeat frequency as one of features for the following analysis.

FFT Transform in Hamming Window. Before we extract the heart rate value, we normalize the values of time domain pixel and impose the Hamming window on the 15–20 s video signal to get a periodic signal. It is assumed that the signal in the Hamming window is changing in cycles. The signals of the left and right parts of the Hamming window can be roughly connected together, and we can conduct FFT transform for the signal in the Hamming window. The expression of Hamming window can be written in the following equation and the length of our Hamming window is 250 points.

$$W(n, \alpha) = (1 - \alpha) - \alpha * cos(2 * pi * n / (N - 1)) \tag{2}$$

In this equation, α is usually set as 0.46. After the Hamming window is imposed, we transform the signal in Hamming window by FFT. For our collected video, the following formula is used to convert the time-varying signal to frequency domain. The maximum value in the frequency domain is the heart rate after the Fourier transform of the 250 time points.

$$X_k = \sum_{n=0}^{N-1} x_n e^{-2\pi jkn/n} \tag{3}$$

In the formula (2), the x_n is the average value of three channels' pixel, and this value changes according to the time n. The X_k represents the value of the discrete FFT transform in the frequency domain.

Blind Source Signal Separation Using ICA. A major problem with IPPG technology is that motion artifacts cause interference. For example, when the content in the box changes not owing to the reflected light of heart beat, just by external outside movement, the quality of the extracted physiological signal can

Table 1. Performance comparison of occluded human detection algorithm specific to different image and signal process methods.

Different methods	Indoor accuracy	Outdoor accuracy	Indoor IoU	Outdoor IoU	Overall accuracy	Overall IoU
Our proposed model	64%	44%	0.19	0.05	54%	0.12
Skin detection	36%	34%	-	-	35%	-
Our model without relevance	44%	40%	0.11	0.04	42%	0.07
Our model without HR ratio	54%	18%	0.14	0.01	36%	0.07
YOLOv4	34%	28%	-	-	31%	-

be greatly affected. We need to reduce this kind of motion error. In this study, the Independent Component Analysis (ICA) is used to reduce the interference of motion artifacts [24–26].

The ICA algorithm assumes that the observed RGB three channels are linear mixture of original sources, i.e. $x_i(t) = \sum_{j=1}^{3} a_{ij} * s_j(t)$, in which $x_i(t)$ refers to the observed signal, $s_j(t)$ refers to the source signal whose distribution is non Gaussian, and a_{ij} referring to different weights, can be re-expressed by matrix as (2):

$$X(t) = AS(t) \tag{4}$$

Our aim is to find a demixing matrix W to retrieve the source signal, which can be written in the following format. The $\hat{s}(t)$ is the approximation of the inverse of source signal.

$$\hat{s}(t) = WX(t) \tag{5}$$

By employing ICA, we can obtain relatively pure signals relative to heart rate and remove environmental noise in the same frequency range. After extracting the heart rate signal, we calculate the heart rate value between 65 bpm to 90 bpm (beat per minute) in the total length of the signal and take this ratio as the feature for target detection.

Spatio-Temporal Interdependent Relationship. We calculate the correlation between different frame signals. If the signals are highly correlated, we take the two signals as one category. For example, if two candidate boxes intersect with the human body at the same time, but overlap partially, the signals extracted by the two boxes should be highly correlated. Based on the correlation algorithm, we can make up some shortcomings of the heart rate ratio feature. If the heart rate value of the real human body is strongly interfered with the light noise, we can refer to the correlation feature to add more potential bounding boxes for further detection.

The correlation between two different signals is defined as follows.

$$r_{xy}(l) = \sum_{n=-\infty}^{n=\infty} x(n)y(n-l) \tag{6}$$

In the formula, xn is the heart signal of one bounding box in time domain and yn is the heart signal of another bounding box.

We calculate the cross-correlation covariance matrix of all signals and select four candidate box positions corresponding to the maximum value and the sub-maximum value. The four corresponding boxes are selected for further detection and we also take it for granted that the locations of these bounding boxes are human.

2.4   Redundant Boxes Reduction

Due to the interference of the shooting process, the candidate boxes of non-human areas will also be detected. Hence, the skin detection algorithm coupled with image morphological operation is applied to improve the detection accuracy. The raw RGB image is first converted into HSV color space and YCbCr space. The threshold segmentation method is then used for the segmentation of foreground and background. The impulse noise and the glued pixels are suppressed by the median filter and the open operation, respectively. After the skin detection, we judge each candidate frame to determine whether there are skin pixels falling into the candidate frame. As long as there are skin pixels falling into the candidate boxes, it is considered that this candidate frame is effective as a human body. If all pixels in the candidate box do not belong to detected skin, we consider this frame to be the background and perform filtering. Through such a background boxes filtering, we achieve the goal of occluded human targets detection.

3   Results and Discussion

The detection accuracy and IoU are applied to validate the performance of the proposed model. If the final left heart rate boxes hit the ground-truth box, the occluded human target is considered to be successfully detected. Otherwise, we consider that the model fails to detect the occluded human target. Table 1 shows the performance of the proposed model validated on the collected videos.

In Table 1, the proposed model outperforms the YOLOv4, with indoor accuracy, outdoor accuracy, and overall accuracy with 64%, 44%, and 54%, respectively. This indicates that the addition of physiological signal feature into the detection pipeline can significantly improve the detection rate of hidden human targets. At the same time, we found that the detection accuracy of indoor environment is 20% higher than the detection accuracy of outdoor environment, suggesting that our model is susceptible to the effects of light. Therefore, in future research, we need to reduce the effect of changing illumination on model performance from an algorithmic or hardware perspective.

To explore the role of each module, we conducted ablation experiments. For outdoor environments, the physiological signal measurement module is very significant for model performance improvement. In indoor environments, the skin detection module contributes more to the model performance improvement.

From the IoU metric, we can also see that the performance of overall model is the best, with the IoU of 0.19, 0.05, and 0.12 for indoor, outdoor, and overall environments, respectively.

The constructed hidden targets recognition model has the following distinct advantages: 1) in an environment where the human body is hidden and obscured by a large area and the human target is relatively small, the YOLOv4 algorithm fails. At this time, the developed model can be competitive. The human body characteristic signal of heart rate can be extracted well, which makes up for the shortcomings of the traditional algorithm in incomplete body features; 2) the developed model can be used to detect the real and false human body target; 3) the equipment requirements of model are not high, and the existing surveillance cameras can carry the model; and 4) there is no need for a large number of prior data for training, that is, no need for tuning neural network. We just input the captured video into our model and then we can get the detection results.

4 Conclusion

In this study, we propose a physiological signals powered hidden human targets detection model to make up for the insufficiency of the detection failure of the YOLOv4 algorithm. The performance of the proposed model is validated by our homemade dataset, and it is superior to the YOLOv4 algorithm with overall accuracy of 54% versus 31%. This model displays a huge potential to be utilized in the field of military rescue, and public security investigation.

References

1. Bochkovskiy, A., Wang, C.-Y., Liao, H.-Y.M.: YOLOv4: optimal speed and accuracy of object detection. arXiv preprint arXiv:2004.10934 (2020)
2. Rubins, U., et al.: Real-time photoplethysmography imaging system. In: Dremstrup, K., Rees, S., Jensen, M.Ø. (eds.) NBC 2011, vol. 34, pp. 183–186. Springer, Heidelberg (2011). https://doi.org/10.1007/978-3-642-21683-1_46
3. Rubins, U., Erts, R., Nikiforovs, V.: The blood perfusion mapping in the human skin by photoplethysmography imaging. In: Bamidis, P.D., Pallikarakis, N. (eds.) XII Mediterranean Conference on Medical and Biological Engineering and Computing, pp. 304–306. Springer, Heidelberg (2010). https://doi.org/10.1007/978-3-642-13039-7_76
4. Chen, M.-Y., Ting, C.-W.: A robust methodology for heartbeat detection in imaging photoplethysmography. In: International Conference on ICT Convergence. IEEE (2013)
5. Zheng, J., et al.: Feasibility of imaging photoplethysmography. In: International Conference on BioMedical Engineering and Informatics, vol. 2. IEEE (2008)
6. Goudarzi, R.H., Mousavi, S.S., Charmi, M.: Using imaging photoplethysmography (iPPG) signal for blood pressure estimation. In: International Conference on Machine Vision and Image Processing. IEEE (2020)
7. Kumar, M., Veeraraghavan, A., Sabharwal, A.: DistancePPG: robust non-contact vital signs monitoring using a camera. Biomed. Opt. Express **6**, 1565–1588 (2015)

8. Allen, J.: Photoplethysmography and its application in clinical physiological measurement. Physiol. Measur. **28**(3), R1–R39 (2007)
9. Du, X., Liu, C., Yu, Y.: Analysis of detection and track on partially occluded face. In: 2009 International Forum on Information Technology and Applications, vol. 3. IEEE (2009)
10. Adar, N., et al.: Detection of partially occluded upper body pose using hidden Markov model. In: 15th Signal Processing and Communications Applications. IEEE (2007)
11. Sohn, K.: Recognition of partially occluded target objects. In: Proceedings of 3rd IEEE International Conference on Image Processing, vol. 3. IEEE (1996)
12. Mirunalini, P., Jaisakthi, S.M., Sujana, R.: Tracking of object in occluded and non-occluded environment using SIFT and Kalman filter. In: IEEE Region 10 Conference. IEEE (2017)
13. Girshick, R., et al.: Rich feature hierarchies for accurate object detection and semantic segmentation. In: Proceedings of the IEEE Conference on Computer Vision and Pattern Recognition (2014)
14. Ren, S., et al.: Faster R-CNN: towards real-time object detection with region proposal networks. IEEE Trans. Pattern Anal. Mach. Intell. **39**(6), 1137–1149 (2016)
15. Shimoni, M., Perneel, C., Gagnon, J.P.: Detection of occluded targets using thermal imaging spectroscopy. In: 2nd Workshop on Hyperspectral Image and Signal Processing: Evolution in Remote Sensing. IEEE (2010)
16. Will, C., et al.: Human target detection, tracking, and classification using 24-GHz FMCW radar. IEEE Sens. J. **19**(17), 7283–7299 (2019)
17. Nunez, A.S., Mendenhall, M.J.: Detection of human skin in near infrared hyperspectral imagery. In: IEEE International Geoscience and Remote Sensing Symposium, vol. 2 (2008)
18. Uto, K., et al.: Hyperspectral band selection for human detection. In: 7th Sensor Array and Multichannel Signal Processing Workshop. IEEE (2012)
19. Milanic, M., et al.: Detection of hypercholesterolemia using hyperspectral imaging of human skin. In: European Conference on Biomedical Optics. Optical Society of America (2015)
20. Zhao, Z.-Q., et al.: Object detection with deep learning: a review. IEEE Trans. Neural Netw. Learn. Syst. **30**(11), 3212–3232 (2019)
21. Pandiya, M., Dassani, S., Mangalraj, P.: Analysis of deep learning architectures for object detection-a critical review. In: IEEE-HYDCON. IEEE (2020)
22. Jonathan, E., Leahy, M.J.: Cellular phone-based photoplethysmographic imaging. J. Biophotonics **4**(5), 293–296 (2011)
23. Anchan, R.: Estimating pulse wave velocity using mobile phone sensors, B.S. dissertation, Edith Cowan University (2011)
24. Poh, M.-Z., McDuff, D.J., Picard, R.W.: Non-contact, automated cardiac pulse measurements using video imaging and blind source separation. Opt. Express **18**(10), 10762–10774 (2010)
25. Ye, P., Wu, X., Gao, D., Deng, S., Xu, N., Chen, J.: DP3 signal as a neuro-indictor for attentional processing of stereoscopic contents in varied depths within the 'comfort zone'. Displays **63**, 101953 (2020)
26. Gao, Z., Zhai, G., Deng, H., Yang, X.: Extended geometric models for stereoscopic 3D with vertical screen disparity. Displays **65**, 101972 (2020)

Adapting on Long-Tail Domains by High Quality Self-training for Object Detection

Duo Li[1,2(✉)], Sanli Tang[1], Binbin Zhang[1], Zhanzhan Cheng[1], Wenming Tan[1], and Xiaokang Yang[2]

[1] Hikvision Research Institute, Hangzhou Hikvision Digital Technology Co., Ltd., Hangzhou, China
{liduo6,tangsanli,zhangbinbin,chengzhanzhan,tanwenming}@hikvision.com
[2] MoE Key Lab of Artificial Intelligence, AI Institute, Shanghai Jiao Tong University, Shanghai, China
xkyang@sjtu.edu.cn

Abstract. Domain shift is a critical challenge when we deploy object detectors to real world applications. Due to the data distribution misalignment between the source and target domains, the detector suffers from a significant performance drop on the target domain. In some situations, the target domain contains a large ratio of objects in a few categories. This long-tail distribution makes it even harder to transfer well from source to target. In this paper, we tackle this categorical distribution difference in domain adaptation using self-training, where the unlabeled images in target domain are tagged with pseudo-labels to train the detector itself. To promote the effect of self-training, we propose SEAT (**S**core **E**nsemble and **A**daptive **T**hreshold), where high quality pseudo-labeled samples are elected by comprehensively analyzing information from multiple aspects. We show that these high quality pseudo-labeled training samples play a critical role in dealing with categorical distribution difference. Experiments on public data sets show the effectiveness of our method.

Keywords: Domain adaptation · Semi-supervised learning · Pseudo-label · Threshold

1 Introduction

Over the years, as the development of deep learning, object detection has been dramatically improved in supervised learning manner. Although plenty of works have achieved good results on public datasets [9,16], there still exists challenges in real-world applications. Domain shift is the major challenge when we deploy the models trained on large scale public datasets to real-world applications. Due to data distribution mismatch, the images in the source and target domains differ in style, illuminance, angle of view, instance size, and categorical distribution. The model degrades on the target domain, although it is well trained on the source domain.

© Springer Nature Singapore Pte Ltd. 2022
G. Zhai et al. (Eds.): IFTC 2021, CCIS 1560, pp. 239–252, 2022.
https://doi.org/10.1007/978-981-19-2266-4_19

Following the assumption that for cross-domain transfer one model should generate representations that the other algorithm cannot identify the input's original domain [2], domain adaptation methods solve domain shift by pulling deep network features of two domains into the same feature space. This is usually done by minimizing the domain shift, such as MMD (Maximum Mean Discrepancy) [17,26], correlation distances [22] and adversarial training [10,25]. Another way is to generate a intermediate domain by transferring images styles from source to target domain which can be used bridge two domains [14,30] (Fig. 1).

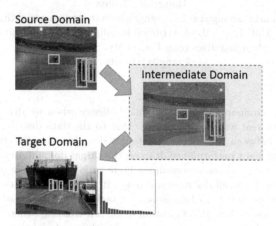

Fig. 1. One classical method of self-training based domain adaptation is creating an intermediate domain before conducting self-training. We find that the self-training degenerates on long-tailed domains. We propose SEAT to solve this problem, where high quality pseudo-labeled samples are generated for self-training.

Although above methods have largely remitted the domain shift of images style difference, the categorical distribution misalignment is still a critical challenge in real-world applications which has not been explored. It is a common situation that the source domain obeys one categorical distribution, but the target domain obeys another categorical distribution. Categorical distribution misalignment has a negative impact on the quality of the pseudo-labels on the target domain. In this paper, we study how to cope with domain shift in object detection where the target domain has different categorical distributions from the source domain. We improve the model on the target domain with self-training approach. Our major contribution is to design an efficient high quality pseudolabel generation module, which is crucial for the self-training process. After careful selection, only part of the pseudolabeled samples are activated in self-training.

We propose SEAT (**S**core **E**nsemble with **A**daptive **T**hreshold), a simple and efficient pseudolabel mining method. In SEAT, the high confidence pseudo-labels are refined for self-training. We use multiple scores apart from the confidence score predicted by the detector itself (SE, Score Ensemble). The threshold to filter in/out unlabeled samples is calculated dynamically according to the data distribution of each class (AT, Adaptive Threshold). First, to provide more information to guide the pseudo-labeled sample mining, we introduce the scores of temporal consistency and augmentation consistency. Second, to deal with the difference of confidence score distribution among categories, we propose an adaptive threshold calculation method. For categories where the confidence scores obeys long-tail distribution, we assume that there are more false positive samples mixed with true positive samples. The thresholds of these categories are set higher to filter out the FP samples. For categories where the confidence scores aggregates around 1 and 0, we assume that there are fewer FP samples mixed with TP samples. The corresponding thresholds are set lower. We have the following contributions:

- We propose SEAT, a novel pseudolabel mining method to improve the self-training for long-tail domain adaptation. Multiple scores are used to help pseudo-label sample selection from the candidates generated by the teacher model, and the dynamic threshold is proposed to deal with class-wise data distribution imbalance of the pseudo-label samples.
- SEAT is a flexible method which can be easily combined with other self-training based domain adaptation methods. And we show SEAT helps to promote the performance of other domain adaptation for object detection methods because it provides more reliable pseudo-label samples for self-training.

2   Related Work

Unsupervised Domain Adaptation. Domain adaptation aims to transfer a model from source domain to target domain, where the data distributions between two domains have an obvious gap. The most popular solution is to learning domain-invariant features. Maximum mean discrepancy (MMD) computes difference of the sample mean value between two domains. If the feature distributions are equal, the MMD is zero. There are also other measurements like correlation alignment (CORAL), contrastive domain discrepancy (CCD) and so on.

Although above methods are applicable for our task, it is still challenging to align feature distributions when the gap is large. Especially, domain adaptation for object detection requires to adapt both classification as well as localization. With a generated intermediate domain, the challenge of data distribution misalignment becomes easier to cope with. [12] generates the intermediate domain with unpaired image-to-image translation. Since the intermediate domain is close to the target domain, self-training is then able to adapt the model trained on the intermediate domain to the target domain. However, [12] does not take categorical distribution difference of the target images, which influences the quality of the pseudolabels. We concentrate on the situation when the target domain images have a long-tail distribution in categories, and focus on conducting high quality self-training.

Semi-supervised Learning. A similar area is semi-supervised learning. Unsupervised Domain Adaptation for Object Detection is different from semi-supervised object detection in two aspects. First, in the problem of DA, the labeled data and unlabeled data have obvious appearance dissimilarity. The main purpose of DA is to learn the domain irrelevant features for both domains [7,8,20]. While in the problem of SSL, the difference between labeled data and unlabeled data is not the concern. The purpose of SSL is to promote the performance of the model with help of unlabeled data. Second, the test set of DA is in the target domain. In SSL, we are concerned about the base data set. Due to above differences, methods for DA usually solves the problem of domain shift by decreasing the feature distribution among two domains [19,28]. On the contrary, SSL methods promotes the performance of the original model by refining the pseudo-labels [5] for self-training or training with carefully designed data augmentation methods [1,27] (Fig. 2).

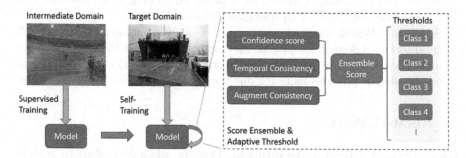

Fig. 2. Framework of our method. In the self-training process on the intermediate domain and the target domain, multiple scores are combined to form an accurate indicator to distinguish positive and negative pseudolabels. Adaptive thresholds are calculated automatically for each class on the target domain.

Semi-supervised learning aims to make use of large scale unlabel data to improve the model where the images are obtained almost for free. Consistency regularization becomes popular in this field because of its effectiveness and flexibility. VAT [18], Temporal Ensemble [15], and Mean-Teacher [24] study semi-supervised image classification with consistency regularization by adding different disturbs to the predictions on the unlabeled data. In CSD [13], consistency regularization is applied to both the classification as well as localization branches. To avoid mismatch of bounding boxes, only horizontal flip is used as the augmentation method to evaluate the consistency on unlabeled images.

Self-training. Self-training is usually used in semi-supervised learning, where the model is first trained on the labeled data to get relatively good representation ability. Then for each unlabeled sample x_u, the model predicts its pseudo-label y_u. Due to the ability limitation of the model, there is usually much noise in the pseudo-labels, which has a large impact on SSL. How to generate high quality pseudo-labeled samples from the unlabeled data becomes an essential problem. MixMatch [3] generates the pseudo-labels using the average predictions of unlabeled images on several augmentations. The unlabeled images are mixed with the labeled images and used for self-training. In Note-RCNN [11], an ensemble of two classification head of Faster-RCNN is used to overcome the disturb from the noisy pseudo-labels. As for object detection, it also turns out to be a powerful strategy to adapt the detectors on unlabeled data with self-training. However, the refinery of the pseudo-labels are rarely noticed and studied. One common coping strategy is to filter out less confident unlabeled samples [13,21,23]. It does help to improve the overall quality of the pseudo-labels, but it ignores the data distribution inconsistency among different classes. Given a static threshold, there exists a high risk to introduce noises to pseudo labels by filtering out many low confident positive samples and keeping high confident negative samples. Another challenge is how to make good use of middle confident unlabeled samples. Samples with confidence scores that are close to the threshold are essential for self-training, since these samples contribute to draw a precise classification boundary. However, the pseudo-labels of these samples convey the most amount of noises than other samples. In STAC [21], high confidence threshold is used to obtain high quality pseudo-labels. However, we argue that a fixed high threshold is not enough due to data distribution difference among categories.

3 Methodology

To reduce the domain gap, CycleGAN is used to transfer the image style from source domain to target domain, thus generates the intermediate domain. Since the pixel-to-pixel transfer does not change the location and class of objects in the images, the ground truth labels of the source domain images holds the same on the intermediate domain. We train a detector on the intermediate domain, and improve this detector by self-training on the intermediate domain. We focus on improving the pseudolabels' quality for self-training.

3.1 Problem Formulation

Given two sets of images $X = \{x_i; i = 1, 2, ..., M\}$ and $U = \{u_j; j = 1, 2, ..., N\}$, where X is the labeled training set on the intermediate domain and U is the unlabeled training set on the target domain. $\{x_i, y_i\}$ corresponds to one pair of labeled training sample, where y_i is the labeled bounding boxes. In the scenario of self-training, pseudo-labels for U are generated by the teacher model. Assume that the teacher generates pseudo-labels $\hat{y}_j^T = T(u_j; \theta_T)$, and the student model has the predictions of the unlabeled data $\hat{y}_j^S = S(u_j; \theta_S)$. Unsupervised loss is then:

$$l_u = \sum_{u_j \in U} l(\hat{y}_j^T, \hat{y}_j^S) = \sum_{u_j \in U} l(T(u_j; \theta_T), S(u_j; \theta_S)) \tag{1}$$

where $l(\cdot)$ is the standard supervised loss function of the object detector. As stated in [13,21], not all of the pseudo-labeled samples are suitable for unsupervised training. Low confident pseudo-labeled samples contain noises and false positive samples which is harmful for the student. Traditional method to get high quality training samples from the unlabeled data is to select samples with highly confident pseudo-label. A uniform threshold is usually used to filter out low confident pseudo-labeled samples, like 0.8.

We argue that there are two problems in this kind of rough division of pseudo-labeled samples, for two reasons. First, confidence score predicted by the detector is not the only indicator of the pseudo-labeled samples. Confidence score itself is only one point view to look at the sample. There are many other ways to check the quality of a sample, for instance, resistance to image noise, similarity to other samples of the same class, consistency during training. Each aspect of the sample reveals only a small part of it. If we come up with a way to find out all the point views and combine all the information together, we get the most accurate judgement on the quality of the sample. Second, uniform threshold is too rough, which does not take category variation into consideration. Due to data distribution difference among categories, the threshold should also be decided separately. To solve above two problems, we propose Score Ensemble (SE) and Adaptive Threshold (AT) to mine high quality pseudo-labeled samples for self-training.

3.2 Score Ensemble

Score is the most simplified signal that reflects our understanding to the world. In object detection, the confidence score is usually used to describe the models understanding of the prediction, good or bad. Although confidence score has already been shown powerful in pseudo-labeled sample mining in previous works, we argue that due to its one-sidedness. Inspired by the idea that weak classifiers can be combined into a strong classifier, we propose Score Ensemble, in which scores are integrated to produce a more powerful indicator of the sample's quality.

Confidence Score. Confidence score is the most popular indicator used to mine high quality pseudo-labeled samples. In Yolov3, confidence score is the combination of the object-ness score which reveals the probability of a bounding box to be foreground and the classification score which reveals the probability that the content in the bounding box belongs to which class (Eq. 2). In Faster-RCNN, the box-head classifies the RPN generated proposals and outputs the confidence scores (Eq. 3). In object detection tasks, confidence score offers the model a basic ability to distinguish true positive samples (TP) from false positive samples (FP).

$$C_i^{FRCNN} = argmin_{p_i} L_{cls}(p_i, p_i^*), \tag{2}$$

$$C_i^{YOLO} = p_i * IOU_{pred}^{truth} \tag{3}$$

p_i^* is the ground-truth label. In previous work, the pseudo-labeled samples are separated into TP and FP with the uniform threshold for all categories (for

Algorithm 1. SEAT for high quality self-training in long-tail domain adaptation.

1: Convert the source domain images to target domain with CycleGAN [31], and the generated images form the intermediate domain.
2: Train the model Π on labeled data X from the intermediate domain.
3: Generate pseudo-labels $Y^T = \hat{y}_j^T, j = 1, 2, ..., N$ for the samples in the unlabeled data set U (target domain) using the model Π.
4: Calculate the adaptive thresholds for each categories following Eq. 7.
5: **for** sample s_i **do**
6:   **if** $s_i \in U$ **then**
7:     Get pseudo-label y_i of s_i. Check the adaptive threshold $\hat{t}_k$ of sample s_i's category.
8:     **if** $scores_i > \hat{t}_k$ **then**
9:       Unsupervised loss calculated by Eq. 1
10:     **end if**
11:   **else**
12:     Supervised loss
13:   **end if**
14: **end for**

instance, 0.9 in [21]). Differently, we use adaptive thresholds for each categories which will be introduced later.

Temporal Consistency Score. We find that with the process of training, the predictions of the model changes over time. Mostly, the false predictions are less stable than the correct predictions. Following this discovery and inspired by [15], we propose the temporal consistency score as another indicator of the pseudo-labeled sample's quality. We record the model during its supervised training process. For the jth epoch, the model is saved as Π_j. The predictions of Π_i on the whole unlabeled sample u_i is written as $\hat{u}_i^j$. For sample u_i, temporal consistency score over multiple models $\{\Pi_j\}$ is calculated as follows:

$$TC_i = \frac{\sum_j C_i^j}{Var[C_i]}, \tag{4}$$

where C_i^j is the confidence score of sample u_i predicted by model Π_j. In [29], multi-model prediction consistency is also used for object detection training sample mining. Different from [29], our temporal consistency does not require additional cut and paste. We are more concerned the agreement degree that multiple models have on each sample, other than the prediction distribution.

Augmentation Consistency Score. It has been proven effective in images classification [15,18,24] that consistency regularization with different augmentations improves the semi-supervised learning. The same conclusion holds for self-training. Instead of directly adding a regularization term, we generate the augmentation consistency scores for the pseudo-labeled samples. Thus, we create another indicator to help distinguishing TPs and FPs. Since some of the samples are not tolerant to the augmentation disturbing, and may produce different predictions, augmentation consistency scores reflect the degree of resistance to different augmentations. Assume there are K types of augmentation written as $f_k(\cdot), k = 1, 2, ..., K$. Augmentation consistency score for sample u_i is calculated as follows:

$$AC_i = \frac{\sum_k \Pi(f_k(u_i))}{Var[\Pi(f_k(u_i))]},\tag{5}$$

where Π is the detector used in self-training. In this work, we use data augmentation strategies like images flip, resize and color transform.

Above scores are ensembled by simply multiplying together:

$$SE_i = C_i \cdot TC_i \cdot AC_i\tag{6}$$

The ensembled score is more distinguishable to positive and negative pseudolabels. For high quality pseudolabel selection, thresholds for each categories are calculated with adaptive threshold module.

3.3 Adaptive Thresholds for Each Category

The quality of unlabel training samples with pseudo-labels play an essential role in self-training. Usually, these training samples are selected according to the confidence score predicted by the detectors. Candidate samples with confidence scores higher than a given threshold like 0.8 are seen as high quality training sample. However, there are two major challenges. First, the confidence score should not be the only indicator of the quality of the training samples. In practice, even if the threshold is set as high as possible, like 0.9, there still exists some high confident false positive samples which significantly brings noise to self-training. More scores that reveals more detailed information from other aspects are needed for high quality sample mining. Second, the confidence scores of unlabeled data does not follow the same distribution of different categories. Setting the same threshold for sample selection is an inaccurate way. For instance, in the same unlabeled data set, there are more highly confident samples of the category CAR than PERSON. In this case, the threshold of the category CAR shall be set higher than that of the category PERSON.

Since the decision boundary is the key for training data selection in self-training, a more accurate thresholding method is essential other than the uniform threshold. With the observation that the data distribution of pseudo-labeled samples for each class are different, we assume that the ideal thresholds for each class should also be different. One challenge is how to figure out the ideal thresholds automatically according to the data distribution of each classes. Since the detectors are usually pre-trained on labeled data, the confidence score is regressed with the supervision of GT labels. The distribution of the confidence scores on the training data tend to gather around 0 or 1. This phenomenon can be explained as follows: when the training process converges, the confidence score prediction loss is small, so they must be around 0 or 1, otherwise the loss will become large. When we calculate the distribution of the confidence scores on the pseudo-labeled data, however, they may not gather around 0 or 1 as close as on the labeled data. It is because the detector has not been trained on the unlabeled data set in supervised manner. We call this the score distribution shift phenomenon. The score distribution shift can be defined as the entropy of the confidence score distribution. Intuitively, when the larger the score shift is, the more noise the pseudo-labeled samples have. The threshold of the category with large score distribution shift should be set higher than that with smaller score distribution shift. We adaptively calculate the threshold for each class with different confidence score shift as follows:

$$\hat{t}_k = argmin_t S_k(t) - \gamma S_k(T), \tag{7}$$

where k is the index of the categories. $S_k(t)$ represents the total number of samples with confidence scores larger than t. γ controls the percentage of samples used to determine the adaptive threshold. Pseudo-labeled samples with confidence scores higher than T are seen as true positive (TP) samples.

4   Experiments

We evaluate our method on public datasets. We transfer from Cityscapes to Foggy-Cityscapes, from Sim10K to Cityscapes, and from Pascal-VOC07 to Pascal-VOC12. The experiment on Cityscapes to Foggy-Cityscapes simulates the situation of weather transfer. The Sim10K dataset contains images that are manufactured by render engine.

Note that all these three target domains (Cityscapes, Foggy-Cityscapes, and VOC12) have long-tail categorical distributions. This setting helps to simulate the real-world challenges of unbalanced category distribution. In Cityscapes and Foggy-Cityscapes, CAR accounts for over 50% among all the eight classes. Top three classes CAR, PERSON, and BICYCLE account for over 90%. In VOC12, PERSON accounts for over 30%, and top three classes account for over 48% among twenty classes. Following previous work, we evaluate the detectors by reporting the average precision under IOU of 0.5 on the datasets.

4.1   Implementation Details

We implement SEAT both Faster RCNN. For Faster-RCNN, we use ResNet-50 as the backbone. Different from previous work, we use FPN in Faster-RCNN. We use MMDetection to construct the networks and design the training process. The models are pretrained on ImageNet.

There are two ways to generate pseudo labels for the unlabeled images, online and offline. Online generation refers to predict pseudo labels while training. Offline generation refers to predict pseudo labels altogether and store the labels in the file, which can be loaded into the memory for training later on. To save calculation resources, we conduct the offline generation in all the experiments for SEAT. We train object detectors with 2 NVIDIA Tesla V100 in 30 epochs with batch size of 8, in which 4 labeled and 4 unlabeled images are sampled randomly from the training set. We use SGD with initial learning rate of 0.0005 to optimize the network. The learning rate is stepped after 15 and 25 epochs.

Table 1. Comparison on Cityscapes to Foggy-Cityscapes. Experiment is conducted on Faster-RCNN. † We re-implement some of previous methods for fair comparison.

Methods	Bus	Bicycle	Car	Motocycle	Person	Rider	Train	Truck	mAP
Baseline	26.0	41.5	43.2	23.4	38.7	45.2	7.60	19.4	30.6
SWDA [20]	36.2	35.3	43.5	30.0	29.9	42.3	32.6	24.5	34.3
SWDA †	45.8	49.2	56.2	31.1	47.0	**57.5**	11.2	21.9	40.0
HTCN [6]	47.4	37.1	47.9	32.3	33.2	47.5	**40.9**	**31.6**	39.8
HTCN †	47.7	48.9	53.3	33.0	44.9	55.7	21.0	26.8	41.4
Intermediate Domain [12] †	51.1	49.5	64.1	32.6	49.1	55.2	13.1	28.7	42.9
ID + SEAT (ours)	51.2	49.5	**64.2**	33.5	49.5	55.5	16.7	30.2	43.8
ID + SEAT-C (ours)	**53.6**	**49.6**	63.5	**36.7**	**50.3**	54.2	27.6	30.8	**45.8**
Oracle	56.7	54.3	75.3	41.8	56.0	62.8	21.4	35.8	50.5

Table 2. Comparison on VOC07 to VOC12. Experiment is conducted on Faster-RCNN. ID is the baseline method, which generates an intermediate domain to close the domain gap, then refine the detector by self-training on the target domain. Our method also makes use of the intermediate domain. We compare the two major components in our method, score ensemble (SE), and adaptive threshold (AT). ST means self-training with universe threshold to select pseudolabels. † We re-implement Intermediate Domain [12] for fair comparison. In the table, 'Oracle' means the model is trained directly on the target domain with the supervised manner.

Methods	ID	SE	AT	mAP
Oracle				69.2
Baseline				65.9
Intermediate Domain + ST [12] †	√			66.0
ID + SE (ours)	√	√		66.8
ID + SEAT (ours)	√	√	√	**67.6**

Table 3. Comparison on Sim10K to Cityscapes. Experiment is conducted on Faster-RCNN. ST means self-training with universe threshold to select pseudolabels. † We re-implement some of previous methods for fair comparison.

Methods	Car
Baseline	18.5
DA [7] †	43.1
SWDA [20] †	47.8
MTOR [4] †	**54.9**
Intermediate Domain [12] †	40.1
ID + ST [12] †	50.6
ID + SEAT (ours)	52.6
ID + SEAT-C (ours)	**53.8**
Oracle	78.5

4.2 Results

Table 1, 2, 3 show the domain adaptation on Cityscapes to Foggy-Cityscapes, VOC07 to VOC12, and Sim10K to Cityscapes, accordingly. For the Cityscapes to Foggy-Cityscapes experiment, we compare with SWDA [20] and HTCN [6]. Since these works only reported results of Faster-RCNN without FPN (sometimes with VGG as backbone), we re-implement the methods under the same settings for fair comparison. As shown in Table 1, our method achieves 43.8, which is higher than all other methods. We also promote our method by adding the class-wise instance level representation invariance regularization between to domains. SEAT-C achieves 45.8, 2.0 higher than SEAT. This shows that self-training based method can be easily combined with representation invariance regularization. For the VOC07 to VOC12 experiment, we achieve 67.6 on mAP (IOU = 0.5), which is 1.7 higher than the baseline. For the Sim10K to Cityscapes experiment, SEAT achieves 52.6 and SEAT-C achieves 53.8. These results outperform DA and SWDA, but MTOR (our re-implement) achieves 1.1 higher than our method. It is not surprising that we do not achieve the best result on Sim10K to Cityscapes. Because in this task, only one class CAR is transferred. Our self-training based method shows its advantage when the categories on the target domain is long-tail distributed. Then the adaptive threshold module finds the best threshold for each class to select pseudolabels.

4.3 Ablation Study

Score Ensemble. Table 2 shows the ablation study of scores used in our method. Comparing ID+ST with ID+SE, we find that score ensemble achieves 0.8 higher result. This shows that the ensembled score help to promote self-training. After applying adaptive thresholds, we achieve 67.6 mAP and get 1.7 mAP over baseline. In our proposed method, we only use three scores, confidence score, augmentation consistency, and temporal consistency. We have proven these scores are all beneficial for the whole system. While a problem naturally arises: what kind of scores are helpful? In our opinion, the scores should provide information from different aspects. Compared with distinguishing accuracy using a score, we are more concerned whether it can provide information other than the confidence score already has.

Understanding Adaptive Thresholds. Threshold is important for self-training, because it is the simplest way to extract high quality pseudo-labeled training samples. In previous works, a static threshold is usually offered for all categories, which causes two side effects. One is that the same threshold for all the categories assumes that the data distributions of each categories are the same, which is not the case for long-tail distributed target domain data. This will cause the mis-split of the pseudo-labeled samples. If the threshold is set too high for one category, the training data is too little. If the threshold is set too low for one category, the noises in the training data are too much. Although the thresholds for each categories can be manually set, it requires plenty of time to figure out all the hyper parameters. Our adaptive thresholds solves above problems by adaptively select suitable thresholds for each class according to the data distribution of the unlabeled data. This method does not require heavy work to adjust parameters, while improves the overall quality of the pseudo-labeled samples.

Apart from the proposed adaptive thresholds by calculating the data distribution on unlabeled data, there is another way to figure out a set of thresholds. In the case where the data distribution on labeled data has little difference to that on unlabeled data, it is fine to calculate the thresholds on labeled data. Then we know whether each pseudo-labeled samples are positive or negative, and can determine more precise adaptive thresholds for each categories. But the assumption of same data distribution on labeled and unlabeled data is not always true. The adaptive thresholds calculated on labeled data has not much difference on our proposed adaptive thresholds on unlabeled data.

Training Samples: Quantity and Quality. To select high quality training data from the pseudo-labeled samples, a high threshold is usually used in self-training. The higher the threshold, the purer is the pseudo-labeled samples. But the threshold cannot be set as high as possible, because number of effective samples decreases as the threshold rises. So the quantity and quality of the training data is contradictory.

5   Conclusion

To deal with the domain shift problem in object detection, we propose a high quality self-training solution. To overcome the challenge that the categories obey long-tail distribution on the target domain, we propose SEAT (**S**core **E**nsemble and **A**daptive **T**hreshold), where high quality pseudo-labeled samples are elected by comprehensively analyzing information from multiple aspects. We show that these high quality pseudo-labeled training samples play a critical role in dealing with categorical distribution difference. To cope with the data distribution difference among categories, the adaptive threshold strategy is used to automatically determine the sample mining threshold for each category. This framework is compatible with feature-invariance based domain adaptation methods. In future work, we will focus on combining with feature-invariance based methods to promote the performance.

References

1. Arazo, E., Ortego, D., Albert, P., O'Connor, N.E., McGuinness, K.: Pseudo-labeling and confirmation bias in deep semi-supervised learning. arXiv preprint arXiv:1908.02983 (2019)
2. Ben-David, S., Blitzer, J., Crammer, K., Pereira, F.: Analysis of representations for domain adaptation. In: Advances in Neural Information Processing Systems (2006)

3. Berthelot, D., Carlini, N., Goodfellow, I., Papernot, N., Oliver, A., Raffel, C.A.: Mixmatch: a holistic approach to semi-supervised learning. In: Advances in Neural Information Processing Systems (2019)
4. Cai, Q., Pan, Y., Ngo, C.W., Tian, X., Duan, L., Yao, T.: Exploring object relation in mean teacher for cross-domain detection. In: Proceedings of the IEEE Conference on Computer Vision and Pattern Recognition (2019)
5. Cascante-Bonilla, P., Tan, F., Qi, Y., Ordonez, V.: Curriculum labeling: self-paced pseudo-labeling for semi-supervised learning. arXiv preprint arXiv:2001.06001 (2020)
6. Chen, C., Zheng, Z., Ding, X., Huang, Y., Dou, Q.: Harmonizing transferability and discriminability for adapting object detectors. In: Proceedings of the IEEE/CVF Conference on Computer Vision and Pattern Recognition (2020)
7. Chen, Y., Li, W., Sakaridis, C., Dai, D., Van Gool, L.: Domain adaptive faster R-CNN for object detection in the wild. In: Proceedings of the IEEE Conference on Computer Vision and Pattern Recognition (2018)
8. Deng, J., Li, W., Chen, Y., Duan, L.: Unbiased mean teacher for cross domain object detection. arXiv preprint arXiv:2003.00707 (2020)
9. Everingham, M., Van Gool, L., Williams, C.K., Winn, J., Zisserman, A.: The pascal visual object classes (VOC) challenge. Int. J. Comput. Vis. **88**, 303–338 (2010)
10. Ganin, Y., et al.: Domain-adversarial training of neural networks. J. Mach. Learn. Res. (2016)
11. Gao, J., Wang, J., Dai, S., Li, L.J., Nevatia, R.: Note-RCNN: noise tolerant ensemble RCNN for semi-supervised object detection. In: Proceedings of the IEEE International Conference on Computer Vision (2019)
12. Inoue, N., Furuta, R., Yamasaki, T., Aizawa, K.: Cross-domain weakly-supervised object detection through progressive domain adaptation. In: Proceedings of the IEEE Conference on Computer Vision and Pattern Recognition (2018)
13. Jeong, J., Lee, S., Kim, J., Kwak, N.: Consistency-based semi-supervised learning for object detection. In: Advances in Neural Information Processing Systems (2019)
14. Kim, T., Jeong, M., Kim, S., Choi, S., Kim, C.: Diversify and match: a domain adaptive representation learning paradigm for object detection. In: Proceedings of the IEEE Conference on Computer Vision and Pattern Recognition (2019)
15. Laine, S., Aila, T.: Temporal ensembling for semi-supervised learning. arXiv preprint arXiv:1610.02242 (2016)
16. Lin, T.-Y., et al.: Microsoft COCO: common objects in context. In: Fleet, D., Pajdla, T., Schiele, B., Tuytelaars, T. (eds.) ECCV 2014. LNCS, vol. 8693, pp. 740–755. Springer, Cham (2014). https://doi.org/10.1007/978-3-319-10602-1_48
17. Long, M., Cao, Y., Wang, J., Jordan, M.: Learning transferable features with deep adaptation networks. In: International Conference on Machine Learning (2015)
18. Miyato, T., Maeda, S.I., Koyama, M., Ishii, S.: Virtual adversarial training: a regularization method for supervised and semi-supervised learning. IEEE Trans. Pattern Anal. Mach. Intell. **41**, 1979–1993 (2018)
19. Pinheiro, P.O.: Unsupervised domain adaptation with similarity learning. In: Proceedings of the IEEE Conference on Computer Vision and Pattern Recognition (2018)
20. Saito, K., Ushiku, Y., Harada, T., Saenko, K.: Strong-weak distribution alignment for adaptive object detection. In: Proceedings of the IEEE Conference on Computer Vision and Pattern Recognition (2019)
21. Sohn, K., Zhang, Z., Li, C.L., Zhang, H., Lee, C.Y., Pfister, T.: A simple semi-supervised learning framework for object detection. arXiv preprint arXiv:2005.04757 (2020)

22. Sun, B., Saenko, K.: Deep CORAL: correlation alignment for deep domain adaptation. In: Hua, G., Jégou, H. (eds.) ECCV 2016. LNCS, vol. 9915, pp. 443–450. Springer, Cham (2016). https://doi.org/10.1007/978-3-319-49409-8_35

23. Tang, P., Ramaiah, C., Xu, R., Xiong, C.: Proposal learning for semi-supervised object detection. arXiv preprint arXiv:2001.05086 (2020)

24. Tarvainen, A., Valpola, H.: Mean teachers are better role models: weight-averaged consistency targets improve semi-supervised deep learning results. In: Advances in Neural Information Processing Systems (2017)

25. Tzeng, E., Hoffman, J., Saenko, K., Darrell, T.: Adversarial discriminative domain adaptation. In: Proceedings of the IEEE Conference on Computer Vision and Pattern Recognition (2017)

26. Tzeng, E., Hoffman, J., Zhang, N., Saenko, K., Darrell, T.: Deep domain confusion: maximizing for domain invariance. arXiv preprint arXiv:1412.3474 (2014)

27. Verma, V., Lamb, A., Kannala, J., Bengio, Y., Lopez-Paz, D.: Interpolation consistency training for semi-supervised learning. arXiv preprint arXiv:1903.03825 (2019)

28. Volpi, R., Morerio, P., Savarese, S., Murino, V.: Adversarial feature augmentation for unsupervised domain adaptation. In: Proceedings of the IEEE Conference on Computer Vision and Pattern Recognition (2018)

29. Wang, K., Yan, X., Zhang, D., Zhang, L., Lin, L.: Towards human-machine cooperation: self-supervised sample mining for object detection. In: Proceedings of the IEEE Conference on Computer Vision and Pattern Recognition (2018)

30. Yu, F., et al.: Unsupervised domain adaptation for object detection via cross-domain semi-supervised learning. arXiv preprint arXiv:1911.07158 (2019)

31. Zhu, J.Y., Park, T., Isola, P., Efros, A.A.: Unpaired image-to-image translation using cycle-consistent adversarial networks. In: 2017 IEEE International Conference on Computer Vision (ICCV) (2017)

Global and Local Feature Based Deep Cross-Modal Hashing

Haibo Yu[1,2], Ran Ma[1,2(✉)], Min Su[1,2], Ping An[1,2], and Kai Li[1,2]

[1] School of Communication and Information Engineering, Shanghai University, 99 Shangda Road, Baoshan District, Shanghai 200444, China
maran@shu.edu.cn
[2] Shanghai Institute for Advanced Communication and Data Science, Shanghai University, 99 Shangda Road, Baoshan District, Shanghai 200444, China

Abstract. In recent years, with the increasing number of different modal data, cross-modal retrieval has come to be an important research task. Deep cross-modal hashing receives increasing attention due to its combination of low storage cost, high search efficiency and strong capability of feature extraction of neural networks. Most of the existing deep cross-modal hashing methods extract the global semantic features of the images and texts to generate hash codes through two independent networks. In this work, we propose a novel method called Global and Local Feature based Deep Cross-Modal Hashing (GLFH). GLFH not only extracts the global features of the images and texts, but also extracts the features of regions containing objects in images and the features of words in texts by introducing the object detection method and the recurrent neural network, respectively. Then the local features of the images and texts are obtained by fusing the region features and the word features with the adaptively learned attention matrix. Finally, the global features and the local features are fused to obtain the richer features of image and text to generate the more robust hash codes. The experimental results on three widely used datasets are significantly surpass other methods, verifying the effectiveness of GLFH.

Keywords: Cross-modal hashing · Deep learning · Global feature and local feature · Attention

1 Introduction

In recent years, with the increasing number of multimedia data such as images and texts, people want to search between multimedia data and get accurate results. Therefore, cross-modal retrieval has attracted increasing attention. The purpose of cross-modal retrieval is to use a certain modal data as a query to search data with similar semantics from another modal [1]. Due to the existence of "heterogeneity" and "semantic gap" [2], the retrieval among different modalities is very challenging. Because of low storage cost and high search efficiency, cross-modal hashing attracts wide attention. Cross-modal hashing generally has two parts: feature extraction and hash learning. In the first part, different

G. Zhai et al. (Eds.): IFTC 2021, CCIS 1560, pp. 253–265, 2022.
https://doi.org/10.1007/978-981-19-2266-4_20

feature extraction methods are used to obtain the features of instances. Early cross-modal hashing relies on hand-crafted features to generate hash codes, in which the process of feature extraction and hash learning are independent and there is no information feedback between them. Therefore, the two processing parts cannot be compatible well with each other. Recent works have introduced deep learning into cross-modal hashing, and cross-modal hashing based on deep learning can achieve better results due to the powerful feature extraction capability. Existing deep cross-modal hashing adopts the convolution neural network (CNN) pre-trained on ImageNet [3], such as VGG [4] and CNN-F [5], to extract the global features, and then embeds the global features into the Hamming space to obtain the hash codes. In fact, besides the global semantic information, there is the more fine-grained information in the images and texts, such as regions in images and words in texts. We should take this local information into consideration. Although the features from low level layers of CNN encode the local information of images or texts, they cannot describe the complete information of the object. As shown in the right picture in Fig. 1, the features extracted from CNN correspond to a series of regions of equal size and shape, which rarely thinks about the content of the image. In fact, people are more likely to focus on the regions containing object instead of equally-sized image regions.

A [man] wearing a light brown [hat,] a white
shirt and brown pants is sitting on a brown
[horse.]

A man wearing a light brown hat, a white
shirt and brown pants is sitting on a brown
horse.

Fig. 1. The local features of CNN corresponding to the regions with the same size and shape (right), and the local features of our method corresponding to the regions containing object, which is more human-like (left).

Based on the idea, we introduce the object detection method to extract region features, which can contain a complete object well, to generate the local features of images. Please note that, for image, the region features are extracted by the object detection method instead of features from CNN in this paper. Then the local features can be obtained through the region features, which can be well compatible with different objects in the images.

In this paper, we recommend a new deep cross-modal hashing referred to as Global and Local Feature based Deep Cross-Modal Hashing (GLFH). Our GLFH not only extracts the global features of the images and texts, but also extracts the local features, which helps to generate more robust hash codes by fully exploiting the correlation between the images and texts from both global and local levels. The main contributions of this paper are as follows: (1) We recommend a new cross-modal hashing method, which not only extracts the global features of the images and texts, but also extracts the region features and the word features to model the relevance between the images and texts at the global and local levels. (2) In order to obtain the region features which can be well compatible with objects in the images, we introduce the object detection method, and fuse the region features with the adaptively attention matrix to obtain the local features of images. (3) Experiments on three widely used datasets show the validity of GLFH, which can significantly improve cross-modal retrieval performance.

2 Related Work

2.1 Deep Cross-Modal Hashing

With the assistance of the powerful feature extraction capability of deep neural network, deep cross-modal hashing can accomplish better results, compared with conventional shallow cross-modular hashing. Therefore, deep cross-modal hashing has gotten increasingly more consideration. Deep Cross-Modal Hashing (DCMH) [6], as one of the earliest methods to apply deep neural network to cross-modal hashing, designs an end-to-end framework to integrate feature extraction and hashing learning. Pairwise Relationship guided Deep Hashing (PRDH) [7] further takes the intra-modal constraints into consideration to boost the retrieval performance. Cross-Modal Hamming Hashing (CMHH) [8] generates hash codes by replacing the inner product restriction with the Hamming distance and adding the focal loss. Self-Supervised Adversarial Hashing (SSAH) [1] uses GAN [9] to maximize the feature distribution consistency between modalities, and add the label network to constrain the generation of hash codes. However, the above methods obtain the instance representations only by the features extracted from the last layer of the deep neural network, which ignores the more discriminative local information in the images and texts.

2.2 Attention

In latest years, the attention mechanism has been applied to many assignments and achieved remarkable results. Some works introduce attention mechanism into cross-modal hashing and achieve satisfactory results. Attention-Aware Deep Adversarial Hashing (HashGAN) [10] to extract the features of important parts of the images and texts by attention mechanism, which enhances the measurement of similarity between the images and texts. Dual Supervised Attention Deep Hashing (DSADH) [11] uses attention mechanism to shrink the gap between the image features and text features and focuses on relevant correlations of the images and texts. Self-Constraining and Attention Hashing (SCAHN) [12] uses attention mechanism to merge the hash representations of different layers in the network to generate high-quality hash codes. Inspired by this, we use attention mechanism to generate a high score for useful regions and words and a low score for the regions and words which should be filtered out.

3 Proposed GLFH

We will introduce the implementation details of GLFH in this section, including formulas, the procedure of feature extraction and hash learning. The structure of our proposed GLFH is illustrated in Fig. 2.

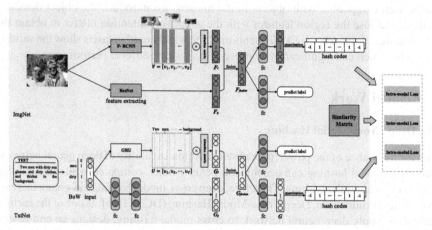

Fig. 2. Our proposed GLFH consists of ImgNet and TxtNet. For ImgNet, we extract the global features F_g through one branch, and extract the local features F_l through another branch. Then F_g and F_l are fused to obtain F_{fusion} and F_{fusion} is fed into two fully-connected layers to obtain the image features F and predict labels, respectively. TxtNet is similar to ImgNet.

3.1 Formulation

Let $O = \{o_i\}_{i=1}^n$ denote the cross-modal dataset with n instances, and each instance is an image-text pair, including an image and the matching text. Let $X = \{x_i\}_{i=1}^n$ and $Y = \{y_i\}_{i=1}^n$ denote image set and text set, respectively. And we use S^{XY}, S^{XX} and S^{YY} to represent the semantic label similarity matrix, where S^{XX} and S^{YY} represent the label similarity among images and texts respectively and S^{XY} represents the label similarity between images and texts. If two instances belong to at least one label, we let $S_{ij}^{\varepsilon\varepsilon} = 1$, otherwise $S_{ij}^{\varepsilon\varepsilon} = 0$, $\varepsilon \in \{X, Y\}$. We use $L \in \{0, 1\}^{n \times c}$ to represent the label matrix, where c is the number of labels. $L_{ij} = 1$ if the ith instance belongs to the jth label, otherwise $L_{ij} = 0$.

Given X and Y, the purpose of GLFH is to generate K-bit hash codes $B^X = \{b_i^X\}_{i=1}^n \in \{-1, +1\}^{n \times K}$ for X and $B^Y = \{b_i^Y\}_{j=1}^n \in \{-1, +1\}^{n \times K}$ for Y. We hope that the hash codes of matched image-text pairs have smaller Hamming distance than the unmatched pairs. Note that $F_g = \{F_{gi*} | i = 1, \cdots, n\} \in \mathbb{R}^{n \times 512}$ and $F_l = \{F_{li*} | i = 1, \cdots, n\} \in \mathbb{R}^{n \times 512}$ denote the global features and the local features of images. Similarly, $G_g = \{G_{gi*} | i = 1, \cdots, n\} \in \mathbb{R}^{n \times 512}$ and $G_l = \{G_{li*} | i = 1, \cdots, n\} \in \mathbb{R}^{n \times 512}$ denote the global features and the local features of texts. $F_{fusion} = \{F_{fusioni*} | i = 1, \cdots, n\} \in$

$\mathbb{R}^{n \times 512}$ and $\boldsymbol{G_{fusion}} = \{\boldsymbol{G_{fusioni*}} | i = 1, \cdots, n\} \in \mathbb{R}^{n \times 512}$ denote the fusion of the global features and the local features of the images and texts. $\boldsymbol{F} = \{\boldsymbol{F_{i*}} | i = 1, \cdots, n\} \in \mathbb{R}^{n \times K}$ and $\boldsymbol{G} = \{\boldsymbol{G_{i*}} | i = 1, \cdots, n\} \in \mathbb{R}^{n \times K}$ are the final representations of the images and texts. $\boldsymbol{B}^X = \{\boldsymbol{B}^X_{i*} | i = 1, \cdots, n\} \in \mathbb{R}^{n \times K}$ and $\boldsymbol{B}^Y = \{\boldsymbol{B}^Y_{j*} | j = 1, \cdots, n\} \in \mathbb{R}^{n \times K}$ are the hash codes by applying the sign function to $\boldsymbol{F}$ and $\boldsymbol{G}$:

$$\boldsymbol{B}^X = sign(\boldsymbol{F}), \boldsymbol{B}^Y = sign(\boldsymbol{G}) \boldsymbol{B}^X, \boldsymbol{B}^Y \in \{-1, +1\}^K \tag{1}$$

3.2 Feature Extraction

Global Feature: For the image, we use Resnet [13] as the basic network to extract the 512-dimension global features $\boldsymbol{F_g}$ by removing the last layer. In order to shorten the training time, we use the parameters pre-trained on the ImageNet to assign initial values of the parameters in Resnet. For the text, we adopt BoW as its representation, and then input the representation into a three-layer fully-connected network ($l \rightarrow 8192 \rightarrow 512 \rightarrow K + c$, l for the length of BoW, K for the length of the hash code and c for the total number of categories) to extract the 512-dimension global features $\boldsymbol{G_g}$.

Local Feature: To obtain more human-like local features, we introduce the object detection method to extract the image local features. Specifically, we use Faster R-CNN [14] with Resnet-101 as the backbone, which is pre-trained on the Visual Genome [15], to extract the region features. As an object detection model, Faster R-CNN can generate the regions containing the object in images and extract the corresponding region features. Each image is fed into Faster R-CNN to generate the anchors with different size and corresponding scores, where the higher the score, the more likely the anchor contains object, and vice versa. Finally, R regions with the highest scores and the corresponding 2048-dimension region features are obtained for each image. In order to make $\boldsymbol{F_l}$ fuse with $\boldsymbol{F_g}$, we convert the dimension of region features into 512 through the full-connection layer, and get the region features $\boldsymbol{V} = [v_1, v_2, \cdots, v_R] \in \mathbb{R}^{512 \times R}$. Then the local features $\boldsymbol{F_l}$ of images are obtained by fusing the region features.

For the text, we first construct a dictionary to store the words in dataset and their corresponding indexes. According to the dictionary, BoW is converted into the sequence $\{w_1, \cdots, w_t, \cdots w_T\}$, where w_t is the index of appearing word and T is the maximum number of words. Then we embed w_t into a vector space by $x_t = \boldsymbol{M} w_t$, where $\boldsymbol{M}$ is the embedding matrix and feed the vectors into the bidirectional GRU (bi-GRU) [16]:

$$h_t^f = \mathrm{GRU}_f(x_t, h_{t-1}^f) \tag{2}$$

$$h_t^b = \mathrm{GRU}_b(x_t, h_{t-1}^b) \tag{3}$$

where h_t^f and h_t^b represent the hidden state of the forward GRU and h_t^b represent the hidden state of the backward GRU as time step t, and we obtain the word features $\boldsymbol{U} = [u_1, u_2, \cdots, u_T] \in \mathbb{R}^{512 \times T}$ by averaging the two hidden states, i.e. $u_t = \frac{1}{2}(h_t^f + h_t^b)$. Then the local features $\boldsymbol{G_l}$ of texts are obtained by fusing the word features.

Attention: We use attention mechanism to filter out the useless regions and words adaptively, and then obtain the local features of the images and texts by fusing the region features and the word features respectively. Specifically, for the ith image, we use linear projection to calculate the scores for each region:

$$A_X = W_X V \qquad (4)$$

where $W_X \in \mathbb{R}^{1 \times 512}$ is the projection matrix. $A_X = [A_{X1j}, \cdots, A_{X1R}] \in \mathbb{R}^{1 \times R}$ is the score matrix where A_{X1j} represents the score of the jth region. Then we aggregate all region features based on the score matrix:

$$F_{li*} = A_X^T V \qquad (5)$$

where F_{li*} is the local feature of the ith image. Such a mechanism can filter out the regions with low scores.

Similarly, for the jth text, we can get its local feature G_{lj*} as follows:

$$G_{lj*} = A_Y^T U, \quad A_Y = W_Y U \qquad (6)$$

where $W_Y \in \mathbb{R}^{1 \times 512}$ is the projection matrix. $A_Y \in \mathbb{R}^{1 \times T}$ is the score matrix where A_{Y1j} represents the score of the jth word.

After obtaining the global and local features, we fuse the global features F_g and local features F_l to get the fusion features F_{fusion} of images and fuse the global features G_g and local features G_l to get the fusion features G_{fusion} of texts:

$$F_{fusion} = F_g + F_l, \quad G_{fusion} = G_g + G_l \qquad (7)$$

3.3 Hash Learning

We fed F_{fusion} into a fully-connected layer with K nodes to get the hash representation F for images, and then obtain B^X by applying a sign function to F. At the same time, F_{fusion} is fed into another fully-connected layer with l nodes to output predicted labels $\widehat{L}^X$.

Similarly, we fed G_{fusion} into two fully-connected layers to output the hash representation G for texts and predicted labels $\widehat{L}^Y$, and then obtain B^Y by applying a sign function to G.

3.4 Loss

The loss of GLFH is composed of inter-modal loss, intra-modal loss, quantization loss and label prediction loss. Here the loss function we used refers to previous works. For example, the first three terms refer to the work of Wang et al. [12], and the last term refers to the work of Peng et al. [11].

In order to measure the similarity between two hash codes, we use the inner product of hash codes as a measure standard, and the probability of S^{XY} under the given hash codes can be formulated as:

$$p\left(S_{ij}^{XY} | \boldsymbol{B}^X{}_{i*}, \boldsymbol{B}^Y{}_{j*}\right) = \begin{cases} \sigma\left(\theta_{ij}^{\boldsymbol{B}^X \boldsymbol{B}^Y}\right) & S_{ij}^{XY} = 1 \\ 1 - \sigma\left(\theta_{ij}^{\boldsymbol{B}^X \boldsymbol{B}^Y}\right) & S_{ij}^{XY} = 0 \end{cases} \tag{8}$$

where $\theta_{ij}^{\boldsymbol{B}^X \boldsymbol{B}^Y} = \frac{1}{2}\boldsymbol{B}^X{}_{i*}\boldsymbol{B}^Y{}_{j*}^T$ and $\sigma(x) = \frac{1}{1+e^{-x}}$. Therefore, the larger the inner product of the two instances, the more similar they are. According to the Formula (8), we can formulate the inter-modal loss as:

$$\mathcal{J}_{inter} = -\sum_{i,j=1}^{n}(S_{ij}^{XY}\theta_{ij}^{FG} - log(1 + e^{\theta_{ij}^{FG}})) \tag{9}$$

where $\theta_{ij}^{FG} = \frac{1}{2}\boldsymbol{F}_{i*}\boldsymbol{G}_{j*}^T$. Note that we calculate the inner product of features to replace the inner product of hash codes because the hash codes are binary which are not conductive to optimization of network parameters. Hence, we can preserve the inter-modal similarity between $\boldsymbol{F}$ and $\boldsymbol{G}$ by optimizing the Formula (9).

Similar to Formula (9), the intra-modal loss of the images and texts can be formulated as:

$$\mathcal{J}_{intra-image} = -\sum_{i,j=1}^{n}(S_{ij}^{XX}\theta_{ij}^{FF} - log(1 + e^{\theta_{ij}^{FF}})) \tag{10}$$

$$\mathcal{J}_{intra-text} = -\sum_{i,j=1}^{n}(S_{ij}^{YY}\theta_{ij}^{GG} - log(1 + e^{\theta_{ij}^{GG}})) \tag{11}$$

where $\theta_{ij}^{FF} = \frac{1}{2}\boldsymbol{F}_{i*}\boldsymbol{F}_{j*}^T$, $\theta_{ij}^{GG} = \frac{1}{2}\boldsymbol{G}_{i*}\boldsymbol{G}_{j*}^T$. The intra-modal loss is defined as:

$$\mathcal{J}_{intra} = \mathcal{J}_{intra-image} + \mathcal{J}_{intra-text} \tag{12}$$

We want to encode semantic label information into the generated hash code. Here uses label prediction loss to generate hash codes with semantic label information, which can be formulated as:

$$\mathcal{J}_{label-image} = -\sum_{i=1}^{n}\left(\boldsymbol{L}_{i*}log\left(\sigma\left(\hat{\boldsymbol{L}}_{i*}^X\right)\right) + (1 - \boldsymbol{L}_{i*})log(1 - \sigma(\hat{\boldsymbol{L}}_{i*}^X))\right) \tag{13}$$

$$\mathcal{J}_{label-text} = -\sum_{j=1}^{n}\left(\boldsymbol{L}_{j*}log\left(\sigma\left(\hat{\boldsymbol{L}}_{j*}^Y\right)\right) + \left(1 - \boldsymbol{L}_{j*}\right)log\left(1 - \sigma(\hat{\boldsymbol{L}}_{j*}^Y)\right)\right) \tag{14}$$

$$\mathcal{J}_{label} = \mathcal{J}_{label-image} + \mathcal{J}_{label-text} \tag{15}$$

Because the image hash representations $\boldsymbol{F}$ and text hash representations $\boldsymbol{G}$ are real-valued, the process of binarization from the hash representations to the hash codes will inevitably cause information loss. To reduce the loss, the quantization loss is defined as:

$$\mathcal{J}_{quantization} = \|\boldsymbol{B}^X - \boldsymbol{F}\|_F^2 + \|\boldsymbol{B}^Y - \boldsymbol{G}\|_F^2 \quad s.t. \; \boldsymbol{B}^X = \boldsymbol{B}^Y = \boldsymbol{B} \tag{16}$$

which can constraint $\boldsymbol{B}^X$ and $\boldsymbol{B}^Y$ to close enough to $\boldsymbol{F}$ and $\boldsymbol{G}$. Please note that we think that the learned hash codes $\boldsymbol{B}^X$ and $\boldsymbol{B}^X$ retain the semantic similarity between images and texts because $\boldsymbol{F}$ and $\boldsymbol{G}$ retain the similarity.

Based on the Formula (8)–(16), the final objective function of GLFH is as follows:

$$\min_{\theta_x, \theta_y, \boldsymbol{B}} \mathcal{J} = \mathcal{J}_{inter} + \mathcal{J}_{intra} + \mathcal{J}_{label} + \mathcal{J}_{quantization} \tag{17}$$

where θ_x and θ_y are parameters of image and text network, respectively, and $\boldsymbol{B}$ is learned unified hash code.

4 Experiment

4.1 Dataset

We validate our model using three extensively used datasets, MIRFLICKR-25K [17], NUS-WIDE [18] and IAPR TC-12 [19]. MIRFLICKR-25K dataset contains 25000 image-text pairs. After deleting the invalid image-text pairs, 20015 pairs are selected and there are 24 unique labels in MIRFLICKR. NUS-WIDE dataset contains 81 unique labels and 269648 image-text pairs. After removing the image-text pairs without labels, in total, we select 190421 pairs that belong to the 21 most-frequent concept labels in our experiment. IAPR TC-12 dataset contains 20000 image-text pairs with 275 semantic labels. Please note that the dataset we use are all multi-label datasets, that is, the image-text pairs in them are annotated by one or more labels. In terms of dataset splitting, for MIRFLICKR-25K and IAPR TC-12, we use 2000 pairs randomly selected from them as the query set, 10000 pairs as the training set, and the rest as the retrieval set. For NUS-WIDE, we randomly select 2100 pairs as the query set, 10500 pairs as the training set and the rest as the retrieval set.

4.2 Implementation Details

Region and Word Features. For the region features, we use Faster R-CNN to extract the features of the top 36 regions with the highest scores for each image. For the word features, for convenience, we intercept the first 30 words from the text with more than 30 words, and fill the text to 30 words for the text with less than 30 words. The parameters to be learned in network are initialized with Gaussian distribution.

Training Strategy. In order to optimize the parameters θ_x, θ_y and $\boldsymbol{B}$, we adopt the alternate learning strategy. In each epoch, we optimize one of the parameters while keeping the other fixed. All parameters are randomly initialized with Gaussian function with a mean value of 0 and a standard deviation of 0.01. We train our GLFH through the Stochastic Gradient Descent (SGD) algorithm, and set the batch size and the number of epoch to 64 and 150, respectively. The initial learning rate of image network and text network are 0.0004 and 0.0005, and reduced by 10 times after every 50 epochs.

4.3 Evaluation

We compare GLFH with other state-of-the-art cross-modal hashing methods, including CMFH [20], STMH [21], SePH [22], DCMH [6], SSAH [1] and SCANH [12]. The first three are based on shallow structure, and the last three are based on deep structure. The deep networks of DCMH and SSAH are CNN-F, and the deep networks of SCANH is Resnet. We replace the deep networks of our method from Resnet to CNN-F to compare with DCMH and SSAH, called GLFH-F. In this paper, Mean Average Precision (MAP) and Precision-Recall (PR) curves are used as evaluation criteria. For the convenience of the following description, we use I2T to symbolize that image query texts and T2I to represent that texts query images.

The MAP values of GLFH and other comparison methods at different hash code lengths are shown in Table 1, and it can be viewed that our proposed GLFH can achieve the optimal performance under different conditions.

Table 1. The MAP values of different methods at different hash code length on three datasets.

Task	Method	MIRFLICKR-25K			NUS-WIDE			IAPR TC-12		
		16 bits	32 bits	64 bits	16 bits	32 bits	64 bits	16 bits	32 bits	64 bits
I2T	CMFH	0.6235	0.6359	0.6487	0.4833	0.4961	0.5092	0.4055	0.4168	0.4238
	STMH	0.6032	0.6219	0.6294	0.4699	0.4856	0.4939	0.3821	0.4023	0.4167
	SePH	0.7021	0.7095	0.7129	0.5964	0.6031	0.6124	0.4429	0.4539	0.4651
	DCMH	0.7325	0.7413	0.7476	0.5857	0.6009	0.6024	0.4519	0.4738	0.4867
	SSAH	0.7819	0.7954	0.8006	0.6136	0.6178	0.6248	0.5289	0.5662	0.5709
	GLFH-F	0.8236	0.8356	0.8446	0.6559	0.6748	0.6967	0.5454	0.5745	0.5971
	SCAHN	0.8098	0.8301	0.8328	0.6416	0.6524	0.6618	0.5413	0.5712	0.5892
	GLFH	**0.8272**	**0.8431**	**0.8525**	**0.6591**	**0.6712**	**0.6735**	**0.5562**	**0.5837**	**0.6092**
T2I	CMFH	0.6347	0.6392	0.6452	0.4935	0.5201	0.5235	0.4038	0.4168	0.4221
	STMH	0.6021	0.6178	0.6259	0.4521	0.4687	0.4791	0.3549	0.3746	0.3998
	SePH	0.7186	0.7201	0.7296	0.5821	0.5925	0.6028	0.4386	0.4597	0.4613
	DCMH	0.7612	0.7716	0.7905	0.6205	0.6452	0.6521	0.5085	0.5279	0.5438
	SSAH	0.7963	0.8050	0.8091	0.6157	0.6208	0.6257	0.5368	0.5582	0.5737
	GLFH-F	0.7970	0.8094	0.8222	0.6541	0.6738	0.6946	0.5285	0.5480	0.5712
	SCAHN	0.8012	0.8132	0.8201	0.6501	0.6512	0.6652	0.5281	0.5560	0.5689
	GLFH	**0.8053**	**0.8233**	**0.8327**	**0.6683**	**0.6812**	**0.6860**	**0.5457**	**0.5679**	**0.5958**

On MIRFLICKR-25K, GLFH surpasses the shallow hashing methods like SePH by 8% to 13%, and the deep hashing methods by 3% to 8%. The MAP of GLFH is also higher than other methods on NUS-WIDE and IAPR TC-12. It shows that the local features can provide finer-grained supplementary information for cross-modal retrieval.

That is, GLFH uses not only global information, but also local information to generate high-quality hash codes.

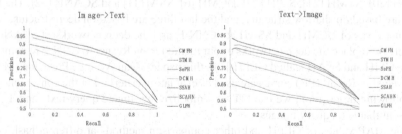

Fig. 3. The PR curves on MIRFLICKR-25K when the hash code length is 16.

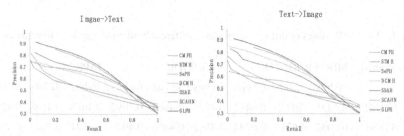

Fig. 4. The PR curves on NUS-WIDE when the hash code length is 16.

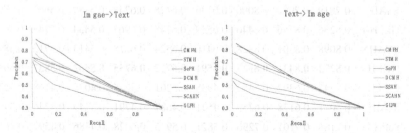

Fig. 5. The PR curves on IAPR TC-12 when the hash code length is 16.

Figure 3, 4 and 5 show the PR curve results of different methods on three datasets when the hash code length is 16. It can be viewed that our GLFH is superior to other comparison methods.

4.4 Ablation Study

To verify the impact of the key components of GLFH, we carry ablation experiments on the MIRFLICKR-25K dataset. The MAP values of ablation experiments are shown in Table 2.

Table 2. The MAP values of ablation study on MIRFLICKR-25K.

Task	Method	MIRFLICKR-25K		
		16 bits	32 bits	64 bits
I2T	**GLFH**	**0.8272**	**0.8431**	**0.8525**
	w/o label	0.8198	0.8350	0.8432
	w/o attn	0.8259	0.8421	0.8476
	w/o label+attn	0.8219	0.8320	0.8422
	Global	0.8135	0.8268	0.8333
	Local	0.8041	0.8154	0.8205
T2I	**GLFH**	**0.8053**	**0.8233**	**0.8327**
	w/o label	0.8011	0.8176	0.8262
	w/o attn	0.8052	0.8199	0.8264
	w/o label+attn	0.8010	0.8151	0.8250
	Global	0.7963	0.8145	0.8197
	Local	0.7962	0.8100	0.8190

Five variants we carefully designed for GLFH are as follows: (a) w/o label denotes removal of the label prediction loss. (b) w/o attn denotes removal of the attention. (c) w/o label+attn denotes removal of the label prediction loss and attention. (d) Global denotes that only global features are used. (e) Local denotes that only local features are used. Through ablation experiments, we can get the impact of each component in GLFH on model performance and verify the effectiveness of complete GLFH.

5 Conclusion

In this paper, we propose Global and Local Feature based Deep Cross-Modal Hashing (GLFH). GLFH introduces the object detection method to extract region features and the recurrent neural network to extract word features, and then fuses the region features and the word features to obtain local features of the images and texts. Moreover, the regions and words useless to retrieval are filtered out through the adaptively learned attention matrix, so that the local features can provide more discriminative information for cross-modal retrieval. Finally, the local features and global features are fused to obtain the features with richer information, and the label prediction loss is used to generate more discriminative hash codes. Extensive experiments demonstrate the effectiveness of GLFH.

Acknowledgements. This work is supported by the National Natural Science Foundation of China under Grant No. 61828105, Chen Guang Project supported by Shanghai Municipal Education Commission and Shanghai Education Development Foundation under Grant No. 17CG41.

References

1. Li, C., Deng, C., Li, N., Liu, W., Gao, X., Tao, D.: Self-supervised adversarial hashing networks for cross-modal retrieval. In: Proceedings of the IEEE Conference on Computer Vision and Pattern Recognition, pp. 4242–4251 (2018)
2. Baltrusaitis, T., Ahuja, C., Morency, L.: Multimodal machine learning: a survey and taxonomy. IEEE Trans. Pattern Anal. Mach. Intell. **41**(2), 423–443 (2019)
3. Deng, J., Dong, W., Socher, R., Li, L., Li, K., Li, F.: ImageNet: a large-scale hierarchical image database. In: Proceedings of the IEEE Conference on Computer Vision and Pattern Recognition, pp. 248–255 (2009)
4. Simonyan, K., Zisserman, A.: Very deep convolutional networks for large-scale image recognition. In: ICLR International Conference on Learning Representation, pp. 1–14 (2015)
5. Chatfield, K., Simonyan, K., Vedaldi, A., Zisserman, A.: Return of the devil in the details: delving deep into convolutional nets. In: Proceedings of the British Machine Vision Conference (2014)
6. Jiang, Q., Li, W.: Deep cross-modal hashing. In: Proceedings of the IEEE Conference on Computer Vision and Pattern Recognition, pp. 3232–3240 (2017)
7. Yang, E., Deng, C., Liu, W., Liu, X., Tao, D., Gao, X.: Pairwise relationship guided deep hashing for cross-modal retrieval. In: Proceedings of the Thirty-First AAAI Conference on Artificial Intelligence, pp. 1618–1625 (2017)
8. Cao, Y., Liu, B., Long, M., Wang, J.: Cross-modal hamming hashing. In: Ferrari, V., Hebert, M., Sminchisescu, C., Weiss, Y. (eds.) ECCV 2018. LNCS, vol. 11205, pp. 207–223. Springer, Cham (2018). https://doi.org/10.1007/978-3-030-01246-5_13
9. Goodfellow, I., Pouget-Abadie, J., Mirza, M., et al.: Generative adversarial nets. In: Proceedings of the 27th International Conference on Neural Information Processing Systems, pp. 2672–1690 (2014)
10. Zhang, X., Zhou, S., Feng, J., et al.: HashGAN: Attention-aware Deep Adversarial Hashing for Cross Modal Retrieval. arXiv preprint arXiv:1711.09347 (2017)
11. Peng, H., He, J., Chen, S., et al.: Dual-supervised attention network for deep cross-modal hashing. Pattern Recogn. Lett. **128**, 333–339 (2019)
12. Wang, X., Zou, X., Bakker, E.M., Wu, S.: Self-constraining and attention-based hashing network for bit-scalable cross-modal retrieval. Neurocomputing **400**, 255–271 (2020)
13. He, K., Zhang, X., Ren, S., Sun, J.: Deep residual learning for image recognition. In: Proceedings of the IEEE Conference on Computer Vision and Pattern Recognition, pp. 770–778 (2016)
14. Ren, S., He, K., Girshick, R., Sun, J.: Faster R-CNN: towards real-time object detection with region proposal networks. IEEE Trans. Pattern Anal. Mach. Intell. **39**(6), 1137–1149 (2017)
15. Krishna, R., et al.: Visual genome: connecting language and vision using crowdsourced dense image annotations. Int. J. Comput. Vis. **123**(1), 32–73 (2017). https://doi.org/10.1007/s11263-016-0981-7
16. Chung, J., Gülçehre, Ç., Cho, K., Bengio, Y.: Empirical evaluation of gated recurrent neural networks on sequence modeling. arXiv preprint arXiv:1412.3555 (2014)
17. Huiskes, M., Lew, M.: The MIR Flickr retrieval evaluation. In: Proceedings of the 1st ACM International Conference on Multimedia Information Retrieval, pp. 39–43 (2008)
18. Chua, T., Tang, J., Hong, R., et al.: NUS-WIDE: a real-world web image database from National University of Singapore. In: Proceedings of the ACM International Conference on Image and Video Retrieval, pp. 1–9 (2009)
19. Escalante, H., Hernández, C., Gonzalez, J., et al.: The segmented and annotated IAPR TC-12 benchmark. Comput. Vis. Image Underst. **114**(4), 419–428 (2010)

20. Ding, G., Guo, Y., Zhou, J.: Collective matrix factorization hashing for multimodal data. In: Proceedings of the IEEE Conference on Computer Vision and Pattern Recognition, pp. 2083–2090 (2014)
21. Wang, D., Gao, X., Wang, X., He, L.: Semantic topic multimodal hashing for cross-media retrieval. In: Proceedings of the International Conference on Artificial Intelligence, pp. 3890–3896 (2015)
22. Lin, Z., Ding, G., Hu, M., Wang, J.: Semantics-preserving hashing for cross-view retrieval. In: Proceedings of the IEEE Conference on Computer Vision and Pattern Recognition, pp. 3864–3872 (2015)

Attentive Feature Focusing for Person Search by Natural Language

Renjie Pan[1,2], Hua Yang[1,2(✉)], Xinxin Yang[1,2], Mao Xiaodong[3], Long Ye[4], and Da Pan[4]

[1] The Institute of Image Communication and Network Engineering, Department of Electronic Engineering, Shanghai Jiao Tong University, Shanghai, China
{rjpan21,hyang,yang-xinxin}@sjtu.edu.cn

[2] Shanghai Key Laboratory of Digital Media Processing and Transmission, Shanghai Jiao Tong University, Shanghai, China

[3] Science and Technology Department of Shanghai Public Security Bureau, Shanghai, China

[4] State Key Laboratory of Media Convergence and Communication, Communication University of China, Beijing 100024, China
{yelong,pdmeng}@cuc.edu.cn

Abstract. Cross-modal Retrieval has made great improvement since social media and artificial intelligence is gradually changing our life style. Human interaction is no longer limited to a single mode. Cross-modal retrieval brings greater portability to users. Extracting more sufficient feature from multimedia data and better fusing the feature have become the focus of academic research. In response to these two issues, this paper applies deep learning as the foundation for person search by natural language, combining CNN and Transformer. Meanwhile, we utilize BERT, the most effective feature extraction network in Natural Language Processing and proposed a network architecture using attention mechanism. The framework is divided into a global branch and a fine-grained branch. At the same time, a human parsing network is designed to classify different parts of the characters to obtain feature representation in attribute level. In the visual-textual alignment, the k-reciprocal sampling algorithm is used to construct a more comprehensive sample pair. The proposed framework has achieved *state-of-the-art* performance in CUHK-PEDES, which proves its great capacity and prospect.

Keywords: Person search by natural language · Cross-modal retrieval · Metric learning

This work was supported in part by National Natural Science Foundation of China (NSFC, Grant No. 61771303, 62171281), Science and Technology Commission of Shanghai Municipality (STCSM, Grant No. 19DZ1209303, 20DZ1200203, 2021SHZDZX0102), SJTU Yitu/Thinkforce Joint Laboratory for Visual Computing and Application, and the Open Research Project of the State Key Laboratory of Media Convergence and Communication, Communication University of China, China (No. MCCSKLMCC2020KF003).

© Springer Nature Singapore Pte Ltd. 2022
G. Zhai et al. (Eds.): IFTC 2021, CCIS 1560, pp. 266–280, 2022.
https://doi.org/10.1007/978-981-19-2266-4_21

1 Introduction

The goal of cross-modal retrieval is to use data from one modality to retrieve another one. The major challenge is measuring the similarity between two modalities. Therefore, a more comprehensive modeling is indispensable during cross-modal retrieval. The current research goal is to design more effective ways to make it more accurate and expandable. Traditional retrieval tasks can only be based on a single modality. For example, in pedestrian re-identification(Re-ID), police officers can only describe the appearance of the suspect based on the verbal description of the witness. In this case, cross-modal retrieval becomes significant in real life.

Whether the model can merge the feature from multi modalities is directly related to the retrieval performance [23]. Taking text-image retrieval as an example, images of different identities may have human characteristics such as hairstyle, facial expression, skin color, tops, bottoms, shoes, bags, etc. Descriptions of images include color, shape, posture, etc. Thanks to deep learning and computer vision, the feature extraction backbone learns abundant feature from images and text such as ResNet [7] and LSTM [8], which solves gradient disappearance generated by RNN [18] and better deal with long sequences. The rich time-domain feature is widely used in the industry. In the past two years, transformer [21] has made a breakthrough in temporal feature representation. In cross-modal retrieval, better fusing two modalities is the main direction of current research.

There are still many challenge in cross-modal retrieval. For example, if a single samples in two modalities share with similar characteristics, chances are that they may be mismatched. This situation is called "mal-positioned matching". In Visual Question Answering (VQA) [3] and image-text retrieval [10], the overall similarity across modalities is measured by the vectors of the image and textual features. The negative sample that is very similar to the positive sample is false positive pair, which makes it difficult for the model to distinguish effectively, thus cannot match them with specific appearance attributes. This problem has made researchers quite confused in recent years, which poses a nontrivial mission for fine-grained interaction between images and text.

This work analyzes the characteristics of existing cross-modal retrieval algorithms and launches an in-depth study of person search by natural language algorithms and proposes a framework using the most advanced backbones, which optimize the text feature extraction capabilities and hence better integrate textual features with image features and improve the comprehensive performance. The main contributions of the work can be summarized as follows:

- **Transformer combined with CNN.** In the image backbone, we fuse CNN with Transformer, which combines both the ability of processing local feature representation and the ability of processing long-term feature representation.
- **BERT as textual feature backbone.** The textual feature backbone uses BERT [5] as the textual feature backbone network, which utilizes its larger vocabulary corpus, pays better attention to the characteristics of long-

sequence, captures more precise semantic information and effectively improves the overall performance.

- **Global-grained branch combined with fine-grained branch.** The local attribute obtained by the Human-parsing network (HRNet) serves as a segmentation block to facilitate each fine-grained branch to create a segmentation map of a specific attribute category. It serves as a knowledge regulator to present the attribute of fine-grained branch. At the same time, contrastive learning is also used in fine-grained branch in order to obtain good embedding of both images and text and to learn excellent feature representations in conjunction with global-grained branch.

2   Related Works

2.1   Cross-Modal Retrieval

Cross-modal retrieval aims at fusing the data between two modalities to accomplish the retrieval task of a given modality and another one. There are plenty of multimedia data such as images, text, voices, videos, physiological signals, etc. Figure 1 shows the cross-modal retrieval framework under common circumstances.

Cross-modal retrieval of images and text requires that both images and text have good feature representation. Traditional image backbone [13] generates local feature representation by detecting key points in the images. Many methods are proposed to handle correlative tasks, which can be generally concluded into two categories: 1) Associative subspace learning [12,24,25,27] and 2) Coupled similarity learning [11,14,19].

The purpose of associative subspace learning is to find an associative latent space where the embedding of images and text can be directly compared. It usually measures the distance based on the characteristics of the two modalities. Andrew et al. proposed Deep Canonical Correlation Analysis (DCCA) [1], which learns complex nonlinear projections of different forms of data to obtain linearly correlated representations. In addition, [27] further extended [1]. But DCCA causes instability of the covariance of each batch will cause eigenvalue problem. Bi-directional ranking loss [12,24,25] optimizes triplet loss [19]. Wang et al. [25] designed a dual-channel nonlinear neural network to extract features of text and images separately, with bi-directional ranking loss as the objective function. Later, [24] used embedded and similarity network to learn a latent semantic embedding, in which the similarity network learned the similarity through the dot product of textual and visual feature matrices. Liu et al. [12] designed the Recurrent Residual Fusion (RRF) module based on the original dual-channel neural network architecture. It draws on residual module idea in ResNet and adds RRF to the network, which makes a better representation of images and text and greatly innovates the previous work.

Coupled similarity learning aims to design a similarity network that can predict image-text matching pairs. In addition to measuring the global-grained similarity between two modalities, many research works are devoted to better matching local regions and textual fragments. Ma et al. [14] introduced CNN for the first time in the image-text retrieval matching problem, proposed m-CNN and segmented the textual content to match the image features. However, it did not pay enough attention to visual fine-grained semantics.

Li et al. [11] compares the feature of a mini-batch with all N samples in another modality. Based on this, CMCE also designed a two-stage network: 1) CMCE loss function, which was designed to learn the identity-aware feature representation of images and texts to obtain ideal text and image feature representations. 2) Further capture fine-grained alignments, which focus more on word-level similarity. The second stage is tightly coupled by CNN-LSTM in order to match remarkable regions and latent text semantics. In addition, the second stage pays more attention to negative samples, so only hard negative samples can enter the second stage for learning, which is a good solution to the negative sample selection strategy. However, it requires hardware of high level and computing power requirements to store samples. Similarly, [19] proposed category prediction to learn the image-text embedding layer. Huang et al. proposed sm-LSTM [14], which includes a multimodal context-modulated attention scheme at each time step. By predicting saliency maps, an image-text pair can be selectively focused on. The representation of the selected pair is obtained based on the predicted saliency map, and then they are compared to measure the local similarity. sm-LSTM focused on the potential information in text through innovative textual feature backbone networks and image instance perception network.

2.2   Person Search by Natural Language

The current cross-modal retrieval between images and text can be categorized into two forms, which are searching by images and natural language. The former can also be termed as Person re-identification (Re-ID).

The typical Re-ID methods refer to the retrieval of the candidates with the highest correlation in the image datasets. However, clear and effective images cannot always be obtained easily, which hinders the application and development of Re-ID. Recently, researchers have focused their attention on re-recognition through text descriptions: recognizing pedestrians through natural language descriptions. At the same time, the model also faces huge challenges such as processing more complicated long and random sentences, and low-quality surveillance images may lead to inconsistent interpretation. In order to solve these problem, [9,12,17] proposed attention mechanism to build a modular connection between visual and textual representation, [15] proposed a cross-modal objective function, and [4] adopted tailoring in order to discover dense visual features, and learns the matching mode at the regional level [30]. In addition, [28] also introduced pose estimation for more details of human body.

It is very important to use appropriate feature representations for image-text retrieval. Many studies have consistently adopted the global image features and only use word segmentation on text description. As a result, some visual cues are ignored in the expression of the fine-grained level and thus visual-textual feature expression is not comprehensive.

For textual feature representation, the phrases serve as the corresponding component of the specific visual cues and is usually the ground truth. Another method is to extract textual features by segmenting the sentence first and then identifying the nominal phrases. Textual attributes are treated as auxiliary tags to supplement the content of image features.

We know that the information we can tell from the text must be greater than or equal to the information expressed by the image. Otherwise, image-text pairs must contain mismatched information and can only be processed as a negative sample. Therefore, whether textual feature is fully discovered completely affects the matching performance. Moreover, there is a fundamental difference between text descriptions even if they look very similar, which brings more difficulty in distinguishing them. Long and random sentences are tend to learn redundant information, which is an urgent problem.

3   Proposed Method

The overall structure of the proposed model is shown in Fig. 1. In global-grained branch, we extract the entire image and the whole text to obtain the global feature representation. Specifically, given an image of a pedestrian, we use ResNet with pre-trained parameters as the basic network. On this basis, we add a Transformer layer, which act as an attention mechanism. Eventually, the visual representation is mapped into an embedding space through a fully connected layer, and the global visual representation $x_g \in R^2$ is obtained. Given a textual description, we segment it first and embed the words into BERT to capture the contextual relations of each words. The hidden states of the antecedent and subsequent word are linked. We obtain the intermediate textual features of all connected hidden states through max-pooling. Then, by mapping the textual representation into the embedding space through a MLP layer, a global-grained textual representation $z_g \in R^{512}$ is generated.

In fine-grained branch, we use Human-parsing network (HRNet) to classify the characters according to different parts of the pedestrians and obtain the fine-grained visual representation; At the same time, the whole sentence are segmented and divided into words. Words are classified into attribute level, which obtains the fine-grained representation of a single word.

3.1   Word Segmentation

Given a natural language description, we use Pytorch transformers to segment the text first. We use BERT as the textual backbone to fully extract textual feature representation. Then, we use Stanford POS tagger to parse and extract the nominal phrases in each text and obtain the global textual information and the fine-grained textual information at the same time.

Then we use a clustering dictionary to extract words with particular information or original attributes in a single sentence. Specifically, we collect a word list of each attribute category, such as "jeans", "sports shoes", etc. We use word

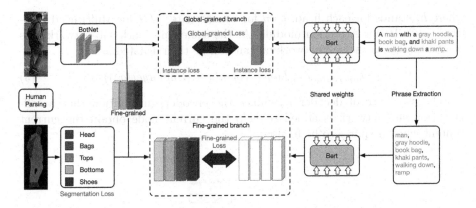

Fig. 1. The proposed architecture is composed of visual and textual input. The image-text embedding learns the joint feature representation and visual-textual alignment module consists of both global and fine-grained branches.

vectors of the same attribute category as anchor embedding. Based on this, the attributes in each category are highly related words and phrases. The extracted attributes are conducive to matching with the classification of human body parts so as to fully achieve a fine-grained analysis. Using clustering to process words at attribute level is one of the innovations of this research.

3.2 Attention Mechanism

Attention mechanism has recently achieved great success in deep neural networks. It was first proposed in machine translation, namely sequence to sequence(seq2seq) tasks. seq2seq treats the last output of the encoder as the input of the decoder, compresses the entire content of the original sequence into a fixed-size vector, which cannot fully mine the information of long sequences. Attention mechanism [2] is one of the core innovations of machine translation. Attention mechanism alleviates this by allowing the decoder to look back at the hidden state of the original sequence, and then provide weight average as an additional input to the decoder, making full use of the output features of each hidden layer in the decoding stage.

Based on Attention mechanism, Transformer also uses an encoder-decoder architecture, but it is more complicated. Whose specific model is shown in Fig. 2. Multi-head self-attention enables current node not only pay attention to the current word, but also obtain the semantics of the context. It uses different linear transformations to project Query, Key and Value, and finally stitches different results together, details as follows:

$$MH(Q, K, V) = Con(h_1, h_2, \ldots, h_h)W^0 \tag{1}$$

$$h_i = Att(QW_i^Q, KW_i^K, VW_i^V) \tag{2}$$

where h_i stands for each head, Con for concatenate, MH for Multi head algorithm and Att for Attention module. At the same time, each sub-network uses residual links, so the sub-network output can be then denoted as:

$$sub_{layeroutput} = LayerNorm(x + (SubLayer(x))) \qquad (3)$$

The structure of decoder resembles the encoder, in addition that a self-attention sub-network is added to help the current node obtain the current content which requires to be focused.

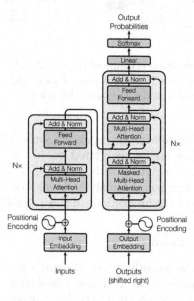

Fig. 2. The architecture of Transformer, where the encoder is made up of six layers with each contains two sub-networks, namely multi-head self-attention mechanism (MSHA) and a fully connected network layer.

Backbone Network with Attention. BERT [5] mainly consists of a stack of multiple Transformer encoders and uses a bidirectional structure to handle classification or regression tasks. With its pre-trained models, we can fine-tune in cross-modal retrieval tasks by learning a more comprehensive textual feature representation. In this work, we also compared bi-LSTM. Extensive experiments show that BERT as the textual backbone network has a great improvement.

Although CNN can effectively capture local information, long-distance dependencies need to be established in visual tasks such as object detection, instance segmentation and key point detection. Vision Transformer (ViT) [6] shows that the dependence of computer vision tasks on CNN is unnecessary, and the direct application of image block sequence converters can perform image classification tasks well. The specific method is to split the image into small blocks and provide the linear embedding sequence of these small blocks as the input. The specific structure is shown in Fig. 3.

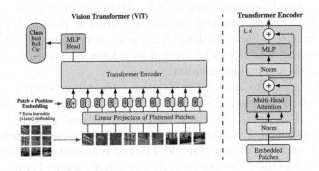

Fig. 3. ViT framework. The image with $(H \times W \times C)$ is flattened into a two-dimensional block, whose size is $(N \times (P^2C))$. Among them, (P, P) is the size of the block, $N = HW/P^2$, where N is block number. Flatten tiles are the input of the encoder and the structure of the decoder is similar to Transformer.

Although ViT first applied Transformer to computer vision, compared with image classification, the size of image is usually larger, hence the application is limited. Besides, dividing images into tiles and expanding them into a line will damage the continuity of information in the horizontal image space. Specifically, the two tiles arranged vertically will be separated by the others after being expanded.

In order to solve these problems, [16,22,29] add a self-attention layer to CNN layers. While fully expressing the local representation, it also pays attention to long sequential information, which makes some substantial progress. [20] designed the following ideas: 1) Preserve the CNN layers to effectively learn coarse feature maps from the image; 2) Design global-grained attention layer to integrate the information captured by CNN. In this way, the advantages of Transformer and CNN are combined and spatial downsampling is performed through convolution so that the attention layer can work more effectively at images with a smaller resolution. In this work, we refer to [20], replace the last three 3×3 convolutional layers of ResNet with MHSA, as is shown in Fig. 3 and 4.

Bottleneck Transformer as the image backbone network learns better image feature representation. In the experiment, we also compared it with the traditional ResNet, which proves Bottleneck Transformer indeed achieved a certain improvement.

3.3 Visual and Textual Semantic Alignment

The image backbone is denoted as $F(x) = BoTNet(x)$, where $x \in (64, 3, 384, 128)$ which represent the batch size, channels and the dimension of the image respectively. Next, we introduce global-grained branch and fine-grained branch, as shown in Fig. 2. $Global = F_{global}(F(x))$, each local feature of fine-grained branch can be expressed as $Fine = F_{fine}(F(x))$.

A segmentation layer is set refer to [26] with fine-grained branches and local attribute representation obtained through the Human parsing network. Each fine-grained branch is supervised to create a segmentation map of a concrete attribute searching list. It can be treated as a knowledge regulator to present the attributes of each fine-grained branch.

The next stage is to learn an associative embedding between two modalities. We introduce contrastive learning and treat the input as a triplet, namely $\langle visual^i, textual^*, textual \rangle$ and $\langle textual^i, visual^*, visual \rangle$, where i means the anchor to be identified, * represents the feature representation corresponding to the ith person, namely a positive sample. The rest represents a randomly selected person irrelevant to the ith person, namely a negative sample. For matching evaluation method, We use cosine similarity to evaluate, which can be specifically expressed as:

$$S_{cosine} = \frac{v_t \cdot t}{\|v\| \cdot \|t\|} \tag{4}$$

For a positive sample $\langle v^i, t^+ \rangle$, larger the similarity, the better. For negative samples, the similarity should be as small as possible. However, simply suppressing the similarity will have constraints on negative samples, so we choose to set a boundary. The goal is to optimize the deviation between S_{cosine}^+ and S_{cosine}^- to be greater than the boundary value, which is also called Relative similarity criterion. It can be denoted as the follows:

$$S_{cosine}^+ \rightarrow 1 \tag{5}$$

$$S_{cosine}^+ - S_{cosine}^- > m \tag{6}$$

We select logistic loss as the loss function, hence the equation above can be simplified as:

$$S_{cosine}^+ - \alpha > 0 \tag{7}$$

$$S_{cosine}^+ - \beta < 0 \tag{8}$$

α is the lower boundary of a positive sample, β is the upper boundary of a negative sample. According to logistic function, the ultimate objective function is:

$$L_{AlignLoss} = \frac{1}{N} \sum_{i=1}^{N} log[1 + e^{-\tau_r(S_i^+ - \alpha)}] + log[1 + e^{-\tau_j(S_i^- - \beta)}] \tag{9}$$

where τ_r and τ_j represents two hyper parameters to control size of the gradient.

One of the prerequisites for correctly retrieving image and text pairs is a large number of positive and negative samples, which can provide effective supervised learning. However, the current mainstream contrastive learning methods select samples belonging to the same category, while only arbitrarily choose negative samples, which has little effect on the matching of global features but suffers from local features. Therefore, to process the information expressed in fine-grained branch, we need to expand the searching space of positive samples to construct a more comprehensive sample pair.

When two images with the same attributes belong to different identities, they can be called "surrogate positive sample". For such samples, how to deal with fine-grained semantic difference is the key point. Subject to the rearrangement technology in the Re-ID, k-reciprocal unsupervised sampling [26] learns to gain attribute-level labels effectively. Specifically, we can extract a batch of visual and textual feature representations from backbone and use k-reciprocal unsupervised sampling to mine the corresponding "surrogate positive samples" of each attribute.

For the instance level, we add cross-entropy loss separately to help learn their discriminative features, that is, the Instance loss. Pixel-level cross-entropy loss is added for the local attribute features obtained through the Human parsing network, which is the Segmentation loss. What's more, in visual-textual alignment, we designed matching loss function in global granularity and fine granularity, namely Global-grained loss and Fine-grained loss. The overall objective function can be specifically denoted as:

$$L_{overall} = L_{instance} + L_{segmentation} + L_{global} + L_{fine} \tag{10}$$

4   Experiments and Results

4.1   Evaluation Dataset

We evaluated the proposed methods on CUHK-PEDES, which is currently the only cross-modal pedestrian retrieval dataset based on natural language description. It consists of 40,206 pictures and 13,003 identities in total. The training set is composed of 34054 images, including 11,003 identities; the validation set is composed of 3078 images, including 1,000 identities; and the test set is composed of 3074 images, including 1,000 identities and at least two descriptions for each.

4.2   Experiment Setup

All the experiments are based on PyTorch. The model used in the experiments was implemented on NVIDIA Tesla V100 and NVIDIA GeForce RTX 3080 GPU. We use Recall@K to evaluate the performance, which means that in the top-K results, at least the percentage of the text description corresponding to the image of a matching person is retrieved.

For images, we use the model shown in Fig. 3 as the backbone, and ResNet-X for comparison. The input image size is 384×128. Adam optimizer and weight decay is set to 4×10^{-5}. Each mini-batch contains 64 image-text pairs. The learning rate is initialized to 2×10^{-4} in the first 40 iterations, and then decay by 0.1 times in the remaining 30 iterations. The hyper parameters of formula 9 are set to $\alpha = 0.6, \beta = 0.4, \tau_r = 10, \tau_j = 40$, respectively.

For attribute level, we use the Human parsing network to divide the visual-textual attributes into five categories: head, upper body, lower body, shoes, and bags. These five categories can describe the appearance of a pedestrian in detail. In Fig. 4, we visualize the body segmentation result, which proves effective performance of our method where different color blocks represent different feature attributes.

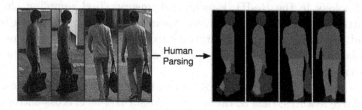

Fig. 4. Segmentation of 5 human body parts

4.3   Comparisons with *State-of-the-Art*

We summarized the global and fine-grained representations, and compared them with the current *state-of-the-art* methods under CUHK-PEDES by using Recall@ K (K = 1, 5, 10). Dual Path [9], CMPM+CMPC [28] designed better joint embeddings to learn the relationship between images and text, while GNA-RNN [?], CMCE [11] and PWM-ATH [4] use attention mechanism to express the relationship between images and text. Without exception, these methods use global representation learning. Compared with ViTAA, we have obtained a more adequate global and fine-grained feature representation after optimizing the backbone network of both images and text, which has improved in all indicators. The specific test results are shown in Table 1.

Table 1. Comparison with *state-of-the-art* methods on CUHK-PEDES

Methods	Feature selection	R@1	R@5	R@10
GNA-RNN	Global	19.05	–	53.64
CMCE	Global	25.94	–	60.48
CMPM+CMPC	Global	49.37	–	79.27
Dual Path	Global	44.40	66.26	75.07
ViTAA	Global+Fine-grained	55.97	75.84	83.52
Proposed method	Global+Fine-grained	**57.98**	**77.37**	**84.84**

The proposed method has improved in all indicators, R@1 is 2% higher than ViTAA, while R@5 is 1.53% higher and R@10 is 1.32% higher.

4.4 Ablation Studies

After analyzing the overall performance of our proposed model, we test each part of the model and use the test results to verify the role of each part. The specific test details are as follows. To test the performance of each part, We still used CUHK-PEDES, and the model is divided into four parts: image backbone network, textual backbone network, global-grained module and fine-grained module.

Image Backbone Network. For the image backbone, we use ResNet-X and our proposed method to test the feature extraction capabilities, while keeping the text backbone network all set to BERT, and the global-grained branch and the fine-grained branch are all retained, The test details are shown in Table 2.

Table 2. Comparison of different image backbones

Backbone selection		R@1	R@5	R@10
Visual	Textual			
ResNet-18	BERT	46.60	69.24	78.36
ResNet-34	BERT	55.96	74.18	84.24
ResNet-50	BERT	55.99	75.84	83.51
Proposed method	BERT	**57.98**	**77.37**	**84.84**

From the table above, the proposed image backbone has achieved the highest retrieval performance under while other modules remain unchanged. The fusion of CNN and MHSA can better extract visual feature representation.

Textual Backbone Network. For the textual backbone, we use LSTM, Bi-LSTM and our proposed method to test the textual feature extraction capability, while keeping the image backbone network all set to BotNet-50, and the global and fine-grained branches are all retained. Test details are shown in Table 3.

Table 3. Ablation studies of different textual backbone network

Backbone selection		R@1	R@5	R@10
Textual	Visual			
LSTM	BotNet-50	55.46	75.14	78.35
bi-LSTM	BotNet-50	55.98	75.85	83.55
Proposed method	BotNet-50	**57.98**	**77.37**	**84.84**

From the results, we can conclude that our textual backbone has achieved better retrieval results than the others, which proves BERT is better than traditional models in textual feature extraction. However, BERT is relatively larger in framework and requires higher computing power and hardware conditions. Compared with LSTM, BERT does better in processing long-sequence information.

Visual-Textual Alignment. The visual-textual alignment can be divided into the following parts: Instance loss, Segmentation loss, Global-grained loss and Fine-grained loss. In order to compare the contribution of each part of the module, we keep one part and remove all the other parts to compare the effect of the individual modules. Test results are shown in Table 4.

Table 4. Ablation studies of visual-textual alignment module

Model selection				R@1	R@5	R@10
Instance	Segmentation	Global	Fine			
*				29.52	51.82	61.57
*	*			30.39	52.71	63.11
*	*		*	32.16	53.91	63.67
*	*	*		54.81	74.02	82.45
*	*	*	*	**57.98**	**77.37**	**84.84**

The results in Table 4 certify that: 1) The purpose of fine-grained loss is to improve the marginal optimization of local feature, which only has a feeble help to the matching process. Similarly, when the segmentation loss is detached, the local attribute feature cannot be fully aligned, leading to a decrease in global-grained module. It can be seen that the segmentation loss and the global-grained loss are indispensable. 2) When both the fine-grained loss and segmentation loss are selected, the performance is greatly improved, indicating that segmentation loss and global-grained loss complement each other well. 3) The last two rows compare the impact of fine-grained loss. It can be seen that the global-grained loss contributes the most, which greatly improves the retrieval effect. After integrating all modules, the performance has been slightly improved, which proves the contribution of fine-grained loss again.

5   Conclusion

In this paper, we design a cross-modal retrieval framework for person search by natural language, adding attention mechanism to both image and textual backbones to more fully discover the features from these modalities. At the same time, on the basis of retaining the CNN layer in the image backbone network, we apply Transformer so as to effectively learn features at attribute level and low-resolution maps from the images, while also using the global self-attention layer to roll the information captured from CNN layers. In this way, the advantages of Transformer and CNN are combined, and spatial downsampling is performed in order that the attention layer can work more effectively at a smaller resolution. Besides, global and fine grained branches contribute to the performance a lot, which proves the idea that both feature from global-grained level and attribute level deserves to be discovered. Experiments on CHUK-PEDES demonstrate that our method outperforms *state-of-the-arts* results. In the future, we will focus on the generalization of this work with tests on other datasets to further elaborate the framework.

References

1. Andrew, G., Arora, R., Bilmes, J., Livescu, K.: Deep canonical correlation analysis. In: International Conference on Machine Learning, pp. 1247–1255. PMLR (2013)
2. Bahdanau, D., Cho, K., Bengio, Y.: Neural machine translation by jointly learning to align and translate. arXiv preprint arXiv:1409.0473 (2014)
3. Cai, G., et al.: Ask&confirm: active detail enriching for cross-modal retrieval with partial query. In: Proceedings of the IEEE/CVF International Conference on Computer Vision (ICCV), pp. 1835–1844, October 2021
4. Chen, T., Xu, C., Luo, J.: Improving text-based person search by spatial matching and adaptive threshold. In: 2018 IEEE Winter Conference on Applications of Computer Vision (WACV), pp. 1879–1887. IEEE (2018)
5. Devlin, J., Chang, M.W., Lee, K., Toutanova, K.: BERT: pre-training of deep bidirectional transformers for language understanding. arXiv preprint arXiv:1810.04805 (2018)
6. Dosovitskiy, A., et al.: An image is worth 16×16 words: transformers for image recognition at scale. arXiv preprint arXiv:2010.11929 (2020)
7. He, K., Zhang, X., Ren, S., Sun, J.: Deep residual learning for image recognition. In: Proceedings of the IEEE Conference on Computer Vision and Pattern Recognition, pp. 770–778 (2016)
8. Hochreiter, S., Schmidhuber, J.: Long short-term memory. Neural Comput. **9**(8), 1735–1780 (1997)
9. Huang, Y., Wang, W., Wang, L.: Instance-aware image and sentence matching with selective multimodal LSTM. In: Proceedings of the IEEE Conference on Computer Vision and Pattern Recognition, pp. 2310–2318 (2017)
10. Jeon, J., Lavrenko, V., Manmatha, R.: Automatic image annotation and retrieval using cross-media relevance models. In: Proceedings of the 26th Annual International ACM SIGIR Conference on Research and Development in Information Retrieval, pp. 119–126 (2003)
11. Li, S., Xiao, T., Li, H., Yang, W., Wang, X.: Identity-aware textual-visual matching with latent co-attention. In: Proceedings of the IEEE International Conference on Computer Vision, pp. 1890–1899 (2017)
12. Liu, Y., Guo, Y., Bakker, E.M., Lew, M.S.: Learning a recurrent residual fusion network for multimodal matching. In: Proceedings of the IEEE International Conference on Computer Vision, pp. 4107–4116 (2017)
13. Lowe, D.G.: Distinctive image features from scale-invariant keypoints. Int. J. Comput. Vis. **60**(2), 91–110 (2004)

14. Ma, L., Lu, Z., Shang, L., Li, H.: Multimodal convolutional neural networks for matching image and sentence. In: Proceedings of the IEEE International Conference on Computer Vision, pp. 2623–2631 (2015)
15. Nam, H., Ha, J.W., Kim, J.: Dual attention networks for multimodal reasoning and matching. In: Proceedings of the IEEE Conference on Computer Vision and Pattern Recognition, pp. 299–307 (2017)
16. Ramachandran, P., Parmar, N., Vaswani, A., Bello, I., Levskaya, A., Shlens, J.: Stand-alone self-attention in vision models. arXiv preprint arXiv:1906.05909 (2019)
17. Reed, S., Akata, Z., Lee, H., Schiele, B.: Learning deep representations of fine-grained visual descriptions. In: Proceedings of the IEEE Conference on Computer Vision and Pattern Recognition, pp. 49–58 (2016)
18. Schmidhuber, J.: Deep learning in neural networks: an overview. Neural Netw. **61**, 85–117 (2015)
19. Schroff, F., Kalenichenko, D., Philbin, J.: FaceNet: a unified embedding for face recognition and clustering. In: Proceedings of the IEEE Conference on Computer Vision and Pattern Recognition, pp. 815–823 (2015)
20. Srinivas, A., Lin, T.Y., Parmar, N., Shlens, J., Abbeel, P., Vaswani, A.: Bottleneck transformers for visual recognition. In: Proceedings of the IEEE/CVF Conference on Computer Vision and Pattern Recognition, pp. 16519–16529 (2021)
21. Vaswani, A., et al.: Attention is all you need. In: Advances in Neural Information Processing Systems, pp. 5998–6008 (2017)
22. Wang, H., Zhu, Y., Green, B., Adam, H., Yuille, A., Chen, L.-C.: Axial-DeepLab: stand-alone axial-attention for panoptic segmentation. In: Vedaldi, A., Bischof, H., Brox, T., Frahm, J.-M. (eds.) ECCV 2020. LNCS, vol. 12349, pp. 108–126. Springer, Cham (2020). https://doi.org/10.1007/978-3-030-58548-8_7
23. Wang, K., Yin, Q., Wang, W., Wu, S., Wang, L.: A comprehensive survey on cross-modal retrieval. arXiv preprint arXiv:1607.06215 (2016)
24. Wang, L., Li, Y., Huang, J., Lazebnik, S.: Learning two-branch neural networks for image-text matching tasks. IEEE Trans. Pattern Anal. Mach. Intell. **41**(2), 394–407 (2018)
25. Wang, L., Li, Y., Lazebnik, S.: Learning deep structure-preserving image-text embeddings. In: Proceedings of the IEEE Conference on Computer Vision and Pattern Recognition, pp. 5005–5013 (2016)
26. Wang, Z., Fang, Z., Wang, J., Yang, Y.: *ViTAA*: visual-textual attributes alignment in person search by natural language. In: Vedaldi, A., Bischof, H., Brox, T., Frahm, J.-M. (eds.) ECCV 2020. LNCS, vol. 12357, pp. 402–420. Springer, Cham (2020). https://doi.org/10.1007/978-3-030-58610-2_24
27. Yan, F., Mikolajczyk, K.: Deep correlation for matching images and text. In: Proceedings of the IEEE Conference on Computer Vision and Pattern Recognition, pp. 3441–3450 (2015)
28. Zhang, Y., Lu, H.: Deep cross-modal projection learning for image-text matching. In: Proceedings of the European Conference on Computer Vision (ECCV), pp. 686–701 (2018)
29. Zhao, H., Jia, J., Koltun, V.: Exploring self-attention for image recognition. In: Proceedings of the IEEE/CVF Conference on Computer Vision and Pattern Recognition, pp. 10076–10085 (2020)
30. Zheng, Z., Zheng, L., Garrett, M., Yang, Y., Xu, M., Shen, Y.D.: Dual-path convolutional image-text embeddings with instance loss. ACM Trans. Multimed. Comput. Commun. Appl. (TOMM) **16**(2), 1–23 (2020)

Video Salient Object Extraction Model Guided by Spatio-Temporal Contrast

Chunhua Li$^{(\boxtimes)}$, Nana Hao$^{(\boxtimes)}$, and Yukun Liu

Hebei University of Science and Technology, Shijiazhuang 050018, China
`1739565759@qq.com`, `haonan0926@126.com`

Abstract. The classical video salient object extraction model has the problems of incomplete salient object extraction and background interference, which limits the application scenarios of video salient object. Video salient object extraction should not only consider the spatial saliency formed by the intrinsic features of video frames, but also consider the temporal saliency formed by motion information. In this paper, a video salient object extraction model based on spatio-temporal fusion is proposed to search salient objects under the guidance of spatio-temporal contrast. Firstly, the priori information about the rough position of prominent targets is determined by adaptive fusion of three-color space contrast and motion contrast along the non-selective path. Then, based on the obtained prior salience cues, the energy function is used to guide the fusion of the underlying significance cues to optimize the interframe salience accuracy. The energy function consists of the foreground extraction item of the current frame and the dynamic position optimization item of the next frame. Finally, a complete video salient object is extracted by the spatio-temporal adaptive fusion using super pixels level and pixels level smoothing optimization twice. Experiments on ViSal, Segtrack-V2 and DAVIS public video saliency datasets show that this model is superior to classical video saliency algorithms in accuracy, reliability and robustness.

Keywords: Spatio-temporal prior · Energy function · Degradation optimization · Video salience

1 Introduction

The visual system is able to quickly capture important objects in the field of vision, a cognitive process that allows humans to easily interpret complex scenes in real time. Saliency detection technology imitates human visual function to analyze and detect the areas of interest in images or videos, and is widely used in practical tasks such as image compression [1], image segmentation [2] and target recognition and detection [3]. In recent years, surveillance system [4], behavior detection [5], target tracking [6], video compression [7] and other application fields put forward the requirements of comprehensive temporal dimension visual

G. Zhai et al. (Eds.): IFTC 2021, CCIS 1560, pp. 281–296, 2022.
https://doi.org/10.1007/978-981-19-2266-4_22

cues detection of salient objects, making video salient object extraction an urgent problem to be solved.

Various target motion modes, complex and changeable video scenes, camera motion and other factors in video sequence increase the difficulty of video saliency detection, making it extremely challenging to improve the accuracy of video saliency detection. Video saliency detection methods can be roughly divided into two categories: one is based on spatial algorithm, the other is based on space-time algorithm. Image saliency detection is directly applied to video data detection based on spatial algorithm. Spatial algorithms are further divided into bottom-up [8, 9] and top-down [10, 11] algorithms for integrating visual cues. Guo [12] builds dense and sparse appearance models with the help of super pixels; Zhu [13] cascades center prior and secret channel prior to obtain significance values of images; and Li [14] proposes a popular sorting significance detection method combining convex hull intersection with super pixels. Although these algorithms have good detection performance in images, they cannot deal with problems caused by motion such as occlusion and motion blur, and the time jitter phenomenon is serious when used in video detection.

In order to ensure time consistency, spatio-temporal algorithm synchronously applies spatial structure features and motion information of images to improve detection performance. Liu [15] extracted video salient targets based on motion histogram detection of temporal saliency and adaptive fusion of spatial saliency. In [16], the motion vector field is used to construct the graph structure and refine the salient information in the propagation process. Wang [17] introduced local and global contrast bias to construct gradient fields and extracted foreground objects with high significance. In [18], geodesic technology was used to construct undirected intra-frame and inter-frame graphs, and skeleton abstract model was used to enhance salience estimation. Zhang [19] proposed a processing method of optical stream vectors based on maximum consistency, which improved the detection performance of significant video targets. However, these algorithms cannot achieve robust low-level clues. Therefore, we use contrast to distinguish conspicuous objects in the scene. Optical flow describes the motion variation caused by the movement of the foreground object itself, the camera movement, or both movements in the video. The modeling of appearance and motion is regarded as global cues at the temporal level to guide the fusion of temporal and spatial salience. Finally, super pixels' level and pixels level optimization form a video saliency detection method suitable for various motion modes and complex scenes.

2   Algorithm Description

The existing algorithm uses optical flow method to detect saliency target movement, but the processing effect is not ideal for the local movement of significant target, the change of sports field is not obvious or has occlusion, which becomes the bottleneck of improving detection accuracy of this kind of algorithm. Aiming at this problem, we put forward a kind of video target detection model, based on the contrast guidance on color contrast and movement as a prior condition on the basis of the contrast model, structure model and dynamic appearance position model, to ensure the consistency of the video sequence, add significant target local movement or the impact of the condition. The block diagram of the algorithm model in this paper is shown in Fig. 1.

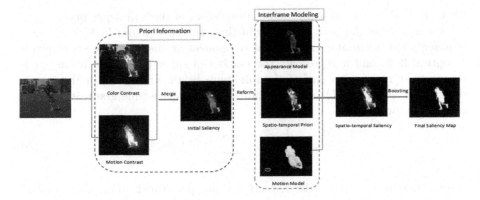

Fig. 1. Algorithm model of this paper

2.1 Contrast Based Prior Information

Human vision mechanism can actively extract the color and motion boundary of the object of interest and quickly lock the prominent target in the complex scene. In this process, both the color difference of discontinuous video frames and the motion change between adjacent frames can become important clues for video salience detection. Optical flow [20] refers to the instantaneous velocity of pixel movement of a moving object in space on the observed imaging plane. Using the optical flow gradient to extract the changes of pixels in the time domain and the correlation between adjacent frames in the image sequence, the object's motion speed can be calculated.

Motion Contrast. In order to overcome the complexity and high time cost of computing optical flow on pixel level, this paper uses super pixels segmentation technology [21] to divide each frame in video frame sequence $I = \{I_1, \ldots, I_k, \ldots\}$ into super pixels set $I_k = \{I_{k,1}, I_{k,2}, \ldots\}$, and calculates the optical flow vector of each frame super pixels by optical flow method. Estimation of optical flow field based on super pixels can reduce computational burden. Since the motion gradient is more reliable than the motion explicit cue [22], here we use the combination of motion gradient and color gradient to generate spatio-temporal gradient to guide the calculation of low-level contrast. The expression of space-time gradient M_k is:

$$M_\mathrm{k} = \|\nabla (I_k)\|_2 \bullet \|v_x, v_y\|_2 \tag{1}$$

where $\nabla (I_k)$ is the color gradient of the super pixels in the frame I_k, (v_x, v_y) is the optical flow vector in the horizontal and vertical directions, $\|\ \|_2$ denotes 1_2- norm, and '$\bullet$' is the Hadamard product. Thus, motion contrast S_M is described as:

$$S_M = \sum_{P_j \in \varphi_i} \frac{\|V_i, V_j\|_2}{\|P_i, P_j\|_2}, \quad \varphi_i \in \{\varepsilon \in \|P_i, P_j\|_2 \le \varepsilon + d\} \qquad (2)$$

where $P_i \in R^2 \times 1$ represents the position center of the i-th super pixels, $P_j \in R^2 \times 1$ represents the position center of the j-th super pixels; $V_i, V_j \in R^{2n} \times 1$ represents the horizontal and vertical component gradients of the super pixels I_k optical flow, and n represents the number of super pixels in a frame; φ_i is the contrast range, d is half of the minimum height and width of the image, that is $d = \frac{1}{2}\min\{W, H\}$. ε is determined by the space-time gradient M_k, the calculation formula is:

$$\varepsilon = \frac{d}{\|\wedge (M_k)\|_0} \sum_{\varepsilon \in \|\varepsilon, i\|_2 \le d} \|\wedge (M_k)\|_0 \qquad (3)$$

where $\|\ \|_0$ indicates that order reduction is not performed; $\wedge()$ is the sampling operation.

Color Contrast. Color is the most intuitive sensory feature of human beings. In the feature extraction method based on image content, color is the first image feature used. By definition of salience, the foreground and background areas should be visually distinct, and the object area should be time continuous between successive frames. Due to different pixels and information in different color spaces, the feature points detected by contrast are also different. The brightness and tone of the color in HSV color space are more obvious, which shows the color difference well. The color distribution in LAB and RGB color space is more uniform, and it contains all the colors that can be recognized by the human eye.

Therefore, in order to improve the integrity and accuracy of the explicit indigenous in the color contrast image, we use the contrast fusion information of the three-color spaces to interpret the visible target. Similar to the calculation of motion contrast, we replace the optical flow gradient vector in Formula (2) with component values in RGB, HSV and LAB in three color Spaces to obtain three color space contrast maps, denoted as:

$$S_{C1} = \sum_{P_i \in \varphi_i} \frac{\|(R_i, G_i, B_i), (R_j, G_j, B_j)\|_2}{\|P_i, P_j\|_2} \qquad (4)$$

$$S_{C2} = \sum_{P_i \in \varphi_i} \frac{\|(H_i, S_i, V_i), (H_j, S_j, V_j)\|_2}{\|P_i, P_j\|_2} \qquad (5)$$

$$S_{C3} = \sum_{P_i \in \varphi_i} \frac{\|(L_i, A_i, B_i), (L_j, A_j, B_j)\|_2}{\|P_i, P_j\|_2} \qquad (6)$$

The intersection of color contrast of the three Spaces was calculated to obtain the final color contrast saliency map S_C, as shown in Fig. 2(g). The obtained saliency map based on color and motion contrast was fused by Hadamard product to obtain the initial saliency estimate S_o.

$$S_O = S_M \cdot S_C \tag{7}$$

The motion information calculated by optical flow is assumed to be constant between video frames, similarly, the brightness of colors within short video frames is also assumed to be constant. Therefore, we use color contrast adjustment of consecutive three frames of video to enhance the robustness of initial significance estimation to obtain the spatio-temporal prior information S_1.

As shown in Fig. 2, bmx (top) with a complex background and dog (bottom) with a target whose color was close to the background were obtained by optical flow method, and optical flow gradient and static gradient were used to guide the motion contrast diagram (f). The contrast of three-color spaces solves the problem of inaccurate positioning of significant objects. The adaptive fusion of spatial cues (g) and temporal cues (f) forms the initial salience estimation (h) to reduce the interference of background noise. The color contrast of three consecutive frames updates and adjusts the initial prior information to further reduce the influence of background.

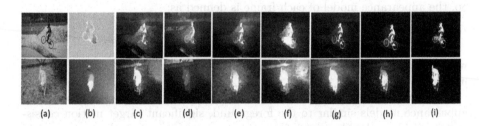

Fig. 2. Realization process diagram of spatio-temporal prior information. (a) video frames; (b) optical flow diagram; (c) RGB color space comparison map; (d) HSV color space contrast map; (e) LAB color space contrast map; (f) motion contrast map S_M; (g) color contrast map S_C; (h) initial significance estimate S_o; (I) space-time prior map S_1. (Color figure online)

2.2   Interframe Modeling

The spatio-temporal prior saliency map reveals the foreground target region, but it is not complete and accurate. In particular, the foreground probability of the boundary region of an object may have a low value due to the over-segmentation process of the super pixels. In addition, inaccurate optical flow estimates may result in incorrect values. Therefore, we refer to the idea of energy function in [18] and adjust the composition of the energy function. The energy function is defined as a pair of space-time prior, foreground model of the current frame and dynamic position model of the next frame. Energy function is used to complement the foreground pixels f in the video frame. For the super pixels $I_{k,n}$ of each frame I_k, the pixels of the prominent target are marked as:

$$S(f) = \left\{ S_1 + \sum_{k,n} M^k\left(f^k\right) + \sum_{k,n} N^k\left(f^k\right) \right\} \cdot \alpha \qquad (8)$$

where M^k marks pixels with similar colors according to their appearance model; N^k is to estimate position prior marker pixels according to the dynamic position model. The α parameter is the weighting of the model and is set according to the characteristics of the video.

Appearance model M^k: to construct the foreground appearance model, we only use pixels from the super pixels connected to the foreground super pixels space of the previous frame, and the significance value is greater than the adaptive threshold, which is defined as the average of the spatio-temporal salience map. This strategy makes better use of the spatio-temporal significance information and minimizes the adverse effects of the pollution foreground in the background area with similar color to the foreground. Since our global appearance model is obtained on the basis of spatio-temporal prior information and has already located significant targets, the background in the appearance model is suppressed for more intuitive observation results [19], as shown in Fig. 3(d). So, the appearance model of each frame is defined as:

$$M^k = S_1 * (S_C + 0.1) \qquad (9)$$

where S_1 is the spatio-temporal prior information, and S_C is the color saliency map after fusion.

Motion model N^k: For clutter-like scenes and background regions with appearance models similar to the foreground, significant target motion consistency provides valuable prior information for locating regions that may contain objects. Therefore, we estimate the position of foreground objects according to the motion information of a few adjacent frames, as shown in Fig. 3(f). For frame I, we accumulate the optical flow gradient in the time window of frame $\pm t$ to obtain relatively long motion information in the foreground region, as shown below:

$$N^k = S_C * 0.5 + S_1 * 0.5 \qquad (10)$$

At the bottom of Fig. 3(b), the edge significance value of the spatio-temporal prior significance map may be lower than the adaptive threshold, resulting in incomplete object region extraction. To solve this problem, appearance model (d) and motion model (f) are added to guide the spatio-temporal salience map to improve the accuracy and robustness of detection.

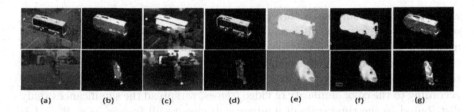

Fig. 3. Modeling process diagram. (a) Video frames; (b) Spatio-temporal prior significance map; (c) Global significance map; (d) The appearance model minus the background; (e) Optical flow diagram; (f) Removing motion models with complex backgrounds; (g) Spatio-temporal saliency map.

2.3 Saliency Optimization

Compared with prior information, the accuracy and robustness of the motion model and appearance model guided by spatio-temporal prior information are greatly improved. However, it can be seen from Fig. 3(g) that background noise still exists. In order to sharpen the boundaries of salient objects and slightly suppress false detection, we perform two smoothing enhancements at the super pixels level and pixels level to complete the refinement of salient images.

In [17,18], the traditional spatio-temporal smoothing method is used, which attempts to reveal the undetected region of the current video frame through the spatio-temporal salience transfer between all video frames belonging to the same video frame batch. As a "many-to-many" smoothing scheme, the final significance value of each super pixels is determined by the weighted average of the objects of all surrounding super pixels on spatial and temporal scales, which is prone to false detection accumulation. Inspired, in this article, we adopt cross frame between super pixels "one-on-one" [23] manner smoothing, which means that all super pixels belong to different frame is arranged together, super pixels have been given a significant degree of coherence and belong to the same time "line" of other super pixels, to overcome the false information accumulation, to a certain extent, inhibit the background noise at the same time.

The foreground objective of the obtained spatio-temporal significance $S(f)$ feature subspace is expressed as $S(f) = \{vec\,(S_1), vec\,(S_2), \ldots vec\,(S_m)\} \in R^{n \times m}$, where n, m are all positive elements, representing the number of hyperpixels per frame and all frames of a given video, respectively, and $vec()$ is vectorization function. According to the degree of homogeneity of flat display, the corresponding color clues are regarded as sparse parts, and the salience of frame I_k is:

$$S(I_k) = \frac{\bar{\beta} - (\bar{\beta} - 1) \cdot N\,(\bar{E}_c)}{\bar{\beta}(m-1)} \sum_{I=1}^{m} G(S(f) \cdot \theta, I) \tag{11}$$

$$\bar{\beta} = G(\beta, I) \tag{12}$$

$$\bar{E}_c = G\,(E_c, I) \tag{13}$$

where $N(\cdot)$ is the normalized function; β equilibrium factor matrix, $G(\cdot)$ represents l_2 distance from the objective function, I is the first column of the distance matrix, ϑ is the selection matrix [24], which codes the corresponding relation constructed between super pixels. The sparse matrix E_c is a good indicator of the difference between correct and incorrect super pixels alignment. Meanwhile, according to the color similarity of video frames, we spread the significance evenly distributed in the time scale of 9 adjacent frames to all frames, $s_l \in R^n \times 1$ is used to represent the temporal prior of 9 adjacent frames, and obtain the final salience value of the j-th super pixels of the I_k video:

$$S_{I_{k,j}} = \frac{s_l \cdot \omega_l + \sum_{I=1}^{m} \omega_I \cdot S_{I_{k-1,j}}}{\omega_l + \sum_{I=1}^{m} \omega_I} \tag{14}$$

where ω_l represents the weight of the previous frame based on l_2 color distance, $\omega_l = e^{-\|c_{l,j}, c_{I,j}\| \sigma}$, ω_I represents the weight of the next frame based on l_2 color distance, and $\sigma = 15$. Finally, the obtained super pixels level saliency map is smooth-optimized at the pixel levels, and the process is the same as formula (11). The final saliency map in Fig. 4(f) is obtained.

Figure 4 shows some examples of the two optimization processes, both of which use the integrity of the spatial domain to solve the salient objects suppressed in contrast and modeling based on the spatio-temporal salient map. For example, Fig. 4(b), the optimization enhancement superposition of different levels finally achieves relatively complete salient objects.

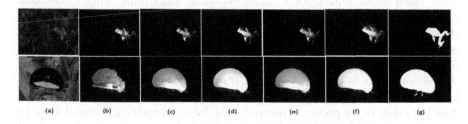

(a)   (b)   (c)   (d)   (e)   (f)   (g)

Fig. 4. Optimization process diagram: (a) original video frame, (b) spatio-temporal salience diagram, (c) super pixels level optimization diagram, (d) super pixels level enhancement diagram after optimization, (e) pixels level optimization diagram, (f) Final salience diagram, (g) Ground-truth diagram.

3   Experimental Results

In this section, a large number of experiments are conducted on the public video saliency data set of ViSal [17], Segtrack-V2 [25] and DAVIS [26], and the algorithm model is compared with 9 classical video saliency detection algorithms, including 6 traditional methods and 3 deep learning models, that is STBP [27] (space-time background prior of SIFT flow), SFLR [23](low-rank coherent space-time fusion), SGSP [16] (super pixels level), SAG [18] (geodesic space-time prior), SGAF [28] (spatio-temporal consistency), MGVS [29] (Bayesian model guided by space-time prior), SCOM [30] (deep spatio-temporal constraint optimization model), MBNM [31] (unsupervised segmentation model of bilateral network), and DLVS [32] (full convolutional network training model).

3.1 Contrast of Subjective Results

ViSal dataset was specifically proposed by Wang [17] for video object detection. This dataset includes 17 challenging video sequences, including highly chaotic backgrounds (horse, man, panda, etc.), various motion modes (fast: car, cat; slow: Boat), The foreground background color difference is small (motorbike, rider, lion, etc.), and mobile camera (gokart, etc.). The videos range in length from 30 to 100 frames.

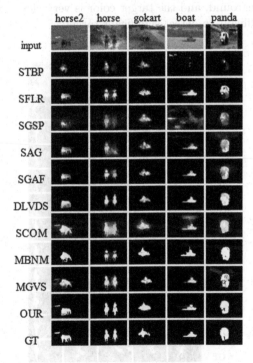

Fig. 5. Results of this model and other 10 algorithms in ViSal dataset.

In Fig. 5, we can intuitively compare the experimental results of various algorithms. Both SGSP and STBP models add motion field factors on the basis of super pixels, simply locate the position of salient targets, do not fully consider the integrity of targets, and the detection effect needs to be improved.

Although the traditional models SAG, SGAF, SFLR, MBNM and the deep learning model DLVDS show relatively robust detection performance in the face of video sequences with complex background, when there are distant targets in the video, such as horse2, the distant cloud will be directly used as background suppression, which poses a threat to the accuracy of the detection results. Although SCOM and MGVS algorithms fully consider the foreground information in the video, when dealing with the situation that the visible target is close to the background color, the detection results will have a lot of noise interference, such as panda. When dealing with complex scenes and videos with foreground and background colors close to each other, the model in this paper can reduce background interference as much as possible while ensuring the integrity of the salient target. The detection performance of the algorithm is better than that of the comparison algorithm, and it is always the closest to the ground truth value.

SegtrackV2 data set includes 14 video sequences, most of which have a very short time period (less than 100 frames), and the background is chaotic and does not change much. Each frame shows the target movement through subtle local changes in the foreground, and the target color is very close to the background color, making it difficult to detect significant targets.

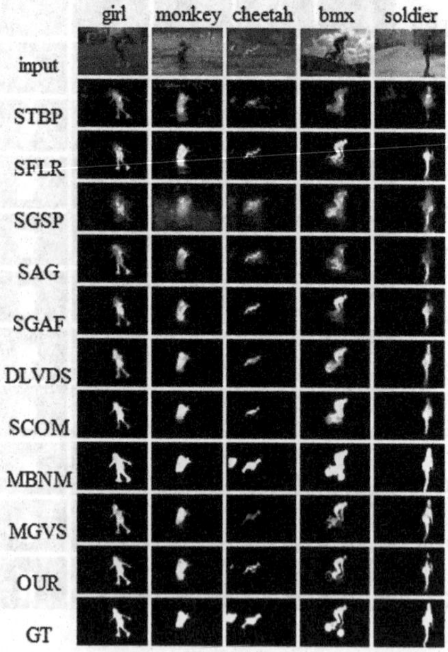

Fig. 6. Results of this model and other 10 algorithms in SegtrackV2 dataset.

As can be seen from Fig. 6, for the fast-moving target cheetah, the video sequence is blurred. The proposed algorithm and MBNM model are superior to other algorithms in target integrity and background suppression. However,

MBNM expands the salient target and ignores the target boundary details. In the face of only local movement of arms and legs of the girl, the other algorithm detection results are one kind of near the head with background noise, cannot clearly detect the complete contour of the girl (such as STBP, SGSP algorithm); the other is to use the hand of small girls as background suppression (such as SFLR, SGAF, DLVS, SCOM, MGVS). Only the proposed algorithm shows relatively stable target extraction performance to deal with various video situations.

The DAVIS dataset consisted of 50 high-resolution videos, and the scenes in the dataset contained a large number of occlusion (bus, etc.), appearance changes (mallard-fly, etc.) and shape distortion (breakdance-flare, etc.), making salient object extraction challenging.

It can be seen from Fig. 7 that in the face of the video train with complex background and close to the foreground color, the proposed algorithm and MBNM algorithm show excellent detection performance. In the face of cars that are not obvious from a distance, the algorithm, SCOM and SFLR show similar detection capabilities. However, when a bus comes all the way, the visible target

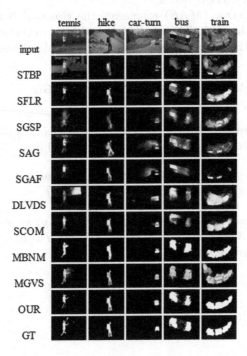

Fig. 7. Results of this model and other 10 algorithms in DAVLS dataset.

is partially occluded. The model in this paper adjusts the detection results by predicting the motion gradient of the next frame and the appearance model of the current frame, so that it is closest to the real ground map. The experimental results in this dataset once again verify that our algorithm can detect salient targets more accurately in challenging situations such as occlusion, appearance changes, small targets, and motion blur.

3.2   Objective to Evaluate

In order to evaluate our algorithm more objectively, we use standard PR curves, mean absolute error (MAE), F-measure (F_m) and S-measure (S_m) values to quantitatively analyze the performance of the algorithm.

PR curve, the abscissa denotes the recall rate and precision as the ordinate, where accuracy means the significant figure in the correct area proportion, the recall rate said significant figure and the correct figure concentrated true value corresponding to the area, the proportion of the curve of the initial value is higher, the more stable with the increase of the recall rate curve indicates algorithm to detect the effect is better.

Mean absolute error (MAE) represents the closeness between the binary graph and the truth graph. The smaller the value is, the closer the two images are to each other, the better the performance of the algorithm. It is defined as:

$$MAE = \frac{1}{W * H} \sum_{x=1}^{W} \sum_{y=1}^{H} |S(x,y) - G(x,y)| \qquad (15)$$

F-measure is used to evaluate the overall performance of the algorithm. A larger value indicates a better algorithm. It can be expressed by the following formula:

$$F_m = \frac{\left(1 + \beta^2\right) precision * recall}{\beta^2 * precision + recall} \qquad (16)$$

where $G(x,y)$ stands for Ground Truth graph, $S(x,y)$ stands for significance graph, and $\beta^2 = 0.3$ is based on experience. W and H correspond to the width and height of the image.

S-measure considers the structural similarity of region and object at the same time. The greater the value of S-measure, the better the detection performance. It is defined as follows:

$$S_m = \mu * S_0 + (1 - \mu) * S_r \tag{17}$$

where S_0 and S_r are the similarity of region perception structure and object perception structure respectively, and μ is the balance factor, set to 0.5.

To ensure the fairness of the experiment, we used codes provided by other algorithm authors to detect salient targets in the video, and obtained PR curves on ViSal, SegtrackV2, DAVIS datasets and performance evaluation tables related to MAE, F_m and S_m.

As shown in Fig. 8, the PR curve of this algorithm is slightly higher than DLVS, SCOM and other algorithms, indicating that under the same recall rate, the accuracy value of this model is higher than other algorithms, and the extracted salient regions are more accurate. With the increase of recall rate, the segmentation threshold gradually decreases, so that more regions are judged as salient regions, so the accuracy of each algorithm decreases. It can be seen from the data comparison results of Table 1 that the algorithm in this paper shows a stable detection ability, and the accuracy and robustness of the algorithm are verified again by comparing the experimental results.

Table 1. Quantitative comparison results by different approaches on ViSal, Segtrack-V2 and DAVIS datasets.

Methods	ViSal			Segtrack-V2			DAVIS		
	$F_m\uparrow$	$S_m\uparrow$	$MAE\downarrow$	$F_m\uparrow$	$S_m\uparrow$	$MAE\downarrow$	$F_m\uparrow$	$S_m\uparrow$	$MAE\downarrow$
$STBP_{17}$	0.580	0.606	0.145	0.658	0.841	0.039	0.615	0.748	0.082
$SFLR_{17}$	0.710	0.826	0.037	0.791	0.895	0.029	0.800	0.870	0.040
$SGSP_{17}$	0.568	0.723	0.129	0.500	0.787	0.082	0.654	0.798	0.097
SAG_{18}	0.593	0.807	0.066	0.648	0.896	0.040	0.593	0.759	0.085
$SGAF_{18}$	0.778	0.842	0.042	0.751	0.858	0.033	0.656	0.735	0.073
$DLVDS_{18}$	0.772	**0.905**	0.030	0.788	0.916	0.025	0.660	0.833	0.066
$SCOM_{18}$	0.591	0.766	0.100	**0.894**	0.918	0.017	0.806	**0.908**	0.033
$MBNM_{18}$	0.764	0.890	0.037	0.831	0.906	0.015	**0.861**	0.887	**0.032**
$MGVS_{19}$	0.564	0.797	0.036	0.778	0.940	0.026	0.790	0.880	0.039
OUR	**0.808**	0.858	**0.029**	0.872	**0.949**	**0.013**	0.808	0.880	**0.032**

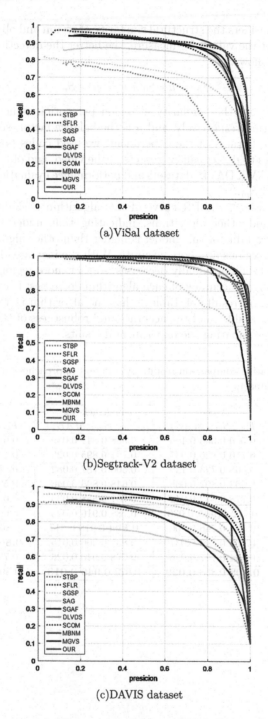

(a)ViSal dataset

(b)Segtrack-V2 dataset

(c)DAVIS dataset

Fig. 8. The PR curve of different algorithms on ViSal dataset (top), Segtrack-V2 dataset (middle) and DAVIS dataset (bottom).

4   Conclusion

In this paper, we propose a contrast guided video salient target extraction model, which does not need to know the size and target shape of the input video in advance. First choose path difference is used to calculate the movement of the video contrast and color contrast, will be based on the contrast of the fused appearance in a prior estimate of time and space as a clue to guide the energy function model and motion model is formed, in the process of removing video to determine the background, using the model and the prior information complement each other and two smooth optimizations to obtain the final saliency goals. We validate our algorithm model in three common data sets and compare it with six traditional algorithms and three deep learning models. Experimental results show that there are salient targets with fast movement, occlusion and deformation in the video, and this paper shows relatively stable detection ability.

References

1. Zheng, B., Zhang, J., Sun, G., et al.: Fully learnable model for task-driven image compressed sensing. Sensors (Basel, Switzerland) **21**(14), 4662 (2021)
2. Wang, K., Kai, W., Wang, C., et al.: Identification of NOx hotspots from oversampled TROPOMI NO2 column based on image segmentation method. Sci. Total Environ. **803**, 150007 (2022)
3. Xue, P., Wu, X., Yin, G., et al.: Real-time target recognition of urban Autonomous Vehicles based on information fusion. J. Mech. Eng. **56**(12), 165–173 (2020)
4. Sultan, S., Jensen, C.D.: Metadata based need-to-know view in large-scale video surveillance systems. Comput. Secur. **111**, 102452 (2021)
5. Lahouli, I., Karakasis, E., Haelterman, R., et al.: Hot spot method for pedestrian detection using saliency maps, discrete Chebyshev moments and support vector machine. IET Image Proc. **12**(7), 1284–1291 (2018)
6. Li, S., Qin, Z., Song, H.: A temporal-spatial method for group detection locating and tracking. IEEE Access **4**, 1 (2016)
7. Rekha, B., Kumar, R., Science, C.: High quality video assessment using salient features. Indonesian J. Electr. Eng. **7**(3), 767–772 (2017)
8. Jian, M., Wang, R., Yu, H., et al.: Saliency detection via robust seed selection of foreground and background priors. In: 2019 Asia-Pacific Signal and Information Processing Association Annual Summit and Conference (APSIPA ASC). IEEE (2019)
9. Li, C., Chen, Z., Liu, C., et al.: Saliency detection: multi-level combination approach via graph-based manifold ranking. In: 13th International Conference on Natural Computation, Fuzzy Systems and Knowledge Discovery (ICNC-FSKD) (2017)
10. Yuan, J.: Application research of RGBD Image Saliency Detection and Pedestrian Detection. University of Science and Technology of China (2019)
11. Zhang, H.: Study on Computing Model of Image saliency. University of Chinese Academy of Sciences (2013)
12. Guo, P., Qiu, J., Liu, W., et al.: Saliency detection via object enhancement and sparse reconstruction. J. Image Graph. **22**(9), 1240–1250 (2017)
13. Zhu, C., et al.: An innovative salient object detection using center-dark channel prior. In:2017 IEEE International Conference on Computer Vision. IEEE (2017)

14. Li, C., Qin, Y., Liu, Y.: Bayesian model saliency detection algorithm based on improved convex hull. Comput. Sci. **42**(01), 30–37 (2021)

15. Liu, Z., Zhang, X., Luo, S., et al.: Superpixel-based spatiotemporal saliency detection. IEEE Trans. Circuits Syst. Video Technol. **24**(9), 1522–1540 (2014)

16. Liu, Z., Li, J., Ye, L., et al.: Saliency detection for unconstrained videos using superpixel-level graph and spatiotemporal propagation. IEEE Trans. Circuits Syst. Video Technol. **27**, 2527–2542 (2016)

17. Wang, W., Shen, J., Shao, L.: Consistent video saliency using local gradient flow optimization and global refinement. IEEE Trans. Image Process. **24**(11), 4185 (2015)

18. Wang, W., Shen, J., Yang, R., et al.: Saliency-aware video object segmentation. IEEE Trans. Pattern Anal. Mach. Intell. **40**(1), 20–33 (2018)

19. Zhang, J., Chen, J., Wang, Q., et al.: Spatiotemporal saliency detection based on maximum consistency superpixels merging for video analysis. IEEE Trans. Ind. Inform. **16**, 606–614 (2019)

20. Tsai, Y., Yang, M., Black, M.: Video segmentation via object flow. In: IEEE Conference on Computer Vision & Pattern Recognition. IEEE (2016)

21. Shen, J., Du, Y., Wang, W.: Lazy random walks for superpixel segmentation (2014)

22. Fu, Q., Yu, X., Hu, W., et al.: A large displacement variational optical flow based on features matching. J. Geom. Sci. Technol. **30**, 54–57 (2013)

23. Chen, C., Li, S., Wang, Y., et al.: Video saliency detection via spatial-temporal fusion and low-rank coherency diffusion. IEEE Trans. Image Process. **26**(7), 3156–3170 (2017)

24. Zeng, Z., Chan, T., Jia, K., et al.: Finding Correspondence from Multiple Images via Sparse and Low-Rank Decomposition. Springer, Heidelberg (2012)

25. Perazzi, F., Pont-Tuset, J., Mcwilliams, B., et al.: A benchmark dataset and evaluation methodology for video object segmentation. In: 2016 IEEE Conference on Computer Vision and Pattern Recognition (CVPR). IEEE (2016)

26. Li, F., Kim, T., Humayun, A., Tsai, D., et al.: Video segmentation by tracking many figure-ground segments. In: IEEE International Conference on Computer Vision (2014)

27. Tao, X., Wei, Z., Han, W., et al.: Salient object detection with spatiotemporal background priors for video. IEEE Trans. Image Process. **26**(7), 3425–3436 (2017)

28. Guo, Y., Li, Z., Yi, L., et al.: Video object extraction based on spatiotemporal consistency saliency detection. IEEE Access **6**, 35171–35181 (2018)

29. Jiang, W., Yang, K., Li, Y.: A video salient object detection model guided by spatio-temporal prior. In: 2019 IEEE Symposium Series on Computational Intelligence (SSCI). IEEE (2019)

30. Chen, Y., Zou, W., Tang, Y., et al.: SCOM: spatiotemporal constrained optimization for salient object detection. IEEE Trans. Image Process. **27**, 3345–3357 (2018)

31. Li, S., Seybold, B., Vorobyov, A., et al.: Unsupervised video object segmentation with motion-based bilateral networks. In: European Conference on Computer Vision (2018)

32. Wang, W., Shen, J., Ling, S.: Video salient object detection via fully convolutional networks. IEEE Trans. Image Process. **27**(1), 38–49 (2017)

Spatial-Temporal Constrained Pseudo-labeling for Unsupervised Person Re-identification via GCN Inference

Sen Ling[1,2], Hua Yang[1,2,3(✉)], Chuang Liu[1,2], Lin Chen[1,2], and Hongtian Zhao[1,2]

[1] The Institute of Image Communication and Network Engineering, Department of Electronic Engineering, Shanghai Jiao Tong University, Shanghai, China
{lingsen971205,hyang,niklaus,SJChenLin,zhaohongtian}@sjtu.edu.cn
[2] Shanghai Key Laboratory of Digital Media Processing and Transmission, Shanghai Jiao Tong University, Shanghai, China
[3] MoE Key Lab of Artificial Intelligence, AI Institute, Shanghai Jiao Tong University, Shanghai, China

Abstract. Most existing unsupervised person re-identification (Re-ID) methods primarily depend on the cluster distance, and merely exploit the available source labeled data to assign pseudo labels for the unannotated data. Whereas, the cluster distance usually fails to adapt to different datasets due to the domain gap. Besides, learning exclusively from the source data can not generate accurate pseudo labels for the lack of the target data information. To address this problem, we propose to exploit the spatial-temporal constraints to facilitate the pseudo label generation process. Specifically, graphs for the labeled source data are constructed and the graph convolution network (GCN) is used to learn graph embeddings. Based on these graph embeddings, the likelihood of linkages between graph nodes is estimated and utilized to assign pseudo labels for the unlabeled data. Then, with the pseudo labels, a smoothed spatial-temporal probability distribution model is generated to amend the likelihood of linkages between graph nodes as well as correct the visual similarity scores for person Re-ID. Finally, we optimize the pseudo label assignment, feature extraction networks, and spatial-temporal model alternatively and iteratively to improve the person Re-ID performance. Comprehensive experiments demonstrate that the proposed method outperforms state-of-the-art methods.

Keywords: Person re-identification · Unsupervised learning · Graph convolutional network · Pseudo-labeling · Spatial-temporal constraints

This work was supported in part by National Natural Science Foundation of China (NSFC, Grant No. 61771303), Science and Technology Commission of Shanghai Municipality (STCSM, Grant Nos. 19DZ1209303, 20DZ1200203, 2021SHZDZX0102), Open Research Project of the State Key Laboratory of Media Convergence and Communication, Communication University of China, China (No. MCCSKLMCC2020KF003), and SJTU Yitu/Thinkforce Joint Laboratory for Visual Computing and Application.

G. Zhai et al. (Eds.): IFTC 2021, CCIS 1560, pp. 297–311, 2022.
https://doi.org/10.1007/978-981-19-2266-4_23

1   Introduction

Person re-identification (Re-ID) aims to match the same person images captured with cross-view cameras. Although existing supervised Re-ID methods [1,22,26, 27] can achieve high performance, they depend on a large amount of high quality labeled data.

It is well-known that annotating large-scale data sets of high quality costs lots of manual efforts. Consequently, the weakly-supervised [13,21] and unsupervised learning methods [4,5,14,17,30] draw considerable attention from researchers because of their low dependence on labeled data.

Many existing unsupervised domain adaption methods [2,11,20] adopt adversarial generative algorithms to transfer the style of images from the source domains into the target domains, yet they neglect the underlying distribution of samples in the target domains. Recent methods utilize pseudo-labeling techniques to fine-tune the Re-ID model in the target domains. Whereas some threshold-based methods [17,24] heavily rely on the available source data distribution, which makes it hard to adapt to different target datasets owing to the domain bias. Additionally, other methods [4,5] generate suboptimal pseudo labels due to inevitable noises and hard examples in target domains.

To solve this problem, some methods [8,12,18] propose to exploit the spatial or temporal information for better clustering. Whereas these methods model the spatial-temporal relationships independent of visual cues, leading to a suboptimal solution.

For better exploitation of spatial-temporal information, we propose to combine the spatial-temporal constraints with visual cues based on the following assumptions. Since there is certain distance between different cameras, the walking speed of pedestrians should be within a reasonable range. If the time interval between the pictures taken by two cameras is very small or very large, but the visual similarity score of these two pictures is high, there is a high probability of misclassification. To this end, we make the most of the pseudo labels predicted by the GCN, camera id numbers, and timestamps information to generate rough spatial-temporal histograms on the target dataset. Motivated by [18], we utilize the Parzen Window method to smooth the rough histogram, and employ the logistic function to normalize the spatial-temporal probability into ultimate similarity scores, which are combined with the likelihood of linkage between nodes in graphs during the process of clustering. In the end, spatial-temporal scores are integrated with visual similarity scores at the evaluation stage.

To validate the effectiveness of our joint model, we conduct comprehensive experiments on multiple datasets. The results confirm that our method outperforms the state-of-the-art methods for unsupervised domain adaptive person Re-ID. Also, ablation studies are conducted to validate the effectiveness of each proposed component.

The main contributions of this paper can be summarized in three aspects:

- We propose a GCN-based network to cluster and generate pseudo labels on an unannotated target domain.

- We use the pseudo labels to generate and smooth spatial-temporal distribution for target domains and utilize spatial-temporal constraints to ameliorate clustering and evaluation.
- We demonstrate the mutual benefits between proposed components during the iterative optimization and their effectiveness through comprehensive experiments.

2 Related Work

We mainly review unsupervised methods for person Re-ID and methods related to spatial-temporal constraints.

Unsupervised Person Re-ID. Unsupervised Re-ID methods [4,5,17,20,25] are proposed for learning tasks in labeled source domains and unlabeled target domains, and many existing unsupervised methods focus on clustering and pseudo-labeling techniques on target datasets. The DBSCAN method [3] is used in [17] to cluster and classify on the unlabeled target datasets. This threshold-based and non-parametric method may bring about false samples. An augmented discriminative clustering technique is designed in [25] to estimate and augment person clusters in target domains and enforces the discrimination ability of Re-ID models with the augmented clusters. However, all the above methods neglect to make the best of unlabeled target data, thus generating suboptimal pseudo-labels owing to the domain difference.

Graph Models for Re-ID. There are some attempts to build graph models [10,22,31] for Re-ID task. A graph representation learning scheme is proposed in [22] fro the contextual interactions between relevant regional features. The pose alignment and the feature affinity connection is utilized to construct adjacency graph and improve feature representation. The work of [10] proposes modeling a query frame and a gallery frame as a graph pair, and then designing the Siamese Residual Graph Convolutional Networks (SR-GCN) to aggregate context information to generate graph similarity as a complement of the original similarity. In this paper, we use GCN to learn graph embedding on labeled source data and assign pseudo labels on the target data, then the pseudo labels are applied for re-training the Re-ID network and generating smoothed spatial-temporal distribution model.

Spatial-Temporal Constraints. Some Re-ID methods use spatial-temporal information explicitly in camera networks [8,12,18,23] to improve Re-ID precision. The distance between cameras is used in [8] to infer the likelihood of person's transit between different cameras. The work of [12] propose a camera matching cost to indicate the connections between cameras and learn the network topology to limit the cameras inquired for matching. The Histogram-Parzen method is used in [18] to approximate the spatial-temporal probability

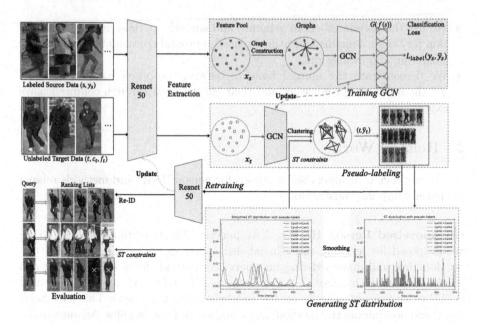

Fig. 1. The framework of our method. First, we train a graph convolutional network with extracted features from source data, then utilize GCN to cluster and label the unannotated target data. Then we use the pseudo labels to re-train the Re-ID network, generate and smooth spatial-temporal (ST) distribution. The ST constraints help clustering on the target data and improve evaluation performance. We iteratively optimize GCN, Re-ID network, and ST model to achieve the best performance.

distribution and integrate visual information and spatial-temporal information into a unified framework. All of the above methods are applied for a single labeled dataset, yet our task is devoted to cross-dataset learning on the unlabeled dataset. Besides, the spatial-temporal models are generated without the Re-ID network and stay immobilized after the initialization stage. By comparison, we use the pseudo labels predicted by the GCN to generate and smooth spatial-temporal distribution in the target domain, then utilize spatial-temporal constraints to ameliorate clustering and evaluation. The Re-ID network, GCN network, and spatial-temporal model are united as an iterative process for promoting each other.

3   The Proposed Method

3.1   Overview

For unsupervised Re-ID, there exists a labeled source domain as the assistant dataset $S = (s, y_s)$ and an unlabeled target dataset $T = (t, c_t, f_t)$, where s and t are images of source and target data respectively. y_s is the ground-truth labels of the source data, and c_t, f_t denote the camera id numbers and timestamps of the target data, respectively. Our method aims to predict pseudo labels $\bar{y}_t$ on the target dataset for re-training the Re-ID network and generate effective spatial-temporal models to improve the performance for GCN clustering and evaluation with the Re-ID network. Figure 1 shows the overall architecture of the proposed method, which contains the following main steps:

(1) Graph Construction and Training GCN on Source Data. Firstly, we construct a graph with the nodes of features extracted from labeled source data, then use GCN to learn the graph embedding.

(2) Pseudo-Labeling on Target Data and Re-training Re-ID Network. We use the trained GCN to cluster features nodes extracted from the target data and predict pseudo labels for the target data. Then the pseudo labels are used to re-train the Re-ID network on target data for the next iteration.

(3) Generating and Smoothing Spatial-Temporal Distribution. In this step, we generate spatial-temporal distribution with the pseudo labels, as well as the camera id numbers and timestamps of target data. Then the Parzen Window method is adopted to smooth it.

(4) Applying Spatial-Temporal Constraints to Improve Clustering and Evaluation. Finally, we apply the logistic function to normalize spatial-temporal distribution, then calculate spatial-temporal similarity scores and combine them with the probability of the connection between feature nodes in clustering, and correct the visual similarity scores calculated by the Re-ID network at the evaluation stage.

By repeating steps (1)–(4) up to a maximum threshold I, the overall model is iteratively updated until the performance of the Re-ID network converges. As a consequence, all the Re-ID network, the GCN model, and the spatial-temporal distribution are optimized reciprocally. The design and analysis of principal components of our joint model will be explicated in the following sections.

3.2   GCN for Clustering and Labeling

In this section, we construct graphs with feature nodes and use GCN to learn the graph embedding. Then the trained GCN is applied for clustering and pseudo-labeling on the target data.

Graph Construction. Firstly, a pre-trained feature learning model $f_{feat}(\cdot)$ is used to extract the features of source data:

$$x_s = f(s), s \in S \tag{1}$$

For simplicity, $f_{feat}(s)$ is denoted as $f(s)$ in brief. The features serve as nodes to form an implicit connected graph $G = (V, E, A)$, with the node set V, edge set E, and the adjacency matrix A, where $x \in V$ and $(x^i, x^j) \in E$. $A(i,j)$ indicates the linkage weight between two nodes x^i and x^j, and $A(i,j) = 0$ denotes that the two nodes are disconnected.

h-hop Linkage. Similar to the approach in [19], we merely link the edge between two feature nodes when their labels indicate the same person, thus converting the clustering process into a binary classification task. Specifically, the linkage likelihood between two arbitrary feature nodes based on their context in a graph. Given a pivot p, the high-order neighbors up to h-hop of p are used as nodes to construct a subgraph. The number of nearest neighbors in the i-th hop is denoted as $k_i, i = 1, 2, ..., h$, and in this paper, h is set as 2, and k_1 as 200, k_2 as 10,

$$N\left(x_h^p\right) = \{x_h^{p_1}, x_h^{p_2}, \cdots, x_h^{p_k}\}, |N\left(x_h^p\right)| = K_h \qquad (2)$$

The K-reciprocal nearest neighbors of x^p is:

$$V\left(x^p\right) = \{x^q \mid (x^q \in N\left(x_1^p\right) \wedge N\left(x_2^p\right))\} \qquad (3)$$

In order to encode the pivot information into the node features, the pivot feature x^p is subtracted to normalize the node features, $X^p = [..., x^q - x^p, ...]$. Then neighboring and non-neighboring features are aggregated by linkage weight of 1 and 0 respectively. Therefore, the adjacency matrix $A^p \in \mathbb{R}^{|V^p| \times |V^p|}$ is defined as:

$$A^p = \begin{cases} 1, & \text{if } x^q \in V(x^p) \\ 0, & \text{otherwise} \end{cases} \qquad (4)$$

Graph Convolution. To utilize the context contained in the graph for determining the linkage between two nodes, we slightly modify the graph convolution networks(GCN) [9] to perform reasoning on the graph G. Formally, a graph convolution network has the following formulation:

$$\bar{Y} = \sigma(\hat{A}XW), \text{ s.t. } \hat{A} = D^{-1}A \qquad (5)$$

where $\bar{Y}$ represents the prediction of node feature matrix. $X \in \mathbb{R}^{N \times d_{in}}$, N is the number of nodes, and d_{in} is the dimension of input node features. W is the learnable weight matrix of the graph convolution layer, and $\sigma(\cdot)$ is the ReLU unit for nonlinear activation. D is the degree matrix of A, where $D(i, j) = \sum_{j=1}^{n} A(i, j)$. After this formula, a fully connected layer is used to compute a two-dimensional vector for binary classification and eventually outputs predicted labels $\bar{y}$.

Cross-Entropy Loss for Optimization. The training process on the source data is identified as a classification task, and GCN is optimized with cross-entropy loss, which is defined by the following formula:

$$L_{\text{label}}\left(y_s^i, \bar{y}_s^i\right) = -\sum_{i=1}^{N_s} y_s^i \log \bar{y}_s^i \qquad (6)$$

where y_s means the provided labels from assistant source data and $\bar{y}_s$ denotes the predicted labels from Eq. 5.

3.3 Unsupervised Person Re-identification

In this section, the trained GCN is used to cluster and predict pseudo labels $\bar{y}_t$ on unannotated target data T, then use pseudo labels to re-train the Re-ID network. $x_t = f(t)$ is set as the feature representation for target data, and the probability of linkage between two arbitrary nodes x_a, x_b is $p_{edge}(a, b)$. Similar to [17], we cluster and generate pseudo labels for the target data. The clustering process is to remove the edges with low linkage probability. Firstly, a threshold th is preset, and edges with linkage probability below the threshold are removed, and the remaining edges with the highest linkage probability form connected clusters. The connected clusters larger than a maximum preset size are selected for the iterative follow-up processing. In the next iteration, the threshold th' used for removing the edges is increased by:

$$th' = th + \alpha(1 - th) \tag{7}$$

where $\alpha \in (0, 1)$. As a result, all the nodes are clustered and given pseudo labels until the queue is empty:

$$\bar{y}_t = GCN(x_t) \tag{8}$$

Then the pseudo labels are utilized to re-train the Re-ID network. The Re-ID network is denoted by R, and the feature extraction function as $f_{feat}(\cdot)$, then the features of the target data t are denoted as $x_t = f_{feat}(t)$. Since the pseudo labels vary during iterations, the Re-ID network is optimized by using a triplet loss [7] instead of a cross-entropy loss:

$$L_{feat} = \sum_{t \in \{T, \hat{T}\}} \left[\|x_t - x_{t^p}\|_2^2 - \|x_t - x_{t^n}\|_2^2 + m \right]_+ \tag{9}$$

$$\text{s.t. } \bar{y}_t = \bar{y}_{t^p}, \bar{y}_t \neq \bar{y}_{t^n}$$

where t^p and t^n are positive and negative pairs for the target data T and the distance threshold m is set to 0.3.

3.4 Spatial-Temporal Models and Constraints

We assume that the time intervals will have a specific priori probability distribution based on the scene, and the time interval distribution can be obtained between any two cameras by counting the camera id numbers and time frame information corresponding to all pedestrian image pairs in the dataset. This probability distribution is used to define a spatial-temporal constraint function, which represents the spatial-temporal similarity between image pairs, then we combine it with the probability of the connection between vertices and neighbors of the graph convolution prediction target data, and correct the visual similarity scores calculated by the Re-ID network at the evaluation stage.

Similar to the method in [18], in order to calculate the spatial-temporal distribution, we count the time intervals of all the image pairs of identical pedestrians under every two cameras, then smooth them with the Parzen Window method.

Specifically, two cameras C_i, C_j capture two images I_a, I_b of a pedestrian P respectively, with corresponding timestamps t_a, t_b. Then the time difference is $\Delta t = t_b - t_a$, hence generates a scatter plot of the time differences corresponding to these two cameras. In order to get the distribution graph with statistical probability, the time differences are divided into many intervals, and each interval δ_t occupies M frames. The spatial-temporal probability within an interval is the same. Then we divide the number of samples in the k_{th} interval by the total number of samples to get a rough spatial-temporal histogram:

$$\hat{p}(k, c_i, c_j) = \frac{n^k}{\sum_l n^l}, k \in N^+ \qquad (10)$$

where n^k denotes the number of image pairs of the same pedestrian, with the time difference satisfying $\Delta t \in ((k-1)\delta_t, k\delta_t)$. Furthermore, Gaussian smoothing and normalization are applied to the histogram:

$$p(k, c_i, c_j) = \frac{\sum_m \hat{p}(k, c_i, c_j) G(m-k)}{\sum_k \hat{p}(k, c_i, c_j)} \qquad (11)$$

where the Gaussian smoothing function is $G(x) = \frac{1}{\sqrt{2\pi}\sigma} e^{\frac{-x^2}{2\sigma^2}}$, normalized factor is $\sum_k \hat{p}(k, c_i, c_j)$. When counting the number of image pairs, we also average the time of multiple appearances of the same person under a certain camera, thus avoiding statistical errors caused by multiple images of this person in a short period of time. We perform the above operation for all cameras to create the spatial-temporal probability distribution D_{ST}.

Since pseudo labels are insufficient and imperfect, and the walking trajectory and velocity of different people vary greatly, the inferred spatial-temporal distribution may contain many flaws.

Therefore, the spatial-temporal probability p_{st} is normalized by using the logistic function:

$$f(p_{st}; \lambda, \gamma) = \frac{1}{1 + \lambda e^{-\gamma p_{st}}} \qquad (12)$$

where λ and γ are constant coefficients, λ is the smoothing factor, and γ is the shrinking factor. The spatial-temporal probability $p_{st} = p(\lfloor \frac{t_b - t_a}{\delta t} \rfloor, c_i, c_j)$, where c_i, c_j are the cameras corresponding to the two samples and t_a, t_b are the corresponding time frames, according to Eq. 11. The normalized spatial-temporal probability is used as a similarity score to constrain the clustering process of GCN and the evaluation by the Re-ID network.

Constraints on Clustering. During the clustering process on target data, trained GCN is used to predict the linkage likelihood between the feature nodes and their neighbors, i.e., the probabilistic output of the node classifier. The probability of linkage between two nodes x_a, x_b is set as $p_{edge}(a, b)$. By multiplying the linkage probability and the normalized temporal probability, the final linkage probability is formulated as:

$$P = p_{edge}(a, b) \cdot f(p_{st}; \lambda, \gamma) \qquad (13)$$

Algorithm 1. Unsupervised Person Re-ID

Input:
    Labeled dataset S with labels Y_s, unlabeled dataset T with camera id numbers c_t and timestamps f_t

Output:
    Learned feature learning network $f(; \theta_R)$ and spatial-temporal distribution D_{ST}

1: pseudo labels $\bar{Y}_t = \varnothing$, iteration $i = 1$;
2: **while** $i \leqslant I$ **do**
3:     Extract features $f(S)$ by $f(; \theta_R)$ on S;
4:     Construct graphs with $f(S)$ and train GCN with $L_{\text{label}}(y_s, \bar{y}_s)$;
    $\theta_{GCN}^{(i)} = \arg\min L_{\text{label}}(y_s, \bar{y}_s; \theta_{GCN}^{(i-1)})$;
5:     Cluster and generate pseudo labels $\bar{Y}_t$ on T by using GCN;
    $\bar{Y}_t = GCN(f(T); \theta_{GCN}^{(i)})$;
6:     Re-train Re-ID network on T with pseudo labels;
    $\theta_R^{(i)} = \arg\min L_{\text{feat}}(f(T), \bar{Y}_t; \theta_R^{(i-1)})$;
7:     Generate spatial-temporal distribution histogram $\hat{D}_{ST}$ with $(\bar{Y}_t, c_t, f_t)$ and use gaussian function $G(\cdot)$ to smooth it;
    $D_{ST} = G_{smooth}(\hat{D}_{ST}(\bar{Y}_t, c_t, f_t))$;
8:     Applying spatial-temporal constraints to improve clustering in the next iteration;
    $P = p_{edge}(a, b) \cdot f(p_{st}; \lambda, \gamma)$;
9: **end while**
10: **return** $f(; \theta_R^I)$ and D_{ST};

In this way, we obtain a set of edges, the weights of which are the fusion of linkage probability and spatial-temporal probability. Therefore, the clustering results are more accurate, and the pseudo labels are closer to ground-truth labels.

Constraints on Evaluation. During the evaluation stage, the re-trained Re-ID network is used to calculate the visual similarity scores between two features x_a, x_b, which is formulated by the reciprocal of the Euclidean norm: $s(x_a, x_b) = \frac{1}{\|x_a - x_b\|_2^2 + \eta}$, where η is a small positive value to prevent the denominator being zero. We combine the visual similarity scores and the normalized temporal probability to get the final similarity scores:

$$s_{eval} = s(x_a, x_b) \cdot f(p_{st}; \lambda, \gamma) \tag{14}$$

Due to the inherent noise in pseudo-labeling, we optimize the Re-ID network R, the label learning network GCN, and the spatial-temporal model alternately. Concretely, R and spatial-temporal model are optimized with the predicted pseudo labels, while with fixed features extracted by R and spatial-temporal constraints, GCN is optimized to learn clustering and pseudo-labeling. This iterative strategy is mutually beneficial for all models, with more accurate pseudo labels, better feature representations of the Re-ID model, and a more practical spatial-temporal model. Our whole person Re-ID framework is concluded in Algorithm 1.

4   Experiments and Analysis

4.1   Datasets Setting

We evaluate proposed method against other state-of-the-art methods on two public person Re-ID datasets, Market-1501 [28] and DukeMTMC-reID [15] datasets. The Market-1501 dataset contains 6 cameras, including 5 high-resolution cameras, and 1 low-resolution camera. Overlap exists among different cameras. Overall, this dataset contains 32,668 annotated bounding boxes of 1,501 identities.

The DukeMTMC-reID dataset is a subset of the DukeMTMC dataset for image-based re-identification. It consists of 8 cameras, 36,411 person images of 1,404 identities in total.

Each image of these two datasets contains its camera id number and frame figure (timestamp). It's important to note, we do not use any labels on the target datasets during training. Cumulative match characteristic (CMC) and Mean average precision (mAP) scores [28] serve as evaluation metrics.

4.2   Implementation Details

The ResNet50 [6] model is set as a feature learning network, which is pretrained on the labeled source dataset. Traditional image augmentation techniques such as cropping, flipping, and random erasing are performed during training. Each input image is uniformly resized to 256×128 pixels. The SGD optimizer with a mini-batch size of 32 is used to train the GCN model, the learning rate is set as 10^{-6}, and momentum is 0.9. The parameter λ is set as 0.2 and γ as 50 for the logistic function to normalize the spatial-temporal constraints. During re-training on the pseudo-labeled target data, the Adam optimizer is applied with a batch size of 128, learning rate of 10^{-6}, and momentum of 0.9.

4.3   Evaluation Results

We compare the proposed algorithm with the baseline and state-of-the-art methods, and the results are shown in Table 1. The Re-ID results are calculated with respect to different CMC rank accuracy ($R = 1, 5, 10$) and mAP. The *Supervised Learning* method only use a ResNet50 as feature extraction network to train on a single labeled dataset. The *Direct Transfer* method trains the Re-ID network on the source annotated dataset, and conducts evaluations directly to the target datasets. It performs badly owing to the huge distinction between different domains. The *Baseline* method [17] clusters and labels the target data based on a non-parametric method, i.e., the DBSCAN scheme [3] which can hardly adapt to the feature representation bias, hence generating suboptimal pseudo labels. In contrast, our method utilizes GCN for clustering and pseudo-labeling, and generates smoothed spatial-temporal distribution as constraints for the pseudo labels, thus having achieved considerable improvements on rank accuracy and

Table 1. Comparison of the proposed method with the state-of-the-arts methods.

Datasets	Duke→Market1501				Market1501→Duke			
Evaluation	R = 1	R = 5	R = 10	mAP	R = 1	R = 5	R = 10	mAP
Supervised Learning	91.6	96.7	98.2	78.2	80.8	90.2	92.8	65.4
Direct Transfer	46.8	64.6	71.5	19.1	27.3	41.2	47.1	11.9
Baseline [17]	75.8	89.5	93.2	53.7	68.4	80.1	83.5	49.0
DG-Net [29]	61.8	–	–	33.6	62.0	–	–	40.7
ECN [16]	75.1	–	–	43.0	63.3	–	–	40.4
SSG [5]	80.0	90.0	92.4	58.3	73.0	80.6	83.2	53.4
AD-Cluster [25]	86.7	94.4	96.5	68.3	72.6	82.5	85.5	54.1
Ours	**90.1**	**96.1**	**97.6**	**69.4**	**78.5**	**86.5**	**89.6**	**64.0**

mAP. Furthermore, the gap of R = 1 is less than 3% between our method and the supervised learning method, confirming the effectiveness of our method.

Additionally, we include comparisons with other unsupervised methods, including DG-Net [29] and ECN [16] that use GANs, and SSG [5] that uses additional grouping information, as well as AD-Cluster [25] that uses density-based clustering and adaptive sample augmentation. Concretely, our method outperforms [25] with 3.4% and 6.1% on R = 1 scores respectively in the Market1501 and Duke datasets, and the gain on mAP reaches 1.1% and 9.9% respectively. The results demonstrate the effectiveness of our method.

4.4 Ablation Study

To prove that our model is robust, we conduct ablation studies to evaluate the effectiveness of different components in our method and hyper parameters of the smoothing factor for smoothing the spatial-temporal distribution.

Effectiveness of GCN Model and Spatial-Temporal Constraints. As is shown in Table 2, we isolate the GCN model and two spatial-temporal constraints for clustering and evaluation to analyze their effectiveness. Firstly, the DBSCAN scheme [3] is used to cluster and label the target data, which replaces the GCN model. The results show that without the GCN model, the performance drops a lot. It proves that our GCN model is effective in clustering and pseudo-labeling, and without accurate pseudo labels, the spatial-temporal model is not qualified to provide valid constraints. Then we remove the spatial-temporal constraints for clustering and evaluation jointly and respectively. The results illustrate that both constraints are indispensable for improving performance.

Learned Spatial-Temporal Models. We compare the spatial-temporal histogram and smoothed spatial-temporal distribution with pseudo labels and actual labels on DukeMTMC-reID datasets, as shown in Fig. 2. The pseudo labels

Table 2. Evaluation of different components in the proposed method. We evaluate the effectiveness of the GCN model, spatial-temporal (ST) constraints in clustering (ST_1) and evaluation (ST_2) in our joint model.

Datasets	Duke→Market1501				Market1501→Duke			
Evaluation	R = 1	R = 5	R = 10	mAP	R = 1	R = 5	R = 10	mAP
Direct Transfer	46.8	64.6	71.5	19.1	27.3	41.2	47.1	11.9
Baseline [17]	75.8	89.5	93.2	53.7	68.4	80.1	83.5	49.0
GCN	83.7	93.2	95.2	60.2	71.7	81.8	85.4	52.6
GCN+ST_1	84.1	93.3	95.5	62.9	73.5	83.4	87.3	55.5
GCN+ST_2	87.3	93.8	95.9	66.7	75.4	85.2	87.8	59.8
GCN+ST_1+ST_2(Ours)	**90.1**	**96.1**	**97.6**	**69.4**	**78.5**	**86.5**	**89.6**	**64.0**

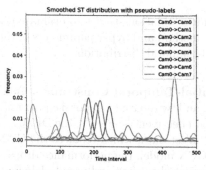

(a) ST histogram with pseudo labels.

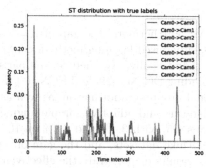

(b) ST histogram with actual labels.

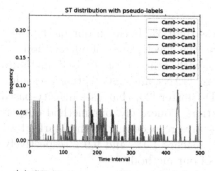

(c) ST distribution with pseudo labels.

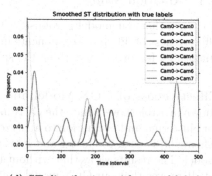

(d) ST distribution with actual labels.

Fig. 2. Spatial-temporal (ST) histogram and smoothed spatial-temporal distribution with pseudo labels and actual labels on DukeMTMC-reID datasets.

are predicted by well-trained GCN. Obviously, the inaccuracy in pseudo labels leads to the discrepancy in the two spatial-temporal histograms. Whereas, the ultimate smoothed two spatial-temporal distribution images appear to be very

Table 3. Evaluation of parameter λ and γ

Datasets		Duke→Market1501				Market1501→Duke			
λ	γ	R = 1	R = 5	R = 10	mAP	R = 1	R = 5	R = 10	mAP
0.1	50	88.1	91.4	94.7	65.4	76.5	82.2	87.1	62.9
0.2	50	**90.1**	**96.1**	**97.6**	**69.4**	**78.5**	**86.5**	**89.6**	**64.0**
0.3	50	86.7	92.5	95.2	66.8	77.7	83.3	87.6	62.7
0.2	40	87.7	93.2	95.2	67.2	75.7	84.8	88.4	63.6
0.2	60	89.3	94.8	95.9	68.7	76.4	85.2	88.9	63.8

similar, confirming that our spatial-temporal model is comparable to the actual spatial-temporal distribution. Besides, the time intervals between images from different pairs of cameras follow different distribution, indicating pedestrians' distinctive temporal patterns of transfer among different locations. This proves that our spatial-temporal model is qualified to filter out the matching pairs with less transferring probability and ameliorate the Re-ID network.

Parameter Sensitivity. As mentioned in Eq. 12, there are two tunable parameters in normalizing spatial-temporal probability scores, i.e., smoothing factor λ and the shrinking factor γ.

We conduct sensitivity experiments on the CMC and mAP scores with respect to different parameters, as shown in Table 3. The results show that the evaluation results fluctuate within a small range for two parameters, and the combination of $\lambda = 0.2$ and $\gamma = 50$ achieves the best performance.

5   Conclusions

In this paper, we utilize graph convolution network (GCN) to cluster and label unannotated data and exploit the spatial-temporal constraints as reliable knowledge to facilitate pseudo labels generation for promoting unsupervised Re-ID. In particular, a smoothed spatial-temporal probability distribution model is generated to amend the likelihood of linkages between graph nodes for clustering process as well as correct the visual similarity scores for Re-ID evaluation. In order to improve performance, we alternatively and iteratively optimize the label and feature learning networks, as well as the spatial-temporal model. Comprehensive experiments show that our model outperforms state-of-the-art methods on unsupervised Re-ID. In the future, we will optimize the clustering network as well as combine the spatial-temporal model with different pseudo labeling methods to handle more general cases.

References

1. Chen, L., Yang, H., Xu, Q., Gao, Z.: Harmonious attention network for person re-identification via complementarity between groups and individuals. Neurocomputing **453**, 766–776 (2021)
2. Deng, W., Zheng, L., Ye, Q., Kang, G., Yang, Y., Jiao, J.: Image-image domain adaptation with preserved self-similarity and domain-dissimilarity for person re-identification. In: Proceedings of the IEEE Conference on Computer Vision and Pattern Recognition, pp. 994–1003 (2018)
3. Ester, M., Kriegel, H.P., Sander, J., Xu, X.: A density-based algorithm for discovering clusters in large spatial databases with noise. In: KDD, vol. 96, pp. 226–231 (1996)
4. Fan, H., Zheng, L., Yan, C., Yang, Y.: Unsupervised person re-identification: clustering and fine-tuning. ACM Trans. Multimed. Comput. Commun. Appl. (TOMM) **14**(4), 1–18 (2018)
5. Fu, Y., Wei, Y., Wang, G., Zhou, Y., Shi, H., Huang, T.S.: Self-similarity grouping: a simple unsupervised cross domain adaptation approach for person re-identification. In: Proceedings of the IEEE/CVF International Conference on Computer Vision, pp. 6112–6121 (2019)
6. He, K., Zhang, X., Ren, S., Sun, J.: Deep residual learning for image recognition. In: Proceedings of the IEEE Conference on Computer Vision and Pattern Recognition, pp. 770–778 (2016)
7. Hermans, A., Beyer, L., Leibe, B.: In defense of the triplet loss for person re-identification. arXiv preprint arXiv:1703.07737 (2017)
8. Huang, W., et al.: Camera network based person re-identification by leveraging spatial-temporal constraint and multiple cameras relations. In: Tian, Q., Sebe, N., Qi, G.-J., Huet, B., Hong, R., Liu, X. (eds.) MMM 2016. LNCS, vol. 9516, pp. 174–186. Springer, Cham (2016). https://doi.org/10.1007/978-3-319-27671-7_15
9. Kipf, T.N., Welling, M.: Semi-supervised classification with graph convolutional networks. arXiv preprint arXiv:1609.02907 (2016)
10. Liu, C., Yang, H., Zhu, J., Li, X., Chang, Z., Zheng, S.: Graph similarity rectification for person search. Neurocomputing **465**, 184–194 (2021). https://doi.org/10.1016/j.neucom.2021.08.136
11. Liu, J., Zha, Z.J., Chen, D., Hong, R., Wang, M.: Adaptive transfer network for cross-domain person re-identification. In: Proceedings of the IEEE/CVF Conference on Computer Vision and Pattern Recognition, pp. 7202–7211 (2019)
12. Martinel, N., Foresti, G.L., Micheloni, C.: Person reidentification in a distributed camera network framework. IEEE Trans. Cybern. **47**(11), 3530–3541 (2016)
13. Meng, J., Wu, S., Zheng, W.S.: Weakly supervised person re-identification. In: Proceedings of the IEEE/CVF Conference on Computer Vision and Pattern Recognition, pp. 760–769 (2019)
14. Qi, L., Wang, L., Huo, J., Zhou, L., Shi, Y., Gao, Y.: A novel unsupervised camera-aware domain adaptation framework for person re-identification. In: Proceedings of the IEEE/CVF International Conference on Computer Vision, pp. 8080–8089 (2019)
15. Ristani, E., Solera, F., Zou, R., Cucchiara, R., Tomasi, C.: Performance measures and a data set for multi-target, multi-camera tracking. In: Hua, G., Jégou, H. (eds.) ECCV 2016. LNCS, vol. 9914, pp. 17–35. Springer, Cham (2016). https://doi.org/10.1007/978-3-319-48881-3_2

16. Sarfraz, M.S., Schumann, A., Eberle, A., Stiefelhagen, R.: A pose-sensitive embedding for person re-identification with expanded cross neighborhood re-ranking. In: Proceedings of the IEEE Conference on Computer Vision and Pattern Recognition, pp. 420–429 (2018)
17. Song, L., et al.: Unsupervised domain adaptive re-identification: theory and practice. Pattern Recogn. **102**, 107173 (2020). https://doi.org/10.1016/j.patcog.2019.107173
18. Wang, G., Lai, J., Huang, P., Xie, X.: Spatial-temporal person re-identification. In: Proceedings of the AAAI Conference on Artificial Intelligence, vol. 33, no. 01, pp. 8933–8940 (2019). https://doi.org/10.1609/aaai.v33i01.33018933
19. Wang, Z., Zheng, L., Li, Y., Wang, S.: Linkage based face clustering via graph convolution network. In: Proceedings of the IEEE/CVF Conference on Computer Vision and Pattern Recognition, pp. 1117–1125 (2019)
20. Wei, L., Zhang, S., Gao, W., Tian, Q.: Person transfer GAN to bridge domain gap for person re-identification. In: 2018 IEEE/CVF Conference on Computer Vision and Pattern Recognition (2018). https://doi.org/10.1109/CVPR.2018.00016
21. Wu, A., Zheng, W.S., Guo, X., Lai, J.H.: Distilled person re-identification: towards a more scalable system. In: Proceedings of the IEEE/CVF Conference on Computer Vision and Pattern Recognition, pp. 1187–1196 (2019)
22. Wu, Y., Bourahla, O.E.F., Li, X., Wu, F., Tian, Q., Zhou, X.: Adaptive graph representation learning for video person re-identification. IEEE Trans. Image Process. **29**, 8821–8830 (2020)
23. Yang, H., Cheng, Z., Chen, L.: Reranking optimization for person re-identification under temporal-spatial information and common network consistency constraints. Pattern Recogn. Lett. **127**, 146–155 (2019)
24. Yu, H.X., Zheng, W.S., Wu, A., Guo, X., Gong, S., Lai, J.H.: Unsupervised person re-identification by soft multilabel learning. In: Proceedings of the IEEE/CVF Conference on Computer Vision and Pattern Recognition, pp. 2148–2157 (2019)
25. Zhai, Y., et al.: Ad-cluster: augmented discriminative clustering for domain adaptive person re-identification. In: Proceedings of the IEEE/CVF Conference on Computer Vision and Pattern Recognition, pp. 9021–9030 (2020)
26. Zhang, J., Wang, N., Zhang, L.: Multi-shot pedestrian re-identification via sequential decision making. In: Proceedings of the IEEE Conference on Computer Vision and Pattern Recognition, pp. 6781–6789 (2018)
27. Zhang, Z., Lan, C., Zeng, W., Chen, Z.: Densely semantically aligned person re-identification. In: Proceedings of the IEEE/CVF Conference on Computer Vision and Pattern Recognition, pp. 667–676 (2019)
28. Zheng, L., Shen, L., Tian, L., Wang, S., Wang, J., Tian, Q.: Scalable person re-identification: a benchmark. In: 2015 IEEE International Conference on Computer Vision (ICCV), Santiago, Chile, pp. 1116–1124. IEEE (2015). https://doi.org/10.1109/ICCV.2015.133
29. Zheng, Z., Yang, X., Yu, Z., Zheng, L., Yang, Y., Kautz, J.: Joint discriminative and generative learning for person re-identification. In: Proceedings of the IEEE Conference on Computer Vision and Pattern Recognition, pp. 2138–2147 (2019)
30. Zhong, Z., Zheng, L., Luo, Z., Li, S., Yang, Y.: Invariance matters: exemplar memory for domain adaptive person re-identification. In: Proceedings of the IEEE/CVF Conference on Computer Vision and Pattern Recognition, pp. 598–607 (2019)
31. Zhou, Q., et al.: Graph correspondence transfer for person re-identification. In: Thirty-Second AAAI Conference on Artificial Intelligence (2018)

A Cross-Modality Sketch Person Re-identification Model Based on Cross-Spectrum Image Generation

Qingshan Chen[1], Zhenzhen Quan[1], Kun Zhao[2], Yifan Zheng[1],
Zhi Liu[1(✉)], and Yujun Li[1(✉)]

[1] School of Information Science and Engineering, Shandong University, Qingdao,
Shandong 266237, China
{liuzhi,liyujun}@sdu.edu.cn
[2] Inspur Electronic Information Industry Co., Ltd., Jinan, Shandong 250101, China

Abstract. Person re-identification (Re-ID) retrieval usually requires the query photo of the target person. However, in the actual crime forensics scene, it is difficult to obtain such photos. This paper studies the problem of Sketch person Re-ID, whose query image is the professional sketch of the target rather than the picture captured by the camera. It is a very challenging problem that sketch only has highly abstracted body outline information. In this paper, a cross-spectrum image generation (CSIG) method is proposed to process the input image, and then the generated image is sent to a dual-stream network model for training. The generalized-mean pooling (GMP) layer is added to the network and the domain invariant features are extracted by weighted regularization triplet (WRT) loss. We validated this method on the Sketch person Re-ID dataset, and the experimental results show that the proposed method outperforms the state-of-the-arts.

Keywords: Sketch person Re-ID · Cross-modality · Cross-spectrum image generation · Deep learning

1 Introduction

The widespread application of video surveillance systems in cities is an indispensable part of smart cities. Person Re-ID is an image retrieval problem that uses computer vision and machine learning methods to match the query photos with the person pictures in the database. In recent years, a large quantity of person Re-ID methods have emerged, and they have achieved a high accuracy rate, even exceeding the level of humans [1–3]. However, they are limited to RGB light images with small illumination changes of the same data type, and cannot be applied to images collected in the real world. At present, cross-modality person Re-ID using multiple types of data for recognition has aroused the interest of many researchers. Due to the inconsistency of data sources and data types, as well as the inconsistency of imaging principles and image quality, cross-modality

© Springer Nature Singapore Pte Ltd. 2022
G. Zhai et al. (Eds.): IFTC 2021, CCIS 1560, pp. 312–324, 2022.
https://doi.org/10.1007/978-981-19-2266-4_24

person Re-ID not only needs to overcome the occlusion, attitude, illumination, and other problems faced by general person Re-ID, also needs to focus on solving the key problem of cross-modality feature matching.

Some crimes in the blind spot of surveillance need to find suspects through the description of witnesses. The portrait expert draws a full-body sketch image of the suspect based on the description of the witness, and uses the sketch image to search in a large number of surveillance videos, which can greatly improve the search efficiency and save time. The difference between Sketch person Re-ID and face recognition is that it faces the entire body instead of facial details.

Due to the huge inter-domain differences, the re-identification of sketch pedestrians faces a huge challenge. Figure 1 shows a partial example of the Sketch person Re-ID dataset. On the one hand, compared to photo, sketch images lack color and texture information and are highly abstract and blurry. On the other hand, because the sketch images are conveyed to the portrait experts through witnesses, a lot of errors will inevitably occur in this process. In addition, sketches are presented in the form of the main view, while pedestrian photos will have angle changes and occlusion due to the change of monitoring perspective. Due to the need for professional portrait experts to draw sketch images, it is very difficult to acquire data sets. So far, the only Sketch person Re-ID dataset [4] contains just 200 pedestrian images. All in all, there is still a big gap between Sketch person Re-ID and general RGB person Re-ID.

We propose a novel end-to-end depth model to solve the challenges faced by Sketch person Re-ID. Ignoring modality specific features and extracting modality shared features is the key to cross-modality person Re-ID. In this paper, we propose a CSIG method, including red spectrum, blue spectrum, green spectrum, red-blue spectrum, red-green spectrum, blue-green spectrum, gray image and RGB image. In this way, the network uses multiple spectrums for training, forcing the network to mine cross-spectrum shared features to correctly identify images of different modalities. Moreover, this method indirectly increases the number of training dataset and makes the model better trained. We use a dual-stream network model as our backbone network. The first two convolutional layers extract modality specific characteristics, and the subsequent convolutional layer parameter sharing is used to extract modality shared features. Then we added a GMP [5] to capture the distinguishing characteristics of different domains, which cannot be achieved by average pooling or maximum pooling. Finally, a WRT loss [6] is adopted to narrow the intra-class distance without introducing additional hyper parameters.

The contribution of this article can be summarized as follows:

(1) A new end-to-end model based on dual-stream network is proposed to solve the Sketch person Re-ID problem. Extensive experiments have proved that our method has achieved the most advanced performance on the Sketch person Re-ID dataset, and the accuracy of Rank-1 has increased by 28.6%.

(2) A CSIG method is proposed, which can efficiently generate images of multiple spectrums to obtain the characteristics of different spectrums, help the network learn to reduce domain gap, and extract modality sharing features.

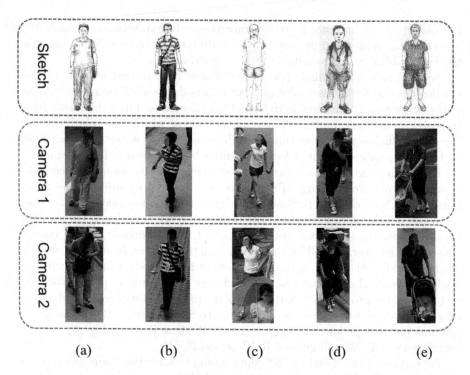

Fig. 1. Examples in Sketch person Re-ID dataset. The first line is the sketch image, the second and third lines are the pedestrian images collected by the two cameras. Sketch person Re-ID faces challenges such as (a and b) posture changes, (c and d) cluttered background, (c and e) partial body occlusion.

In addition, this method indirectly increases the number of datasets, which is conducive to more adequate training of the model.

2   Related Work

In this section, we will introduce the two parts of the existing person Re-ID work which are only based on RGB images and the cross-modality between Sketch-RGB images respectively.

2.1   RGB Person Re-ID

In recent years, with the development of large-scale parallel computing, the application of deep learning algorithms in person Re-ID has achieved better performance [7–9]. Person Re-ID based on RGB focuses on intra-class changes such as posture [10], proportion [9], occlusion [11] and background clutter [12] in the image. Representation learning and metric learning are the two most commonly

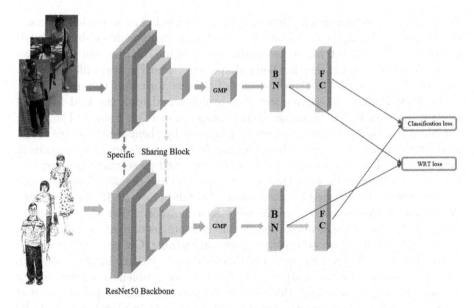

Fig. 2. The overall structure of our proposed approach. The inputs of the dual-stream network model are different spectrum images and sketch images. The parameters of the first two layers of the convolutional network are independent, the parameters of the last three layers are shared. After that, the features are obtained through GMP. Classification Loss is obtained from FC layer, and the batch normalization (BN) features is used for WRT loss.

used methods of person Re-ID. Representation learning treats it as a classification problem, and finally performs similarity matching through a fully connected (FC) layer. There are many ways to extract feature vectors before matching: graph neural networks can use the relationship of global feature vectors to map images to distinguishable feature spaces [13,14]; Self-attention mechanism can explore the similarity between pixels, so that the model can focus on biological features [15,16]; Generating adversarial networks (GAN) can increase data diversity [17,18]; Local feature learning methods can perform fine-grained feature alignment to solve the problems caused by posture changes and occlusions [11,19]. Metric learning to mine the associations between data points can produce more distinctive features. Methods such as contrast loss and triple loss learn to identify features by comparing the feature distances between different samples, narrow the same identity features and push different identity features away.

2.2 Sketch Person Re-ID

The problem of matching between sketch images and RGB images first attracted the attention of scholars in the field of cross-modality face recognition [20,21]. In comparison, the research of pedestrian retrieval based on sketch image and

RGB image is a relatively late development in the field of cross-modality person Re-ID. person Re-ID is based on the retrieval of pedestrian full-body sketch image. Full-body sketch image has more biological information that is not easy to be disguised, such as height, body shape, etc., which is very different from only relying on the partial sketch images of the face for target matching.

In 2018, Pang et al. [4] realized this problem and took the lead in cross-modality person Re-ID based on sketch images and RGB images. The cross-domain adversarial learning framework proposed by them jointly learns cross-modality invariant features such as identity features, contours, and textures in sketches and photos by filtering low-level features and preserving high-level features. In addition, they presented a sketch-photo cross-domain dataset of 200 people, which compensated for the lack of a Sketch person Re-ID dataset. However, Pang method loses part of modality specific information which is beneficial to pedestrian identification, and has no advantages of joint optimization of sketch and pedestrian photo feature expression learning. Gui et al. [22] proposed a model used multi-level feature fusion method and gradient inversion layer to obtain modality invariant features, which solves the problem of cross-modality instance matching. Although this method achieved the highest performance at the time, the Rank-1 accuracy rate could only reach 49% in Sketch person Re-ID dataset.

3   Method

In this section, we first briefly describe the model architecture, and then introduce the CSIG method, GMP module, and WRT loss in detail.

3.1   Model Architecture

Sketch person Re-ID is a challenge due to modality differences. The key to narrowing the gap between modalities and obtaining effective discriminative features is to be able to make full use of the constraints of the common feature space. As shown in Fig. 2, a new end-to-end dual-stream network model designed specifically for Sketch person Re-ID is proposed. Identity feature learning and modality invariant feature learning are the two major components of the network. The identification of pedestrians in different modalities is completed by the learning of identity features, while the modal invariant feature discards the modality-specific information and retains the modality-invariant information to reduce modal differences.

We first process the original image to generate cross-spectrum image, and use the processed RGB image and sketch image as input. For the backbone network of the retrieval task, we chose to use the most popular ResNet-50 [23]. It contains five convolutional blocks. We use the first two convolutional blocks to extract modality specific features, and the parameters are trained independently. We share parameters in the last three convolutional blocks to extract modality invariant features. Then, the features obtained from the last convolution block are passed through a GMP layer. The features are then expanded through a BN layer and a FC layer. The dimension of the fully connected layer is equal to the number of pedestrian identity. The feature behind BN layers will be used in the calculation of WRT loss. The calculation of classification loss directly uses FC features. The final loss is expressed as:

$$\mathcal{L}_{\text{total}} = \mathcal{L}_{id} + \mathcal{L}_{\text{wrt}} . \tag{1}$$

3.2 Cross-Spectrum Image Generation

Although the RGB picture and the sketch picture from the same person have the same physical appearance, the images are very different due to the different composition of the picture. Compared with RGB images, sketch images are highly abstract due to a lack of texture and color information, which is called modality difference in this paper. The RGB image is collected by a color camera in the visible light spectrum, and the sketch image is hand-drawn by a professional artist. From one modality to another, it is inevitable to lose part of the information. Only by extracting the features common to all modalities can the problem of cross-modality person Re-ID be solved.

This paper proposes a CSIG method, which can generate images from multiple different frequency spectra. The color image is obtained by combining the three spectrum channels of the red spectrum, the green spectrum, and the blue spectrum, and contains the characteristics of the different spectrums of the three channels. Given an RGB image, first of all, we can extract the features of the three channels separately, and generate the corresponding spectrum image [24]. Secondly, we can also combine RGB in pairs to generate three different images: R+G, R+B, and G+B. Finally, we added gray images and RGB images to further increase the number of modalities and increase the richness of modalities. The CSIG method proposed in this section can be expressed by the following formula:

$$C \xrightarrow{f} \{R, G, B, RG, RB, GB, X, RGB\}. \tag{2}$$

Where C is the original input image, R is the red channel, G is the green channel, B is the blue channel, X is the gray image, and f is the CSIG function.

Figure 3 shows an example of partial CSIG, where each row represents the same pedestrian. It can be clearly seen that the generated images of seven different frequency spectra exhibit different appearance characteristics. For example, the red shoulder straps in the first row and the part of the logo in the middle of the clothes in the second row disappear in the G and G+B spectrum. This effectively shows that the CSIG method can simulate the appearance change caused by the change of the frequency spectrum. Different spectrum images can provide additional supervision signals during the training process, so that the network can better mine the modality invariant features to distinguish different pedestrians. To maintain consistent, we also performed the same processing on the sketch image.

					Blue	**Red**	**Red**
RGB	Gray	Red	Green	Blue	**+**	**+**	**+**
					Green	**Blue**	**Green**

Fig. 3. Example of CSIG method. The original RGB image is placed in the first column, and the second to the eighth columns are the images generated in the gray spectrum, the red spectrum, the green spectrum, the blue spectrum, the red-green spectrum, the red-blue spectrum, and the green-blue spectrum, respectively. (Color figure online)

3.3   Generalized-Mean Pooling

For most fine - grained image retrieval problems, maximum pooling or average pooling feature extraction is usually used. Maximum pooling is to extract the maximum value from all features of a channel as the overall feature of the graph, while average pooling takes the mean value of all small blocks as the overall feature. As the ReLU activation function is finally included in the general CNN network, the eigenvalues are all positive, which also avoids the problem that positive and negative values cancel each other out. We adopt GMP [5], which is a learnable pooling layer, formulated by

$$\mathbf{f}^{(g)} = \left[f_1^{(g)} \cdots f_k^{(g)} \cdots f_K^{(g)}\right]^{\top}, \quad f_k^{(g)} = \left(\frac{1}{|\mathcal{X}_k|} \sum_{x \in \mathcal{X}_k} x^{p_k}\right)^{\frac{1}{p_k}} \tag{3}$$

where f_k represents the feature map, and K is number of feature maps in the last layer. $\mathcal{X}_k$ is the set of $W \times H$ activations for feature map $k \in \{1, 2, \cdots, K\}$. p_k is a pooling hyper-parameter, which is learned in the back-propagation process [5]. The GMP is between maximum pooling and average pooling. When p_k approaches infinity, it is maximum pooling, and when p_k is equal to 1, it is average pooling.

3.4 Weighted Regularization Triplet

Our final loss function consists of two parts, identity cross-entropy loss and triplet loss. The traditional triplet loss needs to define a margin parameter by itself, and the WRT loss [6] can avoid this problem.

$$\mathcal{L}_{wrt}(x) = \log(1 + \exp(\sum_y w_{xy}^p d_{xy}^p - \sum_z w_{xz}^n d_{xz}^n)) \tag{4}$$

$$w_{xy}^p = \frac{\exp\left(d_{xy}^p\right)}{\sum_{d_{xy}^p \in \mathcal{P}_x} \exp\left(d_{xy}^p\right)}, w_{xz}^n = \frac{\exp\left(-d_{xz}^n\right)}{\sum_{d_{xz}^n \in \mathcal{N}_x} \exp\left(-d_{xz}^n\right)} \tag{5}$$

where (x, y, z) represents a hard triplet within each training batch. For anchor x, $\mathcal{P}_x/\mathcal{N}_x$ is the corresponding positive/negative image. d_{xy}^p and d_{xy}^n are the Euclidean distance of the positive sample pair and the negative sample pair, respectively. The above weighted regularization avoids the introduction of additional margin parameters while following the advantages of optimizing the relative distance between positive and negative sample pairs.

4 Experiments

4.1 Sketch Person Re-ID Dataset

So far, there is only one Sketch person Re-ID data set in the world, which is the PKUsketchRE-ID Dataset proposed by Pang et al. [4]. Figure 1 shows some examples in the dataset. The dataset consists of 200 pedestrian identities, each of which has two RGB images and one sketch image. The two RGB images are taken by two surveillance cameras with cross-view angles during the day. In order to increase the realism of real-world cases, volunteers play the role of witnesses and describe the characteristics of pedestrians in the photos to professional portrait experts after watching the photos for a period of time. The portrait expert draws the sketch image based on the description of the eyewitness, and after many revisions until the eyewitness approves it, the final draft is finalized. The dataset is completed by five artists with different painting styles. In order to maintain consistency with the previous article, for each painting style, we randomly selected 75% of the images for training, and the remaining 25% for testing. Table 1 shows the number of training sets and test sets we selected from each painting style and the total number of sketch pictures in each painting style. Among them, the training set contains a total of 150 people, and the test set contains 50 people.

Table 1. The numbers of sketches in five different painting styles, the last column shows the split of training set/testing set on Sketch person Re-ID dataset.

Style category	Numbers	Training/Testing
(a)	45	34/12
(b)	20	15/5
(c)	80	60/19
(d)	33	25/8
(e)	22	16/6

4.2 Evaluation Protocol

We use the same top K evaluation strategy as Reference 5 to evaluate the proposed model on the Sketch person Re-ID dataset. Rank1, rank5, rank10, and rank20 represent the top 1, 5, 10, and 20 retrieval accuracy, respectively. The final accuracy rate is obtained by averaging the results of ten experiments.

4.3 Implementation Details

The model was implemented using the PyTorch [25] deep learning tool and the Sketch person Re-ID dataset was trained on a single Nvidia Geforce GTX 2080 Ti GPU. The backbone uses the more popular ResNet-50 network. In each training epoch, we randomly select 8 pedestrian identities from the entire dataset. Each identity randomly selects 4 sketch images and 4 RGB images. So each training batch contains 64 pictures, which are 32 RGB images and 32 sketch images. This provides a guarantee for digging out information-rich hard triples from the two modalities, that is, the most difficult positive and negative samples can be selected directly from inter-modality and intra-modality. In this way, the inter-modality and intra-modality changes can be dealt with at the same time. All input images of the two modalities are first adjusted to 288 × 144, and zero-padding random cropping and random horizontal flipping are used for data demonstration. The cropped image size of both modalities is 256 × 128. The initial learning rate as 0.1 on both datasets, and decay it by 0.1 and 0.01 at 20 and 50 epochs, respectively. The total number of training epoch is 160.

4.4 Results

It is compared with a hand-crafted based model and four deep models, a total of five models (since the experimental settings are the same, we directly use the results of the previous article). The final result is the average of ten experiments. Dense-Histogram of Oriented Gradient (HOG) [26] +Local Binary Pattern (LBP)+rank-support vector machines (SVM) is the most representative method based on hand-crafted models. The traditional feature HOG is connected with the auxiliary feature LBP and then the score is ranked by rankSVM. Triplet SN [27] is a network specially designed for the sketch recognition of the free-hand object, which solves the problem of image retrieval based on fine-grained sketches. GN Siamese [28] has two GoogleNet [29] branches, optimized by siamese and classification loss. AFL Net [4] proposes a cross-domain adversarial learning model that can simultaneously learn identity features and domain invariant features. MLD Net [22] uses an end-to-end deep neural network to obtain domain invariant features using multi-level feature fusion modules and gradient inversion layers. The first four models are all pre-trained on the person Re-ID dataset Market-1501 [30]. Our model has achieved good results without this step. During the test, each pedestrian's identity is randomly selected one image as the gallery set. The comparison of all model results is shown in Table 2. As you can see, the rank-1 of our proposed model is 28.6% higher than MLD Net, achieving the best performance. The hand-crafted based model has the worst effect and cannot be used to solve this problem at all. Triplet SN has poor performance because it is used for frontal sketch recognition of objects. Both AFL Net and MLD Net have made some improvements, but the effect is only 49.0%. Our method plays a very good role in bridging the gap between the two domains.

Table 2. Comparison results with other baselines on the Sketch person Re-ID dataset.

Sketch person Re-ID dataset	rank1	rank5	rank10	rank20
Dense-HOG [26] + LBP + rankSVM	5.1%	16.8%	28.3%	37.9%
Triplet SN [27]	9.0%	26.8%	42.2%	65.2%
GN Siamese [28]	28.9%	54.0%	62.4%	78.2%
AFL Net (Vanilla) [4]	34.0%	56.3%	72.5%	84.7%
MLD Net [22]	49.0%	70.4%	80.2%	92.0%
Our model	**77.6%**	**93.0%**	**97.0%**	**98.8%**

4.5   Ablation Study

By using the CSIG method to introduce more modalities of input images, the network is guided to discover more distinctive shared features across all modalities. The GMP layer is used to extract fine-grained features that are domain-invariant. We compared the completed model with the model without the CSIG, only use gray and R, G, B, only use gray and RG, GB, RB, and without GMP on the Sketch person Re-ID dataset, and the results are shown in Table 3. The results show that the CSIG module greatly improves the performance of the model, and use all spectrum modalities to achieve the best performance

Table 3. Ablation study of our modules on Sketch person Re-ID dataset.

Sketch person Re-ID dataset	rank1	rank5	rank10	rank20
Our model without CSIG	54.4%	80.6%	90.8%	95.4%
Our model only with gray and R, G, B	68.4%	93.8%	96.6%	97.4%
Our model only with gray and RG, GB, RB	69.0%	94.4%	98.0%	98.8%
Our model without GMP	65.8%	94.2%	98.0%	98.8%
Our model	**77.6%**	**93.0%**	**97.0%**	**98.8%**

5   Conclusion

In this paper, an end-to-end deep neural network model designed to solve Sketch person Re-ID is proposed. A CSIG method is proposed to process the input image. Different spectral images help the model to extract domain-invariant information and indirectly expand the dataset. Then, the GMP layer is added to the network, which is between maximum pooling and average pooling and can better extract features. The final loss is represented by both classified loss and triplet loss. Through verification on the Sketch person Re-ID dataset, the proposed model can achieve the most advanced performance.

Acknowledgements. This work was supported in part by the Major Fundamental Research of Natural Science Foundation of Shandong Province under Grant ZR2019ZD05, the Key Research & Development Project of Shandong Province under Grant 2019JZZY0-20119, and Joint fund for smart computing of Shandong Natural Science Foundation under Grant ZR2020LZH013. The Sketch Re-ID dataset used in this article was collected under the funding of the National Natural Science Foundation of China.

References

1. Zhu, Z., et al.: Viewpoint-aware loss with angular regularization for person re-identification. arXiv (2019)

2. Xia, B.N., Gong, Y., Zhang, Y., Poellabauer, C.: Second-order non-local attention networks for person re-identification. In: 2019 IEEE/CVF International Conference on Computer Vision (ICCV) (2019)

3. Chen, T., et al.: Abd-net: attentive but diverse person re-identification. arXiv (2019)

4. Pang, L., Wang, Y., Song, Y.-Z., Huang, T., Tian, Y.: Cross-domain adversarial feature learning for sketch re-identification. In: Proceedings of the 26th ACM International Conference on Multimedia, pp. 609–617 (2018)

5. Radenović, F., Tolias, G., Chum, O.: Fine-tuning CNN image retrieval with no human annotation. IEEE Trans. Pattern Anal. Mach. Intell. **41**(7), 1655–1668 (2018)

6. Ye, M., Shen, J., Lin, G., Xiang, T., Shao, L., Hoi, S.C.: Deep learning for person re-identification: a survey and outlook. IEEE Trans. Pattern Anal. Mach. Intell. (2021)

7. Yan, Y., et al.: Learning multi-attention context graph for group-based re-identification. IEEE Trans. Pattern Anal. Mach. Intell. (2020)

8. Ding, C., Wang, K., Wang, P., Tao, D.: Multi-task learning with coarse priors for robust part-aware person re-identification. IEEE Trans. Pattern Anal. Mach. Intell. **44**, 1474–1488 (2020)

9. Hou, R., Ma, B., Chang, H., Gu, X., Shan, S., Chen, X.: Interaction-and-aggregation network for person re-identification. In: Proceedings of the IEEE/CVF Conference on Computer Vision and Pattern Recognition, pp. 9317–9326 (2019)

10. Liu, J., Ni, B., Yan, Y., Zhou, P., Cheng, S., Hu, J.: Pose transferrable person re-identification. In: Proceedings of the IEEE Conference on Computer Vision and Pattern Recognition, pp. 4099–4108 (2018)

11. Luo, H., Jiang, W., Zhang, X., Fan, X., Qian, J., Zhang, C.: Alignedreid++: dynamically matching local information for person re-identification. Pattern Recogn. **94**, 53–61 (2019)

12. Tian, M., et al.: Eliminating background-bias for robust person re-identification. In: Proceedings of the IEEE Conference on Computer Vision and Pattern Recognition, pp. 5794–5803 (2018)

13. Shen, Y., Li, H., Yi, S., Chen, D., Wang, X.: Person re-identification with deep similarity-guided graph neural network. In: Proceedings of the European conference on computer vision (ECCV), pp. 486–504 (2018)

14. Miao, J., Wu, Y., Liu, P., Ding, Y., Yang, Y.: Pose-guided feature alignment for occluded person re-identification. In: Proceedings of the IEEE/CVF International Conference on Computer Vision, pp. 542–551 (2019)

15. Luo, C., Chen, Y., Wang, N., Zhang, Z.: Spectral feature transformation for person re-identification. In: Proceedings of the IEEE/CVF International Conference on Computer Vision, pp. 4976–4985 (2019)

16. Xu, J., Zhao, R., Zhu, F., Wang, H., Ouyang, W.: Attention-aware compositional network for person re-identification. In: Proceedings of the IEEE Conference on Computer Vision and Pattern Recognition, pp. 2119–2128 (2018)

17. Zhong, Z., Zheng, L., Zheng, Z., Li, S., Yang, Y.: Camstyle: a novel data augmentation method for person re-identification. IEEE Trans. Image Process. **28**(3), 1176–1190 (2018)

18. Wei, L., Zhang, S., Gao, W., Tian, Q.: Person transfer gan to bridge domain gap for person re-identification. In: Proceedings of the IEEE Conference on Computer Vision and Pattern Recognition, pp. 79–88 (2018)

19. Wang, G., et al.: High-order information matters: Learning relation and topology for occluded person re-identification. In: Proceedings of the IEEE/CVF Conference on Computer Vision and Pattern Recognition, pp. 6449–6458 (2020)
20. Galoogahi, H.K., Sim, T.: Face photo retrieval by sketch example. In: Proceedings of the 20th ACM International Conference on Multimedia, pp. 949–952 (2012)
21. Zhang, W., Wang, X., Tang, X.: Coupled information-theoretic encoding for face photo-sketch recognition. In: CVPR 2011, pp. 513–520. IEEE (2011)
22. Gui, S., Zhu, Y., Qin, X., Ling, X.: Learning multi-level domain invariant features for sketch re-identification. Neurocomputing **403**, 294–303 (2020)
23. He, K., Zhang, X., Ren, S., Sun, J.: Deep residual learning for image recognition. In: Proceedings of the IEEE Conference on Computer Vision and Pattern Recognition, pp. 770–778 (2016)
24. Fan, X., Luo, H., Zhang, C., Jiang, W.: Cross-spectrum dual-subspace pairing for rgb-infrared cross-modality person re-identification. arXiv preprint arXiv:2003.00213 (2020)
25. Paszke, A., et al.: Pytorch: an imperative style, high-performance deep learning library. Adv. Neural Inf. Process. Syst. **32**, 8026–8037 (2019)
26. Hu, R., Collomosse, J.: A performance evaluation of gradient field hog descriptor for sketch based image retrieval. Comput. Vision Image Underst. **117**(7), 790–806 (2013)
27. Yu, Q., Liu, F., Song, Y.-Z., Xiang, T., Hospedales, T.M., Loy, C.-C.: Sketch me that shoe. In: Proceedings of the IEEE Conference on Computer Vision and Pattern Recognition, pp. 799–807 (2016)
28. Sangkloy, P., Burnell, N., Ham, C., Hays, J.: The sketchy database: learning to retrieve badly drawn bunnies. ACM Trans. Graph. (TOG) **35**(4), 1–12 (2016)
29. Szegedy, C., et al.: Going deeper with convolutions. In: Proceedings of the IEEE Conference on Computer Vision and Pattern Recognition, pp. 1–9 (2015)
30. Zheng, L., Shen, L., Tian, L., Wang, S., Wang, J., Tian, Q.: Scalable person re-identification: a benchmark. In: Proceedings of the IEEE International Conference on Computer Vision, pp. 1116–1124 (2015)

Weakly Supervised Bolt Detection Model Based on Attention Mechanism

Zhenyu Chen[1]([✉]), Lutao Wang[1], Zheng Fei[2], and Yanhong Deng[2]

[1] State Grid Corporation Big Data Center, Beijing 100031, China
czy9907@126.com
[2] Beijing China-Power Information Technology Co., Ltd, Beijing 100089, China

Abstract. At present, a high-precision annotated data set is still the key factor for object detection model to achieve good performance. However, in many practical scenarios such as power production, the high cost of image acquisition and the difficulty of expert annotation make the acquisition of high quality image annotation very time-consuming and laborious. Therefore, a weakly supervised bolt detection model based on attention mechanism is proposed in this paper. Firstly, the method in this paper uses the ability of the attention mechanism to filter information to strengthen the object positioning properties of the convolutional neural network itself, and on this basis, a model capable of rough bolt detection is trained under the weakly supervised bolt data set. Secondly, in view of the problem that the attention mechanism is easy to fall into the local optimal solution during training, the attention saliency maps are expanded by using a method similar to data augment, so as to realize the purpose of decentralizing the focus area of the attention mechanism. The experimental results show that the proposed model can achieve an average accuracy of 76.5% on the weakly supervised bolt data set. Compared with the traditional strongly supervised object detection algorithm, the proposed model can achieve the purpose of training high-quality bolt detection model by only using the low-quality training data set by sacrificing certain accuracy.

Keywords: Weakly supervised bolt detection · Attention mechanism · Expansion of attention saliency map

1 Introduction

The object detection task in the field of computer vision is to identify the target object in the image and determine its position and size, which is one of the basic problems in the field of computer vision. After 2013, with the research and development of deep learning technology, object detection method using convolutional neural network as feature extractor has become the mainstream of object detection methods, and R-CNN [1], Faster R-CNN [2], YOLO [3], SSD [4] and other object detection methods have emerged.

With traditional object detection methods can only be extracted to lower level such as color, texture and shape features of different, the depth of the neural network model using convolution neural network can extract the image characteristics of a higher level

© Springer Nature Singapore Pte Ltd. 2022
G. Zhai et al. (Eds.): IFTC 2021, CCIS 1560, pp. 325–337, 2022.
https://doi.org/10.1007/978-981-19-2266-4_25

of abstraction, which improves the image feature extraction the robustness of this step, it also makes the accuracy and efficiency of object detection model has made breakthrough progress.

As the transmission stage of China's electric power industry, the safe operation of transmission lines is the key to ensure the transmission of electric energy [5]. In the past, in order to ensure the safety of transmission lines, it was necessary for people to climb onto the transmission line for inspection, which was dangerous and inefficient. In recent years, with the advancement of drone inspection technology and the rapid development of computer vision, the safe and efficient method of transmission line detection based on drones has been extensively studied in the field of power systems.

The components that need to be detected on the transmission line, such as fittings and insulators, have achieved good results [6–8]. Because of the large size of fittings and insulators, the differences between different categories are obvious, and it is easy to detect and identify. In contrast, as a kind of fastener, bolts are used to fix all kinds of metal parts and connect all kinds of structural parts on the power transmission line. They are very small and complex. And, they are the most numerous and extensive parts on the power transmission line. These lead to difficulties in bolt inspection tasks. Therefore, bolt detection has always been one of the important research directions in the field of power vision.

In recent years, thanks to the rapid development of deep learning technology, bolt detection tasks based on deep learning have achieved many achievements. Feng et al. [9] uses the traditional object detection method to detect bolts in the transmission line. By constructing the transmission line inspection image data set, the HOG feature of bolts is extracted and the SVM classifier is used to classify the bolts in the inspection image to realize the detection of bolts. Wang et al. [10] introduced auxiliary data to solve the problem of unbalanced samples and proposed a transmission line bolt detection method based on RetinaNet, which achieved good performance. Zhao et al. [11] constructed an automatic detection model for missing defects, AVSCNet, which proposed an unsupervised clustering method for visualizing bolt shapes, and applied this method to build a defect detection model that can learn visual shape differences. Then, three deep convolutional neural network optimization methods are used in the model to perform regression calculation and classification of regional features to obtain defect detection results. Xue et al. [12] proposed a detection method based on the improved Faster R-CNN model for the puncture clamp and its bolts on the transmission line that are easily affected by factors such as light, occlusion, environmental background, and shooting angle. Use flipping, translation, angle rotation and other methods to enhance the data set, and then use a deeper network with a deeper network and a smaller amount of calculation to solve the problem of small bolt size.

However, when deep neural network model is widely used in object detection task, there is still an urgent problem to be solved, that is, the training of a high-quality neural network model often relies on a large number of artificially annotated high-quality training data. In actual power scenarios, it usually takes several months to collect a complete set of annotated bolt data with high specification and quality, including data collection, cleaning, annotation and final arrangement [13]. Moreover, due to the scarcity of data and experts in the field of power, the acquisition cycle and cost of high-quality bolt data sets will be higher, which is also one of the key factors limiting the development of deep learning technology in the field of power. Therefore, it is of great significance and practical value to study how to train a reliable and effective object detection model by using weakly supervised labeling data of low specification.

To solve the above problems, this paper proposes a weakly supervised bolt detection method based on the attention mechanism. The weakly supervised bolt detection method mainly studied in this paper is an object detection model training method based on the weakly supervised bolt data set combined with the attention mechanism.

By imitating the attention mechanism used by human in recognizing things, combined with the object location ability obtained by the convolutional neural network in the deep neural network in extracting image features, the aim of training high-quality bolt detection model on the weakly supervised bolt data set with low specification is realized.

2 Methodology

In this section, we first introduce the attention mechanism, and then introduce in detail the design of bolt detection model based on the attention mechanism and the implementation process of the expansion algorithm of attention saliency map.

2.1 Attention Mechanism

There are two types of common attention mechanisms, one of them is channel attention (Fig. 1), such as SE module [14], and the other one is spatial attention (Fig. 2), such as spatial transformer network [15]. Channel attention aims to learn more discriminative features. Among them, the SE module is a classic channel attention method, which adaptively changes the channel feature response by finding the correlation between channels. Compared with the traditional neural network, this model greatly reduces the amount of calculation. Spatial attention aims to understand more detailed features. The spatial transformer network STN explicitly allows spatial operations on data and allows data to be processed to enhance the geometric invariance of the model. It can be inserted into any existing convolutional model and only a few modifications are required.

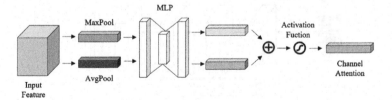

Fig. 1. The structure of channel attention

The attention mechanism can help the model to assign different weights to different parts of the input, extract more critical and more discriminative information, and make the model more accurate. At the same time, it will not bring additional calculations and storage to the model. Attention can be roughly divided into two types: soft attention [16] and hard attention [17]. Soft attention pays more attention to channels and spaces, and soft attention is deterministic. It can use model calculation gradients for forward propagation and reverse update to learn model weights, and can directly generate weights through training. The difference between hard attention and soft attention is that hard attention is more inclined to random prediction, that is, hard attention pays more attention to discrete location information and emphasizes the dynamic changes of the model. Therefore, hard attention is difficult to use end-to-end training methods to form, mostly through reinforcement learning.

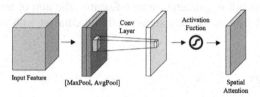

Fig. 2. The structure of spatial attention

In this paper, the attention mechanism we use mainly refers to the spatial soft attention mechanism in deep convolutional neural network.

2.2 Bolt Detection Model Based on Attention Mechanism

The structure of the deep convolutional neural network for weakly supervised bolt detection based on the attention mechanism designed in this paper is shown in Fig. 3. The model is mainly composed of two parts, one is the attention mechanism module surrounded by the red box in the figure, the schematic diagram of the attention mechanism module is shown in Fig. 4, and the other is the classification network part surrounded by the blue box in the figure. The solid and dashed arrows in the figure represent different transmission modes of data streams.

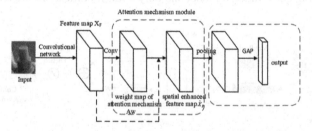

Fig. 3. The structure of the proposed bolt detection model

According to the existence of dotted lines, the whole model can be divided into two different working modes, as follows:

In the first mode, the data shown in Fig. 3 will flow in the direction of both the solid and the dashed arrows. When a bolt image is input, the feature map $X_F \in R^{H \times W \times D}$ is obtained after the feature extraction network, and then the feature map X_F is taken as the input of the attention mechanism module, and the spatial dimension is normalized through a 1×1 convolutional layer. Finally, the weight map of the attention mechanism is output, denoted as $A_W \in R^{H \times W}$. Then multiply the feature map X_F with the weight map of attention mechanism A_W channel by channel to obtain $X_A \in R^{H \times W \times D}$, finally, the enhanced feature map with spatial normalization $\hat{X}_F$ can be obtained by adding feature map X_F with X_A. The formula of attention mechanism module in the model is as follows:

$$Z_{i,j} = F(w^T x_{i,j} + b) \tag{1}$$

$$a_{i,j} = \frac{Z_{i,j}}{\sum_{i,j} Z_{i,j}} \tag{2}$$

w and b in Eq. (1) represent the weight and bias parameters of the 1×1 convolution layer in the attention mechanism module. $x_{i,j}$ represents the feature map corresponding to width and height of i and j, $F(\cdot)$ is the nonlinear activation function, the resulting $Z_{i,j}$ corresponds to the activation values of all points on the feature map $x_{i,j}$. $a_{i,j}$ in Eq. (2) represents the weight map of attention mechanism A_W obtained by the normalization of spatial dimensions of $Z_{i,j}$.

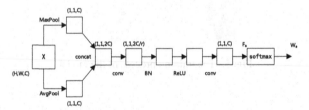

Fig. 4. The schematic diagram of the attention mechanism module

Combined with the above equations, it can be deduced that the spatial enhanced feature map $\hat{X}_F$ is expressed as follows:

$$\hat{X}_{i,j} = (1 + a_{i,j}) x_{i,j} \tag{3}$$

After the spatial enhanced feature map $\hat{X}_F$ is obtained through the above process, on this basis, a global average pooling operation is used to complete the classification task after a down sampling to indirectly achieve the effect of bolt detection, thereby achieving the purpose of weakly supervised bolt detection.

The second mode is called the attention mechanism strengthening training model, which is similar to the first mode above, but in this mode, the data flow will only flow in the direction of the solid arrow. The purpose of this mode is to separately strengthen the ability of training the attention mechanism module to filter the key position information of the object to be detected from the features extracted by the convolutional neural network.

In this mode, the original input bolt image passes through the feature extraction network to obtain the feature map $X_F \in R^{H \times W \times D}$, and then the feature map X_F is taken as the input of the attention mechanism module, and the spatial dimension is normalized through a 1×1 convolution layer. Finally, the weight map of the attention mechanism $A_W \in R^{H \times W}$ is output. After obtaining the weight map of attention mechanism A_W, the model only uses A_W to carry out all subsequent calculations without combining with the original feature map X_F. On the basis of A_W, the model successively completes the image classification task through a layer of convolution layer and global average pooling operation.

The actual training process of this paper is shown in Fig. 5, the bolt data set will first go through the weakly supervised bolt detection model of the first mode. Then the parameters and weights in the convolutional neural network used for feature extraction are frozen, after that, the attention mechanism reinforcement training model of the second mode was used to strengthen the attention mechanism module separately.

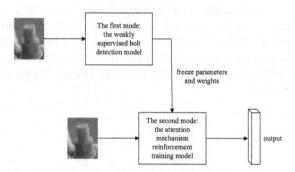

Fig. 5. The training process of the model

2.3 Expansion Algorithm of Attention Saliency Map

After the training process of weakly supervised bolt detection model, the requirements of weakly supervised bolt detection task have been fulfilled to a certain extent. However, during the experiment, after visualizing the attention saliency map output by the attention mechanism module, it can be found that the attention mechanism module still focuses most of its attention on the key local area of the bolt. If the bounding box of the bolt is directly calculated based on this, the bounding box will be too small compared with the actual bounding box, which cannot really meet the requirements of weakly supervision of the bolt detection task.

Therefore, after obtaining the attention saliency map corresponding to the bolt data set, on this basis, the attention saliency map is expanded to a certain extent in a way similar to data augment by referring to the idea of generative adversarial network (GAN) [18]. After this operation, the signal strength of the key local area that the attention mechanism module focuses on is weakened, so that the attention is more distracted to the whole of the object to be detected instead of the part [19–25].

The specific implementation process is as follows: First, the bolt data set S_1 is passed through the above-mentioned weakly supervised bolt detection model training process, and the weakly supervised bolt detection model $Model_a$ based on the attention mechanism is obtained. After the first model $Model_a$ is obtained, all images of the bolt data set S_1 are subjected to weakly supervised bolt detection through model $Model_a$, and the attention saliency map corresponding to each bolt image is obtained. Due to the characteristics of the attention mechanism, the saliency map obtained by the first-round training model will be more inclined to the key local information of the object to be detected, and accurate bolt detection cannot be achieved. For this reason, after obtaining the attention saliency map Att_a corresponding to all images, the signal strength of the focus area of the bolt data set's attention mechanism is weakened to a certain extent based on this. Among them, the weakening method proposed in this paper is as follows: the attention saliency map Att_a and bolt image I_A generated by the model $Model_a$ are calculated by the following equation:

$$I_B = I_A - \alpha \cdot Att_a \cdot I_A \tag{4}$$

In Eq. (4), $I_A \in S_1$ is the image data in the original bolt data set of the input model $Model_a$. And I_B is the bolt image that will be used for model $Model_b$ training after being weakened, and its set is defined as S_2, that is, $I_B \in S_2$. α is the dilution factor, the larger the value is, the stronger the model weakens the attention area of the attention mechanism module.

The process of the expansion algorithm of attention saliency map is shown in Fig. 6. For the bolt image I_A at the left of the first line, it belongs to the original bolt data set S_1. After passing through the model $Model_a$, the attention saliency map Att_a at the right of the first line is obtained. By observing the attention saliency map, it can be found that the attention mechanism module pays most of its attention to a small area in the upper part of the bolt image at this time. In order to disperse the attention, that is, to expand the attention saliency map, the bolt image I_A is weakened by Eq. (4) to get the bolt image I_B processed at the left of the second row.

After obtaining the data set S_2 that has been weakened in the key area, the training process of weakly supervised bolt detection model mentioned above is continued to be used to obtain the second weakly supervised bolt detection model $Model_b$. Since in the process of training model $Model_b$, the image regions that are most easily noticed by the attention mechanism module and are most conducive to the classification and judgment of the attention mechanism module are weakened by the data processing algorithm. So, the attention mechanism module of model $Model_b$ must increase its focus range or reselect some other areas to obtain the amount of information that can complete the classification task. Therefore, with the training of model $Model_b$, we get a new attention mechanism which is completely different from that in model $Model_a$, it has a completely different attention area from the attention mechanism of model $Model_a$. That is, the attention saliency map Att_b of model $Model_b$ in Fig. 6 is quite different from the attention saliency map Att_a of model $Model_a$, and it can be clearly seen that the attention saliency map has been expanded.

By repeating the above process over and over again, a series of different models can be obtained: $Model_a$, $Model_b$, $Model_c$, etc. These models correspond to different

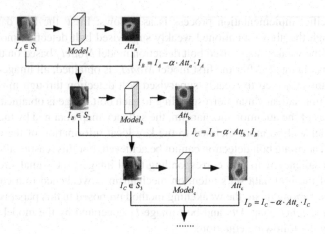

Fig. 6. The process of the expansion algorithm of attention saliency map

attention mechanisms. The attention mechanisms corresponding to these models are different, after enough different attention mechanisms are obtained, merging all the attention saliency maps can enhance the attention range of the attention mechanism module and improve the effect of weakly supervised bolt detection. As the key local area of the original bolt image data is continuously weakened, the area occupied by the object to be detected in the generated training image will also become smaller and smaller, which will eventually result in no object to be detected in the training data. In order to avoid this situation, a suitable condition for terminating the continued expansion of the attention saliency map is required, and the algorithm of this application only needs to train three new models to verify through experiments. The visualization results of the experiment are shown in Fig. 7.

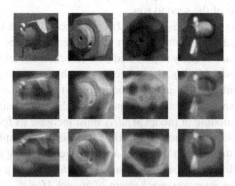

Fig. 7. Visualization of attention saliency map

3 Experiments and Analysis

This section evaluates the performance of the weakly supervised bolt detection model based on attention mechanism proposed in this paper on the bolt data set. Analyze experimental results from both qualitative and quantitative perspectives. The experiments are implemented in the PyTorch 1.0.0 on a machine with two GeForce GTX1080Ti GPUs, CUDA 9.0 and cuDNN v7.

3.1 Datasets

In order to verify the performance of the method proposed in this paper, we prepare two bolt data sets. These images of bolts are all intercepted from samples taken by drone line inspections. One is the low-quality weakly supervised annotation data set for the proposed model, which includes only bolt category information.

We divide bolt images into four categories as shown in Fig. 8(left): the first column (a) is a normal bolt, the second column (b) is a bolt with a missing pin, the third column (c) is a rusty bolt, and the fourth column (d) is a bolt with a missing nut. And the other one is a high-precision annotated data set used in traditional strongly supervised object detection models that not only contains bolt category information but also contains detailed location information of bolts.

(a) normal   (b) pin losing   (c) rusting   (d) nut losing

Fig. 8. The low-quality annotation dataset (left) and the high-precision annotated dataset (right)

As shown in Fig. 8 (right), the dataset contains the location information and category labels of the bolts in the original image. The two bolt data sets each consist of 2000 bolt images, and are divided into training set and testing set according to the ratio of 7:3. Both datasets adopt Pascal VOC dataset structure, the detailed structure of the datasets is shown in Fig. 9. And the original resolution of the transmission line images of the two data sets is 4000 * 4000, and the resolution is cut to 1000 * 1000. When labeling bolts, the size of the labeling box is limited to 128 * 128.

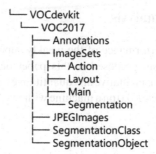

Fig. 9. The structure of the datasets

3.2 Qualitative Experiment

The model trained in this paper is applied to the weakly supervised bolt data set, and the results of the qualitative experiment are shown in Fig. 10. Among them, the first column of Fig. 10 is the original bolt image, the second and third columns represent the saliency maps corresponding to the first and second models $Model_a$ and $Model_b$ respectively, and the fourth column represents the final saliency maps Att_c obtained after termination. The fifth column is the final bolts detection result. As can be seen from the figure, the expansion algorithm of attention saliency map proposed in this paper can effectively distract attention, and can gradually disperse the attention that tends to the local optimal solution to the entire picture, and can achieve the purpose of detecting the bolt.

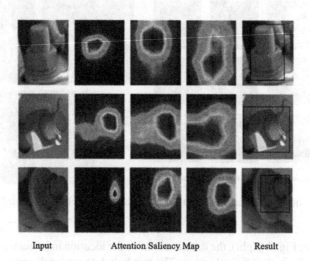

Input   Attention Saliency Map   Result

Fig. 10. The results of the qualitative experiment

3.3 Quantitative Experiment

In order to verify the performance of the proposed method, some algorithms in the object detection field are selected for comparison. Experiments were conducted on the low-quality annotation dataset and the high-precision annotated dataset respectively, and the experimental results are shown in Table 1. It can be seen that in the high-precision annotated dataset, the detection accuracy of the weak supervision bolt detection method in this paper is lower than the other object detection algorithms. However, on the low-quality annotation dataset, the mAP value of the proposed method is higher than the other object detection algorithms. The detection effect of weak supervision is achieved.

Table 1. Comparative experiment on bolt datasets

Methods	mAP	
	High-precision dataset	Low-quality dataset
Faster-RCNN	80.4	77.3
YOLO	78.5	75.2
SSD	81.9	78.4
YOLO v4	84.2	82.2
YOLO X	85.7	83.1
Swin transformer	**86.4**	84.5
ours	76.5	**85.1**

4   Conclusion

Aiming at the problem that the current mainstream object detection algorithms rely heavily on high-precision labeled data sets, a weakly supervised bolt detection model based on attention mechanism is proposed in this paper. Firstly, the method in this paper uses the ability of the attention mechanism to filter information to strengthen the object positioning properties of the convolutional neural network itself, and on this basis, a model capable of rough bolt detection is trained under the weakly supervised bolt data set. Secondly, in view of the problem that the attention mechanism is easy to fall into the local optimal solution during training, the attention saliency maps are expanded by using a method similar to data augment, so as to realize the purpose of decentralizing the focus area of the attention mechanism. And the experimental results show that the purpose of training the bolt detection model only on the low-quality weakly supervised bolt data set that only includes object category information is realized, which has high research significance and practical value.

Acknowledgement. This work was funded by the "Research and application of small-scale hardware defect detection technology for transmission line inspection images based on deep learning and knowledge reasoning" program of the Big Data Center, State Grid Corporation of China (SGCC).

References

1. Girshick, R., Donahue, J., Darrell, S.T., et al.: An enhanced image binarization method incorporating with Monte-Carlo simulation. In: Proceedings of the IEEE Conference on Computer Vision and Pattern Recognition, pp. 580–587 (2014)
2. Ren, S., He, K., Girshick, R., et al.: Faster R-CNN: towards real-time object detection with region proposal networks. arXiv preprint arXiv:1506.01497 (2015)
3. Redmon, J., Divvala, S., Girshick, R., et al.: You only look once: unified, real-time object detection. In: Proceedings of the IEEE Conference on Computer Vision and Pattern Recognition, pp. 779–788 (2016)
4. Liu, W., et al.: Ssd: single shot multibox detector. In: Leibe, B., Matas, J., Sebe, N., Welling, M. (eds.) ECCV 2016. LNCS, vol. 9905, pp. 21–37. Springer, Cham (2016). https://doi.org/10.1007/978-3-319-46448-0_2
5. Zhao, Z., Qi, H., Nie, L.: Research overview on visual detection of transmission lines based on deep learning. Guangdong Electric Power 32(9), 11–23 (2019)
6. Qi, Y., Jiang, A., Zhao, Z., et al.: Detection method of transmission line inspection image fittings based on improved SSD model. Electr. Meas. Instrum. 56(22), 7–12+43 (2019)
7. Zhao, Z., Li, Y., Zhen, Z., et al.: Faster R-CNN typical hardware detection method combining KL divergence and shape constraints. High Volt. Technol. 46(09), 3018–3026 (2020)
8. Zuo, G., Ma, L., Xu, C., et al.: Insulator detection method based on cross-connection convolutional neural network. Autom. Electric Power Syst. 43(04), 101–106 (2019)
9. Feng, M., Luo, W., Yu, L., et al.: A bolt detection method for pictures captured from an unmanned aerial vehicle in power transmission line inspection. J. Electric Power Sci. Technol. 33(4), 135–140 (2018)
10. Wang, K., Wang, J., Liu, G., et al.: RetinaNet algorithm based on auxiliary data for intelligent identification on pin defects. Guangdong Electric Power 32(9), 41–48 (2019)
11. Zhao, Z., Qi, H., Qi, Y., et al.: Detection method based on automatic visual shape clustering for pin-missing defect in transmission lines. IEEE Trans. Instrum. Meas. 69(9), 608–6091 (2020). https://doi.org/10.1109/tim.2020.2969057
12. Xue, Y., Wu, H., Zhang, N., et al.: Detection of insulation piercing connectors and bolts on the transmission line using improved faster R-CNN. Laser Optoelectron. Progress 57(08), 84–91 (2020). https://doi.org/10.3788/LOP57.081008
13. Zhao, Z., Jiang, A., Qi, Y., et al.: Hardware detection of transmission line image based on SSD model embedded with occlusion relation module. J. Intell. Syst. 14(8), 343–348 (2020)
14. Hu, J., Shen, L., Sun, G., et al.: Squeeze-and-excitation networks. In: Proceedings of the IEEE Conference on Computer Vision and Pattern Recognition, pp. 7132–7141 (2018)
15. Jaderberg, M., Simonyan, K., Zisserman, A., et al.: Spatial transformer networks. arXiv preprint arXiv:1506.02025 (2015)
16. Shen, T., Zhou, T., Long, G., et al.: Reinforced self-attention network: a hybrid of hard and soft attention for sequence modeling. arXiv preprint arXiv:1801.10296 (2018)
17. Serra, J., Suris, D., Miron, M., et al.: Overcoming catastrophic forgetting with hard attention to the task. In: International Conference on Machine Learning, pp. 4548–4557. PMLR (2018)
18. Goodfellow, I., Pouget-Abadie, J., Mirza, M., et al.: Generative adversarial networks. arXiv preprint arXiv:1406.2661 (2014)
19. Chen, J., Liu, Z., Wang, H., et al.: Automatic defect detection of fasteners on the catenary support device using deep convolutional neural network. IEEE Trans. Instrum. Meas. 67(2), 257–269 (2017)
20. Fu, J., Zheng, H., Mei, T., et al.: Look closer to see better: recurrent attention convolutional neural network for fine-grained image recognition. In: Proceedings of the 2017 IEEE Conference on Computer Vision and Pattern Recognition, pp. 4438–4446. IEEE, Honolulu (2017)

21. Gao, X., Hoi, S.C.H., Zhang, Y., et al.: Sparse online learning of image similarity. ACM Trans. Intell. Syst. Technol. **8**(5), 64:1-64:22 (2017)
22. Zhu, Y., Zhai, G., Min, X., et al.: The Prediction of saliency map for head and eye movements in 360 degree images. IEEE Trans. Multimedia **22**(9), 2331–2344 (2020)
23. Zhang, Y., Gao, X., Chen, Z., et al.: Mining spatial-temporal similarity for visual tracking. IEEE Trans. Image Process. **29**, 8107–8119 (2020)
24. Zhu, Y., Zhai, G., Min, X., et al.: Learning a deep agent to predict head movement in 360-degree images. ACM Trans. Multimedia Comput. Commun. Appl. (TOMM) **16**(4), 1–23 (2020)
25. Xia, Z., Hong, X., Gao, X., et al.: Spatiotemporal recurrent convolutional networks for recognizing spontaneous micro-expressions. IEEE Trans. Multimedia **22**(3), 626–640 (2020)

Cross Domain Person ReID Based on Symmetric Coding and Pedestrian Similarity

Xingyu Gao[1], Zhenyu Chen[2,3]([✉]), Jingwen Cheng[1], and Zhijun Zhao[1]

[1] Institute of Microelectronics, Chinese Academy of Sciences, Beijing, China
[2] Big Data Center, State Grid Corporation of China, Beijing, China
czy9907@gmail.com
[3] China Electric Power Research Institute, Beijing, China

Abstract. Person re-identification (ReID) aims to find images of the same pedestrian in cross camera scenarios. Recent years have witnessed extensive studies on person ReID by exploiting machine learning techniques under single domain settings. In this paper, we propose a novel cross domain person ReID method based on symmetric coding and pedestrian similarity. Specifically, we first introduce a symmetric coding technique for pedestrian attributes, and compute the attribute similarity matrix. Then, we extract pedestrian features by utilizing convolutional neural networks, and compute the feature similarity matrix. By fusing the pedestrian attribute similarity and pedestrian feature similarity, we obtain the fusion similarity accordingly. The attribute-tensor graph can be represented by the edges composed of the pedestrian similarity, which is produced by pedestrian attribute similarity and pedestrian feature similarity. Finally, the person ReID results can be obtained by similarity ranking. We conduct comprehensive experiments to evaluate the performance of our proposed algorithm for cross domain person ReID tasks, in which the encouraging results validate the efficacy of our proposed cross domain person ReID method.

Keywords: Cross domain · Symmetric coding · Pedestrian similarity · Person ReID

1 Introduction

Recently, person re-identification (ReID) plays an important role in many computer vision applications. Person ReID aims to retrieve images of the same pedestrian from a variety of views in cross camera scenarios, which has been commonly used in the fields of intelligent video surveillance, urban security, and so on. There are two key challenges in this research. One challenge is to efficiently extract the pedestrian features, and the other is to effectively explore similarity functions on the feature space. The person ReID results can be obtained by the similarity ranking for pedestrian images accordingly. Typical features in computer vision

© Springer Nature Singapore Pte Ltd. 2022
G. Zhai et al. (Eds.): IFTC 2021, CCIS 1560, pp. 338–348, 2022.
https://doi.org/10.1007/978-981-19-2266-4_26

include color feature [24], texture feature [18,20], and combined feature [9,32,33]. Most existing similarity functions generally follow supervised learning methods, which are often optimal in multimedia and computer vision communities. Due to the superior performance of convolutional neural networks, deep learning based person ReID methods have attracted much attention from both academic and industrial societies. Recent years have witnessed a surge of active research efforts in person ReID, which applies machine learning techniques to optimize similarity metrics from training data for computer vision applications, such as unsupervised person ReID based on soft pseudo label [6,29], clustering-based person ReID with pseudo labels [3,31], supervised person ReID by exploiting generative adversarial networks [2,11,17], pedestrian attribute based person ReID by utilizing feature alignment [14], adversarial learning based unsupervised person ReID [1,22], and multi-teacher adaptive similarity distillation model based scalable person ReID [28], etc.

Despite being explored extensively, the major shortcoming of existing person ReID schemes is that deep learning methods on single domains often results in decreasing performance under cross domain settings. In addition, many existing person ReID algorithms widely utilize pedestrian visual features, which learns feature representation poorly for various features of training data.

To tackle the above challenges, we propose a novel cross domain person ReID method based on symmetric coding and pedestrian similarity in this paper. First of all, we investigate a symmetric coding technique for pedestrian attributes, and compute the attribute similarity matrix. Furthermore, we employ convolutional neural networks to extract pedestrian features, and compute the feature similarity matrix. By fusing the pedestrian attribute similarity and pedestrian feature similarity, we can obtain the fusion similarity accordingly. The attribute-tensor graph can be represented by the edges composed of the pedestrian similarity, which is produced by pedestrian attribute similarity and pedestrian feature similarity. We exploit unsupervised learning based Graph Sample and Aggregate (GraphSAGE) scheme to train the model. Finally, we obtain the person ReID results by similarity ranking. In summary, the main contributions of this paper include:

- We propose a novel person ReID method by fusing pedestrian feature and pedestrian attribute for cross domain person ReID.
- We introduce a symmetric coding technique for pedestrian attributes which contributes to learn effective feature representation.
- We conduct extensive experiments on person ReID datasets to verify the efficacy of our proposed cross domain person ReID scheme.

The rest of this paper is organized as follows. Section 2 presents our proposed method for cross domain person ReID tasks. Section 3 discusses the experimental results. Finally, Sect. 4 concludes this paper.

2   Methodology

In this section, we present our proposed cross domain person ReID method based on symmetric coding and pedestrian similarity, which consists of three main modules: pedestrian feature extraction, attribute-tensor graph building, and graph neural networks training.

2.1 Pedestrian Feature Extraction

Since supervised learning methods for person ReID on single domains have achieved superior performance, we leverage supervised learning method [19] on source domain to improve person ReID accuracy as much as possible while avoiding overfitting of the model. Specifically, we adopt ResNet50 as the backbone network, and exploit a pre-trained model on ImageNet. The data is augmented by randomly flipping the input pedestrian images. In order to increase the feature size, we change the last stride parameter to 1 in ResNet50, followed by adding batch normalization [12] on the last layer. The global features of pedestrian images are obtained by this network. We then compute center loss [27] and triplet loss [4,5] respectively. The pedestrian labels are smoothed, and we compute the classification loss by cross entropy loss function. We train the model by utilizing Adam optimizer [13] and warmup learning rate. Finally, we obtain the pedestrian features on the target domain by employing the trained model on the source domain.

2.2 Attribute-Tensor Graph Building

We build the attribute-tensor graph by utilizing pedestrian feature and pedestrian attribute. As shown in Fig. 1, we first introduce a symmetric coding technique for pedestrian attributes, and compute the attribute similarity matrix. Then, we extract pedestrian features by utilizing convolutional neural networks, and compute the feature similarity matrix. By fusing the pedestrian attribute similarity and pedestrian feature similarity, we can obtain the fusion similarity accordingly. Finally, the attribute-tensor graph can be represented by the edges composed of the pedestrian similarity, which is produced by pedestrian attribute similarity and pedestrian feature similarity.

Symmetric Coding for Pedestrian Attribute. For the representation of pedestrian attributes, e.g., wearing a hat or not, each attribute is labeled as binary. However, $\{0, 1\}$ coding utilized for encoding attribute vector may lead to the following major drawbacks: (i) It cannot compute Cosine similarity for zero vector. (ii) It may cause inconsistent results for computing Cosine similarity. (iii) The discrimination of produced similarity value is limited by the encoded vector with angles between $0°$ and $90°$.

To address the above problems, we introduce a symmetric coding, i.e. $\{-1, +1\}$, for pedestrian attributes with extended discrimination. The vector angles are expanded between $0°$ and $180°$, and the pedestrian attribute similarity produces value from the range $[-1, 1]$, which contributes to learn effective feature representation of pedestrian attributes.

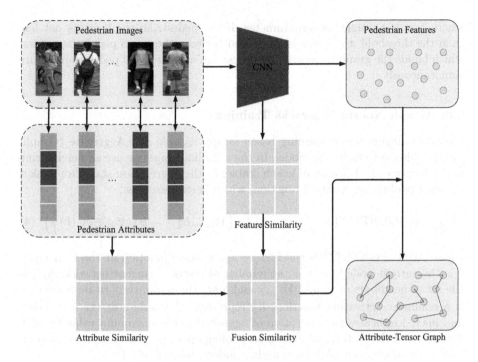

Fig. 1. The pipeline of building the attribute-tensor graph.

Fusion of Pedestrian Attribute and Pedestrian Feature. We build the edges of attribute-tensor graph by fusion similarity, which indicates the relationship between pedestrians for model training.

To formulate the pedestrian similarity learning task, we let $\mathcal{S}(\mathbf{p}_i, \mathbf{p}_j)$ denote the similarity function between any two pedestrian images $\mathbf{p}_i, \mathbf{p}_j$. The attribute similarity between two pedestrians is mathematically expressed as:

$$\mathcal{S}(\mathbf{p}_i^a, \mathbf{p}_j^a) = \frac{\mathbf{p}_i^a \cdot \mathbf{p}_j^a}{\|\mathbf{p}_i^a\| \|\mathbf{p}_j^a\|} \tag{1}$$

where $\mathbf{p}_i^a$ and $\mathbf{p}_j^a$ denote the attribute vector of two pedestrians $\mathbf{p}_i$ and $\mathbf{p}_j$ respectively. Accordingly, the feature similarity between two pedestrians can be computed as:

$$\mathcal{S}(\mathbf{p}_i^f, \mathbf{p}_j^f) = \frac{\mathbf{p}_i^f \cdot \mathbf{p}_j^f}{\left\|\mathbf{p}_i^f\right\| \left\|\mathbf{p}_j^f\right\|} \tag{2}$$

where $\mathbf{p}_i^f$ and $\mathbf{p}_j^f$ denote the feature vector of two pedestrians $\mathbf{p}_i$ and $\mathbf{p}_j$ respectively. We finally produce the pedestrian similarity by exploring a fusion method defined as:

$$\mathcal{S}(\mathbf{p}_i, \mathbf{p}_j) = \mathcal{S}(\mathbf{p}_i^a, \mathbf{p}_j^a) + \alpha \cdot \mathcal{S}(\mathbf{p}_i^f, \mathbf{p}_j^f) \tag{3}$$

where α is the weight hyperparameter. If the pedestrian similarity is not less than the threshold, the edges is connected between these two pedestrian nodes, which builds the graph by leveraging pedestrian attribute and pedestrian feature simultaneously.

2.3   Graph Neural Networks Training

We adopt unsupervised learning based Graph Sample and Aggregate (Graph-SAGE) scheme to train the model. In the sampling stage, we use all neighboring nodes to make the training of graph stable. In the aggregation stage, we exploit the max pooling aggregation function, which is expressed as:

$$h^k_{\mathcal{N}(v)} = \text{AGGREGATE}^{pool}_k = \max\left(\left\{\sigma\left(\boldsymbol{W}_{pool}h^{k-1}_{u_i} + \boldsymbol{b}\right), \forall u_i \in \mathcal{N}(v)\right\}\right) \quad (4)$$

where $\text{AGGREGATE}^{pool}_k$ is the feature aggregation function at the k-th layer. v is the current node, and k is the number of layers of current network. $\mathcal{N}_{(v)}$ is the set of neighbors of v, and $\boldsymbol{W}_{pool}$ and b are the parameters to be trained. σ is a nonlinear activation function. h^k_v represents the node v at the k-th layer, and $\max(\cdot)$ indicates the operation of aggregating the maximum value by each dimension of the feature, i.e., the max pooling operator widely used in convolutional neural networks. We then update hidden feature of v by:

$$h^k_v \leftarrow \sigma\left(\boldsymbol{W}^k \cdot \text{CONCAT}\left(h^{k-1}_v, h^k_{\mathcal{N}(v)}\right)\right) \quad (5)$$

where $\text{CONCAT}(\cdot)$ is the concatenation function. $\boldsymbol{W}^k$ is the weight matrix, and σ is the activation function. We finally learn the similarity representation by utilizing unsupervised graph based loss function [10]. Consequently, the person ReID results can be obtained by similarity ranking.

3   Experiments

In this section, we conduct comprehensive experiments on benchmark datasets to validate the efficacy of our proposed method for cross domain person ReID. Specifically, we first describe the experimental testbed and setup, followed by presenting the experimental results and discussion.

3.1   Experimental Testbed and Setup

In our experiments, we adopt two publicly available person ReID datasets, which have been commonly used for the benchmarks of person ReID tasks. The first testbed is the "Market-1501" dataset [34], which contains 751 identities with 12,936 images for training and 750 identities with 19,732 images for test. Each image has 27 annotated attributes [15]. The second testbed is "DukeMTMC-ReID" dataset [35], which is the subset of "DukeMTMC" dataset [23]. This dataset consists of 702 identities with 16,522 images for training and 1,110 identities with 17,661 images for test. Each image is labeled with 23 attributes [15].

To evaluate the efficiency and effectiveness of our proposed person ReID algorithms, we compare the proposed cross domain person ReID algorithm with various existing representative person ReID algorithms, including the TF-IDF scheme without learning BoW [34], the domain adaptation based scheme SPGAN [2], and pedestrian attributes based learning schemes TJ-AIDL [25] and MMFA [14].

3.2 Experimental Results

Evaluation of Accuracy with Different Layers. Our first experiment is to evaluate the performance with different GraphSAGE layers for cross domain person ReID. Table 1 and Table 2 demonstrate the comparison of accuracy with different GraphSAGE layers on two person ReID datasets. We can draw the observation from the experimental results that the performance of cross domain person ReID achieves the best accuracy with three GraphSAGE layers. This shows the importance of number of layers by applying GraphSAGE techniques for training data. In addition, the network converges by the hyperparameter of pedestrian similarity α between -0.05 and -0.06.

Evaluation of Accuracy with Different Thresholds. The threshold plays a key role for cross domain person ReID, especially in the phase of building graph. The small similarity threshold may lead to the generation of large graph or the large number of layers of GraphSAGE, which causes expensive cost of

Table 1. Comparison of accuracy with different layers for cross domain Person ReID from Market-1501 to DukeMTMC-ReID.

Layer	Rank@1	Rank@5	Rank@10	mAP
1	0.746	0.861	0.902	0.609
2	0.762	0.882	0.922	0.647
3	**0.773**	**0.882**	**0.922**	0.652
4	0.753	0.870	0.917	**0.654**

Table 2. Comparison of accuracy with different layers for cross domain person ReID from DukeMTMC-ReID to Market-1501.

Layer	Rank@1	Rank@5	Rank@10	mAP
1	0.847	0.940	0.961	0.699
2	0.866	0.949	0.971	0.766
3	**0.872**	**0.955**	**0.978**	0.786
4	0.858	0.950	0.975	**0.787**

building graph. Table 3 and Table 4 show the evaluation of accuracy with different similarity thresholds. We can see that the performance achieves the best accuracy for most cases with the similarity threshold 0.75, which demonstrates the importance of the similarity threshold for building graph.

Table 3. Comparison of accuracy with different thresholds for cross domain person ReID from Market-1501 to DukeMTMC-reID.

Threshold	Rank@1	Rank@5	Rank@10	mAP
0.70	0.766	0.882	0.921	**0.654**
0.75	**0.773**	0.882	0.922	0.652
0.80	0.766	0.873	0.915	0.653
0.85	0.755	**0.885**	**0.926**	0.644
0.90	0.743	0.860	0.904	0.640
0.95	0.728	0.857	0.897	0.634

Table 4. Comparison of accuracy with different thresholds for cross Domain person ReID from DukeMTMC-reID to Market-1501.

Threshold	Rank@1	Rank@5	Rank@10	mAP
0.70	0.845	0.934	0.962	0.723
0.75	**0.872**	**0.955**	**0.978**	**0.786**
0.80	0.837	0.937	0.966	0.753
0.85	0.835	0.931	0.964	0.765
0.90	0.845	0.936	0.966	0.776
0.95	0.847	0.940	0.970	0.783

Evaluation of Accuracy with Different Modules. We measure the accuracy of cross domain person ReID with different modules, i.e., symmetric coding module, and pedestrian similarity module. From the results of evaluation of accuracy with different layers and thresholds, we set the layer of GraphSAGE as 3, and the similarity threshold as 0.75. Table 5 and Table 6 show the evaluation of accuracy by different schemes. We draw some observations from the experimental results. First, we can see that the performance of baseline by using $\{0, 1\}$ coding is lower than other schemes. Furthermore, we found that the performance of cross domain person ReID achieves very comparable accuracy with symmetric coding module. Finally, we can conclude that our proposed scheme by exploiting symmetric coding module and pedestrian module achieves the best accuracy, which validates the efficacy of proposed cross domain person ReID scheme.

Table 5. Comparison of accuracy with different modules for cross domain person ReID from Market-1501 to DukeMTMC-ReID. SC: symmetric coding module, PS: pedestrian similarity module.

Method	Rank@1	Rank@5	Rank@10	mAP
Baseline	0.742	0.869	0.908	0.641
Ours w/SC	0.763	0.876	0.918	0.648
Ours w/SC+PS	**0.773**	**0.882**	**0.922**	**0.652**

Table 6. Comparison of accuracy with different modules for cross domain person ReID from DukeMTMC-ReID to Market-1501. SC: symmetric coding module, PS: pedestrian similarity module.

Method	Rank@1	Rank@5	Rank@10	mAP
Baseline	0.849	0.942	0.971	0.762
Ours w/SC	0.861	0.953	0.976	0.779
Ours w/SC+PS	**0.872**	**0.955**	**0.978**	**0.786**

Evaluation of Accuracy by Different Algorithms. Our last experiment is to measure the performance of different person ReID algorithms. Table 7 and Table 8 demonstrate the evaluation of accuracy by different algorithms. We draw several observations from the experimental results. First, we found that all learning based algorithms are able to outperform BoW model by TF-IDF scheme without learning for most cases. Furthermore, we can see that our proposed method outperforms typical unsupervised person ReID algorithms. Finally, we draw the observation that the proposed method achieves better or at least comparable accuracy than state-of-the-art cross domain person ReID approaches, which verifies the effectiveness of our proposed method.

Table 7. Comparison of accuracy by different algorithms for cross domain person ReID from Market-1501 to DukeMTMC-reID.

Method	Rank@1	Rank@5	Rank@10	mAP
BoW [34]	0.171	0.288	0.349	0.083
UMDL [21]	0.185	0.314	0.376	0.073
SPGAN [2]	0.411	0.566	0.630	0.223
TJ-AIDL [25]	0.443	0.596	0.650	0.230
MMFA [14]	0.453	0.598	0.663	0.247
AD-Cluster [30]	0.726	0.825	0.855	0.541
SDA [8]	0.765	0.866	0.897	0.614
MMT [6]	0.780	0.888	0.925	0.651
SpCL [7]	0.829	0.901	0.925	0.688
AWB [26]	0.834	0.917	0.938	0.710
Ours	0.773	0.882	0.922	0.652

Table 8. Comparison of accuracy by different algorithms for cross domain person ReID from DukeMTMC-reID to Market-1501.

Method	Rank@1	Rank@5	Rank@10	mAP
BoW [34]	0.358	0.524	0.603	0.148
ISR [16]	0.403	0.622	–	0.143
SPGAN [2]	0.515	0.701	0.768	0.228
TJ-AIDL [25]	0.582	0.748	0.811	0.265
MMFA [14]	0.567	0.750	0.818	0.274
AD-Cluster [30]	0.867	0.944	0.965	0.683
SDA [8]	0.869	0.944	0.963	0.700
MMT [6]	0.877	0.949	0.969	0.712
SpCL [7]	0.903	0.962	0.977	0.767
AWB [26]	0.929	0.972	0.982	0.806
Ours	0.872	0.955	0.978	0.786

4 Conclusion

In this paper, we propose a novel cross domain person ReID method based on symmetric coding and pedestrian similarity. First of all, we investigate a symmetric coding technique for pedestrian attributes, and compute the attribute similarity matrix. Furthermore, we extract pedestrian features by utilizing convolutional neural networks, and compute the feature similarity matrix. By fusing the pedestrian attribute similarity and pedestrian feature similarity, we obtain the fusion similarity accordingly. Finally, the attribute-tensor graph can be represented by the edges composed of the pedestrian similarity, which is produced by pedestrian attribute similarity and pedestrian feature similarity. Consequently, we obtain the person ReID results by similarity ranking. To evaluate the efficiency and effectiveness of our proposed person ReID algorithms, we compare the proposed cross domain person ReID method with various existing representative person ReID schemes. The experimental results demonstrate that the proposed method achieves better or at least comparable performance than state-of-the-art cross domain person ReID approaches, which verifies the efficiency and effectiveness of our proposed technique.

References

1. Delorme, G., Xu, Y., Lathuilière, S., Horaud, R., Alameda-Pineda, X.: Canu-reid: a conditional adversarial network for unsupervised person re-identification. In: International Conference on Pattern Recognition, pp. 4428–4435 (2021)
2. Deng, W., Zheng, L., Ye, Q., Kang, G., Yang, Y., Jiao, J.: Image-image domain adaptation with preserved self-similarity and domain-dissimilarity for person re-identification. In: Proceedings of the IEEE Conference on Computer Vision and Pattern Recognition, pp. 994–1003 (2018)

3. Fu, Y., Wei, Y., Wang, G., Zhou, Y., Shi, H., Huang, T.S.: Self-similarity grouping: a simple unsupervised cross domain adaptation approach for person re-identification. In: Proceedings of the IEEE International Conference on Computer Vision, pp. 6112–6121 (2019)
4. Gao, X., Hoi, S.C., Zhang, Y., Wan, J., Li, J.: SOML: sparse online metric learning with application to image retrieval. In: Twenty-Eighth AAAI Conference on Artificial Intelligence, pp. 1206–1212 (2014)
5. Gao, X., et al.: Sparse online learning of image similarity. ACM Trans. Intell. Syst. Technol. (TIST) 8(5), 1–22 (2017)
6. Ge, Y., Chen, D., Li, H.: Mutual mean-teaching: Pseudo label refinery for unsupervised domain adaptation on person re-identification. arXiv preprint arXiv:2001.01526 (2020)
7. Ge, Y., Zhu, F., Chen, D., Zhao, R., Li, H.: Self-paced contrastive learning with hybrid memory for domain adaptive object re-id. arXiv preprint arXiv:2006.02713 (2020)
8. Ge, Y., Zhu, F., Zhao, R., Li, H.: Structured domain adaptation with online relation regularization for unsupervised person re-id. arXiv preprint arXiv:2003.06650 (2020)
9. Gray, D., Tao, H.: Viewpoint invariant pedestrian recognition with an ensemble of localized features. In: Forsyth, D., Torr, P., Zisserman, A. (eds.) ECCV 2008. LNCS, vol. 5302, pp. 262–275. Springer, Heidelberg (2008). https://doi.org/10.1007/978-3-540-88682-2_21
10. Hamilton, W.L., Ying, R., Leskovec, J.: Inductive representation learning on large graphs. In: Advances in Neural Information Processing Systems, pp. 1024–1034 (2017)
11. Huang, Y., Wu, Q., Xu, J., Zhong, Y.: SBSGAN: suppression of inter-domain background shift for person re-identification. In: Proceedings of the IEEE International Conference on Computer Vision, pp. 9527–9536 (2019)
12. Ioffe, S., Szegedy, C.: Batch normalization: accelerating deep network training by reducing internal covariate shift. In: International Conference on Machine Learning, pp. 448–456 (2015)
13. Kingma, D.P., Ba, J.: Adam: a method for stochastic optimization. arXiv preprint arXiv:1412.6980 (2014)
14. Lin, S., Li, H., Li, C.T., Kot, A.C.: Multi-task mid-level feature alignment network for unsupervised cross-dataset person re-identification. arXiv preprint arXiv:1807.01440 (2018)
15. Lin, Y., et al.: Improving person re-identification by attribute and identity learning. Pattern Recogn. 95, 151–161 (2019)
16. Lisanti, G., Masi, I., Bagdanov, A.D., Del Bimbo, A.: Person re-identification by iterative re-weighted sparse ranking. IEEE Trans. Pattern Anal. Mach. Intell. 37(8), 1629–1642 (2014)
17. Liu, J., Zha, Z.J., Chen, D., Hong, R., Wang, M.: Adaptive transfer network for cross-domain person re-identification. In: Proceedings of the IEEE Conference on Computer Vision and Pattern Recognition, pp. 7202–7211 (2019)
18. Lowe, D.G.: Object recognition from local scale-invariant features. In: Proceedings of the Seventh IEEE International Conference on Computer Vision, vol. 2, pp. 1150–1157. IEEE (1999)
19. Luo, H., et al.: A strong baseline and batch normalization neck for deep person re-identification. IEEE Trans. Multimedia 22, 2597–2609 (2019)

20. Ojala, T., Pietikainen, M., Harwood, D.: Performance evaluation of texture measures with classification based on kullback discrimination of distributions. In: Proceedings of 12th International Conference on Pattern Recognition, vol. 1, pp. 582–585. IEEE (1994)

21. Peng, P., et al.: Unsupervised cross-dataset transfer learning for person re-identification. In: Proceedings of the IEEE Conference on Computer Vision and Pattern Recognition, pp. 1306–1315 (2016)

22. Qi, L., Wang, L., Huo, J., Zhou, L., Shi, Y., Gao, Y.: A novel unsupervised camera-aware domain adaptation framework for person re-identification. In: Proceedings of the IEEE International Conference on Computer Vision, pp. 8080–8089 (2019)

23. Ristani, E., Solera, F., Zou, R., Cucchiara, R., Tomasi, C.: Performance measures and a data set for multi-target, multi-camera tracking. In: Hua, G., Jégou, H. (eds.) ECCV 2016. LNCS, vol. 9914, pp. 17–35. Springer, Cham (2016). https://doi.org/10.1007/978-3-319-48881-3_2

24. Swain, M.J., Ballard, D.H.: Color indexing. Int. J. Comput. Vision $7(1)$, 11–32 (1991)

25. Wang, J., Zhu, X., Gong, S., Li, W.: Transferable joint attribute-identity deep learning for unsupervised person re-identification. In: Proceedings of the IEEE Conference on Computer Vision and Pattern Recognition, pp. 2275–2284 (2018)

26. Wang, W., Zhao, F., Liao, S., Shao, L.: Attentive waveblock: complementarity-enhanced mutual networks for unsupervised domain adaptation in person re-identification and beyond. arXiv preprint arXiv:2006.06525 (2020)

27. Wen, Y., Zhang, K., Li, Z., Qiao, Yu.: A discriminative feature learning approach for deep face recognition. In: Leibe, B., Matas, J., Sebe, N., Welling, M. (eds.) ECCV 2016. LNCS, vol. 9911, pp. 499–515. Springer, Cham (2016). https://doi.org/10.1007/978-3-319-46478-7_31

28. Wu, A., Zheng, W.S., Guo, X., Lai, J.H.: Distilled person re-identification: towards a more scalable system. In: Proceedings of the IEEE Conference on Computer Vision and Pattern Recognition, pp. 1187–1196 (2019)

29. Yu, H.X., Zheng, W.S., Wu, A., Guo, X., Gong, S., Lai, J.H.: Unsupervised person re-identification by soft multilabel learning. In: Proceedings of the IEEE/CVF Conference on Computer Vision and Pattern Recognition, pp. 2148–2157 (2019)

30. Zhai, Y., et al.: Ad-cluster: augmented discriminative clustering for domain adaptive person re-identification. In: Proceedings of the IEEE/CVF Conference on Computer Vision and Pattern Recognition, pp. 9021–9030 (2020)

31. Zhang, X., Cao, J., Shen, C., You, M.: Self-training with progressive augmentation for unsupervised cross-domain person re-identification. In: Proceedings of the IEEE International Conference on Computer Vision, pp. 8222–8231 (2019)

32. Zhao, R., Ouyang, W., Wang, X.: Unsupervised salience learning for person re-identification. In: Proceedings of the IEEE Conference on Computer Vision and Pattern Recognition, pp. 3586–3593 (2013)

33. Zhao, R., Ouyang, W., Wang, X.: Learning mid-level filters for person re-identification. In: Proceedings of the IEEE Conference on Computer Vision and Pattern Recognition, pp. 144–151 (2014)

34. Zheng, L., Shen, L., Tian, L., Wang, S., Wang, J., Tian, Q.: Scalable person re-identification: a benchmark. In: Proceedings of the IEEE International Conference on Computer Vision, pp. 1116–1124 (2015)

35. Zheng, Z., Zheng, L., Yang, Y.: Unlabeled samples generated by gan improve the person re-identification baseline in vitro. In: Proceedings of the IEEE International Conference on Computer Vision, pp. 3754–3762 (2017)

Top-Down Driver Head Orientation Detection Method Based on Monocular Camera and Virtual Scene Generation

Jiangnan Shi, Jingyu Tang, and Menghan Hu[✉]

Shanghai Key Laboratory of Multidimensional Information Processing,
School of Communication and Electronic Engineering, East China Normal University,
Shanghai 200241, China
mhhu@ce.ecnu.edu.cn

Abstract. Head posture assessment plays a very important role in the fields of driver attention detection, driving behavior analysis, and driving habit analysis. The mainstream head posture assessment methods use cameras to capture all the driver's front face videos, this approach has a natural drawback that it requires a lot of facially sensitive data which is contrary to the increasing awareness of privacy protection. Considering privacy protection, we innovatively apply a monocular camera to acquire an image of the driver's head with top-down shooting view and develop a corresponding TOP OF HEAD ONLY (TOHO) algorithm to estimate the head orientation. Subsequently, the virtual scene generation technique is leveraged to generate diverse model data. The generated data is afterwards used to validate the effectiveness of the proposed TOHO algorithm. The experimental results show that the error of the head attention angle calculated by the proposed algorithm is within 15° compared to the labeled data.

Keywords: Head pose assessment · Driver attention detection · Privacy preservation · Virtual scene generation · Image processing

1 Introduction

In recent years, the popularity of cars in China is increasing significantly [1,2]. The rapid growth of vehicles is inevitably bringing more complex road conditions, and the increased complexity of road conditions will certainly put forward higher requirements on drivers' safe driving behavior [3].

Among the various factors that affect driving safety, driver distraction is particularly critical [4], especially in long-distance driving scenarios where prolonged fatigue can have a significant impact on distraction [5]. In the field of driver attention detection, the driver's head orientation can be an intuitive indicator of the driver's attention status [6]. By detecting the driver's attention orientation and then providing real-time voice alerts on the driver's driving status, dangerous driving behavior due to driver inattention can be minimized. In addition to

© Springer Nature Singapore Pte Ltd. 2022
G. Zhai et al. (Eds.): IFTC 2021, CCIS 1560, pp. 349–360, 2022.
https://doi.org/10.1007/978-981-19-2266-4_27

other driving aids, for example, after reminding the driver of distracted driving behavior, the voice system can participate in providing appropriate navigation and other services for the driver to actively choose to enter the service zone for a rest, thus ensuring safe driving.

Research in the area of driver attention detection and safe driving has been conducted by many researchers and has achieved a number of results. In general, the current researches on driver attention detection are focused on head pose detection and eye movement tracking. Among those studies, Sun et al. established a head posture database containing more than 140,000 head posture images, which is great and positive significance for subsequent head posture evaluation studies [7]. Li et al. investigated the effect of Head-up display on whether experienced drivers or not on safe driving [8], and also investigated the effect of screen layout on in-vehicle information system on safe driving of drivers [9]. He et al. investigated the effect of tunnel lighting environment on driver's visual transient adjustment thus leading to the effect of environment on driving safety [10]. Hansen et al. investigated video-based detection and eye tracking, in which they also presented a detailed historical review of research on eye models [11]. Al-Rahayfeh et al. proposed an evaluation of driver fatigue and gaze classification without monitoring eye movements [12]. John et al. introduced a new approach to eye detection, showing that they used horizontal segmentation of the upper and lower parts of the eye to detect eye states [13]. Sun et al. proposed a lightweight CNN network for head pose detection and obtained good results [14]. Borghi et al. proposed a head pose prediction method based on a deep image architecture, and achieved remarkable results [15]. Ahn et al. proposed a multi-task deep neural network to detect the driver's head pose and showed good environmental adaptation [16]. Zhao et al. proposed a new orientation sensor to detect the absolute motion of the head [17]. Li proposed a joint processing method based on the noisy depth map and the high-resolution RGB map, which takes advantage of both images to achieve the recognition of head pose [18].

The above-mentioned methods require image capture over the entire facial area. This is contrary to the increasing importance of personal data privacy protection by the general public in today's society [19,20], especially since many current software applications can use facial information to synthesize into other scenarios that are difficult to identify, it causes that the misuse of personal facial data will have a bad social impact [21]. The current Chinese local governments, such as Tianjin, pay particular attention to the information security of face data. Therefore, it will be increasingly important that how to extract only local face feature information or even whether it is possible to implement engineering applications without collecting face data.

To protect the security of driver face data and prevent the uncontrolled outflow or even misuse of the collected face data, this paper propose a privacy-preserving driver head orientation detection method. The detection method uses a monocular camera for top-down image data acquisition to capture only the top of the driver's head features. Then, based on the captured non-face features, the image data of non-face features are analyzed and processed by the proposed

TOP OF HEAD ONLY (TOHO) algorithm to achieve the detection of driver's face orientation.

In addition, to collect rich and diverse sample data, the virtual scene generation method is specifically used for data collection, which has the advantages of being more efficient than real-world data collection, i.e., it can acquire a large amount of data in a short time [22], and it has the advantages of being less prone to errors and can be quickly adjusted to specific angles and scenes [23], which can enable algorithms to be quickly evaluated and quickly applied to real world.

2 Methods

2.1 Generation of Virtual Scene Data

To verify the effectiveness of the algorithm in terms of data diversity, it is necessary to obtain test samples of different drivers with different head sizes and different clothing. In this paper, to obtain a large amount of test data, a virtual three-dimensional (3D) modeling environment is used.

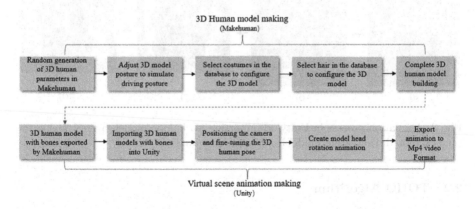

Fig. 1. Block diagram of 3D human modeling and animation production process.

The method described in this paper starts with the use of the software Makehuman to generate a variety of human model data containing a variety of head shapes and costumes to simulate a variety of different drivers. The human model is then animated in the software Unity and output in video format. The flow chart of the model animation process is shown in Fig. 1. The corresponding 3D human model and animation production process are shown in Fig. 2 and Fig. 3, respectively.

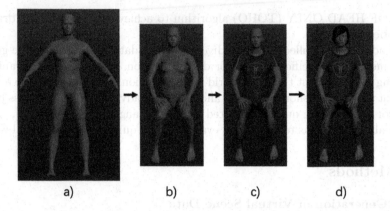

Fig. 2. 3D human modeling process in Makehuman. a) random generation of 3D human parameters, b) simulating driving posture, c) costumes configuration, and d) hair configuration.

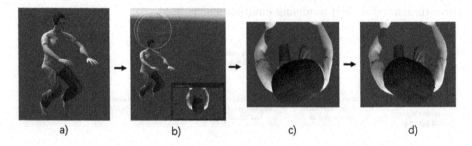

Fig. 3. Animation process in Unity. a) importing 3D human model, b) positioning the camera, c) and d) creating model head rotation animation.

2.2 TOHO Algorithm

By animating the head rotation of multiple human model in Unity, video data simulating the capture of the driver's head in real-time using a monocular camera can be obtained. We intercepted images from the generated videos with different head angles, and then analyzed them by the data analysis procedure shown in Fig. 4.

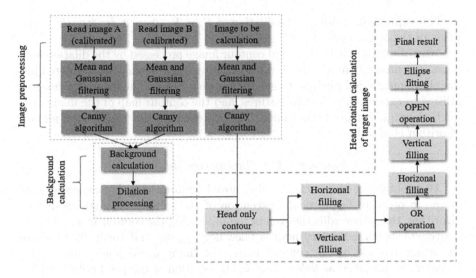

Fig. 4. Flowchart of the TOHO algorithm used in this paper.

To more accurately evaluate the angle of the driver's head orientation, we need to calibrate the images of the driver's head orientation angle. In this paper, 0° and 30° of the driver's head orientation angle are selected as the angles of the calibrated images. Subsequently, the environmental contour images are analyzed and processed based on the two calibrated angles. The two calibration images are first averaged and Gaussian filtered to reduce the noise of the images, and then the contours of the two calibration images are extracted using the Canny algorithm [24], The parameters of the Canny algorithm need to be adjusted according to the actual scene situation to obtain the best performance. After the calculation of the Canny algorithm, we can obtain the contour map of the two calibrated angle images, and then use the frame difference method to identify and extract the common part of the images so as to acquire the background contour images of the environment. Suppose the contour maps of the two calibrated images are A and B respectively, then we can get the contour expression of the background image shows as following

$$Background = (A \cap B) \tag{1}$$

Although Canny operator has good performance in capturing details, in real scenes, short-time light intensity changes and camera shake can introduce distortion, thus reducing the performance of Canny operator. To obtain better extraction results of the background image contour, the background contour image obtained by the frame difference method needs to be processed by the dilation algorithm, so as to reduce the influence of the environmental slight changes and camera shake. The expression of the dilation algorithm is as follows

$$E \oplus F = \{x | [(\hat{F})_x \cap E] \neq \varnothing\} \tag{2}$$

This expression expresses the dilation of E by F, where x denotes the translation of the origin map of F.

After obtaining the background contour image processed by the dilation algorithm, the image C needed for head orientation angle evaluation is entered into the above-mentioned pipeline to get the image contour. The processed image is utilized to extract the effective features, and the contour map of the image with the background removed is obtained. The expression of this background removal algorithm is as follows

$$Contour = C - Background(dilation) \tag{3}$$

After obtaining the background-removed contour map of a specific angle image, in order to facilitate the execution of the subsequent angle estimation algorithm, this paper adds the step of pre-processing the contour image, i.e., the scattered contour boundary map is filled horizontally and vertically to realize the regionalization of the contour map. The filling algorithm of the contour boundary is described as follows: detect the position of the pixel point with the pixel value of 255 at the beginning and the end of the row, then set the pixel value of 255 for those pixels as the single row filling, and fill the row by row to complete the row filling operation. At the same time, the same operation is performed in the vertical direction of the image. The images obtained from this operations are combined with OR logical processing to obtain a horizontal and vertical fill and integration map, and then performing an OPEN operation to obtain a fully filled contour map. After that, the ellipse fitting algorithm is used to estimate the angle of the filled contour map to complete the estimation of the driver's head angle.

Regarding the head angle selection for calibration and the corresponding adaptive algorithm, the general approach is as follows: after the driver enters the cockpit and fastens the seat belt, the camera starts working and captures the driver's head features from the top view only. After the camera starts working, it provides a corresponding tone to remind the driver to look straight ahead at a specified point, at which time the camera collects data as the calibration angle data for the 0° angle of the head, and then prompts the driver to aim the gaze at a second specified point while collecting data, thus completing the calibration angle data for the 30° angle of the head.

3   Results

3.1   Human Modeling Based on Virtual Scene Generation

As shown in Fig. 5. The method described in this paper uses Makehuman and Unity software for 3D human model data production of virtual scenes.

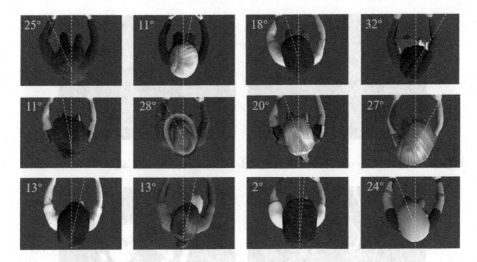

Fig. 5. Examples of 3D model generated by virtual scene generation. The yellow dotted line and the yellow numbers represent the angle calculation baseline and the labeled head angle, respectively.

In this paper, a total of 20 models of human body are newly created and the head shaking action of the model human body is captured separately, and the head shaking range is from 60° left to 60° right. The algorithm calculates the selected single frame images from left to right, and the frame selection interval takes into account the uneven action amplitude and speed of the actual situation, so the acquisition is not done at equal angle intervals (Fig. 5).

3.2   Intermediate Processed Image Based on TOHO Algorithm

The animated video data of the 20 human models will be extracted to a single frame and then calculated step by step according to the above method. The following process results can be obtained. First, Canny algorithm is used to obtain the contour map of the two calibrated angle images, and result map is shown in Fig. 6. Second, the frame difference and dilation algorithm are respectively used to obtain the background contour images of the environment and dilation map of background contour, and the results are shown in Fig. 7. Third, the background removal algorithm is used to acquire the contour map of the image without the background, and the result is shown in Fig. 8. Moreover, the filling algorithm is used to realize the regionalization of the contour map, and the result is shown in Fig. 9. It should be noted that the following results are mainly based on the No. 15 model as an example.

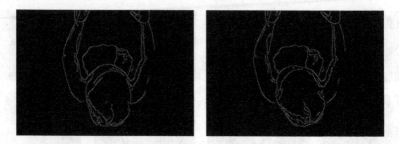

Fig. 6. Contour map of two calibrated angle images after Canny algorithm processing.

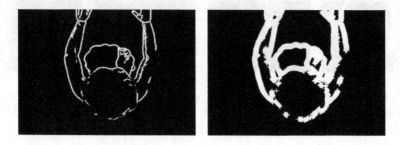

Fig. 7. Background contour map (left) and dilation background contour map (right).

As shown in Fig. 10, the merged map obtained after the horizontal vertical fill and OR logic operations contain a lot of noise outside the head contour. Therefore, we need to use OPEN operation for reducing the noise. After OPEN operation, the relatively good and less noisy head contour map can be obtained (Fig. 11). Finally, we use the ellipse fitting algorithm to estimate the angle of the driver's head rotation, and the result map is shown in Fig. 12.

We can see that the method described in this paper can eventually detect the driver's attention angle without collecting the driver's front face data. Figure 13 demonstrates the performance of TOHO algorithm on 20 generated scenes. The number of 3D scene model indicates the current model, the proportion of error

Fig. 8. Contour map of the two calibrated angle images after removing the background.

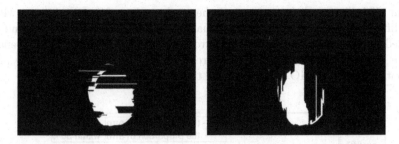

Fig. 9. The filling contour map obtained by the horizontal (left) and vertical (right) filling process respectively.

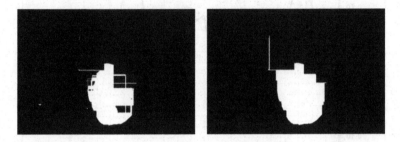

Fig. 10. Parallel set of graphs after horizontal (left) and vertical (right) filling with OR logical operation.

Fig. 11. Pure head contour map with less noise after OPEN logical operation.

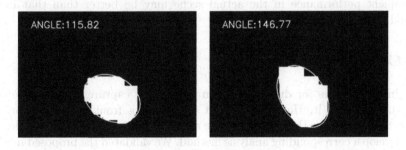

Fig. 12. Head rotation angle image obtained by ellipse fitting algorithm.

within 15° indicates the percentage of the total number of images that are within 15° difference between the angle evaluated by the TOHO algorithm and the marked angle, and the proportion of error within 30% indicates the percentage of the total number of images that are within 30% error between the angle evaluated by the TOHO algorithm and the marked angle.

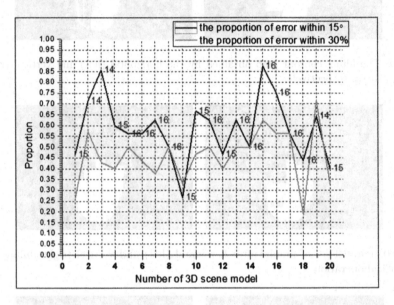

Fig. 13. Performance of TOHO algorithm in generated images from 20 virtual scenes. The data such as 15 and 16 on the edge of the fold line represents the number of samples of the 3D scene model.

As it can be seen from Fig. 13, the algorithm can be accurate up to 88% (No. 15) for some data within 15° error and up to 71% (No.19) for some data within 30% error. Since the data generated by the virtual scene simulates more light shadows than the real world, it will have a very obvious impact on the TOHO algorithm's calculation of the frame difference for the head contour. The subsequent performance in the actual scene may be better than that in the virtual scene.

4   Conclusion

Existing techniques for driver attention monitoring capture positive face data and then analyze it. However, the act of collecting frontal data has privacy protection issues. For this reason, we use a top-down approach for data collection and develop a corresponding analysis method. We validated the proposed method on a virtually generated dataset. The experimental results show that the error of the head attention angle calculated by the proposed algorithm is within 15° compared to the labeled data.

The top-down driver head orientation detection method based on monocular camera and virtual scene generation has a huge application scenario, i.e., this method can complete the attention orientation detection without collecting sensitive data such as human front face features. Generally, when the head is not rotating, the observation range of the human eye is in front of the face, with the eye as the apex of the cone, and the center of the cone axis is composed of the apex of the cone as the end point emitting toward the front of the face, and the cone apex angle formed by the observation range is roughly within 20°. Therefore, when the driver's head starts to turn, it is highly likely that the driver's attention is distracted or the driver is viewing other environmental information, such as shifting the field of view to the rearview mirror. The viewing angle of the left and right mirrors can be recognized by the detection system because of its specific angle and is not considered to be caused by driver distraction. The system extracts and analyzes only the features of the driver's head region, thus enabling a great degree of privacy protection of the driver's biometric data such as face, which has considerable practical value and application prospects. At present, it seems that the method described in this paper can be improved in the following aspects: 1. The ellipse fitting scheme may cause large recognition errors when very individual driver's head shape is positively round from the top to down. 2. The use of the dilation algorithm to dilate the background contour will produce a certain degree of overdetermination, thus causing a reduction of the limited pixels of the background extraction of the subsequent images to be evaluated, and it may reducing the algorithm performance.

References

1. Jin, S.N., Su, L.J.: Forecasting the car penetration rate (CPR) in China: a non-parametric approach. Appl. Econ. **39**(17), 2189–2195 (2007)
2. Pierdzioch, C., Rulke, J.C., Stadtmann, G.: Forecasting US car sales and car registrations in Japan: rationality, accuracy and herding. Japan World Econ. **23**, 253–258 (2011)
3. Wang, Y.-Y., Wei, H.-Y.: Road capacity and throughput for safe driving autonomous vehicles. IEEE Access **8**, 6262 (2020)
4. Araluce, J., et al.: Gaze focalization system for driving applications using OpenFace 2.0 toolkit with NARMAX algorithm in accidental scenarios. Sensors **21**, 1401–1409 (2021)
5. Li, X., Hong, L., Wang, J.-C., Liu, X.: Fatigue driving detection model based on multi-feature fusion and semi-supervised active learning. IET Intell. Transp. Syst. **13**(9), 1401–1409 (2019)
6. Zhao, Z., et al.: Driver distraction detection method based on continuous head pose estimation. Comput. Intell. Neurosci. **2020**, 9606908 (2020)
7. Sun, W., Fan, Y., Min, X., Peng, S., Ma, S., Zhai, G.: LPHD: a large-scale head pose dataset for RGB images. In: International Conference on Multimedia and Expo. IEEE (2019)

8. Li, R., Chen, Y.V., Zhang, L., Shen, Z., Qian, Z.C.: Effects of perception of head-up display on the driving safety of experienced and inexperienced drivers. Displays **64**, 101962 (2020)

9. Li, R., Chen, Y.V., Sha, C., Lu, Z.: Effects of interface layout on the usability of in-vehicle information systems and driving safety. Displays **49**, 124–132 (2017)

10. He, S., Liang, B., Tähkämö, L., Maksimainen, M., Halonen, L.: The influences of tunnel lighting environment on drivers' peripheral visual performance during transient adaptation. Displays **64**, 101964 (2020)

11. Hansen, D.W., Ji, Q.: In the eye of the beholder: a survey of models for eyes and gaze. IEEE Trans. Pattern Anal. Mach. Intell. **32**(3), 478–500 (2010)

12. Al-Rahayfeh, A., Faezipour, M.: Eye tracking and head movement detection: a state-of-art survey. IEEE J. Transl. Eng. Health Med. **1**, 2100212 (2013)

13. John, S.J., Sharmila, S.T.: Real time blink recognition from various head pose using single eye. Multimed. Tools Appl. **77**, 31331–31345 (2018)

14. Sun, J., Lu, S.: An improved single shot multibox for video-rate head pose prediction. IEEE Sens. J. **20**, 12326–12333 (2020)

15. Borghi, G., Fabbri, M., Vezzani, R., Calderara, S., Cucchiara, R.: Face-from-depth for head pose estimation on depth images. IEEE Trans. Pattern Anal. Mach. Intell. **42**(3), 596–609 (2020)

16. Ahn, B., Choi, D.-G., Park, J., Kweon, I.S.: Real-time head pose estimation using multi-task deep neural network. Robot. Auton. Syst. **103**, 1–12 (2018)

17. Zhao, Y., Gorne, L., et al.: An orientation sensor-based head tracking system for driver behaviour monitoring. Sensors (Basel) **17**(11), 2692 (2017)

18. Li, C., Zhong, F., Zhang, Q., Qin, X.: Accurate and fast 3D head pose estimation with noisy RGBD images. Multimed. Tools Appl. **77**, 14605–14624 (2017)

19. Taylor, M.J., Whitton, T.: Public interest, health research and data protection law: establishing a legitimate trade-off between individual control and research access to health data. Laws **9**(1), 6 (2020)

20. Erdos, D.: Beyond "having a domestic"? Regulatory interpretation of European data protection law and individual publication. Comput. Law Secur. Rev. **33**(3), 275–297 (2017)

21. Kuang, Z., Guo, Z., Fang, J.: Unnoticeable synthetic face replacement for image privacy protection. Neurocomputing **457**(2021), 322–333 (2021)

22. Li, X., Wang, K., Tian, Y., Yan, L., Deng, F., Wang, F.-Y.: The paralleleye dataset: a large collection of virtual images for traffic vision research. IEEE Trans. Intell. Transp. Syst. **20**(6), 2072–2084 (2019)

23. Tian, Y., Li, X., Wang, K., Wang, F.-Y.: Training and testing object detectors with virtual images. IEEE/CAA J. Autom. Sin. **5**(2), 539–546 (2018)

24. Canny, J.: A computational approach to edge detection. IEEE Trans. Pattern Anal. Mach. Intell. **8**(6), 679–698 (1986)

An Iris Center Localization Method Based on 3D Eyeball Model and Snakuscule

Jie Tao[✉], Changhua Wang, and Bao Li

Zhejiang Institute of Mechanical and Electrical Engineering CO. LTD., Hangzhou
31000, Zhejiang, People's Republic of China
tj198111200163.com

Abstract. In this paper, we propose a new iris center localization algorithm based on Snakuscule and 3D eyeball model. Firstly, the initial iris center is obtained from the facial feature key-points by face alignment algorithm. Then we reduce the error caused by the low-quality images by judging the state of eye region. We establish a 3D eyeball model, which reflects the geometric relationship among iris center, eye center and iris contour. To further obtain the accurate iris center location, we put forward an improved Snakuscule energy model. The energy value is obtained by initializing a fixed size of Snakuscule model and combining with the 3D eyeball model. The iris contour is updated iteratively according to the energy value, and the final iris center is obtained. Finally, experiments conducted on BioID face dataset validate the effectiveness and superiority of our method. The maximum standard error of the algorithm reached 85.0%, 97.8% and 99.8% respectively for $e \leq 0.05$, $e \leq 0.1$, and $e \leq 0.25$.

Keywords: Iris center localization · Snakuscule model · Eyeball model

1 Introduction

Accurate iris center location algorithm plays an important role in many fields, such as face alignment, gaze estimation and human-computer interaction. Therefore, the stability and accuracy of iris center localization method has certain theoretical research value and practical application significance.

The state of the art iris localization can be assigned to three categories: the feature-based methods [6,7,11], the model-based methods [2,4], and the hybrid methods combining feature and model [9,10,13]. The algorithm presented in this paper is the hybrid algorithms for iris localization. The iris contour is obtained by 3D eyeball model. According to the characteristics of iris, an improved Snakuscule model is used to update the iris contour, so as to locate the center of iris accurately.

The process of iris center localization proposed in this paper is as follows. We use the commercial cameras to record the image of human face in natural light. Face alignment method is used to extract the features of the eye region from the recorded image so as to get the initial iris center. According to the

G. Zhai et al. (Eds.): IFTC 2021, CCIS 1560, pp. 361–372, 2022.
https://doi.org/10.1007/978-981-19-2266-4_28

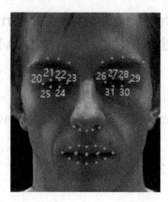

Fig. 1. Feature points of face alignment

features, we judge the state of the open and closed of the eyes, and then the iris center is iteratively updated. To weaken the error of face alignment method, we give a threshold value. When the value is exceeded, the initial iris center is re-positioned and the iterative steps are repeated to get the final iris center.

2   Face Tracking and Detection

In this paper, we apply the facial alignment model which is designed by Xiong [14] to detect human faces. The model can automatically locate facial feature points based on the recorded human faces in given pictures or real-time video frames. The method is a regression algorithm, which gives the initial shape from a given face, and returns the initial shape to the real shape close to the face through constant iteration. This method mainly uses SDM (Supervised Descent Method) to minimize nonlinear least-squares objective function, learn the direction of gradient descent from training data and then establish corresponding regression model. By using the regression model to estimate the direction of gradient, the objective function converges to the minimum value at a very fast speed, and the complex least-squares problem is solved.

As shown in Fig. 1, the green point in the figure is the detected face feature point X, which consists of 5 significant features, namely eyebrow, eye, mouth, nose and face contour. We obtain the feature points of eye region (X[20] – X[31]) by this method. We compute the iris center initial point (u_{ic}, v_{ic}), iris radius (R_i), eye center (u_e, v_e) and eye radius (R_e) according to the eye feature points.

(1) The initial iris center, the iris radius, the eyeball center and the eyeball radius of the left eye can be calculated like this:

$$(u_{lic}, v_{lic}) = \frac{X[21] + X[22] + X[24] + X[25]}{4} \tag{1}$$

$$R_{li} = \frac{|X[21]X[24]| + |X[22]X[25]|}{4} \tag{2}$$

(a) the eyes are open   (b) the eyes are closed

Fig. 2. State of the eye

$$(u_{le}, v_{le}) = \frac{X[20] + X[23]}{2} \tag{3}$$

$$R_{le} = \frac{|X[20]X[23]|}{2} \tag{4}$$

(2) The initial iris center, the iris radius, the eyeball center and the eyeball radius of the right eye can be calculated as follows:

$$(u_{ric}, v_{ric}) = \frac{X[27] + X[28] + X[30] + X[31]}{4} \tag{5}$$

$$R_{ri} = \frac{|X[27]X[30]| + |X[28]X[31]|}{4} \tag{6}$$

$$(u_{re}, v_{re}) = \frac{X[26] + X[29]}{2} \tag{7}$$

$$R_{re} = \frac{|X[26]X[29]|}{2} \tag{8}$$

3   The Update of Iris Center

This paper deals with the two states of eyes when they are closed and open respectively. If the eyes are in a closed state, we directly determine the initial iris center point is the final iris center point; If the eyes are open, the iris center is iteratively updated by combining the iris contour model and the energy model to obtain the final iris center.

3.1   The Judgement of the Eyes State

We use the face alignment to obtain 8 feature points (X21, X22, X24, X25, X27, X28, X30, X31) of the eyelids in the both eye areas. As shown in Fig. 2, when the eyes are opened (as shown in Fig. 2(a)), there is a certain distance between the two feature points of the upper eyelid and the two feature points of the lower eyelid; When the eyes are closed (as shown in Fig. 2(b)), the two feature points of the upper eyelid usually coincide with the two feature points of the lower eyelid.

The judgment of human eye state is as follows: taking the left eye as an example, the distance D_{ud} between the feature points of the upper eyelid (X21, X22) and the feature points of the lower eyelid (X24, X25) are calculated.

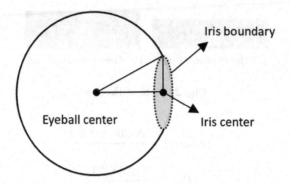

Fig. 3. The model of iris contours

We set a threshold value is –1. If $D_{ud} < -1$, we determine that the eyes are in the closed state at this time, and directly select the initial iris center as the final iris center; if $D_{ud} \geq -1$, we determine that the eyes are open and proceed to the next step. The judgment of the right eye is consistent with the judgment of the left eye.

$$\begin{cases} D_{ud} < -1, \textit{the eyes are closed} \\ D_{ud} \geq -1, \textit{the eyes are open} \end{cases} \tag{9}$$

3.2 The Model of Iris Boundary

As shown in Fig. 3, the 3D coordinate is established at the center of the eyeball, and the Z axis is outside. Assuming that the eyeball center is (X_{ec}, Y_{ec}, Z_{ec}), the iris center is (X_{ic}, Y_{ic}, Z_{ic}). Next the distance from the eyeball center to the iris center can be derived by the following rule.

$$x_{ic}^2 + y_{ic}^2 + z_{ic}^2 = R_e^2 + R_i^2 \tag{10}$$

where R_i and R_e respectively represent the iris and radius of eyeball center (including the left and right eye).

The iris boundary is the intersection of the iris plane and eyeball. Since the normal vector of the iris plane can be composed of the eyeball and iris center. The relationship between the iris plane and the iris boundary could be expressed:

$$(x_{ic} - x_{ec})(x_i - x_{ic}) + (y_{ic} - y_{ec})(y_i - y_{ic}) + (z_{ic} - z_{ec})(z_i - z_{ic}) = 0 \tag{11}$$

where the point in the iris boundary is (x_i, y_i, z_i).

Since the key-points of the iris boundary are on an ellipsoid, which are constrained by the following:

$$\begin{cases} \frac{x_i^2}{a^2} + \frac{y_i^2}{b^2} + \frac{z_i^2}{c^2} = 1 \\ a = R_i \\ b = R_i \\ c = R_e - \sqrt{R_e^2 - R_i^2} \end{cases} \tag{12}$$

Since the information used in the paper comes from the web camera, we turn the coordinates into the camera space. The coordinates of iris boundary can be obtained by combining Eq. 11 and Eq. 12.

$$\frac{(x_i - x_{ec})^2}{a^2} + \frac{(y_i - y_{ec})^2}{b^2} + \frac{\left((x_{ic} - x_{ec})(x_{ic} - x_i) + \frac{(y_{ic} - y_{ec})(y_{ic} - y_i)}{z_{ic} - z_{ec}} + z_{ic} - z_{ec}\right)^2}{c^2} = r_e^2 \tag{13}$$

According to the pinhole model, it is assumed that the spatial point $m(X, Y, Z)$ has the following relationship with the coordinates of pixel points on the recorded image.

1) Convert the camera plane to the image plane

Point $m(X, Y, Z)$ is a point in the camera space, and the point projected onto the image plane is $m(X, Y, f)$. The image plane is perpendicular to the z-axis, and the distance from the projection center is f (f is the focal length of the camera). According to the triangular proportion relationship, we can get $x = \frac{f_x}{z}, y = \frac{f_y}{z}$.

1) Convert the coordinate of image plane to the coordinate of pixel plane

A point in the coordinate of the image plane is (x, y), which is (u, v) in the coordinate of pixel plane, (u_0, v_0) is the center point of the image, and the physical size of each pixel is $dx * dy$, which satisfy the following relationship: $u = \frac{x}{dx} + u_0, v = \frac{y}{dy} + v_0$.

And because of $dx/f \approx dy/y$, $Z_{ic} \approx Z_{ec}$, it is assumed that: $Z_{ic} \cdot (dx/f) \approx Z_{ic} \cdot (dy/f) \approx Z_{ec} \cdot (dx/f) \approx Z_{ec} \cdot (dy/f) \approx 1$. Then, Eq. 10 can be reformulated as

$$(u_e - u_{ic})^2 + (v_{ic} - v_e)^2 + (z_{ic} - z_{ec})^2 = r_e^2 - r_i^2 \tag{14}$$

In the same way, Eq. 13 can be calculated as

$$\frac{(u_e - u_{ic})^2}{a^2} + \frac{(v_i - v_e)^2}{b^2} + \frac{\left(\frac{(u_e - u_{ic})(u_i - u_{ic}) + (v_{ic} - v_e)(v_{ic} - v_i)}{z_{ic} - z_e} + z_{ic} - z_{ec}\right)^2}{c^2} = r_e^2 \tag{15}$$

where u_e, u_i, v_i, and v_e are the input values, $z_{ic} - z_{ec}$ is got from Eq. 14 and (u_i, v_i) is the coordinate of iris boundary on the image plane. The formula can be combined with the energy model in the next section to express the change of the iris boundary when the iris center changes.

3.3   The Model of Snakuscule

In the current iris localization algorithms, deformation contour template based on energy has proved their high accuracy. However, this algorithm needs to

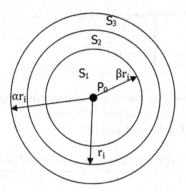

Fig. 4. Structure of a Snakuscule model

Fig. 5. The initialization and convergence of a Snakuscule

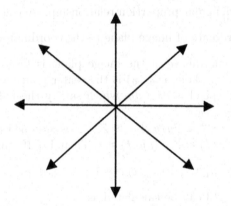

Fig. 6. Directions of the update

constantly update and change the iris radius until the final iris center is found. This template cannot be used for real-time iris center localization in practical application. Therefore, we propose a fixed-radius Snakuscule energy model that significantly reduces the number of iterations, and it is also valid for real-time performance. Since the iris is usually a dark circular in the eye with a low pixel value, we initialize a mobile circular outline-known as Snakuscule, for capturing the iris within the eye.

As shown in Fig. 4, it is the proposed Snakuscule model. In order to reduce the computation, we set a fixed internal radius r_i for the model, where r_i is the initial iris radius obtained by the face alignment method and the size of S_2 is the size of the initial iris boundary region. In this section, α is defined as the ratio from inner radius to outer radius, and β is defined as the ratio from inner radius to reduction.

Figure 5 is the image of the Snakuscule model from the initialization state to the final convergence state. We initialize a Snakuscule with a fixed internal radius of r_i to overlap with part of the iris. Snakuscule works under the influence of local energy gradient. As shown in Fig. 6, Snakuscule can move in eight possible directions, and choose the direction that provides the maximum energy to move. The energy function is as follows:

$$E1 = \iint_{(x,y) \in S3} \frac{p(x,y)}{n} dxdy - \iint_{(x,y) \in S2} \frac{p(x,y)}{n} dxdy \qquad (16)$$

where $S3$ is a circular region with the radius of αr_i, $S2$ is a circular region with the radius of r_i, (x,y) is all points of S, and $p(x,y)$ represents the pixel value. Considering that r_i is obtained by face alignment method, which is different from the actual iris radius. It is possible that the actual iris radius is smaller or larger than r_i, and there are still some noise points in the region of iris boundary after preprocessing of the recorded image. When the actual iris radius is larger, it has no effect on the result. Therefore, we narrow r_i to βr_i and define a circular region $S1$ with the radius of βr_i. The energy function is as follows:

$$E1 = \iint_{(x,y) \in S3} \frac{p(x,y)}{n} dxdy - \iint_{(x,y) \in S1} \frac{p(x,y)}{n} dxdy \qquad (17)$$

Combining Eq. 15 and 16, the energy function of Snakuscule is deduced to be:

$$E3 = E1 + E2 \qquad (18)$$

where α and β are also obtained by face alignment method, take the left eye as an example. Refer to Sect. 3.1 to derive the following:

$$\begin{cases} if \frac{|X[22]X[25]|}{2} > \frac{|X[21]X[24]|}{2} \\ \alpha = \frac{|X[22]X[25]|}{2r_i} + d, \beta = \frac{|X[21]X[24]|}{2r_i} - d \\ else \frac{|X[22]X[25]|}{2} < \frac{|X[21]X[24]|}{2} \\ \beta = \frac{|X[22]X[25]|}{2r_i} - d, \alpha = \frac{|X[21]X[24]|}{2r_i} + d \end{cases} \qquad (19)$$

where d is 0.25, the experimental effect is the best.

There are two main characteristics in the iris: low pixel value in the iris and significant gradient change of iris boundary, so Snakuscule energy function is supplemented:

$$E4 = E5 + h * E6 \qquad (20)$$

where h is a coefficient to balance the E5 and E6. We set it to 0.17 in our experiment.

Iris is usually the darkest area in the eye image, so:

$$E5 = 255 - \iint_{(x,y)\in(x_{ii},y_{ii})} \frac{p(x,y)}{n} dxdy \qquad (21)$$

where (x_{ii}, y_{ii}) is all points of the iris, $p(x, y)$ represents the pixel value, the pixel value in the iris is the lowest, so when E5 takes the maximum value, the region is exactly the iris region.

Iris boundary is usually the area with the largest gradient value, so:

$$E6 = \iint_{(x,y)\in(x_i,y_i)} \frac{g(x,y)}{n} dxdy \qquad (22)$$

where (x_i, y_i) is all points of the iris boundary, and $g(x, y)$ represents the gradient value. Since the gradient value of the iris boundary is usually the largest, this region happens to be the iris boundary area when E6 takes the maximum value.

Combined with Eq. 17 and 18, the final energy function is:

$$E = E3 + E4 \qquad (23)$$

To sum up, we calculate the energy value via the eight-field directions by Eq. 23. When E_{max} is obtained, the iris boundary position is updated in the direction of E_{max}. Repeat the above steps until the moving direction of the two adjacent updates is opposite. At this point, the center of the Snakuscule is the final iris center.

4   The Experimental Results

4.1   Database

To prove the accuracy and robustness of the proposed iris center location method, this paper uses BioID Face Database, which is one of the most challenging databases. BioID database consists of 1521 gray-scale images of human faces from 23 different people. The image is a frontal view including the different scales, face poses, backgrounds and positions. There are many low-quality photos in the database, either taken in dim conditions or seriously reflected by wearing glasses. The ground-truth of left and right eyes is given in the database.

4.2   Evaluation Strategy

To evaluate the accuracy of iris center localization method, we apply the following well-known evaluation measure [3]:

$$e \le \frac{1}{d}max(e_l, e_r) \qquad (24)$$

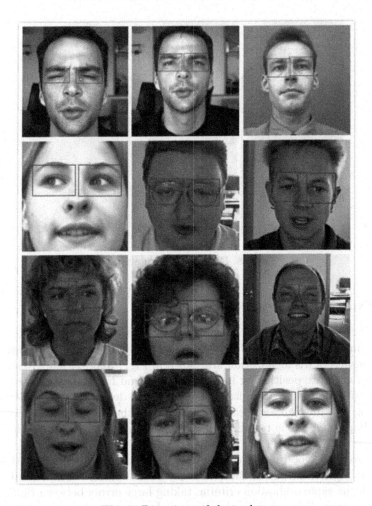

Fig. 7. Directions of the update

where e_l denotes the Euclidean distance between the real left iris center and the detected left iris center. e_r indicates the Euclidean distance between the real right iris center and the detected right iris center. e shows the Euclidean distance between the true position of the left and right iris center. The value of error less than 0.25 means that the distance between the real iris center and the detected iris center is less than the distance between the eye center and the eye corner. The value of error less than 0.1 indicates that the distance between the detected iris center and the real iris center is smaller than the iris radius. The value of error less than 0.05 evinces that the distance between the detected iris center and the real iris center is smaller than the radius of the pupil.

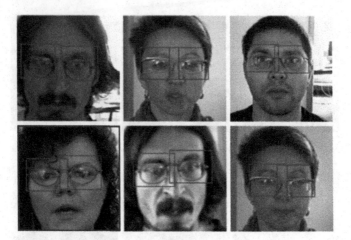

Fig. 8. Directions of the update

4.3   Experimental Result

We exclude some images which the faces cannot be detected. Therefore, a total of 1520 images detected by face alignment method are used for testing. The partial results of iris localization are shown in Fig. 7 and 8. Figure 7 shows some results of accurate positioning in the database, and Fig. 8 shows some results of failed positioning in the database. The model can deal with the problems of the occlusion, illumination and head posture. When the severe occlusion of the eye area is happened or the testers wear glasses, the accuracy of our model may be get worse.

To reveal the good performance of our method, we choose some other state-of-the-art algorithms on the BioID dataset for comparison. These results are all based on the same evaluation criteria, taking large errors between right and left eyes, and normalizing it with the distance between two eye. According to the Table 1, the experimental results of our algorithm can reach 84.3% when the error is less or equal to 0.05, which shows that the algorithm has good accuracy. Compared with the method proposed by Zhang, the accuracy of our method is slightly lower, however, the traversal process in this paper is simpler and requires less time. It is not necessary to locate the iris center by changing the iris radius. When the error is less than or equal to 0.1 and 0.25, our method ranks first and is superior to the majority of the methods.

Table 1. The accuracy of iris center location method proposed in this paper is compared with existing methods

Methods	$e \leq 0.05$	$e \leq 0.1$	$e \leq 0.25$
Niu et al. [11]	75.0%	93.0%	98.0%
Asteriadis et al. [1]	74.0%	81.7%	97.4%
Campadelli et al. [4]	62.0%	85.2%	96.1%
Laddi et al. [9]	81.4%	92.2%	97.5%
Zhang et al. [15]	85.6%	93.6%	99.2%
Kroon et al. [8]	65.0%	87.0%	98.8%
Leo et al. [10]	80.6%	87.3%	93.6%
Timm et al. [12]	82.5%	93.4%	98.0%
Garg et al. [5]	77.6%	88.7%	98.6%
Our method	84.9%	97.6%	99.7%

5 Conclusion

In this paper, a novel iris center localization algorithm based on Snakuscule energy measure is proposed, which combines the geometric relationship of the eyeball model with the characteristics of iris boundary. We use face alignment method to get facial feature points, select the feature to get the initial iris center, and then reduce the error caused by the image by judging the state of the eye region. We consider 8 directions to get the energy value through Snakusucle model combined with 3D eyeball model, and iteratively update the energy value to get the final iris center. This method is evaluated on the BioID database. The experimental results show that the method can solve practical problems well and achieve good accuracy. However, the performance of this method is still not ideal when the large area of glasses reflects almost occludes the eye area. Future work will consider how to solve these noise points and apply the method to practical application as soon as possible.

References

1. Asteriadis, S., Nikolaidis, N., Hajdu, A., Pitas, I.: An eye detection algorithm using pixel to edge information. In: International Symposium on Communications, Control and Signal Processing (2006)
2. Baek, S.J., Choi, K.A., Ma, C., Kim, Y.H., Ko, S.J.: Eyeball model-based iris center localization for visible image-based eye-gaze tracking systems. IEEE Trans. Consum. Electron. **59**(2), 415–421 (2013)
3. Cai, H., Liu, B., Zhang, J., Chen, S., Liu, H.: Visual focus of attention estimation using eye center localization. IEEE Syst. J. **11**(3), 1320–1325 (2015)
4. Campadelli, P., Lanzarotti, R., Lipori, G.: Precise eye localization through a general-to-specific model definition. In: BMVC, vol. 1, pp. 187–196 (2006)

5. Garg, S., Tripathi, A., Cutrell, E.: Accurate eye center localization using snakuscule. In: 2016 IEEE Winter Conference on Applications of Computer Vision (WACV), pp. 1–8. IEEE (2016)

6. Kim, S., Chung, S.T., Jung, S., Oh, D., Kim, J., Cho, S.: Multi-scale gabor feature based eye localization. World Acad. Sci. Eng. Technol. **21**, 483–487 (2007)

7. Koenderink, J.J., Van Doorn, A.J.: Surface shape and curvature scales. Image Vis. Comput. **10**(8), 557–564 (1992)

8. Kroon, B., Hanjalic, A., Maas, S.M.: Eye localization for face matching: is it always useful and under what conditions? In: Proceedings of the 2008 International Conference on Content-based Image and Video Retrieval, pp. 379–388 (2008)

9. Laddi, A., Prakash, N.R.: An augmented image gradients based supervised regression technique for iris center localization. Multimed. Tools Appl. **76**(5), 7129–7139 (2016). https://doi.org/10.1007/s11042-016-3361-y

10. Leo, M., Cazzato, D., De Marco, T., Distante, C.: Unsupervised eye pupil localization through differential geometry and local self-similarity matching. PLoS ONE **9**(8), e102829 (2014)

11. Niu, Z., Shan, S., Yan, S., Chen, X., Gao, W.: 2D cascaded adaboost for eye localization. In: 18th International Conference on Pattern Recognition (ICPR 2006), vol. 2, pp. 1216–1219. IEEE (2006)

12. Timm, F., Barth, E.: Accurate eye centre localisation by means of gradients. Visapp **11**, 125–130 (2011)

13. Zhou, X., Jiaqi Jiang, J.L., Chen, S.: An algorithm for iris center location based on three-dimensional eyeball model and snakuscule. Comput. Sci. **46**(9), 284–290 (2019)

14. Xiong, X., De la Torre, F.: Supervised descent method and its applications to face alignment. In: Proceedings of the IEEE Conference on Computer Vision and Pattern Recognition, pp. 532–539 (2013)

15. Zhang, W., Smith, M.L., Smith, L.N., Farooq, A.: Eye center localization and gaze gesture recognition for human-computer interaction. JOSA A **33**(3), 314–325 (2016)

Video Processing

Optical Flow-Guided Multi-level Connection Network for Video Deraining

Mengyao Li[1], Yongfang Wang[1(✉)], and Zhijun Fang[2]

[1] School of Communication and Information Engineering, Shanghai University, Shanghai 200444, China
yfw@shu.edu.cn

[2] School of Electronic and Electrical Engineering, Shanghai University of Engineering Science, Shanghai 201620, China

Abstract. Video deraining, which aims at removing rain streaks from video, has drawn increasing attention in computer vision task. In this paper, we present an optical flow guided multi-level connection network for video deraining which can effectively take advantage of additional information in frames of the video sequence. Firstly, we utilize optical flow estimation method to extract the motion between two neighboring frames and perform warp operation according to inter-frame motion information to make neighboring frames align with target frame. Then, a multi-level connection network based on encoder-decoder residual block architecture is proposed for removing rain streaks from preceding aligned frames. To better recover background details, multi-level connection is used to effectively utilize the information between different scales. Furthermore, we also introduce hard example mining loss which is beneficial for promoting the performance enhancement of video deraining. Extensive experiments on three public datasets demonstrate that the proposed model achieves the state-of-the-art performance.

Keywords: Video deraining · Multi-level connection · Optical flow

1 Introduction

In daily life, rain often occurs. The images and videos captured in rainy weather will suffer visibility degradation such as detail loss and content distortion. The presence of rain seriously affects the performance of several computer vision tasks, such as object detection, recognition, scene analysis, and person reidentification. Therefore, rain removal has recently attacked considerable attention.

Recently, many algorithms have been presented to improve restoration quality of rain videos. Video deraining methods are mainly divided into the following two categories: hand-crafted prior-based ones, deep learning (DL) based ones. Some methods [1, 2] utilize temporal property of rain to design deraining correlated model, including histogram model and probabilistic model, for rain streaks removal. In [3, 4], a global model is developed in frequency domain for detecting and removing rain or snow. In [5], a low-rank appearance model is proposed to characterize the spatio-temporally related

© Springer Nature Singapore Pte Ltd. 2022
G. Zhai et al. (Eds.): IFTC 2021, CCIS 1560, pp. 375–386, 2022.
https://doi.org/10.1007/978-981-19-2266-4_29

rain streaks for rain removal. Later, many sparsity and low sparse based algorithms [6–8] are presented. As the fast development of deep learning, video deraining has made significant progress. Several convolutional neural networks (CNN) like superpixel alignment [9], recurrent network [10–12], have been introduced to solve the video deraining problem. Aforementioned algorithms are trained with rainy/clean video pairs which is usually synthetic because real rainy/clean video pairs are difficult to collect. Yang et al. presented a self-learning method [13] without requiring paired rainy/clean videos. Although these DL-based methods have improved the quality of restored videos in some cases, there is still a lot of room for progress.

In this paper, we present a flow-guided multi-level connection network (FMLCN) for video deraining. FMLCN contains two parts: optical flow estimation and warping module, and latent frame restoration module. Considering that the inter-frame information plays an important role in video vision task, we present an optical flow estimation module to extract inter-frame motion information, which is used to warp adjacent frames into the target frame. The concatenation of aligned frames and target frame are sent to next module for target frame restoration. Latent frame restoration module is developed on the basis of the encoder-decoder architecture with multi-level connection, which exploit rich scales information to compensate image details.

The main contributions of this paper are summarized as follows:

1. We design a novel CNN based method named FMLCN for video deraining.
2. We introduce multi-level connection between different levels to effectively utilize information across all the scales for image details restoration.
3. Hard flow example mining loss is introduced to further improve the performance of video deraining.
4. The proposed method significantly outperforms the state-of-the-art methods on three synthetic rain video datasets and two real-world rain video sequences.

2   Related Work

2.1   Image Deraining

Single image deraining is a quite ill-posed and challenging problem. To address the problem, many traditional prior-based algorithms have been presented, such as image decomposition [14], discriminative sparse coding [15], bi-layer optimization [16], hierarchical deraining [17], directional group sparse model [18] and gaussian mixture model [19]. Recently, as the rapid growth of deep learning, the deep learning based image deraining algorithms outperform previous traditional methods. Yang et al. present a recurrent rain detection and removal network [20] to progressively remove rain streaks. Later, Li et al. [21] divide the rain removal network into multiple stages. Similar to [21], Ren et al. also presented a multi-stage method [22] for deraining, which is combined by several simple block. Li et al. [23] integrate physics-based network and model-free refine network to bridge the gap between real rain and synthetic rain. Wei et al. [24] present a semi-supervised learning paradigm that adapts to real and diverse rain patterns by transferring from synthetic rain. In order to make the most of the multi-scale collaborative representation of rain streaks, a multi-scale progressive fusion network is presented in [25].

2.2 Video Deraining

Garg and Nayar make attempt for video deraining, and propose several methods [26–28]. Later, several priors of rain streaks are proposed to address video deraining problem. In [29], the temporal and chromatic properties of rain are utilized to detect and remove rain streaks. In [1], temporal and spatial properties of rain streaks are exploited to form a histogram model for image deraining. In [30], intrinsic characteristics of rain streaks are analyzed for eliminating rain streaks. Barnum et al. [3, 4] remove rain or snow based on using physical and statistical model to highlight spatio-temporal frequencies. Ren et al. [6] model sparse and dense components which decomposed by rain streaks separately based on matrix decomposition. Kim et al. [31] train a support vector machine to divide rain maps into outliers and rain streaks, and then remove rain streaks by performing low rank matrix completion and finding the rain maps to exclude outliers. In [7], rain streaks are encoded as stochastic knowledge by using patch-based mixture of gaussian. In [8], Two intrinsic characteristics are introduced into multiscale convolutional sparse coding model. Recently, the development of deep learning significantly promotes the update of video deraining methods. Chen et al. [9] apply superpixel segmentation to align content and remove occlusion, then use a CNN to compensate detail effectively. Liu et al. [10] integrate rain degradation classification, rain removal based on spatial texture representation and background details reconstruction based on temporal consistency to design a joint recurrent rain removal and restoration network. Liu et al. [11] propose a hybrid video rain model including rain occlusions, which is then embedded in a dynamically routed residual recurrent network. In [12], build a two-stage network with dual level flow regularization is built to eliminate rain streaks, which is inverse to the proposed new rain synthesis model. Besides, a self-learning deraining network [13] by utilizing temporal correlation and consistency is proposed. Yue et al. [32] present a semi-supervised video deraining network with dynamic rain generator which is based on the spatial-temporal process in statistics.

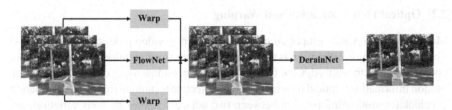

Fig. 1. Framework of optical flow-guided multi-level connection network for video deraining

3 Proposed Method

In this section, Sect. 3.1 introduce the overall network architecture, Sect. 3.2 present optical flow estimation and warping network in detail, Sect. 3.3 clarify the deraining network, Sect. 3.4 specify the loss function used in experiment.

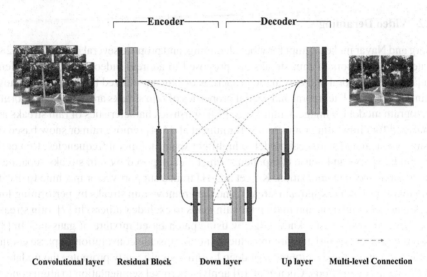

Fig. 2. Framework of multi-level connection network

3.1 Proposed Network Architecture

The overview of the proposed framework is illustrated in Fig. 1. Our framework contains two parts, optical flow estimation and warping network and multi-level connection video deraining network. Video deraining model aims to restore one clean frame from several adjacent rain frames. In the proposed method, an optical flow network is performed to extract motion information between two neighboring frames, then the neighboring frames align with the target frame by utilizing extracted motion information. Finally, the aligned frames are sent to video deraining network for restore clean frame.

3.2 Optical Flow Estimation and Warping

Motion estimation and compensation is widely used in video processing task [33, 34]. Specifically, motion estimation is to extract inter-frame motion information, and motion compensation is to align adjacent frame with the target frame using obtained inter-frame motion information. Optical flow method is an effective technique for motion estimation. It calculates motion information between two adjacent frames by their variations and correlations in the temporal dimension. In our method, PWC-Net [35] is used as the optical flow estimation module. Note that the pretrained model is used to initialize it. Generally, an optical flow estimation module adopts two adjacent frames as input, the estimation process is shown as follows:

$$F_{i \to i+1} = N_f(I_i, I_{i+1}) \tag{1}$$

Where $F_{i \to i+1}$ denotes the optical flow vector field generated from frame I_i to I_{i+1}, N_f is the network used to compute optical flow.

For the warping module, we use the bilinear interpolation to make neighboring frame align with the target frame. The warping process is expressed as follows:

$$J = W_j(I_i, F_{i \to i+1}) \tag{2}$$

Where J is the warped frame, W_j is the warping function, I_i is the neighboring frame.

3.3 Multi-level Connection Network for Video Deraining

In this paper, we present a multi-level connection network for video deraining based on encoder-decoder residual block (ResBlock) architecture. Inspired the great success of encoder-decoder residual block architecture in image deblurring task [36], as illustrated in Fig. 2, the proposed network adopts encoder-decoder residual block as baseline, which also shows excellent performance in video deraining. The encoder part contains three parts, each part contains a convolutional layer followed by three ResBlocks. Note that the last two convolutional layer downsample the feature map to half size while doubles the channel. The decoder part also contains three parts, first two parts contain three ResBlocks followed by a deconvolutional layer, and the last part contains three ResBlocks followed by a convolutional layer. For the deconvolutional layer, the size of feature map doubles and the channels halve. All the ResBlocks include two convolutional layers. The kernel size of all convolutional layer is five, and all convolutional layers are followed by Rectified Linear Units (ReLU) as the activation function.

For the purpose of taking advantage of multi-scale information during the low-level recovery, multi-level connection [37] is introduced to further improve model performance. Based on above all, we propose a multi-level connection video deraining network based on encoder-decoder ResBlock architecture. In the proposed network, features from all scales in the encoder part are aggregated to send to each level of the decoder part. Specifically, the multi-level connection is formed as follows:

$$F^l = \left(\oplus_{i=1}^{3} H_i^l(F_E^i) \right) \oplus F_D^l \tag{3}$$

where F^l is the sum of all multi-level features of encoder and corresponding level feature of decoder, $\oplus$ is the element-wise addition, F_E^l is the output feature at level l in the encoder part, H_i^l is the sampling operation from level i to l, F_D^l is the output feature at level l in the decoder part.

3.4 Loss Function

In our work, the proposed FMLCN is an end-to-end trainable model, we employ two types of loss function to constrain the training of proposed method. We define the total loss function as:

$$\mathcal{L} = \mathcal{L}_1 + \alpha \mathcal{L}_{HEM} \tag{4}$$

where $\mathcal{L}_1$ is mean squared error loss, $\mathcal{L}_{HEM}$ is hard flow example mining loss, α denotes trade-off parameter, empirically set to 2.

Mean Squared Error Loss: We employ mean squared error to compute the difference between the derained frame and ground truth, which is defined as:

$$\mathcal{L}_1 = \|X^{derained} - X^{gt}\| \qquad (5)$$

where $X^{derained}$ is the derained frame, X^{gt} is the corresponding ground truth.

Hard Flow Example Mining Loss: Motivated by [38], we adopt the hard flow example mining mechanism that encourages the model to preserve sharp boundaries. In detail, all pixels are sorted in descending order of the loss function. The top 50% of pixels are identified as hard examples. The random 10% of pixels are labeled as random examples. The hard flow example mining loss is defined as:

$$\mathcal{L}_{HEM} = \left\| \left(M^h + M^r\right) \odot \left(X^{derained} - X^{gt}\right) \right\| \qquad (6)$$

where M^h, M^r are binary masks indicating the hard example regions and random example regions respectively, $\odot$ is element-wise multiply.

4 Experiments

In this section, first, we present the datasets and evaluation metrics, then we demonstrate the effectiveness by comparing with several state-of-the-art deraining methods on three synthetic datasets quantitatively and qualitatively, and finally conduct ablation experiments to verify the significance of several parts in proposed method.

Our experiments are performed using Pytorch on a PC with two Nvidia RTX2080. The patch size of each frame is 256×256 and the batch size is 8. Adam optimizer [39] is adopted to train proposed network with the initial learning rate of 0.0001. For NTURain dataset [9], the learning rate is reduced by every 40 epochs by multiplying with 0.5 and training stops at 110 epochs. For RainSynComplex25 and RainSynLight25 datasets [11], the learning rate reduces every 80 epochs by multiplying with 0.5 and training stops until 180th epochs.

4.1 Datasets and Evaluation Metrics

NTURain: The NTURain contains 8 rain-free video clips of various urban and natural scenes, which are taken from panning with unstable movement and low speed, or car-mount camera with high speed up to 30 km/h. Adobe After Effects is used to synthesize 25 rainy scenes over each video clip. The training set contains 25 rain/clean video clips, and testing set contains 8 rain/clean video clips.

RainSynComplex25: It contains 190 rain/clean video clips for training and 25 rain/clean video clips for testing. And the rain video clips are produced by the probabilistic model [40], sharp line streaks [20] and sparkle noises.

RainSynLight25: The dataset is approximately similar to the RainSynComplex25 dataset. The rain video clips are synthesized just by the probabilistic model [40].

Two commonly used metrics, Peak Signal to Noise Ratio (PSNR) and Structural Similarity (SSIM) [41], are utilized to quantitatively evaluate the restoration results.

4.2 Evaluation on Synthetic Datasets

To study the effectiveness of proposed FMLCN, the proposed FMLCN is compared against several state-of-the-art methods on the above three synthetic datasets: RainSyn-Complex25, RainSynLight25 and NTURain. For FastDerain [42], online multi-scale convolutional sparse coding (OTMS-CSC) [43], superpixel alignment and compensation CNN (SPAC-CNN) [9], semi-supervised video deraining (S2VD) [32], the results are calculated directly from the models provided by authors. For frame-consistent recurrent network (FCRNet), since the source code is not available, we directly copy the numerical results from [12]. Table 1 list quantitative results of all compared methods on RainSynComplex25, RainSynLight25 and NTURain. Values in red indicate the highest and values in blue indicate the second highest. As the Table 1 list, our method obtains highest or at least second highest values of PSNR and SSIM on three synthetic datasets. For dataset NTURain, our method achieved up to 2.63 dB PSNR and 0.0101 SSIM gain compared with S2VD. For dataset RainSynComplex25, our method outperforms FCR-Net, with a gain of 1.19 dB PSNR and 0.065 SSIM. Although the performance of our method is not the best on dataset RainSynLight25, it achieved second highest value in PSNR and SSIM, respectively. It may be related to the 30 missing clips in the training set.

We also provide several visual reconstruction results of all compared methods on the dataset NTURain, RainSynComplex25, and RainSynLight25 in Fig. 3, 4 and 5. As is shown in Fig. 3, 4, 5, our method generates visually more pleasing results, with least remaining rain streaks and abundant details.

Table 1. Quantitative evaluation on three synthetic datasets with different methods. Both PSNR and SSIM are listed.

Dataset	Metric	Fast Derain	SPAC-CNN	OTMS-CSC	S2VD	FCRNet	Ours
NTURain	PSNR	28.70	32.15	27.65	36.48	35.80	39.11
	SSIM	0.8861	0.9440	0.8807	0.9669	0.9622	0.9770
RainSynComplex25	PSNR	25.47	19.75	16.12	16.39	27.72	28.91
	SSIM	0.7635	0.5611	0.4874	0.5306	0.8239	0.8889
RainSynLight25	PSNR	29.99	29.76	24.74	25.45	36.05	34.24
	SSIM	0.8805	0.8843	0.8024	0.8426	0.9676	0.9474

4.3 Evaluation on Real Datasets

To further general validate the robustness of our method, visual comparison of restoration results on real-world video clips are provided. The real-word video dataset is from [9]. Figure 6 shows qualitative performance with compared methods on two real-world video sequences. It can be seen from top row of Fig. 6 that S2VD obvious remained rain streaks, FastDerain and OTMS-CSC removed the majority of rain streaks, SPAC-CNN removed

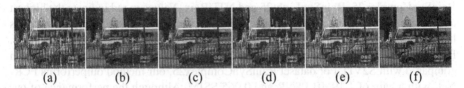

Fig. 3. Visual restoration results on NTURain (a) Input (b) FastDerain (c) SPAC-CNN (d) OTMS-CSC (e) S2VD (f) Ours

Fig. 4. Visual restoration results on RainSynComplex25 (a) Input (b) FastDerain (c) SPAC-CNN (d) OTMS-CSC (e) S2VD (f) Ours

Fig. 5. Visual restoration results on RainSynLight25 (a) Input (b) FastDerain (c) SPAC-CNN (d) OTMS-CSC (e) S2VD (f) Ours

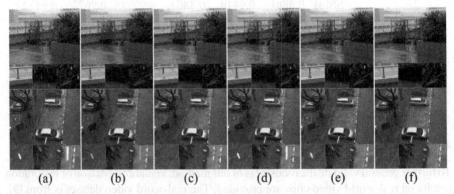

Fig. 6. Visual restoration results on the real-world rain sequences (a) Input (b) FastDerain (c) SPAC-CNN (d) OTMS-CSC (e) S2VD (f) Ours. (Color figure online)

almost all streaks but the railing is discolored as shown in blue cropped box. In contrast, proposed method removed nearly all rain streaks and remained visual pleasing details. For the bottom row of Fig. 6, FastDerain, OTMS-CSC and C2VD remained rain streaks to some extent, SPAC-CNN removed almost all rain streaks but restore rain streak to lane lines as illustrated in blue cropped box. In contrast, our method generated the best visual results both in removing of rain streaks and reconstructing details.

4.4 Ablation Study

In this section, various ablation experiments on different parts are performed to verify the significance of our design choices. All the ablation experiments are conducted on NTURain [9] dataset.

Effectiveness of Optical Flow Estimation and Warping Module. To prove the validity of optical flow estimation and warping module (OFEWM), as a comparison, we directly concatenate three consecutive frames as input for latent frame restoration network, the optical flow estimation and warping module is not used. As the Table 2 shows, the performance of method with optical flow estimation and warping module is significantly superior to the method without optical flow estimation and warping module. It is because that OFEWM can effectively utilize temporal information across frames to improve deraining performance.

Table 2. Ablation study on optical flow estimation and warping module

Methods	PSNR (dB)	SSIM
Without OFEWM	37.55	0.9709
With OFEWM	39.11	0.9770

Effectiveness of Multi-level Connection. In order to demonstrate the validity of multi-level connection on latent frame reconstruction, we experiment by removing multi-level connection on restoration network. As can be seen in Table 3, multi-level connection is beneficial for improving deraining performance with an increase of 0.10 dB in PSNR value and 0.0005 in SSIM value.

Table 3. Ablation study on multi-level connection

Methods	PSNR (dB)	SSIM
Without Multi-level Connection	39.01	0.9765
With Multi-level Connection	39.11	0.9770

Effectiveness of Hard Flow Example Mining Loss. To investigate the effect of hard flow example mining loss function on restoration performance, proposed method with and without hard example mining loss function are trained respectively. As observed in Table 4, PSNR achieved a gain of 0.07 dB and SSIM achieved an improvement of 0.0006.

Table 4. Ablation study on hard flow example mining loss

Methods	$\mathcal{L}_1$	$\mathcal{L}_{FEM}$	PSNR (dB)	SSIM
FMLCN	√		39.04	0.9764
FMLCN	√	√	39.11	0.9770

5   Conclusion

In this paper, we proposed a novel deep CNN which integrates optical flow network and multi-level connection network based on encoder-decoder residual architecture for video rain removal. To effectively utilize temporal information across frames, we introduce an optical flow estimation module to extract inter-frame motion formation which is then used to make neighboring frame align with target frame. The multi-level connection deraining network takes the concatenation of aligned frames and target frame as input to help rain frame reconstruction. Furthermore, in order to restore background details effectively, multi-level connection is employed to restoration module for aggregating the features from all levels. Extensive experiments on synthetic datasets and real-world rain video sequences have verified the effectiveness of proposed video deraining method.

Acknowledgement. This work was supported by Natural Science Foundation of China under Grant No. 61671283, U2033218.

References

1. Zhao, X., et al.: The application of histogram on rain detection in video. In: 11th Joint International Conference on Information Sciences, pp. 382–387 (2008)
2. Tripathi, A.K., Mukhopadhyay, S.: A probabilistic approach for detection and removal of rain from videos. IETE J. Res. **57**(1), 82–91 (2011)
3. Barnum, P., Kanade, T., Narasimhan, S.: Spatio-temporal frequency analysis for removing rain and snow from videos. In: Proceedings of the First International Workshop on Photometric Analysis for Computer Vision-PACV 2007, p. 8 (2007)
4. Barnum, P.C., Narasimhan, S., Kanade, T.: Analysis of rain and snow in frequency space. Int. J. Comput. Vis. **86**(2–3), 256 (2010)
5. Chen, Y.L., Hsu, C.T.: A generalized low-rank appearance model for spatio-temporally correlated rain streaks, In: Proceedings of the IEEE International Conference on Computer Vision, pp. 1968–1975 (2013)

6. Ren, W., et al.: Video desnowing and deraining based on matrix decomposition. In: Proceedings of the IEEE Conference on Computer Vision and Pattern Recognition, pp. 4210–4219 (2017)
7. Wei, W., et al.: Should we encode rain streaks in video as deterministic or stochastic? In: Proceedings of the IEEE International Conference on Computer Vision, pp. 2516–2525 (2017)
8. Li, M., et al.: Video rain streak removal by multiscale convolutional sparse coding. In: Proceedings of the IEEE Conference on Computer Vision and Pattern Recognition, pp. 6644–6653 (2018)
9. Chen, J., et al.: Robust video content alignment and compensation for rain removal in a cnn framework. In: Proceedings of the IEEE Conference on Computer Vision and Pattern Recognition, pp. 6286–6295 (2018)
10. Liu, J., et al.: Erase or fill? Deep joint recurrent rain removal and reconstruction in videos. In: Proceedings of the IEEE Conference on Computer Vision and Pattern Recognition, pp. 3233–3242 (2018)
11. Liu, J., Yang, W., Yang, S., et al.: D3R-Net: dynamic routing residue recurrent network for video rain removal. IEEE Trans. Image Process. **28**(2), 699–712 (2018)
12. Yang, W., Liu, J., Feng, J.: Frame-consistent recurrent video deraining with dual-level flow. In: Proceedings of the IEEE/CVF Conference on Computer Vision and Pattern Recognition, pp. 1661–1670 (2019)
13. Yang, W., et al.: Self-learning video rain streak removal: when cyclic consistency meets temporal correspondence. In: Proceedings of the IEEE/CVF Conference on Computer Vision and Pattern Recognition, pp. 1720–1729 (2020)
14. Kang, L.W., Lin, C.W., Fu, Y.H.: Automatic single-image-based rain streaks removal via image decomposition. IEEE Trans. Image Process. **21**(4), 1742–1755 (2011)
15. Luo, Y., Xu, Y., Ji, H.: Removing rain from a single image via discriminative sparse coding. In: Proceedings of the IEEE International Conference on Computer Vision, pp. 3397–3405 (2015)
16. Zhu, L., et al.: Joint bi-layer optimization for single-image rain streak removal. In: Proceedings of the IEEE International Conference on Computer Vision, pp. 2526–2534 (2017)
17. Wang, Y., Liu, S., Chen, C., et al.: A hierarchical approach for rain or snow removing in a single color image. IEEE Trans. Image Process. **26**(8), 3936–3950 (2017)
18. Deng, L.J., Huang, T.Z., Zhao, X.L., et al.: A directional global sparse model for single image rain removal. Appl. Math. Model. **59**, 662–679 (2018)
19. Li, Y., et al.: Rain streak removal using layer priors. In: Proceedings of the IEEE Conference on Computer Vision and Pattern Recognition, pp. 2736–2744 (2016)
20. Yang, W., et al.: Deep joint rain detection and removal from a single image. In: Proceedings of the IEEE Conference on Computer Vision and Pattern Recognition, pp. 1357–1366 (2017)
21. Li, X., Wu, J., Lin, Z., Liu, H., Zha, H.: Recurrent squeeze-and-excitation context aggregation net for single image deraining. In: Ferrari, V., Hebert, M., Sminchisescu, C., Weiss, Y. (eds.) ECCV 2018. LNCS, vol. 11211, pp. 262–277. Springer, Cham (2018). https://doi.org/10.1007/978-3-030-01234-2_16
22. Ren, D., et al.: Progressive image deraining networks: a better and simpler baseline. In: Proceedings of the IEEE/CVF Conference on Computer Vision and Pattern Recognition, pp. 3937–3946 (2019)
23. Li, R., Cheong, L.F., Tan, R.T.: Heavy rain image restoration: integrating physics model and conditional adversarial learning. In: Proceedings of the IEEE/CVF Conference on Computer Vision and Pattern Recognition, pp. 1633–1642 (2019)
24. Wei, W., et al.: Semi-supervised transfer learning for image rain removal. In: Proceedings of the IEEE/CVF Conference on Computer Vision and Pattern Recognition, pp. 3877–3886 (2019)

25. Jiang, K., et al.: Multi-scale progressive fusion network for single image deraining. In: Proceedings of the IEEE/CVF Conference on Computer Vision and Pattern Recognition, pp. 8346–8355 (2020)

26. Garg, K., Nayar, S.K.: When does a camera see rain? In: Tenth IEEE International Conference on Computer Vision (2005)

27. Garg, K., Nayar, S.K.: Vision and rain. Int. J. Comput. Vis. **75**(1), 3–27 (2007)

28. Garg, K., Nayar, S.K.: Detection and removal of rain from videos. In: Computer Vision and Pattern Recognition (2004)

29. Zhang, X., et al.: Rain removal in video by combining temporal and chromatic properties. In: 2006 IEEE International Conference on Multimedia and Expo, pp. 461–464 (2006)

30. Jiang, T.X., et al.: A novel tensor-based video rain streaks removal approach via utilizing discriminatively intrinsic priors. In: Proceedings of the IEEE Conference on Computer Vision and Pattern Recognition, pp. 4057–4066 (2017)

31. Kim, J.H., Sim, J.Y., Kim, C.S.: Video deraining and desnowing using temporal correlation and low-rank matrix completion. IEEE Trans. Image Process. **24**(9), 2658–2670 (2015)

32. Yue, Z., et al.: Semi-Supervised Video Deraining with Dynamic Rain Generator. arXiv preprint arXiv:.07939 (2021)

33. Pan, J., Bai, H., Tang, J.: Cascaded deep video deblurring using temporal sharpness prior. In: Proceedings of the IEEE/CVF Conference on Computer Vision and Pattern Recognition, pp. 3043–3051 (2020)

34. Wang, Z., et al.: Multi-memory convolutional neural network for video super-resolution. IEEE Trans. Image Process. **28**(5), 2530–2544 (2018)

35. Sun, D., et al.: PWC-Net: CNNs for optical flow using pyramid, warping, and cost volume. In: Proceedings of the IEEE Conference on Computer Vision and Pattern Recognition, pp. 8934–8943 (2018)

36. Tao, X., Gao, H., Shen, X., et al.: Scale-recurrent network for deep image deblurring. In: Proceedings of the IEEE Conference on Computer Vision and Pattern Recognition, pp. 8174–8182 (2018)

37. Park, Y., et al.: MARA-Net: single image deraining network with multi-level connection and adaptive regional attention. arXiv preprint arXiv:.13990 (2020)

38. Xu, R., et al.: Deep flow-guided video inpainting. In: Proceedings of the IEEE/CVF Conference on Computer Vision and Pattern Recognition, pp. 3723–3732 (2019)

39. Kingma, D.P., Ba, J.: Adam: a method for stochastic optimization. arXiv preprint arXiv:.07939 (2014)

40. Garg, K., Nayar, S.K.: Photorealistic rendering of rain streaks. ACM Trans. Graph. **25**(3), 996–1002 (2006)

41. Wang, Z., Bovik, A.C., Sheikh, H.R., et al.: Image quality assessment: from error visibility to structural similarity. IEEE Trans. Image Process. **13**(4), 600–612 (2004)

42. Jiang, T.X., Huang, T.Z., Zhao, X.L., et al.: Fastderain: a novel video rain streak removal method using directional gradient priors. IEEE Trans. Image Process. **28**(4), 2089–2102 (2018)

43. Li, M., Cao, X., Zhao, Q., et al.: Online rain/snow removal from surveillance videos. IEEE Trans. Image Process. **30**, 2029–2044 (2021)

Efficient Wavelet Channel Attention Module with a Fusion Network for Image Super-Resolution

Xiyu Han[1], Jian Ma[1,2,3](✉), Guoming Xu[1], Ping An[3], and Ran Ma[3]

[1] School of Internet, Anhui University, Hefei 230039, China
y20301018@stu.ahu.edu.cn, jianma@ahu.edu.cn
[2] School of Computer Science, Fudan University, Shanghai 200433, China
[3] Key Laboratory of Advance Displays and System Application,
Ministry of Education, Shanghai University, Shanghai 200444, China
{anping,maran}@shu.edu.cn

Abstract. In recent years, deep convolutional neural networks (CNNs) have been generally used in image Super-Resolution (SR) and has made great progress. Nevertheless, the existing CNNs based SR method cannot fully search the background information in the step of feature extraction. Moreover, the later network pursues too much deeper and heavier, thus ignoring the desired performance of SR. To solve the problem, we project a learning wavelets and channel attention network (LWCAN) for image SR. The network mainly comprises three branches. The first part extracts the low-level feature from the input image through two convolution layers and the Efficient Channel Attention (ECA) block. The second part is calculating the second level low frequency wavelet coefficient. The third part is used for forecasting the residual frequency bands of wavelet coefficient. Finally, the reverse wavelet transform is used to reconstruct the SR image from these coefficients. Experiments on the common used dataset prove the effectiveness of our projected LWCAN in the light of visual effects and quantitative metrics.

Keywords: CNNs · Image super-resolution · Efficient channel attention · Wavelet transform

1 Introduction

Single Image Super-Resolution (SISR) means that the reconstruction of visually pleasing high resolution (HR) images from low resolution (LR) images. Applied by the SR technology as a pretreatment step, many advanced visual applications (for instance, medical imaging [1,2], satellite and aerial imaging [3], security and surveillance imaging [4], object detection and recognition [5]) can profit by high-quality reconstructed HR images. The key to this problem is how to pick up useful information with effect from the input LR image. Moreover, how to make use of the extracted feature to rebuild the HR image of fine-detailed is also

© Springer Nature Singapore Pte Ltd. 2022
G. Zhai et al. (Eds.): IFTC 2021, CCIS 1560, pp. 387–400, 2022.
https://doi.org/10.1007/978-981-19-2266-4_30

important. Due to multiple the HR image could be down-sampled to the same LR image, and restoring the HR image from one LR image is a one-to-many mapping relationship, SISR is still a challenging and morbid problem, although that plenty of methods have been projected.

In order to resolve the SR problem, the community researched interpolation and played a significant role in reconstruction in earlier years. Nevertheless, owing to the greatly development of deep learning (DL), the current progress based on DL [6–10] far exceeds the traditional method of interpolation based. As a breakthrough study in the domain of image SR, SRCNN [11] significantly improves the reconstruction performance by using three-layer complete convolutional neural network (CNN). Since then, due to the theory of "the deeper, the better", deeper CNN and generative adversarial networks (GANs) [12] have been proposed. These networks not only achieve excellent reconfiguration performance, but also bring a very large number of network parameters. To solve this problem, the research community focuses on searching lightweight network backbone and recurrent learning [7,13]. However, for the light weight backbone network, it needs careful design, then the network structure could not be too complicated. To recursive learning, owing to its successive structure, the current reasoning of recursive unit need to await the output of the previous reasoning [8,14]. The other side of the shield, most CNN-based methods [15,16] equally treat the channel feature, which lacks adaptability in handling different kinds of information. Recently, channel attention has been used to pick up the low level feature from the LR image of input [17], showing great potential in performance improvement. Nevertheless, not only these methods achieve higher precision, but also bring very high network complexity and very large computational burden.

To sum up, the existing method do not achieve a good balance in the pursuit of network performance, network running time and network parameters. Motivated by this fact, we propose a learning wavelets and channel attention network (LWCAN) to realize image lightweight and accurate super-resolution. The whole network model is mainly made up three parts. In the first part, two convolution layers and an efficient channel attention (ECA) block are used to pick up the low-level feature from the LR image of input without dimensionality reduction. ECA block is modified from SE block [18]. More information about ECA block is described in Sect. 3.2. The second part is composed of a CNN branch, which is used to calculate the second level low frequency wavelet coefficient. The third part consists of an RNN branch. It is mainly composed of several RB (recurrent block) blocks, which uses the method of sharing parameters to lessen the gross amount of the network parameter. This part is used to predict the residual sub-band coefficients of the first and second scale. After predicting the wavelet coefficients of all branches, we use the inverse discrete wavelet transform to reconstruct the last SR results. In order to train the network end to end, we use the real inverse matrix implementation of the wavelet transform with PyTorch Library [19].

Over all, the mainly contribution of work is as follows:

(1) We project a learning wavelets and channel attention network (LWCAN) for SR image. The network predicts the wavelet coefficient of the source image and inverse transforms the predicted wavelet coefficient to obtain the final HR image.

(2) The Efficient channel attention (ECA) block is proposed, it creates channel attention through a fast $1D$ convolution. We add it to our lightweight CNN network for picking up the LR image features better.

(3) The experiments show that our LWCAN network achieves a good balance in three aspects: running time, network parameters and network performance, and surpasses most of the existing SR methods.

2   Related Works

In general, the previous SR models could be separated into two classifications: DL-based and interpolation-based models. In this part, we focus on the DL-based methods which have gotten very popular in recent years in SR and overall performance far exceeds the interpolation-based methods.

2.1   Wavelet-Related SR

Wavelet transform is the traditional image processing means, and has been broadly used in the previous SR field. At an early stage, Ji et al. [20] used the multi-frame information in the wavelet territory to forecast the missing part of wavelet coefficient, and Anbarjafari et al. [21] directly up-sampled the wavelet sub-bands through bicubic interpolation. After that, in the wake of the rapid development of DL, some wavelet transforms based on DL methods have been projected. Huang et al. [22] projected a wavelet based face image SRCNN for small-scale face images. Guo et al. [23] projected DWSR of a deep CNN to forecast the residual wavelet coefficient, these coefficients are between bicubic-up-sampled LR images and counterparts of the HR images. The Multi-level Wavelet-CNN (MWCNN) proposed by Liu et al. [24] uses inverse wavelet transform and the discrete wavelet transform for down-sampling and up-sampling. However, the wavelet correlation SR network inputs a layer of wavelet coefficients of the bicubic-upsampled LR image and outputs a layer of wavelet coefficients of the required image, which could be considered as the thinning process from the wavelet coefficient of the up sampled LR images to the wavelet coefficients of the corresponding HR images. Most importantly, these methods could not give complete play to the advantages of wavelet transform in multi-resolution decomposition, and yet furnish a single up-sampling scale. Not alike the above-mentioned methods, in this study, we directly make the initial LR image as the input image to construct a lightweight network to forecast the wavelet coefficient of the objective images.

2.2   Attention Mechanisms

Attention Mechanism is currently very popular, which has made some progress in enhancing CNN and plays a significant part in various computer fields, such as image restoration, image capture and image recognition. The reason why it is very fashionable is the attention endows models with the capability to distinguish. For instance, in machine translation and speech recognition application, for every word in this sentence gives diverse weights, made the learning of the neural network block becomes more flexible (soft), at the same time attention itself can be as a relationship of alignment, explain the route of the relationship between the input or output sentence, what interpretation model learned knowledge, provides a window for us to open the deep learning black box. In short, they help the network focus on important information while ignoring irrelevant information. Wang et al. [25] projected a residual attention network, based on truck-and-mask attention mechanism for image classification. Hu et al. [18] projected a channel attention learning mechanism (SENet). This network builds the squeeze-and-excitation (SE) blocks to raise the classification precision, and achieved good results. Inspired by SENet, Residual Channel Attention Network (RCAN) [17] introduces a very deep network has channel attention of image SR for the first time, which improves the representation ability of the model. Zhu et al. [26] used U-shaped formation and the residual channel attention block to get superior image SR performance. It is not difficult to see that all the above methods show solicitude for developing complex attention module for superior performance. Different from these methods, in this study, we project ECA block is an effective channel attention for learning low complexity networks. We add ECA block to lightweight networks to achieve better performance.

3   Method

3.1   Overview of the Proposed Model

Nowadays, many DL-based SR methods have well solved the SR problem of small-scale (such as 2× and 3×), but it is still a challenge for large-scale 4×SR. In this paper, LWCAN is mainly designed for large-scale SR. Our detailed network framework is shown in Fig. 1. It is principally separated into three parts. In the first part, two convolution layers pick up the low level feature of input images, and ECA block is added at the end to pick up the low-level features without dimensionality reduction and cross-channel information interaction. In the following second and third parts, our network divides the wavelet coefficients of the target image into a CNN branch and an RNN branch for prediction, and each branch predicts a part of the coefficients. The second part is a CNN branch. The features extracted in the first part forecast the wavelet coefficient ω_2^0 through two convolution layers. In order to reduce the all-out number of network parameters, in the third part, we adopt the idea of recursive neural network and the strategy of sharing parameters, introduce the recurrent block (RB). The third part is composed of RNN branch, which transfer the extracted features to a recurrent block (RB), and then use two convolutions to forecast the remaining three second-level wavelet coefficients (ω_2^1, ω_2^2, and ω_2^3). Then the same RB does the previously extracted features and the underlying features as the input at the same time, then outputs new features through RB, and then predicts a layer of wavelet coefficients (ω_1^1, ω_1^2, and ω_1^3) through a 2× deconvolutional layer and a convolutional layer. All RB blocks have the same weight. Finally, the forecasted wavelet coefficient is reconstructed by 2D IDWT (Inverse Discrete Wavelet Transformation), and the reconstructed image is obtained. For IDWT, we use db1 wavelet function as wavelet filter for experiments.

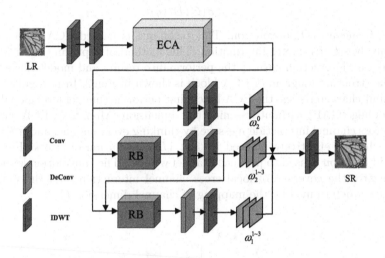

Fig. 1. Overview of the proposed model (LWCAN)

3.2   Efficient Channel Attention (ECA) Block

Our ECA block is improved from SE block. We analyze the impact of channel dimensionality reduction and channel attention learning of crossing channel interaction, and propose ECA block. We believe that the channel and weight need to correspond directly, and avoiding dimensionality reduction is more significant than considering non channel dependence. We use the frequency band matrix W_k to represent the learned channel attention, W_k involves $k \times C$ parameters, and W_k avoids the complete independence of different groups. For weight y_i, we only consider the information interaction between y_i and its k neighbors. The calculation formula is as follows,

$$\omega_i = \sigma(\sum_{j=1}^{k} \omega_i^j y_i^j), y_i^j \in \Omega_i^k \tag{1}$$

the Ω_i^k means the set of k adjacent channels of y_i. In order to further improve performance, all channels can also share weight information,

$$\omega_i = \sigma(\sum_{j=1}^{k} \omega^j y_i^j), y_i^j \in \Omega_i^k \qquad (2)$$

According to the above analysis, a new method is proposed, which can realize the information interaction between channels through $1D$ convolution with convolution kernel size k,

$$\omega = \sigma(C1D_k(y)) \qquad (3)$$

the $C1D$ means $1D$ convolution. This technique is named ECA block, which only involves k parameter information. This method of capturing cross channel information interaction ensures the performance results and model efficiency.

The structure diagram of ECA block is shown in Fig. 2. In particular, given the input characteristics, the ECA block first performs channel level global average pooling (GAP) without lessening the dimension. After that, ECA captures local cross channel interaction message by thinking every channel and it k neighbors, which is effectively realized by fast $1D$ convolution of size k. Finally, a sigmoid function is used to produce channel weights. The convolution kernel size k delegates the coverage of local cross channel interaction, and the weight is adaptively determined by the mapping of channel dimension C.

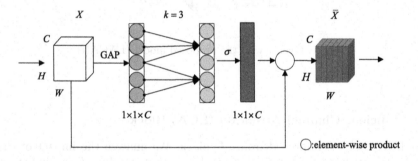

Fig. 2. The frame of the efficient channel attention (ECA) block.

3.3   Loss Functions

In the part, we measured the paired differences between the rebuild HR image and it conforming ground truth value (GT) in two phases and two diversity regions. The loss considers several elements, including the all round pixel distance of the image in spatial region and the difference of texture in wavelet region. The loss component is linearly combined into the total loss as follows,

$$L_{total} = \alpha L_{spatial} + \beta L_{wavelet} \tag{4}$$

For the spatial loss, the mean absolute error (MAE) between the reconstructed result (O) and it corresponding GT(G) is used to lessen the picture element difference in the spatial region after the IDWT. The formula is as follows,

$$L_{spatial} = \|O - G\|_1 \tag{5}$$

For the wavelet loss, differentiate from others SR operations, we just suggest a loss between the output and the ground truth in the spatial region. Before IDWT, we used wavelet loss in wavelet region to preferably a strict the distance between forecasted wavelet coefficients and target wavelet coefficients. Between the predicted wavelet coefficients, using MAE to calculate the wavelet loss is helpful to produce higher frequency and more detailed texture (ω) and its GT counterpart, it could be indicated as,

$$L_{wavelet} = \lambda_2^0 \left\| \omega_2^0 - dwt(G)_2^0 \right\|_1 + \sum_{i=1}^{2} \sum_{j=1}^{3} \lambda_i^j \left\| \omega_i^j - dwt(G)_i^j \right\|_1 \tag{6}$$

where $dwt(\cdot)$ is the mapping function for 2-level 2D discrete wavelet transformation (DWT). $\lambda_2^{0~3}$ and $\lambda_1^{1~3}$ are very important that be the equilibrium weight of the different frequency wavelet coefficients.

4 Experiments

4.1 Datasets and Metrics

DIV2K dataset [27] includes 1000 high-quality natural RGB images, and it is widespread applied to image processing missions. To our experiment, we just apply the 1–900 images in DIV2K as the training data. We employ five standard benchmark datasets: Set5 [28], Set14 [29], B100 [30], Urban100 [31], and Manga109 [32] for evaluation. Two quantitative metrics are used to appraise the SR result. There are the peak signal-to-noise ratio (PSNR) and the structural similarity index (SSIM) [33]. For the sake of contrasting equitable, SSIM and PSNR are barely regarded on the luminance (Y) channel as previous works do. For generating the training data of LR images, we down-sample the high quality images using Matlab function with bicubic interpolation.

All the networks in our experiment in view of 4× SR, the mini-batch size of training is 16, which is used for 2000 epochs. In every iteration, we put a batch of with 40×40 patch size, they are cut from the LR image in the training data stochastic. In order to enhance the data on the fly, we use stochastic flip (vertical and horizontal) and 90 °C rotation, and then send the data to the network. Initialize the network parameter according to [34] and the learning rate 1×10^{-4} by Adam [35] for optimization. Both α and β in Eq. (4) are set to 1.0. All the λ in Eq. (6) are equally set to 1.0. The training code of our LWCAN is made with the PyTorch Library [19] run on a single NVIDIA Quadro RTX 6000 GPU.

Table 1. Comparisons on the number of network parameters and PSNR/SSIM of different SR methods.

Method	Parameters	PSNR/SSIM				
		Set5	Set14	B100	Urban100	Manga109
Bicubic	–	28.42/0.8104	26.00/0.7027	25.96/0.6675	23.14/0.6577	24.89/0.7866
SRCNN [11]	8 K	30.48/0.8628	27.50/0.7513	26.90/0.7101	24.52/0.7221	27.58/0.8555
FSRCNN [16]	13 K	30.71/0.8657	27.59/0.7535	26.98/0.7150	24.62/0.7280	27.90/0.8610
VDSR [36]	666 K	31.35/0.8830	28.01/0.7674	27.29/0.7251	25.18/0.7540	28.83/0.8870
DRCN [37]	1775 K	31.53/0.8854	28.02/0.7670	27.23/0.7233	25.14/0.7510	28.93/0.8854
DWSR [23]	374 K	31.39/0.8833	28.04/0.7669	27.25/0.7240	25.26/0.7548	–/–
MSWSR [38]	1228 K	–/–	28.47/0.7776	27.48/0.7311	25.78/0.7744	30.01/0.8999
LWCAN(Ours)	975 K	32.02/0.8921	28.49/0.7782	27.50/0.7328	25.86/0.7774	30.07/0.9010

4.2 Effectiveness Analysis

To research the robustness and effectiveness of our projected method for image SR, we contrast LWCAN and some typically existing SR methods, and the quantitative result is tabulated in Table 1. It could be found out from the Table 1, the performance indicators of the projected LWCAN model in terms of SSIM and PSNR [33] are better than most comparison methods.

Table 2. Comparisons on the number of network parameters of the SR methods with large model size.

Method	Parameters
EDSR [39]	43.1 M
RCAN [17]	15.6 M
D-DBPN [40]	10.4 M
SRFBN [8]	3.6 M
LWCAN (Ours)	1.0 M

Specially, we compare the proposed LWCAN network with the other seven methods. It could be found out from the Table 1, compared with bicubic, SRCNN [11] and FSRCNN [16], our method has greatly improved the PSNR and SSIM values. For VDSR [36] and DWSR [37], although our network has slightly larger parameters, their PSNR and SSIM also lag behind us. For MSWSR [38], our method parameters are smaller than it, and PSNR and SSIM are larger than them. Meanwhile, our LWCAN is separated into three parts. The parameters of the first part of the convolution layer and ECA block are 326 K, the parameters of the second part of the CNN branch are 178 K, and the parameters of the third part of the RNN branch are 471 K. We also give another comparison, it is the network parameter numbers of SR methods, these methods all have large model size, the result is tabulated in Table 2. As shown in the Table 2, compared with the projected LWCAN method, although these existing methods (EDSR [39], RCAN [17] and D-DBPN [40]) obtain better PSNR/SSIM values, but their network parameters are far greater than the proposed LWCAN method, and then, to make matters worse, the running time is far greater than the proposed LWCAN method. For SRFBN [8], although recurrent learning is applied to reduce the all-out network parameter number, its network parameters and running time are also greater than our network.

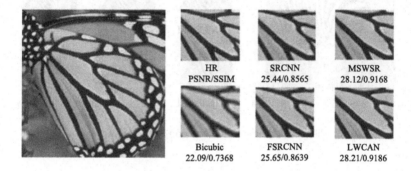

Fig. 3. Visual comparison achieved on Set5 for 4×SR.

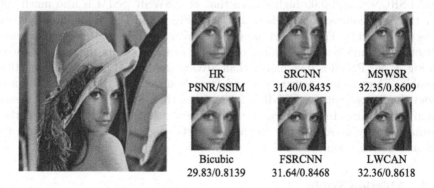

Fig. 4. Visual comparison achieved on Set14 Lenna for 4× SR.

From the visual effect, we compare LWCAN with Bicubic, SRCNN, FSRCNN and MSWSR. We select a picture from the five standard benchmark data sets

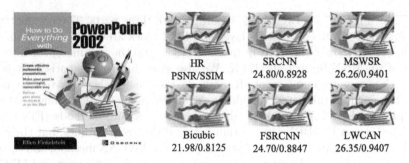

Fig. 5. Visual comparison achieved on Set14 ppt3 for 4× SR

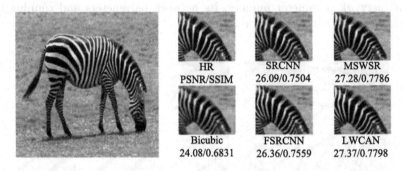

Fig. 6. Visual comparison achieved on Set14 zebra for 4× SR

for comparison. As shown in the figure below, we can see our model is superior to most SR methods in reconstruction performance and comparable to the most advanced methods. As shown in Fig. 3, Fig. 3 is a picture of the Set5 dataset. Numerically, our method is about 3 higher than the PSNR of SRCNN, Bicubic and FSRCNN, and 0.09 higher than that of MSWSR. SSIM is also much better than the comparison method. Figure 4, Fig. 5 and Fig. 6 are three pictures selected on Set14. From the visual effect, our method has better reconstruction effect and clearer texture than the other four methods. From the data, as shown in Fig. 4, our PSNR is 0.96 higher than SRCNN and SSIM is 0.0479 higher than bicubic. Figure 7 is a picture selected from Manga109 dataset. It can be seen from the figure that our PSNR is 2.39 higher than FSRCNN, and it is clearer from the picture. In summary, the experiment result exhibit that our method realizes a very good balance in three aspects: parameters, running time and reconstruction performance.

4.3   Ablation Study

For the sake of verifying the impact of ECA block that we added in feature extraction on the performance of the whole network, we trained two versions of our LWCAN. The first is LWCAN without ECA block, which is represented by LWCAN (without ECA). The second is LWCAN with ECA module. We test

| HR PSNR/SSIM | SRCNN 31.63/0.9269 | MSWSR 34.22/0.9542 |
| Bicubic 27.95/0.8759 | FSRCNN 31.97/0.9251 | LWCAN 34.36/0.9544 |

Fig. 7. Visual comparison achieved on Manga109 for 4× SR

the two trained models on five standard benchmark datasets, and compare the SSIM and PSNR. As shown in Table 3, it can be seen that the network with ECA block has significantly higher SSIM and PSNR values than the network without ECA module, which proves that the ECA block we added is effective.

Table 3. Comparisons on PSNR/SSIM of LWCAN with ECA and without ECA.

Method	PSNR/SSIM				
	Set5	Set14	B100	Urban100	Manga109
LWCAN (without ECA)	31.94/0.8910	28.41/0.7763	27.46/0.7310	25.70/0.7715	29.83/0.8974
LWCAN	32.02/0.8921	28.49/0.7782	27.50/0.7328	25.86/0.7774	30.07/0.9010

5 Conclusion

In this paper, we project a learning wavelets and channel attention network (LWCAN) to realize image lightweight and accurate super-resolution. The network predicts the wavelet coefficients of target images and inverse transforms the predicted wavelet coefficients to obtain the last result. In particular, we use ECA module in feature extraction, which generates channel attention through fast one-dimensional convolution, which improves the performance of the network architecture. Experiment shows that contrast most of the state-of-the-art approaches, LWCAN realizes a superior balance between the network parameter number, reasoning time and rebuild performance. In the future work, we would like to use the algorithm to mobile devices, and consider the combination of ECA and spatial attention module.

Acknowledgment. This work was supported in part by the National Natural Science Foundation of China under Grants 61906118 and AnHui Natural Science Foundation of China under Grants 2108085MF230.

References

1. Shi, W.Z., et al.: Cardiac image super-resolution with global correspondence using multi-atlas patchmatch. In: Mori, K., Sakuma, I., Sato, Y., Barillot, C., Navab, N. (eds.) MICCAI 2013. LNCS, vol. 8151, pp. 9–16. Springer, Heidelberg (2013). https://doi.org/10.1007/978-3-642-40760-4_2

2. Park, H., Son, J.-H.: Machine learning techniques for THz imaging and time-domain spectroscopy. Sens. Basel **21**(4), 1186 (2021)

3. Yıldırım, D., Güngör, O.: A novel image fusion method using IKONOS satellite images. J. Geodesy Geoinf. **1**(1), 75–83 (2012)

4. Gunturk, B.K., Altunbasak, Y., Mersereau, R.M.: Super-resolution reconstruction of compressed video using transform-domain statistics. IEEE Trans. Image Process. **13**(1), 33–43 (2004)

5. Pang, S., Chen, Z., Yin, F.: Convolutional neural network based sub-pixel line-edged angle detection with applications in measurement. IEEE Sens. J. **21**(7), 9314–9322 (2021)

6. Chen, R., Xie, Y., Luo, X., Qu, Y., Li, C.: Joint-attention discriminator for accurate super-resolution via adversarial training. In: Proceedings of the 27th ACM International Conference on Multimedia, pp. 711–719 (2019)

7. Hui, Z., Gao, X., Yang, Y., Wang, X.: Lightweight image super-resolution with information multi-distillation network. In: Proceedings of the 27th ACM International Conference on Multimedia, pp. 2024–2032 (2019)

8. Li, Z., Yang, J., Liu, Z., Yang, X., Jeon, G., Wu, W.: Feedback network for image super-resolution. In: Proceedings of the IEEE/CVF Conference on Computer Vision and Pattern Recognition, pp. 3867–3876 (2019)

9. Jing, P., Guan, W., Bai, X., Guo, H., Su, Y.: Single image super-resolution via low-rank tensor representation and hierarchical dictionary learning. Multimed. Tools Appl. **79**(11), 1–19 (2020)

10. Yang, X., Zhang, Y., Guo, Y., Zhou, D.: An image super-resolution deep learning network based on multi-level feature extraction module. Multimed. Tool Appl. **80**(5), 7063–7075 (2021)

11. Dong, C., Loy, C.C., He, K., Tang, X.: Learning a deep convolutional network for image super-resolution. In: Fleet, D., Pajdla, T., Schiele, B., Tuytelaars, T. (eds.) ECCV 2014. LNCS, vol. 8692, pp. 184–199. Springer, Cham (2014). https://doi.org/10.1007/978-3-319-10593-2_13

12. Goodfellow, I., et al.: Generative adversarial nets. In: Proceedings of the Advances in Neural Information Processing Systems, pp. 2672–2680 (2014)

13. Yu, J.H., et al.: Wide activation for efficient and accurate image super-resolution. In: Proceedings of the IEEE Conference on Computer Vision and Pattern Recognition (2018)

14. Tai, Y., Yang, J., Liu, X.M.: Image super-resolution via deep recursive residual network. In: Proceedings of the IEEE Conference on Computer Vision and Pattern Recognition, pp. 3147–3155 (2017)

15. Dong, C., Loy, C.C., He, K., Tang, X.: Image super-resolution using deep convolutional networks. IEEE Trans. Pattern Anal. Mach. Intell. **38**(2), 295–307 (2016)

16. Dong, C., Loy, C.C., Tang, X.: Accelerating the super-resolution convolutional neural network. In: Leibe, B., Matas, J., Sebe, N., Welling, M. (eds.) ECCV 2016. LNCS, vol. 9906, pp. 391–407. Springer, Cham (2016). https://doi.org/10.1007/978-3-319-46475-6_25

17. Zhang, Y.L., Li, K.P., Li, K., Wang, L.C., Zhong, B.N., Fu, Y.: Image super-resolution using very deep residual channel attention networks. In: Proceedings of the European Conference on Computer Vision, pp. 286–301 (2018)
18. Hu, J., Shen, L., Sun, G.: Squeeze-and-excitation networks. In: Proceedings of the IEEE Conference on Computer Vision and Pattern Recognition, pp. 7132–7141 (2018)
19. Paszke, A., et al.: PyTorch: an imperative style, high-performance deep learning library. In: Proceedings of the Advances in Neural Information Processing Systems, pp. 8024–8035 (2019)
20. Ji, H., Fermüller, C.: Robust wavelet-based super-resolution reconstruction: theory and algorithm. IEEE Trans. Pattern Anal. Mach. Intell. **31**(4), 649–660 (2009)
21. Anbarjafari, G., Demirel, H.: Image super resolution based on interpolation of wavelet domain high frequency subbands and the spatial domain input image. Electron. Telecommun. Res. Inst. **32**(3), 390–394 (2010)
22. Huang, H., He, R., Sun, Z., Tan, T.: Wavelet-SRNET: a wavelet-based CNN for multi-scale face super resolution. In: Proceedings of the IEEE International Conference on Computer Vision, pp. 1689–1697 (2017)
23. Guo, T., Seyed Mousavi, H., Huu Vu, T., Monga, V.: Deep wavelet prediction for image super-resolution. In Proceedings of the IEEE Conference on Computer Vision, pp. 104–113 (2017)
24. Liu, P., Zhang, H., Zhang, K., Lin, L., Zuo, W.: Multi-level wavelet-CNN for image restoration. In: Proceedings of the IEEE Conference on Computer Vision and Pattern Recognition, pp. 773–782 (2018)
25. Wang, F., et al.: Residual attention network for image classification. In: Proceedings of the IEEE Conference on Computer Vision and Pattern Recognition, pp. 6450–6458 (2017)
26. Zhu, L., Zhan, S., Zhang, H.: Stacked u-shape networks with channel-wise attention for image super-resolution. Neurocomputing **345**(14), 58–66 (2019)
27. Agustsson, E., Timofte, R.: Ntire 2017 challenge on single image super-resolution: dataset and study. In: Proceedings of the IEEE Conference on Computer Vision and Pattern Recognition (CVPR), pp. 126–135 (2017)
28. Bevilacqua, M., Roumy, A., Guillemot, C., Alberi-Morel, M.L.: Low-complexity single-image super-resolution based on nonnegative neighbor embedding. In: Proceedings of the British Machine Vision Conference, pp. 1–10 (2012)
29. Zeyde, R., Elad, M., Protter, M.: On single image scale-up using sparse-representations. In: Boissonnat, J.-D., et al. (eds.) Curves and Surfaces 2010. LNCS, vol. 6920, pp. 711–730. Springer, Heidelberg (2012). https://doi.org/10.1007/978-3-642-27413-8_47
30. Martin, D., Fowlkes, C., Tal, D., Malik, J.: A database of human segmented natural images and its application to evaluating segmentation algorithms and measuring ecological statistics. In: Proceedings Eighth IEEE International Conference on Computer Vision, pp. 416–423 (2001)
31. Huang, J.B., Singh, A., Ahuja, N.: Single image super-resolution from transformed self-exemplars. In: Proceedings of the IEEE Conference on Computer Vision and Pattern Recognition, pp. 5197–5206 (2015)
32. Matsui, Y., et al.: Sketch-based manga retrieval using Manga109 dataset. Multimed. Tools Appl. **76**(20), 21811–21838 (2017)
33. Wang, Z., Bovik, A.C., Sheikh, H.R., Simoncelli, E.P.: Image quality assessment: from error visibility to structural similarity. IEEE Trans. Image Process. **13**(4), 600–612 (2004)

34. He, K.M., Zhang, X.Y., Ren, S.Q., Sun, J.: Delving deep into rectifiers: surpassing human-level performance on imagenet classification. In: Proceedings of the IEEE International Conference on Computer Vision, pp. 1026–1034 (2015)

35. Kingma, D.P., Ba, J.: Adam: a method for stochastic optimization. In: Proceedings of the 3rd International Conference for Learning Representations, pp. 1–9 (2015)

36. Kim, J., Lee, J.K., Lee, K.M.: Accurate image super-resolution using very deep convolutional networks. In: Proceedings of the IEEE Conference on Computer Vision and Pattern Recognition, pp. 1646–1654 (2016)

37. Kim, J., Lee, J.K., Lee., K.M.: Deeply-recursive convolutional network for image super-resolution. In: Proceedings of the IEEE Conference on Computer Vision and Pattern Recognition, pp. 1637–1645 (2016)

38. Zhang, H.R., Xiao, J., Jin, Z.: Multi-scale image super-resolution via a single extendable deep network. IEEE J. Sel. Top. Singal Process. **15**(2), 253–263 (2021)

39. Lim, B., Son, S., Kim, H., Nah, S. and Mu Lee, K.: Enhanced deep residual networks for single image super-resolution. In: Proceedings of the IEEE Conference on Computer Vision and Pattern Recognition, pp. 136–144 (2017)

40. Haris, M., Shakhnarovich, G., Ukita, N.: Deep back-projection networks for super-resolution. In: Proceedings of the IEEE Conference on Computer Vision and Pattern Recognition, pp. 1664–1673 (2018)

Traffic Classification Based on CNN-LSTM Hybrid Network

Xuan Kong[1], Congcong Wang[2], Yanmiao Li[3], Jiangang Hou[4],
Tongqing Jiang[5], and Zhi Liu[1(✉)] (iD)

[1] School of Information Science and Engineering, Shandong University,
Qingdao 266237, China
`liuzhi@sdu.edu.cn`
[2] School of Physical and Electronics, Shandong Normal University,
Jinan 250014, China
[3] Center of Information Security, Beijing University of Posts
and Telecommunications, Beijing 100876, China
[4] School of Computer Science and Technology, Beijing Institute of Technology,
Beijing, China
[5] Shandong Gentle Technology Co., Ltd., Jinan, China

Abstract. Network traffic classification is a significant method of network anomaly detection and plays a critical role in cyberspace security.
Accompanied by the rapid development of network traffic diversity, traditional detection methods are not any longer adapt to the complex
network environments. In the article, we use the method of deep learning and present a traffic classification method, which directly operates
on raw traffic data. A hybrid neural network combining 1D CNN and
LSTM network is used for learning the spatial and temporal characteristics of the stream in the meantime, which is verified on the CICIDS2017
dataset. Finally, we applied the model verified on the public data set
to real network traffic, and achieved good results. It can be concluded
from the experimental results that our arithmetic has higher accuracy
on public dataset as well as can be applied to real network environments
to solve real-world problems.

Keywords: Traffic classification · Deep hybrid network · Raw
feature · Real network environment

1 Introduction

In the 21st century, the network is indispensable for our work and life, accompanied by a variety of network space security problems emerge endlessly. With the
vigorous progress of the internet, different kinds of network security issues have
also emerged. For the purpose of solving various puzzlers faced in the development of the internet, it is very urgent and necessary to break network attacks
and solve network security problems by supervising and managing the network.

G. Zhai et al. (Eds.): IFTC 2021, CCIS 1560, pp. 401–411, 2022.
https://doi.org/10.1007/978-981-19-2266-4_31

Accurate and efficient network traffic classification is a key link in network management. As network users pay more attention to data privacy and diversity and complexity of encryption algorithms, network traffic identification is faced with great challenges [1].

According to the type of network application, network traffic classification relates to the classification of two-way UDP flows or TCP flows generated by network communication flows based on the TCP/IP protocol (such as WWW, TFTP, P2P, etc.). Popular speaking, it refers to the process of identifying and categorizing related protocols through the relevant characteristics of network traffic [2].

At the present, the research methods for classifying network traffic can be approximately separated into three categories [3]: port-based methods, DPI(Deep Packet Inspection)-based methods, and flow characteristics-based methods. Port-based classification methods cannot cope with unknown ports. As the network develops, the classification accuracy continues to decrease. DPI-based methods are costly to analyze and cannot cope with encrypted traffic. In the cause of solving the matter of classifying encrypted traffic, a machine learning based classification method was raised on flow characteristics. The machine learning based classification method is mainly designed to extract the key features of encrypted traffic, like data packet arrival time interval, packet length, and build, design, and train classifiers to build models based on the extracted features [4]. This method gets rid of the limitations of the rule-based method [5], but it faces new challenges of manual design features.

Deep learning is an emerging research orientation extended from machine learning. Due to good research results have been achieved in computer vision and other fields, researchers try to use deep learning to classify network traffic. Compared with traditional machine learning methods, deep learning voluntarily chooses features through training, avoiding the tedious process of manually designing features by domain experts, and deep learning has a fairly high learning ability and can learn highly complex patterns. As a result of an end-to-end method, deep learning can learn the non-linear relationship between the original input and the corresponding output instead of resolving the problem of feature selection and classification sub-problems [6]. Based on the above advantages, deep learning has become a very ideal method of traffic classification.

This paper comes up with a hybrid-based deep neural network, which combines convolutional neural network (CNN) and Long Short-Term Memory Network (LSTM) to extracting the temporal and spatial characteristics of network traffic data to improve the accuracy of traffic classification. We have performed numerous sorts of network traffic classification experiments on the CICIDS2017 dataset, and the experimental results demonstrated that the total accuracy of the model reaches 97%, and the accuracy of each attack reaches 90%. Finally, we built a normal network environment and an attack network environment on the virtual machine and collected real network traffic data for classification, which also achieved good results.

The following of the paper is organized as: Sect. 2 presents the related works to traffic classification. Section 3 details the dataset and the methodology of the proposed method. Section 4 presents experimental results and analysis. Section 5 provides conclusions.

2   Related Works

The first breakthrough in deep learning is the Convolutional Neural Network (CNN), which is mainly used for image recognition, face recognition, and the time domain and frequency domain expression of audio and video data. Later, RNN and LSTM networks appeared, and they were applied to speech recognition, natural language processing, and other fields, achieving fine effect [7–9].

In terms of traffic classification, Wang et al. [10] try using deep neural network to operate on encrypted traffic, and the use of stacked autoencoders to automatically study and identify the characteristics of traffic data. Wang et al. [11] proposed a method of transforming traffic data into pictures, using the idea of images to use the CNN network for malware traffic classification.

Yao et al. [12] expressed the data stream as a matrix in the research, using long and short-term memory network and introducing two structures of attention mechanism and hierarchical attention mechanism (HAN) to classify 12 kinds of encryption application traffic. The laboratory results on the common data set prove that the classification accuracy of this method reaches 91.2%.

Lotfollahi et al. [2] put forward a method called Deep Packet, whose feature extraction and classification process can be realized in one institution. Deep Packet uses stacked autoencoders (SAE) and convolutional neural network (CNN) two deep neural network. Experiments show that Deep Packet has achieved better results when using CNN as a classification model.

Zhao et al. [13] put forward to combine the metric learning regularization term with the cross-entropy loss function to conjunctly manage the learning of CNN and improve the feature recognition ability of deep learning. The result proves that the classification performance is great compared with the existing methods.

Dong et al. [14] constructed a deep learning network called CET Analytics to classify application types by combining the payload and statistical characteristics as comprehensive traffic information (CETI) to classify application types. The author verifies the proposed method on the ISCX VPN2016 dataset proves that it can not only effectively classify encrypted applications, but also has high precision and very strong generalization performance.

Gu et al. [15] put forward a new neural network named tree-RNN based on RNN. The principle of the network is to achieve multiple classifiers by distributing large varieties into small varieties, which greatly improves the performance of classification. The verification on the ISCX data set displays that this approach can enhance the accuracy by 4.88% compared with the previous classification method.

Yang et al. [16] proposed a classification framework named AEFETA by combining network anomaly detection with feature self-learning. The advantage of this method lies in that it uses the layered features of network traffic to automatically abstract the characteristics of encrypted applications and directly processes the raw data to achieve end-to-end traffic classification.

3 Proposed Method

In this part, we introduce particularly the dataset put to use in the experiment and the method of preprocessing the data. We designed a traffic classification model based on deep neural network and apply it to network anomaly detection.

The pattern comprises consist of two layers of neural network models. The first layer uses 1D CNN to extract the spatial characteristics of the traffic. The function of this layer network is to abstract the space characteristics of data. The second layer uses the LSTM network to abstract the temporal features of the traffic. After CNN, LSTM is connected, and LSTM plays a major role in the algorithm to abstract the time characteristics of data. These two networks are cascaded into a hybrid network for simultaneous training, therefore the neural network can simultaneously extract the spatial features of the traffic and time characteristics.

3.1 Dataset

As pointed out by Dainotti et al. [17], the lack of shared labeled datasets as test data has greatly hindered the progress of traffic classification research. Many researchers use private data from security companies or manually collected data to conduct experiments, which will reduce the reliability of the results to a certain extent. Moreover, since traditional machine learning methods have higher requirements for feature selection techniques, a large number of common traffic datasets are now feature traffic datasets, rather than original traffic datasets, and these datasets have been in existence for a long time.

KDD CUP1999 and NSL-KDD datasets, which contain some of the latest attacks, are often used in the field of cybersecurity. The two datasets were hand-designed by experts, and a total of 41 features were extracted [18]. And the two data sets have great composability, such as [19].

In this paper, we use the CICIDS2017 dataset, which is relatively new in the field of cyberspace security [18]. The CICIDS2017 data set contains both benign and malicious traffic. The malicious traffic consists of some of the latest common attacks, similar to real-world data (PCAPs). This data set is based on some common protocols, such as HTTP and FTP, to set up an environment to collect traffic. As shown in Table 1, the data was collected for a total of 5 days. Except for the benign traffic collected on Monday, malicious traffic was collected for the remaining four days. The following table lists the attack descriptions collected.

3.2 Data Preprocessing

To convert the primordial data into a format that can be passed to the designed web application, some steps are necessary, commonly known as data preprocessing, including time division, traffic segmentation, traffic cleaning, uniform

Table 1. CICIDS2017 dataset.

Data	Attack
Monday	Normal
Tuesday	Normal + SFTP + SSH
Wednesday	Normal + Dos + Heartbleed Attacks
Thursday	Normal + Web Attack + Infiltration
Friday	Normal + Botnet ARES + Port Scan + DDos

length, image generation, IDX files generation. And Fig. 1 illustrates the specific process mentioned above

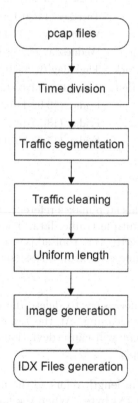

Fig. 1. Data preprocessing process.

(1) Time Division. Time domain segmentation relates to the process of intercepting the PCAP file corresponding to the time from the original PCAP file. This step is the first step to preprocess data. Specifically, we split a large PCAP file into several small PCAP files according to the description document of CICIDS2017. The segmentation is based on the attack time and attack description given in the description document [18]. Table 2 describes the specific descriptions of attacks. This step does not change the file format.

Table 2. Time distribution of CICIDS2017 dataset.

Attack	Time
Normal	Monday
FTP	Tuesday (9:20-10:20)
SSH	Tuesday (14:00-15:00)
Dos	Wednesday (9:47-11:23)
Heartbleed	Wednesday (15:12-15:32)
WebAttacks	Thursday (9:20-10:42)
Infiltration	Thursday (14:19-15:45)
Botnet	Friday (10:02-11:02)
PortScan	Friday (13:55-14:35)
DDoS	Friday (15:56-16:16)

(2) Traffic Segmentation. This step makes reference to slicing the original traffic data and dividing it into multiple traffic data. The process is shown in Fig. 2. In this step, the USTC-TK2016 [11] toolset is used to split the time-divided pcap file into streams and merge them into sessions according to the definition of streams and sessions.

(3) Traffic Cleaning. It is necessary to delete data packets that do not have an application layer during cleaning. At the same time, since duplicate files with exactly the same content will cause deviations in training, only one such duplicate file needs to be kept.

(4) Uniform Length. Uniform length refers to the uniform length processing of the cleaned file according to 784 bytes. When the file's byte length exceeds 784, it will be intercepted. When the file's number of bytes is below 784, it is padded with 0.

(5) Image Generation. This step refers to visualizing the files with a uniform length, that is, converting them into grayscale images. The visualized session is shown in Fig. 3.

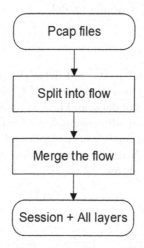

Fig. 2. Traffic segmentation process.

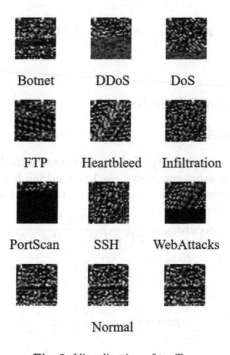

Fig. 3. Visualization of traffic.

(6) IDX Files Generation. This step refers to converting the image into an IDX file and inputting it into the training model.

3.3 Model Description

In this step, we describe the constructed network structure in detail, as shown in Fig. 4. We use a mixture neural network of CNN and LSTM, use CNN to abstract space characteristics of data, and LSTM to abstract time characteristics. The traffic data on flows is one-dimensional, so a one-dimensional CNN is used. Specifically, the two convolutional layers are followed by the pooling layers. After the data is output from CNN network, it is transmitted to LSTM network and finally to the full connection layer.

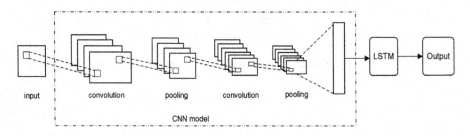

Fig. 4. Architecture of CNN-LSTM.

4 Experiment and Results

4.1 Evaluate Metrics

In order to measure the usability of the model we designed more scientifically, we adopted four indicators commonly used in machine learning to evaluate it: accuracy, precision, recall and F1-scores. They are defined as follows:

$$accuracy = \frac{TP + TN}{TP + TN + FP + FN} \tag{1}$$

$$precision = \frac{TP}{TP + FP} \tag{2}$$

$$precision = \frac{TP}{TP + FN} \tag{3}$$

$$F1 = 2 * \frac{precision \cdot recall}{precision + recall} \tag{4}$$

4.2   Experimental Parameter Setting and Result Analysis

The parameters of the CNN-LSTM network structures are shown in the following: The PyTorch [20] is used as an experiment software framework. We set the batch size to 64 and the epoch to 40. The learning rate changes with the number of iterations.

On the CICIDS2017 data set, we conducted 10 classification experiments with nine types of attack data and benign data, and the accuracy is shown in Fig. 5.

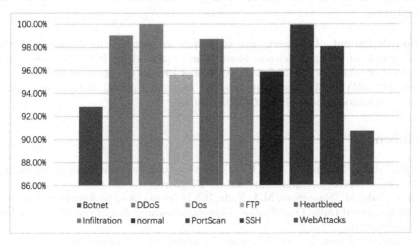

Fig. 5. The accuracy of CICIDS2017 dataset.

Then we conducted experiments on real network traffic and collected normal data and three types of attack traffic. The classification results are shown in Fig. 6.

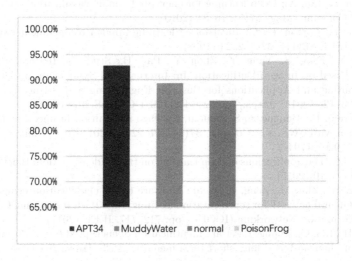

Fig. 6. The accuracy of real traffic.

5   Conclusion

In the paper, we design a traffic classification approach based on deep learning, using CNN to extract the spatial characteristics of the network traffic, and LSTM to extract the temporal characteristics of the network traffic. 10 classification experiments were carried out on a public data set, with an accuracy rate of above 97%. At the same time, real traffic was collected for experiments, and good results were also obtained. This shows that the method we propose can be utilized for intrusion detection in a real network environment, which is of great significance.

Acknowledgment. This work was supported in part by the Major Fundamental Research of Natural Science Foundation of Shandong Province under Grant ZR2019ZD05, the Key Research & Development Project of Shandong Province under Grant 2019JZZY020119, and Joint fund for smart computing of Shandong Natural Science Foundation under Grant ZR2020LZH013.

References

1. Ahmed, M., Mahmood, A.N., Hu, J.: A survey of network anomaly detection techniques. J. Netw. Comput. Appl. **60**, 19–31 (2016)
2. Lotfollahi, M., Siavoshani, M.J., Zade, R.S.H., et al.: Deep packet: a novel approach for encrypted traffic classification using deep learning. Soft. Comput. **24**(3), 1999–2012 (2020)
3. Wang, P., Chen, X., Ye, F., et al.: A survey of techniques for mobile service encrypted traffic classification using deep learning. IEEE Access **7**, 54024–54033 (2019)
4. Wang, M., Cui, Y., Wang, X., et al.: Machine learning for networking: workflow, advances and opportunities. IEEE Netw. **32**(2), 92–99 (2017)
5. Goodfellow, I., Bengio, Y., Courville, A.: Deep Learning. MIT Press, Cambridge (2016)
6. Rezaei, S., Liu, X.: Deep learning for encrypted traffic classification: an overview. IEEE Commun. Mag. **57**(5), 76–81 (2019)
7. Lecun, Y., Bottou, L.: Gradient-based learning applied to document recognition. Proc. IEEE **86**(11), 2278–2324 (1998)
8. Feng, Y., Zeng, S., Yang, Y., Zhou, Y., Pan, B.: Study on the optimization of CNN based on image identification. In: International Symposium on Distributed Computing and Applications for Business Engineering and Science (DCABES), pp. 123–126 (2018). https://doi.org/10.1109/DCABES.2018.00041
9. Ben Fredj, H., Bouguezzi, S., Souani, C.: Face recognition in unconstrained environment with CNN. Vis. Comput. **37**(2), 217–226 (2020). https://doi.org/10.1007/s00371-020-01794-9
10. Wang, Z.: The applications of deep learning on traffic identification. BlackHat USA **24**(11), 1–10 (2015)
11. Wang, W., Zhu, M., Zeng, X., et al.: Malware traffic classification using convolutional neural network for representation learning. In: 2017 International Conference on Information Networking (ICOIN), pp. 712–717. IEEE (2017)
12. Yao, H., Liu, C., Zhang, P., et al.: Identification of encrypted traffic through attention mechanism based long short term memory. IEEE Trans. Big Data (2016)

13. Zhao, L., Cai, L., Yu, A., et al.: A novel network traffic classification approach via discriminative feature learning. In: Proceedings of the 35th Annual ACM Symposium on Applied Computing, pp. 1026–1033 (2020)
14. Dong, C., Zhang, C., Lu, Z., et al.: CETAnalytics: comprehensive effective traffic information analytics for encrypted traffic classification. Comput. Netw. **176**, 107258 (2020)
15. Ren, X., Gu, H., Wei, W.: Tree-RNN: tree structural recurrent neural network for network traffic classification. Expert Syst. Appl. **167**, 114363 (2021)
16. Dainotti, A., Pescape, A., Claffy, K.C.: Issues and future directions in traffic classification. IEEE Netw. **26**(1), 35–40 (2012)
17. Tavallaee, M., Bagheri, E., Lu, W., et al.: A detailed analysis of the KDD CUP 99 data set. In: IEEE Symposium on Computational Intelligence for Security and Defense Applications, pp. 1–6. IEEE (2009)
18. Creech, G., Hu, J.: Generation of a new IDS test dataset: time to retire the KDD collection. In: IEEE Wireless Communications and Networking Conference (WCNC), pp. 4487–4492. IEEE (2013)
19. ASharafaldin, I., Lashkari, A.H., Ghorbani, A.A.: Toward generating a new intrusion detection dataset and intrusion traffic characterization. ICISSp **1**, 108–116 (2018)
20. Paszke, A., Gross, S., Massa, F., et al.: Pytorch: an imperative style, high-performance deep learning library. In: Advances Neural Information Processing System, vol. 32, pp. 8026–8037 (2019)

Enhanced Inter-layer Prediction for SHVC Based on Cross-Layer Adaptive Reference

Xiaoyong Liu[1], Jinghao Yuan[1], Rong Xie[1], Li Song[1,2(✉)], Yanan Feng[3], and Lin Li[3]

[1] Institute of Image Communication and Network Engineering,
Shanghai Jiao Tong University, Shanghai 200240, China
{liuxiaoyong-sjtuee,sjtu_yjh,xierong,song_li}@sjtu.edu.cn
[2] Cooperative Medianet Innovation Center, Shanghai Jiao Tong University,
Shanghai 200240, China
song_li@sjtu.edu.cn
[3] MIGU Co., Ltd., Beijing 100032, China
{fengyanan,lilin}@migu.cn

Abstract. Scalable High Efficiency Video Coding (SHVC) can be potentially applied to broadcasting and multimedia services beneficial from its scalability features. Although the multi-layer architecture of SHVC can adapt to the fluctuation of time-varying networks, the bandwidth usage and error propagation on account of information loss are two critical problems for its applications. On the basis of the performance analysis of an alternative reference structure, we propose a cross-layer adaptive reference (CLAR) algorithm for SHVC motivated by that context. By the means of guided filtering, the original reference pictures of to-be-coded pictures at base layer (BL) is fused with corresponding ones of collocated pictures at enhancement layer (EL) according to conditions of EL picture loss. Experimental results show that the proposed adaptive reference scheme averagely achieves 13.2% overall BD-rate reduction with negligible encoding complexity variation.

Keywords: Scalable high efficiency video coding · Inter-layer prediction · Adaptive reference

1 Introduction

The explosive growth of video data arises out of rapid demands for high frame rate and high definition/ultra-high definition (HD/UHD) video and emerging video types, e.g. panorama video, which leads to more bandwidth requirements and the upgradation of video coding technologies. The ITU-T Video Coding Experts Group (VCEG) and the ISO/IEC Moving Picture Experts Group

Supported by MoE-China Mobile Research Fund Project (MCM20180702), the 111 Project (B07022 and Sheitc No. 150633) and the Shanghai Key Laboratory of Digital Media Processing and Transmissions.

© Springer Nature Singapore Pte Ltd. 2022
G. Zhai et al. (Eds.): IFTC 2021, CCIS 1560, pp. 412–425, 2022.
https://doi.org/10.1007/978-981-19-2266-4_32

(MPEG) are two standardization organizations devoted to video coding standard developments together. They formed the Joint Video Team (JVT) to finalize H.264/Advanced Video Coding (AVC) [1] and the Joint Collaborative Team on video Coding (JCT-VC) for the completion of High Efficiency Video Coding (HEVC) standard [2] with around 50% bit-rate reduction relative to its predecessor H.264/AVC for comparable perceptual video quality. Besides, the new generation video coding standard named Versatile Video Coding (VVC) [3] was finalized by Joint Video Experts Team (JVET) of VCEG and MPEG in July 2020, which achieves around 50% bit-rate reduction over preceding HEVC standard for equal video quality.

The extensions of corresponding video coding standards will be put on the agenda following the finalization of them, where the scalable extension applied to lossy transmission environments is a typical one. Although HEVC addresses the increased video resolutions issue, various devices with different capabilities of displaying and processing exist side by side and require different network conditions. Thus, to further extend HEVC to heterogeneous access networks and make it apply to most video applications, the JVT-CT finalized a scalable HEVC (SHVC) in July 2014 [4]. The functions of SHVC requiring only high-level syntax (HLS) changes comprise spatial scalability, temporal scalability, signal-to-noise ratio (SNR) scalability, bit depth scalability as well as color gamut scalability. With the aid of different inter-layer prediction (ILP) mechanisms from HEVC, the SHVC scheme supports multi-loop solutions and is easily implemented in comparison with the Scalable Video Coding (SVC) extension [5] of H.264/AVC. To work out the issue of additional bit-rate along with the scalable features, this paper refines the reference structure for SNR scalability of SHVC to improve compression efficiency.

The ILP module in the SHVC system architecture is designed for efficient coding and the content variety of reference pictures is beneficial to efficient prediction. The Annex A and U of H.263 and H.264/AVC introduce flexible reference picture selection in motion compensated prediction where the number of reference pictures is up to 16 [6]. The reference picture management refers to the previously decoded reference picture marking process in a decoded picture buffer (DPB). In H.264/AVC, the sliding window process and the memory management control operation (MMCO) process are alternatively used to mark reference pictures. Furthermore, HEVC introduces the reference picture set (RPS) concept in reference picture management which is different to the decoded reference picture marking mechanisms in H.264/AVC in the DPB description, i.e., the relative changes of DPB status for each slice are signaled in H.264/AVC while the complete set of all reference pictures of current or future picture which must be reserved in DPB are signaled in HEVC which avoids the influence of earlier pictures in decoding order on DPB status. The SHVC reference picture management including the RPS concept is mainly same as that in HEVC, except for inter-layer reference pictures. There are three kinds of marks for pictures in the DPB, short-term reference and long-term reference distinguished by temporal distance and nonuse for reference.

A typical scalable layer-based framework enables only that the ELs reference lower layers and the BL can be decoded independently to provide the lowest but still acceptable video quality for networks of varying bandwidth. However, that unilateral reference scheme may result in inefficiency coding for BL if the networks is stable and EL can be decoded normally. Hence, this paper proposes a novel cross-layer adaptive reference (CLAR) architecture based on feedback of the EL loss information. To be exact, The fusion of BL reference pictures of the current to-be-coded BL picture and collocated EL reconstruction pictures is performed to improve the coding efficiency of BL.

The primary contributions of this paper contain two parts. At first, we analyze the reference picture statistics distribution of BL pictures. Then, we propose a novel CLAR algorithm to enhance the inter-layer prediction module by means of adaptively fusing reference pictures from reference picture lists of both BL and EL. In the end, We also conduct confirmatory experiments to validate the effectiveness of CLAR.

The rest of this paper is organized as follows. Section 2 reviews related works to improve the compression efficiency for SHVC. In Sect. 3, elaborate experiments have been conducted to validate the feasibility of our ideas and our proposed CLAR scheme is presented. Experimental results and discussions are given in Sect. 4 and Sect. 5 concludes the paper.

2   Related Works

With respect to traditional means of compression efficiency improvement for SHVC, the temporal correlation among EL pictures as well as the inter-layer correlation between BL and EL pictures are utilized to increase the prediction accuracy of EL coding blocks. Li *et al.* [7] proposed a generalized inter-layer residual prediction (GILRP) method to reduce the prediction error of the EL block by adding its temporal prediction (P_E) with the weighted motion compensation residual ($Resi_B$) of the collocated BL block. The GILRP method achieves 2.9%, 5.1% and 4.9% BD (Bjontegaard Delta)-rate [8] gains on average for RA (random access), LP (Low-delay P) and LB (Low-delay B) configurations respectively. Nevertheless, the rate-distortion check for the optimal weight of $Resi_B$ increases the coding complexity and the access to $Resi_B$ consumes more memory. A low complexity inter-layer residual prediction method [9] was proposed to work out this problem. HoangVan *et al.* refined the merge mode prediction for EL [10] and proposed a joint layer prediction method [11] by combine the BL and EL decoded information, all of which didn't make full use of different video features. In [12], the BL and EL decoded information were adaptively combined with a weighting combination factor estimated by the minimum mean square error (MMSE) criterion.

Additionally, the emerging convolutional neural network (CNN) techniques are utilized to generate virtual reference frames (VRFs) with high quality and high similarity to the to-be-coded frame to improve prediction accuracy [13–17]. In general, adjacent reconstructed frames of the current to-be-coded frame consist of the train set to generate the VRF. In [18], the virtual reference frame generation convolutional neural network (VRFCNN) was proposed to generate the VRF of EL frames. The VRF was obtained by fusion of enhanced BL features and compensated EL features, which can significantly improve compression efficiency. But that method did not take the complexity and the access of EL decoded information into account.

3 Proposed Cross-Layer Adaptive Reference Algorithm

In this section, we refine the prediction structure of BL pictures and explore its effect on the rate-distortion performance. Furthermore, the CLAR algorithm based on guided picture filtering is described, which is utilized to generate the fused BL reference pictures in reconstructed reference picture list.

3.1 Flexible Prediction Structure for SHVC

HEVC test model (HM) defines three configurations which have different prediction structure, i.e., intra-only (AI), Low-delay and RA. One QP value derived by Eq. (1) is specified for every picture, where QP_{PorB} and QP_I denote the QPs of the P/B frame and the IDR/I frame respectively and QP_{offset} denotes the offset of QP of the P/B frame. In the rate control or perceptual optimization, the QP value may be modified to meet the requirements of performance. Considering that the LD configuration fits into real-time communication scenarios better, we only improve the rate-distortion performance in LP coding structure in this paper and it is shown in Fig. 1, where the solid lines with arrow indicate reference relationship for inter prediction. In the current SHVC test model (SHM), the BL and EL pictures use same prediction structure in inter-prediction.

$$QP_{PorB} = QP_I + QP_{offset} \tag{1}$$

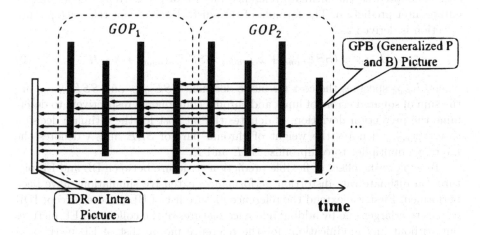

Fig. 1. Prediction structure of LD configuration.

In the Low-delay configuration, the group of picture (GOP) is the basic coding structure for both BL and EL. Each GOP has 4 pictures, the quantization parameters (QP) offset of which are different. The last frame of a GOP has the least QP offset, which indicates its quality is the highest. In the Low-delay reference structure, the reference picture list consists of 4 reference pictures, the proximately previous picture and three previous pictures located at end points of three GOPs (if exist) in ascending order of the distance of each from the to-be-coded picture [19]. The former is called after Ref_1 and the latter are correspondingly expressed as Ref_2, Ref_3 and Ref_4 respectively in the following sections.

The multiple reference pictures selection in HEVC/SHVC can help improve compression efficiency and facilitate error resilience by feedback channels. However, in conventional motion compensation prediction for SHVC, the inter-prediction coding structure of BL and EL is consistent with HEVC and only the collocated reconstructed BL picture is referenced by the EL picture in the inter-layer prediction without taking the feedback information from the client into consideration. It is obvious that the EL picture may be referenced by the BL picture if it is decoded normally to achieve bi-directional inter-layer reference (ILR). Hence the rate-distortion performance of subsequent pictures will be improved both at BL and EL in SNR scalability. The scalable properties of SHVC are realized with only the different high-level syntax (HLS) varied from HEVC, i.e., SHVC inherits the coding tree structure from HEVC, which make it possible to leverage the correlation between BL and EL pictures to further improve compression efficiency.

Generally speaking, short-term reference pictures are more similar to the to-be-coded picture and long-term reference pictures compressed with lower QP have higher quality [15]. The reference picture selection process is a rate-distortion optimization (RDO) process. The rate-distortion cost is calculated for each picture in the reference picture list and that with minimum rate-distortion cost is adopted as the ultimate reference picture of the current CU when executing inter-prediction. The formula of rate-distortion cost for reference picture selection is derived as:

$$J_{mode} = (SSE_{luma} + \omega_{chroma} \times SSE_{chroma}) + \lambda \times R \qquad (2)$$

where J_{mode} specifies the cost for mode decision, SSE_{luma} and SSE_{chroma} are the sum of squared errors of luma and chroma components respectively to determine the prediction deviation, R denotes the bit cost for the ultimate decision case, ω_{chroma} denotes the weight of chroma part of SSE and λ denotes the Lagrange multiplier to compromise SSE and R.

To explore the effect of flexible prediction structure between BL and EL pictures on ultimate rate-distortion performance, extensive simulations have been performed. First, we extend the reference picture list of BL pictures except IDR frames to a larger one by adding reference pictures of the collocated EL pictures but without any modifications for the reference picture list of EL pictures as shown in Fig. 2, wherein the bottom layer is BL, the top layer is EL and the

dotted arrow depicts the generation of the reference picture list extension part
of BL, i.e., the reference picture list of EL pictures is appended to that of BL
ones.

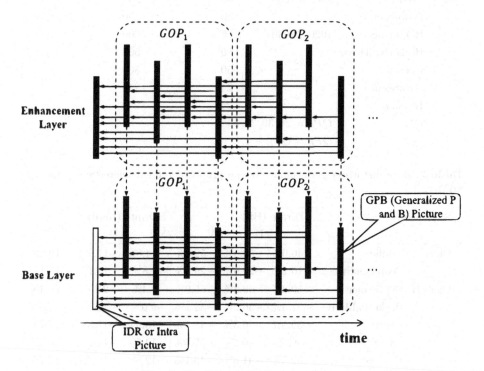

Fig. 2. Flexible prediction structure.

Moreover, we compare the rate-distortion performance of the refined reference scheme with anchor in SNR scalability for LP configuration where only the
first picture is the I frame. The version of SHVC reference software is SHM-
12.4 and all the encoder configurations follow HEVC common test conditions
(CTC) [20]. For more detail, Table 1 summarizes the test conditions, where QP_B
and QP_E denote quantization parameters of BL and EL respectively. Besides,
the common metric BD-rate is used to assess the performance of the proposed
method. The results are shown in Table 2. It can be seen that the rate-distortion
performance of both BL and total layers is improved significantly.

Finally, the average reference percentage of each picture in the BL reference
picture list when encoding 65 frames for every sequence is obtained and shown
in Table 3. $Ref_i(BL)$ and $Ref_i(EL)$ ($i = 1, 2, 3, 4$) denote the reference picture i
of current BL picture from BL and EL, respectively. As a result, the temporally
last pictures at BL and EL have higher temporal correlations with the current
picture and the temporal correlations lessen by degrees along with the increment
of temporal distance.

Table 1. Summary of test conditions

Sequences	Spatial resolution	Frame rate (Hz)	Frame numbers
Traffic	2560 × 1600	30	150
PeopleOnStreet		30	150
BQTerrace	1920 × 1080	60	600
BasketballDrive		50	500
Cactus		50	500
ParkScene		24	240
Kimono		24	240
QP	$QP_B = 26, 30, 34, 38$ $QP_E = QP_B - 4$		

Table 2. Rate-distortion performance of the proposed refined reference scheme with SHM-12.4

Sequences		BD-rate (BL)			BD-rate (total)		
		Y	U	V	Y	U	V
Class A	Traffic	−46.0%	−52.4%	−52.6%	−14.8%	−17.9%	−19.2%
	PeopleOnStreet	−16.2%	−26.9%	−29.0%	−7.8%	−14.1%	−15.1%
Class B	BQTerrace	−50.8%	−66.3%	−65.9%	−9.4%	−21.5%	−25.4%
	BasketballDrive	−27.3%	−36.2%	−32.1%	−9.0%	−12.0%	−11.3%
	Cactus	−39.5%	−46.3%	−45.5%	−13.9%	−17.3%	−17.7%
	ParkScene	−50.3%	−56.2%	−57.3%	−14.5%	−16.2%	−16.9%
	Kimono	−32.5%	−41.6%	−43.7%	−12.8%	−16.4%	−17.7%
Average		−37.5%	−46.5%	−46.6%	−11.7%	−16.5%	−17.6%

3.2 Qualiy Enhancement for BL Reference Pictures

Given the analysis of Subsect. 3.1, the EL picture information can be used to improve the BL and overall rate-distortion performance. Though the multiple hypotheses reference architecture can enrich the content diversity in RPS, the distortion of reconstructed pictures affects the accuracy of block matching for following pictures a lot. This is the main motivation to enhance the quality of reference pictures before performing motion estimation.

In the original quality scalability configuration, the BL pictures quantized by larger QPs have low quality and the collocated EL pictures quantized by smaller QPs have high quality. It's natural to enhance the quality of BL pictures using the collocated EL pictures, but the quality of every pixel is difficult to be measured if we can't get the original lossless video. A fractional gradient-based frame fusion algorithm is proposed in this section and enhanced BL pictures are used as reference pictures of the subsequent to-be-coded BL picture.

Intuitively, the weight factors for pixels in the EL reference picture and the collocated BL reference picture are inversely proportional to their distortion

Table 3. Average reference ratio for every picture in RPS

Sequences	Average block reference ratio							
	$Ref_1(BL)$	$Ref_2(BL)$	$Ref_3(BL)$	$Ref_4(BL)$	$Ref_1(EL)$	$Ref_2(EL)$	$Ref_3(EL)$	$Ref_4(EL)$
BQTerrace	23.95%	7.93%	5.51%	2.57%	33.31%	13.26%	9.25%	4.24%
BasketballDrive	24.31%	1.68%	0.61%	0.24%	62.58%	9.11%	1.07%	0.41%
Cactus	34.16%	4.47%	2.71%	1.01%	54.58%	1.66%	0.71%	0.70%
ParkScene	29.72%	1.98%	0.79%	0.29%	60.23%	5.91%	0.78%	0.30%
Kimono	18.14%	1.00%	0.45%	0.18%	77.67%	1.97%	0.35%	0.25%
Average	26.05%	3.41%	2.01%	0.86%	57.67%	6.38%	2.43%	1.18%

when to take the contribution to the quality of fused pictures as a criterion. In case of original pixel values are available, then their distortions can be expressed as the squared error SE_{BL} between the raw BL reference picture X_{BL} and the corresponding decoded one $\hat{X}_{BL}$, and the squared difference SE_{EL} between the raw EL reference picture X_{EL} and the corresponding decoded one $\hat{X}_{EL}$ respectively, as shown in Eq. (3). These SE values can derive optimal weight values for the fusion of $\hat{X}_{BL}$ and $\hat{X}_{EL}$, i.e., the ideal high quality BL reference picture.

$$SE_{BL} = \left(X_{BL}(x,y) - \hat{X}_{BL}(x,y) \right)^2$$
$$SE_{EL} = \left(X_{EL}(x,y) - \hat{X}_{EL}(x,y) \right)^2 \tag{3}$$

where $X_{BL}(x,y)$ and $\hat{X}_{BL}(x,y)$ denote pixel values at location (x,y) of the original BL reference picture and the corresponding decoded one respectively, and $X_{EL}(x,y)$ and $\hat{X}_{EL}(x,y)$ are defined for EL.

However, the weights computed by the original pixel information at the encoder have to be transferred to the decoder, which is associated with extra bitrate overhead. Instead, a pixel-level picture fusion scheme in which the weights are computed only by the decoded information is proposed in this paper, aiming to avoid the expense of additional bitrate. The guided picture filtering [21] is used to enhance the quality of BL reference pictures and smooth them to maintain the spatial consistency [22] in fusion process.

Firstly, it's assumed that the filtering output picture Q is modeled as the local linear transformation of the guidance picture I for the guided filter. The formula is defined as:

$$Q_i = a_k \times I_i + b_k, \forall i \in \omega_k \tag{4}$$

where (a_k, b_k) are constant linear coefficients corresponding to the local square window ω_k and Q_i and I_i are aligned pixels in local square windows located in Q and I respectively. a_k and b_k can be estimated by minimizing the cost function between the output picture Q and the input picture P as follows:

$$(a_k, b_k) = \arg\min \sum_{i \in \omega_k} \left[(a_k \times I_i + b_k - P_i)^2 + \varepsilon \times a_k^2 \right] \tag{5}$$

where P_i is a pixel in ω_k located in P and ε is the penalty term of a_k.

In the meanwhile, the texture information G_k of the guidance picture I has a hold on the quality of the output picture Q [23] and the Eq. (5) can be revised as Eq. (6).

$$(a_k, b_k) = \arg\min \sum_{i \in \omega_k} \left[(a_k \times I_i + b_k - P_i)^2 \times G_k + \varepsilon \times a_k^2 \right] \qquad (6)$$

Equation (6) can be solved by linear regression [24] and a_k and b_k can be written as:

$$a_k = \frac{G_k \times \left(\frac{1}{N} \sum_{i \in \omega_k} P_i \times I_i - \bar{P}_i \times \bar{I}_i \right)}{G_k \times \sigma + \varepsilon} \qquad (7)$$

$$b_k = \bar{P}_i - a_k \times \bar{I}_i$$

where N is the amount of pixels in ω_k, the $\bar{P}_i$ and $\bar{I}_i$ are mean values of pixels in ω_k of the input picture P and the guidance picture I respectively and σ is the variance of pixels in ω_k of the guidance picture I.

Then, the reference pictures at BL and EL replace the guidance picture I and the input picture P respectively, when we enhance the quality of the BL reference picture. Besides, the gradient is exploited to measure the texture complexity G_k of the picture. To be specific, the more adjacent integer pixels and the smaller step size lead to the higher accuracy, thus the gradients are derived by fractional pixels using DCT-based interpolation filter (DIF) [25] as in [26].

Finally, according to the discussion in Subsect. 3.1, the reference rates of the $Ref_1(BL)$ and the $Ref_1(EL)$ are significantly greater than reference rates of others. Therefore, the reference picture list of the the current to-be-coded BL picture is constructed as Eq. (8). The $Ref_4(BL)$ and $Ref_4(EL)$ with the weakest correlation to the current to-be-coded BL picture are discarded.

$$\hat{Ref_1}(BL) = Ref_1(BL)$$
$$\hat{Ref_2}(BL) = Ref_1(EL)$$
$$\hat{Ref_3}(BL) = F(Ref_2(BL), Ref_2(EL)) \qquad (8)$$
$$\hat{Ref_4}(BL) = F(Ref_3(BL), Ref_3(EL))$$

where $Ref_1(BL)$, $Ref_1(EL)$, $Ref_2(BL)$, $Ref_2(EL)$, $Ref_3(BL)$ and $Ref_3(EL)$ are defined in Subsect. 3.1, $\hat{Ref_1}(BL)$, $\hat{Ref_2}(BL)$, $\hat{Ref_3}(BL)$ and $\hat{Ref_4}(BL)$ are fused reference pictures of the current to-be-coded BL picture after the quality enhancement and $F(\cdot)$ denotes the fusion function based on linear transformation as defined in Eq. (4–7).

4   Experimental Results

The proposed CLAR methodology is integrated into the SHVC reference software SHM-12.4 and all the encoder configurations follow Table 1 under the LP configuration. In the performance assessment process for individual BL, the rate and the distortion of the BL are utilized to evaluate the performance of BL, and as to the total performance, the sum of BL and EL rates together with the distortion of EL are employed. Besides the well-known Peak Signal to Noise Ratio (PSNR) is used to simply evaluate the objective distortion of pictures. Eventually the BD-rate for the proposed CLAR algorithm and the original SHVC anchor is derived by the rate and the distortion to show improvements in two cases, the negative value of which indicates bitrate saving. Table 4 shows BD-rate savings of three components for the CLAR algorithm and the anchor, when all EL pictures are normally decoded. It can be observed that the CLAR algorithm achieves 39.5% luma bitrate saving for single BL and 13.2% overall luma bitrate saving on average. The performance will degrade along with the EL picture loss rate increasing. To demonstrate the overall performance difference between the proposed method and the anchor, several typical rate-distortion curves corresponding to 4 tested QPs are illustrated in Fig. 3, which reflect the proposed method can save more bitrate for equal quality.

Table 4. Rate-distortion performance of the proposed CLAR algorithm with SHM-12.4

Sequences		BD-rate (BL)			BD-rate (total)		
		Y	U	V	Y	U	V
Class A	Traffic	−48.1%	−54.2%	−54.6%	−16.4%	−19.4%	−21.0%
	PeopleOnStreet	−19.6%	−31.1%	−33.2%	−10.2%	−18.1%	−19.1%
Class B	BQTerrace	−50.9%	−67.6%	−67.1%	−8.8%	−22.7%	−26.0%
	BasketballDrive	−30.1%	−38.9%	−35.2%	−11.1%	−14.6%	−14.0%
	Cactus	−41.2%	−47.6%	−47.1%	−14.9%	−18.3%	−19.6%
	ParkScene	−51.8%	−57.7%	−58.7%	−16.1%	−18.2%	−18.8%
	Kimono	−34.8%	−43.9%	−46.0%	−14.7%	−18.5%	−19.9%
Average		−39.5%	−48.7%	−48.9%	−13.2%	−18.5%	−19.8%

To further verify superiority of our CLAR algorithm, the joint layer prediction (JLP) solution [12] and VRFCNN [18] are adopted for comparison, which utilize VRF generation approaches. The comparison results on the BD-rate saving for all tested sequences are listed in Table 5. Our method is superior to other comparative methods in terms of average overall performance and saves more bitrate on most sequences.

The encoding complexity variation ΔT_{Enc} is used to reveal the computation complexity of CLAR defined by Eq. (9), where T'_{Enc} is the encoding time of the proposed solution and T_{Enc} is the encoding time of the anchor. All of the experiments are performed upon a server with Intel (R) Xeon(TM) CPU E5-4627 v3@3.50GHz, 128GB, Windows Server 2012 R2 operating system. Table 6 shows the SHVC encoding variation for every sequence. The temporal merge

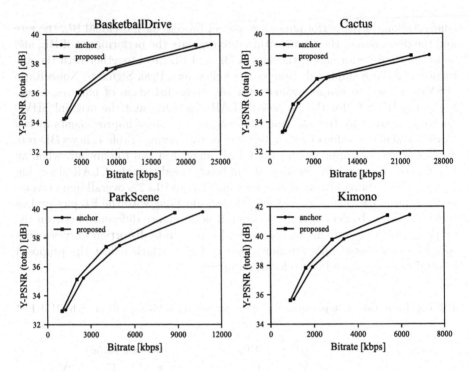

Fig. 3. Rate-distortion comparison for several test sequences.

Table 5. Comparisons of performance over test sequences at four QPs

Sequence		JLP [12] BD-rate (Y)	VRFCNN [18] BD-rate (Y)	Ours BD-rate (Y)
Class A	Traffic	–	−12.3%	−16.4%
	PeopleOnStreet	–	−17.3%	−10.2%
Class B	BQTerrace	−7.6%	−11.1%	−8.8%
	BasketballDrive	−6.8%	−9.2%	−11.1%
	Cactus	3.7%	−12.1%	−14.9%
	ParkScene	–	−8.9%	−16.1%
	Kimono	5.7%	−11.5%	−14.7%
Average		–	−11.8%	−13.2%

mode is disabled if the current to-be-coded BL picture references the EL picture, therefore the encoding time decreases slightly. Meanwhile, the computation complexity of the proposed CLAR algorithm is negligible.

$$\Delta T_{Enc} = \frac{T'_{Enc} - T_{Enc}}{T_{Enc}} \times 100\% \tag{9}$$

Table 6. Encoding time variation resulting from the proposed CLAR algorithm

Sequence		ΔT_{Enc}
Class A	Traffic	−4.4%
	PeopleOnStreet	−5.3%
Class B	BQTerrace	−2.9%
	BasketballDrive	−5.7%
	Cactus	−5.0%
	ParkScene	−5.3%
	Kimono	−5.3%
Average		−4.8%

5 Conclusion

In this paper, we have proposed a cross-layer adaptive reference (CLAR) algorithm considering the frame loss feedback from the decoder mainly intended to improve the coding efficiency of multi-layer SHVC standard. The proposed CLAR solution enhances the quality of BL reference pictures by guided picture filtering while taking texture features of pictures into account. In summary, the proposed algorithm outperforms other relevant state-of-the-art SHVC methods with the average 13.2% overall BD-rate reduction when maintaining the similar picture quality and the computation complexity can be neglected. Moreover, it is scheduled to further extend the proposed scheme to coding unit (CU) level in the future, which will be more effective to volatile network environments.

References

1. Wiegand, T., Sullivan, G., Bjontegaard, G., Luthra, A.: Overview of the H.264/AVC video coding standard. IEEE Trans. Circuits Syst. Video Technol. **13**(7), 560–576 (2003). https://doi.org/10.1109/tcsvt.2003.815165
2. Sullivan, G.J., Ohm, J.R., Han, W.J., Wiegand, T.: Overview of the high efficiency video coding (HEVC) standard. IEEE Trans. Circuits Syst. Video Technol. **22**(12), 1649–1668 (2012). https://doi.org/10.1109/tcsvt.2012.2221191
3. Bross, B., et al.: Overview of the versatile video coding (VVC) standard and its applications. IEEE Trans. Circuits Syst. Video Technol. **31**(10), 3736–3764 (2021). https://doi.org/10.1109/tcsvt.2021.3101953
4. Boyce, J.M., Ye, Y., Chen, J., Ramasubramonian, A.K.: Overview of SHVC: scalable extensions of the high efficiency video coding standard. IEEE Trans. Circuits Syst. Video Technol. **26**(1), 20–34 (2016). https://doi.org/10.1109/tcsvt.2015.2461951
5. Schwarz, H., Marpe, D., Wiegand, T.: Overview of the scalable video coding extension of the H.264/AVC standard. IEEE Trans. Circuits Syst. Video Technol. **17**(9), 1103–1120 (2007). https://doi.org/10.1109/tcsvt.2007.905532
6. Sjoberg, R., et al.: Overview of HEVC high-level syntax and reference picture management. IEEE Trans. Circuits Syst. Video Technol. **22**(12), 1858–1870 (2012). https://doi.org/10.1109/tcsvt.2012.2223052

7. Li, X., Chen, J., Rapaka, K., Karczewicz, M.: Generalized inter-layer residual prediction for scalable extension of HEVC. In: 2013 IEEE International Conference on Image Processing. IEEE (2013). https://doi.org/10.1109/icip.2013.6738321

8. Bjontegaard, G.: Calculation of average PSNR differences between RD-curves. VCEG-M33 (2001)

9. Lim, W., Kim, K., Lee, Y.-L., Sim, D.: Low-complexity inter-layer residual prediction for scalable video coding. J. Real-Time Image Proc. **14**(4), 783–792 (2015). https://doi.org/10.1007/s11554-015-0523-5

10. HoangVan, X., Ascenso, J., Pereira, F.: Improving enhancement layer merge mode for HEVC scalable extension. In: 2015 Picture Coding Symposium (PCS). IEEE (2015). https://doi.org/10.1109/pcs.2015.7170038

11. HoangVan, X., Ascenso, J., Pereira, F.: Improving SHVC performance with a joint layer coding mode. In: 2016 IEEE International Conference on Acoustics, Speech and Signal Processing (ICASSP). IEEE (2016). https://doi.org/10.1109/icassp.2016.7471855

12. Hoangvan, X., Jeon, B.: Joint layer prediction for improving SHVC compression performance and error concealment. IEEE Trans. Broadcast. **65**(3), 504–520 (2019). https://doi.org/10.1109/tbc.2018.2881355

13. Chakraborty, S., Paul, M., Murshed, M., Ali, M.: A novel video coding scheme using a scene adaptive non-parametric background model. In: 2014 IEEE 16th International Workshop on Multimedia Signal Processing (MMSP). IEEE (2014). https://doi.org/10.1109/mmsp.2014.6958823

14. Zhang, X., Tian, Y., Huang, T., Dong, S., Gao, W.: Optimizing the hierarchical prediction and coding in HEVC for surveillance and conference videos with background modeling. IEEE Trans. Image Process. **23**(10), 4511–4526 (2014). https://doi.org/10.1109/tip.2014.2352036

15. Zhao, L., Wang, S., Zhang, X., Wang, S., Ma, S., Gao, W.: Enhanced motion-compensated video coding with deep virtual reference frame generation. IEEE Trans. Image Process. **28**(10), 4832–4844 (2019). https://doi.org/10.1109/tip.2019.2913545

16. Huo, S., Liu, D., Li, B., Ma, S., Wu, F., Gao, W.: Deep network-based frame extrapolation with reference frame alignment. IEEE Trans. Circuits Syst. Video Technol. **31**(3), 1178–1192 (2021). https://doi.org/10.1109/tcsvt.2020.2995243

17. Lee, J.K., Kim, N., Cho, S., Kang, J.W.: Deep video prediction network-based inter-frame coding in HEVC. IEEE Access **8**, 95906–95917 (2020). https://doi.org/10.1109/access.2020.2993566

18. Ding, Q., Shen, L., Yang, H., Dong, X., Xu, M.: VRFCNN: virtual reference frame generation network for quality SHVC. IEEE Signal Process. Lett. **27**, 2049–2053 (2020). https://doi.org/10.1109/lsp.2020.3037683

19. Zhang, M., Zhou, W., Wei, H., Zhou, X., Duan, Z.: Frame level rate control algorithm based on GOP level quality dependency for low-delay hierarchical video coding. Signal Process.: Image Commun. **88**, 115964 (2020). https://doi.org/10.1016/j.image.2020.115964

20. Seregin, V.: Common test conditions for SHVC. JCTVC-X1009 (2016)

21. He, K., Sun, J., Tang, X.: Guided image filtering. IEEE Trans. Pattern Anal. Mach. Intell. **35**(6), 1397–1409 (2013). https://doi.org/10.1109/tpami.2012.213

22. Li, S., Kang, X., Hu, J.: Image fusion with guided filtering. IEEE Trans. Image Process. **22**(7), 2864–2875 (2013). https://doi.org/10.1109/tip.2013.2244222

23. Ren, L., Pan, Z., Cao, J., Liao, J., Wang, Y.: Infrared and visible image fusion based on weighted variance guided filter and image contrast enhancement. Infrared Phys. Technol. **114**, 103662 (2021). https://doi.org/10.1016/j.infrared.2021.103662

24. Draper, N.R., Smith, H.: Applied Regression Analysis. Wiley, Hoboken (1998). https://doi.org/10.1002/9781118625590
25. Lv, H., Wang, R., Xie, X., Jia, H., Gao, W.: A comparison of fractional-pel inter-polation filters in HEVC and H.264/AVC. In: 2012 Visual Communications and Image Processing. IEEE (2012). https://doi.org/10.1109/vcip.2012.6410767
26. Alshin, A., Alshina, E., Lee, T.: Bi-directional optical flow for improving motion compensation. In: 28th Picture Coding Symposium. IEEE (2010). https://doi.org/10.1109/pcs.2010.5702525

Design and Application of Edge Intelligent Recognition Device for Multiple Video Streams in Substations

Xingtao Wang[✉], Xiao Liao, Zhen Qiu, Min Jin, Fan Xu, Wenpu Li,
and Yu Qin[✉]

Academy of Information and Communication Research, State Grid Information
and Telecommunication Group Co., Ltd., Beijing 100052, China
{wangxingtao,qinyu}@sgitg.sgcc.com.cn

Abstract. Substation is an important part of the power grid. Its maintenance is related to the safety and stability of the substation. The contradiction between the increase in the number of substation equipment and the relative shortage of personnel led to the change from manual inspection to intelligent inspection. There are a large number of video cameras in substation, and the video data is generally transmitted to the back-end server for analysis and processing through optical fibers. The channel bandwidth is under pressure and the image recognition efficiency is low. Based on artificial intelligence and edge computing technology, this paper developed the edge intelligent recognition equipment for multiple video streams in substation, designed the intelligent identification algorithms for substation equipment defects. The test and application verification were carried out. The results showed that the real-time collection, online intelligent recognition, and optimized streaming of multiple video streams were realized at the edge. The intelligent level of substation maintenance was significantly improved.

Keywords: Multiple video streams · Artificial intelligence · Defect recognition · Edge computing · YOLOv4

1 Introduction

Substation is an important part of the power grid system, and is the conversion hub of power transmission and distribution. The stable and reliable operation of substation is an important guarantee for the safety of power grid and quality of electricity consumption. The quality and effect of substation operation and maintenance directly determine its safety and reliability. The traditional mode of substation operation and maintenance adopts manual inspection method, which has high working intensity, low efficiency, human uncontrollable factors, and security risks. With the rapid development of large power grid construction, the number of substation equipment increases rapidly, while the number of operation and

G. Zhai et al. (Eds.): IFTC 2021, CCIS 1560, pp. 426–438, 2022.
https://doi.org/10.1007/978-981-19-2266-4_33

maintenance personnel is relatively short, and the workload of equipment operation and maintenance increases sharply. In recent years, the advanced technologies such as artificial intelligence and edge computing developed rapidly. With the continuous advancement of Power Internet of Things and substation digital construction, the substation operation and maintenance put forward higher requirements for intelligent control and lean management of equipment. Unattended smart substation has become an important means to solve the shortage of personnel and intensive management [1–3].

At present, artificial intelligence has been widely applied in substations [4–7], which can realize intelligent identification of substation equipment defects, intelligent control of personnel behavior, and joint autonomous inspection of fixed video camera and inspection robot. Reference [5] carried out substation equipment condition monitoring based on computer vision and deep neural network technology, which can improve the reliability and safety of substation operation. Reference [8] developed a set of temperature early warning system for substation equipment. Through the substation autonomous inspection robot, the infrared temperature measurement and visual images were integrated. The data were uploaded to the background server through wireless WiFi. The artificial intelligence technology was used to process and analyze the data in the remote monitoring system, and the abnormal defect fault was early warning. Reference [9] designed and optimized the Mask-RCNN network, realized the intelligent detection and analysis of substation equipment corrosion, which achieved better accuracy and recall rate than the original Mask-RCNN network. The successful application of artificial intelligence technology in the field of substation improves the efficiency of daily operation and maintenance, and reduces the personnel labor intensity. However, the current video and image data of substation equipment are usually transmitted uniformly to the background server for analysis and processing by from optical fiber or other channels, which increases the cost pressure of communication bandwidth, computing power, and centralized data management. The timeliness and immediacy of data analysis are reduced. In particular, the number of substation video acquisition terminals is large and is still increasing. The quality and resolution of front-end video imaging are continuously improved. The performance requirements of communication channel and background server are higher and higher, and the efficiency of image recognition and processing is greatly reduced, which benefit from computer vision based methods and researches [10–12].

Therefore, based on the artificial intelligence, edge computing, streaming media processing, and deep learning computing acceleration technology, this paper designed an artificial intelligence recognition algorithm model for substation equipment defects, developed an edge intelligent recognition equipment with multiple video streams, and carried out accuracy test and application verification in substations. The functions of real-time acquisition of substation multiple video streams, defect online intelligent recognition, edge computing inference acceleration, and video stream pushing were realized. The device can access up to 32 video streams, complete intelligent recognition and processing on the edge side, reduce the pressure of network transmission bandwidth and server computing sources, and improve the recognition efficiency and timeliness. The efficiency of substation operation and maintenance can be greatly increased to further improve the effectiveness of substation intelligent management.

2   Design of Overall Architecture

The substation multiple video streams edge intelligent recognition equipment can access the multi-channel video devices in the station, and the video streams are framed, decoded, encoded, analyzed, identified, and pushed. The device mainly includes two parts, the interactive control unit and the inference acceleration unit. It has the function of computing acceleration and inference with AI chip, which improves the ability of analysis, calculation and intelligent recognition of videos and images on the edge side. The overall architecture of the device is shown in Fig. 1.

(1) The interactive control unit: This unit is based on the industrial computer processor, adopts the embedded Linux operating system. The Docker container is arranged. It mainly completes the functions of video streams acquisition, frame extraction, network communication, process scheduling, video stream push, and cyber-human interaction, and so on. The unit provides the network and PCIE communication interface, and realizes the scheduling control of the edge calculation in different inference acceleration units for multiple video streams.

(2) The inference acceleration unit: This unit communicates with the interactive control unit through the PCIE interface. The inference acceleration board based on domestic AI processing chip is used. Each inference acceleration unit is configured with three AI chips, and each chip can process three video streams. According to the number of PCIE interfaces in the interactive control unit, each device can configure multiple inference acceleration units. The Faster-RCNN, Yolo, TensorFlow, and other kinds of algorithm model framework are supported to be solidified, called, and accelerated in the unit. A single inference acceleration unit can provide as high as 105.6 TOPs INT8 hashrate and 6.6 TOPs FP32 hashrate, and support high-precision calculation.

The multiple video streams intelligent recognition device accesses the multi-channel cameras through the repeater exchanger. The interactive control unit completes the multiple video data acquisition and frame extraction operation. Based on the memory interaction, the extracted frame image is transferred from the memory of the interactive control unit into the memory of the inference acceleration unit. The artificial intelligence algorithm model is called to analyze and identify the image in the inference acceleration unit. Then the image and video data are compressed by hardware, and the compressed results are forwarded to the memory of the interactive control unit. Finally, the interactive control unit

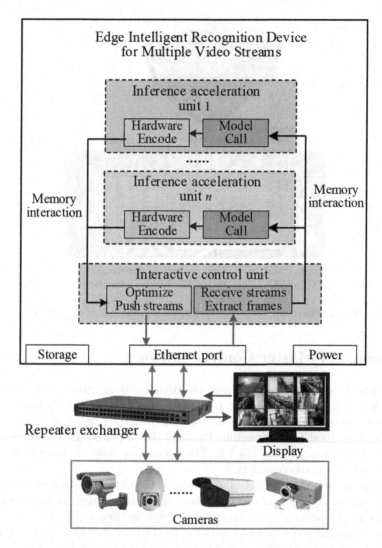

Fig. 1. Overall architecture design of device.

optimizes and pushes the video streams, which are displayed in real time at the master control station.

The hardware structure and interface panel of the device are shown in Fig. 2, which mainly includes power interface, mechanical hard disk, switch button, LED indicators, USB port, RJ45 Ethernet port, inference card channels, VGA port, RS232 port, and so on. The back of the device shell is composed of cover plate with heat dissipation channel, and other parts of the device shell are composed of side cover plates.

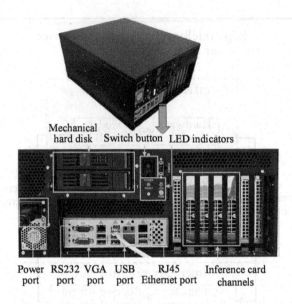

Mechanical
hard disk   Switch button   LED indicators

Power RS232 VGA   USB   RJ45   Inference card
port   port   port   port Ethernet port   channels

Fig. 2. Hardware structure and interface diagram of the device.

3 Design of Master Control Software

The multiple video streams intelligent identification device uses the deep learning network structure of YOLOv4 to realize the intelligent identification of device defects and personnel operation behaviors, and uses the Live555 streaming media server and the Real Time Streaming Protocol (RTSP) to realize the transmission and push of video streams [13,14]. The processing flow of the device master control software is shown in Fig. 3.

Firstly, the interactive control unit collects the video stream data of multiple cameras in the substation, and one frame of the image data is extracted from each five frames of each video stream. The extracted image data is copied to the memory of the inference acceleration unit. In the inference acceleration unit, the YOLOv4 recognition model is called to carry out artificial intelligence calculation and analysis of the image data, in order to realize target recognition such as meter readings, device defects, personnel behaviors, and so on. The results of recognized target categories and coordinates are obtained, which are tagged in the image. Then, the inference acceleration unit encodes the images with identified results in H.264 format by hardware, and pushes the encoded data to the stream queue. If the length of the stream queue is bigger than 1, the head-item is released firstly, so that the current latest image frames are always stored in the stream queue. Finally, the encoded stream queue is copied into the memory of the interactive control unit, which sets up the RTSP server. Based on the Live555 streaming media framework, the multiple video streams are pushed. The user platform can realize real-time identification and display of the multiple video streams through pull operation as the client side.

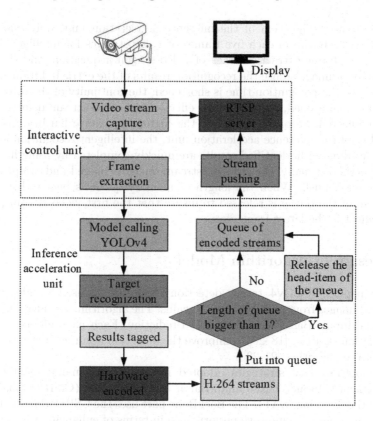

Fig. 3. The processing flow chart of the master control software.

The intelligent recognition and display of multiple video streams in substation require high real-time and low delay of detection and recognition. The stream push strategy of the general Live555 is to put the encoded H.264 data directly into the queue without pre-processing of the queue. When the RTSP client initiates the video stream receiving request, the RTSP server pushes the encoded H.264 video streams according to the sort order in the queue. When the RTSP client does not initiate the video stream request for a long time, the new encoded H.264 stream will be added to the queue until the memory overflows. At this time, if the RTSP client requests to receive the video stream, the encoded 'past state' video stream data in the queue will be decoded and displayed by the client at first. The real-time and display effect are not suitable for the substation intelligent operation and inspection business [15–17].

As shown in Fig. 3, the master control software of the device optimizes the RTSP stream push strategy, which can effectively solve the problem of large time-delay of video display, improve the real-time performance of multiple video streams intelligent recognition, and enhance the adaptability of substation intelligent operation and inspection business. Firstly, according to the performance index and test verification of the inference acceleration unit, only one frame image is extracted from each five frames of video streams for intelligent recognition in the frame extraction stage of video stream acquisition, and the other four frames of images reuse the recognition results of the extracted frame image. By this way, the recognition time is shortened, the continuity of the recognition results are maintained, and the visual effect of the video stream display side is also not affected. Secondly, based on the high-performance hardware processing ability of the inference acceleration unit, the intelligent recognition and the H.264 encoding with identified results are quickly completed by using hardware coding method. Finally, the encoded stream queue is judged and pre-processed before stream push. When the length of memory queue is bigger than 1, the head-item of the queue is released to insure that the first video stream pushed to the client is the latest frame data.

4   Design of Algorithm Model

In this paper, YOLOv4 target detection algorithm is used to identify the extracted images from multiple video streams. The algorithm includes four parts, which are Input, BackBone, Neck, and Prediction. Each part adopts a certain optimization strategy [18–20] to improve the detection accuracy and recognition speed of the algorithm [21,22].

The optimization strategies adopted in Input part mainly include data enhancement Mosaic, Cross mini-Batch Normalization (CmBN), and Self-Adversarial Training (SAT). The BackBone part uses the CSPDarknet53 feature extraction network to improve performance in terms of enhancing learning ability, reducing computational bottlenecks, and reducing memory costs. Backbone uses the Mish activation function to optimize the training stability, the average accuracy, the peak accuracy and so on [23,24], as shown in formula (1).

$$\text{Mish} = x \cdot \tanh(\ln(1 + e^x)) \tag{1}$$

The Neck part mainly adopts the optimization strategies of the Spatial Pyramid Pooling Networks (SPP-Net), the Feature Pyramid Networks (FPN) combined with the Path Aggregation Network (PAN). The SPP-Net can effectively increase the receiving range of backbone features and significantly separate the most important context features. The FPN combined with the PAN can perform parameter aggregation on different detection layers from different backbone layers, which effectively integrates information at all levels [25]. The Prediction part uses CIOU to calculate the BBOX regression loss. The overlap area between the prediction box and the real box, the distance from the center point, and the aspect ratio are all incorporated into the formula, as shown in formula (2). The speed and accuracy of the prediction regression are optimized and improved.

$$\text{CIOU} = \text{IOU} - \frac{(\text{Distance\_2})^2}{(\text{Distance\_C})^2} - \frac{v^2}{(1 - \text{IOU}) + v} \tag{2}$$

Where, IOU is a common indicator in target detection, which is used to reflect the detection effect of prediction box and target box. The Distance_2 represents the Euclidean distance between the center point of prediction box and that of the real box. The Distance_C represents the diagonal distance of the minimum enclosing rectangle between the prediction box and the real box. The is a parameter that measures the consistency of the aspect ratio, which is defined as formula (3).

$$v = \frac{4}{\pi^2}(\arctan\frac{w^{gt}}{h^{gt}} - \arctan\frac{w}{h})^2 \tag{3}$$

CIOU represents the degree of deviation between the prediction box and the real box, and its Loss function is shown as formula (4).

$$\text{Loss}_{CIOU} = 1 - \text{IOU} + \frac{(\text{Distance}\_2)^2}{(Dis\tan ce\_C)^2} + \frac{v^2}{(1 - IOU) + v} \tag{4}$$

At the same time, YOLOv4 optimizes the calculation of IOU to DIOU in the Nms part of the general screening prediction box, which improves the detection effect [26], as shown in formula (5).

$$\text{DIOU} = \text{IOU} - \frac{(\text{Distance}\_2)^2}{(\text{Distance}\_C)^2} \tag{5}$$

5   Test and Application Verification

5.1   The Accuracy Test of the Algorithm Identification

Based on the sample database of substation images of the State Grid, this paper carried out the detection and analysis accuracy tests of the substation device defects, meter reading, personnel behaviors recognition, and other aspects for the intelligent operation and maintenance scenario of substation.

In the training of the algorithm model, the Adam was selected for the optimizer, the learning rate was 10-4, and the batchsize was 6. The test trained a total of 20 epochs, and each epoch was verified on the verification set at the end. Finally, the model with the highest verification accuracy in all epochs was selected for testing. The sample data set contained images under different illumination conditions and shooting perspectives. The images were captured by different devices, and the distance between the image acquisition equipment and the captured instrument was also different. In this paper, the sample data set was divided into the training set, the validation set, and the test set according to the ratio of 7:1:2. The test set contained 2000 samples.

The algorithm model was deployed in the multiple video streams intelligent identification device of substation after completing the model design, compilation, and training. The device was configured three inference acceleration units in the test, and each acceleration inference unit was equipped with three TPU. The identification accuracies of various types of targets based on YOLOv4 are shown in Table 1.

Table 1. The identification accuracy of the substation targets.

Defect type	Subdivision of defect type	Results
State identification	Meter reading anomaly	>97%
	Abnormal oil level and Oil seal of respirator	>96%
	Silica gel discoloration	>98%
	Pressing plate of switch cabinet closed	>97%
	Pressing plate of switch cabinet open	>98%
Defect identification	Meter vague	>94%
	Dial plate broken	>93%
	Shell broken	>75%
	Insulator cracks	>76%
	Insulator rupture	>85%
	Oil contamination of the components surface	>67%
	Oil contamination of ground	>84%
	Metal corrosion	>68%
	Broken of silica gel barrel	>96%
	Abnormal closure of box door	>95%
	Suspended solids hanging	>88%
	Bird's nest	>92%
	Broken of cover plate	>83%
Personnel behaviors identification	No wear safety hat	>94%
	No wear seat belt	>80%
	Break in warning area	>92%
	Nobody in working spot	>94%
	Not wearing overalls	>95%
	Smoking on job site	>85%

5.2   Application Verification of Substation

Up to now, the device has been deployed in 10 substations or converter stations of the State Grid. It can access the video streams collected by the inspection robot, visible light cameras and infrared cameras in the station, and realize the real-time and high-precision intelligent analysis and processing of multiple video streams on the edge side. By deploying different image recognition algorithm models, it can not only identify the visible light images, but also identify the infrared images. It has the intelligent recognition and alarm functions such as real-time monitoring of equipment, intelligent image recognition, personnel safety control, infrared analysis and diagnosis, and environmental safety detection. As shown in Fig. 4, after the high-precision intelligent analysis and processing of the multiple video streams completed by the device at the edge side, the video streams with the identification results were uploaded to the

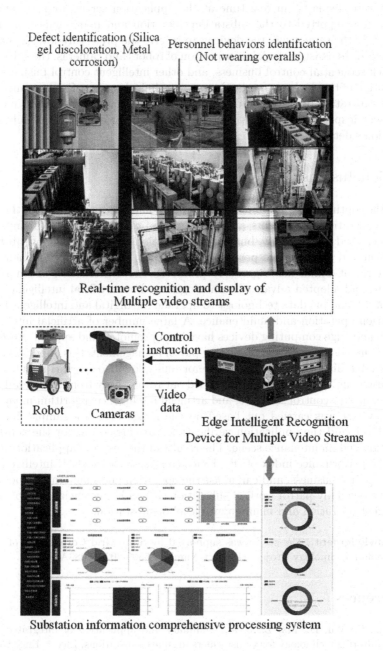

Fig. 4. The application verification of substation.

substation information comprehensive processing system in real time. Then, the results were displayed in real time at the application server, and the analysis results were reported to the substation operation and maintenance personnel in time. At the same time, the device can receive the prefecture-level inspection instructions to assist in the joint inspection of robots and cameras, the substation one-click sequential control business, and other intelligent control business. The application of the device can provide strong technical support for the transformation of substation operation and maintenance from manual inspection mode to intelligent inspection unattended mode, greatly enhance the level of substation operation safety.

6   Conclusions

With the continuous construction of smart grid and new power system, the number of substation equipments and the workload of operation and maintenance have increased dramatically, but the contradiction of the shortage of substation operation and maintenance personnel has become increasingly prominent. The State Grid of China has vigorously promoted the construction of smart substations, and adopted advanced technologies such as artificial intelligence, edge computing, and big data technology to upgrade the digital and intelligent level of substation operation and maintenance. A large number of artificial intelligence devices and edge computing devices have been promoted and applied. According to the demand of substation intelligent patrol management, this paper developed the edge intelligent recognition device for multiple video streams in substation. The design and development were carried out respectively from the overall architecture, master control software, and artificial intelligence algorithm model. The accuracy test was carried out based on the image big data sample library of State Grid, and the application verification was carried out for the substation operation and maintenance scene. The results of the test and application verified that the performance index of the device can meet the needs of intelligent substation patrol business, and can assist the operation and maintenance personnel to carry out daily patrol work of substation. It can be beneficial to support the intelligent operation and maintenance level of substation.

Acknowledgment. The study was supported by State Grid Corporation of China, Science and Technology Project (Project Number: 5500-202017083A-0-0-00).

References

1. Luo, F., Wu, D., Ma, Z., et al.: Summary and application of integrated online monitoring technology for transformers in smart substations. Electr. Eng. **13**, 144–146 (2021)
2. Qian, T.: Research on key technologies of intelligent substation operation and maintenance. School of Electrical Engineering, Shandong University, Shandong (2020)

3. Zhang, C., Lu, Z., Liu, X.: Joint inspection technology and its application in a smart substation. Power Syst. Protect. Control **49**(9), 158–164 (2021)
4. Liu, G., Zhang, L., Wu, D., et al.: Design of intelligent substation patrol inspection system based on head mounted binocular camera. Comput. Measur. Control **28**(2), 235–239 (2020)
5. Wu, D., Tang, X.-B., Li, P., et al.: State monitoring technology of relay protection device in substation based on deep neural network. Power Syst. Protect. Control **48**(05), 81–85 (2020)
6. Wu, X., Wang, Z., Song, K., et al.: Autonomous inspection system of transmission line UAV based on faster RCNN detector. Electr. Power Inf. Commun. Techno. **18**(09), 8–15 (2020)
7. Gao, J.-C., Zhang, J.-H., Li, Y.-N., et al.: Research on insulator burst fault identification based on YOLOv4. Progr. Laser Optoelectron. 1–13 (2021). https://kns.cnki.net/kcms/detail/31.1690.TN.20210409.0942.052.html
8. Zhou, J.-C., Yu, J.-F., Tang, S.F., et al.: Temperature warning system for substation equipment based on mobile infrared temperature measurement. J. Electr. Power Sci. Technol. **35**(01), 163–168 (2020)
9. Wu, T.Q., Dai, M.S., Yang, G., et al.: Corrosion recognition of power equipment based on improved mask-RCNN model. Electr. Power Inf. Commun. Technol. **19**(04), 25–30 (2021)
10. Gao, X., Hoi, S.C.H., Zhang, Y., et al. Sparse online learning of image similarity. ACM Trans. Intell. Syst. Technol. **8**(5), 64:1–64:22 (2017)
11. Yu, Z., Gao, X., Chen, Z., et al.: Mining spatial-temporal similarity for visual tracking. IEEE Trans. Image Process. **29**, 8107–8119 (2020)
12. Xia, Z., Hong, X., Gao, X., et al.: Spatiotemporal recurrent convolutional networks for recognizing spontaneous micro-expressions. IEEE Trans. Multimedia **22**(3), 626–640 (2020)
13. Zeng, T., Huang, D.: A survey of detection algorithms for abnormal behaviors in intelligent video surveillance system. Comput. Measur. Control **29**(7), 1–6 (2021)
14. Han, Y.: Design of multidimensional video monitoring system for Industry 4.0. Comput. Measur. Control **29**(1), 93–96 (2021)
15. Jian, M.: Design and implementation of video surveillance system based on cloud platform. South China University of Technology (2020)
16. Li, W.-F., Lu, J.-T., Lei, W.-L., et al.: Design of real-time video transmission system for mine. Ind. Min. Autom. **46**(02), 18–22 (2020)
17. Wei, C.-Y., Zhang, H.-L.: Design and implementation of mobile phone real-time live broadcast system based on Live555. Comput. Eng. Design **37**(05), 1156–1160 (2016)
18. Gao, X., Hoi, S.C., Zhang, Y., et al. SOML: sparse online metric learning with application to image retrieval. In: Twenty-Eighth AAAI Conference on Artificial Intelligence, pp. 1206–1212 (2014)
19. Zhang, Y., Gao, X., Chen, Z., et al.: Learning salient features to prevent model drift for correlation tracking. Neurocomputing **418**, 1–10 (2020)
20. Tang, G., Gao, X., Chen, Z., Zhong, H.: Unsupervised adversarial domain adaptation with similarity diffusion for person re-identification. Neurocomputing **442**, 337–347 (2021)
21. Wang, Y.-X., Song, H.-S., Liang, H.-X., et al.: Research on vehicle target detection on highway based on improved YOLOv4. Comput. Eng. Appl. **57**(13), 218–226 (2021)
22. Li, P., Liu, Y., Li, X., et al.: A detection method of multi-target for vehicles based on YOLO9000 model. Computer Measur. Control **27**(8), 21–24 (2019)

23. Wang, C.Y., Liao, H.Y.M., Wu, Y.H., et al.: CSPNet: a new backbone that can enhance learning capability of CNN. In: Proceedings of the IEEE/CVF Conference on Computer Vision and Pattern Recognition Workshops, pp. 390–391 (2020)

24. Mish, M.D.: A self regularized non-monotonic activation function. arXiv preprint arXiv:1908.08681 (2019)

25. Xie, Y.-T., Zhang, P.-Z.: Small target detection based on improved YOLOv4 transmission line. Foreign Electron. Measur. Technol. **40**(02), 47–51 (2021)

26. Zheng, Z., Wang, P., Liu, W., et al.: Distance-IoU loss: faster and better learning for bounding box regression. In: Proceedings of the AAAI Conference on Artificial Intelligence, vol. 34, no. 7, pp. 12993–13000 (2020)

Audio and Speech Processing

WebRTcmix - A Cloud-Based API for the Music Programming Language RTcmix

Zhixin Xu[1(✉)] and Yunze Mu[2(✉)]

[1] Institute of Cultural and Creative Industry, Shanghai Jiao Tong University,
Shanghai, China
zhixin.xu@sjtu.edu.cn

[2] College-Conservatory of Music, University of Cincinnati, Cincinnati, USA
muye@mail.uc.edu

Abstract. As the technologies continue to grow, traditional standalone music programming languages and their local IDEs have shown the drawbacks that could not meet people's demands on today's scenes, especially for cross-platform projects. In this works, we investigate a cloud-based API for the music programming language RTcmix based on Google Cloud Run and named it the WebRTcmix. This API will help the users to deploy the music programming language under almost any web-connected environment such as browser apps, mobile apps, games, even single-board computers in no time.

Keywords: Music programming language · RTcmix · Web audio · Cloud computing · API

1 Introduction

Music programming languages have been around as the main tools in the computer music field for decades. From Max Mathew's MUSIC [1] language to modern day's Supercollider [2] even Max/MSP [3], although the platforms have evolved a lot as well as the user's interfaces along with the development of the capabilities of the computers, the principle and main purpose of those languages have not been changed dramatically from then. However, as technologies continue to grow, it not only enhances the capabilities of the platforms but also changes the way people use and develop their applications. In this case, traditional music programming languages have to find another way in addition to standalone and native to make them work for modern scenarios.

Among these music programming languages, RTcmix [4] is not the one that has a huge number of users, it is not even a popular one. Compare to languages such as Supercollider and even Max/MSP, it is easy to incorporate into C/C++ applications with a low degree of data-sharing. The built-in C-style scripting language MINC (stands for "MINC is not C") parser allows users to use C-style code to write the script file, which, for many users, is a straightforward

G. Zhai et al. (Eds.): IFTC 2021, CCIS 1560, pp. 441–452, 2022.
https://doi.org/10.1007/978-981-19-2266-4_34

algorithmic processing experience. The language is also good at scheduling. With these features, although competitors are getting more sophisticated, RTcmix is still valuable for certain scenarios. In the last couple of decades, people have made a lot of efforts to make it fit into modern environments. These new tools increase the flexibility of the language a lot, but are still far from "multi-task". To get it to work for multiple platforms, creating a web API will be an ideal solution.

Some languages such as Csound [5] and Faust [6] have already had their web IDEs. However, in addition to the IDE, the web applications of the language can be extended to more purposes such as generating sound for browser apps, mobile apps, games, even single-board computers. Therefore, instead of making a web IDE for RTcmix, we created a cloud-based API for this language and named it WebRTcmix. This API will help the users to deploy the music programming language under almost any web-connected environment immediately.

2   Related Works

Most of the music programming languages have local IDEs, they are usually cross-platform, providing code highlighting and completion in the editors, working with projects on the file system. Modern programming language IDEs often offer users audio signal and data I/Os such as MIDI, UDP, and TCP/IP, using audio and information systems native to the desktop platforms and rendering sound to disk in real-time. These IDEs including SuperCollider's own IDE, CsoundQt [7] and Cabbage [8] for Csound and ChucK's miniAudicle [9], etc.

RTcmix, however, traditionally didn't have such a widely used environment until John Gibson (Indiana University) developed the RTcmixShell [10]. The language has a rather long history, derived from Paul Lansky's 20-track mixer MIX language written in 1978 ran on VMS in FORTRAN on IBM mainframes. In 1983, it was added with the synthesis function, and renamed CMIX. The MINC parser was added in 1987. In 1995, Brad Garton and Dave Topper created a real-time version with a scheduler, named RTcmix (stands for Real-Time Cmix) [11]. In the past thirty years, many people have helped improve and create new instruments for it, including several IDE-like applications. Gibson's RTcmixShell is one of the most widely used and well-maintained IDEs.

Since graphic programming environments gained tons of users following the success of Max/MSP in the last two decades, music programming has become much more practical especially for composers and musicians who didn't have strong backgrounds in technologies. From then, people who use these languages focus on not only the abilities of sound synthesizing and processing of the languages but also the graphic user's interfaces (GUIs) and compatibilities with external devices such as controllers, sensors and cameras, etc. Some text-based languages like SuperCollider do have the GUI feature that allows people to create interfaces similar to Max, and I/Os for data transform for external devices. Whether a language is worth having these features depends on its orientation. RTcmix, for many years, was always a tool for sound synthesizing and processing, it is not easy to use the language to create an entire project or make live performance, but rather convenient and powerful for generating certain sound. Therefore, the best solution for improving the language will be to make it work coordinately with graphic environments like Max and Pure Data [12].

Brad Garton, along with Dan Trueman and Luke DuBois developed the RTcmix~ [13] ("~" is a specific sign in Max/MSP meaning the signal), which for the most part, gives the solution. The RTcmix~ external for Max and PD encapsulates the RTcmix within Max/MSP and PD, works as a sound synthesis and signal processing object. It can use almost all existing RTcmix instruments and can be used to schedule Max events within RTcmix scripting language and scheduler. The external is also powerful for mathematical and data procedures, which is useful for algorithmic composition. For Max users, the most important feature is that the external can take dynamic controls from other Max objects like numbers and sliders, or external devices. Each RTcmix~ object could take up to 10 dynamic controls from inlets at the same time and connect to the variables of those RTcmix instruments which work with dynamic controls. Users could also dynamically change RTcmix scripts on the fly. Unlike Supercollider and Csound, the standalone version of RTcmix doesn't have a buffer system but only works with disks, which means users cannot create buffers in the language and store sounds for processing. For heavy interactive-oriented projects, that is inconvenient. However, the RTcmix~ works with both disks and the buffer~ object in Max, which gives huge flexibility of the language.

The RTcmix~, along with the iOS compatible iRTcmix [14] and Unity compatible uRTcmix [15], tremendously extend the capabilities of RTcmix as a modern music programming language in today's scenario. However, as the technologies continue to grow, as well as the modern users' demands on multimedia creation and design, cross-platform and multi-task become more and more indispensable. One of the most effective and practical solutions is to build up a web-based environment instead of a local one. Some of the music programming languages have already got their web APIs. The Faust Online Compiler [14] and Csound's Web-IDE are good examples. Web-based IDE is a good practice for cross-platform use of music programming language, but still not unassailable. As mentioned earlier, the music programming language is good at sound synthesis and processing but not quite accessible for certain users since it is code-based. For today's instrument design, game design, music creation for multimedia arts, and even AI music, the ideal situation will be to use it as a core of a sound generation of a project. To achieve the goal, we decided to create an API for RTcmix and put it on the cloud. The benefit of shifting from local to cloud computing is not just transferring the requirement of the ability of the computer to the more powerful web server, but also extending the flexibility of the application design, though there are some challenges such as the need to master multiple languages and operating environment [16].

3   Project Goals

In this work, we investigated an approach based on cloud technologies., trying to design an API to help the users to deploy the music language under any web-connected environment. Specific application scenarios of this API include:

- Music-related interactive web application design~
- Music composition
- Game music design with more possibilities
- Computer music pedagogy and tutorials
- Cross-platform RTcmix project development
- Music-related mobile applications
- SCM based music design

To achieve these targets, we've designed the following features for the API:

- RTcmix score parsing and processing function on the cloud
- Audio file processing
- Support of audio and MIDI processing through Web Audio and Web MIDI APIs
- Support of game design environments
- Updatable variables for processing on the cloud

4   Architecture

The following sections will describe the architecture of the RTcmix API: It describes 1) technologies used; 2) server architecture and implementation; and 3) an example client implementation with RTcmix API, Web Audio, and Web MIDI.

4.1   Technologies

Containerization is a way to let users run more than one application on the same machine. In this way, the application is running in an isolated environment called a container. Each container contains all dependency files and libraries that the application inside needs to function correctly. Multiple containers could be deployed on the same machine and share the resources. With containerization, we would like to create our stack by running services on different containers and then link them together [17]. Docker [18] is a set of platforms as a service (PaaS) products that use OS-level virtualization to deliver software in packages called containers [19]. Based on one or more images that users provide, Docker can spawn multiple containers (Fig. 1).

Using Docker has many advantages for applications like the RTcmix API. It enables reproducible builds (even with older dependencies like RTcmix). It allows for simple deployment and redeployment. In production, additional containers can be spawned and destroyed freely in response to changes in server load allowing reliable horizontal scaling. If a container malfunctions, it can be automatically destroyed and replaced.

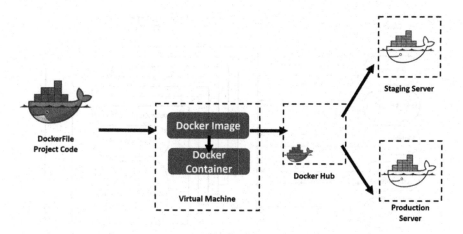

Fig. 1. Docker containerization

For running RTcmix without a server, Google Cloud Run [20] is considered as an indispensable part too. Google Cloud Run is a fully managed serverless execution environment that lets users run stateless HTTP-driven containers, without worrying about the infrastructure. With Cloud Run, you go from a "container image" to a fully managed web application running on a domain name with a TLS certificate that auto-scales with requests in a single command.

Figure 2 shows the outline of the RTcmix API and how it can be used. We built a Docker image with RTcmix on it and used that image to build our web server image which uses Python and Flask, then deployed it to Google Cloud Run. With that finished, clients can send their score files, audio files, and parameters to the server to let the server respond with the resulting audio file. Clients can make as many requests as they need and the Google Cloud Run will spawn as many containers as it needs to keep up.

4.2   Server Architecture and Implementation

Figure 3 illustrates how to build a container from an image. The image was created by adding the commands needed to install RTcmix on the clean Linux image to a Dockerfile. Once created, the image is reusable for anywhere that the user wants to use RTcmix in a Docker container. In this new Dockerfile, set PYTHONUNBUFFERED to true to allow the container to stream logs to the stdout and doesn't need to be explicitly flushed. Reset the default working directory and add the RTcmix command folder to the PATH. Using the RUN command to download and install all needed libraries. Copy the code for RTcmix

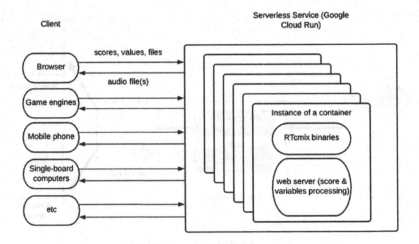

Fig. 2. Getting sever-less service using Google Cloud Run

score processing, web server, and project data and file system under the working directory. Finally, make the container run the python code by default every time it is called.

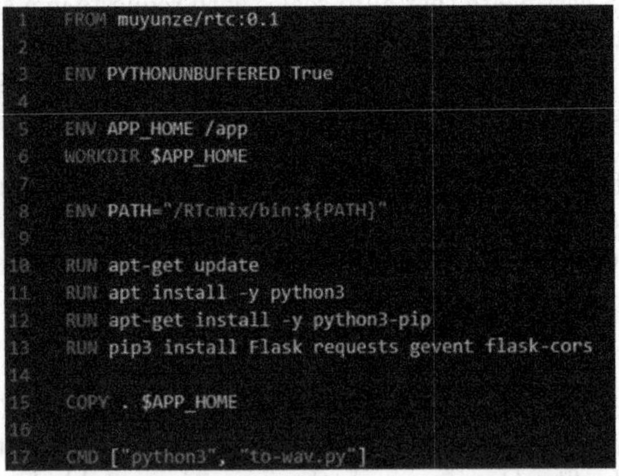

```
1   FROM muyunze/rtc:0.1
2
3   ENV PYTHONUNBUFFERED True
4
5   ENV APP_HOME /app
6   WORKDIR $APP_HOME
7
8   ENV PATH="/RTcmix/bin:${PATH}"
9
10  RUN apt-get update
11  RUN apt install -y python3
12  RUN apt-get install -y python3-pip
13  RUN pip3 install Flask requests gevent flask-cors
14
15  COPY . $APP_HOME
16
17  CMD ["python3", "to-wav.py"]
```

Fig. 3. DockerFile for configuring RTcmix API

Originally, for using RTcmix, users need to create ".sco" file for RTcmix to parse and generate the audio file. Following this idea, the API still allows the user to upload the ".sco" file to the server, process it, and call the RTcmix function to parse it. Figure 4 shows the function.

In the API, we will still need the functions to deal with variables that could be updated. In addition to the "$ variable" like what RTcmix~ has, the API

```
def process_score(input_file, output_path, uploaded_file_path, pitch):
    with open(input_file, "r+") as f:
        old_data = f.read()
        old_data = old_data.replace('webpitch', str(pow(2, (int(pitch)-69)/12)*440))
        f.seek(0)
        f.write('set_option("play = 0")\nrtsetparams(44100, 2)\nrtoutput("' + output_path + '")\n')
        f.write('rtinput("' + uploaded_file_path + '")\n')
        f.write(old_data)

def run_cmix(input_file):
    call('CMIX < ' + input_file, shell=True, timeout=20)
```

Fig. 4. Score processing and RTcmix function recall

also has a "webpitch" variable to deal with the MIDI notes. Different from the standalone version, the user won't be able to customize the sampling rate, bit depth, and buffer size. The benefit of this strategy is that without the flexibility, developers will be able to design their app with an automatic parameter set according to the system situation to avoid errors by unprofessional users.

As a web-based API, a web server is an indispensable part of our RTcmix API. Without developing our bespoke server application, using the Google Cloud Run service on a serverless web application greatly increased the reliability. We use Flask as our web server framework to give the RTcmix API the ability on receiving scores and audio files, process and return the result to the client-side. After deploying all code on the Google Cloud Run platform, the client will be receiving an URL which is the RTcmix API link that is going to be used in the future.

5 Experiments

5.1 A Client Implementation with RTcmix API, Web Audio and Web MIDI

To use the RTcmix API, users need to send score data with variables to it and let RTcmix on the cloud side do all the processing jobs, and fetch the audio data as a blob. With web audio, we can easily turn the blob data into a playable sound:

```
.then(r => URL.createObjectURL(new Blob([r], {type: 'audio/wav'})));
```

Figure 5 shows an example of how to deploy the RTcmix API on a web browser using JavaScript. As we described earlier, the RTcmix API will be able to receive any kind of variables built in the language. From the web browser side, users need to make sure that they are sending the correct data pair with the accurate variable name they set. Figure 6 shows how to set a pitch variable and pair the pitch data from the web browser with it to ensure the RTcmix API is receiving the up-to-date variables on each request. For each variable, it is possible to run some processing on it. For example, in Fig. 6, we request

```
1   const apiURL = 'https://rtcmixapi.a.run.app';
2
3   let formData = new FormData();
4   formData.append('file', new Blob([editor.getValue('\n')], {type : 'text/plain'}), 'file.sco');
5   return fetch(apiURL, {
6   method: 'POST',
7   body: formData,
8   })
9   .then(r => r.arrayBuffer())
10  .then(r => URL.createObjectURL(new Blob([r], {type: 'audio/wav'})));
```

Fig. 5. An example of deploying the RTcmix API in a browser app using JavaScript

```
1   const apiURL = 'https://rtcmixapi.a.run.app';
2
3   function sendScore(pitch) {
4   if(!ctx) init();
5
6   let formData = new FormData();
7   formData.append('file', new Blob([editor.getValue('\n')], {type : 'text/plain'}), 'file.sco');
8   formData.append('pitch', pitch);
9   return fetch(apiURL, {
10    method: 'POST',
11    body: formData,
12  })
13  .then(r => r.arrayBuffer())
14  .then(r => URL.createObjectURL(new Blob([r], {type: 'audio/wav'})));
15  }
```

Fig. 6. Using variables with RTcmix API

the variable "pitch value" from the server-side. With calculation, the variable "pitch" which is supposed to be the MIDI note number from the client-side will be converted to the frequency. The code that converts the MIDI notes number to frequency is:

str(pow(2, (int(pitch)-69)/12*440))

Figure 7 shows how to upload a sound file and let RTcmix API recognize it by pairing the file name and data.

```
1   const apiURL = 'https://rtcmixapi.a.run.app';
2
3   let formData = new FormData();
4   formData.append('sco', new Blob([editor.getValue('\n')], {type : 'text/plain'}), 'file.sco');
5   formData.append('uploadedfile', input.files[0])
6   return fetch(apiURL, {
7   method: 'POST',
8   body: formData,
9   })
10  .then(r => r.arrayBuffer())
11  .then(r => URL.createObjectURL(new Blob([r], {type: 'audio/wav'})));
```

Fig. 7. Uploading an audio file to RTcmix API for processing

Fig. 8. Screen shot of the synthesizer application

With all the features that have been developed so far, we built a web-based synthesizer using the API (Fig. 8). The synthesizer application includes three main parts: 1) RTcmix score editor, 2) score submitting and audio files uploading function, and 3) a MIDI keyboard to recall all sound files generated by the web API.

The RTcmix score editor uses CodeMirror [21] to include line numbers, syntax highlighting, key bindings, and other code editing functionalities. When clicking "Confirm," the browser makes fetch calls for each keyboard key:

```
fetch(apiURL, {method: 'POST', body: formData,})
```

After each fetch is completed, the audio gets assigned to the correct HTML audio element:

```
$('.key').addClass('red');
for(let i=0; i<88; i++) {
((i)=>sendScore(i+21)
.then(r => $('#audios').children().eq(i).attr('src',r))
.then(() => $('.key').eq(i).removeClass('red'))
)(i);
}
```

Event listeners are added for sound playback and can be triggered by clicking on the keyboard on the GUI, hitting on the computer keyboard (a, w, s, e, d, f, t, g, y, h, and j), and pressing MIDI keyboard.

5.2 Results

To evaluate the method that we used to build up the API, we created an RTcmix script using the "GRANSYNTH" instrument and feed it into both the browser application mentioned above and John Gibson's RTcmix shell. Figure 8 shows

450   Z. Xu and Y. Mu

the script running on both two environments. The browser app is on the cloud with the following temporary link to get access to, while the shell is installed locally. To trigger the browser app with a computer keyboard and external MIDI keyboard, we use "webpitch" instead of the variable "pitch" in the original script for the browser app.

https://codepen.io/yunze94/live/6cd17d47b8f62d0fe9663a6710da44b8

After deploying the script, the browser will take some time to download the audio files for all 88 keys, the period is depending on the internet connection. The shell can run the script immediately after deploy, however, it runs only one pitch at the same time, which means the users have to create certain numbers of scripts with different pitch set to play certain numbers of notes. Even with RTcmix~ which could send dynamic controls to the variables, the playing of polyphony is still way complicated than doing the same thing with the API. Figure 10 shows the spectrum plots of both the results of the browser app play 6 polyphony in different octaves at the same time versus the RTcmix shell running the same script that could play only one note back. We can see the difference in the number of spectral contents. For composers and musicians, the browser app provides an intuitional way to create and play both pitched sound and unpitched sound effects with RTcmix (Fig. 9).

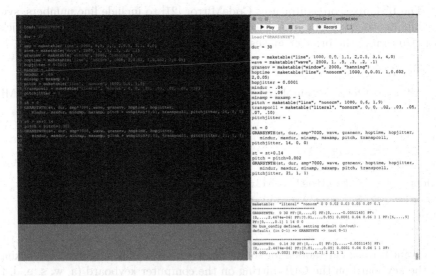

Fig. 9. The same script running on the browser app (left) and the RTcmix Shell (right)

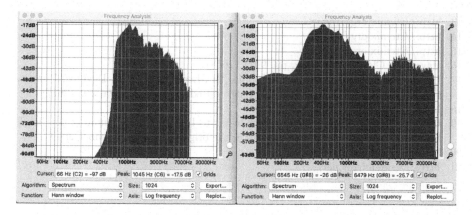

Fig. 10. Spectrum plots of the RTcmix Shell (left) and the browser app (right) running the same script

6   Conclusions

The WebRTcmix provides a cloud-based API for RTcmix users and people who are willing to use RTcmix language to create and process music or sound for browser applications, new instruments, mobile apps, and games, etc. For current RTcmix users who want a handy tool to use, it keeps the MINC syntax and includes the entire RTcmix libraries and frameworks. Compare with the standalone RTcmix and its IDE, despite the huge advantage in flexibility, the API also improved the traditional music programming language's disadvantage on polyphony by sending the scripts to the cloud server and downloading multiple sound files after calculating. For music creators, this feature will provide them with a more intuitive way while using the API for developing or creating music. In the future, we will be able to use the music programming language for more scenarios within the further development of the WebRTcmix.

References

1. Roads, C., Mathews, M.: Interview with max mathews. Comput. Music. J. **4**(4), 15–22 (1980)
2. https://supercollider.github.io/
3. https://cycling74.com/
4. http://rtcmix.org/
5. https://csound.com/
6. https://faust.grame.fr/
7. http://csoundqt.github.io/
8. http://cabbageaudio.com/
9. https://audicle.cs.princeton.edu/mini/
10. https://cecm.indiana.edu/rtcmix/rtcmix-app.html
11. Topper, D.: RTcmix and the open source/free software model. In: ICMC (1999)
12. https://puredata.info/

13. http://rtcmix.org/rtcmi~/
14. http://rtcmix.org/irtcmix/
15. http://rtcmix.org/urtcmix/
16. Hayes, B.: Cloud computing, pp. 9–11 (2008)
17. Uphill, T., Arundel, J., Khare, N., Saito, H., Lee, H., Hsu, C.: DevOps; Puppet, Docker, and Kubernetes - Learning Path, 1st edn. Packt Publications (2017)
18. https://www.docker.com/
19. O'Gara, M.: Ben Golub, Who Sold Gluster to Red Hat, Now Running dotCloud. SYS-CON Media (2013). Archived from the original on 13 September 2019
20. https://cloud.google.com/run
21. https://codemirror.net/

Speech Recognition for Power Customer Service Based on DNN and CNN Models

Yu Yin[✉], Maomao Wu, Xiaodong Wang, and Xiaoguang Huang

State Grid Information and Telecommunication Group Co., LTD., Beijing, China
xtyjy_yy@126.com

Abstract. This paper gives a comprehensive research on the speech recognition technology based on deep learning, combined with the speech data of the electric power professional to build a speech database. Through the study of the speech recognition technology based on deep learning, the acoustic and language models are constructed, and different type speech recognition models are compared especially on the practical effect of the speech recognition model in the electric customer service scene. Specifically, the main works of this paper are as follows: (1) Construct a variety of DNN network-based speech recognition architectures, and analyze the recognition results of various optimization methods; (2) Construction of a text corpus and a speech grid business scenario corpus GS-Data based on meetings and reports; (3) Study the acoustic model and language model construction technology based on deep full-sequence convolutional neural network speech recognition, construct the acoustic model and language model of speech recognition technology; (4) Compare the accuracy of different speech recognition schemes.

Keywords: Speech recognition · DNN-HMM · CNN

1 Introduction

In recent years, artificial intelligence (AI) technology is experiencing a wave of rapid development, especially the continuous innovation of deep learning technology, the continuous accumulation of big data and the steady improvement of computing ability, which also promotes the leap-forward development of artificial intelligence technology [1–5], and also for other fields and applications [6–10]. As one of the most important technologies in the field of AI, speech recognition not only changes the mode of human-computer interaction, and enables human beings to talk to machines in the most natural way, but also has the ability to transform unstructured speech into structured text, which greatly improves the work efficiency of relevant practitioners.

As a key technology to realize intelligent applications such as human computer interaction, speech recognition is mainly developed through signal processing and mode recognition technologies, so that machines can "understand" human sound. Traditional speech recognition technology based on statistical

© Springer Nature Singapore Pte Ltd. 2022
G. Zhai et al. (Eds.): IFTC 2021, CCIS 1560, pp. 453–468, 2022.
https://doi.org/10.1007/978-981-19-2266-4_35

models achieves breakthrough [5] based by Gaussian mixed distribution-hidden Markov model (GMM-HMM). However, this speech recognition system has never been widely recognized and popularized in practical applications, mainly because the accuracy and speed of speech recognition are far from reaching the practical threshold. With the proposed [11] of Deep Belief Networks (DBN), deep neural network (DNN) based research has further promoted the development of speech recognition technology in [12].

Speech recognition technology has gradually emerged out of the traditional GMM-HMM framework, to the deep learning framework represented by the feed forward deep neural network (FFDNN) and convolutional neural network (CNN), and has achieved a good practical effect [13,14]. The DNN-based speech recognition framework replaces the traditional hybrid Gaussian model using a feed-forward neural network structure, using a model to predict all state posterior probability distributions of HMM. Meanwhile, DNN can leverage the knot information contained by context-related speech feature splicing compared to GMM features.

The introduction of the DNN framework into the field of speech recognition has important [15], while the CNN-based speech recognition framework promotes another major improvement in speech recognition technology from another perspective. CNN adopts local receptive field mechanism, which is more robust to interference information, such as noise, speaker changes, etc. Through the accumulation of multiple convolutional layers and pooling layers, CNN network can see very long historical information and future information [16], thus has excellent timing expression ability.

The development of China's national economy has promoted the development of the electric power industry. The automation level and management level of the power system is gradually modernizing. The application requirements of voice technology in power systems have shifted from simple and concise voice alarms to voice human-computer interaction. The application of speech recognition technology in the power system has become indispensable. However, in the field of electric power, the semantic understanding and cognitive technology has not yet formed a general technical framework, and this part requires breakthrough progress. The first is the optimization for professional fields, especially in the electric power field, where there are usually more dedicated vocabulary. Therefore, a customized language business knowledge base is needed to realize the language keyword matching rules for business knowledge points, business handling guidance rules and natural language corresponding rules.

In order to sort out, it also needs to be optimized in terms of query, search, route navigation, etc. Therefore, this paper constructs the data set GS-Data in the electric power field. In order to compare the applicability of DNN-based and CNN-based speech recognition technology in the field of power customer service. Using the first data set GS-Data of power operation customer service we constructed, a variety of DNN and CNN speech recognition models based on DNN are compared and the applicability of different models in electric customer service scenarios are analyzed.

2   Cross-Correlation Technique

2.1   Feed Forward Fully Connected Deep Neural Network

The feedforward fully connected Deep Neural Network (DNN) is essentially a multi-layer sensing machine containing multiple hidden layers.

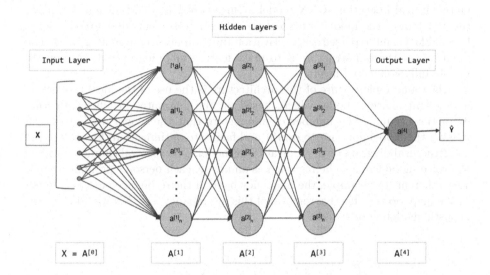

Fig. 1. Schematic structural representation of a DNN

Figure 1 is a schematic diagram of the DNN network structure which contains five hidden layers. The DNN adopts a hierarchical structure, divided into input, hidden and output layers. Nodes in adjacent layers are fully connected, with no connections between nodes in the same layer. The activation values of the hidden layer nodes are the linear weighted sum of the previous layer and the current layer network weights are obtained by the non-linear activation function. For DNN containing L hidden layers, assuming their input is $h^0 = X$, the activation value of its hidden layers can be represented by the following formula:

$$a^l = W^l h^l + b^l (1 < l < L + 1) \tag{1}$$

$$h^l = f(a^l)(1 < l < L) \tag{2}$$

The traditional DNN generally adopts the Sigmoid activation function [17], which is expressed as follows:

$$\sigma(z) = \frac{1}{1 + e^{-z}} \tag{3}$$

2.2 Convolutional Neural Network

Convolutional neural networks (CNN) are another well-known deep learning model that has widespread applications in the image field. The CNN model achieves a more robust characteristic [18,19] by employing local filtering and maximal pooling techniques. The core is performing convolution operations. Convolutional operation is a feature extraction method, which is essentially a mathematical operation. CNN model architecture has a certain unity, that is, the first half of the model is for feature extraction, so generally stacked convolutional layer, interspersed with activation function layer and pooling layer. The main role of the tail structure is to make feature mapping output, so they are mostly fully connected layers.

The remarkable feature of this architecture is the use of the local connection and weight sharing mode, which, based on the guarantee of efficient feature extraction, reduces the number of parameters that the model needs to learn, making the model not easy to overfit and facilitate optimization. Figure 2 shows the structural diagram of the typical CNN model. The spectral characteristics of the voice signal can also be regarded as an image, each person's pronunciation is very different, for example, the frequency band of the resonance peak is different in the map. So the effective removal of this discrepancy by CNN would favor the acoustic modeling of speech.

Fig. 2. The AlexNet architecture

2.3 The Dropout Mechanism

As the number of DNN model layers deepens, its model training causes its reduced generalization ability due to some poor local optima and overfitting to the training data. DNN containing a large number of parameters tend to overfit even with unsupervised pre-training. Traditional BP algorithm uses heavy attenuation normalization and early stop training to control model overfitting. Hinton et al. proposed a dropout strategy that randomly placing some input nodes or hidden layer nodes during each iteration of the network training can prevent mutual adaptation between the network hidden layer nodes, thus effectively preventing the overfitting of the network. Figure 3 is a schematic of dropout, with significant performance improvements obtained in dropout-based training methods in the image classification task as well as a small database of speech recognition. However, dropout tends to greatly slow down the convergence rate of the network, which greatly increases the training time of the network.

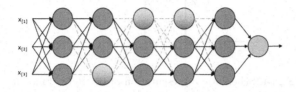

Fig. 3. Schematic representation of the Dropout mechanism

In this paper, we use dropout as a pre-training way to provide a good initialization network for fine-tuning of DNN. Further, this study analyzes the weight characteristics of DNN applied to speech recognition acoustic modeling, and found that the weight of DNN, the higher the sparsity, meaning that the higher the DNN network, the higher the redundancy. Based on this, we propose an intuitive DNN structure with decreasing hidden layer nodes. This structure can effectively utilize the sparse characteristics of the DNN, minimize the number of network parameters without losing the network performance, and speed up the training of the model.

2.4   Linear Rectified Linear Unit

The hidden layer node, as a basic modeling unit of the DNN, usually adopts some nonlinear activation function and performs a nonlinear transformation of the input to obtain the output. Conventional DNN generally adopts the Sigmoid function or Tanh activation function. Using Sigmoid and other function, reverse propagation error gradient, the derivative involves the division, the computation is quite large. For deep networks, the Sigmoid function is easy to show gradient disappearance to completing the training of deep networks.

In this study, Rectified Linear Unit (ReLU) was used to build the RL-DNN model for speech recognition task [20,21]. Figure 4 shows the function diagram of the ReLU. The main advantages of RL-DNN over Sigmoid-DNN are: 1) RL-DNN can achieve better performance than Sigmoid-DNN on many tasks; 2) RL-DNN training converges faster; 3) the output value is 0 when RL-DNN nodes are not activated, which makes the stronger sparsity of the network. The above advantages contributes to the model generalization ability. This study revealed another meaningful property of the RL-DNN. It was found that the RL-DNN based on SGD training can be iteratively updated with a large batch (batch) with reasonable parameter settings. For example, it can be adopted either dozens of times or even hundreds of times larger than the mini-batch normally used for training. Large batch-based SGD training can easily be parallelized through multi-GPU,

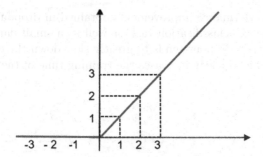

Fig. 4. Schematic representation of the ReLU function

which can significantly improve the training speed of the model. We further propose an optimization method for binding scalar (tied-scalar) normalization for the training of RL-DNN. Thus, it not only make the training stable, but also can improve the performance of the model.

3   Model Construction

3.1   DNN-HMM Acoustic Model

The structure of the DNN-HMM-based acoustic model of speech recognition is shown in Fig. 5. Compared with the traditional GMM-HMM-based acoustic model, the only difference is the use of DNN to replace the GMM to model the observed probability of the input speech signal. In this study, we designed a DNN with 4 hidden layer as shown in Fig. 6, where the input layer is 440 dimensional consists of 40 dimensional Fbank features in series of 11 frames, and 1024 neurons per layer, the activation function is Sigmoid. In the output layer, there are 3335 neurons corresponding to the number of triad states in the GMM-HMM baseline system. The whole network has about 7 million parameters.

The training steps of the DNN-HMM acoustic model in Kaldi are as follows:

(1) Pre-Training: the purpose of pre-training is to better initialize the network parameters, if enough data can also skip pre-training directly for supervised training, DBN pre-training method in the experiment and RBM (Restricted Boltzmann Machine) iterative training 20 times.
(2) Update of the Network Parameters: the entire network was parameter updated with the frame-level annotation information forced aligned the speech data by DNN-HMM, mainly based on the error back-propagation algorithm for stochastic gradient descent. The training included 14 iterations, mini-batch size 256, initial learning rate 0.008, learning rate half the previous iteration, and loss function is frame-level cross-entropy.
(3) Decoding: after the acoustic model training, the Kaldi decoder decoding was called, Then perform an accuracy test on the test set.

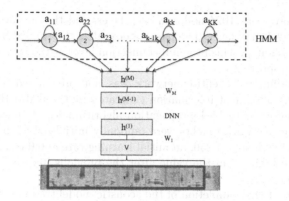

Fig. 5. Schematic representation of the DNN-HMM structure

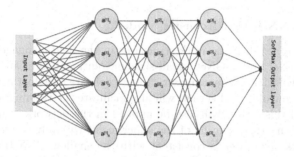

Fig. 6. DNN structure diagram

3.2   Shallow CNN-HMM Acoustic Model

In the shallow CNN-based acoustic model, the front end of the entire network is composed of a convolutional layer and a pooling layer. The convolutional layer obtains the local information of the input feature through the convolution kernel, that is, the information between each dimension in the frame and between each frame. And then hand it over to the pooling layer for generalization processing. The local information in the feature can be better obtained by alternately processing the local information in the feature twice, and then the back-end fully connected layer performs global information integration, and the entire network finally outputs the current feature to which it belongs The status category.

1) Network Parameter: the specific parameters of the network are as follows: The network consists of an input layer, two convolutional layers, and one pooling layer, two fully connected layers, and one softmax layer. The network input is the Fbank feature of multiple frames in parallel, 440 dimensions, 9×1 convolutional core size of C1, 128, movement step of 1, activation function ReLU, output 12832×3 feature Map. S1 layer pooling area size of 4×1, including 1 horizontal movement step, vertical movement step, output 1288×3 Feature Map. C2 convolution core size of $8 \times 34 \times 3$, convolution core 256, and output 2565×1 Feature Map. After grating, the 1280-dimensional vector input full

connection layer has 1024 nodes in each layer, and the output layer is 3335 nodes in the softmax layer. The parameter scale to be trained in the network is about 5 million, of which the full connection layer at the back end accounts for a large proportion.

2) Network Training: the entire network was not pre-trained for supervised directly using alignment information generated by the GMM-HMM baseline system, using an error back-propagation algorithm based on stochastic gradient descent. Network weights were randomly initialized in the (0,1) range, with a mini-batch size of 256, an initial learning rate of 0.008, and the fourth learning rate taking half the value after the previous iteration, with a total of 14 iterations.

3) Decoding: after the completion of the acoustic model training. Then perform an accuracy test on the test set.

3.3   Deep CNN-HMM Acoustic Model

There are many excellent network structures in the field of image recognition, such as GoogleNet and WGNet, small-size convolutional cores are widely used. Small size convolutional cores can extract more delicate local features, and applying small size convolutional kernels will also facilitate the training of deeper network [22], and this design will also be applied in the network structure in this section. To ensure the scientific of the experiment, the fully connected layer in all the network structures is consistent with the shallow CNN-HMM systems, respectively designing several network structures shown in Fig. 7.

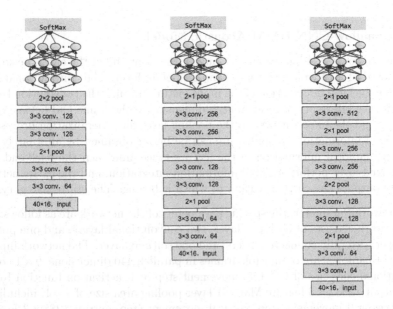

Fig. 7. Plot of the CNN structure of different depths

In Fig. 7, all three network structures adopt the substructure of the pooling layer after 2 convolutional layers, mainly to fully obtain the local information at different positions in the splicing frame features, and to enhance the invariance of the whole network to the voice signal in the time-frequency domain. According to the successful experience in the field of deep learning, with the network depth, the number of Feature Map generated by the convolutional layer increases with the depth, and the information obtained from the original input is richer, which is very beneficial to determine the state of the corresponding speech frame.

All the network structures in Fig. 7 except the output layer activation function is softmax, and all the other hidden layer activation functions are ReLU. The certain sparsity of ReLU can help to train these deeper networks and speed up the convergence rate. Each network consists of two 1024 nodes per layer and one softmax layer with 3335 nodes, with convolutional kernel sizes of 3×3 for all layers and Max Pooling for the pooling layers. The input to each network is the Fbank feature of the network with multiple frames in parallel, namely the feature matrix of 40×16 consisting of 640 dimensions.

The first network has four convolutional layers, C1, C2 and C3, C4 layers have 64,128 convolutional cores each, two pooling layers S1, S2, S1 pooling region size 2×1. Its step lengths are 1 and 2 in horizontal and vertical reverse, S2 pooling region size 2×2 steps 2 respectively, and final S2 output of 1287×4 Feature Map.

The second network has six convolutional layers, C1, C2, C3, C4, C5, C6 has 64, respectively, 128,256 convolutional cores, all steps of 1,3 pooling layers, S1 pooling region size 2×1 its step lengths of 1 and 2 in horizontal and vertical reverse, S2 size 2×2 of 1 and 2, S2 size 2×2, and eventually S2 output 2562×2 Feature Map.

The third network has convolutional layers, C1, C2, C3, C4, C5, C6, 64, 128, 256, 512 nuclear steps of 1, 4 pooling layers S1, S2, S3, S4 pooling regions of 2×1 and 2×2, respectively, and the final S4 output Feature Map of 5123×1.

Each network structures were written by a BrainScript script built into CNTK and Dropour technology was applied to optimize the training of the network using ReLU, with a Dropout ratio of 0.15. Each network was unsupervised pre-trained, directly supervised using GMM-HMM aligned data for supervised training using the mini-batch SGD algorithm, mini-batch value of 256, maximum 30 iterations, initial learning rate of 0.008, and loss function is frame-level cross-entropy.

4   Experimental Results

4.1   Experimental Environment

CNTK is an open-source cognitive computing tool launched by Microsoft, which internally consists of four modules: feature reading, network construction, network training, and execution engine. The feature reading module can support reads such as image, text, and voice features, and certainly a custom feature. The network building module can realize any neural network, and the CNTK provides various component support for the common neural network. The network training module provides gradient training algorithms such as SGD, Adagrad, lbit-SGD, which can seamlessly support the CPU cluster and GPU cluster to greatly improve the training speed of the network. CNTK also offers rich interface in addition to the native Python, C BrainScript interface. In the subsequent experiments in this paper, all acoustic models of the CNN-HMM structures will be trained using CNTK.

Kaldi is a powerful open-source voice recognition system toolbox that provides a complete set of voice recognition tools, supports all mainstream feature extraction such as MFCC and Fbank, as well as more advanced feature processing technologies such as VTLN, CMVN and LDA, supports the training of GMM-HMM and NN-HMM acoustic models, and provides a decoder based on weighted finite state machine design. A prototype of a speech recognition system can be quickly implemented using the rich tools provided by Kaldi, and the Shell scripts can directly call these underlying modules, greatly lowering the threshold for use. In subsequent experiments, Kaldi was mainly used for feature extraction and training of Sigmoid DNN, RL-DNN, GMM-HMM, DNN-HMM acoustic models and decoding.

4.2 Data Preparation

In order to effectively tap the voice data value of electric customer service, improve the quality of electric customer service, and provide technical accumulation for intelligent voice service of electric customer service, it is very important to build a power customer service oriented speech recognition model. We build a GS-Data corpus database using a recording library composed of 95598 customer service personnel recording. The pronunciation database covers 19–29 main age groups, covering the major provinces and cities in the country, among which the gender ratio is 1:1, totaling 209,436 sentences, and all the pronunciation contents are selected from the customer service voice data from 2014–2017.

To avoid the effects of background noise and pronunciation accents, we selected 651 people from the speech library for 80166 pronunciation as cleanly as possible, with 79166 in the training set and 1000 in the test set. The syllable design covers Chinese Yin, Yang, upper, go, soft, child words, a total of about 1904 syllables, and the library marked level is with tone syllables. Some data needs to be prepared before building the identification system using Kaldi, including speech data related to the acoustic model and text data related to the language model.

The information of the modeling unit is stored in photo.txt, and the format is modeling unit, id. Unless otherwise specified, the modeling units in the subsequent experiments of this paper are all consonants and vowels. The pronunciation dictionary is stored in lexicon.txt. The format is tone, syllable initials, and vowels. The function of pronunciation dictionary is to determine the mapping relationship between tone syllables and consonants and vowels. Text is stored in labeling information, and the format is sentence id, labeled content. What is stored in wav.scp is the location information of the original voice data in the format that is sentence id, voice data path information.

Table 1. Experimental data format

File name	Content format
phone.txt	ang2 19
lexicon.txt	ban4 b an4
text	10141051 mai4 diao4 ao4 di2 li2 suo3 ying1 dang4
wav.scp	10221049 home/m/data/data/test/10221049.wav

In order to reduce the difference in model recognition results caused by different data sets, all CNN and DNN speech recognition model models constructed in this paper also use this data set (Table 1).

4.3   Language Model

In this experiment, the language model is constructed using a ternary grammar model, with phone level and trained with the IRSTLM tool, an open-source N-gram language model training tool that is suitable for model training with large data volume. All training corpora in the trial were collected in-laboratory and eventually trained with a language model as shown in Fig. 8, with 2221-gram, 65752-gram and 839463-gram. Each row consists of 3 columns with column 2 as the current gram, the first column is the log probability of the motif appearing, and the third column is the fallback weight.

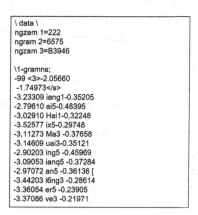

Fig. 8. 3-gram language model

4.4   Feature Extraction

MFCC and Fbank features were extracted for the training and test sets, respectively, for 10 ms in 25 ms per frame, using a Hamming window. The computer-mfcc-feats tool was called to extract the 39 dimensional MFCC feature per frame, the original 13 dimensional plus first order second order difference, without log energy, and the CMVN operation after each frame MFCC was the inverted spectral mean normalized. The compute-fbank-feats tool was called to extract the 40-dimensional Fbank features per napkin (no log energy was used), and the CMVN operation was also performed after extracting each frame of Fbank.

4.5   Analysis of Results

GMM-HMM acoustic model training in Kaldi will first train a single phonic model with the modeling unit, and then base the context extension of the modeling unit, generate the triconic and complete the clustering operation of the triconic, train the GMM-HMM model again as the modeling unit, and then make some special changes to continue training until there is a stable result. Establishing a GMM-HMM baseline system has two purposes: to verify the feasibility of acoustic modeling based on a deep convolutional neural network; most mainly to provide labeled training data for a neural network-based acoustic model, to forcibly align all speech data with the GMM-HMM baseline system, to obtain HMM states corresponding to each frame of speech, and to use the clustered three-tone state (Senone) id as the label information during network training. After training, 3,335 senone tags were generated by GMM-HMM, calling the Kaldi decoder, and the identification results of the GMM-HMM baseline system on the 1,000-sentence test set are shown in Table 2.

We used CNTK, RL-DNN, GNN, GMM-HMM, DNN-HMM and CNN-HMM, to achieve the identification results. To explore the application effect of Deep CNN in speech recognition, we designed the network structure shown in the Fig. 7, with a convolution depth of 4,6, and 7, respectively, and built the corresponding recognition system for experiments. Identification results obtained on the test set are shown in Table 2.

Table 2. Identification results of each identification system on the test set

Sound model type	Factor misknowledge rate
Sigmoid DNN	14.78%
RL-DNN	15.92%
GMM-HMM	24.18%
DNN-HMM	16.64%
CNN-HMM	15.26%

Table 3 is the results of the identification systems at different network depths on the test sets. From Table 3, the acoustic modeling methods based on the neural network hidden Markov hybrid models significantly outperform the traditional hybrid Gaussian hidden Markov models and the Dropout model-based acoustic models. In terms of phoneme error rate, DNN-HMM showed a 7.54% absolute

Table 3. Identification results of the identification systems at different CNN network depths on the test sets

Sound model type	Factor misknowledge rate
GMM-HMM 4-conv	14.84%
DNN-HMM 6-conv	14.02%
CNN-HMM 7-conv	16.25%

reduction from GMM-HMM and a relative decrease of 31.18%, 8.92% and CNN-HMM compared to GMM-HMM. Notably, GMM-HMM here was optimized by discriminative training, while our NN-HMM acoustic model did not perform any discriminative training, indicating that deep neural networks outperformed GMM on complex data sets like speech, that CNN-HMM has a 1.38% absolute reduction than DNN-HMM and an 8.29% relative reduction, indicating that CNN has stronger characterization power than DNN.

From Fig. 9, judging from the frame state classification accuracy, DNN has a state classification accuracy of 61.7515%, and CNN has an absolute improvement of 3.6823% and a relative improvement of 5.9631%. The accurate classification of the states corresponding to the speech frames is the first step in training the acoustic models, and the CNN has a better classification effect than the DNN.

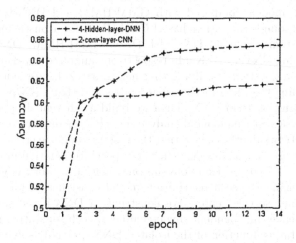

Fig. 9. Speech frame classification accuracy for different networks

In terms of network structure, CNN is more reasonable than DNN. DNN will connect all dimensions of speech features to each neuron, and has a weak ability to capture contextual information between speech frames. CNN can extract local features at different levels through different convolutional cores, to a certain extent, obtain the correlation information between the voice frames can reduce the impact of convolutional noise, downsampling of features through pooling layer can make the network have certain fault tolerance to the offset on the frequency and time domain, and also reduce the amount of data of the network. Convolutional neural network can be said to unify feature-intrinsic information extraction and HMM state classification together, thus achieving better results than DNN. From Table 3, the CNN-HMM misidentification rate of the CNN-HMM and 6 convolution layer 4 decreased by 0.42% and 1.24% compared with the CNN-HMM benchmark system in the 2 convolution layer, respectively. It is seen that with the depth of the convolutional and pooling layers, the phoneme error rate decreased to some extent compared with the 2 convolutional layer CNN-HMM system. However, it is worth noting here that the CNN-HMM misidentification rate of the 7 convolutional layer is 16.25% increased 2.01% from the 2 convolutional layer, and here be because the network is too deep to pass residuals leads to inadequate training of the whole network. Compared to the 2-layer convolution of the CNN-HMM benchmark system, a deeper network can extract more robust features to improve the recognition effect of the system, but if the network is too deep, the insufficient voice data for training will reduce the recognition rate of the whole system.

5   Conclusion

This paper first analyzes the advantages of Sigmoid DNN, RL-DNN, and CNN-HMM acoustic models compared with GMM-HMM and DNN-HMM acoustic models, and expounds the rationality of CNN-HMM for acoustic modeling. Five benchmark systems, Sigmoid DNN, RL-DNN, GMM-HMM, DNN-HMM and CNN-HMM using CNTK and Kaldi, respectively, analyzed experimental results of five benchmark systems, verifying that neural networks are more suitable for acoustic modeling than hybrid Gaussian models and that CNN performs better in speech recognition than DNN. Then we build a different deep convolutional neural network acoustic model and analyze the relationship of recognition performance with network depth to show that the system phoneme error rate decreases to some extent as the network deepens. The speech recognition model construction technology based on deep convolutional neural network is established to solve the problem of speech recognition model construction for the recording data of customer service center. We constructs a DNN-based separation system for the speaker-independent single-channel speech separation problem, and optimizes the target function of the isolated DNN, partially solving some problems existing in the traditional single-channel speech separation techniques, such as the speech replacement problem. However, the effect is still not satisfactory when the characteristics of the speech distribution of the speaker is relatively close, which is also the research direction of forward-step to improve our technical scheme. Speech separation under the proximity of speaker characteristics: for the separation of mixed speech of unknown speakers, because the rich prior information of source signals cannot be obtained, the distribution characteristics can only be learned through mixed signals. However, our proposed system learns its acoustic characteristics through the DNN, and then simulates the speech characteristics of the unknown speaker, but for the speaker characteristics are close, we need to introduce more speaker discriminative information. The future work with this problem are: 1) Increase the amount of data for the training DNN, and increase the information that the DNN can learn by increasing the voice of more speakers and individual speakers seen in the training set; 2) Using other types of neural networks, such as recurrent neural network RNN that can use historical information and bidirectional recurrent neural networks that can use both past and future information, it learns more characteristics by increasing the information that can be seen by the same speaker.

References

1. Gao, X., Hoi, S.C., Zhang, Y., et al.: Sparse online learning of image similarity. ACM Trans. Intell. Syst. Technol. **8**(5), 64:1–64:22 (2017)
2. Zhang, Y., Gao, X., Chen, Z., et al.: Mining spatial-temporal similarity for visual tracking. IEEE Trans. Image Process. **29**, 8107–8119 (2020)
3. Xia, Z., Hong, X., Gao, X., et al.: Spatiotemporal recurrent convolutional networks for recognizing spontaneous micro-expressions. IEEE Trans. Multimed. **22**(3), 626–640 (2020)
4. Abdel-Hamid, O., Mohamed, A.R., Jiang, H., Penn, G.: Applying convolutional neural networks concepts to hybrid NN-HMM model for speech recognition. In: IEEE International Conference on Acoustics (2012)
5. Swietojanski, P., Ghoshal, A., Renals, S.: Revisiting hybrid and GMM-HMM system combination techniques. In IEEE International Conference on Acoustics (2013)
6. Li, W., Chen, Z., Gao, X., et al.: Multimodel framework for indoor localization under mobile edge computing environment. IEEE Internet Things J. **6**(3), 4844–4853 (2019)
7. Gao, X., Chen, Z., Tang, S., et al.: Adaptive weighted imbalance learning with application to abnormal activity recognition. Neurocomputing **173**, 1927–1935 (2016)
8. Gao, X., Hoi, S.C., Zhang, Y., et al. SOML: sparse online metric learning with application to image retrieval. In: Twenty-Eighth AAAI Conference on Artificial Intelligence, pp. 1206–1212 (2014)
9. Zhang, Y., Gao, X., Chen, Z., et al.: Learning salient features to prevent model drift for correlation tracking. Neurocomputing **418**, 1–10 (2020)
10. Tang, G., Gao, X., Chen, Z., Zhong, H.: Unsupervised adversarial domain adaptation with similarity diffusion for person re-identification. Neurocomputing **442**, 337–347 (2021)
11. Mohamed, A.: Acoustic modeling using deep belief networks. IEEE Trans. Audio Speech Lang. Process. **20**, 14–22 (2017)
12. Yu, D., Deng, L.: Signals and communication technology. Automatic Speech Recognition Deep Neural Network Sequence-Discriminative Training. (Chapter 8) 137–153 (2015). https://doi.org/10.1007/978-1-4471-5779-3
13. Qian, Y., Woodland, P.C.: Very deep convolutional neural networks for robust speech recognition. In: Spoken Language Technology Workshop (2017)
14. Ravanelli, M., Omologo, M.: Contaminated speech training methods for robust DNN-HMM distant speech recognition. arXiv:1710.03538 (2017)

15. Liu, C.Z., Zhang, L.: Research on optimization algorithm of convolution neural network in speech recognition. J. Harbin Univ. Sci. Technol. (2016)
16. Zhang, C., Woodland, P.C.: DNN speaker adaptation using parameterised sigmoid and ReLU hidden activation functions. In: IEEE International Conference on Acoustics (2016)
17. Alom, M.Z., Taha, T.M., Yakopcic, C., Westberg, S., Asari, V.K.: The history began from AlexNet: a comprehensive survey on deep learning approaches. arXiv:1803.01164v2 (2018)
18. Hara, K., Saito, D., Shouno, H.: Analysis of function of rectified linear unit used in deep learning. In: International Joint Conference on Neural Networks (2015)
19. Gal, Y., Ghahramani, Z.: Dropout as a Bayesian approximation: representing model uncertainty in deep learning. In: Proceedings of The 33rd International Conference on Machine Learning, ICML'16, vol. 48, pp. 1050–1059 (2016)
20. Qiu, J., Liang, W., Zhang, L., Yu, X., Zhang, M.: The early-warning model of equipment chain in gas pipeline based on DNN-HMM. J. Natural Gas Sci. Eng. **27**, 1710–1722 (2015)
21. Kai, Z., Zuo, W., Gu, S., Lei, Z.: Learning deep CNN denoiser prior for image restoration. In: 2017 IEEE Conference on Computer Vision and Pattern Recognition (CVPR) (2017)
22. Banerjee, D.S., Hamidouche, K., Panda, D.K.: Re-designing CNTK deep learning framework on modern GPU enabled clusters. In: 2016 IEEE International Conference on Cloud Computing Technology and Science (CloudCom) (2017)

Big Data

Big Data

A Review on Financial Robot Process Auto-mining Based on Reinforcement Learning

Cunliang Han[✉], Xiaojun Zhang, Huijuan Jiao, Min Wang, and Tiantian Han

State Grid Huitongjincai (Beijing) Information Technology Co., Ltd., Beijing, China
mengsjtl@163.com

Abstract. In recent years, with the rapid development of science and technology, human society has ushered in the digital information era. Facing the gradually expanding office field and complex business processes, robotics process automation (RPA) technology oriented process auto-discovery and process auto-mining have shown great potential for development. Most of enterprise's financial personnel are also faced with tedious business processes and other situations. Thus, research of the financial robot process auto-mining method based on reinforcement learning becomes particularly important. Based on the traditional financial robot design, through the exploration and understanding of reinforcement learning, the Model-Based strategy optimization algorithm is used to establish a high-frequency business process auto-discovery model. The unmanned underwater vehicle (UUV) autonomous decision-making technology is used to establish an autonomous decision-making model for infrequent business processes, and then the application of natural language understanding and image recognition technology in human-computer interaction is used to study the human-computer high-frequency interaction technology. Finally, based on the time decay model and batch update model, we design a business process mining model for semi-structured data flow, which makes the research of financial robot process automatic mining method complete. The research of automatic mining method of financial robot process based on reinforcement learning will promote the further development of financial automation, and RPA technology will be brilliant in the future.

Keywords: Reinforcement learning · Process auto-mining · High frequency human-computer interaction · Unstructured data · Semi-structured data

1 Introduction

In recent years, with the rapid development of science and technology, we have ushered in the digital information age. China is in the period of digital transformation and upgrading of traditional industries. Driven by the background of the new era, it is also an inevitable development situation to innovate and Reform in the power industry, one of China's traditional industries. There are a lot of repetitive and mechanical basic tasks in the financial management of power grid companies, such as invoice and accounting data verification, reconciliation, invoice verification, etc. these tasks occupy a lot of energy

G. Zhai et al. (Eds.): IFTC 2021, CCIS 1560, pp. 471–484, 2022.
https://doi.org/10.1007/978-981-19-2266-4_36

of financial personnel, and the efficiency and quality of financial processing are affected. Robotics process automation (RPA) uses digital means to replace the repeated things in manual operation, solve the problem of low and medium added value in financial management, and create favorable conditions for promoting the digital transformation of finance. Therefore, the innovation of financial management has increasingly become one of the important links of corporate management.

The financial robot makes use of the automatic processing function of the software to transform the financial management and realize automation and intelligence. For the current mainstream robots, the known business processes are solidified in the robot designer, thus have many shortcomings. Firstly, the interaction between financial personnel and robots is limited to the form of data input and result output, which cannot achieve the purpose of high-frequency interaction on demand; Secondly, the financial personnel don't know which business can be realized by RPA robot. It needs repeated communication and research between the demander and the financial personnel to sort out and mine the business, which is inefficient; Finally, because the design technology and algorithm of RPA robot have not been optimized, and the purpose of being easy to understand and operate has not been achieved, the use of RPA robot must train financial personnel, which has great restrictions in human-computer interaction scenarios such as demonstration, training and promotion. Therefore, the implementation of more intelligent financial management and more scientific deployment of financial robots is an urgent research topic and direction with great needs.

In summary, the significance of optimizing RPA robot technology in financial management lies in: further releasing resources, reducing the demand for a series of communication among personnel, financial personnel and technicians, and promoting financial transformation and upgrading; lay a solid foundation for management, improve the core competitiveness of power grid enterprises and ensure the orderly development of enterprises; integrate intelligent technology and promote enterprise intelligent operation.

2   Business Analysis of Financial Robot

Using the automatic processing function of software, the financial robot can be roughly divided into four development stages. The first stage is defined as virtual helper, and the latter three stages are referred to as virtual labor in a whole. Great progress has been made from the first stage to the second stage. From the second stage, RPA is called robot, which has the ability to replace manpower for business processing [1].

RPA started relatively slowly in Asian market for two main reasons: first, large enterprises have high requirements for data security and system stability. Second, RPA products need to be localized. Enterprises must have their own independent intellectual property rights and core technologies in order to carry out comprehensive customized development and local actions [2].

Coenrad de Jager and Marina Nel of the University of Arkansas studied how to improve the accuracy of automatically obtaining available data from images by tracking image digitization when RPA is combined with optical character recognition (OCR) [3].

In 1959, American scholar B. Shackel published the first literature on man-machine interface in history based on the research on machines to reduce human production fatigue. In terms of natural language interaction, Xie Jiongkun of University of Science and Technology of China has improved the ability of machine to understand natural language by solving three problems: open knowledge semantic extraction with natural language as the carrier, large-scale natural language understanding and the acquisition of a large number of labeled corpus [4]; Dou Ziyi of Carnegie Mellon University and Wang Xing of Tencent artificial intelligence laboratory have improved the performance of natural language processing by using depth representation in neural network [5]. In terms of speech interaction, the speech recognition rate of the speech recognition system developed by iFLYTEK has reached 98%, and has also invested a lot of research in dialect recognition [6].

With the emergence and gradual maturity of information technologies such as big data and artificial intelligence, many enterprises have successively used smart finance to carry out management. For example, State Grid Shanghai electric power company has accelerated the upgrading and transformation of financial management by designing a smart financial system of "smart Finance + power benefit chain". "Smart finance" is the product of the intelligent era and the innovation and continuous development of the traditional financial management model. More and more enterprises will have a deeper understanding of smart finance.

3 Automatic Process Mining of Financial Robot

Process discovery is the process knowledge gained from the event logs common in modern information systems to discover and improve the actual system behavior patterns (expressed in process models). The main focus lies in the following areas:

3.1 Business Process Design Methods and Tools that Match RPA

First, business process design methods and tools for RPA require qualitative analysis capabilities. For example, which business area the process belongs to, and how the upstream and downstream processes are connected. Second, process modeling capabilities are required. Although the requirements in terms of process diagram generation tools to meet the requirements of RPA development are not complicated, the designer's workload increases and the goal can be achieved through research improvements based on the original process diagram. Finally, business value judging capability is required. By automatically checking the delegation relationship between processes and categorizing and evaluating business processes with different scores, the overall return on investment and feasibility can be effectively assessed to support the implementation. The business design methodology flow is shown in Fig. 1.

3.2 Business Process Mining Tools for RPA Data Quantitative Analyze

Process mining technology can play many roles in the field of RPA. Hu Tao of South China University of technology has made a specific research on the consistency checking algorithm of process mining. Through the consistency checking technology, we can quantitatively calculate the matching between the activities in actual production and the

474   C. Han et al.

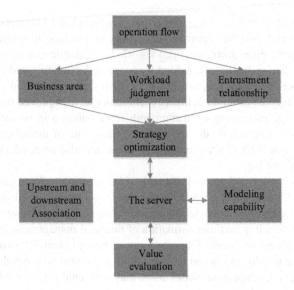

Fig. 1. Business process diagram of matching RPA analysis requirements.

process model, analyze the advantages and disadvantages of the model structure, and provide theoretical support for standardized modeling [7].

In view of the diversity of event logs caused by the complex and changeable operating environment, Yang Liqin and Kang Guosheng of Fudan University used the process mining method based on genetic algorithm to design a business process mining method suitable for a variety of application environments, which solved the application problem of diverse environments, However, how to ensure the correctness of the process model is a problem that needs to be further solved [8]. At the same time, foreign research on process mining is also in full swing. SaaS (software as a server) provided by Celonis, a process mining company, is a product for enterprises to analyze and improve their work processes. It relies on existing ERP (Enterprise Resource Planning) systems such as Salesforce, Sap and Oracle to assist in the analysis of the log data collected. The work process includes extracting data from daily records Find out the key factors and finally reveal the implementation of the company in the business.

4 Reinforcement Learning Based Process Automatic Mining

4.1 Reinforcement Learning

Automatic process discovery starts with process mining. Based on reinforcement learning, the main step is a new application of data mining in workflow management and one of the core elements of financial business process management, mining business processes from the event logs of information systems such as financial control, ERP, warp law, and employee reimbursement in order to establish a process discovery model for financial robots in the power grid industry. This project intends to take the operational behavior profile of financial business personnel as the basis and common financial scenarios as the reference, to deeply study the process mining technology, establish the process discovery model, and realize the automated processing of business processes.

A large amount of semi-structured and unstructured data is generated in the process of system operation and human-machine interaction of financial robots, which is not easy to store but often contains a lot of valuable information. In order to better explore the data value information, we establish a unified data processing scheme based on reinforcement learning principles for unstructured and semi-structured data heterogeneous data in financial scenarios. The focus is on the realization of automatic process mining of semi-structured data and storage and retrieval operations of unstructured data.

4.2 Algorithm Research and Model Establishment

Automatic Process Discovery Technology. As mentioned earlier, the current mainstream robots, which solidify the sorted business rules in the robot designer. Therefore, process auto-discovery technology is essential in intelligent and enhanced financial robots.

Automatic mining model building for high-frequency business processes is established through Model-Based Learning (Model-Based) in reinforcement learning mechanism. Machine learning methods [9, 10] benefit for both related research [11, 12] and applications fields [13, 14] of academic and industry communities in recent years. Reinforcement learning is a branch of machine learning, whose principles are derived from behaviorist theory in psychology, emphasizing environmental change-based to maximize the expected benefits. The Model-Based approach is one of the reinforcement learning mechanisms, which first focuses on environment dynamics by sampling the environment model and then doing value function/strategy optimization based on the learned environment model. In the Model-Based approach, the planning step is crucial, and it is by doing the planning based on the learned model that the efficiency of the whole reinforcement learning algorithm iteration is improved. After completing the modeling of the environment, there are also two paths in the Model-Based approach, one is to generate some simulation trajectories through the learned model, and then optimize the strategy by estimating the value function through the simulation trajectories; the other is to optimize the strategy directly through the learned model, which is also the current route often taken by the Model-Based approach. The more popular is the Model-Based policy optimization series, if the environment model is known, the problem is an optimal control problem; if the environment model is unknown, the optimal solution is obtained by minimizing the mean square error training model and cyclic training model and other algorithms to gradually reduce the error.

Based on the method of Model-Based policy optimization, we design the network self-subject model. By designing office software automation, email automation, document processing automation and browser application automation, we can automate data process mining and analysis to achieve intelligent effect. For finance personnel, they have to deal with a large number of processes and operations every day, and the network self-subject model can extract the processes with high repetitiveness and clear rules from the event logs for finance personnel's daily operations, conduct high-intensity analysis and processing independently, build and verify the automated processes, and verify the

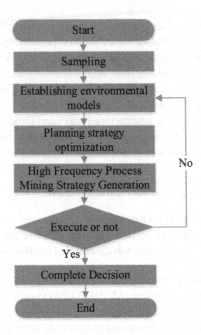

Fig. 2. Model-based policy optimization process.

rationality of the high-frequency process discovery model. The Model-Based policy optimization process is shown in Fig. 2.

In the daily work of finance personnel, besides high-frequency business processes, infrequent business processes are also included. If an intelligent and enhanced finance robot is to be designed, the study of infrequent business processes is also essential. The study of knowledge graph, which is the organization of a large amount of collected data into a knowledge base that can be processed by machines and visualized for presentation, is essentially a large-scale collection of semantic networks whose main purpose is to depict the relationship between entities in the real world through the form of a triad.

The architecture construction of knowledge graph usually includes the processes of data acquisition, knowledge extraction, knowledge fusion, knowledge processing, and knowledge updating. Among them, appropriate knowledge representation techniques are also required from data acquisition to knowledge extraction. Data acquisition techniques are widely used in various fields, and various physical quantities that have been converted into electrical signals are used as the acquired data to collect entity feature values. Finally, the knowledge integration technology is used to reorganize the internal knowledge of the enterprise, remove useless and wrong knowledge, and combine it with the knowledge accumulated by the employees in the enterprise to ensure that the knowledge is well organized and systematic.

After studying the knowledge graph, and algorithmic discretion and screening, the UUV autonomous decision-making technique is used to build an autonomous decision model for infrequent business processes. The knowledge-based UUV autonomous decision model starts from receiving tasks. The autonomous decision system autonomously generates several task scenarios by analyzing the tasks, getting the task requirements, then combining the environmental information obtained by sensors, conducting situation analysis, and querying knowledge such as decision specification constraints, factual constraints and previous successful cases in the knowledge base for prediction. The simulation projection module uses computer simulation technology to simulate and project the decision scheme according to the preset task style template. The effectiveness evaluation and selection module use the predefined effectiveness evaluation model to evaluate each decision solution and finally select the decision solution. If all decision options do not meet the requirements, the system returns to modify the decision options and repeats the process. After completing the mission, the system stores the successful cases as new knowledge in the knowledge base [15]. The UUV autonomous decision process is shown in Fig. 3.

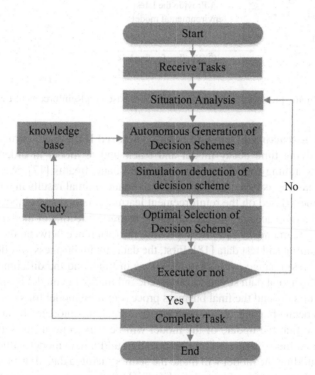

Fig. 3. UUV autonomous decision process.

The establishment of high-frequency business process auto-discovery model and infrequent business process autonomous decision model are two indispensable models in process auto-discovery technology. In this paper, we use Model-Based policy optimization algorithm and UUV autonomous decision technology to explore the process auto-discovery technology in depth, as shown in Fig. 4, and integrate reinforcement learning theory into financial robotics, aiming to break through the traditional robot automation work and further release human resources [16].

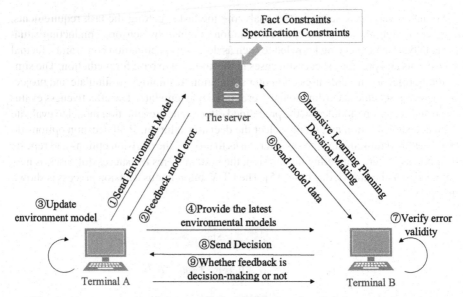

Fig. 4. Automatic process mining of financial robot based on Reinforcement Learning.

Processing of Unstructured Data and Semi-structured Data. Semi-structured data oriented by studying time decay model and batch update model in order to design business process mining model for semi-structured data streams [17]. We know that reinforcement learning is essentially an agent to obtain optimal results in a continuous interaction manner. Based on the reinforcement learning method and objectives, it was decided to build a time decay model to reflect the degree of decline of model metrics on predicted data (i.e., unknown data) by approving the difference between the metrics of the model on training and test data [18]. First, the data stream business is collected, then the business process change extrapolation is done in time, and the difference between the model and the actual data stream is observed, and finally the model is optimized by applying batch update, and the final business process mining model for semi-structured data stream has been obtained. When building the model, it is modeled by an automatic modeling tool so that the update of the model will be very convenient, setting a trigger condition, and the software will automatically build a new model without manual involvement. Building the model will make the semi-structured data flow business more intuitive and enable the study of automatic financial robot process mining methods [19]. The business process mining model building process for semi-structured data streams is shown in Fig. 5.

5   Experiment Results for Process Automatic Mining

5.1   Core Architecture of the Experiment

This research is based on reinforcement learning, and the methods used are all based on reinforcement learning, and the experiments also simulate actual financial scenarios.

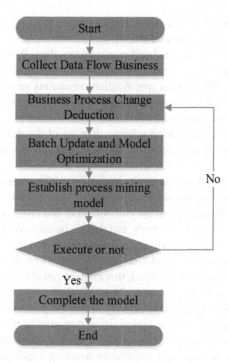

Fig. 5. Establishment of business process mining model.

The core architecture of the experiment is shown in Fig. 6. The core design process is to extract the business process in the event log, get the task requirements, combine the environmental information, through simulation projection and situation analysis, dynamically adjust the terminal server parameters, do prediction with decision specification constraints and factual constraints, and finally evaluate the effectiveness [20]. For each decision solution is evaluated and the final decision solution is selected. If all the decision options do not meet the requirements, then return to modify the decision options and repeat the above process. The experimental results are shown in Fig. 6.

In summary of the above, we present an automatic process mining method for financial robots based on reinforcement learning. This method mainly includes the following six steps:

a) Obtaining the business process information in the event log by sampling to build an environment model, which includes the operational background and the operational environment representing the business or process;

b) Smoothing the collected log data and optimize the value function or strategy for business or process attributes according to the environment model learned after sampling;

c) Establishing a weighting model of primary business decision elements by using the methods of association decision analysis and causal decision analysis, and improving the iteration efficiency of the entire reinforcement learning algorithm by making planning based on the learned model;

d) Dynamic adjustment of terminal server parameters through business criteria, simulation deduction and situation analysis, and algorithm iteration through planning to make predictions with decision specification constraints and fact constraints [21];

e) Evaluating the effectiveness of predictions based on decision-making norm constraints and fact constraints, and evaluating each decision plan;

f) Final choice of decision-making scheme. If none of the decision plans meets the requirements, return to modifying the decision plan and repeat the above process.

This experiment establishes an environmental model by sampling, combining the operational context and operational environment of business processes, using smoothing to process data redundant, business cumbersome, and process complex event logs, effectively extracting normal log records, and using a business decision element weighting model as the primary form of decision optimization, and then iterating through the planning algorithm and business guidelines, etc. for model Optimization [22]. Compared with the traditional model-based method, this method can effectively avoid the random errors generated by normal log records, effectively deal with event logs with complex high and low frequency business, effectively solve the problems of imprecise model optimization and irregular decision optimization that exist in traditional model-based, and compared with automatic process mining in general sense, this method is simpler and training It is more accurate and suitable for handling larger scale data [23].

The purpose of this experiment is to study the automatic process mining method based on reinforcement learning algorithm. The experimental program was developed using JDK1.6 and Eclipse3.4, running on a Windows PC with Intel Xeon 3 GHz CPU and 4G RAM. The core code of the experiment is shown below:

1.	Initialize a policy π_θ and a model f_ϕ.
2.	Initialize an empty dataset D.
3.	**repeat**
4.	Collect samples from the real environment f using π_θ and add them to D.
5.	Train the model f_ϕ using D.
6.	**repeat**
7.	Collect fictitious samples from f_ϕ using π_θ.
8.	Estimate the performance $\eta(\theta; \phi)$.
9.	until the performance stop improving.
10.	until the policy performs well in real environment f.

5.2 Data Analysis of Process Automatic Mining Method

In this experiment, the practicability of reinforcement learning in the process automatic mining method is tested, and the error parameters of gradually determining the decision-making scheme are observed and recorded. See Table 1 for details.

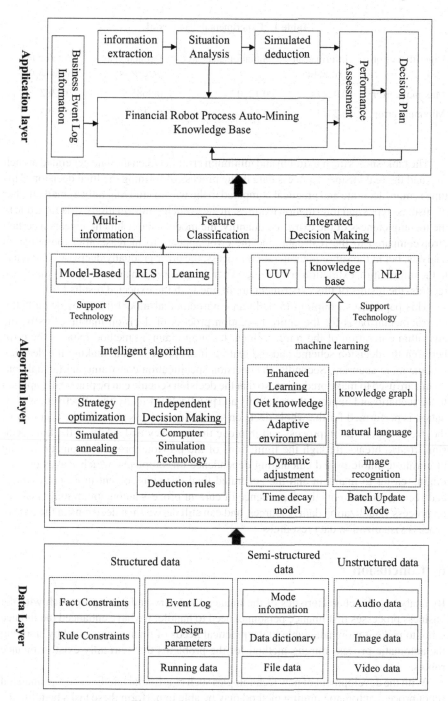

Fig. 6. Experimental core framework.

Table 1. Experimental data record.

Algorithm error	Information extraction	Situation analysis	Deduction and prediction	Analogue simulation
Maximum error	0.0247	0.1220	0.0685	0.0382
Minimum error	0.2514	0.3643	0.3127	0.2785

The table shows the maximum and minimum error between the data generated at each step and the real business process data in the process of forming the final decision. This time is more accurate and practical compared to the way of studying only a small number of business types and information features. In the event log information extraction, due to the incompleteness of the extracted quantity, the model establishment appears a certain error compared to the real data, and the error appears to increase after the situation analysis, but in the subsequent iteration process, the error gradually decreases and tends to the information extraction error value. After the observation and analysis of the above records, the results of this experiment are in line with the expected results [24].

This paper uses sampling to build an environmental model that provides a better environmental basis for the entire formation process of decision making. Firstly, the algorithmic iteration of the reinforcement learning planning method reduces the error between the decision scheme and the real business process data, making the decision scheme more accurate. Secondly, the decision specification constraint and factual constraint are used to make prediction, so that the decision scheme can be practically applied to the scenario and improve the reliability and practicality. Finally, the effectiveness evaluation is performed for the whole decision generation process to verify the accuracy of the decision generation process and improve the accuracy and safety of the final decision. It also breaks through the limitations of the previous process automatic mining of curing technology and calculating dependence on templates, which makes process mining easier to maintain and the generated final decision content more professional and secure; circumvents the dependence of current process automatic mining methods on process visualization data resources, and can still derive final decisions in the case of process visualization data resources.

6   Conclusion

By analyzing the characteristics of the financial industry and getting in touch with the business processes that finance personnel need to handle, we have enhanced the finance robot to make it more adaptable to the practical needs of finance personnel by studying the automatic process mining method for the problems that currently exist in finance robots.

With the development of new technologies such as artificial intelligence, the financial robot process automatic mining method may be able to perform these tasks better in the future, and can better solve the problems of low efficiency of traditional financial robot process planning and limited value of business scenarios to realize the transformation and upgrading of financial management of power grid enterprises and ensure the long-term development of power grid enterprises [25, 26].

References

1. Ma, L., Shen, N., Chen, G.: Application of RPA in the financial field of power grid industry. Technol. Innov. **22**, 16–22 (2018)
2. Sun, Z.: Research and thinking on the application of financial RPA in enterprise groups under the financial sharing mode. Fortune Today **1**, 140–141 (2021)
3. de Jager, C., Nel, M.: Business process automation: a workflow incorporating optical character recognition, approximate string and pattern matching for solving practical industry problems. Appl. Syst. Innov. **2**(4), 210–216 (2019)
4. Zheng, C., Wu, Z., Wen, L.: Detecting concept drift of process models from event logs. Comput. Integr. Manuf. Syst. **25**(4), 830–836 (2019)
5. Hu, X., Wu, Z., Wen, L.: Parallel distributed process mining algorithm based on spark. Comput. Integr. Manuf. Syst. **25**(4), 791–797 (2019)
6. Xie, J.: Research on human-computer interaction oriented natural language understanding. Univ. Sci. Technol. China **1**, 1–90 (2015)
7. Hu, T.: Research on consistency checking algorithm of process mining. South China Univ. Technol. **1**, 1–63 (2015)
8. Yang, L.Q., et al.: Process mining approach for diverse application environments. J. Softw. **26**(3), 550–561 (2015)
9. Gao, X., Hoi, S.C.H., Zhang, Y., et al.: Sparse online learning of image similarity. ACM Trans. Intell. Syst. Technol. **8**(5), 64:1–64:22 (2017)
10. Zhang, Y., Gao, X., Chen, Z., et al.: Mining spatial-temporal similarity for visual tracking. IEEE Trans. Image Process. **29**, 8107–8119 (2020)
11. Xia, Z., Hong, X., Gao, X., et al.: Spatiotemporal recurrent convolutional networks for recognizing spontaneous micro-expressions. IEEE Trans. Multimed. **22**(3), 626–640 (2020)
12. Gao, X., Hoi, S.C.H., Zhang, Y., et al.: SOML: sparse online metric learning with application to image retrieval. In: Twenty-Eighth AAAI Conference on Artificial Intelligence, pp. 1206–1212 (2014)
13. Zhang, Y., Gao, X., Chen, Z., et al.: Learning salient features to prevent model drift for correlation tracking. Neurocomputing **418**, 1–10 (2020)
14. Tang, G., Gao, X., Chen, Z., Zhong, H.: Unsupervised adversarial domain adaptation with similarity diffusion for person re-identification. Neurocomputing **442**, 337–347 (2021)
15. Yu, S., Yao, Y.: Research on autonomous decision-making technology for UUV based on knowledge graph. In: 8th China Command and Control Conference, pp. 425–428. Chinese Institute of Command and Control, Beijing (2020)
16. Boserp, J.C., Vanderaalst, W., Zliobaitei, I.: Dealing with concept drifts in processing mining. IEEE Trans. Neural Netw. Learn. Syst. **25**(1), 154–171 (2014)
17. Weijtes, T., Maruster, L.: Workflow mining: discovering process models from event logs. IEEE Trans. Knowl. Data Eng. **16**(9), 1128–1142 (2004)
18. Weidlich, M., Mendling, J., Weske, M.: Efficient consistency measurement based on behavioral profiles of process models. IEEE Trans. Softw. Eng. **37**(3), 410–429 (2011)
19. Zha, H., Wang, J., Wen, L.: A workflow net similarity measure based on transition adjacency relations. Comput. Ind. **61**(5), 463–471 (2010)
20. Li, B., Wen, M., Li, B.: Research of the scheme for SV direct sampling and GOOSE transmit in the same port in new generation smart substation. Power Syst. Prot. Control **2**(1), 96–101 (2014)

484   C. Han et al.

21. Wang, X., Xu, L., Li, X.: Design and realization of GOOSE decoding module based on FPGA. Power Syst. Prot. Control **43**(24), 101–107 (2015)
22. Cai, T., Li, W., Xie, X.: Condition monitoring and analysis system for intelligent substation functional loop. East China Electric Power **42**(10), 2100–2104 (2014)
23. Wu, G., Cheng, Z., Hao, S.: Application scheme of intelligent substation switch value multi-device sharing. Power Syst. Prot. Control **43**(10), 144–148 (2015)
24. Yang, Y., Gao, X., Zhu, H.: Case study on SCD application based on demo smart substation. Power Syst. Prot. Control **43**(22), 107–113 (2015)
25. Liu, W., Wang, H., Zhang, Y.: Study on message characteristics and communication configuration of process layer network of intelligent substation. Power Syst. Prot. Control **42**(6), 110–115 (2014)
26. Nadeau, D., Sekine, S.: A survey of named entity recognition and classification. Lingvisticæ Investigationes **30**(1), 3–26 (2007)

Enabling Reliable and Secure Data Query Services for the Power Utilities

Qiheng Yuan$^{(\boxtimes)}$, Yingjie Ren, Shenglong Liu, Jingwei Liu, Gang Wang,
Zhongyi Shang, Haifeng Liu, and Xiyang Liu

Big Data Center, State Grid Corporation of China, Beijing, China
yuanqiheng123@gmail.com

Abstract. Data confidentiality and reliable permission management
have always been primary concerns that hinder enterprise customers
from adopting data services of three-party professional providers (e.g.,
Amazon AWS). This situation is especially prominent in the State Grid
Corporation of China (SGCC), in which the data is particularly sensitive.
Accordingly, we hope only authorized users have access to the expected
data, while unauthorized entities, including cloud service providers and
unapproved internal staff, know nothing about the data. In SGCC, we
utilize cloud facilities to maintain our data, and multifold efforts have
been made to achieve these requirements. Specifically, for reliable authority management and access control, we devise an authority separation
mechanism; the data is stored in encrypted form, and we design a set of
mechanisms to enable search and query on encrypted data using searchable encryption and homomorphic encryption. In this paper, we present
architectures, designs, and experiences in launching our systems.

Keywords: Database services · Query processing · Homomorphic
encryption · Authority separation mechanism

1 Introduction

Managing large amounts of data *securely* and *efficiently* has always been an
essential task for the State Grid [28]. Traditionally, access control and permission
management methods have been deployed to protect sensitive data, *e.g.,* users'
personal private information, management personnel information, and financial
information. However, their limited security guarantees make them vulnerable to
attacks, which normally result in terrible consequence [1]. Hence, a more rigorous
method, encryption, is generally taken as a promising solution.

In practice, however, applying cryptography methods for database protection
is in the face of two challenges, which seriously hinder their feasibility. First,
encryption disables any parties to manipulate the data. This implies that any
data query requires the users first to download the entire database, then decrypt
it locally, and conduct data queries on the decrypted data. Downloading the
entire data lies a huge burden for the network transmission. Second, this workflow

© Springer Nature Singapore Pte Ltd. 2022
G. Zhai et al. (Eds.): IFTC 2021, CCIS 1560, pp. 485–499, 2022.
https://doi.org/10.1007/978-981-19-2266-4_37

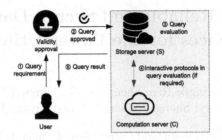

Fig. 1. Architecture and workflow of the data query system.

presents high requirements for the client – it requires each client to have enough storage space to hold the data and has the computational capability to perform queries on the entire dataset (Fig. 1).

Thus, we expect to design a scheme that can perform queries on the encrypted data directly, *i.e.*, do not reveal the data to the server and without downloading the data. Depending on the data type, queries can be divided into two main categories: character-oriented data query and numerical data query. Specifically, a keyword-oriented search is performed to obtain records/data entries containing specific keywords (*e.g.*, to find information on experts whose research interests are "smart grid" and "superconducting DC" in the expert database). On the other hand, when we want to query a specific record to satisfy certain numerical characteristics (*i.e.*, querying the oldest employee with more than 25 years of project review experience), we need to perform calculations (including numerical operations and data comparisons) on specific data records, etc.

In this paper, we build a complete encrypted database query scheme that supports the most common queries. Specifically, for queries that rely only on addition operations, we adopt a somewhat homomorphic encryption scheme to encrypt the data so that the server can perform queries directly on the ciphertext. For complex queries that rely on multiplication operations, we adopt a dual-server architecture, in which two servers that store encrypted data independently work together to make queries. Moreover, we devise an Authority Separation mechanism further to restrict the data exploration of the cloud server, so that the relevant third-party department must approve the user before querying and using the data. Based on the proposed framework, we can mitigate the risk of information leakages caused by unreliable management and employees while maintaining the usability of sensitive data.

2   Preliminary

2.1   Basic Cryptographic Tools

The BCP Crypto-System. BCP cryptosytem [12,23] is quin-tuple (Setup, KeyGen, Enc, Dec and mDec) that consists of the following algorithms:

SetUp(κ): for the security parameter κ, choose a safe prime RSA -modulus $N = qp$ of bit κ, s.t. $p = 2p' + 1$ and $q = 2q' + 1$ for distinct prime p' and q'. Pick a random element $g \in \mathbb{Z}_{N^2}^*$ of order $pp'qq'$ s.t. $g^{p'q'} \mod N^2 = 1 + kN$.

The plaintext space of the crypto-system is $\mathbb{Z}^*$. This algorithm output the public parameters $\texttt{PP} = (N, k, g)$ and the master key is $\texttt{MK}=(p'q')$.

$\texttt{KeyGen(PP)}$: the key generation algorithm which take the public parameter as input and out put the *secret/public* key pairs. For each public-secret key pair, it firstly randomly pick $a \in \mathbb{Z}_{N^2}$ and computes $h = g^a \mod N^2$ and then our put the public key $\texttt{pk} = h$ and secret key $\texttt{sk} = a$.

$\texttt{Enc}_{(\texttt{PP,pk})}(m)$: the encryption algorithm which take the plaintext, the public key and public parameters as input and output the ciphertext. The algorithm firstly pick a random $r \in \mathbb{Z}_{N^2}$ and generate the ciphertext (α, β) as:

$$\alpha = g^r \mod N^2 \text{ and } \beta = h^{(}1 + mN) \mod N^2$$

$\texttt{Dec}_{(\texttt{PP,sk})}(PP)$: the regular decryption algorithm that take the ciphertext, the secret key and public parameters as input and output its corresponding plaintext. In terms a key pair $\texttt{pk} = g^a \mod N^2$ $\texttt{sk}=a$, the ciphertext (α, β), it output the plaintext as:

$$m = \frac{\dfrac{\beta}{\alpha^a} - 1 \mod N^2}{N}$$

$\texttt{mDec}_{(\texttt{PP,pk,mk})}(\alpha, \beta)$: the alternative decryption algorithm which take the public key, the master key, the ciphertext and public parameters as input and output the corresponding plaintext. It first computed $a \mod N$ as:

$$a \mod N = \frac{h^{p'q'} - 1 \mod N^2}{N} \cdot k^{-1} \mod N$$

in which k^{-1} denotes the inverse of k modulo N. Then compute $r \mod N$ as

$$r \mod N = \frac{A^{p'q'} - 1 mod N^2}{N} k^{-1} \mod N$$

Then let δ denote the inverse of $p'q'$ modulo N and compute $\gamma = ar \mod N$. The plaintext is finally computed as

$$m = \frac{(\dfrac{\beta}{g^\gamma})^{p'q'} - 1 \mod N^2}{N} \cdot \delta \mod N$$

The BCP Crypto system has flowing special properties.

1. **Additive Homomorphism.** For the cipertext encrypted using the same public key, the BCP crytosystem satisfies the addictive homomorphism.
2. **Key Homomorphism.** The key homomorphism refers to the property that, if a plaintext is encrypted with the public key $pk = pk_1 \times pk_2$, it can be successfully decrypted with the secret key $sk = sk_1 + sk_2$. Formally, it satisfies

$$m = Dec_{sk_1+sk_2}[Enc_{pk_1+pk_2}(m))]$$

3. **Double Trapdoor.** The BCP cryptosystem provides two independent mechanisms for decryption. Except for decrypting a ciphertext (encrypted with public key p_i) with the corresponding secret key (*i.e.*, sk_i) as the traditional public key cryptosystem does, the BCP cryptosystem allows a master to hold the master key and decrypt ciphertext encrypted by any public-key without knowing its corresponding secret key (*i.e.*, the second trapdoor).

The Goldwasser–Micali Cryptosystem is a bitwise probabilistic (semantically secure) public key encryption scheme based on the quadratic residuosity assumption. It satisfies the additive homomorphic property over $\mathbb{Z}_2$. That is, for two plaintext bit m_1 and $m_2 \in \{0,1\}$,

$$Enc(m_1) \cdot Enc(m_2) \mod N = Enc(m_1 \oplus m_2)$$

As its special bitwise homomorphism, the Goldwasser-Micali Cryptosystem is often used as a basic building block to construct high-level primitives.

2.2 Symbols and Notations

For a plaintext $a \in \mathbb{Z}_{N^2}$ we use $Enc_{pk_A}(a)$ to denote its corresponding ciphertext encrypted by the BCP cryptosystem with public key pk_A. If we do not care which public key is used in encryption, we use [a] to represent the ciphertext of a for short. For a plaintext $b \in \mathbb{Z}_2$, we use $\|b\|$ to denote the corresponding ciphertext encrypted with the Goldwasser-Micali encryption algorithm.

3 Scheme Description

3.1 System Architecture High Level Description

This scheme adopts two non-collusive servers – the storage server $\mathcal{S}$ and the (auxiliary) computing server $\mathcal{C}$. The whole database is stored in server $\mathcal{S}$, and each sensitive attribute (column) is encrypted using BCP cryptosystem with a separate public key, whereas the non-sensitive columns remain in plaintext form. This public key is also stored in the server S along with the ciphertext of this column. The computing server holds the master key mk of the BCP cryptosystem, whereas no data is stored on the computing server.

Operation Modes. As some columns are encrypted whereas some are not, we denote inter-column operations between an encrypted and an unencrypted column as the **[EP]** mode and denote inter-column operations in two encrypted columns as **[EE]** mode. If there is no sensitive column involved, the database management system will execute operations as in the traditional manner, and in this paper, we will not discuss this case. For each operation, if the serve $\mathcal{S}$ gets the encrypted result (which is either used for further operations such as aggregation or used as a final classified result), we denote this case as **[→E]** mode. Likewise, if the serve $\mathcal{S}$ gets the plaintext result (which is normally used for data retrieval such as select clause), we denote this case as **[→P]** mode.

3.2 Scheme Construction

Aggregation. The SUM() operation considers the setting that, given k values $a_1, a_2, ..., a_k$ in one column, it requires to compute the sum $\sigma_a = \sum_{i=1}^{k} a_i$ It serves as the basic step for other aggregation operations such as AGV(), COUNT(), etc.

Actually, as the addictive homomorphism of the BCP cryptosystem, the sum operation within a column can simply achieved by $\mathcal{S}$ independently, without the computing server $\mathcal{C}$ involved.

Addition. [EP→E mode] Given an encrypted column A encrypted with public key pk_A and a non-sensitive column B in the plaintext form, we want to compute the column $C = A + B$, such that each item in C is in encrypted form and can be decrypted with secret key sk_A. Specifically, if a is the element in i-th row of column A and b is the element in i-th row of column B, we want to get c such that $Enc(c) = Enc(a+b)$ This can be achieved by the following two steps (*i.e.*, entire done by $\mathcal{S}$ without interaction)

- Encrypt b with public key pk_A, which will result in $Enc_{pk_A}(b)$.
- based on the addictive homomorphism of the BCP cryptosystem, compute $Enc_{pk_A}(c) = Enc_{pk_A}(a) \cdot Enc_{pk_A}(b)$

[EE →E mode] we want to compute the column $C = A + B$, s.t. each item in C is in encrypted form and can be decrypted by an individual secret key sk_C.

Algorithm 1. The cross-column addition in EE→E mode

Input: The storage server $\mathcal{S}$ holds encrypted column A and B, as well as its corresponding keys pk_A and pk_B; The computing server $\mathcal{C}$ holds the master key mk

Output: Server $\mathcal{S}$ gets the encrypted column C

1: Server $\mathcal{S}$:
2: $pk_C = pk_A \cdot pk_B mod N^2$;
3: **for** i=1 to n **do**
4:    $r_i \xleftarrow{\$} \mathbb{Z}_N$;
5:    $\tau_i \xleftarrow{\$} \mathbb{Z}_N$;
6:    $c_i = \text{ADD}(Enc_{pk_A}(a_i), Enc_{pk_A}(r_i))$;
7:    $d_i = \text{ADD}(Enc_{pk_B}(b_i), Enc_{pk_B}(\tau_i))$;
8: **end for**
9: $C = (c_1, c_2, ..., c_n)$ $D = (d_1, d_2, ..., d_n)$;
10: send pk_A, pk_B, C and D to $\mathcal{C}$;
11: Server $\mathcal{C}$:
12: $pk_C = pk_A \cdot pk_B \ mod N^2$;
13: **for** i=1 to n **do**
14:    $x_i = mDec_{(pk_A, mk)}(c_i)$;
15:    $d_i = mDec_{(pk_b, mk)}(d_i)$;
16:    $z_i = Enc_{pk_C}(x_i + y_i)$;
17: **end for**
18: $Z = (z_1, z_2, ..., z_i)$;
19: send Z to $\mathcal{C}$;
20: Server $\mathcal{C}$:
21: **for** i=1 to n **do**
22:    $e_i = \text{ADD}(z_i, Enc_{pk_C}(-r_i))$;
23:    $t_i = \text{ADD}(e_i, Enc_{pk_B}(-\tau_i))$;
24: **end for**
25: **Output** $T = (t_1, t_2, ..., t_n)$

Multiplication. [EP→E mode] In this setting, given a sensitive column A encrypted by BCP-cryptosystem with public key pk and a none-sensitive column X in plaintext form (with x denoting an item in column X), we want to compute B such that $B = AX$.

Recall that the ciphertext of m under the BCP encryption is in the form of $c = Enc(m) = (\alpha, \beta)$, in which $\alpha = g^r mod \ N^2$ and $\beta = h^r(1 + mN) mod \ N^2$. Thus when multiplay a constant x into the ciphertext c, the storage server just computer $c' = <\alpha^x, \beta^x>$, which will get the ciphertext of xm.(as proved below).

$$xc = <\alpha^x, \beta^x>$$

Algorithm 2. The cross-column multiplication in EE→ E mode

Input: The storage server $\mathcal{S}$ holds encrypted column A and B, as well as its corresponding keys pk_A and pk_B; The computing server $\mathcal{C}$ holds the master key mk

Output: Server $\mathcal{S}$ gets the encrypted column C

1: Server $\mathcal{S}$:
2: $m = \text{ADD}([a], Enc_{pk_A}(-r_1))$;
3: $n = \text{ADD}([b], Enc_{pk_A}(-r_2))$;
4: send pk_A, pk_B, m and n to $\mathcal{C}$;
5: Server $\mathcal{C}$:
6: $pk_C = pk_A \times pk_B$;
7: $x = mDec_{(pk_A, mk)}(m)$;
8: $y = mDec_{(pk_B, mk)}(n)$;
9: $z = Enc_{pk_A}(m \times n)$;
10: send z to Server $\mathcal{S}$:

11: Server $\mathcal{S}$:
12: At this phase the server $\mathcal{S}$ aquires CT_0–the ciphertext of $ab - ar_2 - br_1 + r_1r_2$ encrypted under public key pk_C
13: compute $CT_a = Enc_{pk_A}(ar_2), CT_b = Enc_{pk_B}(br_1)$
14: send CT_a, CT_b to the Server $\mathcal{C}$
15: Server $\mathcal{C}$ decrypt the CT_a and CT_b, re-encrypt them with pk_C, getting CT_a' and CT_b', the ciphertext of ar_2 and br_1 encrypted with the public key pk_C
16: send CT_a' and CT_b' to Server $\mathcal{S}$
17: Server $\mathcal{S}$:
18: $CT_{rr} = Enc_{pk_c}(r_1r_2)$
19: $CT = CT_0 + CT_a' + CT_b' - CT_{rr}$
20: **Output** CT

$$\alpha = g^r mod\ N^2, \beta = h^2(1 + mN) mod\ N^2$$

$$\alpha^a = g^{rax} mod\ N^2$$

$$\frac{\beta^x}{\alpha^{xa}} = \frac{h^{xr}(1 + mN)^x mod\ N2}{g^{rxa} mod\ N^2} = \frac{g^{xar}(1 + mN)^x mod\ N2}{g^{rxa} mod\ N^2} =$$

$$(1 + mN)^x mod\ N^2 = (1 + xmN + C_x^2 mN^2 + ...) mod N^2 = (1 + xmN) mod\ N^2$$

$$Dec = \frac{\frac{\beta^x}{\alpha^{xa}} - 1 mod\ N^2}{N} mod N^2 = \frac{xmN}{N} mod\ N^2 = xm$$

[EE→E mode] Given an encrypted column A (encrypted with pk_A) and column B (encrypted with pk_B), we want to computed $C = A \times B$, such that C is in the encrypt form and can be decrypted by a separate key sk_C. Recall that the ciphertext of BCP cryptosystem is in the form like $< \alpha, \beta >$. We denote the i-th item in column A as $[a] = < \alpha, \beta >$ and the i-th item in column B as $[b] = < \alpha', \beta' >$. The output $[c]$ of Algorithm 2 (*i.e.*, CT) is the ciphertext of $a \times b$ that can be decrypted with secret key $sk_C = sk_A + sk_B$.

Comparison. For the functionality of secure comparison protocol, the server $\mathcal{S}$ holds two values (either both in encrypted form, or one in encrypted and the other in unencrypted form) and hopes to know the relationship (*i.e.*, whether $a \leq b$ or not) among the two numbers. Normally, the server $\mathcal{C}$ is an external service provider that concentrates on providing auxiliary computing service (especially cryptographic operation). Thus, as one design principle, we hope the server $\mathcal{C}$ gets as little information as possible.

As the server $\mathcal{S}$ holds the BCP public key of each column, both EE or EP mode can be transformed to EE mode.

Table 1. Functionality of comparison protocols.

The protocols	Inputs of $\mathcal{S}$	Inputs of $\mathcal{C}$	Protocols' Output
P1: Comparing encrypted data enrypted by same key with plaintext comparison output	$pk, sk_{QR}, [a], [b]$	mk, pk_{QR}	$(a \leq b)?$
P2: Comparing encrypted data enrypted by same key with encrypted comparison output	$pk, pk_{QR}, [a], [b]$	mk, sk_{QR}	$\|(a \leq b)?\|$
P3: Comparing encrypted data enrypted by different keys with plaintext comparison output	$pk_A, pk_B, sk_{QR}, [a], [b]$	mk, pk_{QR}	$(a \leq b)?$
P4: Comparing encrypted data enrypted by different keys with encrypted comparison output	$pk_A, pk_B, pk_{QR}, [a], [b]$	mk, sk_{QR}	$\|(a \leq b)?\|$
P5: Changing encryption schemes	$pk_{QR}, \|t\|$	mk, sk_{QR}	$\|t\|$
P6: Equality test	$pk_A, pk_B, pk_{QR}, [a], [b]$	mk, sk_{QR}	$\|(a = b)\|?$

[**EE→E mode**] Get the BCP-encrypted comparison result, which is normally used for SELECT COUNT(*).

[**EE→P mode**] Get the comparison result in plaintext form. Normally used for directly retrieve the tuples that satisfy the query condition (*e.g.,* SELECT COUNT * where *Production* ≤ *Sells*).

The functionality of comparison protocols in different modes is listed in Table 1.

Equality Test. Similar to the comparison protocol, all cases can be converted to equality test among two encrypted ciphertexts (either encrypted in the same or different keys). As demonstrated in Sect. 3.2, we have composed protocols for encrypted ciphertext comparison, *i.e.,* for two encrypted items $[a]$ and $[b]$, the server $\mathcal{S}$ can get the encrypted or unencrypted bit t indicating whether $a \leq b$. In order to determine whether $a = b$, the servers firstly run the comparison protocol to get the encrypted bit $\|t_1\|$, indicating whether $a \leq b$; and then, ran the comparison to get the encrypted bit $\|t_2\|$ indicating whether $b \leq b$. Note that, during the excursion of these two protocol, the server $\mathcal{S}$ get the encrypt bits whereas the server $\mathcal{C}$ get no information about a and b. Then the server $\mathcal{S}$ computer $\|t\| = \|t_1\| \cdot \|t_2\|$, which equals to $\|t_1 \oplus t_2\|$, and $t_1 \oplus t_2 = 1$ if and only if $t_1 = t_2$ (*i.e.,* when $a \leq b$ and $b \leq a$ satisfies simultaneously, indicating $a = b$).

After acquiring the QR-encrypted comparison result, if we want to get the plaintext of the result, the server $\mathcal{S}$ first generate a random bit τ and blind the QR-encrypted $\|t\|$ with τ and send the blind result to server $\mathcal{C}$. Then, the server $\mathcal{C}$ decrypted the blind equality test result and sent back the decrypted result to $\mathcal{S}$, which will afterward remove the blind factor τ and get the result in plaintext setting (Algorithm 8). Likewise, if the server is required to get BCP encrypted result, then we apply the *Chenging Encryption Schemes* (Algorithm 9).

Unlike theirs, in our scheme, each column is encrypted with BCP cryptosystem of independent keys, and the randomness of each ciphertext is derived from

---

Algorithm 3. Comparing same BCP-key encrypted data with plaintext output

Input:
1: Server $\mathcal{S}$: $pk_A, pk_B, sk_{QR}, [a], [b]$
2: Server $\mathcal{C}$: mk, pk_{QR}
Output: $\mathcal{S}$ get $(a \leq b)$?
3: Server $\mathcal{S}$:
4: $[x] \leftarrow [2^l] \cdot [b] \cdot [a]^{-1} mod\ N^2$;
5: $r \xleftarrow{\$} \{0,1\}^{l+\lambda}$;
6: $[z] \leftarrow [x] \cdot [r]\ mod\ N^2$
7: sent $[z]$ to $\mathcal{C}$;
8: Server $\mathcal{C}$:
9: $z = mDec([z])$;
10: Server $\mathcal{S} : c \leftarrow r\ mod\ 2^l$;
11: Server $\mathcal{C} : d \leftarrow z\ mod\ 2^l$;

12: Using another comparison protocol (DGK protocol) to get $\|t'\|$ (*i.e.*, the ciphertext of t' with Goldwasser-Micali cryptosystem), s.t.

$$t' = \begin{cases} 1, if\ c<d \\ 0, otherwise \end{cases}$$

13: $\mathcal{S}$: encrypt the l-th bit of r getting $\|r_l\|$ and send $\|r_l\|$ to $\mathcal{C}$;
14: $\mathcal{C}$: encrypt the l-th bit of z getting $\|z_l\|$
15: Compute $\|t\| \leftarrow \|t'\| \cdot \|z_l\| \cdot \|r_l\|$
16: send $\|t\|$ to $\mathcal{S}$
17: $\mathcal{S}$: decrypt $\|t\|$ and get the result t

---

the cryptosystem itself. In this way, a random number does not exist that influences all the encrypted data items in a whole tuple, and thus, the Cartesian product is natively supported. Joint is actually performing selection operation on the Cartesian product, and accordingly, it is natively supported.

4   Performance Evaluation

We deployed our system on top of Amazon AWS and Aliyun and conducted a comprehensive performance evaluation of our scheme. Specifically, we deploy the storage server (*i.e.*, server $\mathcal{S}$) on a standard VM (with a dual-core CPU @2.5 GHz, 32-GB memory, and 256-GB SSD storage) rented from Amazon EC2 located at N. Virginia datacenter. The computing server (*i.e.*, server $\mathcal{C}$) is run on Aliyun (Silicon Valley datacenter). Both server $\mathcal{S}$ and server $\mathcal{C}$ are connected with a high-bandwidth network. Our experiments are designed to answer the following two questions:
Q1: What is the efficiency of the building blocks, and
Q2: How practical our proposed method is for typical database query workloads.

To answer Q1 we implement each cryptographic primitive with C++, and we adopt the GMP(https://gmplib.org) and NTL (http://www.shoup.net/ntl/) library for large integer representation and algebraic manipulation. To answer question Q2, we build a prototype based on our design. We use MySQL 5.7.19 as the underlying DBMS. To examine the performance of our scheme in the general setting, we conducted the evaluation with the TPC-H benchmark.

Performance of Each Cryptographic Primitive. We tested each building block used in our scheme (*i.e.*, used in query evaluation). In our experiment, we run the aforementioned algorithms/protocols 50 times and record their average exerting time in Table 2. From Table 2 we can see that all the building blocks

Algorithm 4. Comparing data encrypted by same BCP-key with QR-encrypted comparison output

Input:
1: Server $\mathcal{S}$: $pk_A, pk_B, pk_{QR}, [a], [b]$
2: Server $\mathcal{C}$: mk, sk_{QR}
Output: $\mathcal{S}$ get $\|(a \le b)?\|$
3: Server $\mathcal{S}$:
4: $[x] \leftarrow [2^l] \cdot [b] \cdot [a]^{-1} mod\ N^2$;
5: $r \xleftarrow{\$} \{0,1\}^{l+\lambda}$;
6: $[z] \leftarrow [x] \cdot [r]\ mod\ N^2$
7: sent $[z]$ to $\mathcal{C}$;
8: Server $\mathcal{C}$:
9: $z = mDec([z])$;
10: Server $\mathcal{S} : c \leftarrow r\ mod\ 2^l$;
11: Server $\mathcal{C} : d \leftarrow z\ mod\ 2^l$;

12: Using another comparison protocol (DGK protocol) the server get the $\|t'\|$(*i.e.,* the ciphertext of t' with Goldwasser-Micali cryptosystem), s.t.

$$t' = \begin{cases} 1, if\ c < d \\ 0, otherwise \end{cases}$$

13: $\mathcal{S}$: encrypt the l-th bit of r getting $\|r_l\|$;
14: $\mathcal{C}$: encrypt the l-th bit of z getting $\|z_l\|$ and send $\|z_l\|$ to $\mathcal{S}$;
15: $\mathcal{S}$ compute $\|t\| \leftarrow \|t'\| \cdot \|z_l\| \cdot \|r_l\|$

Table 2. Overhead of each cryptographic algorithm and protocol.

Protocals	$\mathcal{S}$ (ms)	$\mathcal{C}$ (ms)	Network lattency
Homomorphic add	0.74	0.00	0.00
Cross-column add in [EP → E] mode	1.22	0.00	0.00
Cross-column add in [EE→E] mode	4.31	1.12	204.7
Cross-column multiplication in [EP→E] mode	2.53	0.00	0.00
Cross-column multiplication in [EE→E] mode	5.56	4.37	832.1
Comparison in [EE→E] mode	8.43	0.00	0.00
Comparison in [EE→p] mode	4.87	1.77	243.1
Fast comparison	2.21	2.11	242.8
Equality test	9.11	9.72	1523.4
Changing encryption scheme	4.43	2.21	265.4

can be finished in millisecond-level, which indicates that they are efficiently constructed and can be used to build practical query evaluation schemes on an encrypted database.

The TPC-H Benchmark. We run our scheme on TPC-H (version 3.0) benchmark (http://www.tpc.org/tpch). Meanwhile, we also compare the performance of our scheme with CryptDB, a state-of-the-art system for encrypted database queries. There are 22 decision-support queries named Q1 to Q22 in the TPC-H workload, and we select Q1-18 to present the performance evaluation. Among them, some of the workloads (*e.g.,* Q13 and Q16) are so complicated that they cannot be run on both our scheme and CryptDB in encrypted form. We record the running time of each workload and record the total time consumption on Table 3. In general, encrypted data query in both our system and CryptDB takes

Algorithm 5. Comparing data encrypted by different BCP keys with plaintext output

---

Input:
1: Server $\mathcal{S}$: $pk_A, pk_B, sk_{QR}, [a], [b]$
2: Server $\mathcal{C}$: mk, pk_{QR}
Output: $\mathcal{S}$ get $(a \le b)$?
3: Server $\mathcal{S}$:
4: $r_1, r_2 \xleftarrow{\$} \{0,1\}^{l+\lambda}$
5: $[x] = [a] \cdot Enc_{pk_A}(r_1)$
6: $[y] = [b] \cdot Enc_{pk_B}(r_2)$;
7: Sent $[x]$ and $[y]$ to $\mathcal{C}$
8: Server $\mathcal{C}$:
9: $x = mDec_{(mk, pk_A)}([x])$;
10: $y = mDec_{(mk, pk_B)}([y])$;
11: $z = 2^l + y - x$;
12: $d = z \mod 2^l$;
13: Send z to $\mathcal{S}$
14: Server $\mathcal{S}$:
15: $r = r_2 - r_1$;
16: $c = r \mod 2^l$;

17: Using another comparison protocol (DGK protocol) to get $\|t'\|$ (*i.e.*, the ciphertext of t' with Goldwasser-Micali cryptosystem),s.t.

$$t' = \begin{cases} 1, if \ c<d \\ 0, \text{otherwise} \end{cases}$$

18: Server $\mathcal{S}$:
19: encrypt the l-th bit of r getting $\|r_l\|$ and send $\|r_l\|$ to $\mathcal{C}$;
20: Server $\mathcal{C}$:
21: encrypt the l-th bit of z getting $\|z_l\|$;
22: Compute $\|t\| \leftarrow \|t'\| \cdot \|z_l\| \cdot \|r_l\|$
23: send $\|t\|$ to $\mathcal{S}$
24: Server $\mathcal{S}$: decrypt $\|t\|$ and get the comparison result t

---

Table 3. Performance of our scheme under TPC-H workload, compared with CryptDB; "–" denotes the corresponding system cannot work on this workload.

Benchmark	Q1	Q2	Q3	Q4	Q5	Q6	Q7	Q8	Q9
Plaintext	121.51	64.44	81.23	45.33	176.32	62.32	291.27	201.29	672.01
CryptoDB	4860.22	148.23	332.12	182.23	534.34	582.21	973.32	523.23	2932.21
Our scheme	3731.98	127.23	1623.32	164.71	201.23	1243.32	628.23	667.23	2123.21
Benchmark	Q10	Q11	Q12	Q13	Q14	Q15	Q16	Q17	Q18
Plaintext	132.42	56.73	71.20	398.22	72.34	64.23	41.22	3423.32	1187.23
CryptoDB	542.23	263.12	362.12	–	534.32	–	–	17342.66	73238.78
Our scheme	412.31	59.23	372.81	–	342.23	372.23	–	12029.30	36439.91

several times (less than 10 ×) than query on plaintext setting. Only a few of them take longer times (*e.g.*, Q1, Q17 and Q18), but still less than 100× of plaintext data query. Most importantly, we can also see that our scheme achieves a better performance than CryptDB in most cases.

5 Related Works

Encrypted Database. The notion of executing SQL query on encrypted relational database was firstly considered by Hacigümüş *et al.* [16]. They proposed a prospective architecture in which the client outsources his encrypted database along with some additional auxiliary information (*i.e.*, serves as a secure index)

Algorithm 6. Comparing data encrypted by different BCP-key with QR-encrypted comparison output

---

Input:
1: Server $\mathcal{S}$: $pk_A, pk_B, pk_{QR}, [a], [b]$
2: Server $\mathcal{C}$: mk, sk_{QR}
Output: $\mathcal{S}$ get $\|(a \leq b)?\|$
3: Server $\mathcal{S}$:
4: $r_1, r_2 \xleftarrow{\$} \{0,1\}^{l+\lambda}$;
5: $[x] = [a] \cdot Enc_{pk_A}(r_1)$;
6: $[y] = [b] \cdot Enc_{pk_B}(r_2)$;
7: Sent $[x]$ and $[y]$ to $\mathcal{C}$
8: Server $\mathcal{C}$:
9: $x = mDec_{(mk,pk_A)}([x])$;
10: $y = mDec_{(mk,pk_B)}([y])$;
11: $z = 2^l + y - x$;
12: $d = z \mod 2^l$;
13: Send z to $\mathcal{S}$
14: Server $\mathcal{S}$:

15: $r = r_2 - r_1$;
16: $c = r \mod 2^l$;
17: Using another comparison protocol (DGK protocol) the server get the $\|t'\|$(*i.e.*, the ciphertext of t' with Goldwasser-Micali cryptosystem), s.t.

$$t' = \begin{cases} 1 & if \ c{\mathrel{\hat{}}}d \\ 0 & otherwise \end{cases}$$

18: Server$\mathcal{S}$: encrypt the l-th bit of r getting $\|r_l\|$;
19: Server $\mathcal{C}$: encrypt the l-th bit of z getting $\|z_l\|$ and send it to $\mathcal{S}$;
20: Server $\mathcal{S}$: compute $\|t\| \leftarrow \|t'\| \cdot \|z_l\| \cdot \|r_l\|$

Algorithm 7. Equality Test (protocol 4)

Output: $\mathcal{S}$ get $\|u\| = (a = b?)$
1: Using protocol 2 to compute $\|u_1\|$, which is the comparison result of $(a \leq b?)$ encrypted under QR.
2: Using protocol 2 to compute $\|u_2\|$, which is the comparison result of $(b \leq a?)$ encrypted under QR.
3: $\|u\| = \|u_1 \oplus u_2\| = \|u_1\| \cdot \|u_2\|$

---

into the server and can latterly issue the SQL queries to this database. In their scheme, the database is encrypted by a traditional encryption scheme (*i.e.*, symmetric encryption scheme such as DES and AES), and the aforementioned split-and-transformation mechanism is achieved by a delicately designed algebraic framework. Followed by this approach, Hacıgümüs *et al.* proposed a query optimization method in [18] and constructed a secure DBMS that support aggregation query in [17]. However, for the sake of query processing efficiency, DBMS built in this approach only provides very limited notions of data privacy.

Property-Preserving Encryption Approach. In order to accelerate data processing operations meanwhile provide appropriate privacy guarantees, researchers proposed some specific cryptographic primitives that support particular calculations to be performed on encrypted data. Specifically, for example, Order-Preserving Encryption [2,9] enables the ciphertext to maintain the numerical order of its corresponding plaintext, and the Order-Revealing Encryption[11] enables efficient comparison among multiple (randomly-encrypted) ciphertexts. Deterministic encryption [7] have advantage on equality search and match. Using these primitives, Popa *et al.* [25] proposed the first practical system, CryptDB,

---

Algorithm 8. Changing QR-encrypted (equality test) result into plaintext

Input:
1: Server $\mathcal{S} : pk_{QR}, ||t||$
2: Server $\mathcal{C} : sk_{QR}$
Output: $\mathcal{S}$ get $t = (a = b?)$
3: Server $\mathcal{S}$:
4: $\tau \xleftarrow{\$} \{0,1\}$
5: $x' = ||t|| \cdot ||\tau||$

6: Send x' to server $\mathcal{C}$
7: Server $\mathcal{C}$
8: $x = Dec_{QR}(x')$;
9: Send back x to $\mathcal{S}$
10: Server $\mathcal{S}$:
11: $t = x \oplus \tau$

Algorithm 9. Changing Encryption Schemes (Protocol 5)

Input:
1: Server $\mathcal{S} : pk_{QR}, ||t||$
2: Server $\mathcal{C} : sk_{QR}$
Output: $\mathcal{S}$ get $v = [t]$
3: Server $\mathcal{S}$:
4: $x_1 = ||t|| \cdot ||0||$;
5: $x_2 = ||t|| \cdot ||1||$;
6: $r \xleftarrow{\$} \{0,1\}$
7: **if** $r = 1$ **then**
8:     $s_1 = x_1, s_2 = x_2$;
9: **else**
10:     $s_1 = x_1, s_2 = x_1$;
11: **end if**

12: Send s_1 and s_2 tp $\mathcal{C}$
13: Server $\mathcal{C}$:
14: $m_1 = Dec_{QR}(s_1), m_2 = Dec_{QR}(s_2)$;
15: $n_1 = Enc_{pk_A}^{(BCP)}(m_1)$
16: $n_2 = Enc_{pk_A}^{(BCP)}(m_2)$;
17: Send n_1, n_2 to $\mathcal{S}$
18: Server $\mathcal{S}$:
19: **if** $r = 1$ **then**
20:     $v = n_1$;
21: **else**
22:     $v = n_2$
23: **end if**
24: **Output** v;

---

an integrated system that can perform query processing on encrypted data. Afterwards, several systems, like MONOMI [29], are proposed.

FHE and SMPC Based Approach. Fully homomorphic encryption (FHE) [15] is a cryptographic encryption primitive that enables to compute any function on encrypted data. Boneh et al. [10] firstly implement the database-query functionally with a specific homomorphic encryption scheme. This line of work is based on the prerequisite that efficient fully homomorphic encryption schemes exist; nevertheless, the efficiency for FHE is still far more satisfactory. Similarly, SMPC enables multiple distributed parties to jointly compute an arbitrary functionality in an privacy-preserving manner. Secure database systems implemented SMPC include Blindseer [14,22], Arx [24], sharemind [8] and SDB [19,32].

Secure Hardware Based Approach. Secure hardware enclaves (e.g., Intel SGX [13] and Catalyst [21] etc.) promise data confidentiality and secure execution of arbitrary computation. The TrustDB [5,6], constructed with an ordinary commodity cryptographic co-processor, is the first practical outsourced database prototype that supports a subset of SQL operation, and the Cipherbase [3,4] achieves the similar functionality with FPGA serving as the tamper-proof hardware. SGX based systems include include VC3 [26], Ryoan [20] and Opaque [33]. However, the secure hardware may not be as "secure" as it claims [31], and there are lots of effective attacks targeted to hardware that can totally devastate the underlying systems[27,30].

6 Conclusion

Reliable, secure, and trustworthy services are essential for industries with highly sensitive data. In SGCC, we deployed our systems that ensure only authorized users have access to the expected data, while unauthorized entities, including cloud service providers and unapproved internal staff, know nothing about the data. To achieve these goals, we devise an authority separation mechanism, store data in encrypted form, and design a set of mechanisms to enable search and query on encrypted data using searchable encryption (SE) and homomorphic encryption (HE). Experimental and real-work running experiences indicate the practicability of our system.

Acknowledgement. This work is funded by the "Research on Key Technologies for Secure Query on Encrypted Electric Power Data" program of the Big Data Center, SGCC.

References

1. Yahoo! data breaches. https://en.wikipedia.org/wiki/Yahoo!_data_breaches
2. Agrawal, R., Kiernan, J., Srikant, R., Xu, Y.: Order preserving encryption for numeric data. In: Proceedings of SIGMOD, pp. 563–574. ACM (2004)
3. Arasu, A., et al.: Secure database-as-a-service with cipherbase. In: Proceedings of SIGMOD, pp. 1033–1036. ACM (2013)
4. Arasu, A., Eguro, K., Joglekar, M., Kaushik, R., Kossmann, D., Ramamurthy, R.: Transaction processing on confidential data using cipherbase. In: Proceedings of ICDE, pp. 435–446. IEEE (2015)
5. Bajaj, S., Sion, R.: TrustedDB: a trusted hardware based database with privacy and data confidentiality. In: Proceedings of SIGMOD, pp. 205–216. ACM (2011)
6. Bajaj, S., Sion, R.: TrustedDB: a trusted hardware-based database with privacy and data confidentiality. IEEE Trans. Knowl. Data Eng. **26**(3), 752–765 (2014)
7. Bellare, M., Fischlin, M., O'Neill, A., Ristenpart, T.: Deterministic encryption: definitional equivalences and constructions without random oracles. In: Wagner, D. (ed.) CRYPTO 2008. LNCS, vol. 5157, pp. 360–378. Springer, Heidelberg (2008). https://doi.org/10.1007/978-3-540-85174-5_20
8. Bogdanov, D., Laur, S., Willemson, J.: Sharemind: a framework for fast privacy-preserving computations. In: Jajodia, S., Lopez, J. (eds.) ESORICS 2008. LNCS, vol. 5283, pp. 192–206. Springer, Heidelberg (2008). https://doi.org/10.1007/978-3-540-88313-5_13
9. Boldyreva, A., Chenette, N., O'Neill, A.: Order-preserving encryption revisited: improved security analysis and alternative solutions. In: Rogaway, P. (ed.) CRYPTO 2011. LNCS, vol. 6841, pp. 578–595. Springer, Heidelberg (2011). https://doi.org/10.1007/978-3-642-22792-9_33

10. Boneh, D., Gentry, C., Halevi, S., Wang, F., Wu, D.J.: Private database queries using somewhat homomorphic encryption. In: Jacobson, M., Locasto, M., Mohassel, P., Safavi-Naini, R. (eds.) ACNS 2013. LNCS, vol. 7954, pp. 102–118. Springer, Heidelberg (2013). https://doi.org/10.1007/978-3-642-38980-1_7

11. Boneh, D., Lewi, K., Raykova, M., Sahai, A., Zhandry, M., Zimmerman, J.: Semantically secure order-revealing encryption: multi-input functional encryption without obfuscation. In: Oswald, E., Fischlin, M. (eds.) EUROCRYPT 2015. LNCS, vol. 9057, pp. 563–594. Springer, Heidelberg (2015). https://doi.org/10.1007/978-3-662-46803-6_19

12. Bresson, E., Catalano, D., Pointcheval, D.: A simple public-key cryptosystem with a double trapdoor decryption mechanism and its applications. In: Laih, C.-S. (ed.) ASIACRYPT 2003. LNCS, vol. 2894, pp. 37–54. Springer, Heidelberg (2003). https://doi.org/10.1007/978-3-540-40061-5_3

13. Costan, V., Lebedev, I., Devadas, S., et al.: Secure processors part I: background, taxonomy for secure enclaves and Intel SGX architecture. Found. Trends® Electron. Des. Autom. 11(1–2), 1–248 (2017)

14. Fisch, B.A., et al.: Malicious-client security in blind seer: a scalable private DBMS. In: Proceedings of SP, pp. 395–410. IEEE (2015)

15. Gentry, C.: Fully homomorphic encryption using ideal lattices. In: Proceedings of STOC, p. 169. ACM Press (2009)

16. Hacıgümüş, H., Iyer, B., Li, C., Mehrotra, S.: Executing SQL over encrypted data in the database-service-provider model. In: Proceedings of SIGMOD, pp. 216–227. ACM (2002)

17. Hacıgümüş, H., Iyer, B., Mehrotra, S.: Efficient execution of aggregation queries over encrypted relational databases. In: Proceedings of DASFAA, pp. 633–650 (2004)

18. Hacıgümüş, H., Iyer, B., Mehrotra, S.: Query optimization in encrypted database systems. In: Zhou, L., Ooi, B.C., Meng, X. (eds.) DASFAA 2005. LNCS, vol. 3453, pp. 43–55. Springer, Heidelberg (2005). https://doi.org/10.1007/11408079_7

19. He, Z., et al.: SDB: a secure query processing system with data interoperability. Proc. VLDB 8(12), 1876–1879 (2015)

20. Hunt, T., Zhu, Z., Xu, Y., Peter, S., Witchel, E.: Ryoan: a distributed sandbox for untrusted computation on secret data. In: Proceedings of OSDI, pp. 533–549. USENIX Association (2016)

21. Liu, F., Lee, R.B.: Random fill cache architecture. In: Proceedings of MICRO, pp. 203–215. IEEE (2014)

22. Pappas, V., et al.: Blind seer: a scalable private DBMS. In: Proceedings of S&P, pp. 359–374. IEEE (2014)

23. Peter, A., Tews, E., Katzenbeisser, S.: Efficiently outsourcing multiparty computation under multiple keys. IEEE Trans. Inf. Forensics Secur. 8(12), 2046–2058 (2013)

24. Poddar, R., Boelter, T., Popa, R.A.: Arx: a DBMS with semantically secure encryption (2017). https://www2.eecs.berkeley.edu/Pubs/TechRpts/2017/EECS-2017-111.pdf

25. Popa, R.A., Redfield, C., Zeldovich, N., Balakrishnan, H.: CryptDB: protecting confidentiality with encrypted query processing. In: Proceedings of SOSP, pp. 85–100. ACM (2011)

26. Schuster, F., et al.: VC3: trustworthy data analytics in the cloud using SGX. In: Proceedings of S&P, pp. 38–54. IEEE (2015)

27. Shih, M.-W., Lee, S., Kim, T., Peinado, M.: T-SGX: eradicating controlled-channel attacks against enclave programs. In: Proceedings of NDSS (2017)

28. Tu, C., He, X., Shuai, Z., Jiang, F.: Big data issues in smart grid-a review. Renew. Sustain. Energy Rev. **79**, 1099–1107 (2017)
29. Tu, S., Kaashoek, M.F., Madden, S., Zeldovich, N.: Processing analytical queries over encrypted data. In: Proceedings of VLDB, vol. 6, pp. 289–300. VLDB Endowment (2013)
30. Van Bulck, J., Weichbrodt, N., Kapitza, R., Piessens, F., Strackx, R.: Telling your secrets without page faults: stealthy page table-based attacks on enclaved execution. In: Proceedings of USENIX Security. USENIX Association (2017)
31. Weichbrodt, N., Kurmus, A., Pietzuch, P., Kapitza, R.: AsyncShock: exploiting synchronisation bugs in intel SGX enclaves. In: Askoxylakis, I., Ioannidis, S., Katsikas, S., Meadows, C. (eds.) ESORICS 2016. LNCS, vol. 9878, pp. 440–457. Springer, Cham (2016). https://doi.org/10.1007/978-3-319-45744-4_22
32. Wong, W.K., Kao, B., Cheung, D.W.L., Li, R., Yiu, S.M.: Secure query processing with data interoperability in a cloud database environment. In: Proceedings of SIGMOD, pp. 1395–1406. ACM (2014)
33. Zheng, W., Dave, A., Beekman, J.G., Popa, R.A., Gonzalez, J.E., Stoica, I.: Opaque: an oblivious and encrypted distributed analytics platform. In: Proceedings of NSDI, pp. 283–298. USENIX Association (2017)

Research on the Cloud-Edge Service Collaboration and Interaction Technology Oriented for Dispatching and Control Cloud

Dong Liu, Dapeng Li[✉], Yunhao Huang, and Lei Tao

Beijing Key Laboratory of Research and System Evaluation of Power Dispatching Automation Technology, China Electric Power Research Institute, Beijing, China
lidapeng3704@163.com

Abstract. With the continuous promotion of the construction of dispatching and control cloud, the existing service interaction mechanism has network security risks. At the same time, the service deployment is cumbersome, which affects the efficiency of service interaction. Based on the service proxy, cloud-side collaboration is used to complete the service interaction between two levels of clouds, which can improve the efficiency of the service deployment and interaction. On this basis, the overall architecture of the wide-area cloud-edge service collaboration and interaction of the dispatching and control cloud is completed.

Keywords: Dispatching and Control Cloud · Service proxy · Wide-area cloud-edge service collaboration and interaction

1 Introduction

With the advancement of the construction of the dispatching and control cloud, the scale of power grid construction has become larger and larger [1–3], and the control operation of the power grid has the characteristics of a wider range of faults, more decentralized operation control, more business coverage, and greater collaborative work. The dispatching and control cloud adopts two-level deployment $(1 + 27)$ at the national and provincial levels [4–6], and more than 230 source data terminals are connected to the source business system to form an organic whole. Therefore, the support dispatching mode shifts from hierarchical management and control to multi-level coordination [7–9], it is necessary to establish a power grid model data collaboration and hierarchical zoning mechanism, collect multi-party data resources for power generation, transmission, transformation, distribution and use, run through five-level dispatching business, and create an application sharing ecological, standard and opening service system for power operation related parties, both internally for all departments of the company and externally for power generation enterprises, and provide services to users.

In order to better support the construction of the applications of the dispatching and control cloud, the wide-area service interactions between the two-level clouds are required to implement mutual calls between applications. The wide-area service bus

© Springer Nature Singapore Pte Ltd. 2022
G. Zhai et al. (Eds.): IFTC 2021, CCIS 1560, pp. 500–511, 2022.
https://doi.org/10.1007/978-981-19-2266-4_38

has been deployed on the two-level dispatching and control cloud platform. However, through the analysis of the current operation of the wide-area service bus and the interaction of two-level cloud services, it is found that the existing mechanism has hidden network security risks, and at the same time, the service deployment is cumbersome, which affects the efficiency of service interaction [10–13]. It is embodied in the following aspects: firstly, the IP and ports of all services and clients need to be opened to the external network; secondly, two sets of service registration centers which consists of wide area and local, need to be deployed; thirdly, the client and the service need to agree on the content and method (such as online/offline status, service monitoring information), and so on. Therefore, it is urgent to optimize the architecture of the existing wide-area service bus.

By introducing an proxy mechanism, reducing the exposed IP and ports, shielding the internal implementation of the bus, optimizing the service interaction process, so as to improve the overall security of the system and the network [14–19], and also improve the service efficiency of their deployment, interaction, methods and applications [20–26].

In response to the dilemma facing the dispatching and control cloud service interaction, edge computing has been proposed as a new computing paradigm, and has gradually become an emerging computing model that meets the needs of Internet of Everything applications. The cloud-edge collaboration computing model is very suitable for internal and wide-area service interaction mechanisms. The introduction of the cloud-edge collaboration model to the dispatching and control cloud service collaboration interaction can well solve the problems of dispatching and control cloud service interaction mentioned in this article.

Through the above analysis, service collaboration interaction scheme is designed in this paper. Based on the service proxy, cloud-side collaboration is used to complete the service interaction between two levels of clouds, which can improve the efficiency of the service deployment and interaction. On this basis, the overall architecture of the wide-area cloud-edge service collaboration and interaction of the dispatching and control cloud is completed.

2   The Wide-Area Service Proxy Technology

Drawing lessons from the service gateway idea of the Internet microservice architecture and the wide-area service interaction mode of the existing dispatch automation system. In combination with the actual wide-area network architecture and security of the dispatching and control cloud, it is proposed to increase the wide-area service proxy mechanism based on the dispatching and control cloud service bus. All wide-area service requests are uniformly forwarded by the wide-area service proxy cluster, and only the IP and port of the wide-area service proxy node need to be opened between nodes, which avoids the internal network of nodes exposed to the outside caused by the direct interaction of services between nodes.

2.1 Principles of Wide-Area Service Proxy

(1) The service publishing in the agency mechanism

Service publishing process: The service publishing is consistent with the existing mechanism, and the service provider publishes the service to the service registry
through the dubbo bus.

(2) Consumption process in agency mechanism

When the application needs to call the services of other cloud nodes, the client
uses the service bus remote call interface to implement wide-area service calls. The
specific process is as follows:

Service consumption process: the wide area service client first sends a service request
to the local output proxy. After receiving the request, the egress service proxy initiates
a request to the opposite ingress service proxy. After receiving the request, the opposite
ingress service proxy calls the corresponding wide area service through the dubbo bus.
The service result is returned to the ingress service proxy, the ingress service proxy
returns the service result to the local egress service proxy, and the local egress service
proxy returns the service result to the wide area service client. At this point, the service
call is completed. The service proxy architecture of the dispatching and control cloud is
shown in Fig. 1.

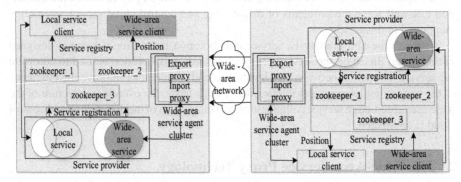

Fig. 1. The service proxy architecture of the dispatching and control cloud

2.2 The Function Module of the Service Proxy

The flow diagram of input/output proxy service of the dispatching and control cloud is
shown in Fig. 2.

(1) The output proxy of the dispatching and control cloud

The output proxy of the dispatching and control cloud receives the calling
request from the client, and forwards the request to the opposite input proxy, at the
same time, it receives the invocation result returned by the opposite input proxy,
and sends the result to the client. The basic functions are as follows:

1) Proxy management and positioning function

The local output management records the status of different opposite-end input proxy, and can locate the corresponding opposite-end input proxy according to the client's request.

2) Proxy cluster management function

The proxy cluster is composed of multiple nodes, and it supports random and QPS methods; when a certain proxy node is abnormal, the cluster will be automatically removed, and client requests and alarms will no longer be accepted.

3) Service result feedback function

The output proxy can forward the client request to the opposite input proxy according to the agreed proxy protocol.

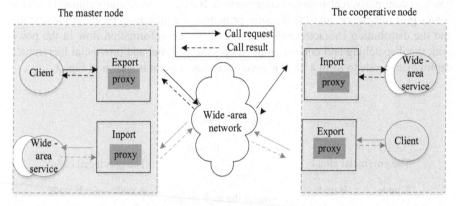

Fig. 2. The flow diagram of input /output proxy service of the dispatching and control cloud

(2) Input proxy of the dispatching and control cloud

The input agent proxy of the dispatching and control cloud receives the calling request of the wide-area client forwarded by the peer output proxy, and calls the local service, returns the service result to the peer output proxy at the same time. The basic functions are as follows:

1) Proxy management and positioning function

The input proxy subscribes to the service information of the dubbo service registry, and calls the corresponding service according to the client's request from the opposite end.

2) Proxy cluster management function

The proxy cluster is composed of multiple nodes, and it supports random and QPS methods; when a certain proxy node is abnormal, the cluster will be automatically removed, and client requests and alarms will no longer be accepted.

3) Service result feedback function
        The input proxy can forward the client request to the opposite output proxy
    according to the agreed proxy protocol.
4) Service whitelist function
        The input proxy sets a whitelist of services, and only allows wide-area
    services on the whitelist to be called by the peer.

3 The Cloud-Edge Service Collaboration and Interaction Technology

The dispatching and control cloud is a cloud service platform for power grid dispatching business. Its architecture design should meet the requirements of power grid control business continuity, real-time and coordination. Based on the business characteristics of power grid integration and the division principle of dispatching business jurisdiction, and the distribution characteristics of energy flow and information flow in the power grid, the dispatching and control cloud adopts the national and provincial hierarchical deployment mode to form a "1 + n" overall architecture, it is shown in Fig. 3.

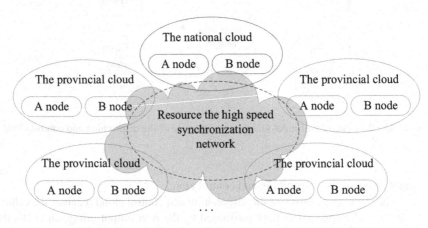

Fig. 3. The architecture of "dispatching and control cloud"

In the whole of dispatching and control cloud, the master node is in the core which is responsible for the management of cloud metadata and dictionary data, and the establishment and collection of the model data. There are n cooperative nodes, which are responsible for the collection of models and data in the province and the synchronization/forwarding of the data of the master node. In order to ensure the high reliability of the dispatching and control cloud, each node adopts the dual-site mode of remote active-active, that is, A and B sites are deployed in different places on the same node to realize the high-speed synchronization of data between sites.

3.1 The Wide-Area Service Interaction Technology

The service bus and service proxy mechanism are used to conduct collaborative interactions of various services between the master node and the collaborative node on the platform of the dispatching and control cloud. Requests and responses of internal services are completed within the node. The requests of wide-area service are uniformly forwarded by the wide-area service proxy cluster. The specific process is shown in Fig. 4.

As shown in Fig. 4, the wide-area service client of the master node sends a service request to the local output proxy firstly. After receiving the request, the output service proxy sends a request to the input service proxy of the cooperative node. then receiving the request, input service proxy of the cooperative node calls the corresponding wide-area service through the service bus and returns the service result to the input service proxy. The input service proxy returns the service result to the output service proxy of the master node. The output service proxy finally returns the service result to the master node wide-area service client.

3.2 The Wide Area Task Scheduling Technology

Task scheduling adopts micro service and wide area service scheduling technology, realizes task wide area scheduling through workflow mechanism, and realizes information interaction through wide area message bus. Its structure is divided into master module, worker module and workflow service. Master server is mainly responsible for task segmentation, task submission monitoring, and monitoring the health status of other master servers and worker servers at the same time. Worker server is mainly responsible for task execution and providing log service; Workflow service is mainly responsible for processing client requests and transmitting information through wide area service bus (Fig. 5).

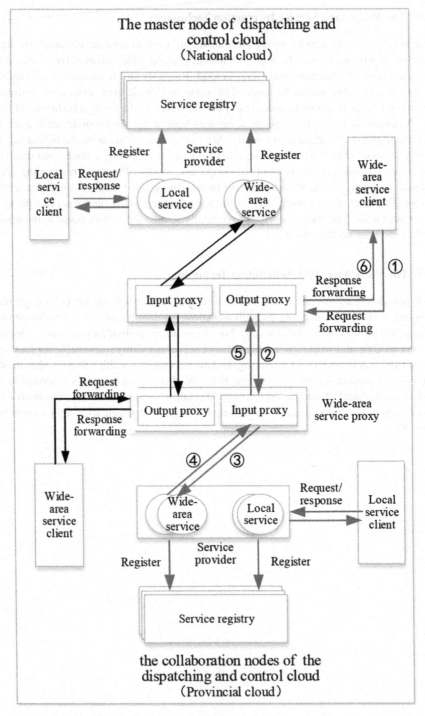

Fig. 4. Interaction architecture of wide area service

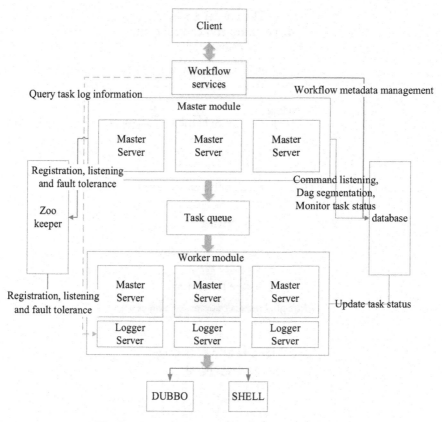

Fig. 5. The architecture of wide area task scheduling

3.3 The Wide-Area Message Interaction Technology

The dispatching and control cloud exchanges data through the message bus. The wide area message transmission is realized through the wide area message agent. The message agent is deployed on the communication proxy server regulating the boundary of each cloud node in the active and standby mode, responsible for the wide area message forwarding and completing the real-time push of messages across nodes. As shown in Fig. 6, this paper takes an application of the leading node sending a message to an application of the cooperative node as an example to illustrate the message transmission process:

(1) The cooperative node application subscribes to the message topic from the message management center;
(2) The master node application sends the wide area message to the local wide area message agent;
(3) According to the subscription relationship between each cooperative node and the message subject, the wide area message agent adds it to the sending queue of the corresponding node and sends it to the opposite end wide area message agent;

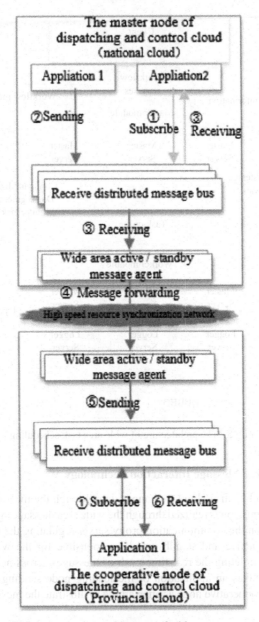

Fig. 6. Interaction architecture of wide area message

(4) After receiving the message, the cooperative node message agent sends the message to the application in the node, so as to complete the real-time transmission of the message across the WAN.

3.4 The Result Analysis

Compared with cloud services, the most direct advantage of wide area edge services of dispatching and control cloud is low latency and high bandwidth. The applications in the edge nodes are located in the same LAN, which can ensure low delay and high bandwidth. The cloud center generally deviates from the user in space. If the data is collected from the source and directly sent to the cloud Center for processing, the delay will be relatively high, and the overall bandwidth of the cloud center will occupy a lot. Table 1 shows the advantages of edge nodes in delay and bandwidth compared with cloud centers in general. This advantage is more obvious for applications requiring high real-time performance.

Table 1. Comparative analysis of delay and bandwidth.

Calculation type	Bandwidth/(Mb.s-1)	Delay/ms
Cloud computing	<155	>100
Edge calculation	>1000	<10

4 Conclusions

In this paper, based on the service proxy, cloud-side collaboration is used to complete the service interaction between two levels of clouds, which can improve the efficiency of the service deployment and interaction. On this basis, the overall architecture of the wide-area cloud-edge service collaboration and interaction of the dispatching and control cloud is completed.

Acknowledgment. This work was supported by R&D project of China Electric Power Research Institute Co., Ltd under Grant No.5242001900CX (Research on the Cloud-edge Wide-area Service Collaboration and Interaction Technology Oriented for Dispatching and Control Cloud).

References

1. Xu, H.: Architecture of dispatching and control cloud and its application prospect. Power Syst. Technol. **41**(10), 3104–3111 (2017)
2. Xu, H.: Structured design and application of power dispatching universal data object for dispatching and control cloud. Power Syst. Technol. **42**(7), 2248–2254 (2018)

3. Xu, H., Sun, S., Ge, Z., et al.: Research and application of architecture and key technologies for power grid real-time dispatching and control data platform. Autom. Electric Power Syst. **43**(22), 157–164 (2019)
4. Shi, W., Sun, H., Cao, J., et al.: Edge computing-an emerging computing model for the internet of everything era. J. Comput. Res. Dev. **54**(5), 907–924 (2017)
5. Caprolu, M., Di Pietro, R., Lombardi, F., et al.: Edge computing perspectives: architectures, technologies, and open security issues. In: Proceedings of 2019 IEEE International Conference on Edge Computing, Milan, Italy: IEEE (2019)
6. Lv, H., Chen, D., Fan, B., et al.: Standardization progress and case analysis of edge computing. J. Comput. Res. Dev. **55**(3), 487–511 (2018)
7. Zhang, J., Zhao, Y., Chen, B., et al.: Survey on data security and privacy-preserving for the research of edge computing. J. Commun. **39**(3), 1–21 (2018)
8. Deng, X., Guan, P., Wan, Z., et al.: Integrated trust based resource cooperation in edge computing. J. Comput. Res. Dev. **55**(3), 449–477 (2018)
9. Si, Y., Tan, Y., Wang, F., Lian, W., Liu, B.: Cloud edge collaborative structure model for power Internet of things. Chin. J. Electr. Eng., 1–9 (2020). https://doi.org/10.13334/j.0258-8013.pcsee.191532
10. Cui, H., Jiang, C., Miu, W., Yang, W., Ma, T., Shen, Y.: Design and implementation of power intelligent IOT system based on edge computing. Power Inf. Commun. Technol. **18**(04), 33–41 (2020)
11. Zhang, S., Tong, J., Zhang, Y., Zhang, M., Lei, Y., Zhu, Y.: Research on edge computing technology for intelligent perception of energy Internet. Power Inf. Commun. Technol. **18**(04), 42–50 (2020)
12. Gong, G., Luo, A., Chen, Z., et al.: Application prospect of edge computing in power demand response business. Power Syst. Technol. **42**(10), 3128–3135 (2018)
13. Sun, Y., Li, X., Liu, Y., et al.: Edge computing terminal equipment planning method for real-time online monitoring service of power grid. In: Proceedings of 2019 IEEE 4th Advanced Information Technology, Electronic and Automation Control Conference, IEEE, Chengdu (2019)
14. Zhao, Z., Liu, F., Cai, Z., et al.: Edge computing: platforms, applications and challenges. J. Comput. Res. Dev. **55**(2), 327–337 (2018)
15. Chen, Z., Li, D., Huang, Y., et al.: A partition coordinated and optimized operation design for power grid wide area coordination and interaction service. In: Proceedings of 2018 2nd IEEE Conference on Energy Internet and Energy System Integration. IEEE, Beijing (2018)
16. Li, Z., Chen, Z., Gao, X., et al.: The fast simulation architecture construction for integrated electric transmission and distribution power grid based on big data platform. In 2021 China International Conference on Electricity Distribution (CICED), pp. 484–489. IEEE (2021)
17. Qi, X., Chen, Z., Li, Z., et al.: Application of non-player character simulation technology in union dispatcher training simulator of multi-level dispatching and control system. In: 2019 IEEE 3rd Conference on Energy Internet and Energy System Integration (EI2), pp. 1676–1681. IEEE (2019)
18. Chen, Z., Li, D., Deng, Z., et al.: The application of power grid equipment plug and play based on wide area SOA. In 2018 IEEE International Conference on Energy Internet (ICEI), pp. 19–23. IEEE (2018)
19. Li, D., Chen, Z., Deng, Z., et al.: A wide area service oriented architecture design for plug and play of power grid equipment. Procedia Comput. Sci. **129**, 353–357 (2018)
20. Chen, Z., Li, D., Cui, C., et al.: A multi-database hybrid storage method for big data of power dispatching and control. In: 2019 IEEE SmartWorld, Ubiquitous Intelligence & Computing, Advanced & Trusted Computing, Scalable Computing & Communications, Cloud & Big Data Computing, Internet of People and Smart City Innovation (Smart-World/SCALCOM/UIC/ATC/CBDCom/IOP/SCI), pp. 502–507 (2019)

21. Qi, X., Chen, Z., Li, D., et al.: Model management and service based power grid multi-agent dispatcher training simulator. In: 2018 2nd IEEE Conference on Energy Internet and Energy System Integration (EI2), pp. 1–9 (2018)
22. Li, W., Chen, Z., Gao, X., et al.: Multimodel framework for indoor localization under mobile edge computing environment. IEEE Internet Things J. **6**(3), 4844–4853 (2019)
23. Zhang, Y., Gao, X., Chen, Z., et al.: Mining spatial-temporal similarity for visual tracking. IEEE Trans. Image Process. **29**, 8107–8119 (2020)
24. Gao, X., Steven, C.H.H., Zhang, Y., et al.: SOML: sparse online metric learning with application to image retrieval. In: Twenty-eighth AAAI conference on artificial intelligence, pp. 1206–1212 (2014)
25. Zhang, Y., Gao, X., Chen, Z., et al.: Learning salient features to prevent model drift for correlation tracking. Neurocomputing **418**, 1–10 (2020)
26. Tang, G., Gao, X., Chen, Z., et al.: Unsupervised adversarial domain adaptation with similarity diffusion for person re-identification. Neurocomputing **442**, 337–347 (2021)

Perspective on Power Smart Customer Service Based on AI

Xiaoguang Huang, Gang Wu, Yu Yin, and Xiaodong Wang[✉]

State Grid Information and Telecommunication Group Co., LTD., Beijing, China
1303875427@qq.com

Abstract. At present, the power customer service system is only used as an auxiliary means of front-line customer service. However, with the continuous development of speech recognition, natural language processing, knowledge graph and other technologies, as well as the continuous integration and application of relevant AI technologies in the field of power customer service, the original customer service mode will be disruptive changed from service scenario and interaction mode. The smart customer service system based on AI technology will further play an important role in improving quality and efficiency, and help state grid to build a first-class energy Internet enterprise. Based on the current situation and future development and application requirements of power customer service AI, relying on the construction results of "two libraries and one platform" of AI of State Grid Corporation, this paper studies the power smart customer service process and key technologies, and analyzes the construction scenario of power smart customer service application from the aspects of service navigation, service quality detection and customer service operation, Support the construction of smart customer service application scenarios and systems of State Grid Corporation.

Keywords: Artificial intelligence · Power customer service · Intelligent service

1 Introduction

With the new round of technological innovations such as the Internet, big data and sensors, major breakthroughs have been made in large-scale computing capabilities and algorithms based on cloud platforms. Computers can already complete more complex tasks independently by virtue of deep learning, and AI has become ubiquitous. In order to grasp the opportunities for the development of AI technology research and application, countries around the world have introduced AI strategies.

Presently, 18 countries and regions including the United States, the United Kingdom, China, Japan, and the European Union have successively launched their own national AI strategic plans to support the development and application of their own AI technology [1]. The technology giants also regard AI as

G. Zhai et al. (Eds.): IFTC 2021, CCIS 1560, pp. 512–527, 2022.
https://doi.org/10.1007/978-981-19-2266-4_39

a strategic fulcrum for future development, and strive to establish an ecosystem of AI services in the cloud. Facebook, Amazon, Google, Baidu and other companies have declared AI as the core of their future business [2]. Currently, AI technology has been deeply applied in many industries. Such as smart security, autonomous driving, smart assistants, smart manufacturing, health-care, e-commerce retail, finance and education, location-based service, etc. [3–13]. The key deployment applications include speech recognition, natural language processing, image recognition, computer vision, autonomous driving, unmanned aerial vehicles, intelligent robots, etc. Among them, industries such as finance, communication operators, and e-commerce retail use AI technologies such as natural language processing, speech recognition, speech synthesis, and multiple rounds of conversations [14,15] to vigorously develop smart customer service robots, intelligent voice portals, online customer service, etc. System construction and application, the application of AI in the field of customer service has broad prospects. Traditional customer service positions are mainly for manual answering of incoming calls.

However, as the demand for customer service continues to increase, the labor and operating costs of the customer service department of enterprises have increased sharply. By introducing an intelligent voice customer service system, using AI and other technical means, combined with the traditional seat service model, creating a full-service smart customer service center can greatly improve service efficiency and reduce labor service costs. Therefore, AI technology is a new way to improve the quality and efficiency of customer service operation management. Customer service is the main entrance of enterprise user information and service information, using AI technology to convert user voice data into a reasonable data format and big data analysis to achieve accurate customer service, improve customer service quality, and improve customer service efficiency. Therefore, the application of AI technology is a new method for deep mining of customer service value information. In the era of consumption upgrading, the traditional IT technology + manual customer service model has been unable to cope with the ever-increasing user scale and service demand.

The application of AI technology saves a lot of costs for enterprises, improves operating efficiency, and becomes an important technical support for modern customers to innovate, qualitatively change, and transform and upgrade means. The application of AI in the customer service industry has accelerated and has become one of the core technologies in the customer service field. It focuses on achieving a better customer service experience, reducing the intensity of a single repetitive work by customer service personnel, and knowledge management based on deep learning, intelligent voice analysis, and smart customer service. Service robots etc. are gradually applied in various vertical industries [16,17], which can greatly improve work efficiency, reduce service costs, and meet the needs of diversified and fragmented services in the new era. Therefore, the application of AI technology is to meet user consumption upgrades. New guarantee of demand.

2   The Application Status and Development Demands of AI in the Field of Customer Service

2.1   Application of AI in the Field of Customer Service Outside the Industry

China Mobile "Jiu Tian" Smart Customer Service Application. The telecommunications industry pays great attention to AI. China Mobile is committed to promoting the implementation of AI, deeply integrating AI technology with the operation scenarios of the telecommunications industry, and achieving close coupling between AI iteration optimization and generation links. China Mobile's AI platform "Jiu Tian" [18] focuses on telecom scenarios, provides basic platforms and core AI service capabilities, and provides scenario-driven end-to-end AI application solutions and implementation guarantees for vertical industries. Relying on this platform, China Mobile has implemented large-scale AI applications in the customer service business area, achieving a 20% increase in the proportion of customer service robots in intelligent services. At the same time, it uses speech recognition, natural language processing and intelligent modeling to achieve intelligent analysis of customer service quality and smart customer service questions and answers.

Alibaba's Customer Service Robot "Xiaomi Yun". Alibab Smart Customer Service Robot Cloud Xiaomi is a conversational robot for enterprises, organizations, and developers [19]. It has 36 preset knowledge packages of subdivisions, supports Chinese and English conversations, and can work online 7 × 24 h. At present, it has covered more than 20 business lines in the Alibaba ecosystem, serving 6 million customers every day, and the problem solving rate has reached 95%. Cloud Xiaomi supports intelligent conversations on different messaging terminals, such as web pages, APPs, and physical robots. Combines big data analysis, natural language processing (NLP) and machine learning (ML) capabilities in one, based on massive multi-industry fields and multi-language knowledge bases, accurately understands dialogues, conducts natural human-computer questions and answers, and provides accurate business analysis Report. Users can use the preset knowledge package of 36 sub-fields, so that Xiaomi Yun can quickly put into actual business. With the use of users, Xiaomi Yun, which has the ability to learn, can continue to evolve the knowledge base to analyze, judge and respond more accurately.

Online Customer Service and Outbound Application of Financial Institutions. With the rapid development of AI, major domestic financial institutions also rely on cutting-edge technology to accelerate the transformation to intelligent services. For example, the "Gongxiaozhi" smart customer service system [20] launched by Industrial and Commercial Bank of China uses AI technology to realize the self-understanding of customer problems and provide the best answers. At the same time, it will recommend corresponding products to customers according to their needs. At present, ICBC has promoted "Gongxi-aozhi" to major service channels such as SMS, e-linking, WeChat, etc., bringing customers a good experience of replying in seconds, within reach, and without interruption. According to statistics, the recognition rate of ICBC's smart customer service has reached 98%, leading the industry. Over the past two years, it has solved 400 million customer-related needs. At present, "Gongxiaozhi" has become an important hub for ICBC to provide external services and strengthen customer contacts, effectively improving customer service efficiency and service levels. China Construction Bank has launched a smart customer service platform "Small and Micro". This customer service system can understand the questions asked by users in voice or text, and provide corresponding answers, thereby realizing automatic response services. In addition, many financial institutions have launched an intelligent outbound call robot system, which can be tailored according to the telemarketing process. By pre-setting the outbound call process in the system, it can complete the marketing of user identity confirmation, marketing guidance, and marketing information confirmation. Moreover, the intelligent outbound robot can use smooth and clear Mandarin, allowing the dialogue to be like a real agent, easily completing most of the repetitive outbound work originally undertaken by humans, greatly reducing operating costs and improving marketing efficiency.

"Smart Customer Service" System of Ping an Group. The "Smart Customer Service" system launched by Ping An Life uses AI technologies such as biometric authentication, big data, and remote video to build a smart service system with full domain coverage, full-process intelligent management, and dynamic and precise risk control. As long as users use the Ping An Jinguanjia APP, they can handle insurance policy business online, and insurance services have since broken the limitations of time and space. Under the "smart customer service" service model, the average processing time for service scenarios such as preservation, claims settlement, and underwriting has been greatly reduced.

Gome Mall Artificial Intelligence Customer Service System. The intelligent robot customer service system Xiaomei independently developed by Gome integrates pre-sales consultation, scene-based shopping guide, knowledge base and other functions. It realizes that 80% of Gome customer service is completed by smart customer service, effectively reducing the repeated answers to basic questions of manual customer service and saving manpower and cost.

2.2   Application of AI in the Field of Electric Power Customer Services

Customer Service Smart Service: Power customer service smart services, relying on the voice recognition, natural language processing, knowledge graph and other AI service capabilities provided by the State Grid Corporation's power AI "two databases and one platform", as well as power voice sample database and power customer service knowledge base, to create power smart customers. The service platform provides simple, clear and efficient self-service customer service for power users, realizes accurate analysis and understanding of power system customer demands, improves the intelligent service level of the State Grid Customer Service Center, and enables power customers to enjoy precision, intelligence, and interaction Efficient and intelligent communication services [21].

Smart Business Hall: At present, most of the business of electric power business halls are mainly handled manually. The business hall business system and business hall self-service robots integrate speech recognition, natural language processing, OCR, knowledge graph, etc. provided by the State Grid Corporation's electric power AI "two databases and one platform". Technology, to realize the functions of self-identification, active guidance, business intelligence explanation and assistance, precise service for customers in the business hall and service hall, improve the efficiency and service quality of customer service in the business hall of the power company, and fully demonstrate the excellent power industry Service level to help the construction of new smart business halls of various power companies of State Grid [22].

2.3 Demands for AI Applications in the Field of Electric Power Customer Service

The application direction of AI in the power industry is mainly through the combination of AI technology with power industry business scenarios, industry knowledge, and industry big data to achieve intelligent, automated and efficient services. With the application of AI in the power system, power customer service is gradually becoming smarter. The main requirements for AI applications in the field of force customer service are as follows:

Omni-Channel Service: At present, there are various channels for electric power customer service. In addition to telephone and web pages, there are also electric power APP, WeChat, Alipay, Weibo, H5, mini programs and other channels. Therefore, it is necessary to build intelligent call centers, online customer service, etc. The multi-in-one smart customer service system, including text + voice customer service robots, realizes omni-channel intelligent services in the field of electric customer service, and meets the needs of customer service, operation management, corporate marketing, and multi-party collaboration.

Intelligent Service: Combine AI technology and add an intelligent interactive environment to IT services to realize online customer service robots, intelligent voice navigation, intelligent insight response, intelligent management and other functions, such as customer sentiment analysis, text content analysis, and intelligent assistance Response, monitoring and early warning of major issues, intelligent work order quality inspection, intelligent scheduling and scheduling, etc., to achieve smart customer service.

Active Service: Intelligent power customers are realizing active and personalized customer service. Based on customer service big data analysis and AI technology, it deeply explores user demand hotspots and pain points, proactively predicts user service needs (such as problem prediction, operation guidelines, etc.), and realizes customer service initiative.

3 Power Smart Customer Service Process and Key Technologies

3.1 Power Smart Customer Service Process

With the construction and application of State Grid's "Two Databases and One Platform", the electric power smart customer service system will adopt the speech recognition, natural language understanding, knowledge base and big data intelligent analysis provided by the State Grid's AI two databases and one platform. This AI technology realizes the flexible access and invocation of multiple service engines, so as to provide users with voice, text, image and other interactive customer service services. The voice data is converted into text information. The semantic understanding engine processes the text information, finds out the accurate answer in the knowledge base, and then converts the text information into voice information through the speech synthesis engine and returns it to the user. The smart customer service system can accurately identify user problems, analyze and understand user intent, is suitable for a variety of power customer service scenarios, provides faster business response capabilities, greatly reduces the labor intensity of manual customer service, effectively reduces enterprise labor costs, and improves customer satisfaction.

The main processing flow of the smart customer service system is shown in the Fig. 1.

The smart customer service system in the power industry usually includes four main parts: a front-end interaction module, a voice recognition module, an intelligent engine module, and a back-end management module. The front-end interactive module mainly realizes the interactive activities between the smart customer service system and the customer. The customer can input requirements in the form of voice or text according to this module, and the smart customer service system outputs the answer to the customer through this module. The voice recognition module recognizes the voice information input by the customer as text information, so as to prepare for the smart customer service system to understand customer needs. The intelligent engine module includes two main functions: information preprocessing and semantic understanding. The semantic understanding function needs to use machine learning algorithms to extract keywords based on a pre-established semantic knowledge base to complete natural language processing. The back-end management module includes functions such as semantic retrieval, optimal matching and answer processing. This module needs to perform semantic retrieval based on the results of the language processing by the intelligent engine module, combined with the established corpus,

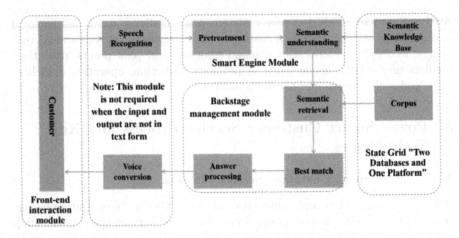

Fig. 1. Main service processes of Smart customer service system.

to find the optimal match for the user's needs, and according to the matching The results collate the answers. Finally, the voice conversion is performed, and the answer of the smart customer service system to the customer is output to the customer through the front-end interactive module to complete the complete process of the smart customer service system.

3.2 Main Key Technologies of Smart Customer Service

Speech Recognition Technology: Speech recognition technology is an important technology in the front end of the smart customer service system, and it is the fundamental guarantee for the machine to correctly identify customer needs. This is a modern technology that converts the input sound signal into the corresponding text or command. Through Speech recognition technology, users can abandon traditional operation devices such as buttons and mice, and give orders directly through language. The task can be completed more easily and quickly by downloading. The smart customer service system first preprocesses the customer's voice. This process mainly includes signal processing such as noise reduction processing, filtering, analog-to-digital conversion, and automatic gain control of the voice signal [23]. Then the preprocessed digital speech signal is input to the feature extraction module, where the feature parameters of the digital speech signal are extracted and compared with the reference pattern library trained by these speech feature parameters, and the voice signal features and The similarity measurement result of the template. Finally, perform post-processing on the voice signal according to the obtained measurement result, and make the computer perform post-processing according to the recognition result, thereby converting the voice signal into text information or corresponding instructions and output. Among them, the reference pattern library and the selected speech signal characteristics are the key steps of the speech recognition system. Only by selecting parameters that can completely and accurately reflect the signal characteristics for feature extraction and pre-training the complete reference pattern library can the effect of speech recognition be guaranteed. The speech recognition process is shown as Fig. 2.

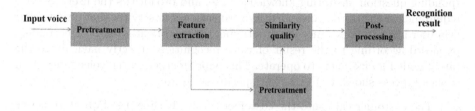

Fig. 2. Speech recognition process of Smart customer service system.

Natural Language Processing Technology: Natural language processing technology is the basis for computers to learn and understand customer intentions based on the results of speech recognition. Natural language processing is a key technology that reflects the intelligence of the Smart customer service system [24], enabling the Smart customer service system to understand customer needs like humans, and provide technical guarantees for customers to process business.

Knowledge Graph Technology: Knowledge graph is a semantic network that reveals the relationships between entities, and it can formally describe things in the real world and their relationships. The knowledge graph of electric power smart customer service is a typical industry knowledge graph [25]. Power smart customer service uses knowledge graph technology, based on the power grid unified business data model specification, and describes the entities and relationships of the power grid business according to the structure of the "nodes" and "edges" in the graph database, and builds a unified business model of the power grid based on the graph data model knowledge graph, which supports the smart customer service system to realize smart customer service such as electric power business guidance and professional knowledge answering.

4   Electric Power Smart Customer Service Application Construction

4.1   Intelligent Voice Navigation

The intelligent voice navigation function can complete all the functional navigation of the self-service voice service in the electric customer service. It can be applied to the three core customer service areas. The first is the intelligent interactive service voice response. After the user speaks his service needs, the system automatically match to the corresponding database and transfer to the corresponding service skill group; the second is intelligent voice service, after the user speaks his business needs, the system automatically jumps to the corresponding question answering knowledge base, and broadcasts the user's Service requirements; the third is user identity verification. For services that need to confirm user identity in advance, after verifying the user identity and corresponding password according to the result of voice recognition, directly navigate to the target node for customers to operate. This paper focuses on the voice interaction service process shown in Fig. 3. The specific steps are:

(1) The customer calls into the customer service hotline, the IVR (Interactive Voice Response) system establishes a path with the voice recognition engine, the IVR system transmits the acquired customer voice to the voice recognition engine, and the voice recognition engine divides the customer voice into sentences through the endpoint rules. Threshold rules assign values to customer's speaking speed and tone.
(2) The speech recognition engine passes the sentence to the natural language processing engine for semantic analysis, and at the same time passes the sentence to the semantic emotion recognition model for keyword matching, and the speech recognition engine transmits the emotion threshold to the speech emotion recognition model for threshold matching.
(3) The natural language processing engine performs keyword translation on the transmitted sentences, obtains service nodes through business model matching, and transmits feedback to the IVR system
(4) Voice emotion recognition and semantic emotion recognition comprehensively analyze customer emotions and return the results to the IVR system. The IVR system matches the emotional service strategy according to the feedback emotional state for service response.
(5) If the customer's emotional priority is higher, transfer to labor or voice comfort according to the emotional service strategy. If the customer's emotional priority is low, the service speech or self-service transfer will be performed according to the service map.

The basic technical components of the intelligent voice navigation system are speech recognition and natural and original processing. With the development of AI technology, deep learning has become the key technology of speech recognition. Compared with the traditional GMM-HMM-based speech recognition framework, it is based on The biggest change of deep learning speech recognition technology is to use DNN to replace GMM model to model the observation probability of speech. The advantages of DNN over GMM are: (1) The use of DNN to estimate the posterior probability distribution of HMM states does not require assumptions about the distribution of speech data; (2) The input features of DNN can be the fusion of multiple features, including discrete or continuous (3) DNN can use the structural information contained in adjacent speech frames. Figure 4 shows the process of speech recognition based on deep learning.

Deep learning models are also key technical methods in natural language processing, such as convolutional neural networks, recurrent neural networks,

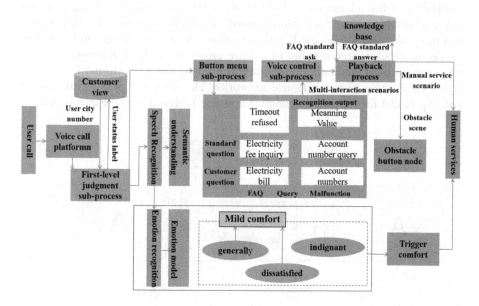

Fig. 3. Process of voice interactive service.

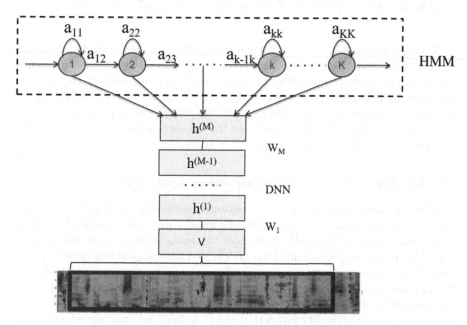

Fig. 4. Speech recognition model structure based on deep neural network

etc., through learning the generated word vectors to complete the process of natural language classification and understanding. Compared with traditional machine learning, natural language processing technology based on deep learning has the following advantages: (1) Deep learning can constantly learn language features based on the vectorization of words or sentences, and master higher-level and more abstract languages Features to meet the natural language processing requirements of a large number of feature projects. (2) Deep learning does not require experts to manually define the training set, and can automatically learn high-level features through neural networks. The structure of a common deep learning model for natural language processing is shown in the Fig. 5 below.

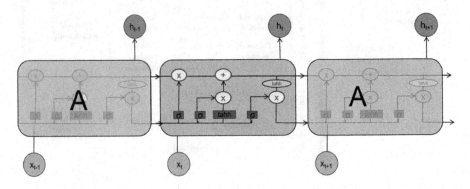

Fig. 5. The basic structure of deep neural networks commonly used in NLP

Through the intelligent voice navigation system, user needs can be accurately divided, user waiting time can be reduced, and the service level of customer service can be improved, thereby enhancing customer satisfaction. At the same time, the intelligent voice customer service system is used as a backup resource for manual services to guide users to use the self-service voice service system when manual is busy, which can increase the connection rate and greatly reduce the pressure of manual agents during busy hours.

4.2 Intelligent Voice Quality Inspection Application

In order to ensure service quality and customer satisfaction, the power customer service industry usually arranges full-time quality inspection agents for quality inspection. The ratio of quality inspectors to agents is usually controlled within 1:30. The quality inspection methods are divided into random inspections, patrol inspections and recordings. monitor. Traditional quality inspection methods have low management scope, high labor costs, and low quality inspection coverage, making it difficult to effectively evaluate the overall service quality. At the same time, the coverage of quality inspection and complaint information is insufficient, and it is difficult to comprehensively provide users with detailed requests to the back-end departments under the large-scale service mechanism.

The voice recognition and voice transcribing module of the electric power smart customer service system can transcribe real-time phone recordings into work orders and text files according to the distinction of user roles, and automatically convert massive recordings into structured indexes for keyword search, screening, and classification and so on, to realize automatic quality inspection, according to the business, the whole process of quality inspection, mining and analysis of valuable information. In addition, through voice recognition, emotion detection and other technologies, increase voice analysis and retrieval and mining, from manual random inspection to automatic full inspection, and improve the level of refined analysis operation and the support effectiveness of tools and the accuracy of quality inspection. Through the monitoring and refining of recording data, we regularly sort out issues related to business processes, management loopholes, product defects, service shortcomings, etc., to provide a basis for improving overall power supply service capabilities and reducing service shortcomings.

4.3 Auxiliary Support for Smart Seats

Automatic voice recognition technology can not only provide support for voice navigation, but also provide effective service assistance support after the customer enters the manual service. The electric power Smart customer service system uses automatic voice recognition technology to recognize customer's service demands in real time during the service process. Through service strategy models and emotion recognition models, it provides agents with real-time and effective information on business error-prone points, business knowledge, and service bans. Service support, and prompt prompts based on customer's emotional changes at the same time, to enhance customer experience perception.

(1) Business service capability support: The voice recognition engine collects real-time voice information from customers and transmits natural language processing engines to extract business keywords and match service strategies. The system provides agents with information delivery or information push templates and related knowledge points according to the service strategy. And mark the error-prone points and push the business entry. The smart customer service system is based on the feedback of the business keywords. The first is to match the service strategy model, which integrates and provides one-click issuance operations to facilitate the completion of the service; the second is to match the error-prone points of the business and the information associated with the knowledge base, which is displayed in an obvious position of the system to support the agents quickly and accurately answer customer questions; the third is to match the business that needs to be accepted, and push the corresponding business processing entry to the portal interface, and the agent can quickly enter the business area through the link to handle the business for the customer.

(2) Customer emotional change reminder: In the customer service process, grasping the customer's complex emotions is the key to improving service perception. According to the emotional service strategy model of the smart customer service system, the customer's emotional state is identified, and real-time

reminders to intervene in comfort, obvious through the system The position promptly reminds the agents of the emotional fluctuations of the customers, and promptly intervenes to calm the emotions of the customers. If the customer's emotions continue to fluctuate, the team leader's desk will give early warning, and at the same time, based on the customer's anger emotion service strategy, appropriate strategic compensation and reassure the customers emotions and reduce the risk of complaints.

4.4   Customer Service Operation Analysis Application

The voice analysis system can convert voice data into text data, and at the same time, through data labeling, formatting, clustering, and analysis and statistics, at the same time, the correlation between data can be established, which can provide a reference for customer service operation management.

By performing feature statistics on the number of occurrences and relevance of context-related words in the semantics, the root cause of the impact on the business can be unearthed. Through root cause analysis, the main purpose and intention of the user's call can be analyzed, so as to sort out and improve the weak links in a timely manner when there are more problems.

In addition, the voice analysis system can add multiple dimensions to analyze the relevance of recordings, including call type, business classification, user level, service content, etc., intelligently and fully data analysis of user satisfaction for each service unit, or different regions, and the customer's service satisfaction with the business. The system displays the development and change trend of each business in a timely manner, so that the operation team can adjust the business development strategy and service strategy in time to promote the overall vitality of the business.

4.5   Power Business Knowledge Base Construction

With the continuous development and use of communication software, the number of customer consultation methods faced by customer services in the power industry is also increasing. In addition to traditional telephone services, it also includes various mobile terminal applications such as consultation, repairs, and electricity. At the same time, the questions asked by customers have gradually become professional and objective. If the business knowledge base of the power industry cannot be established effectively, then the questions asked by customers will not be answered in a timely, accurate and efficient manner, which in turn reduces the accuracy and reliability of the service. In this regard, using artificial intelligence technology to support the construction of electric power smart customer service, while realizing electric power smart customer service, it can establish a complete power service system intelligent knowledge base such as electric power business according to different service areas, different service timeliness, and different service groups. Thesaurus, electric power voice knowledge base, etc., so as to effectively improve the service quality in the field of electric power enterprise customer service. It mainly includes the construction of power business lexicon and language knowledge base.

5 Summary

This paper first introduces the main applications of AI in the field of customer service inside and outside the industry, clarifies the application requirements of AI in the field of electric power customer service, and then analyzes the service process and key technologies of electric power Smart customer service. On this basis, from voice navigation, voice quality inspection, Smart customer service application analysis is carried out in customer service areas such as agent support, customer service voice analysis and power business knowledge base construction, and comprehensively elaborates the application support of AI technology in Smart customer service. The application of smart customer service system in the power industry has huge market potential, but it also faces certain problems and challenges in the development of the industry. Therefore, it is recommended that power companies should actively carry out cooperative research and development and talent reserves, and cultivate power business and information technology. Advanced talents, do a good job of compound talent reserves, and realize the rapid, healthy and sustainable development of enterprise intelligence. Fully understand the advantages and disadvantages of current AI technologies, and establish the correct concept of intelligence and information development. Blindly touting AI technology, and not overly exaggerating the application risks of AI technology, we must make reasonable plans, steadily promote the intelligent process of the power industry, and create a new era of industry development by leveraging AI technology; accelerate the formulation of relevant industry standards and Regulatory system, a new generation of Smart customer service systems must keep up with the trend of the times. Electric power companies must face up to the actual needs of the power industry to promote Smart customer services and create Smart customer services, keep up with the progress of the times, and accelerate the establishment of in line with the development of electric power information and the needs of electricity customers service and supervision system.

References

1. Wan, X.F.: European union releases artificial intelligence white paper: the European road to excellence and trust. Technol. China (9), 4 (2020)
2. Guohong, L.I., Jiang, L., Zhang, C.: Patent situation analysis of key technologies of artificial intelligence. Inf. Commun. Technol. Policy 10(6–9), 44–45 (2019)
3. Li, W., Chen, Z., Gao, X., et al.: Multimodel framework for indoor localization under mobile edge computing environment. IEEE Internet Things J. 6(3), 4844–4853 (2019)
4. Gao, X., Chen, Z., Tang, S., et al.: Adaptive weighted imbalance learning with application to abnormal activity recognition. Neurocomputing 173, 1927–1935 (2016)

5. Tang, G., Gao, X., Chen, Z., Zhong, H.: Unsupervised adversarial domain adaptation with similarity diffusion for person re-identification. Neurocomputing **442**, 337–347 (2021)
6. Zhang, Y., Gao, X., Chen, Z., et al.: Learning salient features to prevent model drift for correlation tracking. Neurocomputing **418**, 1–10 (2020)
7. Chen, J.Z.: The application of artificial intelligence technology in intelligent building. Intell. Build. Smart City **03**(013), 44–45 (2018)
8. Ma, Y., Wang, Z., Yang, H., Yang, L.: Artificial intelligence applications in the development of autonomous vehicles: a survey. Acta Automatica Sinica Engl. Ed. **7**(2), 15 (2020)
9. Li, B., Chai, X., Hou, B., Zhang, L., Liu, Y.: New generation artificial intelligence-driven intelligent manufacturing (ngaiim). In: IEEE SmartWorld, Ubiquitous Intelligence & Computing, Advanced & Trusted Computing, Scalable Computing & Communications, Cloud & Big Data Computing, Internet of People and Smart City Innovation (SmartWorld/SCALCOM/UIC/ATC/CBDCom/IOP/SCI) (2018)
10. Zhang, Y., Gao, X., Chen, Z., et al.: Mining spatial-temporal similarity for visual tracking. IEEE Trans. Image Process. **29**, 8107–8119 (2020)
11. Xia, Z., Hong, X., Gao, X., et al.: Spatiotemporal recurrent convolutional networks for recognizing spontaneous micro-expressions. IEEE Trans. Multimedia **22**(3), 626–640 (2020)
12. Gao, X., Hoi, S.C.H., Zhang, Y., et al.: Sparse online learning of image similarity. ACM Trans. Intell. Syst. Technol. **8**(5), 641–6422 (2017)
13. Gao, X., Hoi, S.C.H., Zhang, Y., et al.: SOML: sparse online metric learning with application to image retrieval. In: Twenty-eighth AAAI Conference on Artificial Intelligence, pp. 1206–1212 (2014)
14. Deng, C., Wang, B., Zhu, L., Ren, Z., Hui, L.I., Feng, J.: Typical applications of artificial intelligence in telecom operation. Inf. Commun. Technol. Policy **7**(14), 34–38 (2019)
15. Cheng, X.: A research on the development of artificial intelligence and consumer finance in china. J. Phys. Conf. 1176, 042073 (2019)
16. Zhu, Y.Y., Dai, C., Chen, Y., Zhuo, L., Liao, Y., Zhao, M.: Design of online power smart customer service system based on artificial intelligence. Mach. Tool Hydraul. **24**(002), 9–14 (2018)
17. Chen, X., Zhao, Y., Zhu, F., Qi, X.: Research on sensitivity and strategy service of customer electricity charge based on big data. Procedia CIRP **83**, 636–641 (2019)
18. Narendra, V.G., Hareesha, K.S.: Recognition and classification of white wholes (ww) grade cashew kernel using artificial neural networks. Acta Scientiarum Agron. **38**(2), 145 (2015)
19. Zhang, J., Wang, Z., Peng, Z.: Analytical model of the piezoresistive behavior of highly compressible sensors made of microporous nanocomposites. Adv. Theory Simul. **7**, 151–164 (2019)
20. Trivedi, J.: Examining the customer experience of using banking chatbots and its impact on brand love: the moderating role of perceived risk. J. Internet Commer. **18**, 91–111 (2019)
21. Xu, J., Zhang, X., Li, J.: Application of artificial intelligence in the field of power systems. In: 2019 4th International Conference on Electrical Engineering, Mechanical Engineering and Automation, pp. 36–41 (2019)
22. Ding, H.: Discussion on construction and characteristics of power smart business hall. Guizhou Electr. Power Technol. **07**, 51–52 (2013)
23. Wang, Z., Ren, H., Xuhai, L.U.: Key technologies of AI in customer service system. Telecommun. Sci. **19**, 121–132 (2018)

24. Zhang, K.: Research on the optimizing method of question answering system in natural language processing. In: 2019 International Conference on Virtual Reality and Intelligent Systems (ICVRIS), pp. 19–33 (2019)
25. Bhattacharya, S., Poray, J.: Application of graph theory in bigdata environment. In: International Conference on Computer, pp. 1–8 (2016)

An Abnormal Data Detection Method Based on Text Classification

Lisha Wu, Zhenyu Chen[✉], and Lutao Wang

Big Data Center, State Grid Corporation of China, Beijing, China
czy9907@126.com

Abstract. With the construction of smart grid and informatization, the power industry has accumulated massive amounts of data. A large amount of equipment status data, user power consumption data, grid operation data, etc. are collected in the grid data center, but there is a lot of noise or abnormal data in these massive data, which affects the follow-up application and analysis. Therefore, for massive data, we need to perform real-time filtering and anomaly detection. According to the State Grid Co., Ltd. technical object type standard rules, this article selects device data in the power industry assets as the experimental objects, and proposes an abnormal data based on text classification. Detection method research, without the need for feature engineering and feature selection, can quickly detect abnormal data to ensure that the corresponding relationship between the types of technical objects and equipment assets is correct. Experimental results show that the proposed method can effectively improve the operating efficiency of anomaly detection and the accuracy of the algorithm, which has practical application value and significance.

Keywords: Text classification · Abnormal data detection · Natural language processing

1 Introduction

With the deep integration and wide application of modern information technology and energy technology such as "Big Data, Cloud, IoT, Mobile and Intelligence", power data has become a strategic resource and core production factor of enterprises, and higher requirements are put forward for the real-time processing and intelligent optimization of massive power data. However, in the process of collecting and storing existing power data, abnormal data or noise will inevitably appear. Therefore, how to accurately and quickly detect abnormal data in real-time power data [1–4] becomes the primary problem to solve.

In many storage scenarios of power data, it is usually necessary to add some tags to the data to indicate a certain characteristic of this data, such as gender, payment type, product type, etc. The main basis for identifying a device asset is the object type field, but in actual data, spaces or random characters (such as 0, etc.) may be entered in this field, and it is more likely that an incorrect code has been entered, these are the conditions

© Springer Nature Singapore Pte Ltd. 2022
G. Zhai et al. (Eds.): IFTC 2021, CCIS 1560, pp. 528–539, 2022.
https://doi.org/10.1007/978-981-19-2266-4_40

we define as exception data. In this context, additional fields are required to determine whether the device type is abnormal. Device descriptions are more reliable as multi-text fields than fields of other numeric types. This method uses text classification [5, 6] technology to extract text information from the equipment asset database to construct a new abnormal data detection method.

In this way, we analyzed the real equipment data, which included a total of 3029,872 pieces of equipment data with as many as 2048 standard classifications. In order to check the proportion of abnormal data, we randomly sampled 1000 items for their manual verification, and the percentage of abnormal codes such as null values and wrong values reached 36%. On the other hand, there is a large amount of electric power terminology in the equipment descriptions, and in this case, to train the classification model for all equipment types, manual annotation of the full amount of data with the assistance of experts in the field of electric power equipment is required. In order to avoid ineffective work, we first validate the idea, starting from the dichotomous classification problem, select the "car" equipment that does not need the assistance of electric power expertise, divide the equipment data into two categories according to whether it is a car, with the equipment description as the feature input and the equipment type as the output, and achieve the purpose of equipment classification by training the model, so as to Detect the wrong classification, omission of classification as car, and the abnormal data that are originally cars but wrongly classified as other types.

2 Related Works

Natural Language Processing (NLP) is an important field in artificial intelligence. Its purpose is to make the computer understand natural language and process it effectively by modeling and analyzing language or semantics. Among them, text classification [7–10] is an important application in the field of natural language processing. The current text classification algorithms are mainly divided into schemes based on machine learning and schemes based on deep learning [11–13]. Among them, the scheme based on machine learning emphasizes extracting features and designing classifiers. First of all, the model will extract the different features contained in the text through expert knowledge or manually designed templates. You can use the general bag of words model (BOW) [14, 15], N-gram model [16] or use keywords. Word frequency feature TF-IDF and so on. Afterwards, the text information is classified based on the obtained features by the classifier. For example, SVM [17], Adaboost [18] and random forest.

Although these methods are effective, they require a lot of manual assistance and cost. In the absence of domain knowledge, deep neural networks can automatically perform feature extraction [19–23] and learning [24–27], providing us with simple and efficient text classification [28–32] and representation learning methods, with performance comparable to machine learning and it is faster, using CNN, RNN and attention mechanism for text classification [14]. Many researchers have improved the performance of text classification for different tasks by improving CNN, RNN and attention, or model fusion and multi-task methods. Among them, FastText [33–35] is a fast text classification algorithm, which is a commonly used algorithm at present. Its characteristics are: it accelerates the training speed and testing speed while maintaining high precision [36];

it does not need pre-trained word vectors, FastText [37] will train the word vectors by itself.

The architecture of FastText model is shown in Fig. 1, where $x_1, x_2,..., x_{N-1}, x_N$ represent the n-gram vector in a text, and each feature is the average value of the word vector. At the same time, FastText, as a subword embedding algorithm, runs faster. The problem is that feature engineering needs to be done, and the classification effect depends on the selection of features.

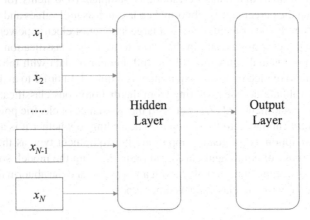

Fig. 1. The diagram of FastText model

3 Anomaly Data Detection Method Based on Text Classification

This paper proposes an anomaly data detection method (Text classification model for anomaly detection, TAD) based on text classification. Without the need for feature engineering and feature selection, it can quickly detect abnormal data to ensure the type of technical objects and equipment assets. The corresponding relationship is correct.

3.1 The Methodology Overview

We construct a deep neural network structure with an input layer, implicit layer, and an output layer in TAD for the input device asset's descriptive text data and annotation information. The input layer includes multiple words in the description text of each device asset, the hidden layer adds the square and average of the input word vector and the N-gram vector, and the output layer is hierarchical softmax and negative sampling (Fig. 2).

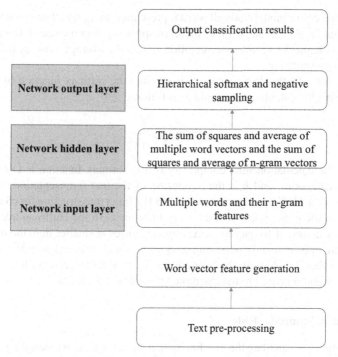

Fig. 2. The method flowchart of the model

3.2 The Workflow of Our Method

First, we preprocess the description text in the input layer, which mainly includes operations such as word segmentation, de-duplication, and de-digital symbols [38]. The exact mode of jieba splitting is used and the device vocabulary in the device object code is added to the lexicon.

After that, we convert the input words into word vectors in the hidden layer. Specifically, we generate a vector for each word in the corpus based on n-gram. We transform the input string into multiple phrases containing different semantics through multi-grammatical processing, and obtain the representation of the input string by modeling these phrases. For example, for the word "book", assuming the value of n is 3, its corresponding ternary phrases are: "<bo", "boo", "ook", "ok>", where "<" means prefix, ">" means suffix. So, we can use these to represent the word "book".

Then, we are inputting the features into the model for training to get the classification model. In the above figure, x_i represents the feature vector of the i-th word in the text. The negative log likelihood function of the model is as follows:

$$-\frac{1}{4}\sum_{n=1}^{N} y_n \log(f(BAx_n))$$

where, A is the corresponding matrix of the word lookup table, and B represents the weight coefficient of the matrix A. After the word representation is obtained through modeling, the entire model finds all word representations x_i, and then sums the squares and averages h_i. At the same time, the corresponding n-gram vector is squared and averaged to obtain the vector representation t_i, and the average value z_j is used as the input text representation.

Finally, we take this text representation z_j into the softmax function of our output layer. The specific calculation formula is as follows:

$$f(z_j) = \frac{e^{z_j}}{\sum_{i=1}^{n} e^{z_i}}$$

where, the calculation time complexity of the softmax function is $O(kh)$, k is the number of categories, and h is the dimension of the text representation. In addition, FastText uses the Huffman algorithm to build a Huffman tree structure for characterizing categories to solve the problem of category imbalance. In the Huffman tree, the depth of the tree structure of frequently occurring categories is smaller than the depth of the tree structure of infrequently occurring categories, which also makes further calculation efficiency higher. In addition, the N-grams model we use can preserve the semantics of the context well compared to the traditional bag-of-words model.

3.3 Negative Sampling Rule

In order to quickly calculate the loss function, we use the negative sampling mechanism to optimize it. For a given positive sample:

$$(\text{context}(w), w)$$

To maximize:

$$g(w) = \prod_{n \in \{w\} \cup NEG(w)} p(u|\text{context}(w), w)$$

Then it should satisfy the following formula:

$$p(u| \text{context } (w)) = \begin{cases} \sigma(X_w^T \theta^u), & L^w(u) = 1 \\ 1 - \sigma(X_w^T \theta^u), & L^w(u) = 0 \end{cases}$$
$$= [\sigma(X_w^T \theta^u)]^{L^w(u)} [1 - \sigma(X_w^T \theta^u)]^{1 - L^w(u)}$$

Therefore, the final loss function is:

$$L = \log \prod_{w \in C} g(w) = \sum_{w \in C} \log g(w)$$

Under the negative sampling rule, that is:

$$P(w) = \frac{[\text{counter}(u)]^{0.5}}{\sum_{u \in D} [\text{counter}(u)]^{0.5}}$$

4 Experimental Results

4.1 Experimental Environment and Dataset

In the testing process of this experiment, the computer configuration environment used in this article is windows system, 16G processor, and 500G solid state drive. This article uses the IntelliJ IDEA development environment for experiments, and uses JAVA language to implement the model algorithm used in this article.

The data in this paper comes from the national grid equipment asset database, which is mainly for equipment asset data, including equipment description, equipment object code, equipment original value, provincial company code and many other fields. In order to select the data related to "car", two query conditions are set, namely, "equipment description" includes "sedan" or equipment object code for " car", and get 8496 samples after taking the set, keeping the two fields of device description and device object code. Next, the manual judgment of whether the sample is a car based on the device description, adding the field "device type", the judgment of yes is marked as 1, otherwise 0. Data samples are shown in Table 1, through the manual marking, the device type of 1 has 8350, the device type of 0 has 119. By comparing the device object code and device type, the abnormal data can be identified and divided into two categories as follows.

Table 1. Car sample data (1: car; 0: non-car)

No.	Description	Object encoding	Type (0 for non-cars, 1 for cars)	Whether it is abnormal (0 is normal, 1 is abnormal)
1	中型客车鲁BD5551	轿车	0	1
2	小轿车川Z23432（生产用车）	-	1	1
3	车管所江铃全顺牌小型普通客车鲁G5U036	轿车	1	0
4	尼桑皮卡工程车（豫MR0963）	轿车	0	1
5	小轿川AMZ835	轿车	1	0
6	六安供电公司电费管理中心摩托车24	轿车	0	1

(1) The device object code is "car" and the device type is "0", that is, other types of equipment data are incorrectly classified as "car".
(2) The equipment object code is non-car or null, and the equipment type is "1", i.e., the data of car type is not marked as type or wrongly classified as other types.

The total number of abnormal data for the 8496 samples was 1672, with an abnormality rate of 19.7%.

In this experiment, we only need two fields, device description and device type, and device type is 1 i.e., positive sample, and 0 is negative sample; these positive and negative samples are randomly divided into training set and test set according to the ratio of 7:3, and the effect of the proposed model is tested on the test set (Table 2).

4.2 Comparison of Model Training Results

Table 2. Comparative analysis of model training results (%)

No	Algorithm model	Accuracy rate	Recall rate	F1 value
1	Naive Bayes	1: 99% 0: 100%	1: 100% 0: 58%	1: 1 0: 74%
2	SVM	1: 100% 0: 96%	1: 100% 0: 72%	1: 1 0: 83%
3	Random forest	1: 0.99% 0: 100%	1: 100% 0: 44%	1: 1 0: 62%
4	XGBoost	1: 100% 0: 90%	1: 100% 0: 72%	1: 1 0: 80%
5	Fasttext	1: 100% 0: 0.96%	1: 100% 0: 75%	1: 1 0: 84%
6	The method of this paper	1: 100% 0: 98%	1: 100% 0: 81%	1: 1 0: 89%
7	The method of this paper (remove the level softmax)	1: 100% 0: 97%	1: 100% 0: 78%	1: 1 0: 86%
8	The method of this thesis (remove the square and average)	1: 100% 0: 97%	1: 100% 0: 80%	1: 1 0: 88%

1) for the model of Naive Bayes:
   Despite the accuracy of the Naive Bayes negative sample is 100%, the recall is only 58%, indicating that this algorithm does not perform well in identifying non-cars. The Parsimonious Bayes algorithm uses a probability calculation where the probability of a positive sample is high with an extremely unbalanced training set of samples P(sedan = True) = 8350/8469 = 0.98. In the case of unknown whether a piece of equipment asset is a car, because the probability of a positive sample in the training set is high, this equipment asset will be classified as a car with a high probability, resulting in a low recall rate of a negative sample.
2) for the model of SVM:
   In SVM, the accuracy rate of negative samples reaches 96%, the recall rate of negative samples reaches 72%, and F1 reaches 0.83. The reason for the good effect of

SVM is that certain words are representative in the positive and negative samples of the training set, such as "Santana" and "Toyota" in the positive sample, and "maintenance", "base", and "base" in the negative sample. These words can be used as support vectors. SVM uses a linear kernel, so most positive and negative samples in the vector space are linearly separable.

3) for models of Random forest and XGBoost [39]:
Both Random Forest and XGBoost use decision tree algorithms, and in the case of very high text analysis dimensions, the depth and number of decision trees required are also very high. The depth of the tree used here is only 10. Perhaps after increasing the depth and number, the accuracy and recall of these two algorithms will increase, but it will also increase the computational complexity.

4) for the model of FastText:
The accuracy, recall and F1 values obtained by FastText on negative samples are 96%, 75%, and 84%, respectively. Compared with other traditional methods, FastText gets a large improvement in the recall rate.

5) for the method of this paper:
According to the comparative analysis of experiments, the method proposed in this paper is obviously better than other algorithms. The accuracy, recall and F1- values of positive samples are 100%, 100%, and 100%. The accuracy, recall and F1-value of negative samples are 98%, 81% and 89%, respectively. Compared with the performance of other algorithms on negative samples, this thesis method has a 4%-66% improvement in recall rate and a 5%-27% improvement in F1-value. The method of adding square sum, hierarchical softmax and negative sampling proposed in this paper are effective in solving the problem of low recall rate.

6) for the method of this paper (remove the level softmax):
After removing the hierarchical softmax, the method in this paper reduces the accuracy of negative samples by 1% compared with the method in this paper, and the recall rate and F1-value are reduced by 3% and 3%, respectively, which effectively proves the proposed method in this paper. Advantages of hierarchical softmax and negative sampling.

7) for the method of this thesis (remove the square and average):
After removing the square and averaging method in this paper, on negative samples, the accuracy rate, recall rate and F1-value are reduced by 1%, 1% and 2% respectively. This shows that the sum-of-squares averaging strategy can effectively affect the judgment effect of the model.

4.3 Result Analysis

In this experiment, we use Naive Bayes, SVM, Random Forest, XGBoost, and Fast-Text as the comparison methods to perform the accuracy, recall, and F1-values on the positive sample (car) and negative sample (non-car). test. The comparative effect of the experiment and the analysis of the results are shown in Table 3. Through experimental comparison, the method proposed in this paper has a better verification effect in negative sample detection, that is, when finding out the wrong classification of cars in other equipment types anomaly detection. Among them, the accuracy rate (100% accuracy of positive samples, 98% accuracy of negative samples), recall rate (positive Sample recall rate is 100%, negative sample recall rate is 81%), F1 value (positive sample value is 1, negative sample value is 89%).

On the other hand, Naive Bayes found only 37 non-car data in the 90,000 data set, but the accuracy rate is relatively high. Most of them are non-car equipment, including "substations" and "switches". The reason why there are only 37 non-cars in the 90,000 data set is that the above training set is not balanced. The accuracy rate here is higher than that of SVM because certain words have a high probability in the negative samples of the training set.

Whether it is the low accuracy rate of SVM on the full amount of data or the low recall rate of Naive Bayes, it is related to the imbalance of data volume and text data processing methods which is a problem we need to consider in the next plan.

Among the comparison methods, FastText is the most similar to the method in this paper. FastText uses multi-layer loss to put all labels, that is, all words, into a Huffman tree and the less frequently they occur the closer the words are to the leaf end. Assuming that there are ten thousand words in the dictionary, the simple softmax is a classification problem of 10,000 categories; assuming that a target word is at position 01001 on the Huffman tree (for example, 0 represents the left subtree and 1 represents the right sub-tree), Then the non-class problem on this sample is five binary classification problems, and it is expected that the predicted word will be more inclined to the correct direction at every position on this path. This method allows FastText to greatly improve the speed of training and prediction, and effectively improves accuracy due to the inclusion of the n-gram model, the order of words is considered, which effectively improves the accuracy.

Although FastText added the n-gram model to increase the order information between words, the length of the overall context is limited, which makes it impossible to capture more order information for words larger than the context window size. Therefore, this test proposes to improve the addition and average method of the mapping layer in FastText to the addition square and average method (see Table 3 for comparison of experiments 6 and 8), and Bing improves the softmax to hierarchical softmax and negative sampling in the output layer (see Table 3 Comparison of experiment 6 and 7). It can be seen from the test results that this method has a certain accuracy improvement effect.

In order to verify the experimental effect of the model proposed in this paper on actual data, we conducted experiments on a dataset of 37848 devices, which are all of sedan type, and through model detection, we found 7983 data mislabeled as "sedan", with an abnormality rate of 21%. For example, a data category for cars is described as "Iveco vans (converted into power cable fault detection and finding vehicles)", and the text classification model found the classification abnormal data, which is not considered to be car data, and the data can be identified as trucks after manual verification.

5 Conclusion

This method aims to propose an abnormal data detection method. The purpose is to face the State Grid Corporation's technical object type standard rules. It can quickly detect abnormal data without the need for feature engineering and feature selection ensuring the correspondence between the type of technical object and equipment assets. The relationship is correct. In this article, we select the sedan objects in the assets of State Grid Corporation for the declassification test. The experimental results show that our proposed method effectively improves the recall rate and F1-value of abnormal data detection.

Acknowledgement. This work is funded by the "Research on short text classification technology based on power equipment master data" program of the Big Data Center, State Grid Corporation of China (SGCC).

References

1. Li, Y., et al.: Monitoring model of electric power information communication system based on SG-CIM. Electr. Power Inf. **10**(10), 35–39 (2012)
2. Hongning, L., Xiaoyun, K., Wensi, H., et al.: Design and application of enterprise database model based on SG-CIM. Inf. Technol. **42**(4), 141–145 (2018)
3. Chalapathy, R., Chawla, S.: Deep learning for anomaly detection: A survey. arXiv pre-print arXiv:1901.03407 (2019)
4. Pang, G., Shen, C., Cao, L., et al.: Deep learning for anomaly detection: a review. ACM Comput. Surv. (CSUR) **54**(2), 1–38 (2021)
5. Asogwa, D.C., et al.: Text classification using hybrid machine learning algorithms on big data. arXiv preprint arXiv:2103.16624 (2021)
6. Li, Q., et al.: A survey on text classification: from shallow to deep learning. arXiv preprint arXiv:2008.00364 (2020)
7. Cai, C.: Research and Application of New Methods of Text Classification. Jiangnan University, Wuxi (2008)
8. Zhao, M., et al.: Research on a network anomaly detection method based on clustering algorithm. Comput. Netw. (2020)
9. Kannan, R., et al.: Outlier detection for text data. In: Proceedings of the 2017 SIAM International Conference on Data Mining. Society for Industrial and Applied Mathematics, pp. 489–497 (2017)
10. Ergen, T., Kozat, S.S.: Unsupervised anomaly detection with LSTM neural networks. IEEE Trans. Neural Netw. Learn. Syst. **31**(8), 3127–3141 (2019)
11. Arshi Saloot, M., Nghia Pham, D.: Real-time text stream processing: a dynamic and distributed NLP pipeline. In: 2021 International Symposium on Electrical, Electronics and Information Engineering, pp. 575–584 (2021)
12. Joshi, R., Goel, P., Joshi, R.: Deep learning for Hindi text classification: a comparison. In: Tiwary, U., Chaudhury, S. (eds.) Intelligent Human Computer Interaction. IHCI 2019. LNCS, vol. 11886, pp. 94–101. Springer, Cham (2020). https://doi.org/10.1007/978-3-030-44689-5_9
13. Shelke, R., Vanjale, S.: A residual network architecture for Hindi NER using Fasttext and BERT embedding layers. NOVYI MIR Res. J. **6**(6), 258–266 (2021)
14. Bojanowski, P., Grave, E., Joulin, A., et al.: Enriching word vectors with subword information. Trans. Assoc. Comput. Linguist. **5**, 135–146 (2017)
15. Joulin, A., et al.: Bag of tricks for efficient text classification. arXiv preprint arXiv:1607.01759 (2016)
16. Habib, M., et al.: AltibbiVec: a word embedding model for medical and health applications in Arabic language. IEEE Access (2021)

17. Xiaoqin, G.: Research on an improved SVM text data classification technology. Bull. Sci. Technol. **28**(4), 70–71 (2012)
18. Schapire, R.E.: Explaining AdaBoost. In: Schölkopf, B., Luo, Z., Vovk, V. (eds.) Empirical Inference, pp. 37–52. Springer, Berlin, Heidelberg (2013). https://doi.org/10.1007/978-3-642-41136-6_5
19. Devlin, J., et al.: Bert: Pre-training of deep bidirectional transformers for language understanding. arXiv preprint arXiv:1810.04805 (2018)
20. Yang, Z., et al.: Hierarchical attention networks for document classification. In: Proceedings of the 2016 Conference of the North American Chapter of the As-sociation for Computational Linguistics: Human Language Technologies, pp. 1480–1489 (2016)
21. Vaswani, A., et al.: Attention is all you need. In: Advances in Neural Information Processing Systems, pp. 5998–6008 (2017)
22. Gao, X., et al.: Sparse online learning of image similarity. ACM Trans. Intell. Syst. Technol. **8**(5), 64:1–64:22 (2017)
23. Zhang, Y., Gao, X., Chen, Z., et al.: Mining spatial-temporal similarity for visual tracking. IEEE Trans. Image Process. **29**, 8107–8119 (2020)
24. Xia, Z., Hong, X., Gao, X., et al.: Spatiotemporal recurrent convo-lutional networks for recognizing spontaneous micro-expressions. IEEE Trans. Multimedia **22**(3), 626–640 (2020)
25. Gao, X., et al.: SOML: sparse online metric learning with application to image retrieval. In: Twenty-eighth AAAI Conference on Artificial Intelligence, pp. 1206–1212 (2014)
26. Zhang, Y., Gao, X., Chen, Z., et al.: Learning salient features to prevent model drift for correlation tracking. Neurocomputing **418**, 1–10 (2020)
27. Tang, G., Gao, X., Chen, Z., Zhong, H.: Unsupervised adversarial do-main adaptation with similarity diffusion for person re-identification. Neurocomputing **442**, 337–347 (2021)
28. Mikolov, T., et al.: Advances in pre-training distributed word representations. arXiv preprint arXiv:1712.09405 (2017)
29. Alghamdi, N., Assiri, F.: A comparison of fastText implementations using Arabic text classification. In: Proceedings of SAI Intelligent Systems Conference, pp. 306–311. Springer, Cham (2019).https://doi.org/10.1007/978-3-030-29513-4_21
30. Santos, I., Nedjah, N., De Macedo Mourelle, L.: Sentiment analysis using convolutional neural network with FastText embeddings. In: 2017 IEEE Latin American Conference on Computational Intelligence (LA-CCI), pp. 1–5. IEEE, (2017)
31. Gaikwad, V., Haribhakta, Y.: Adaptive GloVe and FastText model for Hindi word embeddings. In: Proceedings of the 7th ACM IKDD CoDS and 25th COMAD, pp. 175–179. (2020)
32. Kulai, A., et al.: Emotion analysis of Covid tweets using FastText supervised classifier model. In: 2021 International Conference on Communication information and Computing Technology (ICCICT), pp. 1–6. IEEE (2021)
33. Young, J.C., Rusli, A.: Review and visualization of facebook's fasttext pretrained word vector model. In: 2019 International Conference on Engineering, Science, and Industrial Applications (ICESI), pp. 1–6. IEEE (2019)
34. Giri, R.K., Gupta, S.C., Gupta, U.K.: An approach to detect offence in memes using natural language processing (NLP) and deep learning. In: 2021 International Conference on Computer Communication and Informatics (ICCCI), pp. 1–5. IEEE (2021)
35. Malik, P., Aggrawal, A., Vishwakarma, D.K.: Toxic speech detection using traditional machine learning models and BERT and fasttext embedding with deep neural networks. In: 2021 5th International Conference on Computing Methodologies and Communication (ICCMC), pp. 1254–1259. IEEE (2021)
36. Adewumi, T.P., Liwicki, F., Liwicki, M.: Exploring Swedish & English fastText Embed-dings for NER with the Transformer. arXiv preprint arXiv:2007.16007 (2020)
37. Joulin, A., et al.: Fasttext.zip: Compressing text classification models. arXiv preprint arXiv: 1612.03651 (2016)

38. Rao, J., et al.: Algorithm for using NLP with extremely small text datasets. In: 2018 4th International Conference on Applied and Theoretical Computing and Communication Technology (iCATccT), pp. 1–6. IEEE (2018)
39. Chen, T., Guestrin, C.: Xgboost: a scalable tree boosting system. In: Proceedings of the 22nd ACM SIGKDD International Conference on Knowledge Discovery and Data Mining, pp. 785–794 (2016)

A Data Interaction Mechanism of Multi-market Members in Power Spot Market Based on Blockchain

Shuzhou Wu, Yunhao Huang$^{(\boxtimes)}$, Dapeng Li, Lei Tao, Dong Liu, and Qingbo Yang

Beijing Key Laboratory of Research and System Evaluation of Power Dispatching Automation Technology, China Electric Power Research Institute, Beijing, China
c1000k@163.com

Abstract. Blockchain has the characteristics of smart contract, distributed decision-making, collaborative autonomy, tamper proof high security, openness and transparence. It is suitable for the power spot trading market in terms of operation mode, topology and security protection, and can well support the construction and protection of the power spot trading market. Firstly, this paper expounds the basic principle of blockchain technology. Then, the model architecture of power spot trading market supported by blockchain is studied, and the market transaction process covering the whole process of transaction announcement, transaction declaration, market matching, data deposit and certificate is designed. Finally, based on the application scenario of "multi buyer and multi seller" in the power market, a block chain based power spot market transaction simulation platform is built to realize the efficient distribution and rational utilization of energy, and the feasibility of the transaction mechanism and method is verified by simulation experiments.

Keywords: Blockchain · The dispatching and control cloud · Electricity spot market · Market declaration and disclosure · Transaction deposit

1 Introduction

In March 2015, the State Council of China issued several opinions on further deepening the reform of power system, which required to restore the commodity attribute of power, build a "multi seller-multi buyer" competitive power spot market under the decentralization of transaction part, and strive to form a "source-sale-load" bilateral intraday time-sharing price mechanism reflecting the characteristics of time and location. In the power spot market, the increase of market participants makes the transaction information massive and it is more difficult to manage the power transaction. It is necessary to prevent both parties or third-party intruders from tampering with the transaction data or obtaining private data, and ensure the confidentiality, integrity, tamper proof, traceability, auditability and other information security functions of the data [1].

In recent years, blockchain technology has been widely recognized due to its decentralization, tamper-proof, and traceability characteristics. Tracing the development of

G. Zhai et al. (Eds.): IFTC 2021, CCIS 1560, pp. 540–551, 2022.
https://doi.org/10.1007/978-981-19-2266-4_41

blockchain technology which can be divided into three stages, the 1.0 digital currency era represented by bitcoin; the 2.0 contract era of the combination of digital currency and smart contract represented by Ethereum; the 3.0 application era that provides decentralized solutions for various industries with applications beyond currency and finance [2, 3].

The application scope ranges from currency, finance to energy, technology, information security and other real-life scenarios, relying on the openness, autonomy, security, and anonymity of blockchain technology, and does not rely on third parties or institutions to guarantee credit mechanisms. That solves the problem of trust between network entities and improve the efficiency of the entire network. As a distributed database and decentralized P2P peer-to-peer network, it has the characteristics of smart contracts, distributed decision-making, collaborative autonomy, tamper-proof high security, openness and transparency [4]. It is suitable for the power spot trading market in terms of operation mode, topology and security protection, and can well support the construction and protection of the power spot trading market. From the current research, blockchain technology is still in its infancy in the field of power trading. Yang et.al summarize the typical application scenarios of blockchain in the fields of energy supply, transmission, distribution, consumption and trading, and points out that blockchain will be first applied in the field of energy trading [5]. [6, 7] analyzes the key technologies of blockchain technology applied to automatic demand response from the aspects of workload proof, interconnection consensus, smart contract and information security. Ping et al. proposed a power trading scheme that stores power trading information in the form of smart contract and automatically performs capital transfer [8].

Combined with the development needs of the existing power system, the above works studied the application modes of blockchain technologies such as smart contract, collaborative autonomy and point-to-point trading, but does not deeply analyze the structure of power spot trading market in combination with the scenario of power spot market. Firstly, the basic principle of blockchain technology is expounded in this paper, and analyzes the application mode of blockchain technology from the aspects of consensus accounting, smart contract and business interaction; Then, it studies the model architecture of power spot market supported by blockchain, designs the market transaction process covering the whole process of transaction announcement, transaction declaration and market clearing, and constructs the autonomy and intelligent autonomy of power spot market dispatching and trading under the trend of decentralization of dispatching and trading, Deal with the security and credibility of power spot market transactions participated by multi market entities; Finally, based on the application scenario of "multi buyer and multi seller" in the distributed power market, a distributed power trading platform based on blockchain is built to realize the efficient distribution and rational utilization of energy, and the feasibility of the trading mechanism and method is verified by simulation experiments.

2 The Application Analysis of Blockchain Technology

As a decentralized distributed shared ledger, blockchain realizes chain storage through one-way connection of hash values at the beginning and end of adjacent blocks [6–8].

Each node of the blockchain has a copy of the complete ledger, and any node can view and proofread transaction data in real time. The advantage of distributed storage not only lies in the openness of transactions to effectively maintain data security, but also reduces the cost of purchasing servers. Nakamoto, the initiator of the blockchain concept, has proved that when the illegal computing power is less than 50%, the transaction information on the blockchain cannot be forged and modified [9]. All distributed energy transaction data will be stored on the block body, and the hash algorithm will automatically generate a Merkle tree that stores the hash value of the transaction data [10]. The blockchain structure including murk tree is shown in Fig. 1, it can be seen from the figure that if the transaction data is maliciously tampered with, the corresponding murk tree root hash value will change. In the power market transaction model, the original records such as market subject declaration data, market clearing results and dispatching instruction vouchers are encoded into 64-bit Hash code through standard algorithm (the code corresponds to the original records one by one and cannot be pushed back, stamped with time stamp and put into the blockchain to form historical evidence. Once a user maliciously tampers with the data during the transaction, it will be immediately detected by the upstream and downstream blocks of the chain. All subsequent transaction data will be automatically linked to the legal blocks, and the short chain will become an illegal chain. Therefore, the distributed power market trading system based on blockchain can realize the real-time deposit of certificates, real-time settlement of interests and real-time distribution of subsidies in the trading process. At the same time, P2P direct trading also greatly reduces the intermediate handling fee required.

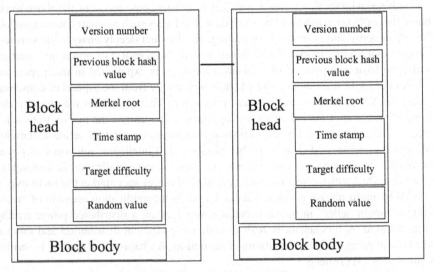

Fig. 1. The Block chain structure diagram

According to the degree of decentralization of blockchain, it can be divided into public chain, alliance chain and private chain. As shown in Table 1, the three blockchains have significant differences in consensus process, node access, security and efficiency.

Table 1. Comparison of three types of blockchain

Type	Public chain	Alliance chain	Private chain
Consensus scope	All nodes	Partially selected nodes	Central node
Read permissions	Open	Open or restricted	Open or restricted
Security	High	Higher	Low
Execution efficiency	Low	Higher	High
Degree of decentralization	Complete decentralization	Partial decentralization	Partial decentralization

The public chain has the highest degree of decentralization, which belongs to complete decentralization. Theoretically, all nodes in the system can participate in the consensus. Therefore, the public chain has high security, which is reflected in that any malicious tampering with data information requires a high proportion of blocks to form a consensus, resulting in high tampering difficulty. At the same time, it is easy to have too many participating nodes and affect the efficiency of consensus. The alliance chain only allows some selected nodes to participate in the consensus, and the transaction data can be used as public data or set as internal data. This feature determines that the alliance chain essentially belongs to a partially decentralized blockchain. This feature makes its security risk relatively increased compared with the public chain, while the execution efficiency is significantly improved, which is more suitable for application scenarios with certain access conditions. Generally, the central node is responsible for the private chain consensus process, which belongs to a partially centralized blockchain architecture. Its data security is relatively low, but it has the characteristics of high execution efficiency. Some special trading occasions are also suitable for private chain mode. From the perspective of network structure, the subjects participating in power market transactions form a partition autonomous mutual isolation network. Therefore, the alliance chain structure is mainly adopted. The power transaction between production and consumption users is to report the transaction power, electricity price and other information to the regional blockchain nodes according to their wishes, and then adopt the cross chain consensus mechanism and update it to all production and consumption user nodes, so as to make the data transparent and open, and all production and consumption users participate in the generation and maintenance of intelligent platform data.

3 Alliance Chain Model for Power Spot Market

Alliance chain model for power spot market the operation of power spot market is restricted by many aspects. For many provinces in developed regions, the power supply in the province is less than the demand, so it is necessary to transfer power from other provinces. When the price in the province is high and the price outside the province is low, the sales of power in the province will be affected. For underdeveloped provinces, the power supply in the province exceeds the demand, and there is a phenomenon of power nest [11]. It is urgent to output the excess power to develop regions for power supply, but the trans provincial transmission distance is long, the loss is large, and the generation of transmission distribution expenses will also increase the transmission cost.

At present, the construction of China's power spot market is mainly divided into inter provincial and intra provincial markets, both of which include power market and auxiliary service market, which are divided into day ahead, day in and real-time markets according to time cycle [12]. Among them, the inter provincial market uses the remaining space of inter regional and inter provincial transmission channels to carry out inter provincial day-to-day and intra day power and power generation rights transactions for the surplus power in the province at the transmission end, so as to meet the needs of renewable energy export, inter provincial surplus and shortage adjustment and the optimal allocation of surplus power in the province at the transmission end throughout the country.

Based on the cross regional contact line plan, the provincial market carries out the spot market in the province, pre clearing in the day before and within the day, formal clearing in the real-time link, and settlement according to the actual implementation results. Of course, the development of spot trading is based on the prediction of the balance of power and electricity in the province. In the process of trading, it is also necessary to repeatedly iterate and accurately coordinate according to the prediction, so as to finally achieve the goal of maximizing social value. Under the framework of the blockchain, each node of the power spot market completes the market demand declaration and matching in chronological order to form the bid winning power/electricity price and transmission and distribution circuit path scheme of the market subject, which improves the fairness and effectiveness of real-time transactions. Since the spot market is mainly aimed at the market transactions in the days ahead and within a few hours, compared with the characteristics of blocks generated every 10 min in in the blockchain [13], the real-time requirements are not high, which can well meet the dispatching and trading needs of the power spot trading market. Due to the high time constraints, the rolling balance of real-time links is not suitable for the application of blockchain technology. Therefore, the electricity spot trading model under the blockchain architecture is shown in Fig. 2.

In Fig. 2, around the day ahead spot market transactions, market entities such as the control center, trading center, regulatory authorities, large industrial users, third-party independent aggregators and comprehensive energy service platform, take the blockchain as the information interaction support to complete the market information announcement, production and consumption/electricity price declaration, centralized balance clearing and information sealing in the market transaction process.

The blockchain identity authentication technology is used to manage the registration and login of market members, and provide identity authentication services for market entities in the form of cloud hosting of digital certificates. After the user completes the market registration, the complete blockchain identity certificate information including deposit certificate "number + user information + public key" is formed through the blockchain key generation mechanism, and the binding relationship between user identity and public key is endorsed to realize blockchain identity authentication.

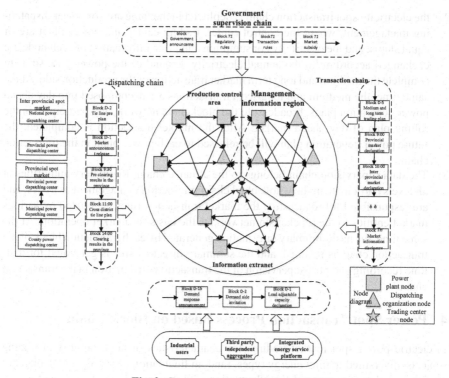

Fig. 2. Power spot trading chain model

Considering the autonomy and isolation of the above market entities accessing the physical network, the structure of alliance chain is adopted, which is composed of dispatching chain, transaction chain and government supervision chain, and the information of each chain is shared with each other.

1) the dispatching chain of the power grid deploys the power grid production control region. According to the inter provincial/provincial market operation mode, the node types include all or part of the national dispatching, network dispatching and provincial dispatching, and the nodes of each dispatching level have equal status. According to the market operation sequence, the dispatching chain issues market announcements to clarify the power grid operation safety constraints, power equipment maintenance plan and power grid load forecasting information, and publish these information to the whole blockchain network; After receiving the declared electricity and electricity price of the power plant and the adjustable load capacity of the user side, carry out centralized matching and clearing, form the bid winning electricity and electricity price of cross regional connecting lines and units in the province, and be responsible for verifying the safety of the clearing scheme. If the transaction is concluded, the transaction power will be distributed according to the order of "generation – transmission – distribution – transformation – consumption" at a specified time and in a specified area.

2) the electricity spot transaction chain is deployed in the large area of power dispatching management, where the control center, trading center and power plant are of equal status, and the electricity consumption and price information of each node are exchanged according to the annual electricity demand of the power grid, so as to complete the medium and long term market transaction of the production side. At the same time, the medium and long-term transactions are decomposed into day ahead power generation plans, broadcast to the blockchain network, and participate in the rolling plan of day ahead market. After the market transaction is completed, the future power generation plan will be released to each power plant in the transaction chain.

3) The data supervision chain belongs to the alliance chain. Regulatory authorities at all levels participate in the whole blockchain transaction management as nodes, and are responsible for broadcasting the market transaction rules negotiated by various market entities to the blockchain network as the basis for market operation. At the same time, the hash summary information generated by each transaction block of the transaction chain is retained, and the summary directory tree is generated for real-time recording and post supervision of the transaction information in the transaction chain.

4   Power Spot Transaction Process Based on Block Chain

In electric power spot market trading, the characteristics of large number of trading subjects, diversified trading energy types, random fluctuation of supply and demand of producers and consumers, real-time fluctuation of electricity price and so on put forward higher requirements for the design of electric power trading mechanism. Referring to the model in Fig. 2, it can be seen that the operation of power spot market based on blockchain mainly depends on the coordinated operation mechanism of dispatching chain and trading chain. It is necessary to analyze the price constraint condition of the trading chain under the clear physical constraint condition of the dispatching chain, and analyze the logical control relationship between them. The specific process is shown in Fig. 3.

1) In the declaration stage of market entities, power plants, large industrial users, load aggregators and other users can submit the demand and quotation of electricity trading on the trading chain. Producers and sellers use an irreversible and easily verifiable SM algorithm to hash and encrypt their own power generation, electricity price and load regulation as sealed quotations, and then broadcast them to the blockchain. This method makes the sealed quotation not only contains the true quotation information that cannot be tampered with, but won't be leaked to other producers and consumers in advance. The encrypted output results of electricity quantity and quotation of market entities are shown in formula (1):

$$D = H(q, p) \tag{1}$$

In formula (1), D is the encrypted declaration data; H is the hash function, using the state secret SM algorithm; q is the declared electricity quantity and p is the real quotation.

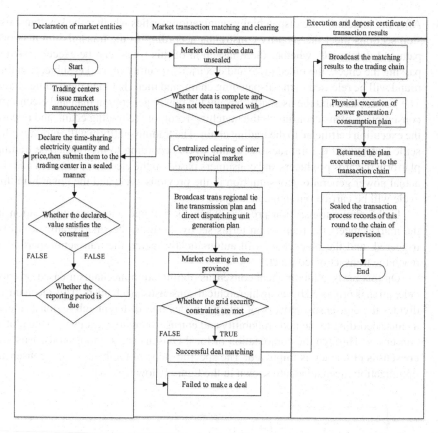

Fig. 3. Power spot transaction flow chart based on block chain

At the same time, the system will test the declared data of market subjects. If the declared amount exceeds the constraint conditions, the demand shall be re-declared within the effective time; otherwise, the transaction stage will be skipped. The data constraints of market entities are shown in formula (2):

$$D_n \leq D_{n,max}, n \in V_d \tag{2}$$

In formula (2), $D_{n,max}$ is the maximum power generation or maximum load regulation mileage of the NTH market entity; V_d is a collection of market subjects.

2) In the market transaction matching clearing stage, check whether the declaration data on the transaction chain is complete and not tampered with. After passing the check, the Inter-provincial market and intra-provincial market centralized bidding to clear will be carry out. That is, power generation demand is placed in the electricity sale queue according to the order of quotation from low to high, and the electricity purchased from the user side is placed in the electricity purchase queue according to the order of high to low, so as to match the clearing. The lowest price of electricity to form the boundary price of this round of trade, as the price of production and consumption side settlement.

3) After the matching, the dispatching organization verifies whether the key transmission sections meet the security constraints according to the transmission network path and determines whether the transaction of this round can be executed. After passing the check, the bided price and electricity quantity of market subjects in this round will be released to the dispatching chain, and then shared to the trading chain.

4) The power plant and the user side execute the power generation plan and electricity consumption plan according to the matching result of the trading chain, and release the execution certificate to the trading chain. The trading platform will automatically settle and reward the transactions in this cycle according to the rules. The trading platform rewards producers and consumers based on the electricity reported and the actual power generation/consumption in the previous cycle and the rewards in this cycle will be carried out in the next cycle.

In the above transaction process, when the volume and price information in the market meets the transaction terms set by the user, the smart contract will be triggered, and the blockchain will automatically match the transaction parties to reach the transaction contract.

On this basis, a hierarchical consensus optimization mechanism based on trust delegation is proposed by using hierarchical consensus mechanism. This mechanism divides the consensus network of internal nodes into different sub regions, selects agents according to the node reliability and entrusts them to participate in the global consensus. Through the combination of local consensus and global consensus, the consensus efficiency is improved. The specific steps of the hierarchical consensus optimization mechanism are shown in the figure below (Fig. 4):

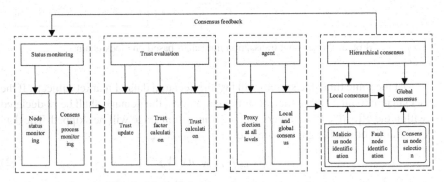

Fig. 4. Blockchain layered consensus mechanism

5 Experimental Results

In order to verify the effectiveness and economy of the mechanism designed in this paper, a distributed power spot transaction simulation platform is built according to the architecture shown in Sect. 2 for transaction simulation test. There are 8 market players in the experimental scenario, including 2 conventional power supplies, 1 energy storage, 1 photovoltaic, 1 controllable industrial load, 2 conventional loads and 1 electric vehicle. The experimental platform sends the power generation and consumption settlement information to the blockchain platform. The blockchain issues and receives vouchers for renewable energy electricity through electronic signature technology, which is divided into power generation and power consumption vouchers. The power generation voucher has the signature of the power generation unit and cannot be traded. It can be used as the basis for accounting. The electricity consumption certificate contains the signature of the power generation unit, the signature of the power purchase unit, transaction time, electricity quantity, electricity price, channel and other information (Table 2).

Table 2. Declaration of market entities

Market subject	Declared quantity/kWh	Quotation/(RMB/kWh)
Conventional power supply A	125	0.598
Conventional power supply B	110	0.582
Energy storage	76	0.458
Photovoltaic	92	0.441
Normal load A	−109	0.612
Normal load B	−66	0.598
Controllable industrial load	−68	0.438
Electric vehicle	−23	0.450

In the simulation test, a transaction cycle is $t = 30$ min, and the producer and consumer submit the transaction declaration demand every 5 min. 0–5 min is the sealed quotation stage; 5–15 min is the market transaction matching stage; 15–30 min is the execution and settlement stage of transaction results.

Since the quotation of conventional load is the highest in the power purchase queue, matching is given priority. In the power sales queue, matching is carried out according to the order of quotation: photovoltaic, energy storage and conventional power supply until the power purchase demand is met, and the quotation of conventional load is higher than that of photovoltaic and energy storage, so the matching can be successful (Table 3).

In addition, since the declared purchase power of 175 kwh for conventional load is greater than the declared total sales power of 168 kwh for photovoltaic and energy storage, the remaining 9 kwh. The total power sales of conventional power supply B are greater than the total power purchase of controllable industrial load and electric vehicle, which shall be settled according to the power purchase price respectively. Conventional power supply has the highest quotation in this round, no matching power purchaser can be found, and the bid winning power is 0.

Table 3. Market transaction matching results

Market subject	Trading electricity/kWh	Transaction price/(RMB/kWh)
Conventional power supply A	0	/
Conventional power supply B	100	0.441
Energy storage	76	0.458
Photovoltaic	92	0.441
Normal load A	−109	0.449
Normal load B	−66	0.463
Controllable industrial load	−68	0.438
Electric vehicle	−23	0.4449

6 Conclusions

In this paper, the characteristics of power spot market transaction is analyzed, based on blockchain, a distributed power spot transaction model is proposed, and the process of market subject declaration, transaction clearing, transaction result execution and settlement is designed. According to the transaction mechanism, a distributed power spot transaction simulation environment is built based on Ethereum. The simulation results verify the rationality of the trading mechanism and promote the consumption of new energy.

Due to the characteristics of decentralization, distrust, programmability and non tampering of blockchain technology, it has broad application prospects in power spot trading. However, the current blockchain technology research and basic theory are still in the primary stage, and issues such as security verification and energy scheduling need to be further explored.

Acknowledgment. This work was supported by R&D project of China Electric Power Research Institute Co., Ltd under Grant No.52420020002K (Research on data management support technology of spot market based on blockchain).

References

1. Zhou, P., Chen, Q., Xia, Q., et al.: Logical analysis of foreign power spot market construction and its enlightenment and suggestions to China. Autom. Electr. Power Syst. (13), 10 (2014)
2. Peters, G.W., Panayi, E.: Understanding modern banking ledgers through blockchain technologies: future of transaction processing and smart contracts on the internet of money (2015)
3. Swan, M.: Blockchain thinking: the brain as a decentralized autonomous corporation [Commentary]. IEEE Technol. Soc. Mag. **34**(4), 41–52 (2015). https://doi.org/10.1109/MTS.2015.2494358
4. Zhou, H., Liu, C., Liu, D., et al.: Research on energy Internet option liberalization transaction. Chin. J. Electr. Eng. (2015)

5. Yang, D., Zhao, X., Xu, Z., et al.: Application status analysis and prospect of blockchain in energy Internet. Chin. J. Electr. Eng. **37**(13), 8 (2017)
6. Li, B., Zhang, J., Qi, B., et al.: Block chain: supporting technology of demand side resources participating in grid interaction. Electr. Power Constr. **38**(3), 1–8 (2017)
7. Yang, X., Zhang, Y., Lu, J., et al.: Blockchain-based automated demand response method for energy storage system in an energy local network. Proc. CSEE **37**(13), 3703–3716 (2017)
8. Ping, J., Chen, S., Zhang, N., et al.: Decentralized transactive mechanism in distribution network based on smart contract. Proc. CSEE **37**(13), 3682–3690 (2017)
9. Nakamoto, S.: Bitcoin: a peer-to-peer electronic cash system. Consulted **75**(8), 1042–1048 (2009)
10. Lee, B., Lee, J.H.: Blockchain-based secure firmware update for embedded devices in an Internet of Things environment. J. Supercomput. **73**(3), 1–16 (2017)
11. Shen, F., Song, Z., Zhang, M., et al.: Research on development of Liaoning power grid based on electric power system reform. Northeast Electr. Power Technol. **38**(5), 1–5 (2017)
12. Song, Y., Bao, M., Ding, Y., et al.: Review of Chinese electricity spot market key issues and its suggestions under the new round of Chinese power system reform. Proc. CSEE **40**(10), 3172–3187 (2020)
13. Göbel, J., Krzesinski, A.E.: Increased block size and Bitcoin blockchain dynamics. In: Proceedings of the 27th International Telecommunication Networks and Applications Conference, Melbourne, VIC, Australia, pp. 1–6. IEEE (2017)

Author Index

Printed in the United States
by Baker & Taylor Publisher Services